THE CERTIFICATE LIBRARY

* * *

FRENCH

THE CERTIFICATE LIBRARY

THIS SERIES of books has been designed to cover the various syllabuses of the Ordinary Level Examination for the General Certificate of Education. The books are equally suitable for all students who wish to improve their standards of learning in the subjects of the various volumes, and together they form an invaluable reference library.

The Editor of each book is an experienced Examiner for one or more of the various Examination Boards. The writers are all specialist teachers who have taught in the classroom the subject about which they write; many of them have also had experience as Examiners.

Each volume is comprehensive and self-contained and therefore has far more than an ordinary class textbook: each has a full treatment of the subject; numerous illustrations; questions on the chapters with answers at the end of the book; and a Revision Summary for each section of the book.

These summaries give the information in a concise and compact way so that examination candidates may easily revise the whole contents of the book—they can soon see how much they readily know, and how much they have forgotten and need to study again. The facts in these summaries serve, therefore, as a series of major pegs upon which the whole fabric of the book hangs.

Advice is given on answering the examination paper and there are questions of examination standard together with suggested answers.

Series Executive Editor
B. E. COPPING, B.A.HONS.

THE CERTIFICATE LIBRARY

★ ★ ★

FRENCH

Edited by

E. G. WEBB, B.A.

Headmaster, Birkenhead Institute

Contributors:

J. H. THOMPSON, M.A.

Deputy Headmaster, Hull Grammar School

R. T. MILES, M.A., B.Sc. (Econ.)

Modern Languages Master, Robert Gordon's College, Aberdeen

L. A. WEBB, B.A.

Formerly Headmaster, Highfields School, Wolverhampton

THE GROLIER SOCIETY LIMITED
LONDON

First published 1965
Reprinted 1968
Reprinted 1971

ISBN 0 7172 7706 2

PREFACE

FRENCH is still the modern foreign language most widely taught in Britain. It is the language not only of our nearest Continental neighbour, one of the most important of European communities, but also the main commercial and cultural language of vast areas in developing Africa.

This volume has been planned to assist the student who wishes to read, write and speak French so as to be able to face the varied tests set by the different examining boards for the Ordinary Level of the General Certificate of Education. It does not cover merely the examination year, but starts from the very beginning; to assist the student working on his own, model versions of the French passages and the exercises are provided, while particular advice is given on tackling the various sections of the examination. Parts I and II of the book are concerned with Grammar; Part III deals with the examination itself: each of these three parts has been written by a practising teacher with years of experience both in the classroom and as an examiner.

The examiners for the different boards have repeatedly pointed out in their reports that many of the candidates who fail do so because they are careless, inaccurate and make poor use of the knowledge they possess. It is hoped that careful attention to the chapters in Part III of this book, which treat the different types of tests set in examinations, will help candidates to make the best use of the knowledge that they have spent so much effort to acquire.

Oral fluency cannot be attained merely by reading and writing. Regular use and repetition aloud of the patterns of speech as they are met is essential. A student can quickly improve his aural perception by listening to speech either on records or on the radio; and he can improve his fluency by reading aloud not only from the literary works of modern French but from the many French newspapers and magazines now available in this country.

E. G. WEBB

CONTENTS

LEARNING A LANGUAGE
Page
9

PRONUNCIATION OF FRENCH
11

PART I by J. H. THOMPSON

Leçon

1 Subject Pronouns; Present Tense of **avoir** and **être**; Definite and Indefinite Articles; Numbers 1-10; Forming Questions; **Une Conversation dans la Cuisine**
17

2 Preposition **à**; First Conjugation Verbs; Negatives; Adjectives— Agreement and Position; Preposition **de** (Possession); Pronoun **on**; Liaison; **Sur le Palier**
26

3 Numbers 11-31; Time; Preposition **de**; **Dans le Jardin**
36

4 Prepositions; Colours; Possessive Adjectives; Second Conjugation Verbs; Questions—Inverted form; **Le Goûter dans le Salon**
44

5 Commands; Questions; Demonstrative Adjectives; Use of Infinitive; **Une Soirée avec des Visiteurs**
54

6 Third Conjugation Verbs; Formation of Adverbs; Days, Months, Dates; Object Pronouns; **Un Jeu de Cartes**
62

7 Verbs—Further Conjugations; Expressions with **avoir** and **faire**; Numerals—Ordinals; **Au Cinéma**
70

8 Perfect Tense; Relative Pronouns; Adjective **tout**; Inversion of Verb; **Au Marché**
78

9 Notes on Perfect Tense; Verbs with **être**; **Un Voyage Triste**
88

10 Reflexive Verbs; Indirect Object—Personal Pronoun; Pronouns **y** and **en**; Order of Pronoun; **La Fête de Madame Girard**
96

11 Future Tense; Future with **aller**; **La Distribution des Prix**
106

12 Disjunctive Pronouns; Pronouns with Commands; Personal Pronouns; **En Vacances**
114

Revision Summary of Grammar
121

PART II by R. T. MILES

13 Imperfect Tense; Uses of the Imperfect Tense; Negative Forms; Age; Prepositions Governing Verbs; **L'École**
137

14 Demonstrative Pronoun; Use of the Demonstrative Pronoun; Further Forms of the Demonstrative Pronoun; Negatives with the Perfect Tense; Negative Forms as Subject; **Les Grands Magasins**
146

15 Conditional Tense; Uses of the Conditional; Idiomatic Use of **venir de**; **Mon voisin**
154

16 Revisions and Completion of Numbers; Collectives; **La France**
162

17 Pluperfect Tense; Dimensions; Irregular Verbs; **Une Promenade en Auto**
172

18 Relative Pronouns; **La Ferme**
180

CONTENTS

Leçon   *Page*

19   Past Historic Tense; Use of the Past Historic Tense; Impersonal Verbs;
      Les Charmes du Camping   190

20   Uses of the Article; **Fin de la Troisième République**   198

21   Omission of the Article; Possessive Pronoun; **Au Bureau**   206

22   Comparison of Adjectives; Comparison of Adverbs; Adjectival Forms;
      En Voyage   214

23   Agreement of Past Participle; Past Participle with Reflexive Verbs; Uses
      of Reflexive Form; Future Perfect Tense; Conditional Perfect Tense;
      Past Anterior Tense; Irregular Plurals of Nouns; **Conversation au Café**   224

24   The Verbs **aller, pouvoir, savoir, vouloir, devoir, faire**; Idiomatic Tense
      Usage; **Une Lettre de Paris**   232

25   **C'est** and **il est**; Questions; Other Uses of Inversion; **Un Crime Effroyable**   242

26   Verb and its Object; Constructions with the Infinitive; **Une Mission
      Dangereuse**   250

27   Subjunctive Mood; Use of Subjunctive; Subjunctive after Certain
      Conjunctions; Sequence of Tenses; **La France Aujourd'hui**   262

      Revision Summary of Verbs   273

PART III by L. A. WEBB

28   French into English   290

29   English into French   303

30   Composition   316

31   Comprehension   325

32   Dictation   339

33   Conversation   343

34   The Examination Paper   349

      Alphabetical List of Special Difficulties   353

      Translation of the Texts   369

      Answers to the Exercises   404

      French-English Vocabulary   461

      English-French Vocabulary   491

      Index   507

      Acknowledgements   512

Coloured Illustrations

	Page		*Page*
La Maison	33	**La Plage**	169
Les Meubles	34	**Les Insectes et Les Oiseaux**	170
Les Vêtements	51	**Les Bâtiments**	187
La Poche et Le Sac à Main	52	**Le Voyage et La Vie Quotidienne**	188
Le Paysage	85	**Le Carrefour**	221
Les Animaux	86	**Les Moyens de Transport**	222
Le Corps Humain	103	**La Famille**	239
La Nourriture	104	**La Papeterie**	240

View of the River Seine in Paris, with the Eiffel Tower beyond.

LEARNING A LANGUAGE

HAVE YOU ever thought what is entailed in learning a language? If you have, you will have realized that there are four basic skills which must be acquired:

> Reading with understanding
> Writing correctly
> Listening with understanding
> Speaking correctly

If we were learning a dead language, it would be enough to develop skill in the first two activities; but French is a living language, so we need to be skilled in the last two as well.

Speaking a language is like performing on an instrument; the language, like the instrument, is there waiting for us, but it takes time to develop the skill needed to manipulate it. However much a man knew about, say, the guitar, we should not call him a guitarist unless he could actually play his guitar, and we should not think a man really qualified in a language unless he could speak it.

So in learning French it is not enough to study with the eye alone; we must also be constantly saying things aloud so that the tongue and the ear become accustomed to the sounds of French. Reading the text and the grammatical examples aloud is therefore an important part of learning the language, and you are given phonetic transcriptions of the words used to enable you to practise the correct pronunciation right from the beginning.

Learning a modern language consists in remembering a very large number of small things. Each thing in itself is easy—for example, the fact that **la main** means *the hand* and that **je suis** means *I am*: there is nothing difficult about that; but it is because there are so many of these small things to learn that French sometimes seems difficult to people with short memories. The things to be learnt consist of points of grammar and of vocabulary. It is as though words are the bricks of a language, and the rules for fitting them together into a building are called the grammar of a language; both are equally important, for a sound knowledge of each is needed to make a solid structure.

Here are some helpful tips to remember as you work through this book:

(a) Learn the article — **le** or **la, un** or **une** — with each new noun, and practise saying them aloud.

(b) Learn the French examples of each new grammatical rule by heart.

Fountains play in the grounds of the Palace of Versailles.

(c) Repeat the verb-tables aloud until you can roll them off the tip of your tongue; let the tongue remember them just as much as the eye.

(d) In this book each illustrated two-page story has the new words listed on the previous two pages; when you first read the stories you will have to refer back repeatedly to these words, but see if you can gradually learn to manage without looking back to the previous pages.

(e) Try to think from the French word straight to the object or idea it represents without translating into English first. There are a number of coloured pages in this book where you can go direct from the idea to the French word representing it, as each page contains a picture of a group of objects, each with the French word underneath and no English translation.

When you have progressed some way with your study of the language, there are various additional things you should do which will help you to learn faster:

1. Use your radio for listening to French radio programmes.
2. Buy a French magazine or newspaper from time to time and see how much of it you can understand (use the pictures to help you). Things like this help to remind you that French is a large part of many people's lives, not just a subject of study.
3. Best of all, go for a holiday in France, so that you can try out your French on the French people you meet.

10

PRONUNCIATION OF FRENCH

THE STUDY of the sounds of human speech is called phonetics, and words as well as being expressed by letters of the alphabet can be expressed by symbols called phonetic symbols. The difference between these two sets of signs is that each letter of the normal alphabet may express different sounds in different words (compare the *c* sound in *cat* and in *cellar*), whereas in phonetics there is one and only one sound represented by each symbol. If a language is pronounced almost exactly as it is spelt, it is called a phonetic language; if however the pronunciation cannot always be deduced from the spelling, it is not phonetic.

French is not a phonetic language — there are many consonants, particularly at the ends of words, that are not pronounced at all. They are there because they were pronounced hundreds of years ago, but in the spoken language they have ceased to be pronounced while they still exist in the spelling. We find the same difficulty with English—in words like *knee, wrong, sight, through.*

Once we become familiar with French, however, we can tell from the general sense of a sentence what each word-ending should be and we then know how to spell it correctly:

I give = **je donne** but *you give* = **tu donnes** with an additional, but silent, **-s**. Both **donne** and **donnes** sound alike.

In order to show exactly which letters are pronounced and which are silent and how each syllable sounds, it is necessary to use a phonetic system with one symbol for each sound and to show the phonetic transcription of each new word. You will see in the Vocabulary to the chapters that the phonetic transcription is given of every word. Furthermore, the two-page stories of the first six chapters also have the phonetic symbols printed below the ordinary text, so that you can see how the words sound in a sentence.

The symbols are those of the International Phonetics Association, those to be found generally in textbooks and dictionaries; they are normally shown enclosed in square brackets.

There are three accents in French: e.g.   é acute accent

                                      è grave accent

                                      ê circumflex accent

and a sign, the cedilla, used to make a **c** soft — ç. The diaeresis ¨ is placed over the second of two vowels if they are to be pronounced separately.

Some of the sounds used in French are also used in English, but many are quite different from any sound used in any English word. One can see that to make some of these sounds a Frenchman uses his whole mouth, his tongue, teeth and lips in quite a different way from an Englishman. He opens his mouth more and makes it wider, and brings his tongue further forward till it touches his top front teeth. If we are going to pronounce French properly we must make our facial gestures as similar to a Frenchman's as possible; we must not be put off by the fact that we have to put our mouths into new and exaggerated shapes to produce the correct sounds.

VOWELS

No.	Phonetic Symbol	Mouth Position and Nearest English Equivalent	Normally Written	Examples
1.	[i]	Draw the corners of the mouth apart tensing the mouth muscles and stretching the lips over the teeth, upper and lower teeth almost touching. (Sound as in *niece, police*.)	i î y	**lis** [li], **nid** [ni] **île** [il] **y** [i], **cycle** [sikl]
2.	[e]	Prepare to make a short sound with the mouth muscles tense and the corners of the mouth half drawn back — the tongue touching the lower teeth lightly. (As in *lay*, but without the final *ee* sound — *lay-ee*.)	e é er ez ai and **et** [e] (= *and*)	**les** [le] **été** [ete] **dîner** [dine] **lisez** [lize] **j'ai** [ʒe], **finirai** [finire]
3.	[ɛ]	Relax the lips, lower the jaw and press the tongue forward against the lower teeth. (As in *bet*.)	è ê et e + two consonants ai ei	**père** [pɛːr] **bête** [bɛːt] **met** [mɛ] **belle** [bɛl] **aime** [ɛm] **peine** [pɛn]
4.	[a]	Draw the lips back against the teeth, with the mouth wide open, keeping the tongue against the lower front teeth. (Between the vowel sound of *mad* and *mud*.)	a à	**madame** [madam] **là** [la] and **femme** [fam]

5.	[ɑ]	Open the mouth wide, keeping the jaw lowered and the tongue low in the mouth. (As in *past*, *palm*.)	a â	**pas** [pɑ] **âme** [ɑːm]
6.	[ɔ]	With the mouth open, lips rounded and tongue flat, force the sound forward as much as possible. (Between sound of *dot* and *dirt*.)	o au u(m)	**dot** [dɔt] **mauvais** [mɔvɛ] **rhum** [rɔm]
7.	[o]	Tense the mouth muscles, round the lips and thrust them forward, keeping the tongue back towards the soft palate. (Between the vowel sound of *so* and *saw*.)	o ô au eau	**sot** [so] **rôle** [roːl] **auto** [oto] **beau** [bo]
8.	[u]	Force the rounded lips as far forward as possible, with the tongue far back in the mouth. (Between sound of *full* and *fool*.)	ou	**foule** [ful], **nous** [nu] and **où** [u]
9.	[y]	Keep the tip of the tongue pressed against the lower teeth and force the rounded lips forward to form a very small circle. (No English equivalent — nearest is the vowel between sound of *tea* and *too*.)	u eu (in the verb avoir)	**tu** [ty] **eu** [y]
10.	[ø]	The lips are slightly less rounded than when saying [o]; keep the tongue behind the lower teeth. (Short sound, as *ir* in *flirt*.)	eu œu	**feu** [fø] **nœud** [nø]
11.	[œ]	Follow the movements for [ɔ], but with the mouth more closed. (Between sound of *pour* and *purr*.)	eu œu œ	**peur** [pœːr] **œuf** [œf] **œil** [œj]
12.	[ə]	This is like a relaxed [œ]. (Short sound, as *a* in *alone*, or second vowel sound in *atom*.)	e	**de** [də], **menu** [məny]
13.	[ɥ]	This is similar to [y] and occurs when **u** is followed by another vowel, usually i. (Similar to first vowel sound in *cruet*.)	u	**lui** [lɥi]

French people sometimes appear to speak through the nose; this is because French has four nasal vowels, and when they are pronounced much air is passed through the nose. The nasal vowels are indicated in spelling by an **n** or an **m** after the vowel: the **n** or **m** are not themselves pronounced separately. There are certain words where they are pronounced, however.

14. [ɛ̃] This is a nasalized [ɛ] with the tongue slightly flattened.

in, im	fin [fɛ̃]
ain, aim	main [mɛ̃]
ein	peint [pɛ̃]
en (after i)	rien [rjɛ̃]

15. [ɑ̃] The mouth should be slightly opened and rounded, the jaw lowered and the tongue quite flat; the sound is projected upwards rather than forwards.

an, am	ample [ɑ̃mpl]
en, em	enfant [ɑ̃fɑ̃]
	temps [tɑ̃]

16. [ɔ̃] This sound is a nasalized fusion of [ɔ] and [o].

on, om	bon [bɔ̃]
	sombre [sɔ̃:br]

17. [œ̃] This sound is the nasalized form of [œ], not of the vowel as it is spelt.

un, um	brun [brœ̃]
	parfum [parfœ̃]

In some words the vowel sound is made longer than usual; this protraction is indicated by : after the phonetic symbol for the vowel:

lire [li:r]	même [mɛ:m]	valeur [valœ:r]
rôle [ro:l]	chaussure [ʃosy:r]	sable [sa:bl]
centre [sɑ̃:tr]	fondre [fɔ̃:dr]	humble [œ̃:bl]

The two sounds which follow are half vowel, half consonant.

18. [j] Produced when **i** or **y** is followed by a vowel; or when **il** or **ill** comes in the body of a word; or **y** comes at the beginning of a word. (As the *y* in *yacht*.)

i	piano [pjano]
il	rail [ra:j]
ill	briller [brije]
y	yeux [jø]

19. [w] Not quite like the English *w*; the sound is drawn in as the lips, which start from the [y] position, are drawn down.

[wa] is the pronunciation for:

oi	trois [trwa]
oê	poêle [pwal]

[wa] is the pronunciation for certain words with **oi**:

oi	boîte [bwat]

[wɛ̃] is the pronunciation for:

oin	loin [lwɛ̃]

CONSONANTS

The consonants are pronounced in much the same way as in English, the exceptions being noted below. Consonants at the ends of French words are usually silent, unless they are followed by an **e** or other vowel.

No.	Phonetic Symbol	Mouth Position and Nearest English Equivalent	Normally Written	Examples
20.	[p]	As in English.	p	**pain** [pɛ̃]
21.	[b]	As in English.	b	**abbé** [abe]
22.	[f]	As in English.	f	**bref** [brɛf]
			ph	**phrase** [frɑːz]
23.	[v]	As in English.	v	**brève** [brɛːv]
24.	[t]	As in English, but with the tongue further forward.	t	**table** [tabl]
			th	**théâtre** [teɑːtr]
25.	[d]		d	**donner** [dɔne]
26.	[s]	As in English.	s	**son** [sɔ̃]
			sc	**scène** [sɛn]
			c before e, i	**cire** [siːr]
			x	**dix** [dis] (when not qualifying a following noun.)
			t before ion	**nation** [nasjɔ̃]
27.	[z]	As in English.	z	**zone** [zoːn]
			s	**rose** [roːz]
28.	[k]	As in English.	k	**kilo** [kilo]
			c before a, o, u	**conte** [kɔ̃ːt]
			ch	**chœur** [kœːr]
			qu, q	**quart** [kaːr]
29.	[g]	As in English.	g before a, o, u	**gare** [gaːr]
				guêpe [gɛːp]

15

30.	[ʃ]	As English *sh* in *share*.	ch	chose [ʃoːz]
31.	[ʒ]	As English *s* in *leisure*.	g j	gilet [ʒilɛ] je [ʒə]
32.	[r]	Rolled with the uvula at the back of the mouth or trilled like the Scots *r* in *Burns*.	r	rouge [ruːz] mère [mɛːr]
33.	[l]	As in English.	l	lait [lɛ]
34.	[m]	Remember that **m** and **n** are often not sounded after a vowel as they usually nasalize the vowel.	m mm	dame [dam] flamme [flaːm]
35.	[n]		n nn	une [yn] canne [kan]
36.	[ɲ]	As the English *n* in *new* or *onion*.	gn	signe [siɲ]

LIAISON

A consonant at the end of a word which is normally silent is sometimes pronounced if the next word begins with a vowel or a mute **h** and the sense runs on from the first word to the second: this practice is called liaison. The degree to which this is done varies almost from speaker to speaker and no rules can ever be laid down for it, but in this book the speech of an educated Frenchman who speaks his language with great care has been taken as the model. Liaisons are indicated by the sign ‿:

nous donnons [nu dɔnɔ̃] but **nous‿allons** [nuzalɔ̃]
les garçons [le garsɔ̃] but **les garçons‿intelligents** [le garsɔ̃zɛ̃tɛliʒɑ̃]

STRESS

When you pronounce an English word of more than one syllable, you give more weight to one syllable than to the others — this is called the accented or stressed syllable. In French, no one syllable in a word is accented any more than the others; in the word **monotonie**, for example, the same amount of stress is given to each syllable, whereas in the same word in English — *monotony* — the stress is on the second syllable.

16

PART I

LEÇON 1

LEARN BY HEART

1. **Quel est votre nom?** *What is your name?*
   kɛl ɛ votrə nɔ̃?
   Mon nom est Robert. *My name is Robert.*
   mɔ̃ nɔ̃ ɛ rɔbɛːr.

2. **Où habitez-vous?** *Where do you live?*
   u abite vu?
   J'habite à Douvres. *I live in Dover.*
   ʒabit a duːvr.

3. **Quel temps fait-il?** *What is the weather like?*
   kɛlː tɑ̃ fɛtil?
   Il fait beau [mauvais]. *It is fine [bad].*
   il fɛ bo [mɔvɛ].

GRAMMAR

SUBJECT PRONOUNS

Because French verbs change their form more than English ones, they have
to be learnt in fixed patterns; the forms required after the personal pronouns
I, you, he, she, it (singular), and *we, you, they* (plural), are set out in that order.

I, we refer to the person or persons speaking (first person).

You refers to the person or persons spoken to (second person).

He, she, it, they refer to persons or things spoken of (third person).

Present tense:

avoir [avwaːr] = *to have*		être [ɛːtr] = *to be*	
j'ai [ʒe]	= *I have*	**je suis** [ʒə sɥi]	= *I am*
tu as [ty a]	= *you have*	**tu es** [ty ɛ]	= *you are*
il a [il a]	= *he has*	**il est** [il ɛ]	= *he is*
elle a [ɛl a]	= *she has*	**elle est** [ɛl ɛ]	= *she is*
nous avons [nuzavɔ̃]	= *we have*	**nous sommes** [nu sɔm]	= *we are*
vous avez [vuzave]	= *you have*	**vous êtes** [vuzɛt]	= *you are*
ils ont [ilzɔ̃]	= *they have*	**ils sont** [il sɔ̃]	= *they are*
elles ont [ɛlzɔ̃]	= *they have*	**elles sont** [ɛl sɔ̃]	= *they are*

Note that (*a*) although **vous** is learned with the plural pronouns, it can in fact be singular as well and refer to one person only. This is because French people use **tu** only when addressing close friends, relatives, children or animals. A French boy would call his teacher **vous**, his school-friend **tu**; (*b*) there is no separate word for *it*; even things in French are either **il** or **elle**; consequently there are two words for *they*, **ils** and **elles**; (*c*) **elle** takes the same verb form as **il**, and **elles** the same as **ils**. In future only the masculine forms will be shown, unless the feminine forms are different.

DEFINITE AND INDEFINITE ARTICLES

There are only two genders in French, masculine and feminine. All nouns have gender; this means that in French all the words for things as well as for people are either masculine (m.) or feminine (f.).

The definite article *the* has two different forms in French, **le** and **la**; **le** is used with masculine nouns, **la** with feminine nouns; the plural of both **le** and **la** is **les**; **le** and **la** before a vowel become **l'**:

le père [lə pɛːr], **les pères** [le pɛːr] = *the father(s)*
la mère [la mɛːr], **les mères** [le mɛːr] = *the mother(s)*
le torchon [lə tɔrʃɔ̃], **les torchons** [le tɔrʃɔ̃] = *the duster(s)*
la nappe [la nap], **les nappes** [le nap] = *the tablecloth(s)*
l'évier (m.) [levje], **les éviers** [lezevje] = *the sink(s)*
l'étagère (f.) [letaʒɛːr], **les étagères** [lezetaʒɛːr] = *the set(s) of shelves*

The indefinite article *a*, *an* also has masculine and feminine forms:

un père [œ̃ pɛːr] = *a father*   **une mère** [yn mɛːr] = *a mother*
un torchon [œ̃ tɔrʃɔ̃] = *a duster*   **une nappe** [yn nap] = *a tablecloth*

Note that **un**, **une** is also the word for *one*, the number, in French.

NUMBERS

In counting aloud	Before a consonant	Before a vowel or mute **h**	
un [œ̃], **une** [yn]			= *one*
deux [dø]		[døz] **deux heures**	= *two*
trois [trwa]		[trwaz] **trois ans**	= *three*
quatre [katr]			= *four*
cinq [sɛ̃ːk]	[sɛ̃]		= *five*
six [sis]	[si]	[siz] **six hommes**	= *six*
sept [sɛt]			= *seven*
huit [ɥit]	[ɥi]		= *eight*
neuf [nœf]	[nœ, nœf]	[nœv] **neuf enfants**	=: *nine*
dix [dis]	[di]	[diz] **dix éviers**	= *ten*

18

GRAMMAR

QUESTIONS

Subject-pronoun + verb statements are easily changed into questions by putting **est-ce que** [ɛs kə] in front. **Dire** [diːr] = *to say, tell,* **je dis** = *I say*:

est-ce que je dis? [ɛs kə ʒə di] = *do I say?* or *am I saying?*
est-ce que tu dis? [ɛs kə ty di] = *do you say?* or *are you saying?*
est-ce qu'il dit? [ɛs kil di] = *does he say?* or *is he saying?*
est-ce que nous disons? [ɛs kə nu dizɔ̃] = *do we say?* or *are we saying?*
est-ce que vous dites? [ɛs kə vu dit] = *do you say?* or *are you saying?*
est-ce qu'ils disent? [ɛs kil diz] = *do they say?* or *are they saying?* Note the -ent verb ending is never pronounced.

Note that (*a*) **que** becomes **qu'** before a vowel: **qu'il(s)** and **qu'elle(s)**; (*b*) the translation here shows that French does not make any distinction between something that is happening now and something that happens periodically, as we do in English, e.g. *I am walking, I walk.*

Questions can also be constructed by putting the verb in front of the subject: this is called inversion; it is usually avoided with **je**:

est-ce que je dis? = *do I say?*   **disons-nous?** [dizɔ̃ nu]
dis-tu? [di ty] = *do you say?* etc.   **dites-vous?** [dit vu]
dit-il? [ditil]   **disent-ils?** [diztil]

Note that when subject-pronouns come after the verb, they are always linked to it by means of a hyphen.

Questions can also be introduced by using interrogative words such as **quand** = *when* and **où** = *where.* Here is a list of French interrogatives:

quand [kɑ̃] = *when.* **Quand est-il sage?** *When is he good?*
pourquoi [purkwa] = *why.*
   Pourquoi sont-elles méchantes? *Why are they naughty?*
où [u] = *where.* **Où sont les parents?** *Where are the parents?*
qui [ki] = *who.* **Qui est jolie?** *Who is pretty?*
que, qu' [kə] = *what.* **Que dit le garçon?** *What does the boy say?*
qu'est-ce que [kɛskə] = *what.*
   Qu'est-ce que le garçon dit? *What does the boy say?*
quel, quelle [kɛl] = *what* or *which* (adjective).
   Quel enfant est sage? *Which child is good?*
combien de [kɔ̃bjɛ̃ də] = *how many, how much.*   [*home?*
   Combien de tapis avez-vous à la maison? *How many carpets have you at*
comment [kɔmɑ̃] = *how, in what way, what . . . like.*
   Comment dites-vous . . . ? *How do you say . . . ?*
quoi [kwa] = *what* (pronoun, after a preposition).
   À quoi est-il occupé? *With what is he occupied?*
Note carefully which of these words require inversion of verb and subject.

19

ANSWERING QUESTIONS

French often uses pronouns in answering questions, as English does. Practise answering with pronouns, as this helps you to learn genders:

Où est le garçon?   **Il est dans le salon.** *He is in the drawing-room.*
Où sont les parents?   **Ils sont dans le jardin.** *They are in the garden.*
Où est la mère?   **Elle est dans la cuisine.** *She is in the kitchen.*
Où sont les nappes?   **Elles sont dans la salle à manger.** . . . *dining-room.*

Note that if a pronoun stands for both masculine and feminine nouns, the masculine plural form is always used: **les parents—ils.**

VOCABULARY

voici [vwasi]   *here is, here are*
la partie [parti]   *part*
de [də]   *of*
la famille [famiːj]   *family*
c'est [sɛ]   *it is* (+ noun)
il y a [il ja]   *there is, there are*
plusieurs [plyzjœːr]   *several*
la pièce [pjɛs]   *room*

la cuisinière

la cuisine [kɥizin]   *kitchen*
le salon [salɔ̃]   *sitting-room*
la salle [sal]   *room*
la salle à manger [sal a mɑ̃ʒe]   *dining-room*
petit [pəti] (m.), **petite** [pətit] (f.)   *small, little*
dans [dɑ̃]   *in*

un évier

la cuisinière [kɥizinjɛːr]   *stove, woman cook*
un évier [evje]   *sink*
le placard [plakaːr]   *cupboard*
une étagère [etaʒɛːr]   *set of shelves*
grand [grɑ̃] (m.), **grande** [grɑ̃d] (f.)   *big, large*
la chaise [ʃɛːz]   *chair*
le plancher [plɑ̃ʃe]   *floor*
beau [bo] (m.), **belle** [bɛl] (f.)   *fine, beautiful*
le tapis [tapi]   *carpet*

la chaise

contre [kɔ̃ːtr]   *against*
le mur [myːr]   *wall*
le buffet [byfɛ]   *sideboard*
la cheminée [ʃ(ə)mine]   *fireplace, chimney*
le canapé [kanape]   *sofa, settee, couch*
le fauteuil [fotœːj]   *armchair*
la femme [fam]   *woman, wife*

le buffet

un or **une enfant** [ãfã]	*child* (m.) or (f.)
le garçon [garsɔ̃]	*boy, waiter*
la fille [fiːj]	*daughter*
la petite fille [pətit fiːj]	*girl*
très [trɛ]	*very*
joli (m.), **jolie** (f.) [ʒɔli]	*pretty*
mais [mɛ]	*but*
souvent [suvã]	*often*
méchant(e) [mɛʃã (m.), -ãt (f.)]	*naughty*
toujours [tuʒuːr]	*always*
sage [saːʒ]	*good, well-behaved*
le soir [swaːr]	*evening*
maman [mamã]	*mother, mummy*
papa [papa]	*father, daddy*
aussi [osi]	*also, as*
même [mɛːm]	*even*
quand [kã]	*when*
bon, bonne [bɔ̃ (m.), bɔn (f.)]	*good*
parce que [pars kə]	*because*
affreux, -euse [afrø (m.), -øːz (f.)]	*awful, horrible*
occupé(e) [ɔkype]	*busy*
le jardin [ʒardɛ̃]	*garden*
que, qu' [kə, k]	*that*
beaucoup de [boku də]	*much, many, a lot of*
le travail [travaːj]	*work*
pour [puːr]	*for*
le frère [frɛːr]	*brother*
ensemble [ãsãːbl]	*together*
voilà [vwala]	*there is, there are*
pauvre [poːvr]	*poor*
si [*si*]	*so, if*
la robe [rɔb]	*dress*
rouge [ruːʒ]	*red*
bleu(e) [blø]	*blue*
coquet, -ette [kɔkɛ (m.), -ɛt (f.)]	*pretty, attractive*
vert(e) [vɛːr (m.), vɛrt (f.)]	*green*
malgré [malgre]	*in spite of, despite*
sale [sal]	*dirty*
le visage [vizaʒ]	*face*
après [aprɛ]	*after*
content(e) [kɔ̃tã (m.), -ãt (f.)]	*pleased, happy*
à [a]	*to, at, on*

le canapé

le fauteuil

la femme

une enfant

le garçon

21

UNE CONVERSATION DANS LA CUISINE

Voici une partie d'une maison. C'est la maison de la famille Girard.
vwasi yn parti dyn mɛzɔ̃. sɛ la mɛzɔ̃ də la famiːj ʒiraːr.

Il y a plusieurs pièces: une cuisine, un salon, une salle à manger. La
il j a plyzœːr pjɛs: yn kɥizin, œ̃ salɔ̃, yn sal a mɑ̃ʒe. La

cuisine est petite: dans la cuisine il y a une cuisinière électrique,
kɥizin ɛ pətit: dɑ̃ la kɥizin il j a yn kɥizinjɛːr elɛktrik,

un évier, une petite table, un réfrigérateur, un placard et une étagère.
œ̃nevje, yn pətit tabl, œ̃ refriʒeratœːr, œ̃ plakaːr e yn etajɛːr.

La salle à manger est spacieuse: elle a une grande table et six chaises;
La sal a mɑ̃ʒe ɛ spasjøːz: ɛl a yn grɑ̃d tabl e si ʃɛːz;

sur le plancher il y a un beau tapis; contre le mur il y a un buffet. Le
syr lə plɑ̃ʃe il j a œ̃ bo tapi; kɔːtr lə myr il j a œ̃ byfɛ. Lə

salon est très grand: il a une belle cheminée, un canapé, et deux fauteuils.
salɔ̃ ɛ trɛ grɑ̃: il a yn bɛl ʃəmine, œ̃ kanape, e dø fotœːj.

Monsieur Girard a une femme et trois enfants (un garçon et deux
məsjø ʒiraːr a yn fam e trwazɑ̃fɑ̃ (œ̃ garsɔ̃ e dø

filles). Les deux petites filles sont très jolies, mais elles sont souvent
fiːj). Le dø pətit fiːj sɔ̃ trɛ ʒɔli, mɛz ɛl sɔ̃ suvɑ̃

méchantes. Est-ce que le petit garçon est toujours sage?
meʃɑ̃t. ɛs kə lə pəti garsɔ̃ ɛ tuʒuːr saːʒ?

22

UNE CONVERSATION DANS LA CUISINE

Un soir   voici la famille Girard   dans la cuisine.   Suzanne dit: "Tu es
œ̃ swaːr vwasi la famiːj ʒiraːr   dã la kɥizin.   syzan   di: "ty ɛ

méchante,   Josette."   Maman et papa disent: "Oui,   Josette est méchante
meʃãt,   ʒɔzɛt."   mamã e papa diz: "wi,   ʒɔzɛt ɛ meʃãt

et Suzanne est méchante aussi;   elles sont méchantes   même quand il y a   un
e syzan ɛ meʃãt osi;   ɛl sɔ̃ meʃãt   mɛːm kãtil j a   œ̃

bon programme   à la télévision."   Josette dit: "Je suis méchante   parce
bɔ̃ prɔgram   a la televizjɔ̃."   ʒɔzɛt di: "ʒə sɥi meʃãt   pars

que le programme   est affreux;   les programmes sont souvent affreux.
kə lə prɔgram   ɛtafrø;   le prɔgram sɔ̃ suvãtafrø.

Maman et papa,   êtes-vous sûrs   que Jacques est toujours sage,   même
mamã e papa,   ɛt vu syr   kə ʒɑːk ɛ tuʒuːr saːʒ,   mɛːm

quand vous êtes occupés   dans le jardin?"   Jacques dit: "Je suis très sage
kã   vuzɛtzokype   dã lə ʒardɛ̃?"   ʒɑːk di: "ʒə sɥi trɛ saːʒ

quand maman et papa sont absents."   Maman et papa disent: "Oui,   nous
kã   mamã e papa sɔ̃tapsã."   mamã e papa diz: "wi,   nu

sommes sûrs   qu'il est sage   quand nous avons   beaucoup de travail   dans
sɔm   syr   kil ɛ saːʒ   kã   nuzavɔ̃   boku də travaːj   dã

le jardin.   Dis-tu aussi,   Suzanne,   que Jacques est sage?   Les petites filles
lə ʒardɛ̃.   di ty osi,   syʒan,   kə ʒɑːk ɛ saːʒ?   le pətit fiːj

ont souvent beaucoup d'affection   pour un frère;   es-tu une exception?"
ɔ̃ suvã boku dafɛksjɔ̃   puːr œ̃ frɛːr;   ɛ ty yn eksɛpsjɔ̃?"

Suzanne et Josette disent ensemble: "Nous disons   qu'il est souvent
syzan e ʒɔzɛt diz ãsãːbl: "nu dizɔ̃ kil ɛ suvã

méchant   et que nous sommes souvent sages.   Voilà!"
meʃã   e kə nu sɔm   suvã saːʒ.   vwala!"

Les pauvres petites filles: Suzanne est si jolie   dans une petite robe rouge
le poːvr pətit fiːj: syzan ɛ si ʒɔli   dãzyn pətit rɔb ruːʒ

et bleue;   Josette est si coquette   dans un petit deux-pièces vert—   et
e blø;   ʒɔzɛt ɛ si kɔkɛt   dãzœ̃ pəti dø pjɛs vɛr—   e

Jacques est si sage,   malgré un visage sale.
ʒɑːk ɛ si saːʒ,   malgre œ̃ vizaːʒ sal.

Après la conversation   les parents et les enfants   sont contents.   Est-ce
aprɛ la kɔvɛrsasjɔ̃   le parã e lezãfã   sɔ̃ kɔ̃tã.   ɛs

que le programme à la télévision   est intéressant?
kə lə prɔgram a la televizjɔ̃   ɛtɛterɛsã?

(*Translation at the end of the book.*)

EXERCISES

I. Answer these questions when you have read the passage on pages 22-23:

1. Où est la petite table?
2. Où est le buffet?
3. Où est la famille Girard?
4. Où sont les petites filles?
5. Dans quelle pièce est la cheminée?
6. Quand sont‿elles méchantes, les‿enfants?
7. Qu'est-ce qu'il y a dans le salon?
8. Combien de fauteuils sont dans le salon?
9. Qui dit que Josette est méchante?
10. Qui dit que Suzanne est méchante aussi?
11. Que dit Jacques?
12. Suzanne est‿une exception; pourquoi?
13. Les parents et les‿enfants sont contents; après quoi?
14. Combien de petites filles y a-t-il? = *are there?*
15. Êtes-vous sage? Oui ou non? = *Yes or no?*
16. Où est le beau tapis?
17. Comment est la cheminée?
18. Comment sont les petites filles?
19. Comment est le salon?
20. Comment est Josette quand le programme est‿affreux?

II. Fill the gap with a suitable verb and then translate the sentences:

1. Est-ce que vous —— que le garçon est méchant?
2. ——-vous plusieurs placards dans la cuisine?
3. Suzanne et Jacques ne —— pas que Josette est sage.
4. Nous ne —— pas toujours contents.
5. Est-ce que les petites filles —— souvent méchantes?
6. —— -ils beaucoup de tapis dans la salle à manger?
7. —— -vous‿occupé dans le jardin?
8. Où —— l'évier et la cuisinière?
9. "Je ne —— pas très petite," dit Suzanne.
10. Il —— une chaise dans le salon.

III. Find in the story the French phrases which mean:

1. In spite of a dirty face.
2. A lot of work.
3. A fine fireplace.
4. Several rooms.
5. Even when there is.

  6. The Girard family's house.
  7. On the floor.
  8. A fine carpet.
  9. Yes, we are sure.
10. In a green two-piece.
11. But they are often naughty.
12. Because the programme is awful.
13. When we have a lot of work.
14. Are you an exception?
15. A good programme on television.

IV. Make a list of all the adjectives in the story; you will notice that French adjectives have more than one form. Write each adjective down with the word it describes and then explain why there are different forms. (Note that whereas in English an adjective comes before the word it describes, in French most adjectives follow the words they describe.)

V. Make a list of words in the passage that mean the same in French and in English. You will find that many French words are commonly used in English: build up a list of these as you come across them in the course of your general reading. Consider carefully how you recognise them as French—clues will be found in both spelling and pronunciation. Here are a few examples to begin with: **chalet, abattoir, fête, façade, communiqué.** What is the difference between a **fiancé** and a **fiancée**?

(Answers at the end of the book.)

Le fiancé et la fiancée.

25

LEÇON 2

LEARN BY HEART

1. **Comment vous appelez-vous?**   *What is your name?*
   kɔmɑ̃   vuzaple   vu?
   Je m'appelle Robert.   *My name is Robert.*
   ʒə   mapɛl   rɔbɛːr.
2. **Êtes-vous blond ou brun?**   *Are you fair or dark-haired?*
   ɛt   vu   blɔ̃   u   brœ̃?
   J'ai les cheveux châtains.   *I have brown [chestnut] hair.*
   ʒe   le   ʃəvø   ʃatɛ̃.
3. **Combien de frères avez-vous?**   *How many brothers have you?*
   kɔ̃bjɛ̃   də   frɛːr   ave   vu?
   J'en ai deux.   *I have two [of them].*   **Je n'en ai pas.**   *I haven't any.*
   ʒɑ̃ne   dø.   ʒə   nɑ̃ne   pɑ.
4. **Quel jour est-ce aujourd'hui?**   *What day is it today?*
   kɛl   ʒuːr   ɛs   oʒurdɥi?
   C'est aujourd'hui lundi.   *It is Monday today.*
   sɛtoʒurdɥi   lœ̃di.

GRAMMAR

THE PREPOSITION **à** = *to, at*

The French preposition **à** [a] = *to, at* is a rather special word because in certain cases it fuses with the definite article to produce a new word. This depends on the number and gender of the following noun:

au [o] *to the, at the* before a masculine singular noun beginning with a consonant.

à la [a la] *to the, at the* before a feminine singular noun beginning with a consonant.

à l' [a l] *to the, at the* before a singular noun beginning with a vowel or mute **h**.

aux [o] *to the, at the* before all plural nouns.

Here are examples with **donner** [dɔne] = *to give* (a first conjugation verb):

Je donne une chaise au garçon = *I give a chair to the boy.*

Tu donnes un fauteuil à la femme = *You give an armchair to the woman.*

Il donne un jouet à l'enfant = *He gives a toy to the child.*

Elle donne le canapé aux parents = *She gives the sofa to the parents.*

We often leave out *to* and say merely: *I give the boy a chair*, where *the boy* really means *to the boy*. French does not do this.

26

GRAMMAR

FIRST CONJUGATION VERBS

The majority of French verbs follow a basic pattern called the first conjugation. Common endings are added to the stem (the part of the verb which does not change). First conjugation verbs are recognized by the infinitive ending **-er**. (The infinitive means *to [do something]*; it cannot have a subject: **avoir** = *to have*, **être** = *to be*, **dire** = *to say*, **gronder** = *to scold*, **aider** = *to help*.)

Present tense of **danser** [dãse] = *to dance* (stem = **dans-**), first conjugation:

je danse [dãs] = *I dance, am dancing, [do dance*

tu danses [dãs] = *you dance*, etc.

il danse [dãs] = *he, she dances*

nous dansons [dãsɔ̃] = *we dance*

vous dansez [dãse] = *you dance*

ils dansent [dãs] = *they dance*

NEGATIVES

French verbs are made negative by putting **ne** [nə] before the verb and **pas** [pɑ] after it: **je suis content** = *I am pleased*, **je ne suis pas content** = *I am not pleased*.

Here is the present tense of **danser** in the negative:

je ne danse pas = *I do not dance*, etc.

tu ne danses pas

il ne danse pas

nous ne dansons pas

vous ne dansez pas

ils ne dansent pas

IRREGULAR VERBS

Present tense of:

prendre [prɑ̃:dr] = *to take*

je prends [prɑ̃]   **nous prenons** [prənɔ̃]

tu prends [prɑ̃]   **vous prenez** [prəne]

il prend [prɑ̃]   **ils prennent** [prɛn]

voir [vwɑːr] = *to see*

je vois [vwa]   **nous voyons** [vwajã]

tu vois [vwa]   **vous voyez** [vwaje]

il voit [vwa]   **ils voient** [vwa]

The negative is formed in the same way: **je ne prends pas** = *I do not take*.

ADJECTIVES—AGREEMENT

On page 25 we noted that adjectives in French have different forms. This is because they must agree in number and gender with the words they describe. Regular adjectives use the masculine singular form as the stem; they add **e** to form the feminine (unless the stem already ends in **e**), and they add **s** to the masculine or feminine to form the plurals. The various forms of irregular adjectives must be learnt separately. Here are the forms of a regular adjective, **petit** [pəti] = *small*, and an irregular one, **beau** [bo] = *fine*:

Masc. sing.   **un beau petit tapis** = *a fine small carpet.*

Fem. sing.   **une belle petite nappe** = *a fine small tablecloth.*

Masc. plur.   **deux beaux petits tapis** = *two fine small carpets.*

Fem. plur.   **deux belles petites nappes** = *two fine small tablecloths*

27

ADJECTIVES—POSITION

We also noted that most adjectives follow the word they describe, but some, including numerical adjectives (note the examples on page 27), come before the words they describe. Those describing proper names come before them and are preceded by the definite article: **le pauvre Jacques** = *poor Jacques*.

POSSESSION

The French do not use apostrophe s (*'s*) as we do to express possession; they always use **de** [də] = *of*: *Suzanne's toy* = **le jouet de Suzanne**.

THE PRONOUN **on**

Un, une = *one* (the number). But when *one* stands for an undefined person the French use the useful word **on** [ɔ̃]. This is a third person singular pronoun and takes the same form of the verb as **il** and **elle**, but it can translate several different English phrases:

    On dit que Jacques est sage = *One says, It is said, People say, They say,*
    —*that Jacques is good.*

LIAISON

Have you noticed this [‿]? In French a silent consonant at the end of a word is pronounced in certain cases if the next word begins with a vowel or mute **h**; the sound is then carried on to the next word. This is liaison: it is shown in this book by ‿. When the consonant is an **s** the sound carried over becomes **z**, when a **d**, the sound becomes **t**. Liaison occurs only where the sense runs on, not, for example, at a comma or full stop: **est‿il** [ɛtil] = *is he*, **les‿enfants** [lezɑ̃fɑ̃] = *the children*, **quand‿il** [kɑ̃til] = *when he.* . . .

VOCABULARY

premier, -ière [prəmje, -jɛːr]	*first*	
un‿étage [etɑːʒ]	*floor, storey*	
encore une fois [ɑ̃kɔːr yn fwa]	*once again*	
la chambre à coucher [ʃɑ̃ːbr a kuʃe]	*bedroom*	
la salle de bain [sal də bɛ̃]	*bathroom*	
le cabinet [kabinɛ]	*water-closet*	
la chambre de débarras [ʃɑ̃ːbr	*boxroom*	
də debarɑ]		**la table de**
		toilette
monter [mɔ̃te]	*to climb, go, come, up*	
un‿escalier [ɛskalje]	*staircase, stairs*	
le palier [palje]	*landing*	
la porte [pɔːrt]	*door*	
entrer [ɑ̃tre]	*to enter, go, come, in*	
le lit [li]	*bed*	
une armoire [armwaːr]	*wardrobe, cupboard*	**la commode**

28

en chêne [ɑ̃ ʃɛn]	*in, made of, oak*	
la table de toilette [tabl də twalɛt]	*dressing-table*	
la commode [kɔmɔd]	*chest of drawers*	
le jouet [ʒwɛ]	*toy*	
en bon ordre [ɑ̃ bɔnɔrdr]	*tidy*	
trop de [tro də]	*too much, too many*	**le jouet**
un illustré [illystre]	*comic paper*	
naturellement [natyrɛlmɑ̃]	*naturally*	
la baignoire [bɛɲwaːr]	*bath*	
le lavabo [lavabo]	*wash-basin*	
laver [lave]	*to wash*	
[dix] fois par jour [(di) fwa par ʒuːr]	*[ten] times a day*	
la poupée [pupe]	*doll*	
laisser [lɛse]	*to leave* (a thing)	**la baignoire**
tout(e) [tu, tut]	*everything, all*	
sous [su]	*under*	
comme [kɔm]	*like, as*	
le singe [sɛ̃ːʒ]	*monkey*	
avec [avɛk]	*with*	
la menace [mənas]	*threat*	
caché(e) [kaʃe]	*hidden*	
derrière [dɛrjɛːr]	*behind*	**le lavabo**
tout de suite [tutsɥit]	*immediately*	
chercher [ʃɛrʃe]	*to seek, look for*	
le petit [pəti]	*little one, little boy*	
trouver [truve]	*to find*	
gronder [grɔ̃de]	*to scold, shout at*	
crier [krie]	*to shout*	
fort(e) [fɔːr, fɔrt]	*loud, strong*	
jouer [ʒwe]	*to play*	**la poupée**
ou [u]	*or*	
fâché(e) [faʃe]	*angry*	
fouetter [fwɛte, fwəte]	*to spank, whip*	
le livre [livr]	*book*	
moi [mwa]	*I* (used apart from verb)	
intéressant(e) [ɛ̃terɛsɑ̃, -ɑ̃t]	*interesting*	
le roman [rɔmɑ̃]	*novel*	
retourner [rəturne]	*to return, go back*	**le singe**
travailler [travaje]	*to work*	

Note that the circumflex accent often shows where there was once an **s** present: **la forêt** (in Latin **forestis**) = *forest*.

29

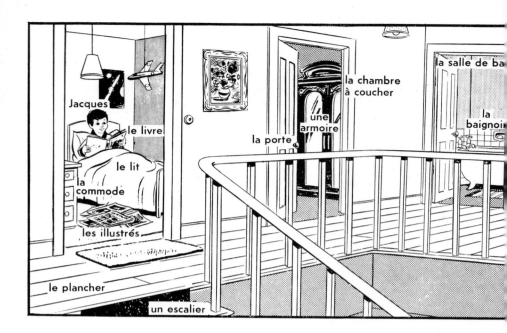

Figure labels: Jacques, le livre, le lit, la commode, les illustrés, le plancher, un escalier, la porte, la chambre à coucher, une armoire, la salle de ba[in], la baignoi[re]

SUR LE PALIER

Voici une autre partie de la maison de la famille Girard: c'est le
vwasi yn oːtr parti də la mɛzɔ̃ də la famiːj ʒiraːr: sɛ lə

premier étage. Il y a encore une fois plusieurs pièces: trois chambres
prəmjɛːretaːʒ. il j a ɑ̃koːr yn fwa plyzjœːr pjɛs: trwa ʃɑ̃br

à coucher, une salle de bain, un cabinet et une chambre de débarras. On
a kuʃe, yn sal də bɛ̃, œ̃ kabinɛ e yn ʃɑ̃br də debaʀa. ɔ̃

monte l'escalier et on arrive sur le palier où on voit six portes; on entre
mɔ̃t lɛskalje e ɔ̃nariv syr lə palje u ɔ̃ vwa si pɔrt; ɔ̃nɑ̃tr

dans la première chambre et on voit un grand lit, un beau tapis, une
dɑ̃ la prəmjɛːr ʃɑ̃br e ɔ̃ vwa œ̃ grɑ̃ li, œ̃ bo tapi, yn

armoire en chêne et une table de toilette. Dans la seconde chambre il y
armwaːr ɑ̃ ʃɛn e yn tabl də twalɛt. dɑ̃ la səgɔ̃ːd ʃɑ̃br il j

a deux petits lits pour les fillettes, une petite commode, une petite
a dø pəti li puːr le fijɛt, yn pətit kɔmɔd, yn pətit

armoire et beaucoup de jouets. On n'entre pas dans la chambre de
armwaːr e boku də ʒwɛ. ɔ̃ nɑ̃tr pa dɑ̃ la ʃɑ̃br də

Jacques parce qu'elle n'est pas en bon ordre: il y a trop de jouets et
ʒaːk pars kɛl nɛ pazɑ̃ bɔnɔrdr: il j a tro də ʒwɛ e

d'illustrés. Dans la salle de bain. il y a naturellement une baignoire et un
dillystre. dɑ̃ la sal də bɛ̃ il j a natyrɛlmɑ̃ yn bɛɲwaːr e œ̃

lavabo   où Madame lave   (dix fois par jour)   le visage sale de . . . qui?
lavabo   u madam laːv   (di fwa par ʒuːr)   lə vizaːʒ sal də . . . ki?

Une petite scène   dans la chambre de Suzanne et de Josette:
yn pətit sɛn   dã la ʃãbr də syzan e də ʒɔzɛt:

Josette: "Je ne vois pas la poupée!   Vois-tu la poupée, Suzanne?   C'est
ʒɔzɛt: "ʒə nə vwa pa la pupe!   vwa ty la pupe, syzan?   sɛ

Jacques   qui prend les jouets   et qui laisse tout   sous les illustrés."
ʒaːk   ki prã le ʒwɛ   e ki lɛs tu   su lezillystre."

Suzanne: "Oui, il est méchant comme un singe.   Il a beaucoup de
syzan: "wi. il ɛ meʃã kɔm œ̃ sɛ̃ːʒ. il a boku də

jouets   mais il n'est pas content   quand il n'est pas avec nous.   Il aime
ʒwɛ   mɛzil nɛ pɑ kɔ̃tã   kãtil nɛ pɑzavɛk nu.   il ɛm

jouer avec la poupée   malgré les menaces de maman. . . ."   (Jacques est
ʒwe avɛk la pupe   malgre le mənas də mamã. . . ."   (ʒaːk ɛ

caché derrière la porte   de la salle de bain.   Monsieur et Madame Girard
kaʃe dɛrjɛːr la pɔrt   də la sal də bɛ̃.   məsjø e madam ʒiraːr

montent l'escalier,   voient les deux petites filles   tout de suite et cherchent
mɔ̃t lɛskalje,   vwa le dø pətit fiːj   tutsyit e ʃɛrʃ

le petit.   Ils trouvent le pauvre Jacques,   ils grondent le pauvre garçon.)
lə pəti.   il truv lə poːvr ʒaːk,   il grɔ̃d lə poːvr garsɔ̃.)

Monsieur Girard: "Suzanne et Josette,   pourquoi criez-vous si fort?
məsjø ʒiraːr: "syzan e ʒɔzɛt,   purkwa krie vu si fɔːr?

Est-ce que Jacques est méchant?   Jacques, pourquoi joues-tu toujours avec
ɛs kə ʒaːk ɛ meʃã?   ʒaːk, purkwa ʒu ty tuʒuːr avɛk

les jouets   de Suzanne ou de Josette?   Je suis fâché et je fouette les petits
le ʒwɛ   də syzan u də ʒɔzɛt?   ʒə sɥi faʃe e ʒə fwɛt le pəti

garçons   qui ne sont pas sages.   Pourquoi ne prends-tu pas un livre?   Maman
garsɔ̃   ki nə sɔ̃ pɑ saːʒ.   purkwa nə prã ty pɑzœ̃ liːvr?   mamã

et moi,   nous prenons un livre intéressant   quand nous n'avons pas trop de
e mwa,   nu prənɔ̃zœ̃ liːvr ɛ̃teresã   kã nu navɔ̃ pɑ tro də

travail;   Josette et Suzanne prennent un livre aussi. . . ."   On donne un
travaːj;   ʒɔzɛt e syzan prɛntœ̃ liːvr osi. . . ."   ɔ̃ dɔn œ̃

grand livre au garçon,   deux beaux livres aux fillettes;   Madame Girard
grã liːvr o garsɔ̃,   dø bo liːvr o fijɛt;   madam ʒiraːr

prend un roman   et le pauvre papa retourne dans le jardin   où il travaille.
prãtœ̃ rɔmã   e lə poːvr papa rəturn dã lə ʒardɛ̃   u il travaːj.

(Translation at the end of the book.)

31

EXERCISES

I. **Répondez aux questions suivantes** (= *Reply to the following questions*):
1. **Où voit-on six portes?**
2. **Où voit-on un grand lit?**
3. **Où voit-on deux petits lits?**
4. **Que voit-on dans la chambre de Jacques?**
5. **Pourquoi n'entre-t-on pas dans la chambre?**
6. **Quel visage est-ce que Mme Girard lave?**
7. **Comment crient-elles, les petites filles?**
8. **Est-ce que Josette cherche une chaise?**
9. **Pourquoi est-elle fâchée?**
10. **Combien de poupées y a-t-il dans la chambre?**
11. **Qui est méchant comme un singe?**
12. **Qui aime jouer avec la poupée?**
13. **Est-ce que Jacques travaille dans le jardin?**
14. **Où est-il caché?**
15. **Qui monte l'escalier?**
16. **Que dit M. Girard?**
17. **Quels garçons est-ce qu'il fouette?**
18. **Quand est-ce que les parents prennent un livre?**
19. **Qu'est-ce qu'on donne à Jacques?**
20. **M. Girard travaille: où?**

II. Translate the questions in Exercise I into good, natural English.

III. Translate into French:
1. I give a book to the boy.
2. I give two large books to the children.
3. We give the girls a little book.
4. We give the beautiful toys to the children.
5. We give the red doll to a good girl.

IV. Write down these sentences putting each adjective in its correct form:
1. **Les (beau) poupées sont sur le lit de Suzette.**
2. **Les tapis (bleu) ne sont pas dans le salon.**
3. **Les petites filles ne sont pas toujours (méchant).**
4. **Suzanne et Josette sont (content).**
5. **M. et Mme Girard ne sont pas souvent (fâché).**
6. **Il y a une chaise (blanc) dans la cuisine.**
7. **La (petit) Suzette crie très fort.**
8. **Il trouve les livres (intéressant).**

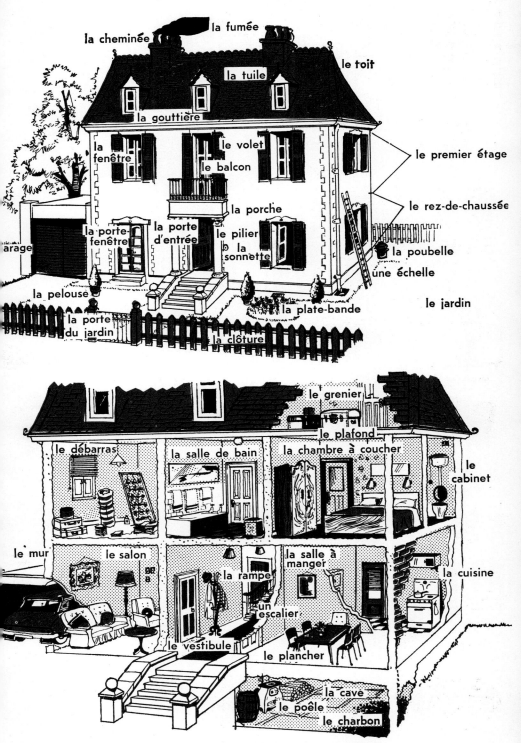

la cheminée · la fumée · le toit · la tuile · la gouttière · le volet · le premier étage · la fenêtre · le balcon · la porche · le rez-de-chaussée · la porte-fenêtre · la porte d'entrée · le pilier · la sonnette · arage · la poubelle · une échelle · la pelouse · la plate-bande · le jardin · la porte du jardin · la clôture

le grenier · le plafond · le débarras · la salle de bain · la chambre à coucher · le cabinet · le mur · le salon · la salle à manger · la cuisine · la rampe · un escalier · le vestibule · le plancher · la cave · le poêle · le charbon

L'EXTÉRIEUR ET L'INTÉRIEUR D'UNE MAISON

une armoire

le fauteuil

le matelas

le secréta

le berceau

le foyer

un oreiller

la table

la bibliothèque

le garde-manger

la pendule

la table
à
ouvrage

le buffet

le garde-robe

le piano

la glace

le porte-
manteau

le tableau

le tabou

le canapé

la prise
de
courant

le tapis

la cheminée

le lampadaire

le radiateur
électrique

le téléphone

la coiffeuse

la lampe

la lampe de bureau

la radio

le télévise

la commode

la couverture

le lit

le drap

le réveil

le tiroir

le coussin

le divan

la machine à coudre

le rideau

un électrophone

VOICI LES MEUBLES QUI SONT DANS LA MAISON

9. Les (beau) tapis sont dans la (grand) chambre.
10. La table, la chaise et le lit ne sont pas très (grand).

V. Insert the appropriate form of the verb and complete each sentence with an expression from the text:

1. Monsieur et Madame Girard (travailler) ——.
2. Nous ne (dire) pas que ——.
3. Les garçons (laisser) tout ——.
4. Ils (prendre) un livre quand ils n'(avoir) pas ——.
5. (Être)-vous toujours occupé ——?
6. (Gronder)-vous souvent les ——?
7. Ils (voir) les chaises ——.
8. Nous (monter) —— et nous (arriver) sur le ——.
9. On (voir) que la baignoire est dans ——.
10. Que (prendre)-tu quand tu n'(avoir) pas trop ——?

VI. Study the picture below and complete the sentences with appropriate prepositions chosen from this list: **à, contre, derrière, avec, sur, de, sous, dans, malgré**.

1. Le garçon est —— la porte.
2. Le livre est —— la table.
3. La poupée est —— la table.
4. Les vêtements sont —— l'armoire.
5. La poupée —— Josette est dans la chambre —— Jacques.
6. Jacques est méchant —— les menaces de Mme Girard.
7. M. Girard n'est pas —— Jacques.
8. La baignoire n'est pas —— la chambre.
9. Qu'est-ce qui est —— le plancher?
10. L'armoire est —— le mur.

(*Answers at the end of the book.*)

LEÇON 3

LEARN BY HEART

1. **Quelle est la date aujourd'hui?**   *What is the date today?*
   kɛl   ɛ la dat   oʒurdɥi?
   C'est aujourd'hui le six mai.   *It is the sixth of May today?*
   sɛtoʒurdɥi   lə sis mɛ.
2. **Que regardez-vous?**   *What are you looking at?*
   kə   rəgarde vu?
   Je regarde le ciel gris.   *I am looking at the grey sky.*
   ʒə rəgard lə sjɛl gri.
3. **Êtes-vous Anglais?**   *Are you an Englishman?*
   ɛt   vu   ɑ̃glɛ?
   Oui, je suis Anglais.   *Yes, I am an Englishman.*
   wi, ʒə sɥizɑ̃glɛ.
4. **Quel âge a votre frère?**   *How old is your brother?*
   kɛl   ɑːʒ a vɔtr frɛːr?
   Il a dix-sept ans.   *He is seventeen years old.*
   il a   disɛt   ɑ̃.

GRAMMAR

NUMBERS—CARDINALS

11	**onze** [ɔ̃ːz]	18	**dix-huit** [dizɥit]	25	**vingt-cinq** [vɛ̃tsɛ̃k]
12	**douze** [duːz]	19	**dix-neuf** [diznœf]	26	**vingt-six** [vɛ̃tsis]
13	**treize** [trɛːz]	20	**vingt** [vɛ̃]	27	**vingt-sept** [vɛ̃tsɛt]
14	**quatorze** [katɔrz]	21	**vingt et un** [vɛ̃te œ̃]	28	**vingt-huit** [vɛ̃tɥit]
15	**quinze** [kɛ̃ːz]	22	**vingt-deux** [vɛ̃tdø]	29	**vingt-neuf** [vɛ̃tnœf]
16	**seize** [sɛːz]	23	**vingt-trois** [vɛ̃ttrwa]	30	**trente** [trɑ̃t]
17	**dix-sept** [disɛt]	24	**vingt-quatre** [vɛ̃tkatr]	31	**trente et un** [trɑ̃t e œ̃]

Note that hyphens are used where there is no **et**; French has only three -*teen* (ten) numbers: **dix-sept, dix-huit, dix-neuf**.

TELLING THE TIME

Once you know these numbers you can tell the time in French. Learn the phrases on the opposite page and note where liaison occurs. Literally, the French **Il est . . . heures** = *It is . . . hours.* **Il est** never changes.

36

Il est six heures   **Il est six heures**   **Il est six heures**   **Il est six heures**
                  cinq   **dix**   **et quart**

Il est sept heures
moins cinq

Il est une heure [yn œːr]
Il est deux heures [døzœːr]
Il est trois heures [trwɑzœːr]
Il est quatre heures [katr œːr]
Il est cinq heures [sɛ̃kœːr]
Il est six heures [sizœːr]
Il est sept heures [sɛt œːr]
Il est huit heures [ɥitœːr]
Il est neuf heures [nœvœːr]
Il est dix heures [dizœːr]
Il est onze heures [ɔ̃z œːr]
    It is twelve o'clock is always:
Il est midi [midi] = *It is noon,*
or **Il est minuit** [minɥi] = *It is*
midnight.

Il est six heures
vingt

Il est sept heures
moins dix

Il est six heures
vingt-cinq

Il est sept heures   **Il est sept heures**   **Il est sept heures**   **Il est six heures**
   moins le quart   **moins vingt**   **moins vingt-cinq**   **et demie**

   Note that **midi** and **minuit** are masculine, hence: **Il est midi et demi,** etc.

IRREGULAR VERBS

aller [ale] = *to go*   **venir** [vəniːr] = *to come*   **faire** [fɛːr] = *to do, make*
je vais [vɛ] = *I go*, etc.   **je viens** [vjɛ̃] = *I come*, etc.   **je fais** [fɛ] = *I do*, etc.
tu vas [va]   **tu viens** [vjɛ̃]   **tu fais** [fɛ]
il va [va]   **il vient** [vjɛ̃]   **il fait** [fɛ]
nous allons [alɔ̃]   **nous venons** [vənɔ̃]   **nous faisons** [fəzɔ̃]
vous allez [ale]   **vous venez** [vəne]   **vous faites** [fɛt]
ils vont [vɔ̃]   **ils viennent** [vjɛn]   **ils font** [fɔ̃]

   Note that the stems of **aller** and **venir** are regular with **nous** and **vous.**

THE PREPOSITION **de** = *of, from, some*

De [də], like **à**, fuses in some cases with the definite article. It becomes **du** [dy] before masculine singular nouns beginning with a consonant, **des** [de] before plural nouns. It has two entirely different meanings:

of the: **La porte du salon est blanche** = *The door of the sitting-room is white.*
La robe de la femme est verte = *The woman's dress is green.*
Le jouet de l'enfant est petit = *The child's toy is small.*
Les livres des enfants sont cachés = *The children's books are hidden.*

some: **Josette a du pain [de la confiture]** = *Josette has some bread [some jam].*
Suzanne a de l'eau [des œufs] = *Suzanne has some water [some eggs].*

Note that (*a*) the singular refers to an amount of something, the plural to a number of objects; (*b*) these sentences refer to real possession, but if the sentence is negative and denies the possession of something, **de** is used on its own without the definite article:

Josette n'a pas de pain [de confiture] = *Josette hasn't any bread [any jam].*
Suzanne n'a pas d'eau [d'œufs] = *Suzanne has no water [no eggs].*

Note carefully other uses and meanings of **de** as you read this book.

VOCABULARY

devant [dəvã]	*in front of*	
cultiver [kyltive]	*to grow*	
la pomme de terre [pɔm də tɛːr]	*potato*	
le chou [ʃu]	*cabbage*	
la carotte [karɔt]	*carrot*	
le navet [navɛ]	*turnip*	**la carotte**
les épinards (m.) [epinaːr]	*spinach*	
près de [prɛ də]	*near [to]*	
le légume [legym]	*vegetable*	
la pelouse [pəluːz]	*lawn*	
le pommier [pɔmje]	*apple-tree*	
loin de [lwɛ̃ də]	*far from*	
autour de [otuːr də]	*around*	
la palissade [palisad]	*fence*	**le navet**
le bois [bwɑ]	*wood*	
ainsi [ɛ̃si]	*thus, in this way*	
le voisin [vwazɛ̃]	*neighbour*	
le chien [ʃjɛ̃]	*dog*	
le voisinage [vwazinaːʒ]	*neighbourhood*	
entre [ɑ̃ːtr]	*between*	
le potager [pɔtaʒe]	*kitchen-garden*	**le chien**

le sentier [sãtje]	*path*	
étroit(e) [etrwa, -wat]	*narrow*	
le bout [bu]	*end*	
le tas [tɑ]	*heap, pile*	
l'herbe (f.) [ɛrb]	*grass*	
la feuille [fœːj]	*leaf*	**la feuille**
mort(e) [mɔːr, mɔrt]	*dead*	
une après-midi [aprɛmidi]	*afternoon*	
un été [ete]	*summer*	
quitter [kite]	*to leave*	
le ballon [balɔ̃]	*ball, football, balloon*	
moi [mwa]	*me, I*	**la grimace**
le bord [bɔːr]	*edge*	
lancer [lãse]	*to throw*	
cadet, -ette [kadɛ, -ɛt]	*younger, junior*	
faire la grimace [fɛːr la grimas]	*to pull a face*	
un, une adversaire [advɛrsɛːr]	*opponent*	
cependant [səpãdã]	*however*	
le fond [fɔ̃]	*bottom, far end*	**la querelle**
maintenant [mɛ̃t(ə)nã]	*now*	
prêt(e) [prɛ, prɛt]	*ready*	
le jeu [ʒø]	*game*	
continuer [kɔ̃tinɥe]	*to continue*	
quelque [kɛlkə]	*some, a few*	
sans [sã]	*without*	
la querelle [kərɛl]	*quarrel, dispute*	
bientôt [bjɛ̃to]	*soon*	**la couture**
demander [dəmãde]	*to ask for*	
le doute [dut]	*doubt*	
la couture [kutyːr]	*dressmaking, needlework*	
avant [avã]	*before*	
le goûter [gute]	*afternoon tea*	
vrai(e) [vrɛ]	*true, real*	
le temps [tã]	*weather, time*	
mauvais(e) [mɔvɛ, -ɛz]	*bad*	**la couturière**
détester [detɛste]	*to hate*	
ne . . . rien [nə . . . rjɛ̃]	*nothing, not anything*	
le fil [fil]	*cotton, thread*	
la joue [ʒu]	*cheek*	
la jambe [ʒãb]	*leg*	
la couturière [kutyrjɛːr]	*dressmaker*	
déchiré(e) [deʃire]	*torn*	**la robe déchirée**

39

la palissade de bois

le potager

le ballon

les légumes

le bord de
la pelouse

le sentier

le pommier

la jambe

l'herbe
verte

DANS LE JARDIN

Derrière la maison   de la famille Girard   il y a un beau jardin: dans le
dɛrjɛːr la mɛzɔ̃   də la famiːj ʒiraːr   il j a œ̃ bo ʒardɛ̃:   dɑ̃ lə

jardin   Monsieur Girard cultive des pommes de terre,   des choux,   des
ʒardɛ̃   məsjø   ʒiraːr kyltiv de   pɔm də tɛːr,   de ʃu,   de

carottes,   des navets   et des épinards.   Les enfants ne jouent pas   près des
karɔt,   de navɛ   e dezepinaːr.   lezɑ̃fɑ̃   nə ʒu pɑ prɛ de

légumes,   ils jouent sur la pelouse   près du pommier,   mais naturellement
legym,   il ʒu   syr la pəluːz   prɛ dy pɔmje   mɛ   natyrɛlmɑ̃

loin de la fenêtre.   Autour du jardin   il y a   une palissade de bois: ainsi
lwɛ̃ də la fənɛːtr.   otuːr dy ʒardɛ̃   il j a   yn palisad də bwa: ɛ̃si

les enfants ne vont pas   dans les jardins des voisins   et les chiens du voisinage
lezɑ̃fɑ̃   nə vɔ̃ pɑ   dɑ̃ le ʒardɛ̃ de vwazɛ̃   e le ʃjɛ̃ dy vwazinaːʒ

ne viennent pas   dans le jardin des Girard.   Entre la pelouse et le potager
nə vjɛn pɑ   dɑ̃ le ʒardɛ̃ de ʒiraːr.   ɑ̃ːtr la pəluːz e lə pɔtaʒe

il y a   un sentier étroit;   au bout,   un tas d'herbe   et de feuilles mortes.
il j a   œ̃ sɑ̃tje etrwa;   o bu,   œ̃ tɑ dɛrb   e də fœːj mɔrt.

Une belle après-midi d'été,   les enfants quittent la maison   et vont dans le
yn bɛl aprɛmidi dete,   lezɑ̃fɑ̃   kit la mɛzɔ̃   e vɔ̃ dɑ̃ lə

jardin   pour jouer avec un ballon   sur la pelouse.   Josette dit: "Jacques,
ʒardɛ̃   puːr ʒwe avɛk œ̃ balɔ̃   syr la pəluːz.   ʒɔsɛt di: "ʒɑːk,

40

viens avec moi! Suzanne, va au bord de la pelouse. Nous‿allons lancer
vjɛ̃ avɛk mwa! syzan, va o bɔːr də la pəluːz. nuzalɔ̃ lɑ̃se

le ballon à Suzanne," dit-elle à Jacques. La sœur cadette du petit garçon
lə balɔ̃ a syzan," ditɛl a ʒɑːk. la sœːr kadɛt dy pəti garsɔ̃

est fâchée; elle fait la grimace parce qu'elle a deux‿adversaires. Cependant
ɛ faʃe; ɛl fɛ la grimas pars kɛl a døzadvɛrsɛːr. səpɑ̃dɑ̃

elle va au fond du jardin et dit: "Jacques et Josette, lancez maintenant
ɛl va o fɔ̃ dy ʒardɛ̃ e di: "ʒɑːk e ʒɔzɛt, lɑ̃se mɛ̃tnɑ̃

le ballon, je suis prête."
lə balɔ̃, ʒə sɥi prɛt."

Le petit jeu continue quelques minutes sans querelles, mais bientôt
lə pəti ʒø kɔ̃tiny kɛlkə minyt sɑ̃ kərɛl, mɛ bjɛ̃to

Suzanne est fatiguée. "Quelle heure est-il?" demande-t-elle. "Il est
syzan ɛ fatige. "kɛl œːr ɛtil?" dəmɑ̃dətɛl. "il ɛ

deux‿heures et demie," dit Josette. "Il est trois‿heures moins le quart,"
døzœːr e dəmi," di ʒɔzɛt. "il ɛ trwazœːr mwɛ̃ lə kaːr."

dit Jacques. Une querelle va sans doute commencer — mais Madame
di ʒɑːk. yn kərɛl va sɑ̃ dut kɔmɑ̃se — mɛ madam

Girard vient dans le jardin; elle dit: "Il est trois‿heures cinq." "Si
ʒiraːr vjɛ̃ dɑ̃ lə ʒardɛ̃; ɛl di: "il ɛ trwazœːr sɛ̃k." "si

tard!" crie Suzanne. "Généralement je fais de la couture avant le goûter."
taːr!" kri syzan. "ʒenɛralmɑ̃ ʒə fɛ də la kutyːr avɑ̃ lə gute."

"Ce n'est pas vrai," dit Josette, "nous faisons de la couture quand le
"sə nɛ pɑ vrɛ," di ʒɔzɛt. "nu fəzɔ̃ də la kutyːr kɑ̃ lə

temps est mauvais. Si tu détestes le jeu, Jacques et moi, nous‿allons
tɑ̃ ɛ mɔvɛ. si ty detɛst lə ʒø, ʒɑːk e mwa, nuzalɔ̃

jouer ensemble. Vas-tu travailler dans la maison?" Suzanne ne dit rien,
ʒwe ɑ̃sɑ̃bl. va ty travaje dɑ̃ la mɛzɔ̃?" syzan nə di rjɛ̃,

elle va avec sa mère dans le salon pour chercher du fil.
ɛl va avɛk sa mɛːr dɑ̃ lə salɔ̃ puːr ʃerʃe dy fil.

À trois‿heures et quart Josette et Jacques aussi sont fatigués: les joues
a trwaʒœːr e kaːr ʒɔzɛt e ʒɑːk osi sɔ̃ fatige: le ʒu̧

de la petite fille sont rouges, les jambes du petit garçon sont sales; et
də la pətit fiːj sɔ̃ ruːʒ, le ʒɑ̃b dy pəti garsɔ̃ sɔ̃ sal; e

(voici le secret) la robe de la petite couturière est déchirée.
(vwasi lə səkrɛ) la rɔb də la pətit kutyrjɛːr ɛ deʃire.

(Translation at the end of the book.)

EXERCISES

I. Write down the French for these times:

1. It is ten past three; at ten past three.
2. It is a quarter to eleven; at a quarter to eleven.
3. It is half-past nine; at half-past nine.
4. It is twenty minutes to twelve; at twenty minutes to twelve.
5. It is a quarter past eight; at a quarter past eight.
6. Between two o'clock and four o'clock.
7. Soon after half-past twelve.
8. Before twenty-five to eleven.
9. It is not five minutes to twelve.
10. It is not thirteen minutes past two.

II. Write down the French for these phrases:

1. Some thread; some wood; some work; some bread.
2. Some needlework; some jam.
3. Some grass; some water.
4. Some vegetables; some leaves; some dogs; some balls.
5. Suzanne hasn't any cotton.
6. Mme Girard hasn't any vegetables.
7. At the bottom of the garden; the boy's toys.
8. At the edge of the lawn; the little girl's dress.
9. The children's toys; the leaves of the vegetables.
10. Some leaves, some wood and some grass.

III. **Répondez aux questions suivantes:**

1. **Comment est le jardin de la famille Girard?**
2. **Comment est le sentier?**
3. **Comment sont les feuilles au bout du sentier?**
4. **Comment sont les joues de la petite fille?**
5. **Comment est la robe de la petite couturière?**
6. **Où sont les légumes de M. Girard?**
7. **Où est le jardin de M. Girard?**
8. **Où est le sentier étroit?**
9. **Où est le fil de la petite Suzanne?**
10. **Où êtes-vous maintenant?**
11. **Qu'est-ce que M. Girard cultive?**
12. **Qu'est-ce que les enfants quittent?**
13. **Qu'est-ce que Josette et Jacques lancent à Suzanne?**
14. **Qu'est-ce que les deux sœurs font quand il fait mauvais?**
15. **Qu'est-ce que la sœur cadette cherche dans le salon?**

16. **Qui cultive les légumes?**
17. **Qui est la sœur cadette?**
18. **Qui est le frère de Josette?**
19. **Qui est la mère du garçon?**
20. **Qui est la petite couturière?**

IV. Complete the gaps in this little story by inserting appropriate times:

Les enfants vont dans le jardin avant ——; ils jouent sur la pelouse entre —— et ——. Mme Girard va dans le potager à —— et regarde les enfants. À —— elle quitte le potager et va sur la pelouse; elle joue avec les enfants. Mais à —— M. Girard retourne à la maison. Mme Girard quitte le jardin cinq minutes après, à ——. À —— le goûter est prêt. La famille regarde la télévision entre —— et ——.

V. Find in the story the French phrases which mean:
1. Some cabbages, some turnips and some spinach.
2. Near to the apple-tree . . . far from the window.
3. The dogs of the neighbourhood do not come into the Girards' garden.
4. A fine afternoon in summer.
5. The little boy's younger sister is angry.
6. The little dressmaker's dress is torn.
7. She pulls a face because she has two opponents.

VI. **Quelle heure est-il?**

1.   2.   3.   4.

5.   6.   7.   8.

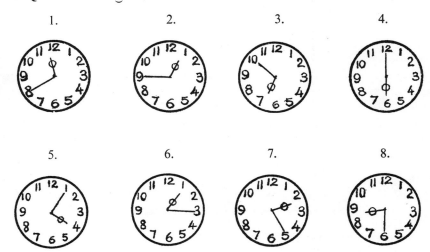

(*Answers at the end of the book.*)

43

LEÇON 4

LEARN BY HEART

1. **À quelle heure vous levez-vous?** *What time do you get up?*
   a kɛl œːr vu ləve vu?
   Je me lève à sept heures et demie. *I get up at half-past seven.*
   ʒə mə lɛːv a sɛtœːr e dəmi.

2. **Avec quoi vous essuyez-vous les mains?** *With what do you wipe your hands?*
   avɛk kwa vuzɛsɥije   vu le mɛ̃?
   Je m'essuie les mains avec une serviette. *I wipe my hands with a towel.*
   ʒə mɛsɥi le mɛ̃ avɛk yn sɛrvjɛt.

3. **Prenez-vous le petit déjeuner en haut?** *Do you have breakfast upstairs?*
   prəne vu lə pəti dejœne ɑ̃ o?
   Non, je le prends dans la salle à manger. *No, I have it in the dining-room.*
   nɔ̃, ʒə lə prɑ̃ dɑ̃ la sal a mɑ̃ʒe.

4. **À quelle heure quittez-vous la maison le matin?** *At what time do you leave*
   a kɛl œːr kite vu la mɛzɔ̃ lə matɛ̃?   *[home in the morning?*
   Je la quitte à neuf heures moins vingt-cinq. *I leave [it] at twenty-five to nine.*
   ʒə la kit a nœvœːr mwɛ̃ vɛ̃tsɛ̃k.

GRAMMAR

PREPOSITIONS
Prepositions in French are very easy to learn because, as in English, they never change their form (with the exception of **à** and **de**). They are used in front of nouns (and verb infinitives), and the simpler ones reveal the position of something: **dans** [dɑ̃] = *in*. **Les légumes sont dans le potager** = *The vegetables are in the kitchen-garden.* Make a list of the prepositions in the preceding vocabulary and complete this list as you read on.

WORDS FOR COLOURS
The words for colours (when used adjectivally) always come after the nouns they describe: **un chien noir**=*a black dog*; **une robe noire**=*a black dress.*

POSSESSIVE ADJECTIVES
The words for *my, your, his, her, its, our, their* (possessive adjectives which are followed by nouns), must be studied carefully.

44

my = **mon** before a masculine singular noun: **mon chien** = *my dog.*

  = **ma** before a feminine singular noun beginning with a consonant: **ma joue** = *my cheek.*

  = **mon** before a feminine singular noun beginning with a vowel or mute **h**: **mon armoire** = *my wardrobe.*

  = **mes** before all plural nouns: **mes livres** = *my books.*

your = **ton, ta, ton, tes,** used like **mon, ma, mon, mes** when you are talking to one person whom you know very well (see p. 18): **Cherches-tu ton père et ta mère?** = *Are you looking for your father and your mother?* (Do not mix up **vous** and **ton, ta** or **tes** in the same sentence.)

You should realise from these examples that it is the noun following the words for *my* and *your* which requires a particular form of these two words: the expression **ma pelouse** reveals that the word **pelouse** is feminine, but not whether the possessor is male or female.

his, her, its = **son, sa, son, ses,** used like **mon, ton,** etc., but note:

son ballon = *his ball, her ball* or *its ball.*

sa chaise = *his chair, her chair* or *its chair.*

ses jouets = *his toys, her toys* or *its toys.*

The identity of the possessor must be quite evident from the story or conversation, otherwise a proper name would have to be used: e.g. **son jardin** = *his* or *her garden,* but we may say instead: **le jardin de M. Girard** or **le jardin de Mme Girard,** if this is necessary to avoid ambiguity.

Note that (*a*) although the word **ses** is plural it only refers to one possessor; (*b*) **son, sa, son, ses** also translate *one's* in a sentence such as *One must not neglect one's garden* = . . . **son jardin.**

our = **notre** before all singular nouns: **notre voisin** = *our neighbour.*

  = **nos** before all plural nouns: **nos voisins** = *our neighbours.*

your (plural or when addressing someone formally) = **votre** before all singular nouns: **votre potager** = *your kitchen-garden.*

  = **vos** before all plural nouns: **vos légumes** = *your vegetables.*

their = **leur** before all singular nouns: **leur maison** = *their house.*

  = **leurs** before all plural nouns: **leurs maisons** = *their houses.*

Note that (*a*) although the word **leur** is sometimes singular in form, sometimes plural **leurs,** it always refers to more than one possessor (contrast **son, sa, ses**); (*b*) **leur** does not require **e** for the feminine.

These possessive adjectives mean real possession to French people. You will realise the importance of this when you see some expressions in French concerning parts of the body: you do not possess a hand in the same sense as you possess a toy or a dress or a pen; the hand is part of you. French people say: **Il lève la main**=*He raises the hand.* **Il secoue la tête**=*He shakes the head.*

IRREGULAR VERBS

Present tense of:

lire = *to read*		**mettre** = *to put*	
je lis [li]	**nous lisons** [lizɔ̃]	**je mets** [mɛ]	**nous mettons** [mɛtɔ̃]
tu lis [li]	**vous lisez** [lize]	**tu mets** [mɛ]	**vous mettez** [mɛte]
il lit [li]	**ils lisent** [liz]	**il met** [mɛ]	**ils mettent** [mɛt]

SECOND CONJUGATION VERBS

The verb **finir** = *to finish* is a common example of the second regular verb pattern which is followed by most verbs whose infinitive ends in **-ir**.

Present tense:	**je finis** [fini]	**nous finissons** [finisɔ̃]
	tu finis [fini]	**vous finissez** [finise]
	il finit [fini]	**ils finissent** [finis]

INVERTED FORM IN QUESTIONS

Est-ce que je finis mon travail?	**Finissons-nous notre travail?**
Finis-tu ton travail?	**Finissez-vous votre travail?**
Finit-il son travail?	**Finissent-ils leur travail?**

Note that regular verbs of the **danser** pattern reveal one complication in the inverted form; this is found in the third person singular, where the letter **t** is introduced to make the construction (i.e. the group of words) easier to say. So **il danse** becomes **danse-t-il?** [dɑ̃sətil], and **elle danse** becomes **danse-t-elle?** Note also that **il va** becomes **va-t-il?**

In the inversion of the third person plural (**ils donnent**) no extra **t** is required; instead there is a liaison and the letter **t** of the otherwise silent **-ent** ending is pronounced: **donnent-ils?** [dɔntil].

VOCABULARY

le membre [mɑ̃:br]	member, limb	
assis(e) [asi, asiz]	seated, sitting	
le repas [rəpɑ]	meal	
manger [mɑ̃ʒe]	to eat	
une heure [œ:r]	hour, time	
le déjeuner [deʒœne]	lunch	**une tranche**
vers [vɛ:r]	towards	**de pain**
affamé(e) [afame]	very hungry, famished	
la baguette [bagɛt]	long loaf	
le pain [pɛ̃]	bread	
la tranche [trɑ̃:ʃ]	slice	
le pot [po]	jar	
la confiture [kɔ̃fity:r]	jam	
le beurre [bœ:r]	butter	**une tablette**
la tablette [tablɛt]	bar, block	**de chocolat**

une tranche de pain

une tablette de chocolat

46

le chocolat [ʃɔkɔla]	*chocolate*	
la pomme [pɔm]	*apple*	
la tasse [tas]	*cup*	
la soucoupe [sukup]	*saucer*	
le sucre [sykr]	*sugar*	
la théière [tejɛːr]	*teapot*	**une pomme**
le thé [te]	*tea*	
devenir [dəv(ə)niːr]	*to become*	
vite [vit]	*quickly*	
froid(e) [frwa, frwad]	*cold*	
cela [s(ə)la]	*that*	
ôter [ote]	*to take off, away*	
le soulier [sulje]	*shoe*	**une tasse**
la pantoufle [pɑ̃tufl]	*slipper*	
répliquer [replike]	*to reply, answer*	
pour changer [puːr ʃɑ̃ʒe]	*for a change*	
le mari [mari]	*husband*	
le lait [lɛ]	*milk*	
distrait(e) [distrɛ, distrɛt]	*absent-minded*	
aujourd'hui [oʒurdɥi]	*today*	**une soucoupe**
tard [taːr]	*late*	
la bouteille [butɛːj]	*bottle*	
expliquer [ɛksplike]	*to explain*	
le pot à crème [pɔta crɛm]	*cream-jug*	
cassé(e) [kase]	*broken*	
hélas [elaːs]	*alas*	
car [kaːr]	*for (giving reason)*	**une théière**
le quotidien [kɔtidjɛ̃]	*daily paper*	
verser [vɛrse]	*to pour, spill*	
le pantalon [pɑ̃talɔ̃]	*trousers*	
la colère [kɔlɛːr]	*anger*	
le journal [ʒurnal]	*newspaper*	
au lieu de [o ljø də]	*instead of*	
la porte-fenêtre [pɔrtfənɛːtr]	*French-window*	**un soulier**
debout [dəbu]	*standing*	
aimer [ɛme]	*to like, love*	
mieux [mjø]	*better*	
la citronnade [sitrɔnad]	*lemonade*	
tacher, la tache [taʃe, taʃ]	*to stain, the stain*	
renverser [rɑ̃vɛrse]	*to knock over, spill*	
emporter [ɑ̃pɔrte]	*to carry, take, away*	**une bouteille**
le roman policier [rɔmɑ̃ pɔlisje]	*detective novel*	**de lait**

47

la cheminée
la porte-fenêtre
le journal
la confiture
le sucre
le lait
le beurre
la baguette
le tapis

LE GOÛTER DANS LE SALON

La famille Girard est dans le salon: **il est quatre heures et demie** et chaque
la famiːj ʒiraːr ɛ dã lə salɔ̃: il ɛ katr œːr e dəmi e ʃak

membre de la famille prend son goûter. Ils ne sont pas assis à la table parce
mãbr də la famiːj prã sɔ̃ gute. il nə sɔ̃ pazasi a la tabl pars

que le goûter n'est pas un repas important; ils mangent beaucoup à l'heure
kə lə gute nɛ pazœ̃ rəpa ɛ̃pɔrtã; il mãʒ boku a lœːr

du déjeuner, vers midi ou midi et demi, et aussi vers sept heures — même
dy deʒœne, vɛːr midi u midi e dəmi, e osi vɛːr sɛtœːr — mɛːm

les enfants ne sont pas souvent affamés quatre heures après leur déjeuner. Sur
lezãfã nə sɔ̃ pa suvã afame katr œːr aprɛ lœr deʒœne. syr

la table il y a une baguette de pain, des tranches de pain, un pot de confiture,
la tabl il j a yn bagɛt də pɛ̃, de trãʃ də pɛ, œ̃ po də kɔ̃fityr,

du beurre, deux tablettes de chocolat, des pommes, six tasses sur des
dy bœːr, dø tablɛt də ʃɔkɔla, de pɔm, si tas syr de

soucoupes, du sucre et une théière. Il n'y a rien sur la théière: le thé
sukup, dy sykr e yn tejɛːr. il nj a rjɛ̃ syr la tejɛːr: lə te

devient très vite froid, mais cela n'a pas d'importance quand le temps est chaud.
dəvjɛ̃ trɛ vit frwa, mɛ s(ə)la na pa dɛ̃pɔrtãs kã lə tã ɛ ʃo.

Monsieur Girard ôte ses souliers, met ses pantoufles et demande: "Où
məsjø ʒiraːr ot se sulje, mɛ se pãtufl e dəmãd: "u

est mon café?" "Il n'y a pas de café," réplique sa femme, "nous_allons
ɛ mɔ̃ kafe?" "il nj a pɑ də kafe," replik sa fam, "nuzalɔ̃

prendre du thé pour changer." (Elle donne une tasse de thé à son mari.)
prɑ̃dr dy te puːr ʃɑ̃ʒe." (ɛl dɔn yn tas də te a sɔ̃ mari.)

"Où est le lait?" demande-t-il. "Oh, je suis distraite aujourd'hui," dit
"u ɛ lə lɛ?" dəmɑ̃dətil. "o, ʒə sɥi distrɛt ojurdɥi," di

Madame Girard. "Jacques, va chercher le lait dans la cuisine!" . . . Une
madam ʒiraːr. "ʒɑːk, va ʃɛrʃe lə lɛ dɑ̃ la kɥizin!" . . . yn

minute plus tard Jacques arrive avec une bouteille de lait et explique que
minyt ply taːr ʒɑːk ariv avɛk yn butɛːj də lɛ e ɛksplik kə

le pot_à crème est cassé. Il donne la bouteille à son père. Hélas, Monsieur
lə pɔta krɛm ɛ kase. il dɔn la butɛːj a sɔ̃ pɛːr. elaːs, məsjø

Girard aussi est distrait, car il lit le quotidien: il renverse du lait sur son
ʒiraːr osi ɛ distrɛ, kaːril li lə kɔtidjɛ̃: il rɑ̃vɛrs dy lɛ syr sɔ̃

pantalon. Malgré sa colère il ne dit rien; il met la bouteille sur la table,
pɑ̃talɔ̃. malgre sa kɔlɛːr il nə di rjɛ; il mɛ la butɛːj syr la tabl,

prend_une serviette et finit l'article qu'il lit dans son journal.
prɑ̃tyn sɛrvjɛt e fini lartikl kil li dɑ̃ sɔ̃ ʒurnal.

Madame Girard gronde ses_enfants parce qu'ils lisent leurs_illustrés au
madam ʒiraːr grɔ̃d sezɑ̃fɑ̃ pars kil liz lœrzillystre o

lieu de manger: Jacques est_assis sur le tapis et sa tasse est sur le plancher,
ljø də mɑ̃ʒe: ʒɑːk ɛtasi syr lə tapi e sa tas ɛ syr lə plɑ̃ʃe,

Josette est_assise sur une chaise près de la porte-fenêtre. Suzanne est debout
ʒɔzɛt ɛtasiz syr yn ʃɛːz prɛ də la pɔrtfənɛːtr. syzan ɛ dəbu

près de la cheminée et loin de la table parce qu'elle n'aime pas le thé et ne
prɛ də la ʃəmine e lwɛ̃ də la tabl pars kɛl nɛm pa lə te e nə

prend pas sa tasse. Elle dit_à sa mère: "J'aime mieux la citronnade. Le
prɑ̃ pa sa tas. ɛl dita sa mɛːr: "ʒɛm mjø la sitrɔnad. lə

thé tache mes robes si je renverse ma tasse."
te taʃ me rɔb si ʒə rɑ̃vɛrs ma tas."

Malgré tout ils finissent leur goûter avant cinq_heures: les_enfants
malgre tu il finis lœr gute avɑ̃ sɛ̃kœːr: lezɑ̃fɑ̃

emportent leurs tasses. "Lavez vos tasses," crie Madame Girard. "Votre
ɑ̃pɔrt lœr tas. "lave vo tas," kri madam ʒiraːr. "vɔtr

papa est fatigué et moi, je lis mon roman policier."
papa ɛ fatige e mwa, ʒə li mɔ̃ rɔmɑ̃ pɔlisje."

(Translation at the end of the book.)

49

EXERCISES

I. Translate the following expressions (check what you write by finding the correct expressions in the story on the previous pages):

1. his (afternoon) tea
2. their lunch
3. his shoes
4. my coffee
5. her husband
6. his cup
7. her cup
8. my dresses
9. your father
10. her mother
11. his father
12. his trousers
13. his anger
14. her children
15. their comic-papers
16. my cup
17. their tea
18. your cups
19. their cups
20. my novel

II. Read the story on the previous pages — then insert suitable prepositions in place of the lines and translate this passage:

Jacques joue dans le jardin —— deux heures et quatre heures —— ses sœurs. —— les menaces de leur mère ils mangent des pommes. —— quatre heures dix, Mme Girard vient —— le potager —— chercher des épinards. Elle voit Jacques —— du pommier. Le petit garçon mange une pomme —— remarquer sa mère. Elle gronde Jacques, mais —— être pénitent le méchant garçon dit que ses sœurs sont —— la maison et qu'elles aussi mangent des pommes. Cinq minutes plus tard Mme Girard trouve Suzanne et Josette —— la porte —— la salle à manger: mais maintenant elles ne mangent pas de pommes, elles mangent la tablette —— chocolat —— Jacques.

III. **Punir** (= *to punish*) is a verb which follows the second regular pattern. Translate:

1. Do they punish their children?
2. You punish your children.
3. Is he punishing his children?
4. We punish our children.
5. I do not always punish my children.
6. Suzanne and Josette punish Jacques.

IV. **Répondez aux questions suivantes** (use pronouns wherever possible):

1. **Est-ce que M. Girard est dans le salon quand il lit le journal?**
2. **Est-ce que Jacques trouve le pot à crème?**
3. **Est-ce que Mme Girard donne une tasse de thé à son mari?**
4. **Où est la famille à quatre heures et demie?**
5. **Où sont les tranches de pain?**
6. **Où est Suzanne quand elle dit: "J'aime mieux la citronnade."**
7. **Qu'est-ce que M. Girard ôte?**
8. **Que met-il?**

le chapeau melon
les lunettes
le mouchoir
le gilet
la poche
le veston
complet
le pantalon
la chaussure
la chaussette

le col
la cravate
la chemise

une écharpe
la botte
la casquette
la pantoufle

le pardessus
le parapluie

le pullover
les bretelles

le pyjama

la robe de chambre

le chapeau de paille
le gant
le ruban
la manche
le bouton
la veste
le tailleur
la jupe

la boucle
la ceinture

le manteau

le sac à main

la robe

un imperméable
le maillot de bain

le chandail

le foulard

le bas

le tablier
la chemise de nuit
la sandale
le soulier

MONSIEUR ET MADAME PORTENT CES VÊTEMENTS

DANS LA POCHE DE MONSIEUR GIRARD

le briquet

une boîte d'allumettes

le permis de conduire

un billet de bar

le canif

la clef

la carte d'abonnement

le mouc

la pipe

la photo[graphie]

le porte-fe

la pièce de monnaie

le tabac

DANS LE SAC À MAIN DE MADAME GIRARD

le rouge à lèvre

la brosse à cheveux

le billet aller et retour

le poud

le carnet de chèques

la pilule

les ciseaux

le flacon de parf

une épingle

le miroir

le peigne

le bonbon

le collier de perles

le porte-monna

LE CONTENU DE LA POCHE DE MONSIEUR ET DU SAC À MAIN DE MADAME

9. Qu'est-ce que Jacques va chercher dans la cuisine?
10. Qu'explique-t-il quand il revient?
11. Qu'est-ce que M. Girard lit?
12. Que renverse-t-il sur son pantalon?
13. Qu'est-ce que M. Girard met sur la table?
14. Que prend-il?
15. Qu'est-ce que les enfants finissent avant cinq heures?
16. Qu'emportent-ils?
17. Qui arrive avec une bouteille de lait?
18. Qui est assise sur une chaise près de la porte-fenêtre?
19. Qui est fatigué?
20. Qui lit un roman policier au lieu de laver les tasses?

V. Write down the French for the following phrases (you will find them in the passage on pages 48 and 49):
1. At dinner-time; towards midday; half-past twelve.
2. Even the children are not often very hungry.
3. Some slices of bread, a jar of jam and some butter.
4. There is nothing on the tea-pot, the tea very quickly becomes cold.
5. There isn't any coffee — we are going to have tea for a change.
6. In spite of his anger, he does not say anything.
7. He finishes the article that he is reading in his paper.
8. Suzanne is standing near to the fire-place and far from the table.
9. Tea stains my dresses if I knock my cup over.
10. In spite of everything, they finish their tea before five o'clock.

VI. In the following sentences change the person mentioned to **je** and rewrite what follows to make perfect sense (as though you yourself were speaking).
1. M. Girard ôte ses souliers et met ses pantoufles.
2. M. Girard finit l'article qu'il lit et prend sa serviette.
3. Jacques est assis sur le tapis et sa tasse est sur le plancher.
4. Suzanne est debout parce qu'elle n'aime pas son thé.
5. Josette est assise sur sa chaise près de son père.

(*Answers at the end of the book.*)

M. Girard ôte ses souliers.   **M. Girard met ses pantoufles.**

LEÇON 5

LEARN BY HEART

1. **Allez-vous en ville par le train, en auto ou à bicyclette?**   *Do you go to*
   ale   vu   ɑ̃   vil   par lə   trɛ̃,   ɑ̃noto   u   a   bisiklɛt?   [*town by train,*
   car or bicycle?
   J'y vais d'habitude en autobus.   *I go there generally by bus.*
   ʒi   ve   dabityd   ɑ̃notɔbyːs.

2. **Combien y a-t-il d'ici à la gare?**   *How far is it from here to the station?*
   kɔ̃bjɛ̃   i   atil   disi   a la   gaːr?
   Il y a à peu près trois kilomètres.   *It is about three kilometres.*
   il   j a a   pø   prɛ   trwɑ   kilɔmɛtr.

3. **Combien de francs faut-il donner au receveur?**   *How many francs is it*
   kɔ̃bjɛ̃   də   frɑ̃   fotil   dɔne   o   rəsəvœːr?   [*necessary to give to*
   the conductor?
   Il faut lui en donner deux.   *One must give [to] him two [of them].*
   il   fo   lɥi   ɑ̃   dɔne   dø.

4. **Descendez-vous de l'autobus au terminus?**   *Do you get off the bus at the*
   dɛsɑ̃de   vu   də lotɔbyːs   o   tɛrminyːs?   [*terminus?*
   Non, j'en descends près de la bibliothèque.   *No, I get off it near the*
   nɔ̃,   ʒɑ̃   dɛsɑ̃   prɛ   də la   bibliɔtɛk.   [*library.*

GRAMMAR

COMMANDS

When you give a direct command in English you use the verb alone without a pronoun before it. French does the same, using the second person singular or plural, without **tu** or **vous**: **Prenez vos tasses!** = *Take your cups!*

(Note that the second person singular is, as always, used only when addressing a close friend, relative, child or animal.)

This general rule is broken in a few irregular verbs and in verbs of the first conjugation (**danser**) which omit the -s from the second person singular:

Donne une tasse à maman, Jacques! = *Give a cup to Mother, Jacques!*
Mes enfants, jouez sur la pelouse! = *Children, play on the lawn!*
Josette, va dans le jardin! = *Josette, go into the garden!*
"Jacques, finis ton goûter!" dit son père = *"Jacques, finish your tea!" says*
his father.

GRAMMAR

QUESTIONS

In some questions in English the noun which is the subject is placed after the verb, e.g. *Is the boy naughty?* In French this cannot be translated word for word. Either **est-ce que** must be used, or the inversion must be kept (to show that it is a question) by introducing a pronoun in addition to the subject. The pronoun to be used is the one which would normally replace the subject, e.g. **il** with a masculine singular subject:

Le garçon est-il méchant? = *Is the boy naughty?*
Sa mère est-elle fatiguée? = *Is his mother tired?*
Ses enfants jouent-ils dans le salon? = *Are his children playing in the sitting-room?*

French does not say *What colour is . . . ?* as English does, but **De quelle couleur est . . . ?** Note that **quelle** is always feminine to agree with **couleur**:

De quelle couleur est ton chien? = *What colour is your dog?*
De quelle couleur sont tes pantoufles? = *What colour are your slippers?*

DEMONSTRATIVE ADJECTIVES

When you are referring to some particular person(s) or thing(s) you often find that you need an introductory expression clearer than *a* or *the*. The words *that, this, those, these* are used in such cases. Basically *this* (singular) and *these* (plural) refer to objects that are near the speaker, *that* (singular) and *those* (plural) to objects that are at a distance from him. The French words, however, do not make this distinction:

ce [sə] = *this, that* before a masculine singular noun beginning with a consonant.
cet [sɛt] = *this, that* before a masculine singular noun beginning with a vowel or mute **h**.
cette [sɛt] = *this, that* before a feminine singular noun.
ces [se] = *these, those* before all plural nouns.

The meaning of these words is usually made more precise by the context or by a gesture: if you say **Prenez cette tasse** = *Take this [that] cup*, you will probably point to the cup in question.

It is very simple however to make a direct contrast between two objects when you want to; place a hyphen and **ci** [si] (short for **ici** = *here*) after the noun to mean *this* or *these*, a hyphen and **là** [la] (= *there*) to mean *that* or *those*:

ce journal-ci = *this newspaper*
cet hôtel-ci = *this hotel*
cette soucoupe-ci = *this saucer*
ces souliers-ci = *these shoes*

ce journal-là = *that newspaper*
cet hôtel-là = *that hotel*
cette soucoupe-là = *that saucer*
ces souliers-là = *those shoes*

55

USES OF THE INFINITIVE

The infinitive, which is the form of the verb given in the vocabulary lists, is most commonly used after another verb: **Il va travailler dans le jardin** = *He is going to work in the garden.* Here are five common irregular verbs which take the infinitive after them:

devoir [dəvwaːr] = *to have to*

je dois [dwa]	**nous devons** [dəvɔ̃]
tu dois [dwa]	**vous devez** [dəve]
il doit [dwa]	**ils doivent** [dwav]

pouvoir [puvwaːr = *to be able to*

je peux [pø]	**nous pouvons** [puvɔ̃]
tu peux [pø]	**vous pouvez** [puve]
il peut [pø]	**ils peuvent** [pœːv]

vouloir [vulwaːr] = *to wish, want to*

je veux [vø]	**nous voulons** [vulɔ̃]
tu veux [vø]	**vous voulez** [vule]
il veut [vø]	**ils veulent** [vœl]

savoir [savwaːr] = *to know [how to]*

je sais [sɛ]	**nous savons** [savɔ̃]
tu sais [sɛ]	**vous savez** [save]
il sait [sɛ]	**ils savent** [sav]

falloir [falwaːr] = *to be necessary to* (this verb is always used impersonally
il faut [fo] = *it is necessary to*   in the third person singular)
Je dois travailler ce soir = *I have to [must] work this evening.*
Elle peut aider sa mère = *She can help her mother.*
Nous voulons déjeuner à midi = *We want to have lunch at midday.*
Tu sais lire = *You can [know how to] read* but **Tu connais Jacques (Paris).**
Il faut cultiver notre jardin = *It is necessary to tend our garden.*

Note that (*a*) **devoir** also translates *must*, **pouvoir** *can* and *may*, which have no infinitive form in English; (*b*) **savoir** = *to know* (a fact) or *to know how to do* something that has been learnt, **connaître** [kɔnɛːtr] = *to know, be acquainted with* a person or place:

je connais [kɔnɛ]	**nous connaissons** [kɔnɛsɔ̃] (this is another commonly
tu connais [kɔnɛ]	**vous connaissez** [kɔnɛse] used irregular verb)
il connaît [kɔnɛ]	**ils connaissent** [kɔnɛs]

VOCABULARY

blanc, blanche [blɑ̃, blɑ̃ʃ]	*white*	⎫
noir(e) [nwaːr]	*black*	
rouge [ruːʒ]	*red*	
bleu(e) [blø]	*blue*	⎬ colour adjectives
jaune [ʒoːn]	*yellow*	
vert(e) [vɛːr, vɛːrt]	*green*	
brun(e) [brœ̃, bryn]	*brown*	⎭
le soir [swaːr]	*[in the] evening*	
rester [rɛste]	*to stay, remain*	

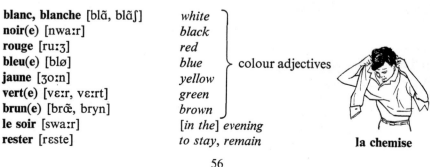

la chemise

56

généralement [ʒeneralmã]	*generally, usually*	
garder [garde]	*to keep [on]*	
les vêtements (m.) [vɛtmã]	*clothes*	
porter [pɔrte]	*to wear, carry*	
pendant [pãdã]	*during*	
la journée [ʒurne]	*day [time]*	
la chemise [ʃmiːz]	*shirt*	
la cravate [kravat]	*tie*	**la cravate**
le chandail [ʃãdaːj]	*sweater*	
la laine [lɛn]	*wool*	
la paire [pɛːr]	*pair*	
la chaussette [ʃosɛt]	*sock*	
le fils [fis]	*son*	
encore [ãkɔːr]	*yet, still, again*	
la culotte [kulɔt]	*trousers, shorts*	
court(e) [kuːr, kurt]	*short*	
à hauts talons [a o talɔ̃]	*high-heeled*	**la laine**
vêtu(e) [vɛty]	*dressed*	
en désordre [ã dezɔrdr]	*untidy*	
tandis que [tãdi(s) kə]	*whilst*	
la coiffure [kwafyːr]	*hair-do, hair-style*	
soigné(e) [swaɲe]	*neat, trim*	
imiter [imite]	*to imitate, copy*	
le, la mannequin [mankɛ̃]	*model, mannequin*	
déjà [deʒa]	*already*	
en bas [ã bɑ]	*downstairs*	**la coiffure**
jusqu'à [ʒyska]	*until, up to, as far as*	
sévèrement [sevɛːrmã]	*sternly*	
chéri(e) [ʃeri]	*dear, darling*	
la carte [kart]	*card, map*	
le bureau [byro]	*writing-desk, office*	
le jeu de cartes [ʒø də kart]	*pack of cards*	
compter [kɔ̃te]	*to count*	
cinquante [sɛ̃kãːt]	*fifty*	**le bureau**
la voix [vwa]	*voice*	
moqueur, -euse [mɔkœːr, -øːz]	*mocking*	
parler [parle]	*to speak*	
trente [trãt]	*thirty*	
Zut! [zyt]	*Oh bother!*	
en haut [ã o]	*upstairs*	
entamer [ãtame]	*start [a conversation]*	
Eh bien! [e bjɛ̃]	*Well!*	**le jeu de cartes**

UNE SOIRÉE AVEC DES VISITEURS

Le soir, après le goûter, les Girard restent généralement à la maison;
lə swaːr, aprɛ lə gute, le ʒiraːr rɛst ʒeneralmã a la mɛzɔ̃;

ils gardent les vêtements qu'ils portent pendant la journée. Quels vêtements
il gard le vɛtmã kil pɔrt pãdã la ʒurne. kɛl vɛtmã

portent-ils? Regardez Monsieur Girard: il porte une chemise blanche,
pɔrtətil? rəgarde məsjø ʒiraːr: il pɔrt yn ʃmiːz blãʃ,

une cravate bleue, un chandail de laine, un pantalon, une paire de
yn kravat blø, ɛ̃ ʃãdaːj də lɛn, ɛ̃ pãtalɔ̃, yn pɛːr də

chaussettes et des souliers noirs ou des pantoufles rouges. Son fils ne
ʃosɛt e de sulje nwaːr u de pãtufl ruːʒ. sɔ̃ fis nə

porte pas‿encore de pantalon, il aime mieux une culotte courte. Madame
pɔrt pɑzãkɔr də pãtalɔ̃, il ɛm mjø yn kylɔt kurt. madam

Girard, comme ses filles, porte une jolie robe verte, blanche, ou jaune
ʒiraːr, kɔm se fiːj, pɔrt yn ʒoli rɔb vɛrt, blãʃ, u ʒoːn

et une paire de souliers à hauts talons. Ils sont bien vêtus — mais les
e yn pɛːr də sulje a o talɔ̃. il sɔ̃ bjɛ̃ vɛty — mɛ le

cheveux du petit Jacques sont‿en désordre, tandis que ses sœurs ont‿une
ʃəvø dy pəti ʒɑːk sɔ̃tã dezɔrdr, tãdis kə se sœːr ɔ̃tyn

coiffure soignée. Elles‿imitent déjà les mannequins.
kwafyr swaɲe. ɛlzimit deʒa le mankɛ̃.

58

Cependant, un soir les parents veulent jouer au bridge; ils invitent des
səpɑ̃dɑ̃, œ̃ swaːr le parɑ̃ vœl ʒwe o bridʒ; ilzɛ̃vit de

voisins, Monsieur et Madame Larivière. Les enfants doivent aller au lit
vwazɛ̃, məsjø e madam larivjɛːr. lezɑ̃fɑ̃ dwavtale o li

à sept heures et quart malgré leurs objections. ("Pourquoi devons-
a sɛtœːr e kaːr malgre lœːrzɔbʒɛksjɔ̃. ("purkwa dəvɔ̃

nous aller au lit maintenant? Pouvons-nous rester en bas jusqu'à
nuzale o li mɛ̃tnɑ̃? puvɔ̃ nu rɛste ɑ̃ bɑ ʒuska

huit heures? Nous sommes toujours sages quand il y a des visiteurs!")
ɥitœːr? nu sɔm tuʒuːr saːʒ kɑ̃til j a de vizitœːr!")

Ces objections finissent quand leur papa dit sévèrement: "Allez au lit
sezɔbʒɛksjɔ̃ finis kɑ̃ lœr papa di sevɛːrmɑ̃: "ale o li

maintenant. Vous savez que vous pouvez lire vos livres et vos illustrés."
mɛ̃tnɑ̃. vu save kə vu puve liːr vo livr e vozillystre."

À sept heures et demie dans le salon: "Prenez cette chaise, Monsieur,"
a sɛtœːr e dəmi dɑ̃ lə salɔ̃: "prəne sɛt ʃɛːz, məsjø,"

dit Monsieur Girard. "Madame peut prendre ce fauteuil, près de la fenêtre.
di məsjø ʒiraːr. "madam pø prɑ̃dr sə fotœːj, prɛ də la fənɛːtr.

Maintenant, chérie," dit-il à sa femme, "il faut trouver les cartes!
mɛ̃tnɑ̃, ʃeri," ditil a sa fam, "il fo truve le kart!

Sont-elles dans le bureau?" "Oui, je peux trouver les jeux de cartes sans
sɔ̃tɛl dɑ̃ lə byro?" "wi, ʒə pø truve le ʒø də kart sɑ̃

difficulté," dit-elle. Cinq minutes plus tard elle retourne et dit: "Il
difikylte," ditɛl. sɛ̃ minyt ply taːr ɛl rəturn e di: "il

faut compter ces cartes, je ne veux pas jouer avec cinquante cartes. Un,
fo kɔ̃te se kart, ʒə nə vø pɑ ʒwe avɛk sɛ̃kɑ̃ːt kart. œ̃,

deux, trois. . . ." "Sais-tu compter jusqu'à cinquante?" demande-t-il
dø, trwa. . . . ." "sɛ ty kɔ̃te ʒuska sɛ̃kɑ̃ːt?" dəmɑ̃dətil

d'une voix moqueuse. "Tu ne dois pas parler quand je compte. Zut!
dyn vwa məkøːz. "ty nə dwa pɑ · parle kɑ̃ ʒə kɔ̃t. zyt!

Cette carte est sale. Chéri, cherche ce jeu de cartes que nous laissons
sɛt kart ɛ sal. ʃeri, ʃɛrʃ sə ʒø də kart kə nu lɛsɔ̃

en haut; elles sont propres." Il va en haut, et sa femme entame une
ɑ̃ o; ɛl sɔ̃ prɔpr." il va ɑ̃ o, e sa fam ɑ̃tam yn

conversation: "Connaissez-vous Madame Lucas? Eh bien, elle connaît. . . ."
kɔ̃vɛrsasjɔ̃: "cɔnɛse vu madam lyka? e bjɛ̃, ɛl kɔnɛ. . . ."

(Translation at the end of the book.)

LEÇON 5

EXERCISES

I. Write down the French for the following:
1. This evening; that sweater; this pack of cards; that writing-desk.
2. This wool; that pair; this voice; that hair-do.
3. These clothes; those socks; these shirts; those ties.
4. This staircase; that staircase; these trousers; that map.
5. That garden; these flowers; this apple-tree; that cupboard.
6. They must; I can; he wishes; he is acquainted with.
7. I know how to; we must; they want to; he must.
8. I must; they know how to; we are acquainted with; you wish.
9. Can he? Do you want to? Is it necessary? Must he?
10. Do we know? Does he want to? Do you know how to? Can they?

II. Fill in with a suitable colour-word in its correct form, and translate:
1. **Le lait est ——.**
2. **L'herbe est ——.**
3. **Le ciel est ——.**
4. **Le chocolat est ——.**
5. **Ma tasse est ——.**
6. **Une carotte n'est pas ——.**
7. **Un chou n'est pas ——.**
8. **Mon chien n'est pas ——.**
9. **La porte de notre salon n'est pas ——.**
10. **Ma cravate n'est pas ——.**

III. Answer these questions (to avoid repetition use pronouns):
1. **De quelle couleur est le lait?**
2. **De quelle couleur est l'herbe?**
3. **De quelle couleur est le ciel?**
4. **De quelle couleur est le chocolat?**
5. **De quelle couleur est votre chemise?**
6. **Les carottes sont-elles noires?**
7. **Un chou est-il bleu?**
8. **Votre chien est-il noir?**
9. **La porte de votre salon est-elle blanche?**
10. **Votre cravate est-elle verte?**

IV. Translate these sentences into French (you can find the correct French for them in the story on the previous two pages):
1. He goes upstairs.
2. Can you count?
3. You can read.
4. Can we stay downstairs?
5. The parents want to play.
6. I can find the packs of cards.
7. It is necessary to count these cards.
8. You must not speak.
9. I do not wish to play.
10. Do you know Mrs. Lucas?

V. **Répondez aux questions suivantes** (use pronouns whenever possible):
1. **Est-ce qu'ils sont soignés, les cheveux de Jacques?**
2. **Où les Girard restent-ils généralement, le soir?**
3. **Où Mme Girard laisse-t-elle un jeu de cartes?**
4. **Qu'est-ce que M. Girard porte?**
5. **Qu'est-ce que les enfants doivent faire à sept heures et quart?**

6. Que disent les enfants à sept heures et quart?
7. Qui porte une chemise blanche?
8. Qui doit aller au lit à sept heures et quart?
9. De quelle couleur sont les robes des sœurs?
10. De quelle couleur sont vos pantoufles?

VI. Complete these paragraphs by inserting suitable adjectives or colour-words; **ce, cet, cette** or **ces**; or a verb. Translate what you have written:

1. **Dans notre salle à manger il y a un grand tapis ——; —— tapis est très beau. Les enfants jouent sur —— beau tapis quand ils ne —— pas jouer dans le jardin.**
2. **Dans notre jardin il y a une —— pelouse ——; —— pelouse est très belle quand l'herbe est ——. Les enfants jouent sur —— belle pelouse, mais ils ne —— pas jouer dans le potager.**
3. **Dans notre potager il y a beaucoup de —— légumes ——; papa cultive —— légumes, quand il n'est pas trop ——! Il dit que nous ne —— pas jouer près de —— légumes. Oui, il ne —— pas faire cela, parce que les légumes qu'on cultive dans les —— potagers sont très ——.**

VII. Give the appropriate command from this list at each point necessary to guide the car to its garage. Try not to let the driver get lost.

Arrêtez! = *Stop!*
Allez tout droit! = *Go straight ahead!*
Tournez à gauche! = *Turn left!*
Tournez à droite! = *Turn right!*
Attention! = *Be careful!*
Attention aux piétons! = *Careful — pedestrians!*
Prenez le premier tournant à gauche! = *Take the first turning to the left!*
Prenez le premier tournant à droite! = *Take the first turning to the right!*

(*Answers at the end of the book.*)

LEÇON 6

LEARN BY HEART

1. **Avez-vous très faim et très soif?** *Are you very hungry and thirsty?*
ave vu trɛ fɛ̃ e trɛ swaf?
Oui, je voudrais bien aller dans ce restaurant. *Yes, I should very much*
wi, ʒə vudrɛ bjɛnale dɑ̃ sə rɛstɔrɑ̃. *[like to go into that*
restaurant.
2. **Ne préférez-vous pas une table sur la terrasse?** *Do you not prefer a table*
nə prefere vu pɑzyn tabl syr la tɛras? *[on the pavement?*
Non, il fait un peu trop froid. *No, it is a little too cold.*
nɔ̃, il fɛtœ̃ pø tro frwa.
3. **Allez-vous commander un bon vin rouge?** *Are you going to order a good*
ale vu kɔmɑ̃de œ̃ bɔ̃ vɛ̃ ruːʒ? *[red wine?*
Oui, je vais consulter le sommelier. *Yes, I am going to consult the wine-*
wi, ʒə vɛ kɔ̃sylte lə sɔməlje. *[waiter.*
4. **Avez-vous bien mangé?** *Have you eaten well?*
ave vu bjɛ̃ mɑ̃ʒe?
Oui, j'ai très bien mangé, et vous? *Yes, I have eaten very well, how*
wi, ʒe trɛ bjɛ̃ mɑ̃ʒe, e vu? *[about you?*

GRAMMAR

THIRD CONJUGATION VERBS

The infinitives of third conjugation verbs end in **-re**, so they can easily be distinguished from the other two conjugations. Here is the present tense of a common third conjugation verb:

perdre [pɛrdr] = *to lose*	**nous perdons** [pɛrdɔ̃] = *we lose*
je perds [pɛːr] = *I lose*, etc.	**vous perdez** [pɛrde] = *you lose*
tu perds [pɛːr] = *you lose*	**ils perdent** [pɛrd] = *they lose*
il perd [pɛːr] = *he loses*	

Note that (*a*) no extra **t** is required in inversion of the third person singular; instead the **d** is pronounced as a **t** in liaison with the following **il** or **elle**: **perd-il?** = *does he lose?* (*b*) In a command the **s** of the second person singular is retained (**rendre** = *to give*) **rends le journal!** = *give back the paper!*

62

IRREGULAR VERBS

The present tenses of irregular -re verbs must be learned separately.

écrire [ekriːr] = *to write*

j'écris [ekri]	**nous écrivons** [ekrivɔ̃]
tu écris [ekri]	**vous écrivez** [ekrive]
il écrit [ekri]	**ils écrivent** [ekriv]

rire [riːr] = *to laugh*

je ris [ri]	**nous rions** [rjɔ̃]
tu ris [ri]	**vous riez** [rje]
il rit [ri]	**ils rient** [ri]

FORMATION OF ADVERBS

Adverbs—words that add to the meaning of verbs, adjectives and other adverbs—are not very difficult in French as they never change their form. In this respect they are like prepositions, and unlike verbs and adjectives.

In English many adverbs are made from adjectives by adding -*ly*: *strong*, *strongly*; in French the most common method is to add **-ment** to the feminine form of the adjective:

fort, forte = *strong*	**fortement** = *strongly*
sévère, sévère = *stern*	**sévèrement** = *sternly*

There is another rule for adjectives ending in **-ant** or **-ent**; these lose the final **-nt** from the masculine form and add the ending **-mment**:

prudent, prudente = *wise*	**prudemment** = *wisely*
constant, constante = *constant*	**constamment** = *constantly*
patient, patiente = *patient*	**patiemment** = *patiently*

Note carefully one of the rare exceptions:

lent, lente = *slow*	**lentement** = *slowly*

Note that (*a*) French differs from English in the positions of adverbs; in French an adverb describing a verb comes immediately after it. One describing an adjective or adverb comes before it as in English:

Ils jouent souvent aux cartes = *They often play cards.*
Elle est extrêmement jolie = *She is extremely pretty.*
Elles chantent très gaiement = *They are singing very gaily.*

(*b*) Many adjectives in French are irregular, i.e. form their feminines by some other means than merely adding **-e**. There are other rules to help with some of these; for example, adjectives ending in **-eux** become **-euse** in the feminine:

heureux, heureuse = *happy*	**heureusement** = *happily*

DAYS, MONTHS AND DATES

Les jours de la semaine [s(ə)mɛn] = *the days of the week*:

lundi [lœ̃di]	= *Monday*	**vendredi** [vɑ̃drədi]	= *Friday*
mardi [mardi]	= *Tuesday*	**samedi** [samdi]	= *Saturday*
mercredi [mɛrkrədi]	= *Wednesday*	**dimanche** [dimɑ̃ːʃ]	= *Sunday*
jeudi [ʒødi]	= *Thursday*		

Les mois (m.) [mwa] = *the months*:

janvier [ʒɑ̃vje]	= *January*	**juillet** [ʒɥijɛ]	= *July*
février [fevrie]	= *February*	**août** [u]	= *August*
mars [mɑrs]	= *March*	**septembre** [sɛptɑ̃:br]	= *September*
avril [avril]	= *April*	**octobre** [ɔktɔbr]	= *October*
mai [mɛ]	= *May*	**novembre** [nɔvɑ̃:br]	= *November*
juin [ʒɥɛ̃]	= *June*	**décembre** [desɑ̃:br]	= *December*

All days and months are masculine and begin with a small letter.
There are three different ways of writing the date in French:
le + number + month: **le neuf septembre** = *[on] September the ninth.*
le + day + number + month: **le jeudi trois mai** = *[on] Thursday, May*
This third way is the form used in letters: *[the third.*
day + number + month: **lundi, six février** = *Monday, February the sixth.*
Note that **le** + day of the week = *on . . .*: **le vendredi** = *on Fridays.*

OBJECT PRONOUNS

Je, tu, il, elle; nous, vous, ils and **elles** are pronouns used as the subject of a verb; there are different forms for most of these pronouns when used as the object of a verb. These direct object forms are:
me [mə], **te** [tə], **le** [lə], **la** [la]; **nous** [nu], **vous** [vu], **les** [le].
Their position in the sentence is very important; they come immediately before the verb (and after the **ne** if the sentence is negative) except in positive commands when they come immediately after it:
Qui me cherche? = *Who is looking for me?*
Un de tes voisins te cherche = *One of your neighbours is looking for you.*
Vous‿avez le ballon. Donnez-le à votre frère! = *You have the ball. Give it to*
your brother!
Où est la bouteille? Ne la donnez pas‿à votre sœur! = *Where is the bottle?*
Qui nous cherche? = *Who is looking for us?* [*Do not give it to your sister!*
Les‿enfants vous cherchent = *The children are looking for you.*
Nous les trouvons dans le jardin = *We find them in the garden.*

Note that (*a*) **nous** and **vous** cannot here be confused with the subject pronouns as the verb ending does not agree with them; (*b*) **le, la** and **les** could not mean *the* before a verb; (*c*) the forms **me** and **te** are not used after verbs.

VOCABULARY

la couleur [kulœ:r]	*colour*, *suit* (in cards)	
une énigme [enigm]	*puzzle*	
le cœur [kœ:r]	*heart*	
le carreau [karo]	*diamond* (cards), *check*	
le trèfle [trɛfl]	*club* (cards), *clover*	**la table**
le pique [pik]	*spade* (cards), *pike*	**de jeu**

64

ce sont (plural of c'est) [sə sɔ̃] *they are*
chaque [ʃak] *each*
ordinaire [ɔrdinɛːr] *ordinary*
c'est-à-dire [sɛtadiːr] *that is to say*
le valet [valɛ] *jack*
la dame [dam] *lady, queen* (cards)
le roi [rwa] *king*
un as [ɑːs] *ace*
la figure [figyːr] *face, picture-card*
jeune [ʒœn] *young*
au bout de [o bu də] *after, at the end of*
apporter [apɔrte] *to bring*
la table de jeu [tabl də ʒø] *card-table*
commencer [à] [kɔmɑ̃se (a)] *to begin [to], start [to]*
couper [kupe] *to cut [down]*
mélanger [melɑ̃ʒe] *to mix, shuffle* (cards)
s'il vous plaît [sil vu plɛ] *please*
distribuer [distribɥe] *to deal*
le quart [d'heure] [kaːr (dœːr)] *quarter [of an hour]*
patiemment [pasjamɑ̃] *patiently*
attentif, -tive [-ment] [atɑ̃tif, -iv *attentive[ly]*
bavarder [bavarde]   [(-mɑ̃)] *to chatter*
admettre [admɛtr] *to admit*
ça, cela [sa, səla] *that*
la remarque [rəmark] *remark*
bref, brève [brɛf, brɛːv] *short, brief*
une annonce [anɔ̃ːs] *bid*
naturel, -elle [natyrɛl] *natural*
le soupir [supiːr] *sigh*
la partie [parti] *part, game*
surtout [syrtu] *especially*
joyeux, -euse [-ment] [ʒwajø, -øːz *gay[ly], joyful[ly]*
trahir [traiːr]   [(-mɑ̃)] *to betray, reveal*
la faiblesse [fɛblɛs] *weakness*
le nombre [nɔ̃ːbr] *number*
le point [pwɛ̃] *point, full-stop, dot*
toi [twa] *you (emphatic)*
ajouter [aʒute] *to add*
oublier [ublie] *to forget*
innocemment [inɔsamɑ̃] *innocently*
une excuse [ɛkskyːz] *excuse, apology*
combien de [kɔ̃bjɛ̃ də] *how much, how many*

**le quatre
de cœur**

**le deux
de carreau**

**le dix
de trèfle**

**le neuf
de pique**

la coiffure

la dame
de cœur

la figure

le roi
de trèfle

la liste
des points

le valet
de carreau

la carte

l'as
de pique

la table de jeu

UN JEU DE CARTES

Dans un jeu de cartes   il y a cinquante-deux cartes différentes.   Vingt-six
dãzœ̃ ʒø de kart   il j a sɛ̃kɑ̃:t   dø kart diferɑ̃t.   vɛ̃t sis

de ces cartes   sont rouges,   les autres sont noires — mais il y a   quatre
də se kart   sɔ̃ ru:ʒ,   lezo:tr   sɔ̃ nwa:r —   mɛzil j a   katr

couleurs en tout!   Pouvez-vous trouver la solution   de cette énigme?   Eh bien,
kulœ:r ɑ̃ tu!   puve vu truve la sɔlysjɔ̃ də sɛt enign?   e bjɛ̃,

il y a treize cœurs,   treize carreaux,   treize trèfles   et treize piques.   Les
il j a trɛ:z kœ:r,   trɛ:z karo,   trɛ:z trɛfl   e trɛ:z pik.   le

trèfles sont noirs,   les piques sont noirs aussi,   mais ce sont des couleurs
trɛfl sɔ̃ nwa:r,   le pik   sɔ̃ nwa:r osi,   mɛ sə sɔ̃ de kulœ:r

différentes!   Dans chaque couleur   il y a neuf cartes ordinaires,   c'est-à-dire
diferɑ̃t!   dɑ̃ ʃak kulœ:r   il j a nœf kart ɔrdinɛ:r,   sɛta di:r

deux jusqu'à dix;   après le dix   nous trouvons le valet,   la dame,   le roi   et
dø ʒyska dis;   aprɛ lə dis   nu truvɔ̃ lə valɛ,   la dam,   lə rwa   e

l'as,   c'est-à-dire les figures,   parce que trois de ces cartes   montrent la
lɑ:s,   sɛta di:r le figy:r,   pars kə trwa də se kart   mɔ̃:tr la

figure (le visage)   d'un jeune homme,   d'une reine   et d'un roi.
figy:r (lə viza:ʒ)   dœ̃ ʒœn ɔm,   dyn rɛn   e dœ̃ rwa.

C'est le vingt-cinq avril   ...il est huit heures du soir.   Que fait Monsieur
sɛ lə vɛ̃t sɛ̃k avril   ...il ɛ ɥitœ:r dyswa:r.   kə fɛ   məsjø

66

Girard? **Il cherche le jeu de cartes;** **au bout de cinq minutes** **il le trouve,**
ʒiraːr? il ʃɛrʃ lə ʒø də kart; o bu də sɛ̃ minyt il lə truv,

il l'apporte au salon **et le met sur la table de jeu.** **"Nous pouvons maintenant**
il lapɔrt o salɔ̃ e lə mɛ syr la tabl də ʒø. "nu puvɔ̃ mɛtnã

commencer à jouer. **Coupez les cartes!"** **Son voisin,** **Monsieur Larivière,**
kɔmãse a ʒwe. kupe le kart!" sɔ̃ vwasɛ̃, məsjø larivjɛːr,

coupe un as. . . . **"Voici les cartes vertes,"** **dit‿il à Madame Larivière.**
kup œ̃naːs. . . . "vwasi le kart vɛrt," ditil a madam larivjɛːr.

"Mêlez-les, s'il vous plaît." **Elle les mélange bien.** **Madame Girard les**
"mele le, sil vu plɛ." ɛl le melãʒ bjɛ̃. madam ʒiraːr le

coupe encore une fois, **et Monsieur Larivière les distribue.** **Ils jouent**
kup ãkɔːr yn fwa, e məsjø larivjɛːr le distriby. il ʒu

pendant‿un quart d'heure **patiemment,** **attentivement,** **sans bavarder. (Il**
pãdãtœ̃ kaːr dœːr pasjamã, atãtivmã, sã bavarde. (il

faut l'admettre, **ils ne jouent pas souvent** **comme ça!)** **Il y a seulement des**
fo ladmɛtr, il nə ʒu pɑ suvã kɔm sa!) il j a sœlmã de

remarques brèves, **des questions,** **des‿annonces,** **et naturellement des**
rəmark brɛːv, de kɛstjɔ̃, dezanɔ̃ːs, e natyrɛlmã de

soupirs. **"Nous perdons la première partie,"** **dit Monsieur Girard.** **"Je**
supiːr. "nu pɛrdɔ̃ la prəmjɛːr parti," di məsjø ʒiraːr. "ʒə

perds toujours le vendredi!" **"Pourquoi perds-tu surtout le vendredi?"**
pɛːr tuʒuːr lə vãdrədi!" "purkwa pɛːr ty syrtu lə vãdrədi?"

demande sa femme, **qui rit joyeusement** **quand il‿ trahit sa petite faiblesse**
dəmãd sa fam, ki ri ʒwajøːzmã kãtil trai sa pətit fɛblɛs

(il est superstitieux). **"Oui, vous perdez,"** **dit Monsieur Larivière,** **"j'écris**
(il ɛ sypɛrstisjø). "wi, vu pɛrde," di məsjø larivjɛːr, "ʒekri

le nombre de points **sur ma feuille de papier.** **Écris-le,** **toi aussi,"**
lə nɔ̃ːbr də pwɛ̃ syr ma fœːj də papje. ekri lə, twa osi,"

ajoute-t-il, **quand‿il voit** **que sa femme n'écrit rien.** **Les deux femmes rient,**
aʒutətil, kãtil vwa kə sa fam nekri rjɛ̃. le dø fam ri,

elles n'écrivent rien, **elles‿oublient le jeu** **pendant quelques‿instants.** **Enfin**
ɛl nekriv rjɛ, ɛlzubli lə ʒø pãdã kəlkəzɛ̃stã. ãfɛ̃

Madame Girard demande innocemment, **"Pourquoi les‿hommes** **cherchent-ils**
madam ʒiraːr dəmãːd inɔsamã, "purkwa lezɔm ʃɛrʃ(ə)til

toujours une excuse **quand‿ils perdent?"**
tuʒuːr yn ɛkskyːz kãtil pɛrd?"

(Translation at the end of the book.)

67

EXERCISES

I. **Vendre** ([vãːdr] = *to sell*) is a regular third conjugation verb like **perdre**. Translate into French:

1. Are you selling your house?
2. Mr. and Mrs. Girard sell their house.
3. Mr. Girard says: Jacques, sell your toys!
4. Is he selling this house?
5. Why do they sell their potatoes?
6. Jacques sells his toys.
7. I sell my vegetables.
8. Do you sell your apples?
9. Josette sells her doll.
10. We sell our carrots.

II. Find in the story the French adverbs which mean:

1. Now
2. Once again
3. Patiently
4. Attentively
5. Often
6. Only
7. Naturally
8. Joyfully
9. Innocently
10. Always
11. Well
12. Especially

Construct adverbs from these adjectives:
13. **Prudent.**   14. **Constant.**   15. **Évident.**   16. **Violent.**

III. Translate each question and insert the missing object pronoun in the answer (e.g. **Où met͜-il la carte? Il met sur la table — Il la met sur la table**); be careful to put it in the proper place, before the verb:

1. **Qui connaît M. et Mme Larivière? Mme Girard connaît.**
2. **Qui lit les livres et les͜ illustrés? Jacques et ses sœurs lisent.**
3. **Qui prend le fauteuil près de la fenêtre? Mme Aubert prend.**
4. **"Qui me cherche?" demande Jacques. "Josette cherche," dit son père.**
5. **"Qui nous cherche?" demandent͜-ils. "Vos parents cherchent," dit le voisin.**
6. **Où mets-tu les cartes? Je mets sur la table.**
7. **Qui vous gronde maintenant? Maman gronde maintenant.**
8. **Connaissez-vous Mme Lucas? Non, je ne connais pas.**
9. **Cherchez-vous le jouet cassé? Non, je ne cherche pas.**
10. **Est-ce que maman nous cherche? Oui, elle cherche.**

IV. Translate into French:

1. Give them to the boys!
2. Do not give them to the girls!
3. Put it on the floor!
4. Do not put it on the table!
5. Scold them!
6. Do not scold us!
7. Here is a cup: put it on the table!
8. Do not put it on the carpet!
9. The twenty-first of March.
10. The sixth of December.
11. The thirtieth of May.
12. The fourteenth of July.
13. The twenty-seventh of August.
14. The sixteenth of February.
15. The fifteenth of June.
16. The first of April.

V. Répondez aux questions suivantes (employez des pronoms pour éviter la répétition des noms):

1. Comment les parents et les voisins jouent-ils pendant un quart d'heure?
2. Comment Mme Girard rit-elle?
3. Comment est M. Girard quand il joue aux cartes?
4. Comment Mme Girard demande-t-elle pourquoi les hommes cherchent une excuse?
5. Où M. Girard porte-t-il les cartes?
6. Où les met-il?
7. Qu'est-ce que M. Girard dit à Mme Larivière?
8. Que faut-il écrire sur une feuille de papier quand on joue aux cartes?
9. Qui mélange les cartes vertes?
10. Qui les distribue?
11. De quelle couleur sont les cœurs?
12. De quelle couleur sont les trèfles?
13. Les piques, sont-ils verts?
14. Est-ce que les carreaux sont bleus?
15. Combien de cartes y a-t-il dans un jeu de cartes?
16. Combien de cœurs y a-t-il?
17. Combien de figures y a-t-il?
18. Combien de mains avez-vous?
19. Combien de crayons avez-vous?
20. Jouez-vous au bridge?

VI. Find in the story the French phrases which mean:

1. Because three of these cards show the face.
2. When he sees that his wife is writing nothing.
3. "Here are the green cards," he says to Mrs. Larivière.
4. Can you find the solution to this puzzle?
5. After five minutes he finds it.

VII. Without using Est-ce que change these sentences into questions:

1. M. Girard est superstitieux.
2. Les enfants de Mme Girard sont souvent très méchants.
3. M. Girard trahit sa petite faiblesse.
4. Les sœurs de Jacques jouent dans le jardin.
5. Le garçon donne une tasse de thé à son père.

(Answers at the end of the book.)

LEÇON 7

GRAMMAR

VERBS—FURTHER CONJUGATIONS

In addition to the three main conjugations there are five other patterns followed by a few verbs. Once you know these the number of apparently irregular verbs seems smaller:

recevoir [rəsəvwaːr] = *to receive*: type recognised by **-cevoir** ending

je reçois [rəswa]	**nous recevons** [rəsəvɔ̃]
tu reçois [rəswa]	**vous recevez** [rəsəve]
il reçoit [rəswa]	**ils reçoivent** [rəswaːv]

Verbs like **recevoir**: **apercevoir** = *to perceive*, **decevoir** = *to deceive, disappoint*, etc.

Note that the cedilla (**ç**) is needed to soften the letter **c** before the hard vowels **a, o** and **u**; no cedilla is needed with the soft vowels **e** and **i**; compare the two sounds in *concentrate*; and in *cat, cot, cut* and *cellar, civil*.

craindre [krɛ̃ːdr] = *to fear*: type recognised by vowel + **-indre** ending

je crains [krɛ̃]	**nous craignons** [krɛɲɔ̃]
tu crains [krɛ̃]	**vous craignez** [krɛɲe]
il craint [krɛ̃]	**ils craignent** [krɛːɲ]

Verbs like **craindre**: **atteindre** = *to reach*, **peindre** = *to paint*, etc.

conduire [kɔ̃dɥiːr] = *to lead, drive*: type recognised by **-uire** ending

je conduis [kɔ̃dɥi]	**nous conduisons** [kɔ̃dɥizɔ̃]
tu conduis [kɔ̃dɥi]	**vous conduisez** [kɔ̃dɥize]
il conduit [kɔ̃dɥi]	**ils conduisent** [kɔ̃dɥiz]

Verbs like **conduire**: **construire** = *to build*, **cuire** = *to cook*, **produire** = *to produce*, **traduire** = *to translate*, etc.

mentir [mɑ̃tiːr] = *to tell lies*: like **finir** except in the present and imperfect

je mens [mɑ̃]	**nous mentons** [mɑ̃tɔ̃]
tu mens [mɑ̃]	**vous mentez** [mɑ̃te]
il ment [mɑ̃]	**ils mentent** [mɑ̃t]

Verbs like **mentir**: **dormir** = *to sleep*, **partir** = *to depart, set out*, **sentir** = *to feel, smell* [*of*], **servir** = *to serve*, **sortir** = *to go, come out*, etc. Note that unlike the **finir** type, these verbs do not add **-iss** to the stem in the imperfect tense.

ouvrir [uvriːr] = *to open*: considerably different from the **finir** type

j'ouvre [uvr]	**nous ouvrons** [nuzuvrɔ̃]
tu ouvres [uvr]	**vous ouvrez** [vuzuvre]
il ouvre [uvr]	**ils ouvrent** [ilzuvr]

70

Verbs like **ouvrir: couvrir** = *to cover*, **découvrir** = *to discover*, **offrir** = *to offer*, **souffrir** = *to suffer*, etc.

EXPRESSIONS WITH **avoir** AND **faire**

Many common French expressions for a state of mind or body use **avoir** and a noun, where English uses the verb *to be* with an adjective. Learn these French expressions carefully; remember that the noun does not change, so do not try to make it agree with the subject like an adjective:

avoir faim = *to be hungry*	**avoir soif** = *to be thirsty*
avoir chaud = *to be hot*	**avoir froid** = *to be cold*
avoir raison = *to be right*	**avoir tort** = *to be wrong*
avoir honte = *to be ashamed*	

Nous avons faim mais nous n'avons pas soif = *We are hungry but not thirsty.*
Elle a raison mais vous avez tort = *She is right but you are wrong.*

Test your grasp of phonetic symbols by writing these down against the appropriate words: frwa, ɔt, ʃo, fɛ̃, tɔːr, rɛzɔ̃, swaf.

French expressions for the weather again avoid the verb *to be* and use **faire** = *to make, do*: **Quel temps fait-il?** = *What is the weather like?* Literally this means *What weather is it making?* Learn these possible answers:

Il fait chaud = *It is hot.*	**Il fait beau** = *It is fine.*
Il fait froid = *It is cold.*	**Il fait mauvais** = *It is bad.*
Il fait jour = *It is [day] light.*	**Il fait de la brume** = *It is misty.*
Il fait nuit = *It is dark.*	**Il fait du brouillard** = *It is foggy.*

Note that although **faire** is used in all these cases, when **le temps** is used as the subject it must be followed by the verb **être**: **Le temps est beau** = *The weather is fine*, but **Il fait beau** = *It is fine.*

NUMERALS—ORDINALS

Ordinals (e.g. *second*) are made by adding **-ième** to the cardinal number (e.g. *two*): **deux** + **-ième**, **deuxième** [døzjɛm] = *second*; but note:

quatrième [katriɛm] = *fourth*	**treizième** [trɛzjɛm]	= *thirteenth*
cinquième [sɛ̃kjɛm] = *fifth*	**quatorzième** [katɔrzjɛm]	= *fourteenth*
neuvième [nœvjɛm] = *ninth*	**quinzième** [kɛ̃zjɛm]	= *fifteenth*
onzième [ɔ̃zjɛm] = *eleventh*	**seizième** [sɛzjɛm]	= *sixteenth*
douzième [duzjɛm] = *twelfth*	**dix-septième**	= *seventeenth*

You will see from these that a final -e is lost before **-ième.**

Note that (*a*) **premier, première** = *first*; **unième** is used only in **vingt et unième** = *twenty-first*, **trente et unième** = *thirty-first*, etc.; (*b*) **second, seconde** is sometimes used instead of **deuxième.**

Remember that these are numerical adjectives and come before the nouns they describe, e.g. **le troisième programme, la sixième répétition**, etc.

VOCABULARY

un hiver [ivɛːr]	*winter*
le vent [vɑ̃]	*wind*
le nuage [nɥaːʒ]	*cloud*
pleuvoir [plœvwaːr]	*to rain*
l'aube (f.) [oːb]	*dawn*
elle-même [ɛl mɛːm]	*herself*
le rhume de poitrine [rym də pwatrin]	*chest-cold*
le médecin [mɛtsɛ̃, mɛdsɛ̃]	*doctor*
le printemps [prɛ̃tɑ̃]	*spring*
doux, douce [du, dus]	*mild, gentle*
faire une promenade [prɔmnad]	*to go for a walk*
la campagne [kɑ̃paɲ]	*country*
seul(e) [sœl]	*alone*
le pré [pre]	*meadow*
la rivière [rivjɛːr]	*river*
d'habitude [dabityd]	*usually*
dehors [dəɔːr]	*outside*
l'obscurité (f.) [ɔpskyrite]	*darkness*
en plus [ɑ̃ ply(s)]	*in addition*
agréable [agreabl]	*pleasant*
le souper [supe]	*supper*
le quartier [kartje]	*district*
le confort [kɔ̃fɔːr]	*comfort*
au coin du feu [o kwɛ̃ dy fø]	*by the fireside*
le microbe [mikrɔb]	*germ*
la grippe [grip]	*influenza*
attraper [atrape]	*to catch*
la salle de cinéma [sal də sinema]	*cinema hall*
la saison [sɛzɔ̃]	*season*
d'ailleurs [dajœːr]	*moreover*
en voiture [ɑ̃ vwatyːr]	*by car*
gagner [gaɲe]	*to win*
une entrée [ɑ̃tre]	*entrance*
le billet [bijɛ]	*ticket*
le bureau de location [lokasjɔ̃]	*box-office*
la place [plas]	*seat, public square*
le balcon [balkɔ̃]	*balcony*
une ouvreuse [uvrøːz]	*usherette*
le pourboire [purbwaːr]	*tip*
le salaire [salɛːr]	*wage[s]*

le nuage

le médecin

le billet

une ouvreuse

réclamer [reklɑme]	*to demand*	
un écran [ekrɑ̃]	*screen*	
la publicité [pyblisite]	*advertisement*	
dernier, -ière [dɛrnje, -ɛːr]	*last*	
la représentation [rəpresɑ̃tasjɔ̃]	*performance*	
assez tard [ase taːr]	*quite late*	
peut-être [pøtɛːtr]	*perhaps*	
étudier [etydje]	*to study*	**la cathédrale**
un entr'acte [ɑ̃trakt]	*interval*	
le foyer [fwaje]	*foyer, entrance hall*	
le verre [vɛːr]	*glass*	
favori, -ite [favɔri, -it]	*favourite*	
durer [dyre]	*to last*	
le mot [mo]	*word*	
défense de [defɑ̃ːs də]	*it is forbidden to*	
retenir [rətniːr]	*to retain, keep, hold*	
tout le monde [tu lə mɔ̃ːd]	*everybody, everyone*	**la porte d'entrée**
mille [mil]	*thousand*	
un assassinat [asasina]	*murder*	
la poursuite [pursɥit]	*chase*	
la bagarre [bagaːr]	*brawl*	
le héros [ero]	*hero*	
satisfait(e) [satisfɛ, -ɛt]	*satisfied*	
la sortie [sɔrti]	*exit*	
une hymne nationale [im(n) nasjɔnal]	*national anthem*	**le verre**
remettre [rəmɛtr]	*to put on again*	
le pardessus [pardəsy]	*overcoat*	
ajuster [aʒyste]	*to adjust*	
soigneusement [swaɲøːzmɑ̃]	*carefully*	
le manteau de fourrure [mɑ̃to də furyːr]	*fur coat*	
		l'auto
le givre [ʒiːvr]	*frost*	
recouvrir [rəkuvriːr]	*to cover*	
la chaussée [ʃose]	*roadway*	
le trottoir [trɔtwaːr]	*pavement*	
glissant(e) [glisɑ̃, -ɑ̃t]	*slippery*	
sain(e) et sauf(-ve) [sɛ̃ (sɛn) e sof (soːv)]	*safe and sound*	
le mystère [mistɛːr]	*mystery*	
la porte d'entrée [pɔrt dɑ̃tre]	*front door*	
éclairé(e) [eklɛre]	*lit up*	**le vol**

73

le bureau de location

une ouvreuse

la torche électrique

AU BALCON

le billet

le manteau de fourrure

le pardessus

le foyer

AU CINÉMA

M. et Mme Girard sont bien contents de rester à la maison le soir parce que le temps est mauvais. C'est l'hiver: il ne neige pas, mais il fait très froid, il fait du vent. Les nuages sont si noirs qu'il va sans doute pleuvoir avant l'aube. En hiver les Girard ne sortent pas souvent après le goûter; ils reçoivent des amis deux ou trois fois par semaine. Mme Girard reçoit tant d'amis au lieu de sortir elle-même parce qu'elle souffre souvent des rhumes de poitrine. Le médecin dit qu'elle ne doit jamais sortir après la tombée de la nuit quand il ne fait pas beau et chaud. En été et au printemps elle souffre moins quand l'atmosphère n'est pas si humide. Mme Girard ne craint pas les soirs doux et en été elle fait souvent une promenade après le dîner; elle ne ment pas quand elle dit qu'elle aime mieux la campagne que le théâtre ou le cinéma.

Généralement elle sort seule par la porte du jardin, traverse les prés et prend un petit sentier qui conduit à la rivière. Elle rentre d'habitude avant dix heures; elle ne veut pas rester dehors quand il fait nuit parce qu'elle craint l'obscurité. En plus elle a souvent faim et soif après une promenade agréable, en conséquence elle mange des biscuits et boit du chocolat avant d'aller au lit. S'il n'est pas trop occupé M. Girard sert ce petit souper pendant que sa femme va regarder les enfants qui dorment.

Cependant, une semaine du mois de février il y a un film policier au cinéma du quartier. Madame veut le voir, mais son mari qui aime le confort au coin du feu objecte: "Je crains les microbes de la grippe qu'on attrape dans les salles de cinéma à cette saison. Et toi, chérie, ne crains-tu pas le froid quand tu sors?" Mme Girard répond: "Moi, je ne sors jamais en hiver, je reste à la maison toute la journée. D'ailleurs, tu peux nous conduire en voiture et ainsi nous ne craignons pas le mauvais temps." Mme Girard gagne.

À l'entrée du cinéma M. Girard prend les billets au bureau de location, deux places de balcon. L'ouvreuse les conduit à leurs fauteuils, à l'aide de sa torche électrique. M. Girard donne à cette jeune femme un pourboire de cinquante centimes, car dans les cinémas français les ouvreuses ne reçoivent pas de salaire. Si l'on oublie de donner un pourboire, l'ouvreuse le réclame, souvent d'un ton agressif! Il est neuf heures moins vingt, mais sur l'écran il y a seulement de la publicité, car en France les cinémas commencent leur dernière représentation assez tard, peut-être vers neuf heures moins le quart.

Voici enfin un film documentaire sur les cathédrales de France. M. Girard étudie l'architecture et il aime beaucoup ce film qui le met de bonne humeur. À l'entr'acte ils retournent au foyer où M. Girard offre à sa femme un verre de sa liqueur favorite. L'entr'acte dure vingt minutes, par conséquent il a le temps de fumer une cigarette. On ne peut pas fumer pendant la représentation car sur les murs du cinéma on voit les mots "Défense de fumer".

Après l'entr'acte M. et Mme Girard retournent à leurs places. Le film principal commence à neuf heures et demie et retient l'attention de tout le monde. Il y a mille incidents dramatiques, plusieurs assassinats, des vols, des poursuites, une bagarre, et une scène où le héros sauve la belle dame (la victime!) à la dernière minute.

À la fin de la représentation les spectateurs satisfaits vont vite vers la sortie pour quitter le cinéma tout de suite — ils ne doivent pas chanter leur hymne nationale! M. Girard remet son pardessus et sa femme ajuste soigneusement son manteau de fourrure, car il fait très froid dehors.

Il est maintenant près de minuit et du givre recouvre la chaussée et les trottoirs. Quand ils sont bien installés dans l'auto (une belle Citroën bleue) Mme Girard dit: "Conduis lentement, chéri. Je crains les routes glissantes." Naturellement il conduit avec précaution et après quelques minutes ils arrivent sains et saufs à la maison. Mais quel est ce mystère? . . . La porte d'entrée est ouverte, la maison est éclairée!

(*See notes on the next page. Translation at the end of the book.*)

LEÇON 7

NOTES ON THE TEXT

Le soir = *in the evening*; **aimer mieux** (literally, *to like better*) means *to prefer*; **en conséquence** = *consequently*; **à l'aide de** = *with the help of*; **centime,** a small unit of French money, fifty are roughly ninepence; **l'on: l'** is used with **on** before **si, où,** etc., to avoid an awkward sound; **d'un ton** = *in a tone of voice*; **de bonne humeur** = *in a good mood*; **par conséquent** = *therefore, so*; **une Citroën,** a well-known French make of car. Note that many French phrases seem similar to English ones but have different prepositions.

EXERCISES

I. **Répondez aux questions suivantes:**

1. Quels sont les mille incidents du film policier?
2. Comment M. Girard conduit-il son auto quand il fait nuit?
3. Comment une ouvreuse demande-t-elle souvent un pourboire?
4. Où le petit sentier conduit-il?
5. Qu'est-ce que M. Girard prend à l'entrée du cinéma?
6. Que voit-on sur les murs du cinéma?
7. Qui conduit M. et Mme Girard à leurs fauteuils?
8. Qui sauve la belle dame à la dernière minute?
9. De quelle couleur est le givre?
10. De quelle couleur sont les prés?
11. Combien de centimes l'ouvreuse reçoit-elle?
12. Combien d'incidents dramatiques y a-t-il dans le film principal?
13. Pourquoi Mme Girard mange-t-elle des biscuits après une promenade?
14. Pourquoi M. Girard ne veut-il pas aller au cinéma?
15. Pourquoi Mme Girard ajuste-t-elle son manteau de fourrure?

II. Write out in full the present tense of these verbs (see pages 70 and 71):

1. **apercevoir** = *to perceive.*
2. **peindre** = *to paint.*
3. **partir** = *to depart.*
4. **souffrir** = *to suffer.*
5. **réduire** = *to reduce.*
6. **joindre** = *to join.*

III. Translate into French:

1. I am hungry but I am not thirsty.
2. He is right, but his sister is wrong.
3. Are you hungry and thirsty? Are your friends hungry too?
4. They are not cold in the cinema, in spite of the weather.
5. When it is raining you cannot go to the cinema.
6. When it is foggy we cannot see where we are driving.
7. When it is not cold, they do not wear a coat.

76

8. They like the first film but they do not like the second film.
9. Are you not cold in the sitting-room when there is no fire?
10. Why is it warm in the kitchen and cold in the dining-room?

IV. Write out this passage replacing the infinitives in brackets with the correct forms of the verbs:

La partie de bridge (continuer). Cette fois Mme Larivière (donner) les cartes. Après les annonces, ils (jouer) vite. M. Girard (gagner) le premier pli, le deuxième pli, le troisième pli . . . onze plis, et au moment où il (ramasser) le douzième pli Mme Girard (crier), "Je n'(avoir) plus de cartes, je (voir) la dame de cœur sur le tapis près de la cheminée." Son mari (entendre) ses mots et il (être) sur le point d'(exprimer) son dépit quand elle (dire): "Ne (craindre) rien, mon chéri. C'(être) une petite plaisanterie. Je (mentir). Je t'(offrir) mes excuses." Les invités (rire) de bon cœur; M. Girard (rire) aussi. Il ne (craindre) pas les plaisanteries de sa femme, il ne (craindre) plus de (perdre) ses treize plis. Ils (reprendre) la partie; tous les quatre (être) heureux. Ils (jouer) pendant une heure presque sans (ouvrir) la bouche. M. Girard (parler) le premier; il (dire): "J'(avoir) soif. Nous (pouvoir) aller dans la salle à manger boire du café chaud. On ne (pouvoir) pas (rester) ici, ce salon (sentir) le tabac."

(Le pli = *trick*; le dépit = *resentment*; la plaisanterie = *joke*; un invité = *guest*; de bon cœur = *heartily*; reprendre = *to continue*; presque = *almost*; la bouche = *mouth*; le tabac = *tobacco*; au moment où = *at the moment when*; être sur le point de = *to be about to*.)

V. Translate the passage in Exercise IV, then rewrite the passage as though you were M. Girard telling the story. Be careful to make all the necessary changes of number and gender and person of the verb.

VI. Test your memory of the first seven lessons with these revision exercises:
1. Write out the time at each five minutes between eight and nine o'clock.
2. Write out the page numbers between ten and thirty using ordinal, not cardinal, numbers, e.g. **la dixième page, la onzième page**, etc.
3. Write down the French for as many objects as you can think of that you might see in a garden, e.g. **la pelouse, la carotte**, etc.
4. Write down the names of ten objects, each with a colour adjective describing it. Remember that colour adjectives always come after their nouns.
5. Learn by heart the first paragraph of the text in Lesson 1. Write it out from memory and check it. Pay attention to accents (seventeen in all).

(*Answers at the end of the book.*)

LEÇON 8
GRAMMAR

PERFECT TENSE

When a verb describes an action that took place in the past, the verb is put in a special form called the past tense: *I kicked, I ate*; *I kick, I eat* is the present tense. The most common past tense in French is **le passé composé** = *perfect tense* which is a compound tense, i.e. it consists of more than one word and is like our perfect tense, *I have kicked*, but it also translates our simple past *I kicked*, as French has no simple past tense used in conversation. It is formed with the past participle, which is a special form of the verb, preceded by the present tense of **avoir** = *to have* (compare English):

peser [pəze] = *to weigh*, past participle **pesé** [pəze] = *weighed*

j'ai pesé = *I weighed, have weighed, have been*	**nous avons pesé**
tu as pesé [*weighing*, etc.	**vous avez pesé**
il a pesé	**ils ont pesé**

Note that this also translates the continuous perfect which is common in English conversation: *I have been weighing the potatoes* = **J'ai pesé les pommes de terre**. Do not use three separate words in French.

Once you have learnt this pattern you can easily form the perfect tense of any verb provided you know how to form the past participle; here are rules and examples for forming these:

First conjugation:	verb stem + **é**	**chanté, donné**
Second conjugation:	verb stem + **i**	**fini, choisi**
Third conjugation:	verb stem + **u**	**vendu, perdu**
recevoir type:	-cevoir becomes -çu	**reçu, aperçu**
craindre type:	-indre becomes -int	**craint, atteint**
conduire type:	-uire becomes -uit	**conduit, construit**
mentir type:	regular second conjugation	**menti, dormi**
ouvrir type:	-rir becomes -ert	**ouvert, couvert**

Irregular verbs:	**avoir, eu**	**battre, battu**	**connaître, connu**
courir, couru	**devoir, dû**	**dire, dit**	**écrire, écrit**
être, été	**faire, fait**	**falloir, fallu**	**lire, lu**
mettre, mis	**pouvoir, pu**	**prendre, pris**	**rire, ri**
savoir, su	**suivre, suivi**	**voir, vu**	**vouloir, voulu**

Note that the past participle must agree like an adjective with any direct object which precedes it. There are three constructions where this occurs:

78

(a) Where the direct object is a pronoun:
   Où sont les fleurs? Je les ai mises sur la table (**mises** agrees with **les**).
(b) In questions introduced by the adjectives **quel, quelle**, etc.:
   Quels livres a-t-il choisis? = *What books has he chosen?*
(c) In adjectival relative clauses describing a preceding noun:
   Les livres que j'ai choisis = *The books that I have chosen.*

RELATIVE PRONOUNS

Relative clauses are those introduced by relative pronouns, of which the most common are **qui** and **que**. We have seen many relative clauses in the first seven lessons and they are not difficult to understand, but it is very important to get the difference between these two words absolutely clear:

qui = *who, which, that*, when it is the subject of the verb which follows;
que (**qu'** before a vowel or mute **h**) = *whom, which, that*, when it is the direct object of the verb which follows — this is true whether the noun it denotes is masculine or feminine, singular or plural, person or thing:

   Le marchand qui vend les carottes = *The tradesman who sells the carrots.*
   Les carottes qui sont dans la cuisine = *The carrots that are in the kitchen.*
   Le marchand que j'ai vu hier = *The tradesman whom I saw yesterday.*
   La carotte qu'il a mangée = *The carrot which he has eaten.*
Note that English often leaves out the pronoun: *The carrot he has eaten.*

THE ADJECTIVE **tout**

Tout = *all*, is irregular and usually comes before **le, la, les**:

tout le vin = *all the wine*	**tous les vins** = *all the wines*
toute la maison = *the whole house*	**toutes les maisons** = *all the houses*

INVERSION OF THE VERB

After direct speech, expressions such as *he says, the boy said*, must be inverted in French. Note the difference in construction between this kind of inversion and that used in questions:

"J'ai mangé toutes les pommes," dit-il (or **a-t-il dit**), or **a dit le garçon.**
"I have eaten all the apples," he says (or *he said*), or *said the boy.*
Pronoun subjects come before the past participle, noun subjects after it.

IRREGULAR VERBS

battre [batr] = *to beat*	**courir** [kuriːr] = *to run*	**suivre** [sɥiːvr] = *to*
je bats [ba]	**je cours** [kuːr]	**je suis** [sɥi] [*follow*
tu bats [ba]	**tu cours** [kuːr]	**tu suis** [sɥi]
il bat [ba]	**il court** [kuːr]	**il suit** [sɥi]
nous battons [batɔ̃]	**nous courons** [kurɔ̃]	**nous suivons** [sɥivɔ̃]
vous battez [bate]	**vous courez** [kure]	**vous suivez** [sɥive]
ils battent [bat]	**ils courent** [kuːr]	**ils suivent** [sɥiv]

79

VOCABULARY

le magasin [magazɛ̃]	*large shop, store*
faire ses provisions [prɔvizjɔ̃]	*to do one's shopping*
le marché [marʃe]	*market*
en plein air [ɑ̃ plɛ̃nɛːr]	*in the open air*
la halle [al]	*covered market*
le commerçant [kɔmɛrsɑ̃]	*merchant, tradesman*
un étalage [etalaːʒ]	*stall*
le fermier [fɛrmje]	*farmer*
le paysan, la -anne [peizɑ̃, -an]	*peasant*
le village [vilaːʒ]	*village*
voisin(e) [vwazɛ̃, -in]	*neighbouring*
le fruit [frɥi]	*fruit*
le marchand [marʃɑ̃]	*merchant*
baisser le prix [bɛse lə pri]	*to lower the price*
attirer [atire]	*to attract*
un acheteur [aʃtœːr]	*buyer*
partout [partu]	*everywhere, all round*
les gens (m.) [zɑ̃]	*people*
faire ses commissions [kɔmisjɔ̃]	*to do one's errands*
la chose [ʃoːz]	*thing*
la ville [vil]	*town, city*
au milieu de [o miljø də]	*in the middle of*
la foule [ful]	*crowd*
une église [egliːz]	*church*
ensuite [ɑ̃sɥit]	*then, next*
autre [otr]	*other*
la ménagère [menaʒɛːr]	*housewife*
acheter [aʃte]	*to buy*
la poire [pwaːr]	*pear*
vieux, vieille [vjø, vjɛj]	*old*
peser [pəse]	*to weigh*
la balance [balɑ̃ːs]	*scales*
le panier [panje]	*basket*
cher, chère [ʃɛːr]	*dear*
suggérer [sygʒere]	*to suggest*
garantir [garɑ̃tiːr]	*to guarantee*
défendre [defɑ̃ːdr]	*to defend*
merci [mɛrsi]	*thank you*
la réponse [repɔ̃ːs]	*answer, reply*
parcourir [parkuriːr]	*to go all over*
enfin [ɑ̃fɛ̃]	*at last*

le fermier

une église

la poire

la balance

le poisson

doré(e) [dɔre]	*golden*	
gros, grosse [gro, gro:s]	*big, fat*	
appeler [aple]	*to call*	
raisonnable [rɛzɔnabl]	*reasonable, sensible*	
le poisson [pwasɔ̃]	*fish*	
le bœuf [bœf]	*ox, bullock, beef*	**le bœuf**
le poulet [pulɛ]	*chicken*	
longtemps [lɔ̃tɑ̃]	*[for] a long time*	
soudain [sudɛ̃]	*suddenly*	
le tambour [tɑ̃bu:r]	*drum*	
curieux, -euse [kyrjø, jø:z]	*curious, strange*	
entourer [ɑ̃ture]	*to surround*	
le produit [prɔdɥi]	*product*	**le tambour**
approcher [aprɔʃe]	*to come closer*	
la goutte [gut]	*drop*	
l'eau (f.) de vaisselle [o də vɛsɛl]	*dish-water*	
une assiette [asjɛt]	*plate*	
la coutellerie [kutɛlri]	*cutlery*	**une assiette**
propre [prɔpr]	*clean*	
merveilleux, -euse [mɛrvɛjø, -jø:z]	*marvellous*	
économe [ekɔnɔm]	*thrifty*	
écouter [ekute]	*to listen to*	
le boniment [bɔnimɑ̃]	*salesman's patter*	
un_intérêt [ɛ̃terɛ]	*interest*	
sourire [suri:r]	*to smile*	
facile à duper [fasil a dype]	*gullible*	**la coutellerie**
la demi-douzaine [dəmi duzɛn]	*half a dozen*	
le bouquet d'œillets [bukɛ dœjɛ]	*bunch of carnations*	
orner [ɔrne]	*to decorate*	
rentrer [rɑ̃tre]	*to return home, re-enter*	

la grand'rue [grɑ̃ ry]	*main street*	
remarquer [rəmarke]	*to notice*	
la terrasse [tɛras]	*open-air café*	
rempli(e) de [rɑ̃pli də]	*full of*	**le bouquet d'œillets**
habiter [abite]	*to live in, dwell*	
de loin [də lwɛ̃]	*from a distance*	
anxieux, -euse [ɑ̃ksjø, -ø:z]	*anxious*	
abuser de [abyse də]	*to take advantage of*	
la soirée [sware]	*evening*	
passer [pɑse]	*to spend* (time)	
le lecteur, la -trice [lɛktœ:r, -tris]	*reader*	**le lecteur**

AU MARCHÉ

Deux ou trois fois par semaine, au lieu d'aller dans les magasins pour faire ses provisions, on va au marché. Le marché est en plein air ou dans les halles. Beaucoup de commerçants ont un étalage au marché et aussi les fermiers et les paysans viennent des villages voisins apporter leurs légumes, leurs fruits, leurs œufs et cætera. Quand il fait beau temps, il y a beaucoup de monde au marché et les commerçants vendent leurs marchandises rapidement, mais quand il pleut ils doivent souvent baisser leurs prix pour attirer les acheteurs.

Mme Girard ne va pas souvent au marché avec ses enfants parce que, quand elle ne regarde pas, ils courent partout ou suivent distraitement les gens qui font leurs commissions. Si elle gronde Jacques, il répond: "Je te suis, maman, mais je veux regarder toutes les choses intéressantes sur les étalages. De toute façon je cours vite si je te perds, parce que je n'aime pas rester seul au milieu de cette foule."

Dimanche dernier il y a eu marché à la ville. Mme Girard a été seule à l'église de bonne heure et ensuite, comme beaucoup d'autres ménagères, elle a été au marché qu'on trouve toujours sur la place de l'église. Ce matin-là, elle a acheté des épinards, des poires et un melon pour le repas de midi. "Combien, les épinards?" a-t-elle demandé. "Un franc cinquante le kilo, madame."

Et la vieille paysanne a pesé un kilo d'épinards sur sa balance. Madame Girard les a mis dans son panier. Ensuite elle a vu de beaux melons.

"Combien, ce melon, monsieur?" "Deux francs, ma petite dame," a répondu le marchand. "Oh! mais il est encore vert, c'est trop cher," a suggéré Mme Girard. "C'est un melon de la Charente, garanti," a répliqué le marchand, qui a voulu à tout prix défendre ses marchandises. "Non, merci, je n'aime pas les melons verts," a été la réponse de Mme Girard. Elle a parcouru le marché et a enfin trouvé un beau melon doré . . . moins cher que le melon vert et aussi gros!

Puis Mme Girard a vu plusieurs marchands de poisson, qui l'ont appelée; malgré les prix raisonnables elle n'a rien acheté, parce que sa famille ne mange pas souvent de poisson, surtout le dimanche — les enfants aiment mieux du bœuf ou du poulet. . . . Heureusement pour elle sa conversation avec les marchands de poisson n'a pas duré longtemps: soudain, dans un coin du marché un homme a battu le tambour et la foule curieuse a entouré son étalage.

"Mesdames, messieurs," a-t-il dit, "je vous offre un produit sensationnel, à un prix sensationnel. Approchez, venez plus près! Quelques gouttes de ce liquide dans votre eau de vaisselle et toutes vos assiettes, toute votre coutellerie, tous vos verres sont propres en un clin d'œil. Et vous, monsieur, vous pouvez laver votre voiture en cinq minutes avec ce liquide merveilleux. À titre publicitaire, je ne vous donne pas une bouteille, mais deux bouteilles pour le prix d'une! Je ne demande pas trois francs, non, deux francs soixante-cinq."

Mme Girard, qui est économe, a écouté le boniment avec intérêt, mais elle a souri. Elle n'est pas facile à duper et elle a quitté cet étalage aussi sans rien acheter. Pour finir son marché elle a enfin acheté une demi-douzaine d'œufs et aussi un bouquet d'œillets (qui vont orner le buffet de la salle à manger).

Elle a quitté le marché vers midi et quart pour rentrer à la maison. Dans la grand'rue qu'elle a dû suivre, elle a remarqué les terrasses des cafés déjà remplies de monde, car c'est dimanche et on ne travaille pas, excepté les pauvres marchands. Enfin Mme Girard a atteint l'avenue où elle habite et de loin elle a vu ses enfants à la fenêtre de leurs chambres. Elle est toujours un peu anxieuse quand elle sort sans les enfants, parce qu'on sait qu'ils abusent de leur liberté! Il ne faut pas oublier la soirée que M. et Mme Girard ont passée au cinéma . . . mais, cher lecteur, chère lectrice, qu'est-ce que les enfants ont fait ce soir-là? C'est un secret que je vais garder — vous devez trouver vous-même la solution de ce problème. . . .

(*See notes on the next page. Translation at the end of the book.*)

NOTES ON THE TEXT

Son, sa, ses = *one's*, when used with the pronoun **on**; **temps** = *weather*, it may be added to expressions like **Il fait beau**, without altering the meaning; **beaucoup de monde** = *a lot of people* (compare **tout le monde**); **de toute façon** = *in any case*; **marché** is used without the article in certain expressions; **de bonne heure** = *early* (compare the English idiom *in good time*); **a été au marché** = *went to the market*, the perfect tense of **être** is sometimes used instead of **aller** to mean *has gone, have gone* or *went*; **le kilo[gramme]**, a French measure which is approximately 2¼ *lbs.*; **de beaux melons, des** is always reduced to **de** before adjectives (see p. 36); **la Charente**, the name of a river and department, i.e. county, in south-west France; **à tout prix** = *at all costs*; **messieurs** = *gentlemen*, this is the plural of **monsieur**, i.e. **mon sieur** = *my lord* (note that the possessive adjective is made plural in this noun and compare **mesdames**); **en un clin d'œil** = *in the twinkling of an eye*, **en cinq minutes** = *in five minutes*, **en** = *within* when used with expressions of time; **à titre publicitaire** = *as a special offer*; **son marché** = *her shopping in the market*; **à la maison** = *to* or *at home*; **vous-même** = *yourself*, adding **même** to a pronoun makes it emphatic (compare **moi-même** = *myself*, and see p. 114).

When you have learned all these phrases thoroughly, read the text through again testing your memory of them.

EXERCISES

I. **Répondez en français aux questions suivantes:**

1. **Comment est le melon que Mme Girard a choisi?**
2. **Comment sont les terrasses des cafés?**
3. **Comment est Mme Girard quand elle choisit ses provisions?**
4. **Où les enfants courent-ils au marché?**
5. **Où Mme Girard écoute-t-elle le boniment du marchand?**
6. **Où voit-on les terrasses?**
7. **Qu'est-ce que les enfants aiment manger le dimanche?**
8. **Que dit le monsieur qui vend le liquide merveilleux?**
9. **Qui a appelé Mme Girard?**
10. **Qui a pesé les épinards que Mme Girard a voulu acheter?**
11. **Qui a mis les épinards dans le panier?**
12. **De quelle couleur sont les épinards?**
13. **Combien d'œufs Mme Girard a-t-elle acheté?**
14. **En combien de minutes peut-on laver sa voiture avec le liquide merveilleux?**
15. **Pourquoi Mme Girard a-t-elle acheté le bouquet de fleurs?**
16. **Pourquoi Mme Girard n'aime-t-elle pas aller au marché avec les enfants?**
17. **Pourquoi les gens vont-ils aux cafés?**

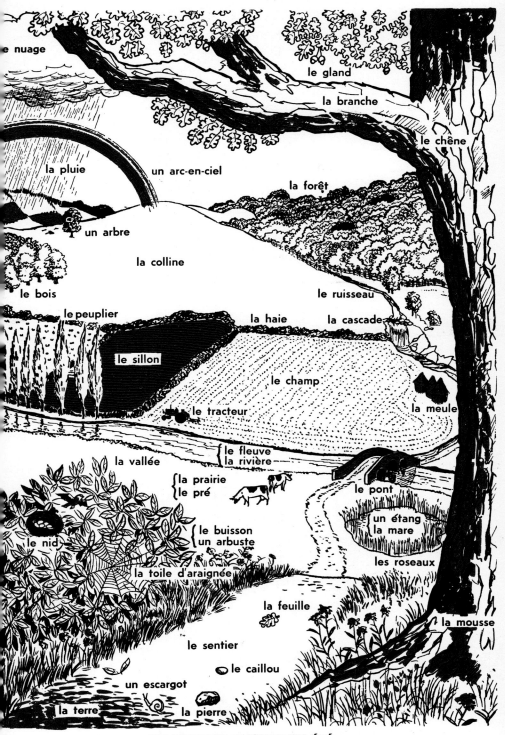

le nuage
le gland
la branche
le chêne
la pluie
un arc-en-ciel
la forêt
un arbre
la colline
le bois
le ruisseau
le peuplier
la haie
la cascade
le sillon
le champ
la meule
le tracteur
le fleuve
la vallée
la rivière
la prairie
le pré
le pont
le buisson
un arbuste
un étang
la mare
le nid
les roseaux
la toile d'araignée
la feuille
la mousse
le sentier
le caillou
un escargot
la terre
la pierre

UN PAYSAGE PAISIBLE EN ÉTÉ

RENCH—F

un agneau

un âne

le bœuf

le chat

la chèvre

le chien

le lapin

le cheval

le mouton

le porc, le cochon

la vache

le veau

la baleine

le chameau

la chauve-souris

un élépha

le hérisson

le lièvre

le lion

un écureuil

le loup

un ours

le cerf

le phoque

le r

le renard

le serpent

le singe

la souris

le tigre

LES ANIMAUX DE LA FERME ET LES ANIMAUX SAUVAGES

EXERCISES

18. À quelle heure Mme Girard a-t-elle quitté le marché?
19. À quelle heure va-t-on généralement à l'église?
20. À quelle heure avez-vous commencé à répondre à ces questions?

II. Re-read the text in Lesson 7 and then write a short account in French in the present tense to explain why M. and Mme Girard found the lights on and the door open.

III. Write out in full the perfect tenses of: **lire, écrire, mettre, être, avoir** and **pouvoir**.

IV. Translate into French:

1. All the boys
2. All the cake
3. All the pears
4. All the baskets
5. All the people
6. All the melon
7. All the crowd
8. All the week
9. All the tradesmen
10. All the peasant-women

V. Complete these sentences by adding the right agreement to the past participle where necessary; then translate them, putting any relative clause in brackets:

1. Je ne peux pas trouver les légumes qu'elle a acheté.
2. Ne peux-tu pas trouver les provisions que j'ai acheté?
3. Il ne peut pas trouver les pommes que vous avez pesé.
4. Ne pouvons-nous pas manger les melons dorés que maman a trouvé?
5. "Quelles poires avez-vous mis sur l'étalage aujourd'hui?" demande sa femme.
6. Les marchandises que les paysans ont vendu au marché, je ne les ai pas trouvé trop sales.
7. L'auto que votre père a acheté la semaine dernière, je l'ai vu pour la première fois devant votre maison.
8. "Combien de poulets avez-vous vendu cette semaine?" a-t-elle demandé.
9. Elle les a acheté au marché qu'il y a eu dimanche.
10. La poupée que Jacques a cassé n'a pas de jolies robes.

(Answers at the end of the book.)

LEÇON 9

GRAMMAR

MORE ABOUT THE PERFECT TENSE

The most important thing to remember about the perfect tense is that it is **avoir** (which is here called the auxiliary verb) which is affected by, and must agree with, the subject; the past participle agrees with the direct object only if the latter precedes the verb. It is only the auxiliary verb which is affected by inversion and by the negative, as you will see from these examples:

ai-je vendu? = *have I sold?* or *did I sell?* or *have I*	**avons-nous vendu?**
as-tu vendu? [*been selling?* etc.	**avez-vous vendu?**
a-t-il vendu?	**ont‿ils vendu?**

je n'ai pas fini = *I have not finished*, etc.	**nous n'avons pas fini**
tu n'as pas fini	**vous n'avez pas fini**
il n'a pas fini	**ils n'ont pas fini**

Note that the participle position is unaffected by negative questions:

n'ai-je pas fini? = *have I not finished?* etc.	**n'avons-nous pas fini?**
n'as-tu pas fini?	**n'avez-vous pas fini?**
n'a-t-il pas fini?	**n'ont‿ils pas fini?**

Even when the sentence contains an adverb it sometimes comes between the auxiliary verb and the past participle:

N'avez-vous pas‿encore fini? *Have you not yet finished?*

VERBS CONJUGATED WITH être

There are some verbs which form their perfect not with **avoir**, but with **être**; they have an important difference, which is that the past participles of these verbs agree with their subjects like adjectives. This group of verbs includes twelve common verbs with compounds (most are verbs of motion):

arriver (arrivé) = *to arrive*	**partir (parti)** = *to leave, depart*
aller (allé) = *to go*	**venir (venu)** = *to come*
entrer (entré) = *to enter, go, come, in*	**sortir (sorti)** = *to go, come, out*
descendre (descendu) = *to go, come, down*	**monter (monté)** = *to go, come, up*
rester (resté) = *to stay, remain*	**tomber (tombé)** = *to fall*
mourir (mort) = *to die*	**naître (né)** = *to be born*

Compounds of **entrer** and **venir**: **rentrer (rentré)** = *to return, come back home*; **devenir (devenu)** = *to become*; **revenir (revenu)** = *to come back.*

88

Here is the perfect tense in full of one of these verbs:

je suis arrivé, arrivée = *I arrived*, etc.   **nous sommes arrivés, arrivées**
tu es arrivé, arrivée   **vous êtes arrivé(s), arrivée(s)**
il est arrivé   **ils sont arrivés**
elle est arrivée   **elles sont arrivées**

Note that it is the subject with which the participle agrees, thus with **vous** it can be singular: "**Ah, vous êtes arrivée,**" **dit-il à la dame.**

These verbs also differ from those conjugated with **avoir** in that they never take a direct object: where the English verb has a direct object the problem is solved in French by introducing a preposition:

Il est entré dans la maison = *He entered the house.*
Il est sorti de la maison (or **Il a quitté la maison**) = *He left the house.*
Il est parti de la ville (or **Il a quitté la ville**) = *He left the town.*

A few of these verbs are sometimes used transitively (i.e. with a direct object), but when this happens (*a*) they have a different meaning, (*b*) they must be conjugated with **avoir**:

Il a descendu la valise = *He took* (or *brought*) *down the suitcase.*
Il a descendu la rivière = *He went* (or *came*) *down the river.*
J'ai sorti mon mouchoir = *I took* (or *brought*) *out my handkerchief.*

Note that **Il a couru dans la maison** = *He ran about in the house.* **Dans** does not always mean *into* when used with a verb of motion, unless the verb is conjugated with **être**.

IRREGULAR VERBS

mourir [muriːr] = *to die* **naître** [nɛːtr] = *to be* **vivre** [viːvr] = *to live*
je meurs [mœːr]   **je nais** [nɛ]   [*born* **je vis** [vi]
tu meurs [mœːr]   **tu nais** [nɛ]   **tu vis** [vi]
il meurt [mœːr]   **il naît** [nɛ]   **il vit** [vi]
nous mourons [murɔ̃]   **nous naissons** [nɛsɔ̃]   **nous vivons** [vivɔ̃]
vous mourez [mure]   **vous naissez** [nɛse]   **vous vivez** [vive]
ils meurent [mœːr]   **ils naissent** [nɛs]   **ils vivent** [viv]

Perfect tense (**mourir** and **naître** conjugated with **être**, **vivre** with **avoir**):

je suis mort(e)   **je suis né(e)**   **j'ai vécu**
tu es mort(e)   **tu es né(e)**   **tu as vécu**
il est mort   **il est né**   **il a vécu**
elle est morte   **elle est née**   **elle a vécu**
nous sommes mort(e)s   **nous sommes né(e)s**   **nous avons vécu**
vous êtes mort(e)(s)   **vous êtes né(e)(s)**   **vous avez vécu**
ils sont morts   **ils sont nés**   **ils ont vécu**
elles sont mortes   **elles sont nées**   **elles ont vécu**

VOCABULARY

il y a ... [il j a]	... *ago*
la tante [tɑ̃t]	*aunt*
aîné(e) [ɛne]	*elder, eldest*
sonner [sɔne]	*to ring*
le papier [papje]	*paper*
presque [prɛsk]	*almost*
la nouvelle [nuvɛl]	*news*
le facteur [faktœːr]	*postman*
distribuer [distribɥe]	*to deliver* (letters)
chaque [ʃak]	*each, every*
plus vite [ply vit]	*more quickly*
le messager [mɛsaʒe]	*messenger*
n'importe quel, -lle [nɛ̃pɔrt kɛl]	*any, whatever*
triste [trist]	*sad*
décider [de + infin.] [deside (də)]	*to decide* [*to*]
chez [ʃe]	*to, at, the house of*
un enterrement [ɑ̃tɛrmɑ̃]	*burial, funeral*
malheureusement [malœrøzmɑ̃]	*unfortunately*
avoir besoin de [avwaːr bəzwɛ̃ də]	*to need, have need of*
le voyage [vwajaːʒ]	*journey*
le chemin de fer [ʃəmɛ̃ də fɛr]	*railway*
aussitôt [osito]	*immediately*
la gare [gaːr]	*station*
regarder [rəgarde]	*to look at*
un horaire [ɔrɛːr]	*time-table*
le départ [depaːr]	*departure*
une arrivée [arive]	*arrival*
inscrit(e) [ɛ̃skri, -it]	*written, inscribed*
une affiche [afiʃ]	*notice-board, poster*
à l'intérieur de [a lɛ̃terjœːr də]	*inside*
le bureau de renseignements [byro də rɑ̃sɛɲmɑ̃]	*enquiry office*
convenable [kɔ̃vnabl]	*suitable*
puis [pɥi]	*then, next*
faire une valise [fɛːr yn valiːz]	*to pack a suitcase*
emmener [ɑ̃mne]	*to take, lead, away*
un ami, une amie [ami]	*friend*
gris(e) [gri, griz]	*grey*
le chapeau [ʃapo]	*hat*
en signe de deuil [ɑ̃ siɲ də dœːj]	*as a sign of mourning*
dedans [dədɑ̃]	*in, into* [*it*]

le facteur

le messager

un horaire

une affiche

le kiosque

le billet aller et retour [bijɛ ale e rətuːr]	return ticket	
le guichet [giʃe]	ticket-office	
attendre [atɑ̃ːdr]	to wait [for]	
en retard [ɑ̃ rətaːr]	late	
la salle d'attente [sal datɑ̃t]	waiting-room	
la banquette [bɑ̃kɛt]	seat, bench, form	
la gravure [gravyːr]	print, picture	**la gravure**
pittoresque [pittɔrɛsk]	picturesque	
le haut-parleur [o parlœːr]	loudspeaker	
le quai [ke]	platform	
montrer [mɔ̃tre]	to show	
le contrôleur [kɔ̃trolœːr]	ticket-collector	
poinçonner [pwɛ̃sɔne]	to punch, clip	
d'abord [dabɔːr]	first of all, at first	**le haut-parleur**
à destination de [a dɛstinasjɔ̃ də]	going to, bound for	
en voiture! [ɑ̃ vwatyːr]	all aboard!	
souterrain(e) [sutɛrɛ̃, -ɛn]	underground,	
la voie [vwa]	track [subterranean	
le rapide [rapid]	express train	
ne . . . jamais [nə . . . ʒamɛ]	never	
hors de [ɔːr də]	out of	
bas, -sse [bɑ, bɑs]	low	**le passage à**
grimper [grɛ̃pe]	climb	**niveau**
la marche [marʃ]	step	
le niveau [nivo]	level	
la portière [pɔrtjɛːr]	carriage-door	
le chef de gare [ʃɛf də gaːr]	station-master	
le sifflet [siflɛ]	whistle	
puissant(e) [pɥisɑ̃, -ɑ̃t]	powerful	
lent(e), lentement [lɑ̃, lɑ̃ːt(əmɑ̃)]	slow, slowly	
tirer [tire]	to pull	**la vache**
croiser [krwaze]	to cross, pass by	
un autorail [otoraːj]	diesel rail-car	
le passage à niveau [pasaːʒ a nivo]	level crossing	
la vache [vaʃ]	cow	
le bois [bwɑ]	wood	
un arrêt [arɛ]	stop	
un omnibus [ɔmnibyːs]	slow (stopping) train	
desservir [desɛrviːr]	to serve, clear the table	
le pays [pe(j)i]	land, country, district	**le bois**
le car, un autocar [kaːr, otokaːr]	motor-coach	

91

UN VOYAGE TRISTE

Il y a deux semaines une vieille tante de Mme Girard (la sœur aînée de son père) est morte. Ce matin-là, à dix heures et demie, le garçon télégraphiste a sonné à la porte; il a donné un papier bleu à Mme Girard. Elle a eu peur, parce que ce papier bleu est un télégramme et on a presque toujours peur quand on reçoit ainsi une nouvelle. Le facteur distribue les lettres et les paquets chaque matin, mais il faut distribuer les télégrammes plus vite. Un messager spécial les apporte à n'importe quelle heure de la journée.

Quand Mme Girard a lu la triste nouvelle écrite sur le papier bleu, elle a décidé d'aller chez son oncle pour l'enterrement. Malheureusement son mari ne peut pas la conduire en auto, car il a besoin de la voiture pour aller à son travail. Que va-t-elle faire? Elle doit faire le voyage par le chemin de fer.

Aussitôt elle est allée à la gare pour regarder l'horaire des trains. Les heures de départ et d'arrivée sont inscrites sur de grandes affiches à l'intérieur de la gare. On peut aussi les demander au bureau de renseignements. Mme Girard a enfin trouvé un train convenable, puis elle est rentrée à la maison pour faire sa petite valise.... Elle n'a pas pu emmener les enfants qu'une de ses amies a gardés pendant les trois jours de son absence.

Le moment du départ est arrivé. Mme Girard a mis un manteau gris et un chapeau noir en signe de deuil. Le taxi est arrivé, elle est montée dedans et bientôt elle est descendue devant la gare. Elle a pris un billet aller et retour au guichet. Elle a dû attendre parce que le train est arrivé en retard. Pour passer le temps elle a acheté une revue au kiosque et est allée dans la salle d'attente. Tout autour de cette salle il y a des banquettes et sur les murs des gravures qui représentent les coins pittoresques de la France où on peut aller par le train.

Enfin à midi et demi le haut-parleur de la gare a annoncé le train de Mme Girard. Elle est sortie vite sur le quai et a montré son billet au contrôleur qui l'a poinçonné. D'abord elle n'a pas pu trouver son train. Le haut-parleur a répété "Attention, attention! Messieurs les voyageurs, à destination de X . . . Y . . . Z, en voiture, s'il vous plaît, au quai numéro trois." Pour arriver à ce quai il faut prendre le passage souterrain, parce qu'on ne doit jamais traverser la voie; même si on regarde toutes les voies avant de traverser, les rapides passent si vite qu'on n'est jamais hors de danger.

Pour être sûre d'attraper le train, Mme Girard a donné un pourboire à un porteur qui a porté sa valise et qui l'a conduite directement à un comparti-ment de seconde classe. Elle est montée dedans tout de suite (. . . il faut dire "est montée" car le quai est bas et on doit grimper trois marches pour arriver au niveau des compartiments). Le porteur a fermé la portière et à une heure moins vingt-sept le chef de gare a donné un coup de sifflet. La puissante locomotive a commencé lentement à tirer les quatre voitures; le train a croisé un autorail et un train de marchandises, a traversé un passage à niveau, et en une minute a quitté la gare. Deux kilomètres plus loin il est entré dans un tunnel.

La pauvre Mme Girard n'aime pas les tunnels parce qu'il fait noir et la fumée de la locomotive entre par les fenêtres. Naturellement elle aime mieux admirer la campagne où elle n'a jamais vécu (. . . elle est née dans une ville industrielle au centre de la France); elle aime regarder les vaches dans les prés, la rivière qu'on traverse sur un viaduc, et les bois sombres à l'horizon.

Au bout de deux heures et demie son train est arrivé à sa destination: il y a eu beaucoup d'arrêts parce qu'un omnibus doit desservir toutes les petites villes et tous les villages du pays. Fatiguée et triste, Mme Girard a quitté la gare pour chercher un car.

(See notes on the next page. Translation at the end of the book.)

NOTES ON THE TEXT

Il y a deux semaines = *two weeks ago* (compare **Il y a un an** = *a year ago*); **écrite,** when the past participle is used as an adjective in this way it must always agree with its noun (compare **les spectateurs satisfaits** in the passage in Lesson 7); **a gardés** = *looked after*; **prendre un billet** = *to buy a ticket*; **a donné un coup de sifflet** = *blew the whistle*; **un train de marchandises** = *goods-train*. **Les haut-parleurs:** when a compound noun is made from an adverb and a noun (as here) only the noun changes. If it is made from two nouns (or an adjective and a noun) then the two halves agree and both take plural endings where applicable (e.g. les plates-bandes).

EXERCISES

I. **Répondez aux questions suivantes:**

1. **Comment est la nouvelle que Mme Girard a lue sur le papier bleu?**
2. **Où Mme Girard a-t-elle décidé d'aller?**
3. **Où a-t-elle pris son billet à la gare?**
4. **Qu'est-ce que Mme Girard a trouvé avant de rentrer à la maison?**
5. **Que fait le chef de gare avant le départ du train?**
6. **Qui apporte les télégrammes que le facteur ne peut pas distribuer?**
7. **De quelle couleur sont les télégrammes en Angleterre (*England*)?**
8. **Pourquoi Mme Girard a-t-elle mis un chapeau noir?**
9. **Quand faut-il regarder l'horaire dans une gare?**
10. **Combien de temps le voyage de Mme Girard a-t-il duré?**

Construct ten questions using vocabulary from the passage and these interrogative words and phrases. Then answer your own questions:

11. **Comment**
12. **Où**
13. **Que**
14. **Qui**
15. **Qu'est-ce que**
16. **Pourquoi**
17. **Combien**
18. **Quel**
19. **Quelle**
20. **De quelle couleur**

II. Write out the perfect tenses of these verbs: **sonner, partir, emmener, garder, avoir, tomber, demander, distribuer, devenir, rester.**

III. Find in the passage the French phrases which mean:

1. Two weeks ago.
2. She was afraid.
3. To her uncle's house.
4. In order to pack her small suit-case.
5. She had to wait.
6. Where one can go by train.
7. Within one minute.
8. Where she has never lived.
9. After two and a half hours.
10. All the little towns and villages.
11. Her father's eldest sister.
12. At any hour of the day.
13. He needs the car.
14. She got into it.
15. In order to while away the time.
16. To be sure of catching the train.
17. Through the windows.
18. On the horizon.
19. There were a lot of stops.
20. To look for a motor-coach.

EXERCISES

IV. When you have learned by heart the constructions in the Grammar section, translate these sentences into French, paying attention to the agreement of the past participle where necessary:

1. Have you not taken them to their uncle's house? (Use **emmener**.)
2. The information that she asked for is on the notice-board.
3. The telegrams that the special messenger delivered are on the table.
4. Why did he not keep the tickets that you gave to his wife?
5. They have not yet eaten all the pears that she bought a week ago.

V. Translate into French:

1. She arrived with her brother at half-past six in the evening.
2. They entered the station at a quarter to three.
3. We did not stay on the platform until five minutes to eight.
4. Why did the old lady fall on to the track?
5. They went to the enquiry office at a quarter past twelve.
6. Did she not leave before (**avant**) the arrival of the taxi.
7. We went out of the house at twenty-five minutes to eleven.
8. He took out his ticket in order to show it to the ticket-collector.
9. The porter took down all the cases, because she is tired.
10. They leave the station because there is no train until (**avant**) mid-day.

VI. Re-write the passage from "**Quand Mme Girard . . .**" to "**la salle d'attente,**" replacing Mme Girard by yourself. Begin "**Quand j'ai lu . . .**".

VII. If you would like to visit France describe, using the perfect tense, an imaginary train journey from your home in Paris. Use some of this vocabulary:

Le train de Versailles = *the train to Versailles*; **louer une place** = *to book a seat* (**place louée** = *seat reserved*); **les Grandes Lignes** = *main lines*; **les lignes de banlieue** = *suburban lines*; **un billet simple pour** = *a single ticket for*; **une demi-place** = *half-fare* (**payer demi-place** = *to pay half-fare*); **la consigne** = *left-luggage office*; **la station** = *underground station* (**le Métro** = *underground railway*); **le wagon-lit** = *sleeping-car*; **le wagon-restaurant** = *dining-car*; **le fourgon** = *guard's van*; **tirer la sonnette d'alarme** = *to pull the communication cord*; **contrôler les billets** = *to check the tickets*; **le filet à bagages** = *luggage-rack* (**les bagages** [m.] = *luggage*); **enregistrer les bagages** = *to send luggage*; **le bulletin de bagages** = *luggage-ticket*; **bagages non accompagnés** = *luggage in advance*; **une correspondance** = *connection*.

(Answers at the end of the book.)

95

LEÇON 10

GRAMMAR

REFLEXIVE VERBS

These verbs have one and the same person (or persons) as subject and object. If you say, "*I wash myself*," you are using a reflexive verb: you are both the person doing the washing and the object being washed. Many ordinary verbs which take an object can be made reflexive; **laver** [lave] = *to wash* is one of them: **Je lave le bébé** = *I wash the baby.* **Je me lave** (reflexive) = *I wash myself.*

The pronouns used with these verbs are called reflexive pronouns; they are the same as normal object pronouns except for the third person, **se** [sə]. Here are the present and perfect tenses of a reflexive verb:

se laver = *to wash oneself* (note the third person pronoun with the infinitive)

je me lave = *I wash myself*	**je me suis lavé(e)** [lave] = *I washed*
tu te laves = *you wash yourself*	**tu t'es lavé(e)** [*myself*, etc.
il se lave = *he washes himself*	**il s'est lavé**
elle se lave = *she washes herself*	**elle s'est lavée**
nous nous lavons = *we wash ourselves*	**nous nous sommes lavé(e)s**
vous vous lavez = *you wash yourself*(*-ves*)	**vous vous_êtes lavé(e)(s)**
ils se lavent = *they wash themselves*	**ils se sont lavés**
elles se lavent = *they wash themselves*	**elles se sont lavées**

Note that all reflexive verbs are conjugated with **être**, but that the past participle agrees with the reflexive pronoun, except when this is an indirect object (see following page).

Note that (*a*) the plural forms of the reflexive verb can have more complex meanings in which the subject is not precisely identical with the direct object. **Nous nous voyons** may be translated in three different ways: *we see ourselves* or *we see each other* (two people involved) or *we see one another* (several people involved). In the two latter no one person sees himself.

(*b*) Reflexives are much commoner in French than in English and must be used often when there is no reflexive idea in English (we usually say *I have washed*, not *I have washed myself*); learn these examples:

Je me souviens de ce jour-là = *I remember that day.*
La porte se ferme = *The door closes.*
Il se fâche = *He becomes angry.*

96

(c) The idea of *becoming* is often expressed by a reflexive: **Je me suis fatigué** = *I became tired, got tired, tired* (**devenir** is incorrect here).

INDIRECT OBJECT PERSONAL PRONOUNS

me = *to me*: **Il me donne le livre** = *He gives the book to me.*
te = *to you*: **Je te rends ton chapeau** = *I give you back your hat.*
lui = *to him, her*: **Tu lui dis ton nom** = *You tell him your name.*
nous = *to us*: **Elle nous écrit souvent** = *She often writes to us.*
vous = *to you*: **Nous vous montrons notre maison** = *We show you our house.*
leur = *to them*: **Vous leur offrez des pommes** = *You offer them some apples.*

You will see that these are the same as the direct object pronouns except for **lui** and **leur**. In the first sentence **le livre** is the direct object of the verb and **me** is the indirect object. Like most pronouns these precede the verb except in a positive command.

Note that (*a*) **à** is not needed in French and *to* is often omitted in English; (*b*) the past participle never agrees with the indirect object: **Elle s'est lavé les mains** = *She has washed her hands* (*the hands to herself*); here **se** is indirect object. But: **Elle s'est lavée** = *She washed herself*; here **se** is feminine direct object and **lavée** must agree with it.

THE PRONOUNS y AND en

y [i] = **à** + a noun: **Va-t-il à la gare à midi? Non, il y va à une heure** = *Does he go to the station at mid-day? No, he goes there at one o'clock.*
en [ã] = **de** + a noun: **Trouve-t-il du pain? Oui, il en trouve dans la cuisine** = *Does he find some bread? Yes, he finds some in the kitchen.*

These are not personal pronouns; they are applied only to things. Basically **y** = *to it*, but it can also mean *on it*, *in it*, etc.; in fact it can stand for **sur**, **dans** or any preposition of place, and can often be translated *there*. **En** = *of it*, *of them* or *some*. Analyse all the uses of **y** and **en** in the following text and decide what words they stand for.

Note that (*a*) **y** cannot be used with **il y a** in the same sentence; (*b*) there is no past participle agreement with **en** as it is not a direct object.

ORDER OF PRONOUNS

If a sentence has more than one of these pronouns, they take this order:

me						
te		le		lui		
se	before	la	before		before y	before en
nous		les		leur		
vous						

Le marchand le leur donne = *The tradesman gives it to them.*
Sa mère nous les a donnés = *His mother has given them to us.*

VOCABULARY

souhaiter [swɛte]	*to wish*	
un anniversaire [anivɛrsɛːr]	*birthday*	
la fête [fɛːt]	*name-day*	
le prénom [prenɔ̃]	*Christian name*	
le nom [nɔ̃]	*name*	
célébrer [selebre]	*to celebrate*	**le calendrier**
le jour où [ʒuːr u]	*the day when*	
le calendrier [kalɑ̃drje]	*calendar*	
un an, une année [ɑ̃, ane]	*year*	
fêter [fɛte]	*to celebrate, keep as a festival*	
le vœu [vø]	*vow, wish*	
le cadeau [kado]	*present, gift*	
la vitrine [vitrin]	*shop-window*	
le, la fleuriste [flœrist]	*florist*	
la pancarte [pɑ̃kart]	*notice, placard*	
annoncer [anɔ̃se]	*to announce*	
le matin [matɛ̃]	*morning*	
se lever [sə ləve]	*to get up, rise*	**la vitrine**
cueillir [kœjiːr]	*to pick, gather, pluck*	
piétiner [pjetine]	*to trample, stamp on*	
la plate-bande [platbɑ̃ːd]	*flower-bed, grass-border*	
puisque [pɥiskə]	*since*	
nouer [nwe, nue]	*to knot, tie*	
le ruban [rybɑ̃]	*ribbon*	
s'écrier [sekrie]	*to cry out, exclaim*	
faire semblant de [fɛːr sɑ̃blɑ̃ də]	*to pretend to*	
surpris(e) [syrpri, -iːz]	*surprised*	
embrasser [ɑ̃brase]	*to embrace, kiss*	
le paquet [pakɛ]	*parcel, packet*	
gentil, -ille [ʒɑ̃ti, -iːj]	*pleasing, nice, kind*	**la plate-bande**
le gant [gɑ̃]	*glove*	
aller bien avec [ale bjɛ̃navɛk]	*to match, go well with*	
exemplaire [egzɑ̃plɛːr]	*exemplary*	
faire la cuisine [fɛːr la kɥizin]	*to do the cooking*	
dîner [en ville] [dine (ɑ̃ vil)]	*to dine [out]*	
la truite [au bleu] [trɥit (o blø)]	*[blue] trout*	
enchanté(e) [ɑ̃ʃɑ̃te]	*delighted*	
le cygne [siɲ]	*swan*	
un oiseau [wazo]	*bird*	
gracieux, -euse [grasjø, -øːz]	*graceful*	**le ruban**
sembler [sɑ̃ble]	*to seem, appear*	

se salir [sə saliːr]	to become, get, dirty	
bien frais, fraîche [bjɛ̃ frɛ, frɛʃ]	nice and cool	
ici [isi]	here	
mettre un couvert [mɛtr œ̃ kuvɛːr]	to lay a place	
le potage [pɔtaːʒ]	soup	
prenons! [prənɔ̃]	let us have, take!	**la paquet**
la tomate [tɔmat]	tomato	
le plat [pla]	dish	
aux petits pois [o pəti pwɑ]	with green peas	
le baba au rhum [baba o rɔm]	rum-baba	
agréer [agree]	to agree to, accept	
d'une voix persuasive [vwa [pɛrsɥaziːv]	in a persuasive voice	**la truite**
approuver [apruve]	to approve of	
le choix [ʃwa]	choice	
du moins [dy mwɛ̃]	at least	
se réserver [sə resɛrve]	to reserve for oneself	
le vin [vɛ̃]	wine	
le sommelier [sɔməlje]	wine-waiter	**le couvert**
lui-même [lɥi mɛːm]	himself	
mûre réflexion [myːr reflɛksjɔ̃]	careful thought	
commander [kɔmɑ̃de]	to order	
la carafe [karaf]	decanter	
le vin rosé [vɛ̃ roze]	light table-wine	
le plateau [plato]	tray	
d'argent [darʒɑ̃]	[made] of silver	
le citadin [sitadɛ̃]	city-dweller, townsman	**le potage**
se ranger à [sə rɑ̃ʒe a]	to agree with	
lourd(e) [luːr, lurd]	heavy, close, sultry	
se rendre à [sə rɑ̃ːdr a]	to go to .	
se contenter de [sə kɔ̃tɑ̃te də]	to be satisfied with	
la bière [bjɛːr]	beer	
la limonade [limɔnad]	lemonade	**le plateau**
frais, fraîche [frɛ, frɛʃ]	fresh, cool	
la hâte [ɑːt]	haste	
une addition [adisjɔ̃]	bill	
poliment [pɔlimɑ̃]	politely	
néanmoins [neɑ̃mwɛ̃]	nevertheless	
se promener [sə prɔmne]	to go for a walk	
le soleil couchant [sɔlɛːj kuʃɑ̃]	setting sun	
refléter [rəflete]	to reflect	**le soleil couchant**
la paix [pɛ]	peace	

99

LA FÊTE DE MADAME GIRARD

En France on souhaite les anniversaires, mais surtout on souhaite les fêtes. Qu'est-ce qu'une fête? Eh bien, presque chaque prénom est aussi le nom d'un saint (ou d'une sainte). On doit célébrer une fête le jour où l'on trouve le nom de ce saint sur le calendrier, parce que, chaque jour de l'année, l'église fête un saint (qu'on appelle "le saint du jour"). Ainsi la fête de St. Michel est le vingt-neuf septembre: ce jour-là tous les garçons qui s'appellent Michel reçoivent des vœux et des cadeaux de leurs parents et de leurs amis. Dans la vitrine d'une fleuriste il y a souvent une petite pancarte qui annonce quelle fête il faut célébrer.

Mme Girard s'appelle Anne-Marie: sa fête se souhaite le vingt-six juillet. Le matin de ce jour-là les enfants se sont levés de bonne heure et sont allés en secret cueillir un bouquet de fleurs au jardin. Jacques a même piétiné les plates-bandes, mais puisque c'est la fête de maman son père ne l'a pas grondé!

Josette a noué un beau ruban autour du bouquet, et ensuite les trois enfants sont entrés dans la salle à manger et se sont écriés: "Maman, je te souhaite une bonne fête!" Mme Girard a fait semblant d'être surprise et a embrassé les enfants. Puis M. Girard est entré et a dit à sa femme: "Bonne fête, chérie." Il lui a donné un petit paquet qu'elle a ouvert tout de suite. "Oh! mais tu es trop gentil, René! Quels beaux gants! Quelle jolie couleur! Ils vont bien avec mon manteau bleu."

Mais M. Girard (quel mari exemplaire!) a une autre surprise pour sa femme. "Tu fais la cuisine tous les jours," a-t-il dit, "mais ce soir nous allons dîner au restaurant de la Truite."

Ils y sont arrivés vers huit heures. Puisqu'il fait chaud à cette heure au mois de juillet, ils ont pu rester dehors sur la belle terrasse, assis près de la rivière. Mme Girard a été enchantée de voir deux cygnes sur l'eau ... elle aime regarder ces oiseaux gracieux qui ne semblent jamais se salir. "Il fait bien frais ici," a-t-elle dit, "tandis qu'en ville il fait presque toujours trop chaud."

Au bout de quelques instants un garçon est venu leur donner un menu et mettre deux couverts sur la nappe blanche. "Choisis, chérie," a dit M. Girard. "Je ne veux pas de potage," dit-elle. "Prenons une salade de tomates pour commencer, et puis la truite au bleu, puisque c'est la spécialité de la maison. Comme plat principal, prenons des pigeons aux petits pois. Et mon dessert favori, le baba au rhum. Tu veux bien, chéri, n'est-ce pas?" a demandé Mme Girard, d'une voix persuasive.

Son mari a agréé (il approuve toujours le choix de sa femme — du moins le vingt-six juillet!), mais il s'est réservé le choix des vins et en a demandé la liste. Le sommelier l'a apportée lui-même. Après mûre réflexion M. Girard a finalement commandé une carafe de vin rosé que le garçon a servie sur un beau plateau d'argent.

Ce soir-là, il y a eu beaucoup de monde au restaurant, car beaucoup de citadins se rangent à l'opinion de Mme Girard: c'est-à-dire, il fait trop chaud et trop lourd en ville, et après une journée passée dans un bureau ou dans un magasin ils se rendent à la Truite pour être en plein air pendant quelque temps, au bord de l'eau. Tous n'ont pas commandé un repas car c'est assez cher et ce n'est pas jour de fête pour tout le monde! Ils se sont contentés d'un verre de bière ou de limonade bien fraîche.

Sans hâte, M. et Mme Girard ont mangé leur dîner de fête; après le dessert ils ont bu une tasse de café noir, puis M. Girard a demandé l'addition. Le garçon n'a pas pu l'apporter tout de suite, mais quand il est arrivé à leur table cinq minutes plus tard il s'est excusé si poliment que M. Girard lui a donné néanmoins un pourboire généreux. Ensuite sa femme et lui se sont promenés sur le petit chemin qui suit la rivière et ont admiré le soleil couchant reflété dans l'eau. L'immense paix du soir est descendue sur la nature et bientôt il leur a fallu rentrer à la maison.

(*See notes on the next page. Translation at the end of the book.*)

LEÇON 10

NOTES ON THE TEXT

En France = *in France*, several French prepositions may mean *in*, e.g.
dans une boîte = [*enclosed*] *in a box*, **à Paris** = *in Paris* (towns and cities),
en France (feminine countries), **au Canada** (masculine countries), **dans deux**
heures = *in two hours* (*after two hours have elapsed*); **le jour où** = *the day*
when, **où** has this meaning when preceded by an expression of time; **Quelle**
jolie couleur! = *What a pretty colour*! **un, une, des** are not used in exclamations
beginning with **quel(le)**, e.g. **Quelle jolie fleur!** = *What a pretty flower*!;
Prenons! = *Let us take*! the first person plural of the present tense, is used as a
command or exhortation (see p. 115); **aux petits pois** = *with green peas*, note
the use of **à** in descriptive phrases, e.g. **le garçon aux cheveux noirs** = *the*
boy with black hair; **Tu veux bien, n'est-ce pas?** = *You don't mind, do you?*;
il approuve = *he approves of*, note the French verbs which need a preposition
to complete the translation in English, e.g. **chercher** = *to look for*; **sa femme**
et lui = *he and his wife*, **il** cannot be used as part of a plural subject, the
emphatic pronoun **lui** must be used instead (see p. 114); **le soleil couchant**
reflété dans l'eau, past participles are often used in descriptive phrases,
sometimes as adjectives, sometimes representing relative clauses, i.e. **le**
soleil qui est reflété dans l'eau.

EXERCISES

I. **Répondez en français aux questions suivantes:**
   1. **Comment le garçon s'est-il excusé?**
   2. **Où les citadins se rendent-ils souvent quand il fait trop lourd en ville?**
   3. **Qu'est-ce que le garçon a donné à M. Girard au bout de quelques instants?**
   4. **Qu'est-ce que M. Girard a dit à sa femme?**
   5. **Que lui a-t-elle répondu?**
   6. **Qu'est-ce qu'on donne généralement à un garçon après un repas?**
   7. **Est-ce que M. Girard a donné un pourboire au garçon?**
   8. **Pourquoi lui en a-t-il donné un?** (en = *of them*).
   9. **Qui a apporté la liste des vins? Qui a apporté la carafe de vin?**
  10. **De quelle couleur sont les cygnes? Y a-t-il des cygnes noirs?**
  11. **À quelle heure les Girard sont-ils arrivés à la Truite?**
  12. **Quel dessert Mme Girard a-t-elle choisi?**
  13. **Pourquoi a-t-elle fait ce choix?**
  14. **Combien de cygnes y a-t-il sur l'eau?**
  15. **Où les Girard se sont-ils promenés après le repas?**
  16. **Quel temps a-t-il fait, le soir où** (= *when*) **les Girard sont allés à la Truite?**
  17. **Quelle est la date de la fête de Mme Girard?**
  18. **Sur quoi le garçon a-t-il apporté le vin rosé?**
  19. **Les Girard se sont-ils contentés d'un verre de bière!**
  20. **Pourquoi, le vingt-six juillet, ne s'en contentent-ils pas?**

102

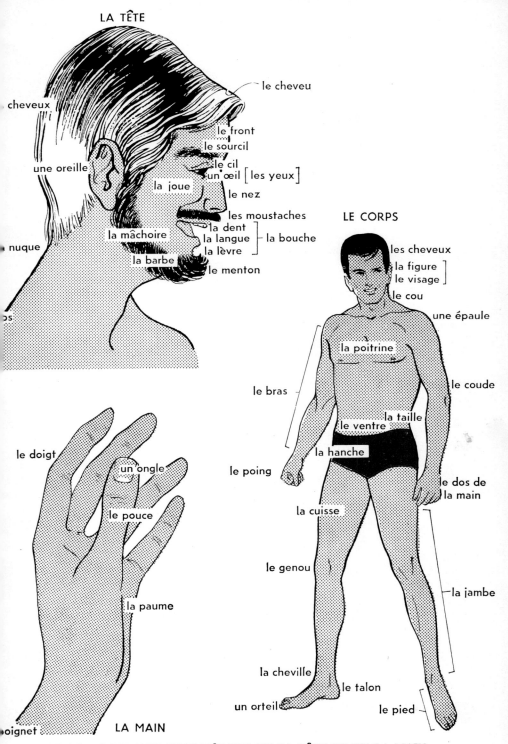

LA TÊTE

le cheveu
cheveux
le front
le sourcil
une oreille
le cil
un œil [les yeux]
la joue
le nez
les moustaches
la dent
la mâchoire
la langue ⎤
la lèvre ⎦ la bouche
la barbe
le menton
nuque
os

LE CORPS

les cheveux
la figure ⎤
le visage ⎦
le cou
une épaule
la poitrine
le coude
le bras
la taille
le ventre
la hanche
le poing
le dos de la main
la cuisse
le genou
la jambe

LA MAIN

le doigt
un ongle
le pouce
la paume
la cheville
le talon
un orteil
le pied
oignet

LE CORPS HUMAIN AVEC DÉTAILS DE LA TÊTE ET DE LA MAIN

AU MARCHAND DE LÉGUMES	AU MARCHAND DES QUATRE SAISONS	À LA POISSONNERIE	À LA LAITERIE	À L'ÉP

AU MARCHAND DE LÉGUMES

une asperge

la carotte

le chou

le chou-fleur

le concombre

les haricots verts

la laitue

un oignon

les petits pois

le poireau

la pomme de terre

la tomate

AU MARCHAND DES QUATRE SAISONS

un ananas

la banane

la cerise

le citron

la fraise

la raisin

les noix

une orange

la pêche

la poire

la pomme

la prune

À LA POISSONNERIE

les coquillages

le poisson

À LA BOUCHERIE

le lapin

le poulet

la viande

À LA CHARCUTERIE

le jambon

le lard

le pâté de foie

une côtelette de porc

la saucisse

le saucisson

À LA LAITERIE

le beurre

la crème

le fromage

le lait

un œuf

À LA BOULANGERIE

la brioche

le croissant

le pain

le petit pain

À LA PATISSERIE

le gâteau

la tarte aux pommes

À L'ÉP

les de con

le ca

la co

la far

l'huile

les

le ri

le se

le

le

le vin

LA NOURRITURE QU'ON PEUT ACHETER AUX MARCHANDS

EXERCISES

II. Write out in full the perfect tenses of: **se contenter, se rendre, se fatiguer, se souvenir, se salir.**

III. Translate these sentences into French:
1. I have not given a tip to that waiter because he has not served us.
2. I have not given him a tip because I haven't enough money.
3. I have not given it to him because the wine is not very cool.
4. He brings the wine to the Girards; he does not bring them a glass of beer.
5. Why does he not bring it to them immediately?
6. Does the wine-waiter bring it to the Girards when they enter?
7. You have seen me, but you have not seen them.
8. You went to the station but I did not go there.
9. You drank a lot of red wine, but I did not drink any.
10. My friend gave them to us, you did not sell them to us.
11. I did not give her that present; her aunt sent it her.
12. Is the cup on the table? Yes, Jacques put it there ten minutes ago.
13. She gave them some when they came back from the restaurant.
14. They always dirty each other when they play together near the water.
15. They always embrace, even when they see each other in the street.

IV. Make a list of your typical daily activities, putting each action in the perfect tense (using **avoir, être** and reflexive verbs) and introducing each sentence with a particular time, e.g.:

À sept heures je me suis reveillé (se reveiller = *to wake up*).
À sept heures dix je me suis levé.
À sept heures et quart je me suis habillé (s'habiller = *to dress oneself*).
À sept heures vingt je me suis lavé.
À sept heures et demie j'ai pris mon petit déjeuner (= *breakfast*).
À huit heures et demie je suis allé en ville.

Practise composing sentences in French by writing a French diary of this type; use as many new expressions and constructions as you can.

V. Construct a series of questions parallel to the sentences in Exercise IV, but using different times for each sentence, e.g.

Est-ce que je me suis reveillé à midi?
Me suis-je levé à minuit?

(Answers at the end of the book.)

LEÇON 11

GRAMMAR

FUTURE TENSE OF REGULAR VERBS

This tense is the easiest one to learn because its stem in most cases consists of the infinitive of the verb, to which the future endings are added. Here are the future tenses of the first and second conjugations:

je donnerai [dɔnəre] = *I shall give, shall be giving* **je finirai** = *I shall finish*
tu donneras [dɔnəra] = *you will give*, etc. **tu finiras** [etc.
il donnera [dɔnəra] = *he will give* **il finira**
nous donnerons [dɔnərɔ̃] = *we shall give* **nous finirons**
vous donnerez [dɔnəre] = *you will give* **vous finirez**
ils donneront [dɔnərɔ̃] = *they will give* **ils finiront**

The future of the third conjugation is formed in the same way except that the **-e** of the infinitive is dropped before the future endings: **vendre** [vɑ̃:dr] = *to sell*, **je vendrai** = *I shall sell*, etc. Beware of confusing [**nous**] **donnerons** and [**ils**] **donneront**, which are pronounced the same but spelt differently.

FUTURE TENSE OF IRREGULAR VERBS

aller, j'irai	être, je serai	prendre, je prendrai
avoir, j'aurai	faire, je ferai	recevoir, je recevrai
battre, je battrai	falloir, il faudra	rire, je rirai
conduire, je conduirai	lire, je lirai	savoir, je saurai
connaître, je connaîtrai	mentir, je mentirai	suivre, je suivrai
courir, je courrai	mettre, je mettrai	venir, je viendrai
craindre, je craindrai	mourir, je mourrai	vivre, je vivrai
devoir, je devrai	naître, je naîtrai	voir, je verrai
écrire, j'écrirai	ouvrir, j'ouvrirai	vouloir, je voudrai

Conduire, **craindre**, etc., set the pattern for other verbs of their types.

Note that (*a*) the future tense in English is ambiguous in the second and third persons. *Will you help me?* can be a simple future meaning *Are you going to help me?* or it can express *Are you willing to help me?* — in French this would be **Voulez-vous m'aider?** (*b*) The future can have a continuous meaning, which often sounds more natural in English, e.g. **Que ferez-vous à neuf heures ce soir? Je lirai sans doute un roman** = *What will you be doing at nine o'clock this evening? I shall doubtless be reading a novel.* (*c*) The present

106

tense is sometimes used for an immediate future as in English: **Nous partons demain** = *We are leaving tomorrow.* (*d*) One type of adverbial time clause uses the present in English (the future is implied) but takes the future in French: **Quand nous arriverons à la gare demain, il nous faudra attendre une correspondance** = *When we arrive at the station tomorrow, we shall have to wait for a connection.*

FUTURE WITH aller

French has an identical expression to ours with the verb *to go*, to express intention or future action. Here the verb loses its basic idea of motion:

Je vais leur écrire une lettre = *I am going to write them a letter.*

Tu vas m'aider cette après-midi, n'est-ce pas? = *You are going to help me* (The pronouns come after **aller**, before **aider**.) [*this afternoon, aren't you?*

IRREGULAR VERBS

boire = *to drink*	**croire** = *to believe, think*	**cueillir** = *to pick, gather*
p.p. **bu**, fut. **je boirai**	p.p. **cru**, fut. **croirai**	p.p. **cueilli**, fut. **cueillerai**
je bois [bwa]	**je crois** [krwa]	**je cueille** [kœj]
tu bois [bwa]	**tu crois** [krwa]	**tu cueilles** [kœj]
il boit [bwa]	**il croit** [krwa]	**il cueille** [kœj]
nous buvons [byvɔ̃]	**nous croyons** [krwajɔ̃]	**nous cueillons** [kœjɔ̃]
vous buvez [byve]	**vous croyez** [krwaje]	**vous cueillez** [kœje]
ils boivent [bwav]	**ils croient** [krwa]	**ils cueillent** [kœj]

s'asseoir = *to sit, sit down*, p.p. **assis**, fut. **je m'assiérai**

je m'assieds [asje]	**nous nous asseyons** [asejɔ̃]
tu t'assieds [asje]	**vous vous asseyez** [aseje]
il s'assied [asje]	**ils s'asseyent** [asej]

These verbs are irregular only in the present and future tenses:

jeter = *to throw*	**lever** = *to raise*	**espérer** = *to hope*	**essuyer** = *to wipe*
je jette	**je lève**	**j'espère**	**j'essuie**
tu jettes	**tu lèves**	**tu espères**	**tu essuies**
il jette	**il lève**	**il espère**	**il essuie**
nous jetons	**nous levons**	**nous espérons**	**nous essuyons**
vous jetez	**vous levez**	**vous espérez**	**vous essuyez**
ils jettent	**ils lèvent**	**ils espèrent**	**ils essuient**

Note that the stem varies in the first and second persons plural (i.e. where the ending is pronounced). Future tenses are formed from the singular stem except when the infinitive has an acute accent (formed regularly): **je jetterai, lèverai, essuierai,** but **j'espérerai.** Verbs whose infinitives end in ə + consonant + er are like **jeter** or **lever**; verbs ending in **-uyer, -oyer** and (usually) **-ayer** are like **essuyer. Envoyer** (= *to send*) and its compounds are like **essuyer** except for the futures, **j'enverrai,** etc.

107

VOCABULARY

le début [deby]	*beginning*
tenir (like **venir**) [təniːr]	*to hold, keep*
suivant(e) [sɥivã, -ãt]	*following*
les grandes vacances [grãd vakãːs]	*the summer holidays*
penser à, de [pãse a, də]	*to think of, about*
la plage [plaːʒ]	*beach, seaside resort*

la plage

augmenter [ɔgmãte]	*to increase*
faire des dépenses [depãːs]	*to incur expenses*
neuf, neuve [nœf, nœv]	*new*
tel, telle [tɛl]	*such*
mettre de côté [mɛtr də kote]	*to save, put aside*
le fonds [fɔ̃]	*funds, savings*
économiser [ekɔnɔmize]	*to economise*
autant que [otã kə]	*as much as*

la montagne

la dizaine de [dizɛn də]	*about ten*
meilleur(e) [mɛjœːr]	*better*
une idée [ide]	*idea*
marier, marié(e) [marje]	*to marry, married*
beaucoup de place [boku də plas]	*a lot of room*
respirer [rɛspire]	*to breathe*
pur(e) [pyːr]	*pure*
la montagne [mɔ̃taɲ]	*mountain*
s'amuser bien [samyze bjɛ̃]	*to have a good time*
tout (adverb) [tu]	*quite, entirely*

le conifère

le bord de la mer [bɔːr də la mɛːr]	*the seaside*
en outre [ãnuːtr]	*besides*
se faire vieux, vieille [vjø, vjɛj]	*to grow old*
le lendemain [de] [lãdmɛ̃ (də)]	*the next day, day after*
un oncle [ɔ̃ːkl]	*uncle*
posséder (like **espérer**) [pɔsede]	*to possess*
le fromager [frɔmaʒe]	*cheesemonger, -maker*

un écolier

l'est (m.) [ɛst]	*east*
la Suisse [sɥis]	*Switzerland*
la pâture [pɑtyːr]	*pasture*
le rocher [rɔʃe]	*rock*
le conifère [kɔnifɛːr]	*conifer, cone-bearing tree*
la fin [fɛ̃]	*end*
revoir [rəvwaːr]	*to see again*
le neveu [nəvø]	*nephew*
un écolier, une -ière [ekɔlje, -jɛːr]	*schoolboy, -girl*
parfois [parfwa]	*sometimes, now and then*

une écolière

un événement [evɛnmã]	*event*	
la fillette [fijɛt]	*girl*	
le trimestre [trimɛstr]	*term*	
l'année scolaire [ane skɔlɛːr]	*school year*	
le prix [pri]	*prize*	
une école [ekɔl]	*school*	
fréquenter [frekãte]	*to frequent, go to*	une école
habillé(e) de [abije də]	*dressed in*	
la robe de fête [rɔb də fɛːt]	*best dress*	
précis(e) [presi, -iz]	*precise, precisely*	
se rassembler [sə rasãble]	*to assemble*	
surveiller [syrvɛje]	*to supervise*	
la maîtresse [mɛtrɛs]	*schoolmistress*	
le banc [bã]	*seat, bench*	
la cour [kuːr]	*court, -yard*	
une estrade [ɛstrad]	*stage*	la maîtresse
reconnaître [rəkɔnɛːtr]	*to recognise*	
le maire [mɛːr]	*mayor*	
la directrice [dirɛktris]	*headmistress*	
le devant [dəvã]	*front*	
dans l'intervalle [dã lɛ̃tɛrval]	*meanwhile*	
donc [dɔ̃ːk]	*so, therefore*	
le chant [ʃã]	*song, singing*	
exécuter [ɛgzekyte]	*to perform*	le chant
la (société) chorale [(sɔsjete) kɔral]	*choral society, choir*	
se mettre à [sə mɛtr a]	*to begin to*	
assidu(e) [asidy]	*assiduous*	
la conduite [kɔ̃dµit]	*conduct*	
relié(e) [rəlje]	*bound*	
le calcul [kalkyl]	*arithmetic*	
un accessit [aksɛsit]	*certificate of merit*	
le dessin [dɛsɛ̃]	*drawing*	le livre relié
une allocution [allɔkysjɔ̃]	*short speech, address*	
féliciter [de] [felisite (də)]	*to congratulate [on]*	
au cours de [o kuːr də]	*during, in the course of*	
maintenir (like venir) [mɛ̃tniːr]	*to maintain*	
la rentrée [rãtre]	*return [to school]*	
avoir lieu [avwaːr ljø]	*to take place*	
se reposer, reposé(e) [sə rəpoze]	*to rest, rested*	
reprendre [rəprãːdr]	*to resume*	
le, la camarade [kamarad]	*[school-]friend*	le dessin
préférer (like espérer) [prefere]	*to prefer*	

une école

la maîtresse

le chant

le livre relié

le dessin

109

LA DISTRIBUTION DES PRIX

Un soir, au début de l'été, M. Girard et sa femme ont tenu la conversation suivante. "Les grandes vacances seront bientôt là, chérie! Y as-tu pensé? Que ferons-nous cette année?" "Oui, j'y ai pensé," a répondu Mme Girard, "peut-être irons-nous sur une petite plage de Normandie, comme l'an dernier." "Mais les hôtels ont augmenté leurs prix au printemps, tu sais. Et nous avons fait pendant l'hiver de grandes dépenses: nous avons acheté un tapis neuf pour le salon et un réfrigérateur. Quand on achète de telles choses, on ne peut pas mettre beaucoup d'argent de côté. J'espère du moins que nous aurons assez de fonds pour de modestes vacances, parce que moi, j'essaie toujours d'économiser autant que possible. Nous ne pourrons pas rester dans un hôtel plus d'une dizaine de jours." "Ah! non, alors! Moi, j'aime les longues vacances. Et c'est aussi meilleur pour les enfants. . . . J'ai une idée. J'écrirai à l'oncle Julien pour demander s'il pourra nous recevoir dans son chalet. Qu'en penses-tu? Ses enfants sont mariés et il a maintenant beaucoup de place." "Mais oui, cela pourra se faire, si ton oncle accepte. Nous pourrons y passer un mois, peut-être. Les enfants respireront l'air pur de la montagne et ils s'amuseront bien, tout autant qu'au bord de la mer, j'en suis sûr. En outre, l'oncle Julien se fait vieux et je l'aiderai dans son travail. Cela me changera du bureau," dit M. Girard.

Le lendemain de cette conversation, Mme Girard a écrit à son oncle qui possède un chalet de fromager dans le Jura. Le Jura est une chaîne de montagnes, à l'est, entre la France et la Suisse. C'est une région très pittoresque de pâtures, de rochers et de bois de conifères. Avant la fin de la semaine une réponse affirmative est venue. L'oncle Julien a écrit qu'il sera très content de revoir ses neveux et nièces. Sa femme, tante Louise, préparera leurs chambres pour la fin de juillet. M. Girard n'a qu'un mois de vacances. Les enfants, comme tous les écoliers, ont deux mois et demi de vacances en été. (C'est bien long, parfois, se dit Mme Girard!) Mais maintenant tout est décidé, ils passeront le mois d'août ensemble à la montagne.

Cependant, avant les grandes vacances il y a eu un événement important pour les deux fillettes. À la fin du troisième trimestre de l'année scolaire, il y a eu la distribution des prix à l'école que fréquentent Suzanne et Josette. Ce jour-là, toutes les petites filles sont venues à l'école habillées de leur robe de fête. À onze heures précises elles se sont rassemblées, surveillées par les maîtresses, et se sont assises sur des bancs dans la grande cour. Au bout de la cour sur une estrade couverte d'un tapis rouge, elles ont reconnu Monsieur le Maire et Madame la Directrice. Et qu'est-ce qu'il y a sur la longue table de bois sur le devant de l'estrade? Naturellement, beaucoup de livres — ce sont les livres de prix.

Dans l'intervalle les parents et les frères des élèves sont arrivés et se sont assis sur des chaises derrière les fillettes. Tout est donc prêt et la cérémonie annuelle va commencer. Après un chant exécuté par les membres de la chorale, la directrice s'est mise à lire la longue liste des élèves qui ont gagné des prix par leur travail assidu et leur bonne conduite. Chaque petite fille s'est levée de son banc et est allée recevoir un beau livre relié des mains du maire. Suzanne a eu le premier prix de calcul et le deuxième prix d'excellence. Josette a eu seulement le deuxième prix de chant et un accessit de dessin, mais elle a été néanmoins bien contente et a souri de loin à ses parents.

Avant la fin de la cérémonie Monsieur le Maire a fait une petite allocution pour féliciter toutes les élèves de leur succès au cours de l'année passée et pour les encourager à maintenir leurs efforts. Puis la chorale a chanté une deuxième fois et la directrice a remercié le maire et les parents. Elle a ajouté: "J'espère que vous passerez de bonnes vacances. La rentrée aura lieu le quinze septembre et vous reviendrez toutes reposées et prêtes à reprendre le travail."

Comme toutes leurs camarades Suzanne et Josette ont quitté l'école à midi et demi avec leurs parents. Elles préfèrent toujours oublier les derniers mots de la directrice. Vivent les vacances!

(*See notes on the next page. Translation at the end of the book.*)

NOTES ON THE TEXT

Peut-être: if this introduces a sentence the subject and verb must be inverted (this does not alter the sense); **neuf** = *new* in the sense of *brand-new*, otherwise it is **nouveau**; **-aine** can be added to several numbers to make them approximate, e.g. **une centaine de maisons** = *about a hundred houses*; **c'est meilleur**: note that **c'est**, not **il est**, is correct when **être** is used in this way with an indefinite subject; **Mais oui**: **mais** is often added for emphasis; **un mois de vacances** = *a month's holiday*, French idiom makes this an expression of quantity; **la montagne**, singular often used for plural, e.g. **en montagne, à la montagne** = *in the mountains*; **Monsieur le . . .** note the French formal idiom; **de** = *with* after **couvert** (= *covered*), **rempli** (= *filled*), etc.; **dernier** (= *last*) comes before the noun it describes when it means *last of a series*, after it when it means *previous*; **Vivent les vacances!** = *Three cheers for the holidays!* (literally — *Long live the holidays!*)

Note carefully the different uses of **là** and **faire**.

EXERCISES

I. **Répondez en français aux questions suivantes:**

1. **Comment sont les livres de prix que reçoivent Suzanne et Josette?**
2. **Où les Girard ne pourront-ils pas passer les grands vacances?**
3. **Qu'est-ce que Mme Girard écrit à son oncle Julien?**
4. **Que lui répond-il dans la lettre qui arrive avant la fin de la semaine?**
5. **Est-ce que M. Girard va avoir deux mois et demi de vacances?**
6. **Pourquoi les Girard ne pourront-ils pas aller au bord de la mer?**
7. **De quelle couleur sont les robes de fête des jeunes filles?**
8. **À quelle heure les fillettes se sont-elles rassemblées?**
9. **À quelle heure Suzanne et Josette sont-elles rentrées à la maison?**
10. **Quel événement important a eu lieu avant les grandes vacances?**
11. **Quel temps fait-il généralement au mois d'août?**
12. **Qui va préparer les chambres dans le chalet de l'oncle Julien?**
13. **De quoi le maire a-t-il félicité les écolières?**
14. **Combien de prix la petite Suzanne a-t-elle reçus?** (See en, p. 97.)
15. **Pourquoi y a-t-il beaucoup de place dans le chalet de l'oncle de Mme Girard?** (See y, p. 97.)

II. Make sure you know by heart the futures of **donner** and **finir** (p. 106), then write out in full the future tenses of these verbs:

commencer, faire, courir, vouloir, venir, devoir, recevoir, vendre, voir, savoir.

EXERCISES

III. Find in the passage the French phrases which mean:

1. More than about ten days.
2. What do you think about it?
3. That will be possible.
4. The long holidays will soon be here.
5. Have you thought about them?
6. Perhaps we shall go to a small seaside resort in Normandy.
7. During the winter we incurred a lot of expenses.
8. That will give me a change from the office.
9. The school that Suzanne and Josette attend.
10. The headmistress began to read the long list.
11. I hope that you enjoy your holidays.
12. Next term begins on the fifteenth of September.
13. I am sure of it.
14. Uncle Julian is growing old.
15. Dressed in their best dresses.

IV. Translate into French:

1. We shall pick some flowers in the woods.
2. We are going to leave in half an hour, at a quarter to eight.
3. I shall wipe my hands (literally, the hands to me) in the bathroom.
4. He will doubtless hope that you will save some money.
5. They always throw their hats on to the settee.
6. At the end of the week she buys a lot of vegetables.
7. I get up at half-past seven when I have to go to the office.
8. I shall sit down behind the pupils if there are enough chairs.
9. When he arrives this evening I shall be preparing his supper.
10. They think that you drink too much tea after your meals.

V. Using the future tense and a time of day in each sentence, describe what you will probably be doing at fifteen different times tomorrow, e.g.:

Demain matin je me réveillerai vers sept heures et quart.
Je me lèverai à sept heures et demie.

VI. Translate into French, taking care with pronoun order and position:

1. I shall not give it to them tomorrow.
2. Will they not finish them before a quarter to eight?
3. They went into the courtyard and saw there the mayor and his wife.
4. He has gathered some flowers but he will not give them any (**en**).
5. Will they not give them to us after the holidays?

(Answers at the end of the book.)

LEÇON 12

GRAMMAR

DISJUNCTIVE PRONOUNS

Special forms of the personal pronouns, called disjunctives, are needed
when they are used other than as subject or object (direct or indirect):

(a) after prepositions:

avec moi = *with me*	**après nous** = *after us*
pour toi = *for you*	**malgré vous** = *in spite of you, of*
sans lui = *without him*	**contre eux** = *against them* [*yourself*
avant elle = *before her*	**près d'elles** = *near* [*to*] *them*

(b) as part of a plural subject with another pronoun or noun:

Mon ami et moi (nous) sommes allés au cinéma = *My friend and I went
to the cinema* (**nous** sums up **Mon ami et moi** but is not obligatory).

Ton ami et toi (vous) n'avez pas vu ce film = *You and your friend did
not see that film.*

Son ami et lui (ils) ont été malades = *He and his friend were ill.*

Elle et moi, nous ne sommes pas rentrés avant une heure du matin = *She
and I did not come back until one o'clock in the morning.*

Toi et eux, vous avez vu ce film cette après-midi, n'est-ce pas? = *You
and they saw this film this afternoon, didn't you?*

Sa mère et elle sont rentrées tard = *She and her mother came back late.*

(c) as a one-word answer to a question:

Qui a acheté les billets? Moi = *Who bought the tickets? I did.*

(d) after the verb **être**:

C'est moi qui ai fait cela.	**C'est nous qui avons fait cela.**
C'est toi qui as fait cela.	**C'est vous qui avez fait cela.**
C'est lui, elle, qui a fait cela.	**Ce sont eux, elles, qui ont fait cela.**

(e) in comparisons:

Je suis plus grand que lui = *I am taller than him* [*than he is*].

(f) for emphasis; they are then sometimes called emphatic pronouns:

Moi, je n'ai rien mangé depuis midi = *I have eaten nothing since midday.*

Eux, ils ne veulent jamais sortir le soir = *They never want to go out in
the evening* (said perhaps with a touch of scorn).

Note that the third person forms usually refer to people; compare: **J'y
pense** = *I think of it* and **Je pense à lui** = *I am thinking of him* and note

these useful adverbial forms: **dedans** = *in it, them,* **dessus** = *on it, them,* **dessous** = *below, beneath, underneath it, them.*

PRONOUNS WITH COMMANDS

In Lesson 5 we learnt the second person imperative (command) forms of the verb; we can also add the first person plural:

Donne! Donnez! = *Give*! **Finis! Finissez!** = *Finish*! **Vends! Vendez!** = *Sell*!
Donnons! = *Let us give*! **Finissons!** = *Let us finish*! **Vendons!** = *Let us sell*!

The singular of **-er** verbs retains the **-s** if followed by **y** or **en**:
Donnes-en à ton_ami! = *Give some to your friend*! **Vas-y!** = *Go there*!

The imperatives of **avoir, être, savoir** and **vouloir** are irregular:
Aie! Ayez! = *Have*! **Sois! Soyez!** = *Be*! **Sache! Sachez!** = *Know*!
Ayons! = *Let us have*! **Soyons!** = *Let us be*! **Sachons!** = *Let us know*!
Veuillez! = *Be so good as to . . .* ! is followed by the infinitive.

In positive commands the pronouns follow the verb and are linked to it with hyphens; **moi** and **toi** replace **me** and **te** and come after the others. In negative commands the pronouns are normal and precede the verb:

Donnez-les-moi! = *Give them to me*! **Ne me les donnez pas!** = *Do not give,* etc.
Vend-le-lui! = *Sell it to him*! **Ne le lui vend pas!** = *Do not sell,* etc.

Note that reflexive verbs are quite normal in the imperative: **Assieds-toi!** = *Sit down*! **Ne vous_asseyez pas!** = *Don't sit down*! **Asseyons-nous!** etc.

TABLE OF PERSONAL PRONOUNS

Subject	Direct object	Indirect object	Reflexive	Disjunctive (emphatic)
je	me	me	me	moi
tu	te	te	te	toi
il	le	lui	se	lui
elle	la	lui	se	elle
nous	nous	nous	nous	nous
vous	vous	vous	vous	vous
ils	les	leur	se	eux
elles	les	leur	se	elles

Note that there is an indefinite disjunctive pronoun **soi** which is also reflexive: **On travaille pour soi** = *One works for oneself*

IRREGULAR VERBS

plaire [plɛːr] = *to please,* p.p. **plu,** fut. **plairai**
je plais [plɛ]   **nous plaisons** [plɛzɔ̃]
tu plais [plɛ]   **vous plaisez** [plɛze]
il plaît [plɛ]   **ils plaisent** [plɛz]

valoir [valwaːr] = *to be worth*, p.p. **valu**, fut. **vaudrai**

je vaux [vo]	**nous valons** [valɔ̃]
tu vaux [vo]	**vous valez** [vale]
il vaut [vo]	**ils valent** [val]

VOCABULARY

s'installer [sɛ̃stale]	*to settle in, down*
le mal du pays [mal dy pe(j)i]	*homesickness*
gâter [gɑte]	*to spoil*
pourvu que [purvy kə]	*provided that*
exercer [ɛgzɛɪsɛ]	*to exercise*
le poumon [pumɔ̃]	*lung*
se plaire à [sə plɛːr a]	*to enjoy, take pleasure in*
brave [braːv]	*brave, good, worthy*
au cœur tendre [o kœːr tɑ̃ːdr]	*tender-hearted*
son pesant d'or [sɔ̃ pəzɑ̃ dɔr]	*one's weight in gold*
les environs (m.) [ɑ̃virɔ̃]	*surroundings*
ainsi [ɛ̃si]	*so, for example*
le champignon [ʃɑ̃piɲɔ̃]	*mushroom*
la variété [varjete]	*variety, kind*
comestible [kɔmɛstibl]	*edible, eatable*
la quantité [kɑ̃tite]	*quantity*
facilement [fasilmɑ̃]	*easily*
une espèce [ɛspɛs]	*kind, species*
vénéneux, -euse [venenø, -øːz]	*poisonous*
la recherche [rəʃɛrʃ]	*searching*
se baisser [sə bɛse]	*to stoop, bend down*
ramasser [ramase]	*to pick up*
le pas [pɑ]	*step*
juste [ʒyst]	*just, fair*
le coquin [kɔkɛ̃]	*rogue, rascal*
se retourner [sə rəturne]	*to turn round*
la grenouille [grənuːj]	*frog*
bien [bjɛ̃]	*well, good*
s'approcher de [saprɔʃe də]	*to approach*
de près [də prɛ]	*closely, from close to*
taquin(e) [takɛ̃, -in]	*teasing, teasingly*
se sauver [sə sove]	*to run away*
à toutes jambes [a tut ʒɑ̃ːb]	*as fast as one's legs can carry one*
le chenapan [ʃnapɑ̃]	*rogue, rascal*
la plaisanterie [plɛzɑ̃tri]	*joke*

**le champignon
comestible**

**le champignon
vénéneux**

la grenouille

le loup

116

lâcher [lɑʃe]	*to let go of, release*	
le projectile [prɔʒɛktil]	*missile*	
le loup [lu]	*wolf*	
valoir la peine [valwaːr la pɛn]	*to be worth the trouble*	
le long de [lɔ̃ də]	*along*	
pendant que [pɑ̃dɑ̃ kə]	*while*	
entendre [ɑ̃tɑ̃ːdr]	*to hear*	**un‿échafaudage**
jusqu'à ce que [ʒyskas(ə) kə]	*until*	
un‿arbre [arbr]	*tree*	
le buisson [bɥisɔ̃]	*bush*	
prochain(e) [prɔʃɛ̃, -ɛn]	*next*	
interrompre [ɛ̃tɛrɔ̃ːpr]	*to interrupt*	
à tour de rôle [a tuːr də roːl]	*in turn*	
la patience [pasjɑ̃ːs]	*patience*	
peu de [pø də]	*few, not much*	**la neige**
en chemin [ɑ̃ ʃmɛ̃]	*on the way*	
en haut de [ɑ̃ o də]	*at the top of*	
s'exclamer [sɛksklame]	*to exclaim*	
un‿échafaudage [eʃafodaːʒ]	*scaffolding*	
là-bas [la bɑ]	*down, over there*	
le saut de ski [so də ski]	*ski-jump*	
la pente [pɑ̃ːt]	*slope*	
la neige [nɛːʒ]	*snow*	
le villageois, la -oise [vilaʒwa, -waːz]	*villager*	**la piste**
faire du ski [fɛːr dy ski]	*to go ski-ing*	
la piste [pist]	*track, ski-run*	
à toute vitesse [a tut vitɛs]	*at full speed*	
le tremplin [trɑ̃plɛ̃]	*spring-board*	
promettre [prɔmɛtr]	*to promise*	
pour l'instant [puːr lɛ̃stɑ̃]	*for the moment*	
manquer [mɑ̃ke]	*to miss*	**le tremplin**
se dépêcher [sə depeʃe]	*to hurry [up]*	
à l'heure pour [a lœːr puːr]	*in time for*	
le miel [mjɛl]	*honey*	
comme d'habitude [kɔm dabityd]	*as usual*	
quotidien, -ienne [kɔtidjɛ̃, -jɛn]	*daily*	
poser, se poser [poze, sə poze]	*to ask, to be asked*	
se fatiguer [sə fatige]	*to tire oneself, become tired*	
se coucher [sə kuʃe]	*to go to bed, lie down*	
dès [dɛ]	*from, as early as*	**le miel**
la miette [mjɛt]	*crumb*	

117

La montagne, un arbre, le bois, le chalet, la pente, le pré, la grenouille, la fleur, le buisson, le champignon

EN VACANCES

La famille Girard est arrivée au chalet de l'oncle Julien le deux août, vers trois heures et demie de l'après-midi. Ils s'y sont installés très vite. À la montagne, chez la tante Louise, les enfants n'ont jamais le mal du pays, parce qu'elle les gâte. Pourvu qu'ils se taisent au cours des repas et pendant la nuit la tante Louise ne les gronde presque jamais. Elle croit que les enfants ont besoin d'exercer leurs poumons et leurs membres! Elle se plaît à les voir jouer; c'est une brave femme au cœur tendre — son mari et elle croient que les enfants valent leur pesant d'or!

Samedi, neuf août: les Girard ont déjà passé une semaine chez leur oncle. M. Girard surtout aime faire des excursions dans les environs et les enfants sont allés plusieurs fois avec lui explorer les coins pittoresques du pays. Ainsi, mardi dernier, il les a emmenés dans les bois pour chercher des champignons de toutes sortes et de toutes les couleurs, car en France il y a beaucoup de variétés de champignons comestibles. Les gens n'ont pas peur de les cueillir en grandes quantités parce qu'ils reconnaissent facilement les espèces vénéneuses. Ils n'en ont pas beaucoup trouvé ce jour-là — mais, au bout d'une heure de recherches Jacques s'est baissé tout à coup et a ramassé quelque chose. Suzanne, quelques pas derrière lui, a crié: "Qu'est-ce que tu as trouvé?" "Viens voir, ma sœur!" a répondu le coquin. "Ce n'est pas un champignon, j'en suis sûr." M. Girard s'est retourné, a ri et a dit: "Ça, c'est une grenouille, tu sais très bien, Jacques." La pauvre Josette aussi s'est approchée d'eux et l'a regardée de près. "Ah, moi, j'en ai peur," a-t-elle dit. "Jette-la vite, Jacques." Mais lui, taquin, a fait semblant de lancer la grenouille à sa sœur qui s'est sauvée à toutes jambes. "Sois sage, chenapan," a crié M. Girard, "si tu la lui lances, tu regretteras ta plaisanterie." Jacques a lâché son "projectile" et a crié: "Reviens, Josette, n'aie pas peur! Jouons au loup, puisque ça ne vaut pas la peine de chercher des champignons aujourd'hui. Tu seras le loup, papa. Commençons à chanter: 'Promenons-nous le long du bois pendant que le loup n'y est pas. Loup, y es-tu? Que fais-tu? Entends-tu?'" "Je mets ma chemise," a répondu le "loup" et les enfants ont continué à chanter, à quelque distance de lui, jusqu'à ce que le "loup" a dit: "Je mets mon chapeau et je viens vous manger." Alors les enfants se sont sauvés derrière les arbres et les buissons, mais M. Girard les a finalement attrapés. "La prochaine fois c'est moi qui serai le loup," a dit Jacques. "Ce ne sera pas toi," a insisté Josette. "Taisez-vous," a interrompu leur père, "vous le serez à tour de rôle, mais ayez de la patience."

À quatre heures ils sont retournés au chalet avec très peu de champignons, mais grand appétit. En chemin ils sont arrivés en haut d'un pré. Suzanne a couru devant et soudain elle s'est exclamée: "Qu'est-ce que c'est, papa, cet échafaudage de bois que je vois là-bas?" "Eh bien, le pré est en pente et l'échafaudage que tu vois est un saut de ski. Cet hiver, quand il y aura beaucoup de neige, les villageois feront du ski, et des touristes aussi viendront peut-être pour les sports d'hiver. Votre oncle m'a dit qu'il y a quelques bonnes pistes de ski dans les environs. Les skieurs agiles montent en haut de la pente, la descendent à toute vitesse, et arrivés en bas ils sautent du tremplin." "Papa," a dit Suzanne, "revenons cet hiver pour faire du ski, nous aussi!" "Peut-être, dans un an ou deux," a promis M. Girard. "Pour l'instant, retournons vite au chalet. Il est près de cinq heures. Les paysans et les fermiers apporteront bientôt leur lait chez l'oncle Julien et nous manquerons le goûter. Dépêchez-vous, les enfants."

Heureusement ils sont arrivés à l'heure pour le bon goûter de pain, de beurre et de miel que la tante Louise et Mme Girard leur ont préparé. Comme d'habitude la question quotidienne se pose: "Qu'est-ce qu'on va faire demain, maman?" "Ne soyez pas trop impatients, mes petits. Vous allez passer tout un mois en montagne, ne vous fatiguez pas dès la première semaine! Allez vous coucher de bonne heure, parce que papa et moi voulons descendre au village. L'oncle Julien m'a dit qu'il y a des amis qui nous ont invités à passer une soirée chez eux. Jacques, ne mange pas trop vite! Ramasse toutes les miettes!"

(*Translation at the end of the book.*)

119

EXERCISES

I. **Répondez aux questions suivantes:**

1. Où les villageois dans le Jura font-ils du ski en hiver?
2. Qu'est-ce que Jacques a fait semblant de lancer à sa sœur?
3. Pourquoi Suzanne veut-elle revenir dans le Jura en hiver?
4. De quelle couleur sont les grenouilles?
5. À quelle heure les Girard sont-ils arrivés chez l'oncle Julien?
6. Où les enfants se sont-ils sauvés du "loup"?
7. Combien de semaines la famille Girard va-t-elle passer en montagne?
8. Qui a préparé le goûter de M. Girard et des enfants?
9. Avez-vous jamais (= *ever*) fait du ski en France ou en Suisse?
10. Est-ce que les grenouilles sont comestibles? Où les mange-t-on?

II. Find in the passage the French for:

1. On the second of August, towards half-past three in the afternoon.
2. Provided that they keep quiet during meals and at night.
3. Josette also approached them and took a close look at it.
4. It is not worth the trouble looking for mushrooms today.
5. The children carried on singing, a little distance from him.
6. Next time I shall be wolf.
7. They did not find a lot that day.

III. Translate into French:

1. Without me.
2. For them (f.).
3. Near us.
4. On it.
5. In spite of themselves (f.).
6. Against them (m.).
7. I am thinking of him.
8. It is I who helped them.
9. It is you whom they invited.
10. It is he whom they listened to.
11. It is she who found them.
12. It is we whom you heard.
13. It is you who ate them.
14. It is they (m.) whom he caught here.
15. It is they who picked them (f.).
16. My friend and I went there with my father.
17. He and his friend did not arrive there late.
18. They and we arrived together before the end of the first film.
19. I believe that you are right but they will think that you are wrong.
20. Give me some bread and some honey, please (if it please you)!
21. Give it to them!
22. Give me that cup!
23. Do not give them to me!
24. Wash yourself in the bathroom!
25. Let us not give it to them!
26. Let us wash ourselves in the river!
27. Let us be good (**sage**)!
28. Do not be impatient!
29. Give some to your brother!
30. Let us not be afraid!

(*Answers at the end of the book.*)

REVISION SUMMARY OF GRAMMAR

ARTICLES

Page

DEFINITE ARTICLE 18

    le, la, les = *the*

le jardin	(masculine noun)
la maison	(feminine noun)
l'arbre	**l'** before any noun beginning with a vowel or
l'homme	mute **h**
le haut	**le** or **la** before an aspirate **h,** when the letter **h** is
la hache	thought of as a consonant
le onze	special case

    PLURAL in all cases: **les** — **les hommes**

INDEFINITE ARTICLE 18

    un, une = *a* or *an*

un jardin	(masculine noun)
une maison	(feminine noun)
un homme	(masculine noun)
une fleur	(feminine noun)

    PLURAL: **des** = *some*

    des jardins

    des arbres

    Il y a des arbres et des fleurs dans le jardin.

PARTITIVE ARTICLE 38, 207

    du, de la, de l', des = *some, any*

du pain	(masculine noun)
de la crême	(feminine noun)
de l'argent	(noun beginning with a vowel or mute **h**)
des maisons	(plural nouns)

    Sur la table il y a des gâteaux, du pain et de la crême.

After a negative: **de**

J'ai du pain	**je n'ai PAS DE pain**
Dans le jardin il y a des arbres	**il n'y a PAS D'arbres**

Before a plural adjective: **de**

    Des pommes but **DE belles pommes**

USE OF THE ARTICLE

The definite article must be used before—

Nouns in a general sense:	**Le fer est un métal.**
Abstract nouns:	**La patience est une vertu.**
But use the indefinite articles if the noun has an adjective:	**Il montra un courage extraordinaire.**
Languages:	**Le latin est difficile.**
But not after **parler**:	**Il parle français.**
and **en**:	**En italien.**
Countries:	**La France est un beau pays.**
But not after **en**:	**En Russie** = *to* (or *in*) *Russia.*
Or **de** (with countries of the feminine gender):	**Il vient de France** = *He comes from France.*
With masculine countries use **à**:	**Au Japon** = *to* (*in*) *Japan.*
	Aux États-Unis = *in* (*to*) *the U.S.*
With proper names preceded by an adjective:	**La petite Marie**
With titles:	**Le roi Édouard** but **Monsieur Lebrun**
With parts of the body when the object of a verb:	**Elle s'est cassé le bras**
For seasons:	**Le printemps** = *spring*
For mountains and rivers:	**Le Mont Blanc**
For weights and quantities:	**Cinq francs la douzaine**
In certain expressions:	
aller à l'école	*to go to school*
aller à l'église	*to go to church*
aller au marché	*to go to market*
l'année dernière	*last year*
la semaine prochaine	*next week*
garder le silence	*keep silent*
se mettre au travail	*to set to work*
faire la queue	*to queue*

The article is omitted—

In certain expressions:	**avoir peur, avoir faim, avoir soif, avoir chaud (froid), avoir raison (tort), avoir besoin de, à cheval, à bicyclette, en auto.**	206
After a negative:	**je n'ai pas de crayon.**	
In adjectival phrases:	**un courage de lion.**	
In apposition:	**Paris, capital de la France.**	
Numerical titles:	**Henri Huit.**	

		Page
In enumerations:	Hommes, femmes, enfants — tous périrent.	206
Notices, headings, advertisements, proverbs:	Défense d'afficher. Maison à vendre.	
Nationalities:	Elle est Française.	207
and professions:	Il est soldat but C'est un bon soldat.	
After quantities:	combien d'élèves? trop de fautes.	

except after **la plupart** (*the majority*); **bien** (= **beaucoup**)
   la plupart des gens; bien des erreurs.   206

| After: | couvert de; plein de; rempli de; quel! — quelle histoire!
ni . . . ni — je n'ai ni crayon ni papier.
jamais standing before the subject — Jamais homme ne fut si triste.
en — en haut de (except in a few phrases: en l'air; en l'absence de; en l'honneur de; en l'espace de). | 207 |

NOUNS

GENDER

Masculine or feminine: **le jardin, la maison**   18

PLURAL, add **s**: **les jardins, les maisons**; but not if ending in **s**, **x**, or **z**:

le tapis	**les tapis**
la voix	**les voix**
le nez	**les nez.**

Add **x** to **-eau**:

le chapeau   les chapeaux   226

And to certain words ending in **-ou, -au, -eu**:

le chou   les choux, etc.

al becomes **aux**:

le général   les généraux

123

COMPOUND NOUNS   94, 207
la salle à manger   **les salles à manger**
(the prepositional part à manger must be left as it is).
l'après-midi   **les après-midi**
(après cannot have a plural and midi is a singular idea).
la porte-fenêtre   **les portes-fenêtres**
(both nouns)
le haut-parleur   **les haut-parleurs**
(haut is an adverb here)
la plate-bande   **les plates-bandes**
(adjective plus noun)

NOUNS WITH MORE THAN ONE MEANING   21, 207
le garçon   = *boy* or *waiter* or *bachelor*
le côté   = *side* or direction.
l'histoire   = *story* or *history*.

SINGULAR FOR PLURAL AND PLURAL FOR SINGULAR   47, 149
le pantalon = *trousers*
les meubles = *furniture*

FEMININES OF NOUNS   216
From verbs: **marcher**   **le marcheur**   **la marcheuse**
                                    la vendeur   **la vendeuse**, etc.
Not from verbs: **acteur**   **actrice**
Change of word: **homme**   **femme**
                   monsieur   **dame**
                   bœuf   **vache**, etc.

ADJECTIVES

AGREEMENT BETWEEN NOUN AND ADJECTIVE   27
un livre vert   **des livres verts**   **le livre est vert**
une tasse verte **des tasses vertes**   **les tasses sont vertes**
No extra e for the feminine if word ends in e: **jeune, jeune** but
add e to é: **damné, damnée.**
Adjectives with the following endings double the consonant: 215

-el:	**mortel**	**mortelle**
-eil:	**pareil**	**pareille**
-en:	**quotidien**	**quotidienne**
-et:	**cadet**	**cadette**
-on:	**bon**	**bonne**

except:	complet	complète
	inquiet	inquiète
	discret	discrète

Note also:

-er:	cher	chère
	premier	première

meilleur, intérieur, extérieur, supérieur, inférieur become **meilleure,** etc.

All other adjectives ending in **-eux** become **-euse** in the feminine:

	heureux	heureuse

Irregular feminine forms: 216

blanc	blanche	long	longue	frais	fraîche
favori	favorite	faux	fausse	gros	grosse
sec	sèche	aigu	aigüe	gras	grasse

Special masculine forms before a vowel or mute **h**: 216

vieux	vieil (homme)	fem. vieille
beau	bel (ami)	belle
nouveau	nouvel	nouvelle
fou	fol	folle

PLURAL, add **s**, unless the word ends in **s, z, x**:

-al becomes **aux**:	spécial	spéciaux
Except	fatal	fatals

ADJECTIVES USED AS NOUNS 216

le petit = *the little boy*	les riches = *rich people*
la petite = *the little girl*	un quotidien = *a daily newspaper*

DEMONSTRATIVE ADJECTIVES 55

ce, cet	} *this, that*	ce monsieur, cet homme
cette		cette femme
ces	*these, those*	ces gens

To distinguish between *this* and *that*:

cette maison-ci et cette maison-là

INTERROGATIVE ADJECTIVES 55, 244

quel?	quelle?	} *which?*
quels?	quelles?	*what?*

Quelle heure est-il?

Quels livres a-t-il choisis?

In exclamations:

Quel joli jardin! = *What a pretty garden!*

Quelle femme! = *What a woman!*

POSSESSIVE ADJECTIVES

Masculine	Feminine	Plural		
mon	ma	mes	=	*my*
ton	ta	tes	=	*your*
son	sa	ses	=	*his, her, its, one's*
notre	notre	nos	=	*our*
votre	votre	vos	=	*your*
leur	leur	leurs	=	*their*

The possessive adjective agrees in gender with the noun:

son mari = *her husband*
sa femme = *his wife*
son nom = *his name, her name, its name, one's name*

With a feminine noun beginning with a vowel or mute **h**, use **mon, ton, son**:

une adresse	mon adresse
une amie	ton amie

INDEFINITE ADJECTIVES 79

Masculine	Feminine	
tout	toute	*each, all every*
tous	toutes	
tous les garçons		*all the boys*
nous tous		*all of us* (pronounce s of **tous**)
aucune(e) ⎫		*no* (take **ne** before the verb)
nul(le) ⎭		
autre		*other*
certain(e)		*certain*
chaque		*each*
même		*same*
plusieurs		*several*
quelque		*some*

POSITION 28

Usually after the noun: **les fleurs sauvages**
Except: **beau, bon (meilleur), excellent, gros, haut** (usually), **jeune, joli, long, mauvais, petit, vieux, vilain**
Un beau garçon.

CHANGE OF MEANING WITH POSITION 298

un brave homme ≐ *a worthy man*
un homme brave = *a courageous man*
la pauvre femme = *the wretched woman*
la femme pauvre = *the poverty-stricken woman*

	Before		After
cher	= *beloved*	(noun)	*expensive*
dernier	= *final*	(noun)	*just passed*
grand	= *great*	(noun)	*tall*
même	= *same*	(noun)	*very*
propre	= *own*	(noun)	*clean*

COMPARISON OF ADJECTIVES 214

grand	**plus grand**	**le plus grand**
grande	**plus grande**	**la plus grande**
grands	**plus grands**	**les plus grands**
grandes	**plus grandes**	**les plus grandes**
(or grand	**moins grand**	**le moins grand, etc.)**

Alternate forms:

mauvais	**plus mauvais**	**le plus mauvais**
	or pire	**le pire**
petit	**plus petit**	**le plus petit**
	or moindre	**le moindre**

Irregular form:

bon, bonne, meilleur(e)   **le (la) meilleur(e)**
la belle ville   **la plus belle ville**
la ville intéressante   **la ville la plus intéressante**

COMPARISON WITH SOMETHING ELSE 114

. . . plus âgé que . . .
. . . moins intelligent que . . .
. . . aussi riche que . . .
. . . pas si riche que . . .

SUPERLATIVE

l'homme le plus riche du monde (de = *in*) **but un homme des plus**   214
intelligents = *a most intelligent man.*

NUMERALS

CARDINAL NUMBERS

18, 36, 162

0 zéro	15 quinze	60 soixante
1 un, une	16 seize	61 soixante et un(e)
2 deux	17 dix-sept	70 soixante-dix
3 trois	18 dix-huit	71 soixante et onze
4 quatre	19 dix-neuf	72 soixante-douze
5 cinq	20 vingt	80 quatre-vingts
6 six	21 vingt et un(e)	81 quatre-vingt-un(e)
7 sept	22 vingt-deux	90 quatre-vingt-dix
8 huit	23 vingt-trois, etc.	100 cent
9 neuf	30 trente	101 cent un(e)
10 dix	31 trente et un(e)	200 deux cents
11 onze	40 quarante	201 deux cent un(e)
12 douze	41 quarante et un(e)	1000 mille
13 treize	50 cinquante	2000 deux mille
14 quatorze	51 cinquante et un(e)	

In dates **mil** is often used for *thousand*. Hence 1964 is **mil neuf cent soixante-quatre** (or, **dix-neuf cent soixante-quatre**).

ORDINAL NUMBERS

71, 163

1st premier, -ère	11th onzième
2nd second(e) or deuxième	12th douzième, etc.
3rd troisième	21st vingt et unième
4th quatrième	22nd vingt-deuxième
5th cinquième	30th trentième
6th sixième, etc.	40th quarantième, etc.
9th neuvième	70th soixante-dixième
10th dixième	100th centième

Ordinals are placed before the noun: **le troisième livre**

DATES

64

Le premier janvier.
Le deux février.
Le trois mars.
Le vingt et un avril, etc.

KINGS

163

Charles Premier
Henri Deux
Louis Quartorze, etc.

FRACTIONS

    un demi = *a half (as a fraction)*   **le tiers** = *one-third*

    la moitié = *half (a quantity)*   **les trois quarts** = *three-quarters*

    une demi-heure = *a half-hour*   **un cinquième** = *a fifth*

COLLECTIVES 16:

    une paire   **une trentaine**

    une huitaine   **une quarantaine**

    une dizaine   **une cinquantaine**

    une douzaine   **une soixantaine**

    une quinzaine   **une centaine**

    une vingtaine   **un millier**

As these are nouns they must be followed by **de**: **une dizaine de copies**

TIME 36, 37

    une heure

    une heure dix

    une heure et quart

    une heure et demie

    deux heures moins le quart

    midi et demi

    minuit

DIMENSIONS 173

Expressed with **avoir** or **être**:

    Cette table a deux mètres de long.

    Cette table a deux mètres de large.

    Cette table a deux mètres de haut.

    Cette table a deux mètres de long sur trois de large.

    Cette table est longue de deux mètres.

    Cette table est large de deux mètres.

    Cette table est haute de deux mètres.

    L'eau a deux mètres de profondeur.

    L'eau est profonde de deux mètres.

    La planche a 2 centimètres d'épaisseur.

    La planche est épaisse de 2 centimètres.

    Il est plus long d'un centimètre.

PRONOUNS

Subject	Object (*including Reflexive*)					Disjunctive (*Emphatic*)
je	me					moi
tu	te					toi
il	se	le	lui			lui
elle	se	la	lui			elle
nous	nous			y	en	nous
vous	vous					vous
ils	se	les	leur			eux
elles	se	les	leur			elles

The above table shows the order when there are two object pronouns
to the verb:

    Je vous le donne. Elle la leur dit. Il y en a.

    (See page 259 for the order after an imperative.)

    y = *to it, at it, there*

    en = *from it, of it, some, any*

Disjunctive pronouns are used: 114

After a preposition:	Il est parti avec elle.
On their own:	Qui est là? Moi.
For emphasis:	Lui, il aime le cinéma.
After être:	C'est lui. Ce sont elles.
In comparisons:	Tu es plus jeune qu'eux.
In double subjects:	Lui et moi, nous irons par le train.
If the direct object pronoun is other than le, la, les:	Je me suis présenté à eux.

INTERROGATIVE PRONOUNS

19, 243

Qui est arrivé? Qui est-ce qui est arrivé?	= *Who?*
Qui cherchez-vous? Qui est-ce que vous cherchez?	= *Whom?*
Avec qui est-il allé au cinéma?	= *With whom?*
Qu'est-ce qui est dans la boîte?	= *What?* (Subject)
Que dit-il? Qu'est-ce qu'il dit?	= *What?* (Object)
Avec quoi fait-il cela?	= *With what?*

lequel?   laquelle?   =   *Which one?*

lesquels?   lesquelles?   =   *Which ones?*

Lequel de ces hommes est le plus riche?

Achetez des fleurs. Lesquelles?

quel?   quelle?   ⎫
quels?   quelles?   ⎬ = *Which?*   17
Quel est votre sport favori?

POSSESSIVE PRONOUNS   208

The possessive pronoun agrees in gender and number with the noun
it stands for:

Sa maison est plus grande que la mienne (= ma maison).
His house is bigger than mine.

	Masculine singular	Feminine singular	Masculine plural	Feminine plural
mine	le mien	la mienne	les miens	les miennes
yours	le tien	la tienne	les tiens	les tiennes
his, hers, its	le sien	la sienne	les siens	les siennes
ours	le nôtre	la nôtre	les nôtres	les nôtres
yours	le vôtre	la vôtre	les vôtres	les vôtres
theirs	le leur	la leur	les leurs	les leurs

à and **de** can be combined with the above:
au mien, du sien, aux nôtres, des vôtres

RELATIVE PRONOUNS   79, 180,

Qui = *who, that, which*, subject of the verb following and referring to   181
    person(s) or thing(s) in the main clause.
    Le marchand qui est vieux reste à la maison.
    Les pommes qui sont mûres se vendent vite.

Que (qu') = *whom, that, which* (often omitted in English), direct object
    of the following verb, referring to person(s) or thing(s) in the main
    clause.
    J'aime la maison que vous avez achetée.
    Note that the past particle **achetée** agrees with the preceding direct
    object **que**, which is feminine, since it stands for **la maison**.
    (Do not confuse the relative **que** with the conjunction **que: On dit
    que vous êtes malade.**)

Qui is used after a preposition when standing for a person:
    L'ami avec qui il est allé au cinéma a pris les billets.

Lequel, lesquels   ⎫ are also used for persons and things after a
Laquelle, lesquelles ⎬ preposition:

L'ami avec lequel il est allé au cinéma
La plume avec laquelle il a écrit la lettre
L'homme auquel vous parliez

Page

Dont = *of whom, whose, of which*: 180
    L'homme dont vous avez vu le fils
    La difficulté dont vous parlez

Où in expressions of time and place 102, 181
    La chambre où il a laissé ses jouets
    The room in which he left his toys
    Le jour où nous avons visité votre oncle
    The day on which we visited your uncle

DEMONSTRATIVE PRONOUNS 55, 146
    celui   **celle** = *the one* *this one*, etc.   **ceci** = *this* 147
    ceux   **celles** = *the ones* *these*, etc.   **cela** = *that*

This pronoun must be followed by a relative clause beginning with qui or que, by de, -ci or -là.
    Celui qui est sur la table est à moi.
    Celui que vous cherchez est parti.
    Ma montre et celle de mon frère.
    Prenez ceux-ci, pas ceux-là.

ADVERBS

Adverbs follow the verb but precede adjectives or other adverbs: 63
    Elle va souvent au marché.
    Elle est très contente.
    Elle ne court pas très vite.
The adverb can come at the beginning of the sentence for emphasis:
    Hier elle est allée au marché.
Adverbs (and words) of quantity are followed by **de**:
    beaucoup de choses
    un kilo de pommes
    un tas de boue
    plus d'argent
    rien de bon
    tant d'articles

FORMATION OF ADVERBS FROM ADJECTIVES 63
Add **-ment** to the feminine form of the adjective:
    cruel   **cruelle**   **cruellement**
For adjectives in **-ant** and **-ent** change **-ant** to **-amment**, **-ent** to **-emment**:
    constant   **constamment**
    prudent   **prudemment**

When the adjective ends in a vowel, add **-ment** to the masculine form:

   poli   poliment

But

assidu	assidûment	gentil	gentiment
précis	précisément	gai	gaiement
bref	brièvement	fou	follement
énorme	énormément		

Also

| bon | bien | | mauvais | mal |

ADVERBIAL PHRASES   76, 84

à la maison	= *at home*
tout de suite	= *at once*
d'ailleurs	= *moreover*
de loin	= *from a distance*
en outre	= *besides*
de près	= *closely*
d'abord	= *first of all*
d'un ton sévère	= *sternly*
d'une manière facile	= *easily*

NEGATIVE ADVERBS   139, 147

ne . . . pas	= *not*	Je n'ai pas vu le livre.
ne . . . point	= *not at all*	Je n'ai jamais vu le livre.
ne . . . jamais	= *never*	Je n'ai rien vu.
ne . . . rien	= *nothing*	
ne . . . plus	= *no more*	
ne . . . personne	= *nobody*	

COMPARISON OF ADVERBS   214

| vite | plus vite | le plus vite |

Elle marche le plus vite.

Note the irregular forms:

bien	mieux	le mieux
mal	pis	le pis
beaucoup	plus	le plus
peu	moins	le moins

COMPARISONS   114

Il est plus âgé que moi.

Il est moins intelligent que son frère.

Il est aussi riche que son voisin.

Il n'est pas si riche que son voisin.

PREPOSITIONS

Repeat **à** and **de** before each word they refer to: 26, 38, 44

Il a donne dix pommes à un garcon et à une fillette.

Il parle de la femme et des enfants.

à and **de** fuse with **le** and **les**:

au garçon   aux garçons   du garçon   des garçons

Some adjectives are always followed by a preposition:

content de   prêt à

Learn the preposition that follows when learning the adjective.

Compound prepositions:

le long de	**le long du trottoir**
près de	**près de la gare**
au lieu de	**au lieu de rester**

No preposition after certain verbs: 250

regarder	= *to look at*	**payer**	= *to pay for*
chercher	= *to look for*	**approuver**	= *to approve of*
demander	= *to ask for*	**écouter**	= *to listen to*

The infinitive follows all prepositions except **en**: 139, 285

pour donner	= *in order to give*
(au lieu) de vendre	= *instead of selling*
(commence) à ecrire	= *begins to write*
sans finir	= *without finishing*
avant de partir	= *before departing*
après avoir dormi	= *after sleeping*
après être tombé	= *after falling*
en sortant	= *on going out*

Prepositions different in French: 252

sous la pluie	= *in the rain*
dans la rue	= *in, along, down the street*
habillé de	= *dressed in*
chez	= *at the shop (house) of*

Il prend un livre dans le tiroir.

He takes the book out of the drawer.

Elle prend une tasse sur la table.

She takes a cup off the table.

Location: 102

à quelque distance de la gare

à deux milles de la mer

à Londres (town or city)

en Angleterre (country of feminine gender)

au Canada (country of masculine gender)

Time: No preposition in—

dimanche	=	*on Sunday*
le dimanche	=	*on Sundays*
le jour où	=	*the day when*
l'après-midi	=	*in the afternoon*
le matin	=	*in the morning*
samedi matin	=	*on Saturday morning*

from:

Il a emprunté le livre à son père.
He has borrowed the book from his father.

Similarly:

prendre	= *to take*		**acheter**	= *to buy*	251
voler	= *to steal*		**cacher**	= *to conceal*	

Jouer: 251

jouer au tennis
jouer du violin
jouer un rôle

CONJUNCTIONS

Joining words and phrases:

et	= *and*	**mais**	= *but*
ou	= *or*	**que**	= *that*
ainsi	= *so, thus*		

Expressing a reason:

parce que	= *because*	**puisque**	= *since*
comme	= *as*	**car**	= *for*

Specifying a time:

quand	= *when*	**lorsque**	= *when*
pendant que	= *while*	**comme**	= *as*
tandis que	= *whilst, whereas*	**depuis que**	= *since*
après que	= *after*	**aussitôt que**	= *as soon as*

Introducing a condition:
si = *if*, **s'il, s'ils** but **si elle, si elles, si on** or **si l'on**

Subjunctive after: 265, 266

pour que	= *so that*	**avant que**	= *before*
jusqu'à ce que	= *until*	**quoique**	= *although*
sans que	= *without*	**pourvu que**	= *provided that*

de peur que ... ne = { *for fear that* / *lest* }

INTERJECTIONS

Unconnected grammatically with the rest of the sentence.   57

Zut!	=	*Oh, bother!*
Dites donc!	=	*I say!*
Hélas!	=	*Alas!*
Eh bien!	=	*Well!*

Note:

Par exemple!	=	*The idea! Really!*
Mon Dieu!	=	*Oh dear! Good heavens!*

VERBS

See Revision Summary beginning on page 273.

PART II

THIS PART of the book completes the study of basic French grammar and leads the student up to the stage where he should be able to tackle the "O" level work in the next part of the book.

The standard now becomes harder as the student should be able by now to work with more confidence and to stand on his own feet. For this reason the setting-out of these chapters is more formal and the exercises for each chapter include a simple composition to lead the student into the way of thinking and expressing his own thoughts in French.

Help with French pronunciation is still given in the form of phonetic transcriptions of new words, and the reading texts are followed immediately by notes. The vocabularies, however, are not as comprehensive as in Part I: words which are like English words and the meanings of which the student can easily guess have been left out, but they can be found in the general vocabulary at the back of the book, to which the student should refer for their genders and forms.

LEÇON 13

GRAMMAR

THE IMPERFECT TENSE

The imperfect tense is so called because the action it describes is not one which is finished (as in the perfect tense), but one which is continuous or repeated. It is formed by taking off the **-ons** ending from the first person plural present tense and adding the imperfect ending **-ais**, etc. Here are the imperfect tenses of the first three conjugations:

donner = *to give*; first person plural, present tense = **donnons**

je donnais [dɔnɛ] = *I was giving, used to give,*	nous donnions [dɔnjɔ̃]
tu donnais [dɔnɛ]	[etc. vous donniez [dɔnje]
il donnait [dɔnɛ]	ils donnaient [dɔnɛ]

finir (finissons) = *to finish*

je finissais [finisɛ] = *I was finishing,* etc.	nous finissions [finisjɔ̃]
tu finissais [finisɛ]	vous finissiez [finisje]
il finissait [finisɛ]	ils finissaient [finisɛ]

vendre (vendons) = *to sell*
je vendais [vãdɛ] = *I was selling,*   **nous vendions** [vãdjɔ]
tu vendais [vãdɛ]   [etc.   **vous vendiez** [vãdje]
il vendait [vãdɛ]   **ils vendaient** [vãdɛ]

There is only one exception to this way of forming the imperfect. This i
with the verb **être**, which forms the imperfect from the stem **ét-**:

j'étais [etɛ] = *I was, used to be,* etc.   **nous étions** [etjɔ]
tu étais [etɛ]   **vous étiez** [etje]
il était [etɛ]   **ils étaient** [etɛ]

All other irregular verbs are regular in the imperfect, but note that verbs i
-cer require a cedilla before the hard vowel **a**, and verbs in **-ger** require an
for the same reason, e.g. **commencer** and **manger**:

je commençais [kɔmãsɛ] = *I was*   **je mangeais** [mãʒɛ] = *I was eating*
tu commençais [kɔmãsɛ] [*beginning*   **tu mangeais** [mãʒɛ]
il commençait [kɔmãsɛ]   **il mangeait** [mãʒɛ]
nous commencions [kɔmãsjɔ]   **nous mangions** [mãʒjɔ]
vous commenciez [kɔmãsje]   **vous mangiez** [mãʒje]
ils commençaient [kɔmãsɛ]   **ils mangeaient** [mãʒɛ]

English has various different forms which are all translated by the imperfec
tense in French. Note carefully these uses of the imperfect tense:

(*a*) to express what used to happen habitually:
  Tous les jours il allait à l'école = *Every day he used to go to school*
(*b*) to express what was happening while something else was happening:
  Il jouait pendant que je travaillais = *He was playing while I was*
                         [*working.*
(*c*) to express what was happening when something else took place:
  Il écrivait quand je suis entré = *He was writing when I entered.*
(*d*) to describe the past state of a person or thing:
  L'élève était malade = *The pupil was ill.*
  Il pleuvait = *It was raining.*

It is also used in certain idiomatic constructions which should be noted when
they occur, e.g. **Sans moi, il tombait** = *But for me, he would have fallen*; and
in the **si** (= *if*) clause of conditional sentences (see p. 154).

Distinguish carefully between the imperfect and the perfect tenses. The
imperfect is a descriptive tense; it describes the background against which
actions in a story take place. The actions themselves are expressed by the
perfect tense (or by the past historic, which will be learned later):

  **J'ai rencontré mon ami dans la rue; il avait l'air malade. Il m'a dit qu'il
  avait un rhume.**

  I met my friend in the street; he looked ill. He told me that he had a cold.

138

GRAMMAR

NEGATIVE FORMS

ne ... point = *not at all*
ne ... plus = *no more, no longer*
ne ... jamais = *never*
ne ... personne = *nobody* (when object of the verb)
ne ... rien = *nothing* (when object)
ne ... aucun(e) = *not a, no* (when qualifying object)

Note also: **ne ... que** = *only* (which is used in the same way). These forms are used in the same way as **ne ... pas** = *not*; the **ne** is placed immediately before the verb, the second part immediately after it:

Il ne pleut plus à verse = *It is no longer pouring (with rain).*
Je ne vois personne = *I see nobody.*
Il ne dit rien = *He says nothing.*
Cela n'a aucune importance = *That has no importance.*
Nous n'avons que deux livres = *We have only two books.*

EXPRESSING AGE

In certain expressions concerning age, the verb **avoir** is used:

Quel âge avez-vous? = *How old are you?*
J'ai quinze ans = *I am fifteen.*
Il avait vingt͜ ans = *He was twenty years of age.*

It is also possible to say: **Je suis͜ âgé de quinze ans** = *I am fifteen*; **Elle était͜ âgée de vingt͜ ans**, etc.

Note that **âgé** here is an adjective, not to be confused with the noun **âge** above.

PREPOSITIONS GOVERNING VERBS

All prepositions (except **en**) which govern a verb are followed by the infinitive in French:

pour arriver = *in order to arrive*
au lieu de dire = *instead of saying*
en train de frapper = *in the act of striking*
sans parler = *without speaking*

After **après** the past infinitive is used:

après͜ avoir parlé = *after speaking*
après͜ être arrivé = *after arriving*
après s'être couché = *after going to bed*

After **en** the present participle is used:

en sortant = *on going out*
en s'habillant = *while dressing*

139

VOCABULARY

se rappeler [sə raple]	*to remember*
le lycéen [liseɛ̃]	*secondary schoolboy*
tant de [tɑ̃ də]	*so much, so many*
oser [oze]	*to dare*
l'enfance (f.) [ɑ̃fɑ̃:s]	*childhood*
en tout cas [ɑ̃ tu kɑ]	*in any case*
sauf [sof]	*except*
avaler [avale]	*to swallow*
le lycée [lise]	*secondary school*
saluer [salɥe]	*to greet*
causer [koze]	*to chat*
la cloche [klɔʃ]	*bell*
un, une élève [elɛ:v]	*pupil*
l'ennui (m.) [ɑ̃nɥi]	*trouble, worry, boredom*
le professeur [prɔfɛsœ:r]	*schoolmaster*
raconter [rakɔ̃te]	*to relate*
se tromper [sə trɔ̃pe]	*to make a mistake*
la matière [matjɛ:r]	*subject*
figurer [figyre]	*to appear, figure*
le grec [grɛk]	*Greek*
l'allemand (m.) [almɑ̃]	*German*
ni . . . ni [ni . . . ni]	*neither . . . nor*
évident(e) [evidɑ̃(t)]	*plain, obvious*
la mémoire [memwa:r]	*memory*
apprendre [aprɑ̃:dr]	*to learn*
obtenir [ɔptəni:r]	*to obtain, get*
parfait(e) [parfɛ(t)]	*perfect, excellent*
le bulletin [byltɛ̃]	*report*
au risque de [o risk də]	*at the risk of*
paraître [parɛ:tr]	*to appear*
peu [pø]	*not very*
le nègre [nɛ:gr]	*negro*
le problème [prɔblɛm]	*problem*
la langue [lɑ̃:g]	*tongue, language*
vivant(e) [vivɑ̃(t)]	*living, modern* (of languages)
un électrophone [elɛktrɔfon]	*electric gramophone*
quelquefois [kɛlkəfwa]	*sometimes*
le cahier [kaje]	*exercise-book*
ou bien [u bjɛ̃]	*or else*
la dictée [dikte]	*dictation*
avouer [avwe]	*to confess*

le lycéen

le lycée

la cloche

le bulletin

140

le paradis [paradi]	*Paradise*
le devoir [dəvwaːr]	*homework*
misérable [mizɛrabl]	*wretched*
au sujet de [o syʒɛ də]	*about*
une injure [ɛ̃ʒyːr]	*insult*
supporter [sypɔrte]	*to endure, put up with*
de long en large [də lõ ã larʒ]	*to and fro*
la bêtise [bɛtiːz]	*silly thing*
brandir [brãːdir]	*to brandish*
une épée [epe]	*sword*
frapper [frape]	*to strike*
quant à [kãt a]	*as for*
le proviseur [prɔvizœːr]	*headmaster*
véritable [veritabl]	*regular, real*
le tyran [tirã]	*tyrant*
rarement [rarmã]	*rarely*
le couloir [kulwaːr]	*corridor*
à la recherche de [a la rəʃɛrʃ də]	*in search of*
généralement [ʒenɛralmã]	*generally*
se soucier de [sə susje də]	*to worry about*
alors [alɔːr]	*then*
présenter [prezãte]	*to offer*
pitoyable [pitwajabl]	*wretched, pitiful*
s'appliquer [saplike]	*to apply oneself*
gaspiller [gaspije]	*to waste, squander*
ennuyer [ãnɥije]	*to annoy*
profiter de [prɔfite də]	*to take advantage of*
le tableau noir [tablo nwaːr]	*blackboard*
le coup de pied [ku də pje]	*kick*
le mal [mal]	*harm*
une attaque [atak]	*attack*
essayer [esɛje]	*to try*
le poing [pwɛ̃]	*fist*
en train de [ã trɛ̃ də]	*in the act of*
formidable [fɔrmidabl]	*mighty, fearsome*
se fâcher [sə faʃe]	*to get angry*
la punition [pynisjõ]	*punishment*
la phrase [fraːz]	*sentence*
sans faute [sã foːt]	*without fail*
autrement [otrəmã]	*otherwise*
coupable [kupabl]	*guilty*

le nègre

la langue

un électrophone

une épée

le coup de pied

141

L'ÉCOLE

Je ne suis plus jeune, hélas! mais je me rappelle très bien le temps où j'étais écolier. Que la vie d'un lycéen était triste! C'est ce que je croyais du moins en ce temps-là; et aujourd'hui, après tant d'années, je n'ose pas dire si les impressions que je garde de mon enfance sont justes ou non. En tout cas, je me rappelle très bien que tous les jours, sauf le dimanche, il fallait se lever de bonne heure, s'habiller, se laver aussi vite que possible, avaler une tasse de café et sortir de la maison à la hâte pour ne pas arriver en retard à l'école.

Arrivé au lycée, on entrait dans la cour, on saluait ses amis, on causait avec eux mais, à un moment donné, la cloche sonnait et tous les élèves entraient en classe.

C'est à ce moment-là que commençaient les ennuis. Il fallait faire attention tout le temps même si la leçon n'était pas très intéressante. Mais j'ai l'impression que pendant la leçon d'histoire, par exemple, quand le professeur racontait d'une voix monotone les glorieux exploits de l'empereur Napoléon, il y avait des élèves qui pensaient à ce qu'ils allaient faire pendant les vacances. Peut-être que je me trompe.

Que de matières à étudier! Au programme figuraient les mathématiques, le grec, le latin, l'anglais, l'allemand, etc. Je n'ai ni le temps ni l'intention d'en faire une liste complète. Il est évident qu'il faut avoir une bonne mémoire pour apprendre tant de choses et obtenir des mentions ''parfait'' dans ses bulletins. Au risque de paraître peu modeste je peux dire que j'avais oujours une bonne note en anglais. Mais je n'aimais pas les mathématiques; e les trouvais toujours si difficiles. Le soir mon père m'aidait à faire mes devoirs et je l'écoutais sans rien comprendre. Un jour le professeur m'a dit pour rire: "Votre père commence à faire des progrès."

Du matin au soir nous travaillions comme des nègres. Nous faisions des calculs et des problèmes. Nous étudiions les langues vivantes —mais, quand 'étais jeune, les professeurs n'avaient pas d'électrophone. Quelquefois nous prenions des notes dans nos cahiers ou bien nous écrivions sous la dictée du professeur. Très souvent nous lisions à haute voix dans un livre de texte. Je dois avouer que, pour ma part, je trouvais la prononciation anglaise très difficile. J'espère bien que ce n'est pas l'anglais qu'on parle au paradis! Après avoir travaillé dur toute la journée, le soir il fallait faire des devoirs. Quelle vie misérable!

Que dirai-je au sujet des professeurs? Ils étaient presque toujours de mauvaise humeur. Ils posaient tant de questions difficiles. De temps en temps ils disaient des injures que nous supportions en silence. Un de nos professeurs, en particulier, était vraiment terrible. Il se promenait de long en large, un gros livre à la main. Quand un élève disait une bêtise ou ne répondait pas assez vite à une question, ce professeur se mettait en colère et brandissait son livre comme une épée. Nous tremblions de terreur car nous croyions qu'il allait frapper notre malheureux camarade.

Quant à M. le Proviseur, n'en parlons pas— c'était un véritable tyran. Mais heureusement nous ne le voyions que très rarement quand il se promenait dans les couloirs à la recherche d'une victime. Nous étions certains qu'il était généralement trop occupé dans son bureau pour se soucier de nous.

Dans notre classe (j'avais alors quatorze ans et j'étais en quatrième) il y avait un méchant élève qui s'appelait François. Très souvent il arrivait en retard à l'école et le professeur le grondait. François présentait des excuses pitoyables et le professeur n'était pas très content. Au lieu de s'appliquer à ses études, ce même François gaspillait son temps et ennuyait le professeur. Parfois il profitait du moment où le professeur écrivait au tableau noir pour donner un coup de pied à son voisin Victor.

Ce dernier était un élève sage qui ne faisait jamais de mal à personne mais il ne supportait pas avec résignation les attaques de François. Souvent il essayait de se défendre. Malheureusement le professeur se retournait à ce moment-là et voyait Victor, le poing levé, en train de frapper le formidable François. Le professeur se fâchait tout rouge. "Que fais-tu là?" criait-il. "Je vais te donner une punition. Écris deux cents fois la phrase: 'Je dois rester tranquille en classe.' Tu me donneras ta punition demain matin sans faute. Autrement. . . ." Il ne terminait jamais la phrase. Malheureux Victor! Ce ne sont pas toujours les coupables qui souffrent.

(See notes on the next page. Translation at the end of the book.)

NOTES ON THE TEXT

Que la vie d'un lycéen était triste! = *How sad a schoolboy's life was!* Note the order of words and this use of **que** in an exclamation. Compare the same use of **que** below in **Que de matières . . . !** = *What a lot of subjects . . . !* **Combien de** can also be used in this way as an exclamation, = *How many . . . !* **Aussi . . . que** = *as . . . as*, e.g. **aussi facile que** = *as easy as*; **d'une voix monotone** = *in a monotonous voice*, but note **à voix basse, à voix haute**; **peut-être que** = *perhaps*: if **peut-être** is the first word in a sentence it must be followed by **que** or the verb inverted, e.g. **Peut-être est-il . . .** ; **un livre à la main** = *with a book in his hand*; **en quatrième** = *in the third form* (not *fourth*) because in a **lycée** the first year is called **la sixième**, the second **la cinquième**, etc.; note the prepositions which follow these verbs: **penser à** = *to think of*; **répondre à** = *to answer*; **profiter de** = *to profit by*; **se soucier de** = *to care about*.

EXERCISES

I. Answer in French:

1. **Comment était la vie d'un lycéen selon l'auteur?**
2. **Que faisait-on quand on arrivait au lycée?**
3. **Que faisait le professeur quand il se fâchait?**
4. **Les professeurs étaient-ils généralement de bonne humeur?**
5. **Comment s'appelait le mauvais élève?**

II. Translate into English:

1. **Je n'ai que deux livres et je n'ai pas de plume.**
2. **Il ne dit rien au professeur parce qu'il est coupable.**
3. **Il n'allait pas au marché le lundi: il restait à la maison.**
4. **Je quittais la maison de bonne heure pour ne pas arriver en retard.**
5. **L'élève était en train de recopier son devoir.**
6. **Le méchant garçon cachait une souris dans son pupitre.**
7. **Mon père avait un gros bâton à la main.**
8. **Lorsque nous sommes sortis, il pleuvait.**
9. **Je sais qu'elle n'a vu personne dans la rue.**
10. **Il me pose toujours la même question. Que c'est ennuyeux!**

III. Replace the words underlined by pronouns, e.g. **Je vois l'élève—Je le vois**:

1. **Je ne voyais jamais cette femme dans la rue.**
2. **Cet après-midi nous allons en ville.**
3. **Nous avons vu six lettres dans la boîte.**
4. **Donnez les cahiers au professeur.**

5. Ils ont dit la vérité à leurs parents.
6. Ne parlez pas à cet homme-là.
7. Il faut profiter du temps pour étudier l'anglais.
8. Combien de crayons avez-vous dans votre poche?

IV. Change the infinitives in brackets into the correct forms of the imperfect tense:

Tous les jours Mme Dubois (se lever) de bonne heure, (se laver) dans la salle de bain et (descendre) à la cuisine préparer son petit déjeuner. Le matin elle ne (manger) pas beaucoup. Après le petit déjeuner elle (laver) la vaisselle et (faire) le ménage. Vers dix heures et quart elle (sortir) pour aller en ville faire des emplettes. Elle (prendre) l'autobus au coin de la rue et (descendre) près de la gare. Elle (aller) droit au marché où elle (acheter) des légumes, des fruits et des œufs. Elle (revenir) chez elle à onze heures et quart et (commencer) à préparer le repas de midi.

V. Translate into French:

1. During the holidays we used to go to the seaside.
2. I am not guilty. I have never done any harm to anybody.
3. From time to time he would write a word on the blackboard.
4. Every day in class we used to read aloud.
5. I am going to ask you a very simple question.
6. My friend was thinking of the holidays when the teacher entered.
7. At that time we were studying English and German.
8. Arriving at school at half-past eight, we would go into the yard.
9. After finishing his work the man used to wash and go home.
10. The teacher used to scold the pupils when they said foolish things.

VI. Write a short composition entitled **"En classe,"** using the imperfect tense as far as possible. Begin **"Tous les jours. . . ."** Here are some useful phrases and vocabulary: **préparer un examen** = *to prepare for an exam*; **se présenter à un examen** = *to sit for an exam*; **échouer à un examen** (also **être collé**) = *to fail an exam*; **réussir à un examen** (also **être reçu**) = *to pass*; **être faible en** = *to be weak in*; **le thème** = *prose composition*; **la version** = *translation into mother tongue*; **négliger ses études** = *to neglect one's studies*; **la bonne conduite** = *good conduct*; **un interne** = *a boarder*; **un externe** = *a day-pupil*; **surveiller la classe** = *to supervise the class*; **le baccalauréat (le bachot)** = *the school-leaving examination*; **la rentrée des classes** = *the return to school after the holidays*; **la lecture** = *reading*; **faire une conférence** = *to give a lecture*.

(*Answers at the end of the book.*)

LEÇON 14

GRAMMAR

THE DEMONSTRATIVE PRONOUN

Pronouns are words used instead of nouns, **il** for **Paul**, **elle** for **Marie**. But sometimes we wish to use a pronoun to point out a particular person or object, and for that we use the demonstrative pronoun **celui**, etc.:

	Masculine	Feminine	
Singular	**celui** [səlɥi]	**celle** [sɛl]	= *this one, that one*
Plural	**ceux** [sø]	**celles** [sɛl]	= *these, those*

(These pronouns must be carefully distinguished from the demonstrative adjectives, **ce**, etc., which are, of course, followed by their nouns.) The demonstrative pronoun takes the gender of the noun for which it stands:

le livre becomes **celui**   **la plume** becomes **celle**
les livres becomes **ceux**   **les plumes** becomes **celles**

USES OF THE DEMONSTRATIVE PRONOUN

There are two common uses of the demonstrative pronoun by itself; the first is when it is followed by a relative clause (e.g. one introduced by **qui** or **que**):

Celui qui est riche n'est pas toujours heureux = *He who is rich is not always happy.*
Celle que vous voyez là-bas est très jolie = *The one* (e.g. **la maison**) *which you see over there is very pretty.*
Ceux qui sont pauvres n'ont pas d'amis = *Those who are poor have no friends.*
Celles dont il parle ne sont pas polies = *Those* (*women*) *he is speaking about* (*of whom he is speaking*) *are not polite.*

You will notice that where the pronoun stands for a thing rather than for a person (e.g. the second example) the noun for which it stands must have preceded it somewhere in the conversation.

The second use of the demonstrative is where it is followed by the preposition **de**:

Voici mon livre. Où est celui de mon frère? = *Here is my book. Where is my brother's* (*that of my brother*)?

When it is not used in either of these two ways **celui**, etc., must be followed by -ci or -là and must still agree with the noun it refers to:

Donnez-moi' celui-là! = *Give me that one!* (e.g. **ce livre**).

Celle-ci est très petite = *This one is very small* (e.g. **cette boîte**).

Celui-ci, etc., means *this one*, **celui-là** means *that one*; but **celui-ci** also sometimes translates *the latter* and **celui-là**, *the former*:

Voici Jeanne et Pierre; celui-ci a onze ans, celle-là en a douze = *Here are [Jeanne and Peter; the former is twelve, the latter eleven.*

Note that *the latter* is always mentioned first in French because **celui-ci** refers to the nearest noun.

FURTHER FORMS OF THE DEMONSTRATIVE PRONOUN

There are different forms of the demonstrative pronoun used when the object indicated has not been named. These are **ceci** [səsi] = *this* and **cela** [səla] = *that*, which do not have different gender and number forms as they have no nouns to agree with. **Cela** is contracted in familiar speech or writing to **ça**. These words are often used to contrast two unnamed objects:

Voulez-vous ceci ou cela? = *Do you want this or that?*

Cela est joli; je préfère ceci = *That is pretty*; *I prefer this.*

Pouvez-vous faire ça? = *Can you do that?*

Ceci refers to a statement which follows, **cela** to one which precedes it:

Rappelez-vous ceci: je compte sur vous! = *Remember this: I count on you!*

Je compte sur vous: rappelez-vous cela! = *I count on you: remember this!*

NEGATIVES WITH THE PERFECT TENSE

In the perfect tense (and other compound tenses to be learnt later) **point**, **plus**, **jamais** and **rien** come before the past participle, while **personne** always follows it:

Je ne l'ai plus revu = *I did not see him any more.*

Elle n'est jamais revenue = *She never came back.*

Nous n'avons rencontré personne = *We met nobody.*

Remember that **pas** must not be used in sentences with these forms.

NEGATIVE FORMS AS SUBJECT

Personne ne . . . , rien ne . . . , aucun (plus noun) **ne . . .** can be used as the subject of a sentence:

Personne ne m'a vu = *Nobody saw me.*

Rien n'est arrivé = *Nothing happened.*

Aucun avion n'a été perdu = *No aircraft has been lost.*

Note that **ne . . . jamais** is sometimes inverted for emphasis:

Jamais il ne le fera = *He will never do it.*

VOCABULARY

un établissement [etablismɑ̃]	*establishment*
la qualité [kalite]	*quality*
la commodité [kɔmɔdite]	*convenience*
le salon de coiffure [salɔ̃ də kwafyːr]	*hairdressing saloon*
le salon d'essayage [salɔ̃ desɛjaːʒ]	*fitting room*
assister à [asiste a]	*to watch, be present at*
le défilé [defile]	*parade*
le tour [tuːr]	*tour, walk round*
la rue [ry]	*street*
bondé(e) [bɔ̃de]	*packed*
un édifice [edifis]	*building*
situé(e) [sitɥe]	*situated*
la mode [mɔd]	*style, fashion*
exposer [ɛkspoze]	*to display*
la pêche [pɛːʃ]	*fishing*
le regard [rəgaːr]	*look, attention*
le moyen [mwajɛ̃]	*means*
se diriger [sə diriʒe]	*to make one's way*
la caisse [kɛs]	*packing-case*
le discours [diskuːr]	*speech*
l'extérieur (m.) [ɛksterjœːr]	*outside*
s'arrêter [sarɛte]	*to stop*
le comptoir [kɔ̃twaːr]	*counter*
dresser [drɛse]	*to set up*
le vendeur [vɑ̃dœːr]	*salesman*
la vertu [vɛrty]	*virtue*
miraculeux, -euse [mirakylø, -øz]	*miraculous*
disposer [dispoze]	*to have at one's disposal*
enthousiaste [ɑ̃tuzjast]	*enthusiastic*
Mon Dieu! [mɔ djø]	*Good heavens!*
le rez-de-chaussée [redʃose]	*ground floor*
la chaleur [ʃalœːr]	*heat*
bousculer [buskyle]	*to jostle*
coudoyer [kudwaje]	*to elbow*
le côté [kote]	*side*
nombreux, -euse [nɔmbrø, -øːz]	*numerous*
ranger [rɑ̃ʒe]	*to set out*
le rayon [rɛjɔ̃]	*department*
la papeterie [paptri]	*stationery*
le crayon [krɛjɔ̃]	*pencil*

le défilé

la pêche

le comptoir

le vendeur

148

le stylo à bille [stilo a biːj]	*ball-point pen*	
le savon [savɔ̃]	*soap*	
parfumé(e) [parfyme]	*scented*	
la pâte dentifrice [pɑːt dɑ̃tifris]	*toothpaste*	
la boîte [bwat]	*box*	**le stylo à bille**
la poudre [puːdr]	*powder*	
la brosse [brɔs]	*brush*	
un ascenseur [asɑ̃sœːr]	*lift*	
le meuble [mœbl] [vizjɔ̃]	*piece of furniture*	
le poste de télévision [pɔst də tele-]	*television set*	
sérieux, -euse [serjø, -øːz]	*serious*	
un escalier roulant [ɛskalje rulɑ̃]	*escalator*	
la brochure [brɔʃyːr]	*pamphlet*	**le savon**
tout en haut de [tutɑ̃ o də]	*right at the top of*	
le bâtiment [bɑtimɑ̃]	*building*	
la comptabilité [kɔ̃tabilite]	*book-keeping*	
la dactylo [daktilo]	*typist*	
le comptable [kɔ̃tabl]	*book-keeper, accountant*	
le gérant [ʒerɑ̃]	*manager*	
un écriteau [ekrito]	*notice*	
livrer [livre]	*to deliver*	
le domicile [dɔmisil]	*private house*	
la livraison [livrɛzɔ̃]	*delivery*	**la pâte dentifrice**
la banlieue [bɑ̃ljø]	*suburbs*	
en comparaison de [ɑ̃ kɔ̃parezɔ̃]	*in comparison with*	
une époque [epɔk]	*time*	
le solde [sɔld]	*remnant, sale*	
la queue [kø]	*tail, queue*	
se précipiter [sə presipite]	*to rush*	
une armée [arme]	*army*	
se disputer [sə dispyte]	*to contend for*	
une occasion [ɔkazjɔ̃]	*bargain, opportunity*	
par mégarde [par megard]	*inadvertently*	**un ascenseur**
le chemin [ʃmɛ̃]	*path*	
harmonieux, -euse [armɔnjø, -øːz]	*harmonious*	
publicitaire [pyblisitɛːr]	*advertising* (adj.)	
le cas [kɑ]	*case*	
le renseignement [rɑ̃sɛɲmɑ̃]	*information*	
en effet [ɑ̃nefɛ]	*indeed*	
coûter [kute]	*to cost*	
déguster [degyste]	*to taste*	
gratuitement [gratɥitmɑ̃]	*for nothing, free*	**la dactylo**

LES GRANDS MAGASINS

Dans presque toutes les villes il y a un grand magasin. Si la ville est assez importante, il y en a même plusieurs. Ces magasins sont des établissements immenses où l'on peut acheter des marchandises de toutes sortes. Ceux qui sont riches et ceux qui préfèrent des articles exclusifs de la plus haute qualité ne vont pas, en général, faire des achats aux grands magasins. Dans les grands magasins tout est arrangé pour la commodité et le confort des clients. On y trouve généralement un restaurant, un salon de coiffure et des salons d'essayage. On peut même assister à un défilé de mannequins si on trouve cela intéressant.

Aujourd'hui nous allons faire un petit tour en ville. Nous visiterons un tel magasin et peut-être que nous y ferons des emplettes. Prenons l'autobus au coin de la rue là-bas. . . . Pas celui-là — il est bondé — le suivant . . . ça y est!

Une demi-heure plus tard nous nous trouvons sur le trottoir devant les vitrines d'un grand magasin, vaste édifice situé dans une des rues principales de la ville. Nous restons quelque temps à admirer les robes de la dernière mode, exposées à l'étalage — ou, si les robes ne nous disent rien, ce sont peut-être les articles de pêche ou de sport qui attirent nos regards. Mais tout est assez cher et justement aujourd'hui nous n'avons pas les moyens d'acheter ces choses-là. Nous nous dirigeons vers l'entrée mais d'abord il faut passer devant un homme monté sur une chaise ou une caisse. Celui-ci gesticule et semble faire un discours. Arrêtons-nous un moment pour l'écouter. . . . À l'extérieur des grands magasins on voit souvent des comptoirs

150

dressés sur le trottoir où des vendeurs récitent les vertus des miraculeux produits qu'ils offrent au public. Si l'on dispose du temps nécessaire, on peut s'amuser à bon marché à regarder les merveilleuses démonstrations faites par ces vendeurs enthousiastes. Naturellement, on n'est pas obligé de croire tout ce qu'ils disent. . . .

Nous voici enfin dans le magasin. Mon Dieu! que de monde au rez-de-chaussée! Quelle chaleur! Les gens se bousculent et se coudoient. De tous côtés on voit de nombreux comptoirs où sont rangées des marchandises de toutes sortes. Par exemple, au rayon de la papeterie on vend du papier à lettres, des crayons de toutes les couleurs et des stylos à bille tandis qu'au rayon des articles de toilette il y a du savon parfumé, de la pâte dentifrice, des boîtes de poudre, des brosses etc. Mais prenons l'ascenseur pour monter au premier étage. Là nous trouvons le rayon des meubles et celui de la radio et de la télévision. Nous faisons le tour et notre curiosité est bientôt satisfaite. Nous avons besoin d'un nouveau poste de télévision mais, comme je l'ai déjà dit, nous sommes à court d'argent. Il me semble que nous ne sommes pas des clients sérieux. Tant pis! Pour monter au deuxième prenons l'escalier roulant. C'est ici le rayon des livres — romans, dictionnaires, cartes. Attendez un moment. Je vais acheter cette brochure-là, celle que vous voyez tout au fond.

Tout en haut du bâtiment se trouvent le restaurant et la section de la comptabilité où travaillent les dactylos et les comptables. Quant au gérant on ne le voit que très rarement; il est trop important pour gaspiller son temps à causer avec les clients.

Comme nous descendons l'escalier nous lisons sur un écriteau: "On livre à domicile". En ville et dans la banlieue les livraisons se font tous les jours, même deux fois par jour mais dans les villages des environs on ne livre les marchandises qu'une ou deux fois par semaine.

Il y a certainement beaucoup de monde dans ce magasin aujourd'hui mais en comparaison de l'époque des soldes ce n'est rien du tout. Dès les premières heures du matin les femmes font la queue à la porte du magasin. Quand on ouvre, elles se précipitent en avant comme une armée d'Amazones pour se disputer les meilleures occasions. Malheur à celui qui se trouve par mégarde dans leur chemin!

Dans certains magasins une musique peu harmonieuse est diffusée par des haut-parleurs installés dans la maison à des points stratégiques. De temps en temps la musique fait place à une voix humaine qui fait des annonces publicitaires. Heureusement que ce n'est pas le cas dans ce magasin. . . . Mais regardez l'heure. Il se fait tard. Sortons d'ici en passant devant le bureau de renseignements. En effet, notre journée n'a pas coûté très cher et tout à l'heure nous avons dégusté du vin — gratuitement!

(*See notes on the next page. Translation at the end of the book.*)

NOTES ON THE TEXT

Note these expressions with **faire**: **faire un tour** = *to go for a stroll*; **faire des emplettes** (f.) or **des achats** (m.) = *to make purchases*; **faire le tour de** = *to go round*; **faire la queue** = *to queue up*. Note also: **ça y est** = *that's it*; **cela ne me dit rien** = *I don't care for that*; **à bon marché** = *cheap(ly)*; **de tous côtés** = *on all sides*; **être à court de** = *to be short of*; **tant pis** = *so much the worse*, compare **tant mieux** = *so much the better*; **au fond** = *at the back*; **il se fait tard** = *it is getting late*.

EXERCISES

I. Répondez aux questions en français:

1. Combien de grands magasins y a-t-il dans votre ville?
2. Que veut dire "bondé"? Employez ce mot dans une phrase.
3. Que voit-on à la devanture (*front*) d'un magasin?
4. Comment s'appelle celui qui fait un discours?
5. Est-ce que les gens polis se bousculent?
6. Nommez quelques-uns des articles qu'on peut voir dans un grand magasin.
7. Qu'est-ce qu'on prend pour monter au troisième étage?
8. Où se trouve le restaurant?
9. Est-ce que le gérant vend les marchandises?
10. Faites-vous d'habitude des réclamations (*complaints*) dans un magasin?

II. Translate into English:

1. J'ai lu ces livres-ci mais je n'ai pas lu ceux-là.
2. Voici deux robes: celle-ci est rouge, celle-là est bleue.
3. Cet élève-là est celui à qui j'ai parlé dans la cour.
4. Quelles fleurs sont les plus jolies? Celles-ci.
5. Celui dont vous parlez est un vaurien (*good-for-nothing*).
6. Celle qui est assise dans le fauteuil est la tante de Jacques.
7. On y voit le père et l'oncle; celui-ci est plus âgé que celui-là.
8. Quel stylo préférez-vous? Celui-ci.
9. Le complet (*suit*) de Jean est bleu, celui d'André est gris.
10. Ceux qui travaillent bien font des progrès.

III. Insert suitable negative forms:

1. Il ne pleuvait —— quand je suis sorti.
2. Je n'ai vu —— dans la rue quand je suis arrivé.
3. Aujourd'hui ils n'ont —— fait d'amusant.
4. Il promet de ne —— dire.
5. Je n'avais —— vingt francs dans ma poche.

Insert suitable prepositions:

6. Au lieu —— répondre il a commencé —— pleurer.
7. —— avoir regardé sa montre, il est sorti —— magasin.
8. Il écrivait quelques mots —— tableau noir.
9. C'est un mauvais père: il ne se soucie pas —— ses enfants.
10. Il ne voulait pas répondre —— la question.

IV. Replace the words underlined by pronouns:
 1. L'orateur a fait un discours à l'assemblée.
 2. Cet après-midi j'ai assisté à la conférence.
 3. Montrez votre nouveau stylo à votre père.
 4. Nous avons vu une bicyclette sur le trottoir.
 5. Le vendeur donne les paquets aux clients.

V. Translate into French:
 1. We see a lot of people on the ground floor.
 2. The furniture department is on the second floor.
 3. I am going to buy the dictionary which I see on the counter.
 4. He goes into town twice a day.
 5. I shall be there at half-past seven without fail.
 6. The young women are standing in a queue at the door.
 7. From time to time I see one of my friends in town.
 8. Show me the article in question, please.
 9. On the pavement people jostle and elbow one another.
 10. I can't afford to buy a television set as I am short of money.

VI. Composition: describe any department store with which you are familiar. Introduce some of these expressions: **de temps en temps** = *from time to time*; **avoir besoin de** = *to need*; **un vendeur poli et serviable** = *a polite and obliging salesman*; **faire des affaires d'or** = *to do a roaring trade*; **acheter en gros (en détail)** = *to buy wholesale (retail)*; **acheter à bon marché** = *to buy cheap*; **vendre cher (à prix fixe)** = *to sell dear (at fixed prices)*; **acheter au comptant (à crédit)** = *to buy for cash (by instalments)*; **pour mille francs de marchandises** = 1,000 *francs worth of goods*; **un grand choix de mar-** **chandises** = *a great choice of goods*; **faire un (son) choix** = *to make a (one's) choice*; **n'avoir que l'embarras du choix** = *to have so (too) much to choose from*; **rendre la monnaie d'un billet** = *to give change for a note*; **la réclame au néon** = *neon sign* (for advertising).

(Answers at the end of the book.)

LEÇON 15

GRAMMAR

THE CONDITIONAL TENSE

I shall give is a future tense. But if we say *I should give*, there is something indefinite about the statement; the certainty of the giving depends on whether a certain condition is fulfilled, so to show the doubt involved we use a special tense called the conditional. The conditional tense is formed by adding the imperfect tense endings (-ais, -ais, -ait, etc.) to the future stem, which in the case of regular verbs is the infinitive (-re verbs drop the -e):

donner = *to give*, fut. **donnerai**	fut. **finirai**	fut. **vendrai**
je donnerais [dɔnərɛ] = *I should*	**finirais** [finirɛ]	**vendrais** [vãdrɛ]
tu donnerais [dɔnərɛ] [*give*, etc.	**finirais** [finirɛ]	**vendrais** [vãdrɛ]
il donnerait [dɔnərɛ]	**finirait** [finirɛ]	**vendrait** [vãdrɛ]
nous donnerions [dɔnərjɔ̃]	**finirions** [finirjɔ̃]	**vendrions** [vãdrjɔ̃]
vous donneriez [dɔnərje]	**finiriez** [finirje]	**vendriez** [vãdrje]
ils donneraient [dɔnərɛ]	**finiraient** [finirɛ]	**vendraient** [vãdrɛ]

Conditional tenses of verbs which are irregular in the future stem:

aller, j'irais	**s'asseoir, je m'assiérais**	**avoir, j'aurais**
courir, je courrais	**cueillir, je cueillerais**	**envoyer, j'enverrais**
être, je serais	**faire, je ferais**	**mourir, je mourrais**
pouvoir, je pourrais	**savoir, je saurais**	**tenir, je tiendrais**
venir, je viendrais	**vouloir, je voudrais**	

Note that other verbs in -oir drop the -oi- of the infinitive to form the future stem, e.g. **devoir**, conditional **je devrais**. Note also: **j'appellerais, j'achèterais, je préférerais, je jetterais**.

USES OF THE CONDITIONAL

Six uses are given here of which the most common are (i), (ii) and (iii):

(i) In the main clause of a conditional sentence:

S'il arrivait en retard, je ne le verrais pas = *If he arrived late, I should not see him.*

Si cela était vrai, je ne partirais pas = *If that were true, I should not leave.*

Note that in this kind of conditional sentence the verb after **si** is always in the imperfect tense.

(ii) In reported speech to represent the future of direct speech (a kind of future in the past):

Direct speech: **Il dit: "Je ne le ferai pas"** = *He says: "I shall not do it."*

Reported speech: **Il a dit qu'il ne le ferait pas** = *He said that he would not do it.*

(iii) In clauses of time in reported speech:

Il a dit qu'il le ferait quand il serait en ville = *He said he would do it when he was in town.*

(iv) Tentative statements:

Il s'agirait d'un crime = *It would appear to be a question of a crime.* This tense is used when a speaker is uncertain as to the truth of a statement and does not wish to commit himself; it is very common in newspapers.

(v) After **quand** or **quand même** with the meaning of *even if*:

Quand (même) il le dirait cent fois, je ne le croirais pas = *Even if he said it a hundred times, I should not believe it.*

(vi) Idiomatically in this type of sentence:

Il le dirait cent fois que je ne le croirais pas = *Even if he said it a hundred times, I should not believe it.*

You will see that in (iii), (v) and (vi) both verbs are conditional.

Note that (*a*) the conditional of **savoir, je saurais,** is often equivalent to **je peux** = *I can*; (*b*) the meaning of **devoir** is less strong in the conditional: **Vous devez le faire** = *You must do it.* **Vous devriez le faire** = *You ought to do it*; (*c*) the conditional must not be used to translate such sentences as: *Every day we would go to market* = **Tous les jours nous allions au marché.** Here *would go* means *used to go*, so the imperfect tense is used.

IDIOMATIC USE OF **venir de**

Literally **venir de** = *to come from*; if you come from doing something, then you have just done it. **Venir de** + the infinitive is used to translate *have just* or *had just done* (*something*). Only two tenses of **venir** can be used in this construction: the present for *have just* and the imperfect tense for *had just*:

Je viens de lui parler = *I have just spoken to him.*

Nous venons d'y arriver = *We have just arrived there.*

Je venais de lui parler = *I had just spoken to him.*

Nous venions d'y arriver = *We had just arrived there.*

Vient de paraître! (literally *comes from appearing*) = *Just published*!

VOCABULARY

loquace [lɔkwas]	*talkative*
apercevoir (like **recevoir**) [apɛrsəvwaːr]	*to catch sight of*

155

lorsque [lɔrskə] *when*

paisiblement [pɛziblmã] *peacefully*

tout son possible [tu sɔ̃ pɔsibl] *everything in one's power*

éviter [evite] *to avoid*

se moquer de [sə mɔke də] *to make fun of, baffle*

avoir envie de [avwaːr ãvi də] *to have an inclination to*

achever (like lever) [aʃve] *to finish*

poli(e) [pɔli] *polite*

répondre [repɔːdr] *to reply*

le salut [saly] *greeting*

le salut

sacré(e) [sakre] *confounded*

bavard(e) [bavaːr, -ard] *talkative, chatterbox*

s'attendre à [satãːdr a] *to expect* [(noun)

en train [ã trɛ̃] *in one's stride*

ajouter [aʒute] *to add*

le commentaire [kɔmãtɛːr] *commentary, comment*

passer en revue [pɑse ã rəvy] *to review*

le gouvernement [guvɛrnəmã] *government*

actuel, -elle [aktɥɛl] *present* (NOT actual)

la manière [manjɛːr] *manner*

le produit
alimentaire

drôle [droːl] *funny*

un esprit [ɛspri] *spirit, mind, wit*

borné(e) [bɔrne] *narrow, limited*

informé(e) [ɛ̃fɔrme] *informed*

le produit alimentaire *foodstuff*
   [prɔdɥitalimãtɛːr]

d'accord [dakɔːr] *agreed*

la politique [pɔlitik] *policy, politics*

interrompre [ɛ̃tɛrɔ̃ːpr] *to interrupt*

le discours [diskuːr] *speech*

le scandale [skãdal] *scandal*

le fonctionnaire

mettre fin, un terme, à [mɛtr fɛ̃, *to put a stop to*
   œ̃ tɛrm, a]

un abus [aby] *abuse*

chasser [ʃase] *to drive away, sack*

sur-le-champ [syrlʃã] *at once*

le fonctionnaire [fɔ̃ksjɔnɛːr] *civil servant*

corrompre [kɔrɔ̃ːpr] *to corrupt*

s'enrichir [sãriʃiːr] *to get rich*

permettre à quelqu'un de + infin. *to allow someone to do*
   [pɛrmɛtr a] *something*

la torpeur

le citoyen, la -enne [sitwajɛ̃, -ɛn] *citizen*

franchement [frɑ̃ʃmɑ̃]	*frankly*
moindre [mwɛ̃:dr]	*least*
dont [dɔ̃]	*of whom, of which*
s'agir de [saʒi:r də]	*to concern, be a matter of*
s'endormir [sɑ̃dɔrmi:r]	*to go to sleep*
évidemment [evidamɑ̃]	*evidently*
se rendre compte de [rɑ̃:dr kɔ̃:t]	*to realize*
la torpeur [tɔrpœ:r]	*drowsiness*
fournir [furni:r]	*to provide*
la somme [sɔm]	*sum*
pareil, -ille [parɛ:j]	*similar, such*
le contribuable [kɔ̃tribyabl]	*taxpayer*
pauvre [po:vr]	*poor*
un, une imbécile [ɛ̃besil]	*fool*
émigrer [emigre]	*to emigrate*
triompher de [triɔ̃fe də]	*to triumph over*
au moins [o mwɛ̃]	*at least*
un impôt (sur le revenu) [ɛ̃po]	*tax (income)*
augmenter [ɔgmɑ̃te]	*to go up, increase*
de jour en jour [də ʒu:r ɑ̃ ʒu:r]	*from day to day, daily*
follement [fɔlmɑ̃]	*madly, wildly*
à l'aise [a lɛ:z]	*comfortably*
la guerre [gɛ:r]	*war*
éclater [eklate]	*to burst, break out*
à present [a prezɑ̃]	*nowadays*
un état [eta]	*state*
se lasser [sə lɑse]	*to tire*
le désastre [dezastr]	*disaster*
l'avenir (m.) [avni:r]	*future*
à coup sûr [a ku sy:r]	*doubtless*
penché(e) [pɑ̃ʃe]	*leaning*
la bêche [bɛʃ]	*spade*
la clôture [kloty:r]	*fence*
la circonstance [sirkɔ̃stɑ̃:s]	*circumstance*
tout à coup [tutaku]	*suddenly*
le cri [kri]	*cry*
perçant(e) [pɛrsɑ̃, -ɑ̃t]	*shrill*
plutôt [plyto]	*rather, on the whole*
agacer [agase]	*to annoy*
empêcher quelqu'un de + infin. [ɑ̃peʃe]	*to prevent someone from doing something*
avoir pitié de [avwa:r pitje də]	*to be sorry for*

la somme

un imbécile

la guerre

la bêche

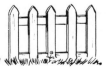

la clôture

157

MON VOISIN

Mon voisin s'appelle M. Durand. C'est un homme très loquace et malheureusement il lui arrive de temps en temps de m'apercevoir lorsque je travaille paisiblement dans mon jardin. Je vous assure que je fais tout mon possible pour l'éviter mais mon voisin se moque de tous mes efforts.

"Bonjour, monsieur," me dit-il, "ça va?" Généralement je n'ai aucune envie de lui parler et je préférerais achever mon travail. Mais il faut être poli, n'est-ce pas? — et après tout, c'est mon voisin. . . . Sans me laisser le temps de répondre à son salut, ce sacré bavard me demande: "Avez-vous lu le journal d'aujourd'hui?" Je sais bien qu'il ne s'attend pas à une réponse de ma part et je me tais. "N'avez-vous pas vu, monsieur, que. . . ."

Le voilà en train et il commence à raconter tout ce qu'il y a dans le journal. Mais ce n'est pas tout; il y ajoute des commentaires de sa façon. Il passe en revue tous les membres du gouvernement actuel. Alors il me dit d'un air tout à fait sérieux que si lui, Durand, était premier ministre il arrangerait les choses d'une manière bien différente. "Si j'étais premier ministre . . ." — voilà ce qu'il dit toujours. Figurez-vous, Durand premier ministre! Ce serait drôle. Je ne sais pas du tout pourquoi il aime faire des suppositions aussi absurdes. Petit commerçant d'une cinquantaine d'années, il a l'esprit borné. Il est bien informé en ce qui concerne les produits alimentaires, d'accord; mais en matière de politique il est très ignorant.

Mais je vous demande pardon, cher lecteur, je viens de faire une digression et d'interrompre le beau discours de M. Durand. "C'est un vrai scandale," dit-il en parlant de je ne sais quoi. "Si j'étais premier ministre, je mettrais bientôt fin à de tels abus. Je chasserais sur-le-champ tous ces fonctionnaires corrompus qui ne pensent qu'à s'enrichir. Je ne leur permettrais pas de duper les bons citoyens qui doivent travailler du matin au soir. Je les jetterais tous en prison. D'ailleurs, avez-vous lu combien cela va coûter?'' Franchement, non. Je n'en ai pas la moindre idée parce que je ne sais même pas ce dont il s'agit. Je m'ennuyais et j'étais prêt à m'endormir.

"Cela va coûter beaucoup d'argent,'' continue-t-il, évidemment sans se rendre compte de ma torpeur. "Et qui va fournir une somme pareille? Nous, les contribuables — pauvres imbéciles que nous sommes. Il y a dix ans j'ai voulu partir en Amérique. Mais c'est ma femme. Vous savez ce que c'est que les femmes! Elle ne voulait pas partir. Si nous avions émigré en ce temps-là, nous serions riches aujourd'hui et peut-être que dans un pays où le mérite triomphe de tous les obstacles je serais au moins sénateur à l'heure qu'il est. Tandis que dans ce pays-ci les impôts augmentent presque de jour en jour. C'est le gouvernement qui gaspille follement notre argent. Si j'étais ministre j'y mettrais un terme. Dans le temps les choses allaient mieux: on vivait à l'aise. Mais par le temps qui court . . . je ne sais pas ce que nous allons devenir. Et notre politique extérieure, c'est un scandale. Je viens de lire dans le journal que la guerre va éclater d'un jour à l'autre. Si nos hommes politiques étaient plus intelligents et plus prudents, nous ne nous trouverions pas à présent dans un si triste état.'' Mon voisin ne se lasse pas de parler des désastres qui nous menacent. "L'avenir est sombre,'' reprend-il, "mais moi, je dis toujours qu'il faut prendre les choses du bon côté. Il y a des gens qui voient tout en noir. Vous en connaissez à coup sûr. Et les jeunes, monsieur. Qu'est-ce que nos grands-pères diraient s'ils vivaient aujourd'hui? Ils croiraient que le monde est devenu fou. . . . Tous ces jeunes gens qui fument, qui dansent, qui boivent trop de vin et qui n'aiment pas travailler. On dirait aussi qu'ils ne se lavent jamais — et des cheveux longs comme ça! C'est abominable. Je n'ai presque plus le courage de vivre. D'ailleurs je viens d'apprendre que la semaine prochaine. . . .''

Pendant qu'il parle, je reste debout penché sur ma bêche près de la clôture. De temps en temps je fais "oui'' ou "non'' selon les circonstances. J'espère seulement que je ne dis pas "oui'' quand je devrais dire "non.'' Il est si facile de se tromper.

Tout à coup un cri perçant se fait entendre. "Louis, où es-tu? Que fais-tu? Viens ici.'' "Pardon, monsieur, je vous quitte,'' dit mon voisin d'un ton qui me semble plutôt triste. "C'est ma femme qui m'appelle. Je dois rentrer tout de suite. Au revoir, monsieur. . . .'' Et il se dirige à pas lents vers la maison. En effet, mon voisin m'agace quelquefois lorsqu'il m'empêche de travailler mais je connais un peu sa femme et . . . j'ai pitié de mon malheureux voisin.

(*See notes on the next page. Translation at the end of the book.*)

NOTES ON THE TEXT

Ça va? (familiar) = *How are you? How goes it?*; **de sa façon** = *of his own invention*; **d'un air sérieux** = *with a serious look*; **dans le temps** = *in times past, in the old days*; **par le temps qui court** = *nowadays, in these days*; **voir tout en noir** = *to take a gloomy view of everything* (cf. the opposite — **voir tout en rose**); **ce que nous allons devenir** = *what is going to become of us* (literally what we are going to become); **à pas lents** = *with slow steps* (cf. **à grands pas** = *with great strides*).

EXERCISES

I. Répondez aux questions en français:

1. Comment s'appelle mon voisin?
2. Quel défaut a-t-il?
3. Aimez-vous lire le journal du soir?
4. Que pense M. Durand des membres du gouvernement?
5. Que ferait-il s'il était premier ministre?
6. Quel était son métier?
7. Connaissez-vous des personnes qui ont l'esprit borné?
8. Que feriez-vous si vous étiez millionnaire?
9. Connaissez-vous des gens bavards? Que veut dire "bavard"?
10. Iriez-vous en France si vous aviez assez d'argent?

II. Translate into English:

1. S'il pleut demain, je n'irai pas en ville.
2. Même si elle était riche, elle ne serait pas heureuse.
3. Le train qui vient d'entrer en gare n'est pas celui que nous attendons.
4. Je ne lui répondrais pas s'il me posait une question.
5. S'il pleuvait à verse, elle ne sortirait pas.
6. Je devrais faire mes devoirs mais je dois aller en ville.
7. La table qui se trouve au fond de la salle est en bois de chêne.
8. La chambre où il y avait deux grands lits était au bout du couloir.
9. L'homme que nous venons de quitter est commerçant.
10. Hier soir mon voisin a assisté à un concert en ville.

III. Replace the words underlined by pronouns:

1. J'ai aperçu <u>mon voisin</u> qui travaillait dans son jardin.
2. Nous avons perdu <u>cinq balles</u>.
3. Je vais <u>à la gare</u> tous les matins.
4. Que pensez-vous <u>de notre politique extérieure</u>?
5. Il garde <u>tous ses timbres</u> dans un album.

160

IV. Give singular and plural of each verb in the person and tense stated:
   1. Third present: **appeler, jeter, se plaire, apercevoir, souffrir, devoir.**
   2. First imperfect: **être, se taire, jeter**; second future: **savoir, aller, tenir.**
   3. Second conditional: **vouloir, s'asseoir**; third fem. perfect: **pouvoir, tomber.**

V. Insert the correct form of the conditional in place of the infinitive:
   1. Je (vouloir) aller au théâtre ce soir.
   2. Que (faire)-vous si vous aviez beaucoup d'argent?
   3. Il a dit qu'il (venir) quand il (être) en ville.
   4. Nous (devoir) faire toujours notre devoir.
   5. Elle ne savait pas s'il (aller) en France.
   6. (Pouvoir)-vous me rendre ce service?
   7. Que (dire)-il, si je le trompais?
   8. Elle (chercher) partout qu'elle ne le (trouver) pas.
   9. S'il arrivait en retard, que (dire) le maître?
   10. Il voulait savoir s'ils (arriver) à temps.

VI. Translate into French:
   1. From time to time he sees me in the garden.
   2. I don't feel like talking to you today.
   3. Without giving me time to answer, he got angry.
   4. I do not know what I should do without you.
   5. They have just learnt that the prime minister will arrive soon.
   6. The book which I have just found is red.
   7. They must work from morning till night. What a pity! (**dommage** m.)
   8. He went into the house and found that his uncle had just left.
   9. I don't even know what it is all about.
   10. They ought to be polite even if they are rich.

VII. Composition: describe in French how you met a neighbour in town, and the conversation that followed. Use some of these expressions: **avoir lieu** = *to take place*; **par un beau jour de printemps** = *on a fine spring day*; **être de bonne (mauvaise) humeur** = *to be in a good (bad) mood*; **il y a quelques jours** = *a few days ago*; **il aime à s'entendre parler** = *he likes to hear himself talking*; **avoir la langue bien pendue** = *to have the gift of the gab* (**pendre** = *to hang*); **parler affaires** (f.), **boutique** (f.) = *to talk business, shop*; **perdre patience** (f.) = *to lose patience*; **être à bout de patience** = *to be at the end of one's tether*; **cela va sans dire** = *that goes without saying*; **le lendemain matin** = *the following morning*; **à vrai dire** = *as a matter of fact.*

(Answers at the end of the book.)

LEÇON 16

GRAMMAR

REVISION AND COMPLETION OF NUMBERS

In previous chapters we learnt the early numbers both cardinal (e.g. *one, two*) and ordinal (which give the order in which things occur and are adjectives, e.g. *first, second*). Here are further lists of cardinals and ordinals.

CARDINAL NUMBERS

1 = **un, une**	16 = **seize**	71 = **soixante et onze**
2 = **deux**	17 = **dix-sept** ...	72 = **soixante-douze** ...
3 = **trois**	20 = **vingt**	80 = **quatre-vingts**
4 = **quatre**	21 = **vingt et un**	81 = **quatre-vingt-un** ...
5 = **cinq**	22 = **vingt-deux** ...	90 = **quatre-vingt-dix**
6 = **six**	30 = **trente**	91 = **quatre-vingt-onze** ...
7 = **sept**	31 = **trente et un**	100 = **cent**
8 = **huit**	32 = **trente-deux** ...	101 = **cent un** ...
9 = **neuf**	40 = **quarante**	200 = **deux cents**
10 = **dix**	41 = **quarante et un** ...	201 = **deux cent un** ...
11 = **onze**	50 = **cinquante**	1.000 = **mille** ...
12 = **douze**	51 = **cinquante et un** ...	2.000 = **deux mille** ...
13 = **treize**	60 = **soixante**	1.000.000 = **un million** ...
14 = **quatorze**	61 = **soixante et un** ...	2.000.000 = **deux millions,** etc.
15 = **quinze**	70 = **soixante-dix**	

(*For pronunciation, see pp.* 18 *and* 36.)

Note that (*a*) **et** is used only in 21, 31, 41, 51, 61, 71; (*b*) when a unit follows **quatre-vingts** the -s is dropped, e.g. 83 = **quatre-vingt-trois**: the same applies to the plural of **cent**, e.g. 300 = **trois cents**, 303 = **trois cent trois**; (*c*) **mille** never takes an -s, 5.000 = **cinq mille**. In dates **mil** is used for 1,000, hence 1965 = **mil neuf cent soixante-cinq** (or **dix-neuf cent soixante-cinq**); (*d*) hyphens are used only between tens and units, e.g. **dix-huit**; (*e*) **cent** and **mille** are never preceded by the indefinite article **un**, *one hundred and ten* = **cent dix**, *one thousand* = **mille**; (*f*) there is no elision before **huit** and **onze**, e.g. **le huit septembre, le onze mai**; (*g*) the -s of **quatre-vingts** and of **cents** is dropped when the number is placed after the noun and takes the place of an ordinal (adjective), e.g. *page* 200 = **page deux cent**; (*h*) **million** is a noun and

162

is followed by **de**, e.g. **un million de soldats** = *a million soldiers*; (*i*) thousands are marked off by a full-stop, decimals by a comma, e.g. 2.075,5 = 2,075·5.

ORDINAL NUMBERS

1*st* = **premier, -ière**	9*th* = **neuvième ...**
2*nd* = **deuxième, second(e)**	20*th* = **vingtième**
3*rd* = **troisième**	21*st* = **vingt et unième ...**
4*th* = **quatrième**	30*th* = **trentième ...**
5*th* = **cinquième ...**	100*th* = **centième**

Note that (*a*) except for 1*st* and the form **second** [zgɔ̃] the ordinals are formed by adding -**ième** to the cardinals and dropping the final -**e** where it exists, but note also the spelling of **cinquième** and **neuvième**; (*b*) **deuxième** must be used in compounds, e.g. 22*nd* = **vingt-deuxième**: **second** generally means *second of two*; (*c*) ordinals precede the noun, e.g. **la première maison**; (*d*) ordinals are not used in dates except for the first of the month, e.g. **le premier avril, le deux avril**, etc.: the same applies to titles, e.g. **François Premier** but **Louis Quatorze**; (*e*) ordinals are used for fractions (**le sixième**) except: ½ = **la moitié**, ⅓ = **le tiers**, ¼ = **le quart**, ¾ = **les trois quarts**.

COLLECTIVES

une paire [pɛːr]	= *a pair*
une huitaine [ɥitɛn]	= *about eight*
une dizaine [dizɛn]	= *about ten*
une douzaine [duzɛn]	= *a dozen*
une quinzaine [kɛ̃zɛn]	= *about fifteen*
une vingtaine [vɛ̃tɛn]	= *about twenty*
une trentaine [trɑ̃tɛn]	= *about thirty*
une quarantaine [karɑ̃tɛn]	= *about forty*
une cinquantaine [sɛ̃kɑ̃tɛn]	= *about fifty*
une soixantaine [swasɑ̃tɛn]	= *about sixty*
une centaine [sɑ̃tɛn]	= *about a hundred*
un millier [milje]	= *about a thousand*

Note that (*a*) as these are all nouns they must be followed by **de** when linked with a following noun, e.g. **une douzaine d'œufs** = *a dozen eggs*; (*b*) **une huitaine** is sometimes used to mean *week* (i.e. **huit jours**) and **une quinzaine** to mean *fortnight* (i.e. **quinze jours**); **quarantaine** also = *quarantine*; (*c*) note the various idiomatic expressions you will come across, e.g. **avoir passé la quarantaine** = *to be over forty* (*years of age*); (*d*) this list contains all the collectives in -**aine** (with one rare exception) and you should not invent others: *about* with other numbers is expressed by **environ**, e.g. **environ cinquante-cinq** = *about fifty-five*.

163

VOCABULARY

s'étendre [setãdr]	*to extend*	
depuis [dəpɥi]	*from, since*	
le nord [nɔːr]	*north*	
l'Espagne (f.) [ɛspaɲ]	*Spain*	
le sud [syd]	*south*	
confiner à [kɔ̃fine a]	*to border on*	
l'Allemagne (f.) [almaɲ]	*Germany*	**la station**
l'Italie (f.) [itali]	*Italy*	**balnéaire**
l'ouest (m.) [wɛst]	*west*	
faire face à [fɛːr fas a]	*to face*	
l'Angleterre (f.) [ãglətɛːr]	*England*	
à travers [a travɛːr]	*across*	
l'Atlantique (m.) [atlãtik]	*Atlantic Ocean*	
l'Amérique (f.) [amerik]	*America*	
le point de vue [pwɛ̃ də vy]	*point of view*	
relier [rəlje]	*to link, connect*	
la ligne [liɲ]	*line*	
la capitale [kapital]	*capital (city)*	
border [bɔrde]	*to border on*	**le charbon**
un océan [ɔseã]	*ocean*	
la Méditerranée [mediterane]	*Mediterranean Sea*	
à la fois [a la fwa]	*at one and the same time*	
le paysage [peizaːʒ]	*landscape, scenery*	
ne . . . guère [nə gɛːr]	*hardly* (cf. ne . . . plus]	
jouir de [ʒwir də]	*to enjoy*	
la station balnéaire [stasjɔ̃ balneɛːr]	*seaside resort*	
un étranger [etrãʒe]	*stranger, foreigner*	
la frontière [frɔ̃tjɛːr]	*frontier*	
protégé(e) [prɔteʒe]	*protected*	**l'énergie**
la valeur [valœːr]	*value*	**hydro-électrique**
défensif, -ive [defãsif, -iːv]	*defensive, as a defence*	
les Pays-Bas [pe(j)ibɑ]	*Low Countries*	
un envahisseur [ãvaisœːr]	*invader*	
autrefois [otrəfwa]	*formerly*	
un habitant [abitã]	*inhabitant*	
la Grande-Bretagne [grãːdbrətaɲ]	*Great Britain*	
les États-Unis (m.) [etazyni]	*United States*	
la Russie [rysi]	*Russia*	
la Chine [ʃin]	*China*	
la superficie [sypɛrfisi]	*area*	
carré(e) [kare]	*square*	**une aciérie**

la station
balnéaire

le charbon

l'énergie
hydro-électrique

une aciérie

le Royaume-Uni [rwajoːmyni]	*United Kingdom*	
plus de [ply də]	*more than*	
à cause de [a koːz də]	*because of*	
un équilibre [ekilibr]	*balance, equilibrium*	
se nourrir [sə nuriːr]	*to feed oneself*	
suffire à [syfiːr a]	*to suffice, cope with*	
le besoin [bəzwɛ̃]	*need*	
produire (like **conduire**) [prɔdɥiːr]	*to produce*	**la soie**
le charbon [ʃarbɔ̃]	*coal*	
la tonne [tɔn]	*ton (1,000 kilos)*	
l'énergie (f.) **hydro-électrique**	*hydro-electric power*	
[enɛrʒi idrɔelɛktrik]		
la houille [uːj]	*coal*	
en abondance [ãnabɔ̃dãːs]	*in abundance*	
la mesure [məzyːr]	*extent*	
le manque [mãːk]	*lack*	
la plupart [plypaːr]	*majority, most part*	
une aciérie [asjeri]	*steel-works*	
ainsi que [ɛ̃si kə]	*as well as*	**le blé**
la filature [filatyːr]	*spinning-mill*	
se trouver [sə truve]	*to be situated*	
la soie [swɑ]	*silk*	
une automobile [otɔmɔbil]	*motor-car*	
la marque [mark]	*mark, brand, make*	
entier, -ière [ãtje, -jɛːr]	*whole*	
le blé [ble]	*corn, wheat*	
la betterave à sucre [bɛtrav a sykr]	*sugar-beet*	
subvenir à [sybvəniːr a]	*to provide for*	
l'élevage (m.) [ɛlvaːʒ]	*stock-farming*	
célèbre [selɛbr]	*famous*	**le tabac**
le fromage [frɔmaːʒ]	*cheese*	
le tabac [taba]	*tobacco*	
indigène [ɛ̃diʒɛn]	*native*	
chacun, -une [ʃakœ̃, -yn]	*every, each man*	
le goût [gu]	*taste, liking*	
apprécier [apresje]	*to value, appreciate*	
le gourmet [gurmɛ]	*epicure*	
le monde [mɔ̃ːd]	*world*	
terminer [tɛrmine]	*to end*	
un aperçu [apɛrsy]	*outline, sketch*	
faire remarquer [fɛːr rəmarke]	*to point out*	
la cuisine [kɥizin]	*kitchen, cooking*	**le monde**

165

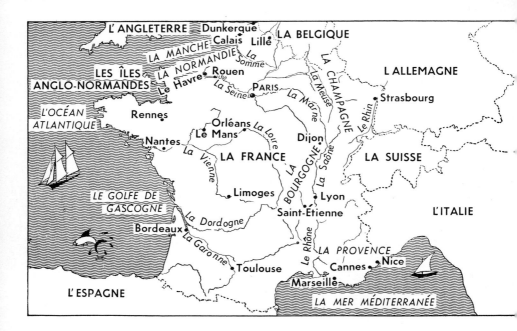

LA FRANCE

La France s'étend depuis la Belgique au nord jusqu'à l'Espagne au sud
— environ 900 (neuf cents) kilomètres. À l'est elle confine à l'Allemagne, à
la Suisse et à l'Italie. Comme à l'ouest elle fait face à l'Angleterre et, à
travers l'Atlantique, à l'Amérique, la France est très avantageusement placée
du point de vue commercial. Si l'on regarde une carte des chemins de fer,
on verra que tous les ports de l'ouest sont reliés directement à Paris, d'où
partent des lignes de chemin de fer vers toutes les capitales de l'Europe.
D'ailleurs, de tous les pays du Continent seules la France et l'Espagne bordent
et l'Océan Atlantique et la Méditerranée. On peut donc dire que la France
est à la fois un pays du nord et un pays méditerranéen. Comme on peut s'y
attendre, elle présente une grande variété de climats et de paysages. Le
climat de la Normandie, par exemple, n'est guère différent de celui du sud de
l'Angleterre tandis que la Provence (au sud-est de la France) jouit d'un climat
méditerranéen. Tout le monde a entendu parler de Cannes, de Nice et d'autres
stations balnéaires où des étrangers opulents se reposent au soleil.

Au point de vue militaire les frontières de la France sont protégées au sud
et à l'est par les Pyrénées, les Alpes, les Vosges et les Ardennes. Mais à
l'âge atomique on se demande si les montagnes ont toujours une valeur
défensive. C'est tout au nord, à travers les plaines des Pays-Bas que
les envahisseurs sont entrés autrefois en France. Les Français n'oublieront
pas les invasions de 1870 (dix-huit cent soixante-dix), de 1914 (dix-neuf cent
quatorze) et de 1940 (dix-neuf cent quarante).

LA FRANCE

La France a quarante-cinq millions d'habitants; la Grande-Bretagne en a cinquante millions. En comparaison des États-Unis, de la Russie et de la Chine, l'Angleterre et la France sont de petits pays. La superficie de la France est de 551.000 (cinq cent cinquante et un mille) kilomètres carrés; celle du Royaume-Uni est de 245.000 (deux cent quarante-cinq mille).

56% (cinquante-six pour cent) de la population française habite des villes. Pour la Grande-Bretagne la proportion est de 80% (quatre-vingts pour cent). On peut donc dire qu'une grande partie (presque la moitié) de la population française est rurale tandis qu'en Angleterre c'est tout le contraire. En France il n'y a pas beaucoup de grandes villes: il y en a seulement huit qui comptent plus de 200.000 (deux cent mille) habitants. Après Paris qui, avec sa banlieue, a près de cinq millions d'habitants, les villes les plus importantes sont Marseille, Lyon, Bordeaux, Lille, Saint-Étienne, Nantes, Nice, Toulouse, Strasbourg et le Havre. À cause de cet équilibre économique entre l'industrie et l'agriculture la France ne se voit pas dans la nécessité d'importer de grandes quantités de produits agricoles pour se nourrir.

Au point de vue industriel la France ne peut pas suffire à tous ses besoins. Elle ne produit que les trois quarts du charbon nécessaire à son industrie et par conséquent elle doit importer une quinzaine de millions de tonnes de charbon par an. Néanmoins il faut remarquer que l'énergie hydro-électrique (qu'on appelle quelquefois "la houille blanche" et que la France possède en abondance) compense dans une certaine mesure le manque de charbon. La plupart des aciéries ainsi que les principales filatures de coton et de laine se trouvent au nord mais Lyon est le centre le plus important pour la soie. Il faut mentionner aussi l'industrie automobile dont le centre est Paris. Les marques Citroën, Renault, Peugeot etc. sont connues dans le monde entier.

Quant à l'agriculture on peut dire que la France cultive assez de blé, de pommes de terre et de betteraves à sucre pour subvenir à ses besoins. L'élevage est important en Normandie et en d'autres régions de la France. Et tout le monde connaît les célèbres fromages français tels que le Camembert, le Brie et le Roquefort. On cultive aussi le tabac et les Français, semble-t-il, préfèrent le produit indigène au tabac importé des États-Unis. Chacun son goût!

En matière de vins la France n'a pas de rival. Nous connaissons tous les vins de Champagne, de Bordeaux et de Bourgogne, appréciés par les gourmets du monde entier. Mais il est permis de croire que les Anglais préféreraient leur bière même si le vin se vendait à très bon marché.

Pour terminer cet aperçu économique nous ferons remarquer que le tourisme représente pour la France des revenus importants. Le climat doux, la grande variété du paysage et la cuisine française y sont certainement pour quelque chose.

(*See notes on the next page. Translation at the end of the book.*)

LEÇON 16

NOTES ON THE TEXT

Au nord, au sud, à l'est, à l'ouest = *in the north, in the south*, etc.; **et . . . et** = *both . . . and* (cf. **ou . . . ou** = *either . . . or*); **la superficie est de 551.000 km.** — note the **de**: when **être** is followed by a number (as complement) **de** is required before it; **chacun (à) son gout** = literally *each to his taste*, i.e. *there is no accounting for tastes*; **nous connaissons tous** = *we all know*: when **tous** stands on its own as a pronoun the **-s** is pronounced [tuːs]; **y sont certainement pour quelque chose** = *have something to do with it*.

EXERCISES

I. Répondez aux questions en français:
1. Quel pays se trouve au nord de la France?
2. Et quel pays se trouve au sud?
3. Quelle est la superficie de la France?
4. Quel pourcentage de la population française habite des villes?
5. Est-ce que la France produit tout le charbon dont elle a besoin?
6. Qu'est-ce qui compense le manque de charbon?
7. Où se trouvent les filatures principales?
8. Pour quelle boisson la France est-elle célèbre?
9. Est-ce qu'on boit beaucoup de thé en France?
10. Irez-vous en France l'année prochaine?

II. Translate into English:
1. Bruxelles est à 270 km. de Paris à vol d'oiseau.
2. La somme perdue était de mille francs.
3. Après avoir attendu dix minutes, il est parti.
4. Je me demande s'ils peuvent faire cela.
5. Que ne ferais-je pour ma mère?
6. L'auberge se trouve à quelque deux cents mètres de la place.
7. Je dois acheter une douzaine d'œufs frais.
8. Elle est partie passer une quinzaine au bord de la mer.
9. Si je ne me trompe, il est mort en 1958.
10. En Belgique au lieu de dire "soixante-dix" on dit "septante".

III. Write out in full:
1. 15, 21, 81, 101, 201, 75, 96, 80, 87, 384, 39, 42, 51, 68, 91, 2.555, 472, 991.
2. 1st April 1920; 30th October 1960; 14th July 1789; 4th August 1914; 3rd September 1939.
3. $\frac{1}{2}$, $\frac{2}{3}$, $\frac{3}{4}$, $\frac{5}{6}$, $\frac{8}{9}$, $\frac{9}{10}$, $\frac{11}{12}$, $\frac{13}{14}$, $\frac{15}{16}$, $\frac{20}{21}$. (Remember that most fractions are expressed by ordinals, e.g. $\frac{5}{12}$ = **cinq douzièmes**.)

168

le ciel

la mouette

le drapeau

le phare

...avire

une île

l'horizon

la falaise

...tée

la mer

le nageur

la vague

le rocher

la baigneuse

le brise-lames

...longeur

une ombrelle

la serviette
de bain

le transatlantique
(le transa)

le peignoir
de bain

le sable

la tente

...piscine

l'algue

le château
de sable

la cabine de
plage

...e crabe

le maillot
de bain

la glace

le filet

le coquillage

le caleçon
de bain

la pelle

le seau

la promenade

LA PLAGE AU BORD DE LA MER

une abeille

une alouette

le scarabée

le corbeau

le faisan

une araignée

le rouge-gorge

la guêp

un aigle

le hibou

la fourmi

une hirondelle

le merle

le héron

le moineau

la mouette

la mouche

le paon

le perroque

la perdrix

le rossignol

la cigale

le papillon

le canard

la colombe

le coq

une oie

la poule

le poussin

le pigeon

le dindon

LES INSECTES, LES OISEAUX SAUVAGES ET CEUX DE LA BASSE-COUR

IV. Using the collectives, translate:

1. About twenty men.
2. About fifty towns.
3. A dozen pens.

4. About a hundred soldiers.
5. Thousands of pounds.
6. He has turned fifty.

V. Replace the infinitive by the correct form of the conditional:

1. **Si j'avais mille livres, je (être) riche.**
2. **Qui le (croire) s'il disait cela?**
3. **Que ne (faire) je pour elle?**
4. **S'il pleuvait à verse, je (rester) à la maison.**
5. **Est-ce qu'on (pouvoir) le faire en deux heures?**
6. **S'il remontait la rue, je le (voir) tout de suite.**
7. **Si j'en avais assez, j'en (envoyer) un paquet à mon ami.**
8. **Il (avoir) tort s'il disait cela.**
9. **Si elle faisait attention, elle (poser) des questions.**
10. **On (avoir) dit qu'il était fou.**

VI. Translate into French:

1. In France they grow wheat, potatoes, sugar-beet and tobacco.
2. The motor industry must also be mentioned.
3. In England 80% of the population lives in towns.
4. Where do rich foreigners spend their holidays?
5. If I have enough money, I shall go to France next year.
6. The area of the country is five hundred and fifty-one thousand sq. kms.
7. I wonder where he was last week.
8. If you are going to Spain you cross the French frontier at Hendaye.
9. Because of the weather he did not go to his aunt's house yesterday.
10. They drink coffee in France but I know some Frenchmen who like tea.

VII. Write a short composition on **La France**. Here is some useful vocabulary:
la Manche = *English Channel*; **le Pas de Calais** = *Straits of Dover*; **la falaise** = *cliff*; **séparé(e) de** = *separated from*; **le fleuve** = *river*; **prendre sa source** = *to rise* (of rivers); **couler** = *to flow*; **la vallée** = *valley*; **la Seine, la Loire, la Garonne, le Rhône, le Rhin** (names of French rivers); **la figue** = *fig*; **le citron** = *lemon*; **un abricot** = *apricot*; **le raisin** = *grapes*; **une olive**; **une orange**; **le touriste**; **la cathédrale**; **la beauté** = *beauty*; **visiter les monuments** = *to see the sights*; **le réseau** = *network* (of railway); **le chiffre** = *figure, number*; **en temps de paix** (f.), **de guerre** (f.) = *in peacetime, wartime*; **y compris** = *including*; **une industrie** = *industry*; **les matières premières** = *raw materials*; **les ressources** (f.) = *resources*.

(Answers at the end of the book.)

LEÇON 17

GRAMMAR

THE PLUPERFECT TENSE

The pluperfect is a compound tense like the perfect, but it is used to express an idea one stage further back in the past, e.g. perfect tense — *I have given,* pluperfect tense — *I had given.* It is formed with the past participle and the imperfect tense of **avoir** or **être**:

j'avais donné = *I had given,* etc.	**j'avais fini**	**j'avais vendu**
tu avais donné	**tu avais fini**	**tu avais vendu**
il avait donné	**il avait fini**	**il avait vendu**
nous avions donné	**nous avions fini**	**nous avions vendu**
vous aviez donné	**vous aviez fini**	**vous aviez vendu**
ils avaient donné	**ils avaient fini**	**ils avaient vendu**

The same verbs which took **être** in the perfect tense (see p. 88) also take it in the pluperfect. These are:

(i) **aller, arriver, descendre, entrer, monter, mourir, naître, partir, rester, sortir, tomber, venir,** when used intransitively (without a direct object).

(ii) compounds of (i) when used intransitively, e.g. **remonter** = *to climb up again,* **repartir** = *to set out again,* **retomber** = *to fall back,* **devenir** = *to become*:

j'étais revenu(e) = *I had come*	**nous étions revenu(e)s**
tu étais revenu(e) *back,* etc.	**vous étiez revenu(e)(s)**
il était revenu	**ils étaient revenus**
elle était revenue	**elles étaient revenues**

(iii) **demeurer** (when it = *to remain*) and **retourner** (when it = *to go back*).

(iv) all reflexive verbs:

je m'étais lavé(e) = *I had washed*	**nous nous étions lavé(e)s**
tu t'étais lavé(e) *(myself),* etc.	**vous vous étiez lavé(e)(s)**
il s'était lavé	**ils s'étaient lavés**
elle s'était lavée	**elles s'étaient lavées**

Note that (*a*) the same rules apply for the agreement with the past participle as in the perfect tense (see p. 88), i.e. participles of **avoir** verbs agree with the preceding direct object, those of **être** verbs agree in general with the

172

subject; (*b*) **depuis** (= *since*) with the imperfect has the force of a pluperfect, as does the imperfect of **venir de**, e.g. **Il parlait depuis cinq minutes quand je suis arrivé** = *He had been talking for five minutes when I arrived.* **Il venait d'entrer quand on a sonné** = *He had just come in when someone rang the bell.*

EXPRESSING DIMENSIONS

Dimensions are expressed in French either with **avoir**:

Cette table a deux mètres de long
Cette table a deux mètres de longueur } = *This table is two metres long.*

Cette table a un mètre de large
Cette table a un mètre de largeur } = *This table is one metre wide.*

Cette table a un mètre de haut
Cette table a un mètre de hauteur } = *This table is one metre high.*

These individual measurements may be combined in this way:

Cette table a deux mètres de long sur un mètre de large sur un mètre de haut = *This table is two metres long by one metre wide by one metre high.*

Note also these examples:

Ce lac a vingt mètres de profondeur = *This lake is twenty metres deep.*

Cette planche a trois centimètres d'épaisseur = *This plank is three centimetres thick.*

or with **être**:

Cette table est longue de deux mètres.
Cette table est large d'un mètre.
Cette table est haute d'un mètre.
Ce lac est profond de vingt mètres.
Cette planche est épaisse de trois centimètres.

When used with nouns they keep **de**:

Une table longue de deux mètres = *A table two metres long.*
Un lac profond de vingt mètres = *A lake twenty metres deep.*

When used as a measure of difference they also keep **de** (cf. English *by*, e.g. *taller by two inches*):

Il est plus grand de deux pouces = *He is two inches taller.*

IRREGULAR VERB

Nettoyer [nɛtwaje] = *to clean*, is not really an irregular verb, but like others ending in **-yer** has unusual forms which must be specially learned.

Present tense: **je nettoie**   **nous nettoyons**
                tu nettoies   **vous nettoyez**
                il nettoie   **ils nettoient**

Future: **je nettoierai**, etc.
Conditional: **je nettoierais**, etc. (cf. **essuyer**, p. 107).

173

VOCABULARY

faire plaisir à [fɛːr plɛziːr a]	*to please*
le plaisir [plɛziːr]	*pleasure*
accompagner [akɔ̃paɲe]	*to accompany*
une offre [ɔfr]	*offer*
la voiture [vwatyːr]	*vehicle, car*
la station-service [stasjɔ̃sɛrvis]	*petrol station*
faire le plein de [fɛːr lə plɛ̃ də]	*to fill up with*
l'essence (f.) [ɛsɑ̃ːs]	*petrol*
le pare-brise [parbriz]	*windscreen*
rouler [rule]	*to roll, run along*
la grand'route [grɑ̃rut]	*highway*
la vitesse [vitɛs]	*speed*
sans cesse [sɑ̃ sɛs]	*ceaselessly*
se repentir de [sə rəpɑ̃tiːr də]	*to repent of*
indiquer [ɛ̃dike]	*to point out*
la droite [drwat]	*right (hand side)*
la gauche [goːʃ]	*left (hand side)*
la colline [kɔlin]	*hill*
profond(e) [prɔfɔ̃, -ɔ̃d]	*deep*
le lac [lak]	*lake*
la grange [grɑ̃ːʒ]	*barn*
la foudre [fudr]	*thunderbolt, lightning*
ainsi de suite [ɛ̃sidsɥit]	*so forth*
le conducteur [kɔdyktœːr]	*driver*
le sens inverse [sɑ̃ːs ɛ̃vɛrs]	*opposite direction*
furieux, -euse [fyrjø, -øːz]	*furious*
le coup [ku]	*blow, blast*
le klaxon [klaksɔ̃]	*hooter*
un éclair [eklɛːr]	*flash of lightning*
le panneau de signalisation [panodə [siɲalizasjɔ̃]	*traffic-sign*
ralentir [ralɑ̃tiːr]	*to slow down*
une émotion [emosjɔ̃]	*emotion, feeling*
un aviateur [avjatœːr]	*pilot*
le moteur [mɔtœːr]	*engine*
la panne [pan]	*breakdown*
abandonner [abɑ̃dɔne]	*to abandon*
un avion [avjɔ̃]	*aeroplane*
prévoir [prevwaːr]	*to foresee*
le danger [dɑ̃ʒe]	*danger*
affronter [afrɔ̃te]	*to face*
tuer [tɥe]	*to kill*

la station-service

le lac

le klaxon

un aviateur

174

le loisir [lwazi:r]	*leisure*
se presser [sə prɛse]	*to hurry*
ce n'est pas la peine [sə nɛ pɑ la	*it is not worth while*
le coup d'œil [ku dœ:j] [pɛn]	*glance*
furtif, -ive [fyrtif, -i:v]	*furtive*
un indicateur de vitesse [ɛ̃dikatœ:r	*speedometer*
də vitɛs]	

la panne

le permis de conduire [pɛrmi də	*driving licence*
auparavant [oparavɑ̃] [kɔ̃dɥi:r]	*previously*
critique [kritik]	*critical*
couvert(e) de [kuvɛ:r, -ɛrt də]	*covered with*
la pluie [plɥi]	*rain*
déraper [derape]	*to skid*
heurter [œrte]	*to run into*
le poteau télégraphique [pɔto	*telegraph post*
un hôpital [ɔpital] [telegrafik]	*hospital*
la chance [ʃɑ̃:s]	*luck*

un avion

s'écouler [sekule]	*to elapse*
le compagnon [kɔ̃paɲɔ̃]	*friend*
renifler [rənifle]	*to sniff*
brûler [bryle]	*to burn*
marquer [marke]	*to mark*
le sens unique [sɑ̃:s ynik]	*one-way (traffic)*
interdit(e) [ɛ̃tɛrdi, -it]	*forbidden*
le stationnement [stasjɔnmɑ̃]	*parking*
le pneu [pnø]	*tyre*
la roue [ru]	*wheel*

un indicateur de vitesse

le phare [fa:r]	*headlamp, lighthouse*
examiner [ɛgzamine]	*to examine*
calme [kalm]	*calm*
à son insu [a sɔnɛ̃sy]	*unknown to him, to her*
serrer [sɛre]	*to grip, pull on*
le frein [frɛ̃]	*brake*
la fumée [fyme]	*smoke*
observer [ɔpsɛrve]	*to observe*
la tâche [tɑ:ʃ]	*task*

le poteau télégraphique

brusquement [bryskəmɑ̃]	*abruptly*
doubler [duble]	*to overtake* (cars)
vivement [vivmɑ̃]	*quickly*
aveugle [avœgl]	*blind*
pacifique [pasifik]	*peace-loving*
un inconnu [ɛ̃kɔny]	*stranger*

le pneu

175

le panneau

le pare-brise

la voiture

le phare

6517·LG 75

le conducteur

un inconnu

la roue

la chaussée

PROMENADE EN AUTO

Un jour mon ami M. Leblanc m'a demandé si cela me ferait plaisir de
l'accompagner pour une petite promenade en auto. Comme il faisait beau
temps j'ai accepté son offre avec plaisir. M. Leblanc possède une belle voiture.
Nous sommes partis de chez lui vers dix heures du matin et nous sommes allés
directement à une station-service où nous avons fait le plein d'essence.
Après avoir nettoyé le pare-brise nous nous sommes mis en route.

Nous avions bientôt quitté la ville et roulions sur la grand'route à une
vitesse considérable. Mon ami parlait sans cesse et ne semblait pas faire
attention à la route. Je commençais déjà à me repentir d'avoir accepté
son offre. Nous roulions au milieu de la route qui avait plusieurs mètres de
large et de temps en temps M. Leblanc tournait la tête pour m'indiquer
quelque chose à droite ou à gauche. "Vous voyez cette colline là-bas? Elle
a deux cents mètres de haut," ou bien "Ce lac à côté du bois est profond de
cinquante mètres. Cette grange-là a été frappée par la foudre il y a six
mois" . . . et ainsi de suite. C'est sans doute à cause de cela que les
conducteurs qui venaient en sens inverse donnaient de furieux coups de
klaxon. Mais M. Leblanc ne s'en souciait pas. Il disait en effet: "Ces
gens-là font beaucoup de bruit et ils vont beaucoup trop vite. Ce n'est pas
comme ça qu'il faut conduire."

De temps en temps nous passions comme un éclair devant des panneaux
de signalisation — "Attention", "Travaux", "Passage à niveau" — mair

nous ne ralentissions pas. Je comprends maintenant les émotions de l'aviateur qui, le moteur en panne, se prépare à abandonner son avion perdu.

J'avais dit à ma femme avant de partir que je reviendrais le soir vers six heures. Je ne prévoyais pas à ce moment-là les dangers que j'allais affronter au cours de la journée. "Nous avons le temps," dis-je enfin à mon ami qui semble vouloir me tuer. "C'est la première fois que je viens par ici et je voudrais avoir le loisir de regarder autour de moi." "Il faut nous presser," répond-il. "Je voudrais arriver à Moulins avant midi. D'ailleurs le paysage par ici n'est pas très beau. Ce n'est pas la peine de perdre du temps." J'ai jeté un coup d'œil furtif sur l'indicateur de vitesse. Nous faisions cent kilomètres à l'heure. Mon Dieu!

Je venais de me rappeler que M. Leblanc avait obtenu son permis de conduire seulement six mois auparavant. La situation devenait critique. D'ailleurs le ciel était maintenant couvert de nuages et il commençait à tomber une pluie fine. Si notre voiture dérapait nous courions le danger de nous heurter contre un arbre ou un poteau télégraphique. Au lieu d'être chez moi à six heures du soir, je serais à l'hôpital — si j'avais de la chance. J'ai décidé de donner une leçon à mon ami et de faire quelque chose tout de suite.

Cinq minutes s'écoulent. Tout à coup je demande d'un air innocent: "Vous ne sentez rien, monsieur? Il me semble qu'il y a quelque chose qui ne va pas." Mon compagnon renifle. "En effet," répond-il, "ça sent le brûlé. Je vais m'arrêter tout de suite." "Pas ici," lui dis-je, "un peu plus loin." Nous étions à l'entrée d'une petite ville et la chaussée n'était pas très large. Après être entrés dans une rue étroite marquée "Sens unique" nous nous arrêtons juste devant un panneau de "Stationnement interdit." Mon ami descend aussitôt de voiture et commence à inspecter pneus, roues, phares. Il examine le moteur avec attention. Moi, j'étais calme: je savais bien ce qu'il y avait. À son insu, j'avais serré le frein à main. Ne me demandez pas maintenant comment je l'ai fait. Je ne vais pas vous le dire. M. Leblanc ne pouvait pas découvrir la cause de la fumée que nous avions observée avant de nous arrêter. Enfin, moi aussi, j'étais descendu de voiture et j'aidais mon ami dans sa tâche. "Allons," lui dis-je enfin, "continuons notre route. Conduisez avec soin. N'allez pas trop vite et tout ira bien."

Aussitôt dit, aussitôt fait. Nous nous sommes remis en marche — un peu brusquement peut-être et soudain — patatras! Une autre voiture qui était en train de nous doubler nous avait heurtés d'une manière violente. "Espèce d'imbécile," crie l'autre conducteur en descendant vivement de voiture. "Êtes-vous aveugle? . . ." Il me semblait que cet homme-là était fâché contre nous et comme je suis un homme pacifique j'ai quitté mon ami qui se disputait avec l'inconnu. Je suis rentré par le train — sain et sauf. Je ne suis pas un héros: je veux simplement mourir dans mon lit.

(*See notes on the next page. Translation at the end of the book.*)

NOTES ON THE TEXT

(Faire) une promenade en auto, à bicyclette, en bateau, etc. = *(to go for) a run in a car, on a bicycle, for a sail in a boat,* etc.; se mettre en route, en marche = *to start off*; jeter un coup d'œil = *to cast a glance* (cf. un coup de fouet = *a lash with a whip*, un coup de pied = *a kick*, un coup de vent = *a gust of wind*, un coup de fusil = *a rifle-shot*, un coup d'épée = *a sword-thrust*, un coup de main = *a helping hand*); ça sent le brûlé = *there is a smell of burning*; aussitôt dit, aussitôt fait = *no sooner said than done.*

EXERCISES

I. Answer in French:

1. Qu'est-ce que M. Leblanc avait?
2. À quelle heure avons-nous quitté la maison?
3. Quelle était la hauteur de la colline?
4. Pourquoi les autres conducteurs donnaient-ils de furieux coups de klaxon?
5. Qu'est-ce qu'on devrait faire en approchant d'un passage à niveau?
6. Qu'est-ce que j'avais dit à ma femme avant de partir?
7. Est-ce agréable quand une voiture dérape?
8. Quel est le contraire de "large"?
9. Qu'est-ce que j'ai fait pour attirer l'attention de mon ami?
10. L'autre conducteur était-il de bonne humeur après l'accident?

II. Translate into English:

1. Il était allé chercher une planche longue de trois mètres.
2. Quelles sont les dimensions de cette chambre?
3. Cette chambre a huit mètres de long sur six mètres de large sur quatre mètres de haut.
4. Voilà un mur haut de six pieds.
5. Le petit garçon qui était tombé à l'eau était âgé de six ans.
6. Hélas! nous nous étions égarés dans le bois.
7. Qu'avait-il fait pour mériter une punition si sévère?
8. Nous nous étions mis en route sans penser à ce qui pourrait arriver.
9. Aviez-vous remarqué que la pauvre femme pleurait?
10. Qu'auriez-vous dit si vous aviez vu quelqu'un qui conduisait comme un fou?

III. Give (1) first person singular and (2) third person feminine plural pluperfect of:

aller	avoir	connaître	devoir	dire	écrire	être
faire	se lever	lire	naître	partir	pouvoir	prendre
rire	savoir	tomber	venir	voir	vouloir	

IV. Replace by pronouns the words underlined:
1. **La reine n'a pas vu le héros.**
2. **Tous les jours j'allais chez mon oncle.**
3. **Il a donné son stylo à son camarade.**
4. **Nous avons mis une vingtaine de poissons dans le bassin.**
5. **Donnez-moi le paquet tout de suite. Ne laissez pas tomber le paquet.**

V. Supply a suitable word in place of the dash:
1. **Mon —— conduisait une —— rouge.**
2. **Nous —— assez —— pommes, merci.**
3. **J'ai dit —— garçon boucher —— apporter la viande avant midi.**
4. **L'auto filait à —— vitesse.**
5. **Sa figure —— couverte —— encre.**

VI. Translate into French:
1. This room is 25 feet long.
2. The lake is 5 metres deep.
3. The plank is 3 centimetres thick.
4. He had arrived too late.
5. The dining room is 40 metres by 20 metres.
6. At the end of the park is a wall 8 feet high.
7. His box is only 10 centimetres long.
8. She had not finished the work.
9. He sat down in order to rest.
10. They had given the children money.

VII. Translate into French:
1. In summer it is pleasant to go for a run in the car.
2. You must stop when you see the red traffic lights (**le feu**).
3. Where is your driving-licence? There is a policeman coming.
4. Towards ten o'clock the rain began to fall.
5. I was beginning to get angry for we were going too fast.
6. It is not worth while going out this evening; let us stay at home.
7. Ten minutes passed. Suddenly he said: "There is a smell of burning."

VIII. Composition: write a connected story in the past tense based on this:
Par un beau jour d'été M. Lafleur sort faire une promenade en auto — M. Lafleur est professeur d'université — très distrait — son auto s'arrête — M. Lafleur en descend — examine le moteur et les bougies (f. = *plugs*) — découvre enfin qu'il n'y a plus d'essence — sort un bidon (= *can*) vide du coffre (= *boot*) il se dirige vers le village voisin — par hasard rencontre un ami — cause un peu avec lui — continue son chemin — écoute en extase les oiseaux qui gazouillent (= *to warble*) — arrivé au village, il prend l'autobus et rentre — surprise de sa femme quand il entre portant le bidon.

(*Answers at the end of the book.*)

LEÇON 18

GRAMMAR

RELATIVE PRONOUNS

We have already learnt about **qui** and **que** (see p. 79); as well as revising these we shall now study some additional forms of the relative pronoun.

qui (subject) = *who, which, that*
que, qu' (object) = *whom, which, that*
These forms refer to persons or things and are singular or plural.
L'homme qui y travaille = *The man who works there.*
Les livres que je lis = *The books which I read.*

Note that (*a*) the relative cannot be omitted in French, cf. English: *the books I read*; (*b*) **qui** does not drop the **i** before a vowel: **l'homme qui entre, mon ami qui invite**; (*c*) after a preposition **qui** can be used only of persons: **l'homme à qui il parle** = *the man to whom he speaks*; (*d*) the verb after **qui** must be in the same person as the antecedent: **nous qui sommes si pauvres** = *we who are so poor*, **vous qui m'écoutez** = *you who are listening to me.*

ce qui, ce que (subject, object) = *what* (i.e. *that which*)
Ce qui est cher est quelquefois mauvais = *What is dear is sometimes bad.*
Ce que vous dites est vrai = *What you say is true.*

quoi = *which*
A kind of neuter used after prepositions; it refers to the whole of the preceding clause.
L'orateur a terminé son discours, après quoi nous sommes sortis = *The speaker ended his speech, after which we came out.*

dont (singular or plural) = *of whom, of which, whose*
Les choses (gens) dont je parle = *The things (people) I am speaking of.*
La maison dont le toit est rouge = *The house whose roof is red.*
L'homme dont j'admire le père = *The man whose father I admire.*

Note that (*a*) the order differs from English in the type of sentence where *whose* + noun is the object of the dependent clause: **l'homme dont je connais la sœur** = *the man whose sister I know*, **la lettre dont j'ai vu la copie** = *the letter the copy of which I have seen*; (*b*) it can be seen from the examples in (*a*) that **dont** must immediately follow the word to which it refers and that the object of the relative clause must follow the verb of that clause.

Note that (*a*) **dont** is not always translated *of which*; sometimes it means *from which*: **le lieu dont vous venez** = *the place from which you come*; (*b*) sometimes **dont** represents various other uses of **de**: **la charrue dont il se sert pour labourer** = *the plough he uses to plough with*, **le cadeau dont il est très content** = *the gift he is very pleased with* (or *with which he is very pleased*).

lequel (m.), **laquelle** (f.), (singular) = *which*
lesquels (m.), **lesquelles** (f.), (plural) = *which*
   These are used after prepositions for persons or things and agree with the preceding noun; **qui** also is used for persons, e.g. **l'homme à qui. . . .**
   Le crayon avec lequel j'écris = *The pencil with which I write.*
   La maison dans laquelle il demeure = *The house in which he lives.*
   Les abus contre lesquels il lutte = *The abuses he fights against.*

auquel, auxquels, auxquelles
duquel, desquels, desquelles
   The prepositions **à** and **de** combine with **lequel**, etc., to give these forms.
   Le port auquel il se dirige = *The port to which he is going.*
   Les lettres auxquelles je fais allusion = *The letters to which I refer.*
   L'endroit duquel vous venez = *The place from which you come.*
   Les villes desquelles ils viennent = *The towns from which they come.*
   However, as these forms are rather awkward, **dont** (of persons and things) and **de qui** (of persons only) are preferred to **duquel, de laquelle**, etc.

Note that **dont** cannot be used in sentences of the type preposition + *whose* + noun because, as we said above, **dont** must always come immediately after (never before) the noun to which it refers. Here **duquel**, etc., are used:
   L'homme au fils duquel (or **de qui**) **j'ai donné un jouet** = *The man to whose* [*son* (literally *to the son of whom*) *I gave a toy.*
   La femme à la fille de laquelle (or **de qui**) **il a envoyé des fleurs** = *The woman* [*to whose daughter he sent flowers.*

où (usually) = *where*
   Can be used as a relative of place and occasionally of time (*in which, on which, to which*, etc.).
   Le port où il va = *The port to which he goes.*
   La maison où il habite = *The house in which he lives.*
   La ville d'où il vient = *The town from which he comes.*
   Le jour où cela est arrivé = *The day on which that took place.*

Note these miscellaneous expressions: **Qui plus est** = *What is more* (here **qui** = **ce qui**); **Voilà qui est amusant** = *That is amusing*; **Il a de quoi vivre** = *He has enough to live on*; **Il n'y a pas de quoi** = *Don't mention it* (in reply to an expression of thanks).

VOCABULARY

la ferme [fɛrm]	*farm*	
comprendre [kɔ̃prɑ̃ːdr]	*to consist of, comprise*	
une écurie [ekyri]	*stable*	
une étable [etabl]	*cow-shed*	
la porcherie [pɔrʃəri]	*pigsty*	
loger [lɔʒe]	*to lodge, quarter*	
le cheval [ʃəval]	*horse*	
le porc [pɔːr]	*pig*	
le foin [fwɛ̃]	*hay*	
le hangar [ɑ̃gaːr]	*open shed*	
la charrette [ʃarɛt]	*cart*	**le foin**
le bûcher [byʃe]	*wood-shed*	
le séjour [seʒuːr]	*stay*	
dur(e) [dyːr]	*hard*	
traire [trɛːr]	*to milk*	
le champ [ʃɑ̃]	*field*	
à peine [a pɛn]	*scarcely*	
un endroit [ɑ̃drwa]	*place*	
la terre [tɛːr]	*land, earth*	
semer (like **lever**) [səme]	*to sow*	**la charrette**
la graine [grɛn]	*seed*	
la croissance [krwasɑ̃ːs]	*growth*	
récolter [rekɔlte]	*to harvest*	
la moisson [mwasɔ̃]	*harvest (of cereals)*	
détruire (like **conduire**) [detrɥiːr]	*to destroy*	
le bétail [betaːj]	*cattle*	
remplir [rɑ̃pliːr]	*to fill in, fill up*	
la bête [bɛːt]	*animal*	
malade [malad]	*ill*	**le bûcher**
le vétérinaire [veterinɛːr]	*veterinary surgeon*	
redouter [rədute]	*to dread*	
la maladie [maladi]	*disease*	
convaincre [kɔ̃vɛ̃ːkr]	*to convince*	
l'orge (f.) [ɔrʒ]	*barley*	
l'avoine (f.) [avwan]	*oats*	
le verger [vɛrʒe]	*orchard*	
fruitier, -ière [frɥitje, -jɛːr]	*fruit-bearing*	
le poirier [pwarje]	*pear-tree*	**le vétérinaire**
le cerisier [srizje]	*cherry-tree*	
juteux, -euse [ʒytø, -øːz]	*juicy*	
décrire (like **écrire**) [dekriːr]	*to describe*	

le valet de ferme [valɛ də fɛrm]	*farm-labourer*	
la fermière [fɛrmjɛːr]	*farmer's wife*	
la poule [pul]	*hen*	
le canard [kanaːr]	*duck*	
une oie [wa]	*goose*	
la volaille [vɔlaːj]	*poultry*	
la basse-cour [bɑskuːr]	*farmyard*	
le ménage [menaːʒ]	*household*	
la rigueur [rigœːr]	*rigour*	**l'orge** (f.)
la vie [vi]	*life*	
mener (like **lever**) [məne]	*to lead*	
remplacer [rãplase]	*to replace*	
la besogne [bzɔɲ]	*task*	
se servir de [sə sɛrviːr də]	*to make use of*	
la charrue [ʃary]	*plough*	
la herse [ɛrs]	*harrow*	**l'avoine** (f.)
surprendre [syrprãːdr]	*to surprise*	
ridé(e) [ride]	*wrinkled*	
faire partie de [fɛːr parti də]	*to be a part of*	
fiévreux, -euse [fjevrø, -øːz]	*feverish*	
scruter [skryte]	*to scan*	
le ciel [sjɛl]	*sky*	
gâter [gɑte]	*to spoil*	
la perte [pɛrt]	*loss*	
la meule [møːl]	*stack, rick*	**la fermière**
une odeur [odœːr]	*smell*	
la tempête [tãpɛːt]	*storm, wind*	
abattre (like **battre**) [abatr]	*to knock down*	
ravager [ravaʒe]	*to devastate*	
la gelée [ʒle]	*frost*	
nuisible [nɥizibl]	*harmful*	
la lutte [lyt]	*struggle*	
faire du bien à [fɛːr dy bjɛna]	*to do good to*	**la charrue**
la nourriture [nurityːr]	*food*	
le jambon [ʒãbɔ̃]	*ham*	
réveiller [revɛje]	*to waken*	
meugler [møgle]	*to low*	
hennir [ɛniːr]	*to neigh*	
en somme [ã sɔm]	*in short*	
aboyer (like **envoyer**) [abwaye]	*to bark*	
la symphonie pastorale [sɛ̃fɔni pastɔral]	*pastoral symphony*	**la herse**

la grange
le hangar
le verger
une étable
une écurie
la porcherie
le tracteur
la charrette
le valet de ferme
la fermière
la poule
le canard
la volaille

LA FERME

L'année dernière je suis allé passer quelques semaines chez un fermier qui est un ami de mon père. Sa ferme qui se trouve à quelques kilomètres de notre ville n'est pas très grande. Elle comprend une habitation où demeure le fermier avec sa famille, une écurie, une étable et une porcherie. Dans l'étable on loge les vaches, dans l'écurie les chevaux et dans la porcherie les porcs. Il n'y a rien d'extraordinaire à cela, n'est-ce pas? On garde le foin et le blé dans des granges. Il y a aussi un hangar sous lequel on met les charrettes et les voitures. Près du hangar se trouve un bûcher où l'on serre le bois à brûler.

Pendant mon séjour j'ai remarqué que la vie du fermier est assez dure. Il doit se lever de bonne heure, souvent avant l'aube, pour aller traire les vaches. Quand il fait beau temps il travaille toute la journée aux champs. À peine a-t-il quelquefois le temps de revenir à la maison prendre ses repas. On les lui apporte à l'endroit où il est occupé. Il travaille au soleil et sous la pluie. Il laboure la terre, il sème les graines, il en surveille la croissance et plus tard il récolte la moisson. Il y a mille tâches qu'il doit faire. Il répare sans cesse les clôtures détruites par le vent et le bétail; il remplit des formulaires dont il reçoit des douzaines tous les mois. Chaque semaine il va au marché vendre ses bêtes ou en acheter d'autres. Il profite de l'occasion, il est vrai, pour bavarder un peu avec ses amis en ville et boire un petit verre avec eux au café. Quand ses animaux tombent malades il fait venir le vétérinaire. Naturellement il redoute les maladies qui pourraient causer la mort de centaines

184

de ses bêtes. Comme je n'ai passé que trois semaines à la ferme, évidemment je n'ai pas pu observer tout le travail qui se fait au cours de l'année. Mais j'en ai assez vu pour me convaincre que la vie du fermier est très laborieuse.

Le fermier dont je parle cultive le blé, l'orge et l'avoine aussi bien que les pommes de terre, les navets et d'autres légumes. Il a aussi un verger où l'on voit des arbres fruitiers — pommiers, poiriers et cerisiers. Tout le monde aime les belles pommes rouges et les poires juteuses, n'est-ce pas? Mais malheureusement lorsque je suis à la campagne et que je suis entouré d'arbres qui portent de beaux fruits je n'ai envie de rien manger. Voilà qui est curieux.

Naturellement le fermier ne pourrait pas faire à lui seul tout le travail que je viens de décrire. Il est aidé de quelques valets de ferme. Ceux-ci, comme ils ne sont pas très nombreux, habitent la même maison que lui et mangent à la même table: ils vivent tous en famille.

Quant à la fermière, elle s'occupe des poules, des canards et des oies, c'est-à-dire, de toute la volaille de la basse-cour — et de tous les travaux du ménage. La fermière doit être une femme robuste pour supporter les rigueurs d'une vie pareille. Je me demande quelquefois ce que feraient nos jeunes femmes de la ville si elles étaient obligées de mener une telle vie.

De nos jours le tracteur commence à remplacer les bêtes pour les besognes agricoles. Cependant on se sert toujours en France des bœufs pour tirer la charrue ou la herse. D'ailleurs les femmes travaillent aux champs autant que les hommes, ce qui pourrait surprendre les touristes étrangers qui parcourent le pays en voiture. Ces fortes paysannes, ridées, bronzées par le soleil font partie, pour ainsi dire, du paysage français.

La saison des foins est une période d'activité fiévreuse. On travaille aux champs du matin au soir et le fermier scrute anxieusement le ciel. Il craint la pluie qui pourrait tout gâter et lui causer des pertes considérables. Quant au foin qu'on doit laisser dehors, on en fait des meules. Quelle bonne odeur que celle d'un champ dans lequel on vient de couper l'herbe!

Assis le soir au coin du feu, le fermier me parlait quelquefois des malheurs qui le menacent de temps en temps et auxquels il faut toujours s'attendre. Il me parlait de la tempête qui abat les arbres et qui ravage les champs; de la gelée qui tue les plantes et des insectes nuisibles qui mangent tout. En effet, sa vie est une lutte continuelle contre la Nature.

Mon séjour à la ferme m'a fait du bien. La nourriture y était saine et abondante. Le jambon, le beurre et le fromage y avaient un goût délicieux. Et je mangeais à ma faim! Je m'amusais bien toute la journée. Le matin, il était impossible de rester au lit. On était réveillé à l'aube par le joyeux chant des oiseaux. Dans la cour on entendait les vaches qui meuglaient, les chevaux qui hennissaient et les chiens qui aboyaient. C'était, en somme, une véritable symphonie pastorale.

(See notes on the next page. Translation at the end of the book.)

NOTES ON THE TEXT

À quelques kilomètres de — note the use of à in this expression (cf. *The village is* 40 *kms. from Paris* = Le village est à 40 km. de Paris); rien d'extraordinaire = *nothing extraordinary*: the de is essential (cf. quelque chose d'intéressant = *something interesting*); aussi bien que = *as well as*; manger à sa faim = *to eat one's fill.*

EXERCISES

I. Answer in French:

   1. Quels animaux trouve-t-on à l'étable?
   2. Avec quoi laboure-t-on la terre?
   3. Pourquoi le fermier va-t-il au marché?
   4. Que fait-on quand un animal est malade?
   5. Quelles céréales est-ce que le fermier cultive?
   6. Comment s'appellent ceux qui aident le fermier?
   7. Qu'est-ce que c'est qu'une besogne?
   8. Qu'est-ce que le fermier fait en ville?
   9. Pourquoi le fermier craint-il la pluie?
  10. Où est-ce qu'on met le blé après l'avoir coupé?

II. Translate into English:

   1. Je ne sais pas ce qu'ils sont devenus.
   2. Le fermier dont il parle est un homme riche.
   3. Le stylo avec lequel il écrit en ce moment est à moi.
   4. Les principes pour lesquels il lutte sont excellents.
   5. Il n'y va plus. Voilà qui est étrange.
   6. Il y a de quoi vous faire enrager.
   7. Les événements auxquels vous faites allusion ont eu lieu l'année dernière.
   8. Vous qui vous plaignez tout le temps ne travaillez pas assez fort.
   9. Le fils de mon voisin lequel vient de passer son examen est un élève paresseux.
  10. Les assistants parmi lesquels il y avait quelques agents ennemis se conduisaient d'une manière désordonnée.

III. Give these verb forms:

   1. Third person plural present: recevoir, dire, prendre, vaincre, naître, lire, mettre, faire, semer, pouvoir.

bliothèque

le bureau de poste

la caserne

flèche

la chaumière

le château

la cathédrale

une école

le clocher

la fabrique, une usine

un hôpital

église

le palais

le phare

un appartement

la tour

immeuble

la mairie, l'Hôtel de ville

le moulin à vent

le théâtre

LES BÂTIMENTS QU'ON TROUVE DANS LA VILLE

LES BAGAGES

la courroie

un appareil
photographique

la ficelle

le co

le filet

la boîte

le carton
à chapeaux

une
étiquette

le porte-
monnaie

la caisse

la corde

la malle

le porte-feuille

le p

le sac
de montagne

le paquet

le sac de voyage

la valise

la serv

le
à

LES RÉCIPIENTS

la bouillotte

une assiette

le bol

la boîte
de conserves

la bouteille

la c

le paquet de cigarettes

la cruche
(le pot)

la corbeille à papier

le cendrier

la casserole

un étui à
cigarettes

le pot

la tasse

la soucoupe

le vase

un étui à lunettes

la coupe
à champagne

le plat

le v

CE DONT ON A BESOIN POUR LE VOYAGE ET POUR LA VIE QUOTIDIENNE

2. First person plural future: **devoir, courir, cueillir, envoyer, mourir, faire, savoir, ouvrir, être, aller.**
3. First person singular conditional: **venir, voir, boire, aller, avoir.**
4. Past participle: **lire, venir, devoir, écrire, voir, pouvoir, vouloir, faire, mettre, prendre.**

IV. Insert suitable relative pronouns in the spaces:

1. **La ferme à —— je passe mes vacances n'est pas grande.**
2. **Il a soupé à neuf heures, après —— il s'est couché.**
3. **La femme pour le fils d —— il a fait tant de sacrifices l'estime beaucoup.**
4. **Le marchand —— la femme est si méchante n'est pas heureux.**
5. **Les élèves à —— j'avais donné des conseils m'ont fait un petit cadeau.**

V. Translate into French:

1. This barn is part (**faire partie**) of the farm you see over there.
2. The farmer of whom I am speaking is a very industrious man.
3. Nowadays the tractor is beginning to replace oxen.
4. They work from morning to night cutting (**à couper**) the corn.
5. He cannot do all that on his own. It is impossible.
6. He dreads bad weather which causes him considerable loss.
7. It is necessary to get up early, a thing which I detest.
8. In his vegetable garden he grows potatoes, carrots and turnips.
9. Every week I go to the market to sell my cows or to buy what I need.
10. On the farm one can hear the cows lowing, the horses neighing and the dogs barking.

VI. Composition: describe a holiday spent on your uncle's farm. Here are some useful phrases and vocabulary: **le mouton** = *sheep*; **le veau** = *calf*; **un agneau** = *lamb*; **la chèvre** = *goat*; **brouter l'herbe** = *to graze*; **bêler** = *to bleat*; **la prune** = *plum*; **la cerise** = *cherry*; **la fraise** = *strawberry*; **passer ses vacances** (f.) = *to spend one's holidays*; **donner un coup de main** = *to give a helping hand*; **pondre des œufs** = *to lay eggs*; **le coq chante** = *the cock crows*; **cocorico** or **coquerico** = *cock-a-doodle-doo.*

(*Answers at the end of the book.*)

LEÇON 19

GRAMMAR

THE PAST HISTORIC TENSE

The past historic is a literary tense used to express a single completed action in the past. It often takes the place of the perfect (compound past) tense in novels, history, newspapers, etc., but never in letters or conversation.

The past historic of regular verbs is formed by dropping the infinitive ending -er, -ir, or -re, and adding to the stem the endings: -ai, -as, -a, -âmes, -âtes, -èrent for -er verbs; -is, -is, -it, -îmes, -îtes, -irent for -ir and -re verbs:

je donnai [dɔne] = *I gave*, etc.	**je finis** [fini]	**je vendis** [vãdi]
tu donnas [dɔna]	**tu finis** [fini]	**tu vendis** [vãdi]
il donna [dɔna]	**il finit** [fini]	**il vendit** [vãdi]
nous donnâmes [dɔnam]	**nous finîmes** [finim]	**nous vendîmes** [vãdim]
vous donnâtes [dɔnat]	**vous finîtes** [finit]	**vous vendîtes** [vãdit]
ils donnèrent [dɔnɛːr]	**ils finirent** [finiːr]	**ils vendirent** [vãdiːr]

USE OF THE PAST HISTORIC

The past historic must be carefully distinguished from the imperfect tense; the imperfect expresses what used to happen or was happening when something else took place, whereas the past historic tense states the actions as they occurred.

The past historic answers the question: what happened next? Imagine a story to be taking place in a setting: the description of the scenery or of the characters will be in the imperfect tense (e.g. *the sky was blue, the sun was shining, the man was wearing a green coat . . .*) while the actions of the characters will be in the past historic (e.g. *he entered, he met his friend, he fell down . . .*). As you will notice, the difference between the imperfect and the past historic tenses is exactly the same as between the imperfect and the perfect (note the difference in the first example):

Il pleuvait quand il sortit = *It was raining when he went out.*

Il vint, il vit, il vainquit = *He came, he saw, he conquered.*

Tous les jours il allait au parc mais un jour il remarqua que le banc n'était plus là = *Every day he used to go to the park but one day he noticed that the bench was no longer there.*

190

IRREGULAR VERBS (PAST HISTORIC)

Some verbs form the past historic in **-us, -us, -ut, -ûmes, -ûtes, -urent**, e.g.:

avoir = *to have*	être = *to be*	recevoir = *to receive*
j'eus [y] = *I had*, etc.	**je fus** [fy] = *I was*, etc.	**je reçus** [rəsy] = *I received*, etc.
tu eus [y]	**tu fus** [fy]	**tu reçus** [rəsy]
il eut [y]	**il fut** [fy]	**il reçut** [rəsy]
nous eûmes [ym]	**nous fûmes** [fym]	**nous reçûmes** [rəsym]
vous eûtes [yt]	**vous fûtes** [fyt]	**vous reçûtes** [rəsyt]
ils eurent [yːr]	**ils furent** [fyːr]	**ils reçurent** [rəsyːr]

These verbs also form the past historic in **-us**, etc.:

boire, je bus	connaître, je connus	courir, je courus	croire, je crus
devoir, je dus	falloir, il fallut	lire, je lus	mourir, je mourus
plaire, je plus	pleuvoir, il plut	pouvoir, je pus	savoir, je sus
se taire, je me tus	valoir, je valus	vivre, je vécus	vouloir, je voulus

These verbs form the past historic in **-is**, etc., on an irregular stem:

s'asseoir, je m'assis	conduire, je conduisis (also **introduire**, etc.)	
craindre, je craignis	dire, je dis	écrire, j'écrivis
faire, je fis	mettre, je mis	naître, je naquis
prendre, je pris	rire, je ris	voir, je vis

Venir and **tenir** (= *to hold*), which follows the same pattern, are very irregular:
vins [vɛ̃], **vins** [vɛ̃], **vint** [vɛ̃], **vînmes** [vɛ̃ːm], **vîntes** [vɛ̃ːt], **vinrent** [vɛ̃ːr].

Note these regular past historics: **je dormis** = *I slept*, **je suivis** = *I followed*.

IMPERSONAL VERBS

Impersonal verbs are those with a vague third person singular subject **il** referring to no expressed noun. Many are connected with weather or time:

Il pleut = *It is raining.*	**Il gèle** = *It is freezing.*
Il neige = *It is snowing.*	**Il grêle** = *It is hailing.*
Il tonne = *It is thundering.*	**Il dégèle** = *It is thawing.*
Il fait du vent = *It is windy.*	**Il fait des éclairs** = *It is lightning.*

Il fait froid, chaud, frais, lourd = *It is cold, warm, cool, heavy.*
Il fait beau, mauvais temps = *It is fine, bad weather.*
Il est deux heures et demie = *It is half past two.*

il faut = *it is necessary*	**il s'agit de** = *it is a question of*
il y a = *there is, are*	**il vaut mieux** = *it is better*

Sometimes **il** anticipates the real subject (but it always stays singular):

il est + adjective + **que: il est vrai que . . .** = *it is true that . . .*
il viendra des hommes = *there will come men*
il arrivera un malheur = *an accident will happen*

VOCABULARY

la joie [ʒwa]	*joy*
la nature [natyːr]	*nature*
se réveiller [sə revɛje]	*to awake, wake up*
le soleil levant [sɔlɛːj ləvɑ̃]	*rising sun*
dorer [dɔre]	*to gild*
le rayon [rɛjɔ̃]	*ray*
magique [maʒik]	*magic*
l'aurore (f.) [ɔrɔːr]	*dawn*
pousser un soupir [puse œ̃ supiːr]	*to heave a sigh*
déposer [depoze]	*to put down*
le camping [kɑ̃piŋ]	*camping*
réfléchir [refleʃiːr]	*to reflect, think*
s'adresser à [sadrɛse a]	*to address*
en face de [ɑ̃ fas də]	*facing*
le congé [kɔ̃ʒe]	*leave, holiday*
c'est dommage de [sɛ dɔmaːʒ də]	*it is a pity to*
à vrai dire [a vrɛ diːr]	*to tell the truth*
pratique [pratik]	*practical*
un, une enthousiaste [ɑ̃tuzjast]	*enthusiast*
consentir à [kɔ̃sɑ̃tiːr a]	*to consent to*
pêle-mêle [pɛlmɛl]	*higgledy-piggledy*
le coffre [kɔfr]	*boot* (of car)
la tente [tɑ̃ːt]	*tent*
la corde [kɔrd]	*rope*
le piquet [pike]	*peg*
un ustensile [ystɑ̃sil]	*utensil*
débrancher [debrɑ̃ʃe]	*to disconnect*
le radiateur [radjatœːr]	(electric) *fire*
aussi (+ inverted verb) [osi]	*so*
faire demi-tour [fɛːr dəmituːr]	*to turn back*
remettre en ordre [rəmɛtr ɑ̃nɔrdr]	*to put straight again*
la route nationale [rut nasjɔnal]	*main road*
prêter attention à [prɛte atɑ̃sjɔ̃ a]	*to pay attention to*
un auto-stoppeur [otostɔpœːr]	*hitch-hiker*
agiter [aʒite]	*to wave*
désespéré(e) [dezɛspere]	*desperate*
jusque-là [ʒyskla]	*so far, there*
la parole [parɔl]	*word*
froncer [frɔ̃se]	*to knit* (one's brow)
le sourcil [sursi]	*eyebrow*
réussir à [reysiːr a]	*to succeed in*

le soleil levant

le coffre

le radiateur

un auto-stoppeur

192

le matériel [materjɛl] — material, *implements*
haleter (like lever) [alte] — *to pant*
le maillet [majɛ] — *mallet*
plus d'une fois [ply dyn fwa] — *more than once*
écraser [ekrɑze] — *to crush*
le pouce [puːs] — *thumb*
le juron [ʒyrɔ̃] — *swear-word*
entre-temps [ɑ̃trətɑ̃] — *meanwhile*
le tronc [trɔ̃] — *trunk*
s'introduire [sɛ̃trɔdɥiːr] — *to worm one's way*
ramper [rɑ̃pe] — *to crawl*
la patte [pat] — *paw*, *foot*
la posture [pɔstyːr] — *posture*
digne [diɲ] — *dignified, worthy*
fort peu de [fɔːr pø də] — *precious little*
se retirer [sə rətire] — *to withdraw*
se débrouiller [sə debruje] — *to shift for oneself*
mécontent(e) [mekɔ̃tɑ̃, -ɑ̃t] — *displeased*
la nuit [nɥi] — *night*
frais, fraîche [frɛ, frɛʃ] — *chilly, fresh*
de plus [də ply] — *moreover*
désagréable [dezagreabl] — *unpleasant*
claquer [klake] — *to slam* (door), *to flap*
la toile [twal] — *canvas*
souffler [sufle] — *to blow*
horriblement [ɔrribləmɑ̃] — *horribly*
gémir [ʒemiːr] — *to moan*
s'inquiéter [sɛ̃kjete] — *to worry, upset oneself*
prier de [prie də] — *to beg to*
fatigué(e) [fatige] — *tired*
la faute [foːt] — *fault*
le sol [sɔl] — *ground*
se rendormir [sə rɑ̃dɔrmiːr] — *to go back to sleep*
le dormeur, la -euse [dɔrmœːr, -øːz] — *sleeper*
de nouveau [də nuvo] — *again*
tremper [trɑ̃pe] — *to soak*
un os [ɔs] — *bone*
la protestation [prɔtɛstasjɔ̃] — *protest*
entendre raison [ɑ̃tɑ̃dr rɛzɔ̃] — *to listen to reason*
entêté(e) [ɑ̃tɛte] — *obstinate*
ne . . . guère [nə . . . gɛːr] — *scarcely*
enrhumé(e) [ɑ̃ryme] — *having a cold*

le sourcil

le pouce

la nuit

le dormeur

un os

193

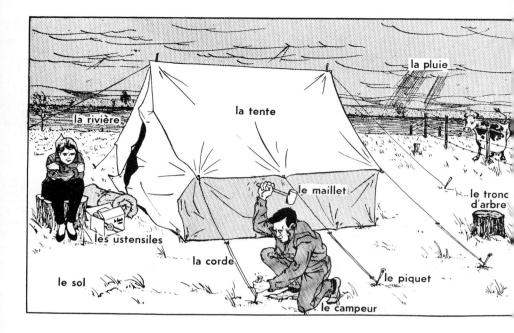

la pluie

la tente

la rivière

le maillet

le tronc
d'arbre

les ustensiles

la corde

le sol

le piquet

le campeur

LES CHARMES DU CAMPING

"Quelle joie de se trouver à l'aube au milieu de la Nature qui se réveille! Le soleil levant dore le ciel de ses rayons magiques. Les oiseaux saluent l'aurore de leur chant joyeux. . . ." M. Leclerc poussa un soupir et déposa son livre — "Le Camping pour Tous". Il réfléchit quelques moments après quoi il s'adressa à sa femme qui était assise en face de lui. "Dis donc, est-ce que tu aimes le camping? J'ai envie d'aller passer quelques jours à la campagne au bord d'une rivière que je connais. Comme tu le sais, j'ai un congé de trois jours et ce serait dommage de rester à la maison. Qu'en dis-tu? Veux-tu bien m'accompagner?"

À vrai dire, Mme Leclerc, femme très pratique, n'était pas une enthousiaste du camping mais comme elle voulait faire plaisir à son mari elle consentit à partir avec lui. Deux heures plus tard, après avoir jeté pêle-mêle dans le coffre de la voiture tente, cordes, piquets, ustensiles de cuisine — enfin tout ce qui peut assurer une vie confortable au milieu des champs loin de toute civilisation, ils se mirent en route.

Au bout de dix minutes de voyage Mme Leclerc dit à son mari qu'elle avait oublié de débrancher le radiateur électrique. Aussi firent-ils demi-tour et revinrent à la maison. Tout étant enfin remis en ordre à la satisfaction de Madame, ils se remirent en route. Ils roulèrent deux heures sur la route nationale et M. Leclerc ne prêta aucune attention aux quelques auto-stoppeurs qui agitaient la main avec une énergie désespérée. Arrivés enfin à l'endroit où ils comptaient passer trois jours délicieux, ils s'arrêtèrent et descendirent de voiture. "C'est bien ici," dit M. Leclerc à sa femme, "qu'il faut laisser la voiture mais il nous faudra traverser trois champs pour arriver au bord de la rivière. Nous devons tout porter jusque-là." En entendant ces paroles Mme Leclerc fronça les sourcils mais elle ne dit rien. Une heure plus tard, après avoir traversé et retraversé les champs trois fois, ils avaient enfin réussi à déposer tout le matériel au bord de la rivière. "Viens," dit M. Leclerc en haletant, "il faut maintenant dresser la tente." Il prit le maillet et donna des coups furieux sur les piquets. Plus d'une fois il était près de s'écraser le pouce. Cependant, après beaucoup d'efforts et non sans quelques petits jurons que nous passerons sous silence, il réussit à dresser la tente. Entre-temps, sa femme qui, comme presque toutes les femmes ne comprenait rien à ces choses-là, s'était assise sur un tronc d'arbre en pensant qu'elle aimerait mieux être à la maison où il faisait plus chaud. M. Leclerc s'introduisit en rampant sous la tente et Mme suivit son mari à quatre pattes — posture peu digne quand il s'agit d'une dame entre deux âges.

Il y avait fort peu de place sous cette tente-là et Mme Leclerc qui se trouvait dans l'impossibilité d'aider son mari se retira aussitôt, le laissant se débrouiller tout seul — ce dont il n'était pas trop mécontent. Mais elle ne resta pas longtemps dehors. La nuit tombait et il faisait frais. De plus, il se levait un vent désagréable qui faisait claquer la toile et les cordes. Elle rentra vite sous la tente. Après avoir bavardé pendant une demi-heure, nos deux campeurs s'endormirent. Mais le vent soufflait de plus en plus fort et de grosses gouttes de pluie commencèrent à tomber sur la tente en faisant un bruit formidable. Impossible de dormir dans ces conditions. "J'ai horriblement froid," gémit Mme Leclerc, "et j'espère que tu as bien dressé la tente. Autrement. . . ." "Ne t'inquiète pas," répondit son mari d'un ton brusque. "Tu t'attends toujours à quelque malheur. À la campagne ce n'est pas comme à la maison, tu sais. Essaie de dormir, je t'en prie. Moi, je suis fatigué." "Ce n'est pas ma faute quand même," reprit Mme Leclerc qui, comme toutes les femmes, voulait avoir le dernier mot même au milieu de la nuit. "D'ailleurs, je trouve que le sol est très dur." À la fin ils se rendormirent.

Quelques heures passèrent. Dehors il pleuvait à verse et de temps en temps quelques gouttes tombaient sur les dormeurs. Cela finit par les réveiller de nouveau. "Ciel!" s'écria Mme Leclerc, "je suis trempée jusqu'aux os. Je ne reste plus ici. Allons passer ce qui reste de la nuit dans la voiture." Et c'est ce qu'ils firent malgré les protestations de M. Leclerc. Car faire entendre raison à une femme entêtée, ce n'est guère possible.

Jusqu'à présent M. Leclerc n'a pas pu connaître les vrais plaisirs du camping car, dès le lendemain matin, sa femme et lui revinrent à la maison, enrhumés tous deux.

(*See notes on the next page. Translation at the end of the book.*)

NOTES ON THE TEXT

Une femme entre deux âges (or, **d'un certain âge**) = *a middle-aged woman*; **de plus en plus fort** = *stronger and stronger*; **pleuvoir à verse** = *to pour with rain*; **quand même** (equivalent to **tout de même**) = *all the same*; **trempé jusqu'aux os** = *soaked to the skin*; **à quatre pattes** = *on all fours* (**la patte** = *paw*).

EXERCISES

I. Answer in French:

1. Qu'est-ce que M. Leclerc avait envie de faire?
2. Pourquoi Mme Leclerc consentit-elle à partir?
3. Qu'est-ce qu'ils mirent dans le coffre de l'auto?
4. Est-ce que Mme Leclerc aida son mari à dresser la tente?
5. Quel temps faisait-il pendant la nuit?
6. Qu'est-ce qui réveilla les dormeurs?
7. Que dit Mme Leclerc à ce moment?
8. Pourquoi Madame voulait-elle retourner dans la voiture?
9. Est-ce que M. Leclerc était content de dormir dans la voiture?
10. Que firent-ils le lendemain matin?

II. Translate into English:

1. Il pleuvait à verse quand ils se mirent en route.
2. Il est impossible de savoir s'il est mort ou non.
3. Arrivés au village, ils descendirent à l'auberge.
4. Un coup de fusil se fit entendre dans la forêt.
5. Il avait cinquante ans quand il alla à Paris.
6. Comme il était fatigué, il s'endormit aussitôt.
7. Un malheur vint troubler notre vie paisible.
8. Il fit trop de fautes dans son devoir.
9. Il est quelquefois agréable de passer la nuit sous la tente.
10. Un jour il arriva une lettre qui attrista mon ami.

III. Give (1) third person singular; (2) first person plural; (3) third person plural of the past historic tense of these verbs: **aller, être, prendre, monter, répondre, faire, avoir, recevoir, devoir, conduire, rougir, attendre, venir, mettre, ouvrir.**

IV. Replace the infinitive by the correct form of either the past historic or the imperfect tense, as necessary in each case:

En ce temps-là Jean (être) assez jeune; je crois qu'il (avoir) huit ans. Son père (travailler) dans un bureau qui (se trouver) de l'autre côté de la ville. Un jour que son père (être) sorti, un étranger (se présenter) à la porte et (demander) d'un ton brusque si c'(être) bien là que (demeurer) M. Lekeux. Jean (répondre) que oui. Alors l'inconnu (demander) s'il (être) visible. Jean (dire) que non et (expliquer) que son père (être) en ville. L'inconnu (dire) qu'il attendrait son retour et il (pénétrer) dans la maison sans plus de façons. Jean qui (être) tout petit (avoir) peur de cet homme énorme. Celui-ci (sortir) de sa poche un paquet de cigarettes, (frotter) une allumette et (allumer) une cigarette. Puis, il (se mettre) à examiner la pièce. Jean (se demander) s'il (aller) voler quelque chose.

V. Translate into French:

1. It is half past three.
2. At a quarter to four.
3. At half past twelve (midnight).
4. At eight p.m.
5. At seven a.m.
6. It is a quarter past six.
7. It is twenty past nine.
8. It is necessary to do it.
9. It is windy.
10. What is it all about?

VI. Translate into French:

1. "I am soaked to the skin," said the camper.
2. To tell the truth, I am not very keen on camping.
3. It was windy and pouring with rain when they arrived at the village.
4. So saying, he slammed the door and left the house.
5. Night was falling when they stopped at the hotel.
6. She quickly got into the tent because it was cold outside.
7. They were both very tired and soon fell asleep.
8. He consented to work in the garden till five o'clock.
9. He took a box of matches from his pocket and struck one match.
10. It is a question of getting home before the return of my father.

VII. Write a composition (past tense) based on this outline:

Un jour d'été — deux amis — partir de bonne heure à bicyclette — pédaler pendant deux heures — chercher un champ convenable — commencer à dresser la tente — ne pas remarquer le taureau qui broute l'herbe — le taureau s'approche — fuite précipitée des deux campeurs — la bête écrase la tente — retour des deux amis à la maison.

(*Answers at the end of the book.*)

LEÇON 20

GRAMMAR

USES OF THE ARTICLE

In this lesson and in the following one we shall study in more detail the uses of the definite article **le, la** and **les** and of the indefinite article **un** and **une** (plural **des**). Although these are often the same as English usage there are some important differences where the article is included in French and omitted in English and vice versa.

The definite article must precede:

(i) abstract nouns and nouns indicating all of a class or kind:

La patience est une vertu = *Patience is a virtue.*
La vieillesse est triste = *Old age is sad.*
Le fer est un métal = *Iron is a metal.*

but abstract nouns followed by an adjective are preceded by the indefinite article:

Il montra un courage extraordinaire = *He showed extraordinary [courage.*

(ii) proper names preceded by an adjective and titles (except **monsieur, madame,** etc.):

Le petit Jean = *Little John.*
Le roi George = *King George.*
Le maréchal Sabatier = *Marshal Sabatier.*
La jeune Marie = *Young Mary.*
Le docteur Leroy = *Dr. Leroy.*

(except when you are speaking to someone directly, e.g. **Bonjour, docteur Leroy.** But if **monsieur** is used as well, the definite article must be inserted, e.g. **Bonjour, monsieur le docteur.**).

(iii) names of countries, languages, mountains and rivers:

La France est un beau pays = *France is a beautiful country.*
Le russe est une langue difficile = *Russian is a difficult language.*
J'étudie le français = *I am studying French.*
Le Mont Blanc est en France = *Mont Blanc is in France.*
La Tamise est un fleuve anglais = *The Thames is an English river.*

but note these exceptions; the article is omitted:

(*a*) after **en** (= *to, in*) and **de** (= *from*) + feminine names of countries:

Je vais en Allemagne = *I am going to Germany.*

Il vient de France = *He comes from France.*

(*b*) if the name of the language follows **en** or **parler**:

Dites cela en français. = *Say that in French.*

Parlez-vous allemand? = *Do you speak German?*

(but this rule is generally broken if **parler** is qualified by an adverb:

Il parle bien le français = *He speaks French well.*)

Note that with masculine names of countries **à** + the article is used instead of **en**, and **de** is used with the article:

Il voyage au Japon = *He is travelling in Japan.*

Il arrive des États-Unis = *He is just back from the United States.*

(iv) parts of the body (the article replaces a possessive adjective):

Elle s'est cassé le bras = *She has broken her arm.*

Levez la main! = *Raise your hand!*

(v) seasons:

Le printemps est une belle saison = *Spring is a fine season.*

(Note that **au printemps** = *in spring*, **en été** = *in summer*, **en automne** = *in autumn*, **en hiver** = *in winter*.)

(vi) days of the week (to translate *on —days*):

Il nous rend visite le dimanche = *He visits us on Sundays.*

(vii) units of weight, quantity, etc., when expressing a price:

Deux francs la douzaine = *Two francs a dozen.*

Un franc la pièce = *One franc each.*

(viii) some expressions which do not require the definite article in English:

aller à l'école = *to go to school*	**souhaiter la bonne année** = *to wish a*
aller à l'église = *to go to church*	*[happy New Year*
aller au marché = *to go to market*	**se mettre au travail** = *to set to work*
à l'hôpital = *in hospital*	**l'année prochaine (dernière)** = *next*
avoir le temps = *to have time*	**au secours!** = *help!* *[(last) year*
garder le silence = *to say nothing*	**à l'assassin!** = *murder!*
mettre le feu à = *to set fire to*	**au revoir!** = *good-bye!*

IRREGULAR VERBS

fuir [fɥiːr] = *to flee, fly*; future **je fuirai** [fɥiːre]; part participle **fui** [fɥi]; past historic **je fuis** [fɥi], etc. (likewise **s'enfuir** = *to flee, escape*).

je fuis [fɥi] = *I flee*	**nous fuyons** [fɥiɔ̃]
tu fuis [fɥi]	**vous fuyez** [fɥie]
il fuit [fɥi]	**ils fuient** [fɥi]

VOCABULARY

la république [repyblik]	*republic*
le pacte [pakt]	*pact*
envahir [ãvaiːr]	*to invade*
la Pologne [pɔlɔɲ]	*Poland*
provoquer [prɔvɔke]	*to provoke*
mondial(e) [mɔ̃djal]	*world* (adj.)
déclarer [deklare]	*to declare*
vainement [vɛnmã]	*in vain*
un agresseur [agrɛsœːr]	*aggressor*
le territoire [tɛritwaːr]	*territory*
le conflit [kɔfli]	*conflict*
la défaite [defɛt]	*defeat*
héroïque [erɔik]	*heroic*
la résistance [rezistãːs]	*resistance*
les armements (m.) [armǝmã]	*armaments*
un ennemi [ɛnmi]	*enemy*
se dépêcher de [sǝ depɛʃe dǝ]	*to hasten to*
regagner [rǝgaɲe]	*to regain*
la ligne [liɲ]	*line*
le système [sistɛm]	*system*
se livrer à [sǝ livre a]	*to engage in*
un espoir [ɛspwaːr]	*hope*
l'horreur (f.) [ɔrrœːr]	*horror*
s'emparer de [sãpare dǝ]	*to take possession of*
une fois de plus [yn fwa dǝ plys]	*once more*
empêcher (de) [ãpɛʃe dǝ]	*to prevent (from)*
la troupe [trup]	*troop*
franchir [frãʃiːr]	*to cross*
neutre [nøːtr]	*neutral*
le commencement [kɔmãsmã]	*beginning*
se rendre [sǝ rãdr]	*to surrender*
se battre [sǝ batr]	*to fight*
grâce à [grɑːs a]	*thanks to*
une arrière-garde [arjɛːrgard]	*rear-guard*
la flotte [flɔt]	*fleet*
s'embarquer [sãbarke]	*to embark*
s'établir [setabliːr]	*to establish oneself*
encombré(e) de [ãkɔ̃bre dǝ]	*encumbered with*
se réfugier [sǝ refyʒje]	*to flee, take refuge*
la panique [panik]	*panic*
épargner [eparɲe]	*to spare*

les armements

les troupes

la flotte

le vainqueur

200

le sort [sɔːr]	*fate, lot*	
Varsovie [varsɔvi]	*Warsaw*	
démoraliser [demɔralize]	*to demoralise*	
complètement [kɔ̃plɛtmɑ̃]	*completely*	
guider [gide]	*to guide*	
la crise [kriːz]	*crisis*	
selon [səlɔ̃]	*according to*	
le terme [tɛrm]	*term*	
le vainqueur [vɛ̃kœːr]	*victor*	**le symbole**
divisé(e) [divize]	*divided*	
la zone [zoːn]	*zone*	
comprendre [kɔ̃prɔ̃ːdr]	*to understand, include*	
le chef [ʃɛf]	*chief, leader*	
le symbole [sɛ̃bɔl]	*emblem*	
la croix [krwa]	*cross*	
correct(e) [kɔrɛkt]	*correct, proper*	
éveiller [evɛje]	*to arouse*	**la croix**
une hostilité [ɔstilite]	*hostility*	
le choc [ʃɔk]	*shock, impact*	
en état de [ɑ̃neta də]	*in a fit state to*	
le Juif, la Juive [ʒɥif, ʒɥiːv]	*Jew, Jewess*	
priver de [prive də]	*to deprive of*	
le droit [drwa]	*right*	
le signe [siɲ]	*mark*	
distinctif, -ive [distɛ̃ktif, -iːv]	*distinguishing*	**le Juif**
une autorité [otɔrite]	*authority*	
émettre (like **mettre**) [emɛtr]	*to issue*	
le billet de banque [bijɛ də bɑ̃ːk]	*bank-note*	
réel, -elle [reɛl]	*real, actual*	
rendre [rɑ̃ːdr]	*to make, render*	
légal(e) [lɛgal]	*legal*	
le pillage [pijaːʒ]	*pillage*	
séduit(e) [sedɥi, -ɥit]	*lured, charmed*	**le billet de banque**
le désir [deziːr]	*desire*	
collaborer [kɔlabɔre]	*to collaborate*	
le maître [mɛːtr]	*master*	
fidèle [fidɛl]	*faithful*	
la liberté [libɛrte]	*liberty*	
l'indépendance (f.) [ɛ̃depɑ̃dɑ̃ːs]	*independence*	
libre [libr]	*free*	
saboter [sabɔte]	*to sabotage*	
une usine [yzin]	*factory*	**une usine**

201

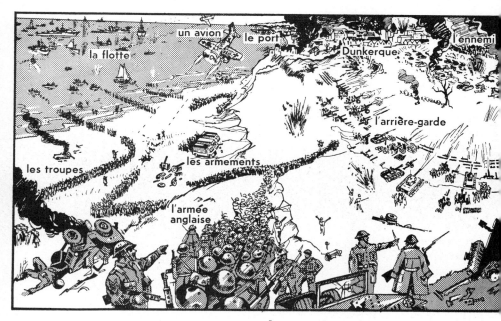

la flotte — un avion — le port — Dunkerque — l'ennemi — l'arrière-garde — les armements — les troupes — l'armée anglaise

FIN DE LA TROISIÈME RÉPUBLIQUE

Le 1 septembre 1939 les Allemands qui venaient de signer un pacte de non-agression avec la Russie envahirent la Pologne — ce qui provoqua la Seconde Guerre mondiale. Le 3 septembre la Grand-Bretagne et la France déclarèrent la guerre au Troisième Reich, après avoir vainement demandé aux agresseurs de se retirer du territoire polonais. Ce conflit allait durer presque six ans jusqu'à la défaite de l'Allemagne en 1945. L'héroïque résistance de la Pologne ne dura que quelques mois et les Alliés qui manquaient d'armements modernes n'osèrent pas attaquer l'ennemi. Il est vrai que les Français gagnèrent quelques kilomètres carrés de territoire allemand mais lorsque la Pologne fut vaincue ils se dépêchèrent de regagner la ligne Maginot, vaste système de fortifications qui protégeaient la frontière française.

Pendant l'hiver de 1939 il n'y eut presque pas d'activité militaire. Les Allemands en profitèrent pour se livrer à la propagande dans l'espoir de démoraliser leurs adversaires. Ils y réussirent dans une certaine mesure. Les Français n'avaient pas oublié les horreurs et les pertes de la guerre de 1914. Au mois d'avril de l'année suivante (1940) Hitler s'empara du Danemark et de la Norvège; une fois de plus les Alliés n'avaient pas pu empêcher l'attaque. Mais c'est le 10 mai 1940 que la guerre commença pour de bon à l'ouest: les troupes allemandes franchirent les frontières de la Hollande, de la Belgique et du Luxembourg — pays neutres qui avaient espéré rester en dehors du conflit. C'était le commencement de la guerre-éclair qui allait écraser la France en moins de deux mois. Le 27 mai les Belges, à bout de forces, se rendirent. Les Anglais qui se battaient aux côtés des Belges durent se retirer et gagner le port de Dunkerque où grâce aux efforts de l'arrière-garde et de la flotte ils purent s'embarquer et rentrer en Angleterre.

Entre-temps, le gouvernement français avait abandonné Paris et s'était établi à Bordeaux. Les routes étaient encombrées de réfugiés qui fuyaient devant l'ennemi et les avions allemands semaient partout la panique et la mort. Le 14 juin les Allemands entraient à Paris qu'on avait déclaré ville ouverte pour lui épargner le sort de Varsovie et de tant d'autres villes. La perte de la capitale que les Allemands n'avaient pas pu prendre au cours de la Grande Guerre démoralisa complètement l'armée française. Le premier ministre Reynaud fit place au maréchal Pétain, héros de la Première Guerre mondiale. Mais Pétain était vraiment trop vieux (il avait quatre-vingts ans passés) pour guider la France dans une crise pareille. Il demanda un armistice aux Allemands, lequel fut signé le 22 juin à Compiègne dans le wagon de chemin de fer où les Allemands avaient signé celui de 1918. Selon les termes de cet armistice les vainqueurs permettaient à la France de garder son empire colonial et sa flotte et de maintenir une armée de cent mille hommes. Mais le pays fut divisé en deux zones et les Allemands occupèrent celle du nord qui comprenait d'ailleurs toute la côte atlantique.

Un général français qui ne voulait pas abandonner la lutte contre les ennemis de son pays se réfugia en Angleterre où il devint le chef de tous les Français qui avaient pu gagner le Royaume-Uni. Le général de Gaulle appela son armée "La France Libre" et adopta comme symbole la croix de Lorraine.

Au commencement de l'occupation les Allemands se montrèrent assez polis et corrects pour ne pas éveiller l'hostilité de la population. Mais, une fois revenus du premier choc du désastre national, les vaincus comprirent clairement le sort qui les attendait. Les Allemands commencèrent à envoyer en Allemagne tous ceux qui étaient en état de travailler. Dès le début de l'occupation les Juifs furent privés de la plupart de leurs droits civils et obligés de porter des signes distinctifs. Enfin la nourriture vint à manquer car Hitler avait dit que, si toute l'Europe devait mourir de faim, les Allemands seraient les derniers à passer par là. Les autorités allemandes émirent des billets de banque sans valeur réelle grâce auxquels l'armée d'occupation pouvait acheter à très bon marché ce qui restait dans les magasins. De cette manière on rendit "légal" le pillage du pays.

Un certain nombre de Français séduits par l'ambition et le désir de s'enrichir consentirent à collaborer avec leurs nouveaux maîtres mais en général les vaincus restèrent fidèles à leurs traditions de liberté et d'indépendance. Ainsi naquit la Résistance qui, avec l'aide des Anglais et des Français libres, allait saboter les chemins de fer, les ports et les usines dont se servaient les Allemands. . . . La Troisième République était morte mais la France vivait toujours.

(*See notes on the next page. Translation at the end of the book.*)

NOTES ON THE TEXT

La ligne Maginot, vaste système . . . — when a noun is an apposition to another the article is omitted (cf. **de la Belgique et du Luxembourg — pays neutres**); **il avait quatre-vingts ans passés** = *he was over eighty*; **à passer par là** (literally = *to pass by there*) = *to suffer such a fate.*

EXERCISES

I. Answer in French:

1. **Quand est-ce que la Seconde Guerre mondiale éclata?**
2. **Que firent les Allemands pendant l'hiver de 1939?**
3. **Qu'est-ce que les Français n'avaient pas oublié?**
4. **Combien de temps les Allemands mirent-ils à écraser la France?**
5. **Où signa-t-on l'armistice?**
6. **Quand est-ce que la guerre commença pour de bon à l'ouest?**
7. **Quelle zone fut occupée par les Allemands?**

II. Translate into English:

1. **Le vendredi je vais généralement au marché.**
2. **Il parle français comme une vache espagnole.**
3. **Traduisez ce morceau en italien.**
4. **On lui coupa la tête parce qu'il s'était battu contre le roi.**
5. **Ces pommes combien coûtent-elles? Un franc le kilo.**
6. **Le capitaine Dupont arriva en Allemagne le sept mai.**
7. **De nos jours le nylon est utilisé dans de nombreuses industries.**
8. **Il tomba amoureux de la belle Isabelle.**
9. **Prenez garde! Je suis à bout de patience.**
10. **Quand il était en Suisse il nous écrivit quelques lettres.**

III. Give these verb forms:

1. Third person singular and plural past historic: **envahir, demander, protéger, commencer, naître, appeler, pouvoir, vouloir, écrire, fuir, être, avoir.**
2. First person singular and plural conditional: **être, venir, jeter, écrire, faire, pouvoir, appeler, tenir, savoir, s'asseoir.**
3. Second person singular and plural pluperfect: **dire, courir, se lever, arriver, mettre, prendre, pouvoir, descendre, couvrir, monter.**

IV. Replace the infinitive by the correct form of the past historic, the imperfect or the pluperfect as required:

Ce jour-là il ne (faire) pas beau temps. Soudain il (commencer) à pleuvoir à verse. Pierre (se dépêcher) pour arriver à la maison car il (vouloir) parler

avec son frère. **Quand il (rentrer) il (trouver) que celui-ci (sortir) faire une commission pour leur maman. Jean (ce [être] son frère) (revenir) peu de temps après. Pierre lui (parler) du vieux matelot qu'il (rencontrer) au port et il lui (répéter) tout ce que le vieillard lui (raconter). Pierre (expliquer) aussi qu'il (ne pas pouvoir) trouver le jeune homme qu'ils (rencontrer) la veille. Son frère le (écouter) avec intérêt mais il ne (dire) rien. Cinq minutes plus tard les deux frères (quitter) la maison à l'insu de leur mère qui (travailler) dans la cuisine.**

V. Translate into French:

1. I speak French and now I am studying German.
2. It is said that Germany has become a rich country.
3. Put up your hands if you know what this word means.
4. He sprained (**fouler**) his foot while playing tennis.
5. On Thursdays we always go to the theatre.
6. In spring the weather is often fine. That's why I like spring.
7. King Edward VII was born in 1841.
8. Tomorrow I shall leave for Spain where it is always hot in summer.
9. After lunch he went for a walk in the country.
10. Copper is a reddish metal, isn't it?

VI. Translate into French:

On September 1st the Germans attacked Poland. On September 3rd Great Britain and France declared war on Germany. Thus began the Second World War. The resistance of Poland did not last long and the Germans soon occupied all the country. On May 10th, 1940, Hitler attacked in the west. The German troops crossed the frontiers of Holland and Belgium. The Allied armies were not able to stop the Germans and the Belgians surrendered. The British Army had consequently to retire towards Dunkirk where, thanks to the Royal Navy, it was able to embark and return to England.

VII. Either: write a composition (based on the text) dealing with the Second World War up to the fall of France; or: narrate an exploit of the Resistance of which you have read. Here is some useful vocabulary: **marcher à pas de loup** = *to creep stealthily*; **faire sauter un bâtiment** = *to blow up a building*; **faire dérailler un train** = *to derail a train*; **le plastic** = *plastic explosive*; **la mitraillette** = *sub-machine gun*.

(Answers at the end of the book.)

LEÇON 21

GRAMMAR

OMISSION OF THE ARTICLE

In Leçon 20 we considered uses of the article; we shall now consider the only important cases where the article is omitted.

The definite article is omitted after **en** except in certain expressions, e.g.: **en l'air** = *in the air*; **en l'absence de** = *in the absence of*; **en l'honneur de** = *in honour of*.

No article is used:

(i) in a number of set expressions, many with **avoir**:
   avoir peur, faim, soif, froid, chaud, raison, tort, honte = *to be afraid, hungry, thirsty, cold, warm, right, wrong, ashamed*; **avoir envie** = *to want*; **demander pardon** = *to ask forgiveness*; **à cheval** = *on horseback*; **à bicyclette** = *on a bicycle*; **à bord** = *on board* . . . etc.

(ii) in adjectival phrases and expressions such as **couvert de** = *covered with* where the **de** is not closely connected with the article:
   un courage de lion = *the courage of a lion*
   un professeur de français = *a French teacher* (i.e. teacher of French)
   couvert de poussière = *covered with dust*
   une caisse pleine de pommes = *a crate full of apples*
   (i.e. **de** + **du, de la** or **des** becomes **de** in phrases of this last kind).

(iii) in enumerations, notices, proverbs, advertisements, book titles, etc.:
   Hommes, femmes, enfants, tous périrent = *Men, women, children, all perished.*
   Maison à vendre = *House for sale.*
   Pierre qui roule n'amasse pas mousse = *A rolling stone gathers no moss.*

(iv) after expressions of quantity unless the noun is qualified by a clause:
   une douzaine d'œufs = *a dozen eggs*; **beaucoup de monde** = *many people*; **combien de soldats?** = *how many soldiers?*
   but: **Combien des soldats que vous‿avez vus . . . ?** = *How many of the soldiers that you saw . . . ?*
   Note that **bien de** (= *many*) and **la plupart de** (= *the greater part of*) always have the article added to the **de**: **bien des soldats** = *many soldiers*; **la plupart des‿élèves** = *most of the pupils.*

206

(v) before the second of two nouns in apposition (i.e. a noun standing for a person or thing identical with that indicated by the first noun):

Paris, capitale de la France = *Paris, the capital of France*
Le bûcheron, homme trapu et vigoureux, travaillait dur dans la forêt = *The woodcutter, a squat and sturdy man, used to work hard in the forest.*

(vi) before a numerical title:
Henri Huit = *Henry the Eighth*
Louis Quatorze = *Louis the Fourteenth*

The indefinite article is omitted:

(i) before nationalities or professions standing as a predicate, unless the noun is accompanied by an adjective:

Il est soldat = *He is a soldier.*
Il est Allemand = *He is a German.*
Il a été nommé ministre = *He has been made a minister.*
but: **Il est devenu un médecin célèbre** = *He became a famous doctor.*

(ii) after exclamatory **quel**, and after **ni ... ni ...** (= *neither ... nor ...*) and **jamais** (when it stands before the subject):

Quelle histoire! = *What a story!*
Quelle chance! = *What luck!*
Je n'ai ni plume ni crayon = *I have neither pen nor pencil.*
Jamais homme ne fut si malheureux = *Never was a man so unhappy.*

The indefinite and partitive articles (**du, de la, des**) become **de** after a negative:

Je n'ai pas de crayon = *I have no pencil.*   [*no eggs.*
Je n'ai pas de fromage et tu n'as pas d'œufs = *I have no cheese and you have*
The partitive article is replaced by **de** alone when it comes before a noun preceded by an adjective (but this rule is often broken in the singular):

Il y avait là de grandes maisons = *There were big houses there.*
Il vend de bon vin = *He sells good wine* (but: **Il vend du bon vin** in everyday conversation).
And note: **Il vend des vins rouges** = *He sells red wines.*

Note that the full partitive article must be used before (*a*) compounds composed of adjective and noun, e.g. **grand-père**; (*b*) adjective and noun where, as a result of long usage, they form a single idea, e.g. **petits pois**:

des grands-pères = *grandfathers*	**des petits pois** = *green peas*
des petits pains = *rolls*	**des jeunes gens** = *young men.*

THE POSSESSIVE PRONOUN

These pronouns, like possessive adjectives (**mon, ton,** etc., p. 45), agree in number and gender with the thing possessed, not the possessor.

Masc. sing.	Fem. sing.	Masc. pl.	Fem. pl.	
le mien [mjɛ̃]	**la mienne** [mjɛn]	**les miens** [mjɛ̃]	**les miennes** [mjɛn]	= *mine*
le tien [tjɛ̃]	**la tienne** [tjɛn]	**les tiens** [tjɛ̃]	**les tiennes** [tjɛn]	= *yours*
le sien [sjɛ̃]	**la sienne** [sjɛn]	**les siens** [sjɛ̃]	**les siennes** [sjɛn]	= *his, hers*
le nôtre [noːtr]	**la nôtre** [noːtr]	**les nôtres** [noːtr]	**les nôtres** [noːtr]	= *ours* [*its*
le vôtre [voːtr]	**la vôtre** [voːtr]	**les vôtres** [voːtr]	**les vôtres** [voːtr]	= *yours*
le leur [lœːr]	**la leur** [lœːr]	**les leurs** [lœːr]	**les leurs** [lœːr]	= *theirs*

Voici ma plume; où est la tienne? = *Here is my pen; where is yours?*
J'aime mes souliers et aussi les vôtres = *I like my shoes and yours too.*

Note that (*a*) to express mere ownership the disjunctive pronoun is commonly used: **Ces souliers sont à moi** = *These shoes are mine* (the possessive would only be used here for emphasis); (*b*) **de** and **à** fuse as usual with **le** and **les** before possessive pronouns, e.g. **Mon hôtel est trop loin; allons au vôtre** = *My hotel is too far; let us go to yours.*

VOCABULARY

demeurer [dəmœre]	to live, reside	
arriver à l'heure [arive a lœːr]	to arrive punctually	
aller de travers [ale də travɛːr]	to go wrong	
le réveil [revɛːj]	alarm-clock	
savoir au juste [savwaːr o ʒyst]	to know exactly	
un époux, une épouse [epu, epuːz]	husband, wife	
aimable [ɛmabl]	pleasant	
saisir [sɛziːr]	to seize	**le réveil**
la serviette [sɛrvjɛt]	brief-case	
le bras [bra]	arm	
précipitamment [presipitamɑ̃]	precipitately	
bien entendu [bjɛ̃nɑ̃tɑ̃dy]	of course	
reconduire [rəkɔ̃dɥiːr]	to take, lead back	
le résultat [rezylta]	result	
sur son compte [syr sɔ̃ kɔ̃ːt]	on his account	**la serviette**
méticuleux, -euse [metikylø,-øːz]	very careful, particular	
ponctuel, -elle [pɔ̃ktɥɛl]	punctual	
taper à la machine [tape a la [maʃin]	to type	
classer [klɑse]	to file	
coller [kɔle]	to stick	
le timbre [tɛ̃ːbr]	stamp	
une enveloppe [ɑ̃vlɔp]	envelope	**le timbre**

208

énergiquement [enɛrʒikmã]	*energetically, hard*	
avoir l'habitude de [avwaːr	*to be in the habit of*	
assez [ase] [labityd də]	*sufficiently, rather*	
sèchement [sɛʃmã]	*dryly*	
un‿œil, des‿yeux [œːj, jø]	*eye, eyes*	
accrocher [akrɔʃe]	*to hang, hook up*	
le clou [klu]	*nail*	**les yeux**
le grand livre [grã livr]	*ledger*	
la poussière [pusjɛːr]	*dust*	
communiquer [kɔmynike]	*to inform*	
le patron [patrɔ̃]	*boss*	
un‿ogre [ɔgr]	*ogre*	
fumer, la fumée [fyme, fyme]	*to smoke, smoke*	**le clou**
la pipe [pip]	*pipe*	
répandre [repãːdr]	*to spread*	
rassembler [rasãble]	*to gather together*	
le courage [kuraːʒ]	*courage*	
particulier, -ière [partikylje, -jɛːr]	*private*	
tousser [tuse]	*to cough*	
affreusement [afrøːzmã]	*frightfully*	
ironique [irɔnik]	*ironic*	**un ogre**
se garder de [sə garde də]	*to take care not to*	
le coffre-fort [kɔfrfɔːr]	*safe*	
la clef [kle]	*key*	
la confiance [kɔ̃fjãːs]	*confidence*	
la veille [vɛːj]	*day before, eve*	
un‿habit [abi]	*suit*	
la poche [pɔʃ]	*pocket*	**la pipe**
regretter [rəgrɛte]	*to be sorry*	
infiniment [ɛ̃finimã]	*extremely*	
balbutier [balbysje]	*to stammer*	
confus(e) [kɔ̃fy, -fys]	*confused*	
rougir [ruʒiːr]	*to blush*	
la honte [ɔ̃ːt]	*shame*	
hurler [yrle]	*to yell*	**la clef**
une entrevue [ãtrəvy]	*interview*	
le geste [ʒɛst]	*gesture*	
le soulagement [sulaʒmã]	*relief*	
le commis [kɔmi]	*clerk*	
le motocycliste [mɔtɔsiklist]	*motor-cyclist*	
la moto [mɔto]	*motor-cycle*	
sa vie durant [sa vi dyrã]	*his whole life long*	**le motocycliste**

209

le pardessus
le bras
un habit
la poche
le comptable
le téléphone
le coffre-fort
les grands livres
le chef
une enveloppe
les lettres

AU BUREAU

M. Duval demeurait dans la banlieue de Paris. Comme il n'avait pas de voiture, il prenait chaque matin le train pour aller en ville où il travaillait dans un bureau. Il quittait la maison à sept heures et demie et arrivait à la gare à huit heures moins le quart. Le train entrait en gare à huit heures moins dix. Généralement tout allait bien, M. Duval attrapait son train et arrivait à l'heure au bureau. Mais lundi dernier tout alla de travers. Pour commencer, M. Duval se leva tard: il n'avait pas entendu le réveil ou celui-ci n'avait pas sonné. Il n'y a pas moyen de le savoir au juste. En tout cas il dut déjeuner à la hâte. Pendant qu'il mangeait, son épouse, femme très aimable mais un peu bavarde, lui dit qu'il pourrait faire quelques commissions pour elle en ville. M. Duval l'écouta avec patience, saisit son pardessus, prit sa serviette sous le bras et sortit précipitamment de la maison — après avoir embrassé sa femme, bien entendu.

Son petit chien sortit avec lui et le suivit le long de la route, en aboyant de plaisir. Malgré cela M. Duval continua son chemin sans se soucier du chien. Mais soudain l'idée lui vint que sa femme ne serait pas très contente s'il arrivait quelque malheur au chien. Il fit demi-tour et reconduisit l'animal à la maison. Les trains partent à l'heure; résultat net: il manqua le sien et dut attendre le suivant. Que de monde il y avait sur le quai ce matin-là! M. Duval acheta un journal et se mit à lire. Au bout d'un quart d'heure le train entra en gare et M. Duval trouva une place dans un compartiment pour fumeurs. Il n'était pas du tout content.

Il arriva enfin au bureau mais il avait au moins une demi-heure de retard et tout le monde commençait à s'inquiéter sur son compte parce qu'on savait que M. Duval était un employé méticuleux et ponctuel.

Il entra donc au bureau. Dans la pièce principale il y avait des dactylos qui tapaient des lettres à la machine et un jeune homme qui classait des papiers et qui collait des timbres sur des enveloppes. Tout le monde travaillait très énergiquement— et en silence. Voilà ce qui surprit M. Duval qui savait très bien que les dactylos avaient l'habitude de bavarder toute la journée. Il entra en disant "Bonjour". On répondit assez sèchement à son salut et on ne leva pas les yeux pour le regarder. "Ho! Ho!" pensa M. Duval, "cela n'annonce rien de bon." Il accrocha son pardessus et son chapeau à un clou, passa entre les tables et gagna la sienne où il se mit au travail. Il allait ouvrir un grand livre tout couvert de poussière— M. Duval était comptable — lorsque le garçon de bureau s'approcha de lui et lui communiqua que le patron voulait lui parler tout de suite. Le chef, qui s'appelait M. Ledoux, était un homme féroce et de grandes moustaches noires ornaient sa figure d'ogre. D'ailleurs il fumait une pipe qui répandait un nuage de fumée dans toute la pièce.

Rassemblant tout son courage, M. Duval frappa à la porte du bureau particulier du chef et entra. Aussitôt il se mit à tousser affreusement. Jamais homme ne fut si malheureux! "Ah! bonjour, monsieur," dit le patron d'un ton ironique. "On m'a dit que vous étiez en retard. Est-ce que cela arrive souvent?"— "Tous les cinq ans," pensa M. Duval, mais il se garda bien de le dire à haute voix. "Je voulais ouvrir le coffre-fort," continua le chef, "mais vous en avez les clefs." C'était vrai. Comme M. Duval jouissait de la confiance de ses chefs, il avait le droit d'avoir la clef du coffre-fort où l'on gardait les livres et les documents importants. En l'absence de M. Duval on n'avait pas pu travailler. Quel ennui! Le pauvre M. Duval, tout confus, se mit à chercher dans ses poches mais il n'y trouva rien. Mon Dieu! La veille il avait changé d'habit et les clefs étaient toujours dans la poche de son habit gris et celui-là était à la maison. Que faire? "Je le regrette infiniment, monsieur le patron, mais. . . ." "Donnez-les-moi tout de suite," dit brusquement M. Ledoux qui n'écoutait pas et qui examinait quelques lettres qu'il avait devant lui. "Mais, monsieur," balbutia M. Duval très confus et rougissant de honte, "je les ai oubliées." "Comment?" hurla l'autre. M. Duval garda le silence. Heureusement, un coup de téléphone vint mettre fin à l'entrevue et le patron indiqua d'un geste impatient à M. Duval qu'il devait se retirer. Celui-ci poussa un soupir de soulagement et sortit.

Il réfléchit un moment puis il alla trouver un des commis qui était motocycliste. Celui-ci partit à moto chercher les clefs et revint avec elles au bout de vingt minutes. . . . Je suis sûr que, sa vie durant, M. Duval n'oubliera jamais le jour où il laissa ses clefs à la maison. Quel malheur pour un tel homme!

(See notes on the next page. Translation at the end of the book.)

NOTES ON THE TEXT

Que de monde! = *What a lot of people!* — note this use of **monde** (= *world*), cf. **nous avons du monde ce soir** = *we have company this evening*; **avoir une demi-heure de retard** = *to be half an hour late*, **demi** does not agree when it precedes the noun; **la pièce** = *room*, but can also = *coin, cask, patch, piece* (in chess, etc.) — 20 **fr. la pièce** = 20 *frs. each*; **changer de** = *to change* (for something of the same sort), e.g. **changer d'avis** = *to change one's mind*, **changer de place** = *to change one's seat*, **changer de train** = *to change trains*, **changer de ton** = *to change one's tune*, but **changer un billet de banque** = *to change a note*; **Que faire?** = *What is (was) to be done?* — the infinitive is often used to ask this type of shortened question.

EXERCISES

I. Answer in French:

1. **Pourquoi M. Duval prenait-il le train tous les matins?**
2. **Où travaillait-il?**
3. **Qu'est-ce qui arriva lundi dernier?**
4. **Que font les dactylos?**
5. **Où est-ce que M. Duval accrocha son pardessus?**
6. **Que lui dit le garçon de bureau?**
7. **Décrivez le chef.**
8. **Qu'est-ce que M. Duval avait oublié?**
9. **Pourquoi M. Duval toussait-il?**
10. **Qu'est-ce qui mit fin à l'entrevue?**

II. Translate into English:

1. **Nous n'avons pas d'argent. C'est dommage.**
2. **Ce jour-là il n'y avait que des jeunes gens dans la piscine.**
3. **Il avait tout perdu — maison, meubles et argent.**
4. **Le jeune homme voulait être soldat mais son père s'y opposait.**
5. **Le cambrioleur ne portait ni revolver ni couteau.**
6. **Il était si content qu'il jeta son chapeau en l'air.**
7. **Comme il était étranger tout le monde se méfiait de lui.**
8. **La plupart des ouvriers étaient Italiens.**
9. **En arrivant à l'atelier elle s'est mise au travail.**
10. **Tout à coup le nageur cria: "Au secours!" et disparut sous l'eau.**

III. Give the third person singular and plural of the past historic tense of:
boire, conduire, dire, être, lire, porter, pouvoir, savoir, suivre, venir.

IV. Substitute the possessive pronoun **le mien, la mienne, le tien, le sien,** etc., for the words underlined:

1. **Ils ont déjà fait <u>leur tâche</u>.**
2. **Avez-vous vu <u>notre auto</u>?**
3. **Prêtez-moi <u>votre crayon</u>; j'ai perdu <u>mon crayon</u>.**
4. **Voici ma bicyclette. Où est <u>votre bicyclette</u>?**
5. **<u>Ma cravate</u> est sur la commode.**
6. **Il a pris <u>son chapeau</u> et il est sorti.**
7. **Elle est arrivée avec <u>ses parents</u>.**
8. **<u>Les enfants</u> ont perdu <u>leur balle</u>.**
9. **Il a rencontré <u>vos sœurs</u>.**
10. **Tu as cassé <u>ton jouet</u>.**

V. Translate into French:

1. He has made many errors.
2. Alas! we have no money.
3. There were a lot of people in the street.
4. I am thirsty: I feel like drinking something.
5. He threw his hat in the air. What an idiot!
6. He replied that he was not a Frenchman.
7. "You are wrong," said the teacher. And the teacher is always right.
8. Every Wednesday he goes to market.
9. He was eating some green peas.
10. How many books have you?

VI. Translate into French:

He rose late and had a hurried breakfast. He kissed his wife, seized his hat and his umbrella and left the house. He had to hurry to catch his train which left at half past eight. The train entered the station as he was buying his ticket. He showed his ticket to the ticket-inspector and rushed towards a carriage. That morning there were a lot of people on the platform and it was not easy to find a seat. He succeeded, however.

VII. Write a composition (in past tenses) based on this outline:

M. Leblanc travaille dans un bureau — un jour il est assis à travailler quand on frappe à la porte — il crie "Entrez" et un jeune homme entre — celui-ci demande à voir le chef — M. Leblanc croit reconnaître quelqu'un que le chef ne veut pas voir — il fait toute sorte d'excuses — il dit que le chef vient de sortir — le jeune homme a l'air étonné — à ce moment le chef sort de son bureau et salue cordialement l'inconnu — c'est son neveu!

(Answers at the end of the book.)

213

LEÇON 22

GRAMMAR

COMPARISON OF ADJECTIVES

Adjectives in French form the comparative (e.g. *bigger*) and superlative (e.g. *biggest*) in this way:

Masc.	**grand** = *big*	**plus grand** = *bigger*	**le plus grand** = *biggest*
Fem.	**grande**	**plus grande**	**la plus grande**
Pl.	**grand(e)s**	**plus grand(e)s**	**les plus grand(e)s**, etc.
	jeune = *young*	**plus jeune** = *younger*	**le plus jeune** = *youngest*, etc.

One adjective, **bon**, is completely irregular:

bon, -nne = *good*   **meilleur(e)** = *better*   **le meilleur, la -e** = *best*

Some adjectives have alternative irregular forms, sometimes with a slightly different meaning:

mauvais = *bad* $\left.\begin{array}{l}\textbf{plus mauvais}\\ \textbf{pire}\end{array}\right\}$ = *worse* $\left.\begin{array}{l}\textbf{le plus mauvais}\\ \textbf{le pire}\end{array}\right\}$ = *worst*

petit = *small* $\left\{\begin{array}{l}\textbf{plus petit} = smaller\\ \textbf{moindre} = lesser\end{array}\right.$ $\left\{\begin{array}{l}\textbf{le plus petit} = smaller\\ \textbf{le moindre} = least\end{array}\right.$

Note the use of **moins** to diminish the strength of the adjective, e.g.:

fort = *strong*   **moins fort** = *less strong*   **le moins fort** = *least strong*

Note these uses of the comparative and superlative (*in* after a superlative is translated by **de**):

de plus en plus grand = *bigger and bigger*
de moins en moins froid = *less and less cold*
l'homme le plus grand = *the tallest man*
la fille la moins intelligente = *the least intelligent girl*
C'est l'homme le plus riche du monde = *He is the richest man in the world.*
le plus grand bâtiment de la ville = *the biggest building in the town*

COMPARISON OF ADVERBS

Adverbs are compared in the same way as adjectives:

vite = *fast*   **plus vite** = *faster*   **le plus vite** = *fastest*
tristement = *sadly* **plus tristement** = *more sadly* **le plus tristement** = *most sadly*
fort = *loudly*   **moins fort** = *less loudly*   **le moins fort** = *least loudly*

Note that the superlative **le** is invariable: **Elle marche le plus vite quand elle est heureuse** = *She walks fastest when she is happy.*

214

GRAMMAR

These adverbs have irregular comparative and superlative forms:

bien = *well*	**mieux** = *better*	**le mieux** = (*the*) *best*
mal = *badly*	**pis** = *worse*	**le pis** = (*the*) *worst*
beaucoup = *much*	**plus** = *more*	**le plus** = (*the*) *most*
peu = *little*	**moins** = *less*	**le moins** = (*the*) *least*

Note these uses of the comparative and superlative (*than* = **que**):
De plus_en plus vite = *Faster and faster.*
Plus je me repose, plus je me sens fatigué = *The more I rest, the more tired*
Elle est plus_intelligente que moi = *She is more intelligent than I.* [*I feel.*
Il est plus grand que son frère = *He is taller than his brother.*
Il est moins grand que sa sœur = *He is not as tall as his sister.*
Il est plus stupide que vous ne croyez = *He is more stupid than you think.*
(**ne** is added to the **que** clause when the first clause is affirmative).

Equality (*as . . . as*) = **aussi . . . que** in the affirmative, **si . . . que** in the negative:
Il est_aussi riche que son père = *He is as rich as his father.*
Il n'est pas si grand que son père = *He is not as tall as his father.*

Do not confuse the true superlative with *most* when it means *very*:
Il était très fâché = *He was most annoyed.*
Il travaille très diligemment = *He works most diligently.*

ADJECTIVAL FORMS

To form the feminine most adjectives add **-e** to the masculine unless it already ends in **-e**:
petit, petite = *small*   **poli, polie** = *polite*
fatigué, fatiguée = *tired*   **jeune, jeune** = *young*
Adjectives ending in—
(i) **-f** change the **-f** to **-v** before adding **-e**:
    actif, active = *active*   **vif, vive** = *lively*
(ii) **-er** add a grave accent to the **-e-** before adding **-e**:
    premier, première = *first*   **fier, fière** = *proud*
(iii) **-eux** form the feminine in **-euse**:
    heureux, heureuse = *happy*   **joyeux, joyeuse** = *joyous*
(iv) **-n, -s, -t, -el** usually double the last letter and add **-e**:
    bon, bonne = *good*   **gras, grasse** = *fat*
    muet, muette = *dumb*   **solennel, solennelle** = *solemn*

Some adjectives in **-et** form the feminine in **-ète**:
complet, complète = *complete, full*   **inquiet, inquiète** = *uneasy*
discret, discrète = *discreet*   **secret, secrète** = *secret*

215

Most adjectives ending in **-eur** add **-e** but adjectives (and nouns) based on verbs change **-eur** to **-euse**:

meilleur, meilleure = *better*   **majeur, majeure** = *major*
flatteur, flatteuse = *flattering*   **rêveur, rêveuse** = *dreamy*

Note the irregular forms of these adjectives:

beau, bel, belle = *beautiful*   **long, longue** = *long*
fou, fol, folle = *mad*   **bref, brève** = *short*
mou, mol, molle = *soft*   **gentil, gentille** = *nice, kind*
nouveau, nouvel, nouvelle = *new*   **frais, fraîche** = *fresh*
blanc, blanche = *white*   **favori, favorite** = *favourite*
franc, franche = *frank*   **public, publique** = *public*
doux, douce = *sweet, gentle*   **turc, turque** = *Turkish*
jaloux, jalouse = *jealous*   **grec, grecque** = *Greek*
roux, rousse = *russet*   **vieux, vieil, vieille** = *old*

Note that **beau, fou, mou, nouveau** and **vieux** have a second masculine form used before a vowel or mute **h-**:

un vieil ami = *an old friend*   **un fol espoir** = *a foolish hope*
un vieil homme = *an old man*

but:

un vieux héros = *an old hero* (here the **h-** is aspirated).

Note that adjectives form their plurals in the same way as nouns, except that a few ending in **-al** form the masculine plural in **-als**: **fatal, fatals; final, finals; natal, natals; naval, navals.**

VOCABULARY

voyager [vwajaʒe]   *to travel*
instruit(e) [ɛ̃strɥi, -ɥiːt]   *educated*
l'étranger [etrɑ̃ʒe]   *foreigner, foreign parts*
la tortue [tɔrty]   *tortoise*
le contrôle [kɔ̃troːl]   *inspection*
le passeport [paspɔːr]   *passport*
une épreuve [eprœːv]   *test, ordeal*
le bateau [bato]   *boat*
le matelot [matlo]   *sailor*
la passerelle [pasrɛl]   *gangway*
tonner [tɔne]   *to thunder*
le débarquement [debarkmɑ̃]   *disembarkation*
se présenter [sə prezɑ̃te]   *to appear, call at*
à son aise [a sɔnɛːz]   *at one's leisure*

la tortue

le passeport

216

la falaise [falɛːz]	*cliff*	
s'éloigner [selwaɲe]	*to recede*	
peu à peu [pø a pø]	*little by little*	
un espace [ɛspas]	*place* (in boat, etc.)	
restreint(e) [rɛstrɛ̃, -ɛ̃ːt]	*restricted*	
la religieuse [rəliʒjøːz]	*nun*	
un aspect [aspɛ]	*appearance*	
le teint [tɛ̃]	*complexion*	
foncé(e) [fɔ̃se]	*dark*	**le porteur**
le compatriote [kɔ̃patriɔt]	*compatriot*	
en vue de [ɑ̃ vy də]	*with a view to*	
escalader [ɛskalade]	*to climb*	
un amoureux, une -euse [amurø, -øːz]	*sweetheart*	
la consommation [kɔ̃sɔmasjɔ̃]	*drink*	
les spiritueux (m.) [spiritɥø]	*spirits*	
s'affairer [safɛre]	*to bustle about*	**la valise**
débarquer [debarke]	*to disembark*	
se borner à [sə bɔrne a]	*to confine oneself to*	
le quai [ke]	*quay*	
le porteur [pɔrtœːr]	*porter*	
la valise [valiːz]	*suitcase*	
lâcher prise [lɑʃe priːz]	*to let go*	
disparaître [disparɛːtr]	*to disappear*	
le numéro [nymero]	*number*	
le douanier [dwanje]	*customs officer*	**le douanier**
ennuyeux, -euse [ɑ̃nɥijø, -øːz]	*boring, tiresome*	
le soupçon [supsɔ̃]	*suspicion*	
la déroute [derut]	*rout*	
par miracle [par miraːkl]	*by a miracle*	
la tête [tɛːt]	*head*	
l'acier (m.) [asje]	*steel*	
le bruit [brɥi]	*noise*	
filer [file]	*to go along*	**la tête**
vertigineux, -euse [vɛrtiʒinø, -øːz]	*dizzy*	
le mécanicien [mekanisjɛ̃]	*engine-driver*	
quand même [kɑ̃ mɛːm]	*all the same*	
le voyageur [vwajaʒœːr]	*traveller*	
troubler [truble]	*to disturb*	
entendre [ɑ̃tɑ̃dr]	*to hear, mean*	
le grondement [grɔ̃dmɑ̃]	*rumble*	
le portefeuille [pɔrtəfœːj]	*wallet*	**le portefeuille**

217

le matelot
le bateau
la grue
le voyageur
la religieuse
la falaise
la passerelle
le quai

EN VOYAGE

Les Trotter étaient Anglais et ils aimaient voyager. M. Trotter était un homme bien instruit tandis que sa femme n'était pas du tout comme les femmes que j'ai décrites jusqu'ici. C'était la femme la plus aimable du monde et elle n'était pas plus bavarde qu'une autre. Il y a deux ans ils décidèrent d'aller passer leurs vacances d'été en Suisse. Quoi de plus agréable qu'un petit séjour à l'étranger? Ils se rendirent un beau matin à la gare terminus et prirent le train de Douvres, où il y avait une queue. Au bout d'un quart d'heure la queue commença à avancer mais plus lentement qu'une tortue. C'était le contrôle des passeports. Ils supportèrent cette épreuve sans difficulté et montèrent enfin sur le bateau. "Première classe à droite, deuxième classe à gauche," criait un matelot qui se trouvait près de la passerelle et qui empêchait ceux qui avaient des billets de deuxième d'entrer au salon de première. Il semblait y attacher la plus grande importance.

Trois quarts d'heure plus tard le bateau quitta le port. M. et Mme Trotter allèrent s'installer confortablement dans des fauteuils mais presque tout de suite les haut-parleurs semés partout à bord commencèrent à tonner. On annonça en bon anglais et en mauvais français qu'il fallait obtenir immédiatement des cartes de débarquement et que pour cela il fallait se présenter au bureau du bateau. M. Trotter se leva et s'y dirigea. Tout en attendant il regardait à son aise les falaises blanches d'Angleterre s'éloigner peu à peu.

Il y avait plus de monde à bord que M. Trotter n'en avait jamais vu dans un espace si restreint. Il y avait des jeunes et des vieux, des Anglais et des étrangers, des religieuses et des femmes d'aspect bien différent.

M. Trotter reconnut facilement les étrangers parce qu'ils avaient en général le teint plus foncé que celui de ses compatriotes et beaucoup d'entre eux semblaient habillés en vue d'escalader des montagnes. Il y en avait aussi plusieurs qui donnaient l'impression d'être des amoureux. Pour passer le temps, M. et Mme Trotter allèrent prendre une consommation mais ils durent faire la queue parce qu'il y avait tant de personnes qui achetaient des cigarettes et des spiritueux— marchandises qui coûtent beaucoup moins cher en haute mer qu'à terre. Déjà on voyait au loin les côtes de France. Tout le monde s'affairait en demandant aux matelots: "Par où est-ce qu'on va débarquer?" Les matelots ne le savaient pas et ils se bornaient à répondre: "Cela dépend". De petites queues commencèrent à se former partout.

Vingt minutes plus tard le bateau était au quai. Les passerelles furent mises en position mais personne ne débarqua. Soudain, une armée d'hommes vêtus de bleu se précipitèrent à bord en criant "Porteur." Un de ces porteurs s'empara des valises de M. Trotter malgré les protestations de ce dernier qui ne voulait pas lâcher prise et qui répétait sans cesse: "Non, merci. Non, merci." Mais probablement ce porteur-là ne comprenait pas très bien le français car il disparut avec les valises après avoir dit: "Trente-quatre." C'était son numéro.

On débarqua enfin mais cela prit du temps. "Rien à déclarer?" demandaient les douaniers qui n'avaient pas l'air très pressé. M. Trotter trouva ces formalités aussi ennuyeuses en France qu'en Angleterre. Mais personne n'éveilla les soupçons des douaniers et on se dirigea à toute vitesse vers le train. On aurait dit une armée en déroute. Il fallait choisir entre trois trains et pas un employé à voir. . . . Installés confortablement dans le train numéro deux marqué "Bâle", M. et Mme Trotter se regardèrent avec satisfaction. Par miracle, leurs valises étaient dans le filet au-dessus de leurs têtes. Mais le départ du train se fit attendre. M. Trotter avait remarqué qu'en France les locomotives étaient plus grandes qu'en Angleterre. Les banquettes de deuxième classe étaient plus dures que celles des trains anglais et les voitures étaient en acier. À cause de cela on entend plus de bruit qu 'en Angleterre.

Enfin le train se mit en marche et bientôt il filait à une vitesse vertigineuse. M. Trotter se demandait si le mécanicien ne se dépêchait pas d'arriver chez lui pour quelque raison de famille urgente. Mais les heures passèrent lentement quand même.

Il était une heure du matin et tous les voyageurs dormaient. Soudain un bruit infernal troubla le calme de la nuit. (Quand je dis "calme" j'entends par là cette espèce de grondement monotone particulier aux trains.) C'était le contrôleur qui ouvrait la portière en criant: "Billets, si vous plaît!" Une heure du matin, c'est l'heure favorite des contrôleurs. À moitié endormi, M. Trotter dut chercher les billets dans son portefeuille. . . .

(See notes on the next page. Translation at the end of the book.)

NOTES ON THE TEXT

Les Trotter — Christian and family names are invariable in the plural, e.g. **les Durand** = *the Durands*, **les Marie** = *the Marys*; **jusqu'ici** = *up to now* — it can also = *as far as this*; **à l'étranger** = *abroad*; **le départ . . . se fit attendre** (literally = *the departure made itself to be waited for*) = *the departure was delayed*; **en acier** = *of steel* — **en** often indicates the material of which something is made; **j'entends par là** = *I mean by that* — **entendre** sometimes = *to understand*; **à moitié endormi** = *half-asleep*, cf. **à moitié cuit** = *half-cooked*.

EXERCISES

I. Answer in French:

1. Où est-ce que les Trotter décidèrent d'aller passer leurs vacances?
2. À quelle gare se rendirent-ils?
3. Dans quel port est-ce qu'ils s'embarquèrent?
4. Pourquoi achetait-on des cigarettes à bord?
5. Que fit un des porteurs? Et que font les douaniers?
6. Où est-ce qu'on contrôle les passeports?
7. À quoi ressemblait la foule de voyageurs qui se dirigeait vers les trains?
8. Où met-on les valises en entrant dans un compartiment?

II. Translate into English:

1. Au cirque nous avons vu la plus grosse femme du monde.
2. Il est beaucoup plus âgé que son frère.
3. La ville que j'habite est un peu plus grande que Rennes.
4. Elle est moins intelligente que sa sœur aînée.
5. L'élève a fait plus de fautes qu'il ne dit.
6. À mesure que nous avancions la forêt devenait de plus en plus épaisse.
7. Il fait moins froid ici que dehors.
8. Plus nous travaillons plus nous gagnons d'argent.
9. Nous n'avons pas la moindre chance d'arriver au sommet.
10. On me dit que depuis les neiges du mois dernier l'état de la route est pire que jamais.
11. Criez moins fort. On pourrait bien vous entendre.
12. Le train filait de plus en plus vite.
13. Il faudra vous lever de meilleure heure.
14. Elle portait des souliers neufs et elle en était très fière.
15. Il n'y a rien de pire qu'une femme à la fois laborieuse et sotte.

III. Give the feminine of these adjectives: **secret, actuel, gros, dernier, poli, jeune, fatigué, vif, malheureux, inquiet, bon, doux, public, fou, nouveau, favori, bref, vieux, long, frais.**

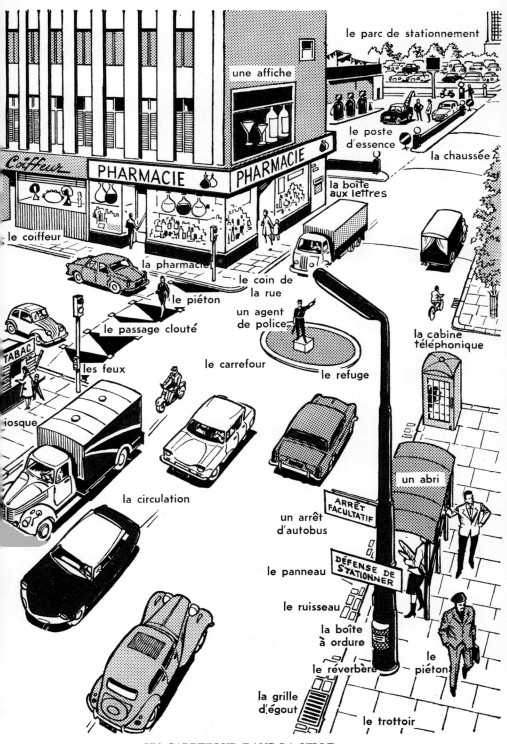

le parc de stationnement

une affiche

le poste d'essence

la chaussée

Coiffeur

PHARMACIE   PHARMACIE

la boîte aux lettres

le coiffeur

la pharmacie

le coin de la rue

le piéton

un agent de police

la cabine téléphonique

le passage clouté

le carrefour

les feux

le refuge

TABAC

iosque

un abri

la circulation

ARRÊT FACULTATIF

un arrêt d'autobus

DÉFENSE DE STATIONNER

le panneau

le ruisseau

la boîte à ordure

le réverbère

le piéton

la grille d'égout

le trottoir

UN CARREFOUR DANS LA VILLE

NCH—O

LES VAISSEAUX

le bateau
(le canot à rames)

le canoë

le bateau
de pêche

le chaland

le paquebot

le sous-marin

le radeau

le transatlantique

le yacht

le voilier

LES VOITURES

un autobus
(un bus)

un autocar
(un car)

une automobile
(une auto)

la bicyclette

le fiacre

le cam

le tramway

la charrette

la motocyclette

le taxi

le fourgon

le scooter

la poussette

le traîneau

le ballon

un avion

la brouette

la voiture d'enf

le Métro

le train

LES MOYENS DE TRANSPORT DE LA VIE MODERNE

IV. Give the comparative and superlative of: **grand, bon, mauvais, haut, petit**; and of these adverbs: **peu, vite, bien, mal, beaucoup.**

V. Give the first person singular and third person plural of (1) the past historic and (2) the imperfect tense of: **se diriger, boire, commencer, faire, ouvrir, venir, vouloir, dire, écrire, tenir.**

VI. Translate into French:

1. She is older than her brother.
2. I have less money than you.
3. Run faster! We are already late.
4. He is the richest man in the world.
5. That merchant is richer than you think.
6. This one is not so rich as you think.
7. The more he reads, the more he knows.
8. He met his old friend in the street.
9. That old man is as clever as his son.
10. That old bicycle is heavier than mine.

VII. Translate into French:

As they had decided to go and spend their holidays abroad, they went one day to the terminus and took the train for Dover. What a crowd there was on the platform! However, they found some seats in the train and soon they were comfortably seated in a compartment. But it was very warm (in it). The train took (**mettre**) about two hours to reach the port. They got out of the train and stood in a queue for ten minutes. After the passport examination they were able to go on to the boat. It is pleasant to cross the English Channel when the weather is fine and when (**que**) the sea is calm. That day it was warm and there was no wind. The crossing lasted less than two hours. They said later that they had never spent a more pleasant day.

VIII. Write a composition (in past tenses) based on this outline:

Un monsieur est assis dans un train — un autre monsieur entre dans le compartiment et met ses valises dans le filet — le nouveau venu sort aussitôt — il ne revient pas — le train se met en marche — le premier monsieur regarde les valises — le train s'arrête à une gare — le monsieur, croyant que l'autre avait manqué le train dépose les valises sur le quai et explique tout à un employé — le train se remet en marche — un quart d'heure plus tard l'autre monsieur revient — il est très fâché quand il voit que ses valises ne sont plus là.

(*Answers at the end of the book.*)

LEÇON 23

GRAMMAR

AGREEMENT OF THE PAST PARTICIPLE

When used as an adjective, the past participle agrees in number and gender with the noun or pronoun which it qualifies, like any adjective:

Les pages déchirées = *The torn pages.*
La page est déchirée = *The page is torn.*
Les femmes fatiguées = *The tired women.*
Nous sommes fatigué(e)s = *We are tired.*

In compound tenses with **avoir** it never agrees with the subject:

Elle a porté = *She has carried.*
Nous avons fini = *We have finished.*

The past participle with **avoir** agrees in number and gender with a preceding direct object (but never with an indirect object). There are three ways in which an object may precede the verb:

(i) as an object pronoun:

Je les ai vus (e.g. **les hommes**) = *I have seen them* (m.).
Je les ai vues (e.g. **les femmes**) = *I have seen them* (f.).

(ii) as a relative pronoun:

Les fautes qu'il a faites = *The mistakes which he made.*
La dame que j'ai rencontrée = *The lady whom I met.*

(iii) as the object of an exclamation or question:

Quelles femmes avez-vous vues? = *Which women did you see?*
Quelle surprise il a eue! = *What a surprise he had!*

Note that (*a*) **en** is not considered as a direct object for purposes of agreement: **J'en ai vu quelques-unes** = *I have seen a few of them* (f.); (*b*) when the verb is an impersonal verb the past participle does not agree with a preceding direct object: **Quelle panique il y a eu!** = *What a panic there was!*

The special group of twelve verbs conjugated with **être**, i.e. **aller, venir,** etc. (p. 88) have their participles agreeing with the subject:

Elle est arrivée = *She has arrived.*   **Nous sommes partis** = *We departed.*

but some of these verbs may be used transitively in which case they are conjugated with **avoir** and the participle agrees regularly with the object:

Elle a descendu l'escalier = *She came down the stairs.*

224

Les marches qu'elle a descendues = *The steps which she came down.*
Elles ont monté leurs bagages = *They took up their luggage.*

THE PAST PARTICIPLE WITH REFLEXIVE VERBS

The past participle of a reflexive verb (as in the case of verbs with **avoir**) agrees with the preceding direct object, and therefore with the reflexive pronoun if this is the direct object, but not if it becomes the indirect object:

Elle s'est lavée = *She washed herself.*
Elle s'est dépêchée = *She hurried.*
Elle s'est lavé les mains = *She washed her hands* (= *the hands to herself*).
Elle s'est cassé la jambe = *She broke her leg.*

In the case of reflexive verbs which have no reflexive counterpart in English the reflexive pronoun is usually the direct object:

Elles se sont écriées = *They exclaimed.*
Elles se sont tues = *They kept silent.*

In some sentences the past participle agrees with a relative pronoun as direct object, while a reflexive pronoun is also present as indirect object:

Les lettres qu'elles se sont écrites = *The letters they wrote to each other.*
Les promesses qu'ils se sont faites = *The promises they made to each other.*

(Note that in English we often leave out the relative pronoun *which*.)

USES OF THE REFLEXIVE FORM

Apart from its true reflexive use (e.g. **il se rase** = *he shaves himself*), reflexive verbs are used idiomatically in various other ways:

(i) in a reciprocal sense (meaning *each other*, *one another*, etc.):
   Ils s'aiment (l'un l'autre) = *They love each other.*
   Ils se regardent tous trois = *They all three look at one another.*

(ii) where English frequently uses the verb in the passive voice (French does not use the passive form as often as English does):
   Cela se voit quelquefois = *That is sometimes seen.*
   Cela se comprend = *That is understood.*

Note that many verbs are reflexive in French, but not in English, including:

se dépêcher = *to hurry*	**se tromper** = *to be mistaken*
s'ennuyer = *to get bored*	**se rappeler** = *to recall*
se fâcher = *to get angry*	**se souvenir de** = *to remember*

Here are three compound tenses which do not occur very frequently:

FUTURE PERFECT TENSE

Formed with the future of **avoir** or **être** + the past participle:
j'aurai donné = *I shall have given*, **je serai arrivé, je me serai couché**, etc.

It states what will have happened:

Il aura attendu une semaine = *He will have waited a week.*
Quand vous serez arrivés, je partirai = *When you have arrived, I shall leave.*

CONDITIONAL PERFECT TENSE

Formed with the conditional of **avoir** or **être** + the past participle:
j'aurais donné = *I should have given*, **je serais arrivé, je me serais couché**, etc.
It is used in the same types of sentence as the ordinary conditional tense:
Tu l'aurais trouvé s'il avait parlé = *You would have found him if he had spoken.*
Je la mangerais dès que je l'aurais acheté = *I should eat it when I had bought*
Selon mon livre, il y serait mort = *According to my book, he died there.* [*it.*

PAST ANTERIOR TENSE

Formed with the past historic of **avoir** or **être** + the past participle:
j'eus donné = *I had given*, **je fus arrivé, je me fus couché**
It is used to translate the English pluperfect after conjunctions of time (e.g.
quand, lorsque) when the verb in the main clause is past historic:
Après qu'elle eut dîné, elle s'assit = *After she had dined, she sat down.*
Quand elle se fut lavée, elle sortit = *When she had washed, she went out.*

PLURALS OF NOUNS

There are exceptions to the rule that the plural is formed by adding
-s. Nouns ending in:
    (i) **-s, -x, -z** remain unchanged: **la voix, les voix** = *voice(s)*.
    (ii) **-au, -eu** and a few in **-ou** add **-x** instead: **le bijou, les bijoux** = *jewel(s)*.
    (iii) **-al** change **-al** to **-aux** (with a few exceptions): **le cheval, les chevaux** =
    horse(s).
    (iv) These are irregular: **un œil, les yeux** = *eye(s)*; **le ciel, les cieux** =
    heaven(s).

VOCABULARY

le rendez-vous [rãdevu]	*appointment*	
la mairie [mɛri]	*town-hall*	
convenu(e) [kɔ̃vny]	*agreed, appointed*	
le café-crème [kafekrɛm]	*coffee with cream*	
la demoiselle [dəmwazɛl]	*young lady*	**la semelle**
surprenant(e) [syrprənã, -ãːt]	*surprising*	
la beauté [bote]	*beauty*	
le défaut [defo]	*fault, defect*	
avare [avaːr]	*miserly*	
tôt [to]	*soon*	
l'électricité (f.) [elɛktrisite]	*electricity*	**le feu**

226

marcher [marʃe]	*to walk*	
user [yze]	*to wear out*	
la semelle [səmɛl]	*sole* (of shoe)	
le parc [park]	*park*	
le feu [fø]	*fire*	
allumer [alyme]	*to light*	
une allumette [alymɛt]	*match*	**une allumette**
le sac à main [sak a mɛ̃]	*handbag*	
là-dedans [ladədã]	*in it*	
s'exécuter [segzekyte]	*to comply, pay up*	
de mauvaise grâce [də movɛz graːs]	*grudgingly*	
le receveur [rəsəvœːr]	*conductor* (of bus)	
fouiller [fuje]	*to rummage*	**le sac à main**
le soin [swɛ̃]	*care, attention*	
le trajet [traʒɛ]	*journey, trip*	
le pied [pje]	*foot*	
un individu [ɛ̃dividy]	*individual*	
la mine [min]	*appearance*	
faire la quête [fɛːr la kɛːt]	*to take a collection*	
le Chinois [ʃinwa]	*Chinaman*	
une âme [aːm]	*soul*	**le receveur**
sensible [sãsibl]	*sensitive*	
la pitié [pitje]	*pity*	
un orphelin [ɔrfəlɛ̃]	*orphan*	
la monnaie [monɛ]	*money, change*	
mal à propos [mal a prɔpo]	*at the wrong time*	
la nièce [njɛs]	*niece*	
la musique [myzik]	*music*	**le pied**
avertir [avɛrtiːr]	*to warn*	
recommander [rəkɔmãde]	*to advise*	
maniaque [manjak]	*fussy, faddy*	
la porcelaine [pɔrsəlɛn]	*china*	
s'extasier [sɛkstazje]	*to go into raptures*	
s'évaporer [sevapɔre]	*to evaporate*	
la rosée [roze]	*dew*	**la monnaie**
le lever du soleil [ləve dy sɔlɛːj]	*sunrise*	
juger [ʒyʒe]	*to judge*	
abréger [abreʒe]	*to cut short*	
désobligeant(e) [dezɔbliʒã, -ãːt]	*disagreeable, rude*	
froisser [frwase]	*to offend, hurt*	
une horloge [ɔrlɔːʒ]	*clock*	
au revoir [o rəvwaːr]	*good-bye*	**la porcelaine**

227

CONVERSATION AU CAFÉ

Deux jeunes filles qui se connaissaient depuis leur enfance s'étaient donné rendez-vous à trois heures au Café Royal en face de la mairie. Elles s'y rencontrèrent à l'heure convenue et après avoir regardé la liste des consommations elles commandèrent deux cafés-crème. Quand le garçon eut apporté les tasses de café, les deux demoiselles qui avaient beaucoup de choses à se dire commencèrent à bavarder. La conversation tomba sur les jeunes gens, ce qui n'est pas surprenant lorsque ce sont deux jeunes filles qui se parlent. Mais ce jour-là elles ne parlaient ni de la beauté ni des vertus de ces messieurs mais de leurs défauts.

"J'ai un ami," disait Mlle Lucienne, "qui est si avare qu'il se couche tôt le soir pour économiser l'électricité. Je suis convaincue qu'en marchant il fait de grands pas pour ne pas user les semelles de ses souliers. Un jour, je suis sortie avec lui pour faire une promenade. Nous avions l'intention de visiter un parc qui ne se trouve pas très loin de chez moi. En quittant la maison il m'a demandé si je pouvais lui donner du feu pour allumer une cigarette qu'il avait obtenue d'un ami. Je lui ai offert une allumette que j'avais trouvée au fond de mon sac à main. Avec mille excuses il m'a expliqué qu'il ne pouvait pas m'offrir une cigarette parce qu'il ne lui en restait plus. Comme nous passions devant un kiosque il m'a demandé d'acheter un journal parce qu'il y avait là-dedans un article qu'il voulait lire. Je me suis exécutée de mauvaise grâce. Aussitôt il s'est emparé du journal que je n'ai plus revu. Puis, nous nous sommes dirigés vers l'arrêt pour attendre l'autobus. Celui-ci est enfin arrivé et nous y sommes montés. Le receveur s'est approché de nous et mon ami s'est mis à fouiller dans ses poches. "Quel ennui!" dit-il enfin, "j'ai changé d'habit et j'ai laissé mon argent à la maison. Est-ce que tu pourrais prendre les billets?" Heureusement que j'avais dans mon sac quelques francs que mon père m'avait donnés la veille et j'ai payé les billets. Mon ami les a pris et il les a examinés avec soin. Il m'a expliqué que j'aurais pu prendre des billets moins chers et qu'alors nous serions descendus à tel ou tel endroit pour faire le reste du trajet à pied. Enfin nous sommes descendus de l'autobus et nous sommes entrés dans le parc. Là, nous avons vu un individu de mauvaise mine. Cet homme faisait la quête pour les petits Chinois. Or, Julien — c'est le nom de mon ami — a le cœur tendre, il faut l'avouer. C'est une âme sensible. Pris de pitié pour les petits orphelins de Chine, Julien a donné à l'homme une pièce de monnaie russe. Quant au monsieur, tu peux imaginer la tête qu'il a faite!"

"Ce que tu me dis là est très intéressant," répondit Yolande, "mais je vais te parler de Lucien. Il n'était pas avare mais il avait un autre défaut: il parlait toujours mal à propos. Un jour, j'étais avec lui chez ma vieille tante. Or, ma tante est assez riche et elle n'a pas d'autre nièce que moi. Mais elle n'aime rien de ce qui est moderne — ni les maisons ni les meubles, ni les livres ni la musique. J'en avais averti mon ami Lucien et je lui avais recommandé de ne pas dire ce qu'il ne faut pas à une vieille tante maniaque. Eh bien, nous étions donc assis à prendre le thé. J'admirais la belle porcelaine de ma tante. 'Qu'en penses-tu?' ai-je dit en m'adressant à mon ami. 'Ce n'est pas exactement de la dernière mode,' a-t-il répondu. Je lui ai jeté un regard furieux et je lui ai lancé un coup de pied sous la table. De telles choses ne se disent pas. J'ai remarqué tout de suite que ma tante était fâchée mais elle était trop polie pour se disputer avec Lucien. Plus tard, nous parlions du salon et des meubles. Ma tante s'extasiait devant un vieux buffet en bois de chêne. 'J'aime les meubles d'un goût plus simple,' a dit Lucien. J'étais hors de moi. Je voyais ma fortune future s'évaporer devant mes yeux comme la rosée au lever du soleil. En conséquence, j'ai jugé prudent d'abréger notre visite surtout lorsque Lucien s'est mis à exposer des idées politiques que ma tante a toujours eues en abomination. Naturellement, je ne te raconte pas toutes les choses désobligeantes que Lucien a dites ce jour-là. J'en ai trop honte. En tout cas, je n'ai pas voulu le revoir depuis. Après tout, il ne faut pas froisser une vieille tante riche. Cela ne se fait pas."

Les deux jeunes filles regardèrent l'heure à l'horloge de la mairie d'en face. Il se faisait tard. Aussitôt qu'elles eurent payé l'addition (n'oubliant pas de donner un pourboire au garçon) elles sortirent du café, se dirent au revoir et chacune rentra chez elle.

(*See notes on the next page. Translation at the end of the book.*)

LEÇON 23

NOTES ON THE TEXT

Donner du feu = *to give a light* (for a cigarette); **la tête qu'il a faite** = *the look on his face* (**faire une tête** = *to look glum*); **hors de moi** = *beside myself* (with grief, anger, etc.); **avoir quelque chose en abomination** = *to loathe something*; **il se faisait tard** = *it was getting late.*

EXERCISES

I. Answer in French:

1. Depuis quand les deux jeunes filles se connaissaient-elles?
2. De quoi parlaient les jeunes filles?
3. Quel défaut l'ami de Lucienne avait-il?
4. Où est-ce qu'un autobus s'arrête?
5. Qui est-ce que Lucienne et son ami avaient rencontré dans le parc?
6. Et Lucien, quel défaut avait-il?
7. Qu'est-ce que la vieille tante n'aimait pas?
8. Pourquoi la tante était-elle fâchée?
9. Pourquoi Yolande était-elle furieuse?
10. Quelle heure est-il à votre montre?

II. Translate into English:

1. Quels livres avez-vous achetés ce matin?
2. Elle a sorti un mouchoir de sa poche.
3. La religieuse que j'avais vue une fois chez ma tante est morte le mois dernier.
4. Nous l'avons vue qui sortait de la gare.
5. Quand je leur ai dit qu'il était déjà midi et demi, ils se sont dépêchés.
6. Elle est arrivée à Paris il y a deux mois.
7. Je me rappelle que Jean s'ennuyait toujours quand on lui contait des histoires.
8. Dès que le train fut parti elle rentra à la maison.
9. Vous vous trompez, monsieur, je ne m'appelle pas Durand.
10. Si je n'avais pas manqué le train de six heures, je serais arrivée plus tôt.
11. Vous voyez bien qu'il triche: voilà les cartes qu'il a jouées.
12. Elle est devenue folle et elle s'est coupé la gorge.
13. La lettre que j'ai reçue ce matin vient de Berlin.
14. Où sont vos amies? — Nous les avons vues sur la plage.
15. On dit que pendant la guerre il travaillait en Suisse.

III. Give the third person feminine singular of (1) future perfect; (2) conditional perfect; (3) past anterior tenses of: **se dépêcher, voir, venir, dire, monter, conduire, écrire, arriver, faire, lire.**

230

IV. Replace by pronouns the words underlined:
1. **Oui, j'ai une allumette.**
2. **Donnez la lettre à Charles!**
3. **Il m'a donné un coup de pied.**
4. **Il y a un oiseau sur le toit.**
5. **Il va nous dire la vérité.**
6. **Hier soir nous sommes allés au cinéma.**
7. **N'envoyez pas ce cadeau au professeur!**
8. **Qui veut aller en ville avec Pierre?**
9. **Elle nous avait montré le chemin.**
10. **Nous n'avons pas vu de fleurs au marché.**

V. Translate into French:
1. She rushed (**se précipiter**) towards the door to see the car.
2. We shaved this morning before leaving.
3. He broke his leg while he was in Switzerland.
4. It is said that it will be fine in July.
5. The plank which I have brought is three metres long.
6. We are tired and do not wish to play cards.
7. I am always bored when I go to my uncle's.
8. You are mistaken. My sister is older than I.
9. I remember the house where I was born.
10. When she had prepared lunch we sat down to table.

VI. Translate into French (using the perfect tense whenever possible):

We entered the café and sat down at a table near the window. The waiter presented himself and we ordered two cups of coffee. The waiter brought them and placed them on the table. He asked us if we wished to play cards. We said (**que**) no. We began to chat and I told a story which I had read a few days ago. My friend laughed and he, too, began to tell stories. We were having a good time. However, as it was getting late, we asked for the bill, gave the waiter a tip and left the café. We caught the bus at the corner of the street.

VII. Write a composition (in the past tense) based on this outline:

Un petit garçon pleure dans la rue — un vieux monsieur s'arrête — lui demande ce qu'il a (= *what is the matter with him*) **— le petit répond qu'il a perdu deux francs — le monsieur veut le consoler — lui donne deux francs — le petit recommence à pleurer — le monsieur en demande la raison — le petit garçon répond qu'il s'est trompé et qu'il a perdu dix francs.**

(*Answers at the end of the book.*)

LEÇON 24

GRAMMAR

THE VERBS **aller, pouvoir, savoir, vouloir, devoir, faire**

We shall now consider in more detail the ways in which these six verbs (p. 56) are used in combination with the infinitives of other verbs.

aller = *to go* and also, to express a future, = *to be going to, be about to*:
Je vais le faire tout de suite = *I am going to do it right away.*

pouvoir = *to be able to, be permitted to* and also *can, may*:
Je peux le faire = *I am able to do it.*
Puis-je fermer la porte? = *May I close the door?*   [*o'clock.*
Il pourrait arriver avant trois heures = *He could, might, arrive before three*
Il aurait pu le faire avant de partir = *He could, might, have done it before*
                                                                    leaving.
Note that (*a*) the first person singular form **puis** is always used in an inverted question form in the place of **peux-je** and is found in the negative without **pas**: **Je ne puis le comprendre** = *I cannot understand it*; (*b*) **pouvoir** = *to be able to* (*do something*) when there is no physical obstacle to the action: **Je peux jouer au tennis ce soir** = *I can play tennis this evening.*

savoir = *to know, know how to* and also *can* when this implies having learnt how to (do something):
Je sais jouer au tennis = *I can play tennis* (have learnt how to do so).
Il sait jouer du piano = *He can play the piano.*
Note that in a negative conditional form (without **pas**) **savoir** = *cannot*: **Je ne saurais le dire** = *I cannot say.*

vouloir = *to wish*:
Je ne veux pas me coucher = *I do not want to go to bed.*
Il voudrait voir ce film = *He would like to see that film.*
Do not confuse *would* — conditional, with *would* = *was willing*:
Il ne le ferait pas même si on le lui demandait = *He would not do it even if he*
                                                            were asked (conditional).
Il ne voulait pas le dire = *He would not* (*was unwilling to*) *say.*
Il n'a pas voulu le faire = *He wouldn't* (*refused to*) *do it.*

232

The imperative **veuillez** = *be good enough to, kindly*:
    Veuillez fermer la porte = *Kindly close the door.*

Vouloir bien is often used in the interrogative form in this sense, i.e. as a polite command or request:
    Voulez-vous bien attendre un moment? = *Be good enough to wait a moment.*

Je veux bien = *I don't mind* or *by all means*, in answer to a question:
    Venez-vous avec nous? Je veux bien = *Are you coming with us? I don't mind.*
Note that the future tense of **vouloir** is used in this expression: **Faites comme vous voudrez!** = *Do as you please!*

devoir expresses (i) compulsion, inevitability (= *must*); (ii) futurity (= *am to*):
    Je dois partir tout de suite = *I must go at once* (i); *I am to go at once* (ii).
    Vous devez avoir faim = *You must be hungry* (i).
    J'ai dû le faire = *I had to do it* (i), or *I must have done it* (i).
    Je devrai le faire demain = *I must do it tomorrow* (i).
    Elle devait prendre le train de cinq heures = *She was to (was supposed to)*
                                   catch the five o'clock train (ii).
In the conditional tense **devoir** = *ought*:
    Je devrais lui écrire = *I ought to write to him.*
    J'aurais dû lui répondre = *I ought to have (should have) answered him.*
    Elle devrait être déjà ici = *She ought to be here by now.*
Note that it is **devoir** which changes tense; the second verb is always a present infinitive, whereas *must* occurs only in the present tense in English.

faire = *to do, make* and also *to cause to, to have (something done)*:
    Je le fais venir = *I make him come, I send for him.*
The infinitive sometimes takes on a passive meaning:
    Il fera réparer la bicyclette = *He will have the bicycle repaired.*
    Je me suis fait couper les cheveux = *I have had my hair cut.*

IDIOMATIC TENSE USAGE

In some constructions the tense differs from that used in English:
    Je viens de le dire = *I have just said so.*
    Elle venait de sortir = *She had just gone out.*

Depuis, **il y a**, **voici** and **voilà** take similar tense constructions to **venir de**:
    Depuis quand êtes-vous ici? = *How long have you been here?* (literally =
        Since when are you here? — present tense because you are still here).
    Je suis ici depuis une heure = *I have been here an hour.*
    Il attendait depuis une demi-heure = *He had been waiting for half an hour.*

Note that as with **venir de**, the only tenses possible in this construction are the present and the imperfect tense.

These sentences can be recast using **il y a, voici** or **voilà**:

Il y a, Voici, Voilà une heure que je suis ici = *I have been here an hour.*

Il y avait une demi-heure qu'il attendait = *He had been waiting for half an hour.*

Do not confuse **il y a** as used above with **il y a** = *ago*: [*ago.*

Il est arrivé chez nous il y a deux ans = *He arrived at our house two years* Note this construction with **il y a** + a compound tense with **ne**: **Il y a deux ans que je ne l'ai vu** = *I have not seen him for two years.*

Si sometimes = *whether*, in which case any tense of the indicative can follow:

Je ne sais pas s'il vient, s'il viendra, s'il est venu = *I don't know if he is coming, if he will come, if he came.*

Je ne savais pas s'il venait, s'il viendrait, s'il était venu = *I didn't know if he was coming, if he would come, if he had come.*

Si sometimes = *if*, in which case neither the future nor conditional tenses can be used in the **si** clause:

S'il pleut, je ne sortirai pas = *If it rains, I shall not go out.*

S'il pleuvait, il ne viendrait pas = *If it rained, he would not come.*

S'il était venu, il m'aurait vu = *If he had come, he would have seen me.*

Quand = *when*; after **quand** and other conjunctions of time (except **avant que**) the future tense must be used if future is implied in the time clause:

Il le fera quand il viendra = *He will do it when he comes.*

but:

Je croyais qu'il le ferait quand il viendrait = *I thought he would do it when he came.*

(Note that when the main verb is in the past tense the verb in the time clause becomes conditional.)

VOCABULARY

la quinzaine [kɛ̃zɛn]	*fortnight*
la lumière [lymjɛːr]	*light*
le logement [lɔʒmɑ̃]	*accommodation*
bâtir [batiːr]	*to build*
une île [il]	*island*
bossu(e) [bɔsy]	*hunch-backed*
un amour [amuːr]	*love*
un invalide [ɛ̃valid]	*disabled soldier*

la lumière

234

le tombeau [tɔ̃bo]	*tomb, vault*
ancien, -ienne [ãsjɛ̃, -jɛn]	*ancient*
négligé(e) [negliʒe]	*neglected, slovenly*
le peintre [pɛ̃tr]	*painter*
se dresser [sə drɛse]	*to rise, stand*
le soldat [sɔlda]	*soldier*
le chef-d'œuvre [ʃɛdœːvr]	*masterpiece*
contenir [kɔ̃tniːr]	*to contain*
un objet d'art [obʒɛ daːr]	*work of art*
à fond [a fɔ̃]	*thoroughly*
s'impatienter [sɛ̃pasjãte]	*to get impatient*
construire [kɔ̃strɥiːr]	*to construct, build*
une exposition [ɛkspozisjɔ̃]	*exhibition, show*
là-haut [lao]	*up there*
une antenne [ãtɛn]	*aerial*
le vertige [vɛrtiːʒ]	*giddiness*
détacher [detaʃe]	*to tear off*
le carnet [karnɛ]	*book (of tickets, etc.)*
commode [kɔmɔd]	*convenient*
revenir [rəvəniːr]	*to cost, amount to*
le métro [metro]	*underground railway*
une affluence [aflyãːs]	*flow, crowd, rush*
le parcours [parkuːr]	*run, trip*
afficher [afiʃe]	*to display (a bill)*
la correspondance [kɔrɛspɔ̃dãːs]	*connection (railway)*
attention! [atãsjɔ̃]	*look out, careful!*
inutile [inytil]	*useless*
le portillon [pɔrtijɔ̃]	*automatic gate*
se fermer [sə fɛrme]	*to shut (itself)*
ramer [rame]	*to row*
le canot [kano]	*small boat*
le bouquiniste [bukinist]	*secondhand bookseller*
le bouquin [bukɛ̃]	*old book*
perché(e) [pɛrʃe]	*perched*
le sommet [sɔmɛ]	*summit*
dominer [dɔmine]	*to dominate, overlook*
fameux, -euse [famø, -øːz]	*famous*
régner [rɛɲe]	*to pervade, reign*
bizarre [bizaːr]	*quaint, odd*
un avis [avi]	*opinion*
sous peu [su pø]	*shortly*
cordialement [kɔrdjalmã]	*heartily, sincerely*

une île

le tombeau

le chef-d'œuvre

une antenne

une affluence

le canot

la cathédrale

un étalage

le bouquin

le soldat

la touriste

le peintre

le bouquiniste

le trottoir   un invalide

UNE LETTRE DE PARIS

Cher Charles,

Comme il y a assez longtemps que je ne vous ai vu, je ne me rappelle pas si je vous ai dit que j'allais passer une quinzaine à Paris. Eh bien, voilà déjà huit jours que je me trouve dans la Ville-lumière. J'y suis arrivé lundi dernier et j'ai trouvé un logement chez un de mes amis à Bécon-les-Bruyères. J'ai eu de la chance car je ne pourrais payer le prix d'un hôtel. À Paris tout est assez cher.

Je sors tous les jours visiter les monuments de la ville. Hier j'ai admiré Notre-Dame, la grande cathédrale gothique bâtie sur une île au milieu de la Seine. Cela m'a fait penser au célèbre roman de Victor Hugo où il raconte l'histoire du bossu Quasimodo et l'amour de celui-ci pour la belle Esméralda. J'ai visité aussi l'Hôtel des Invalides où se trouve le tombeau de Napoléon et le Panthéon où sont enterrés beaucoup de Français célèbres.

Aujourd'hui je me suis promené au Quartier Latin, un des quartiers les plus anciens de Paris. C'est là que se trouve l'Université de Paris connue sous le nom de la Sorbonne. On y voit souvent des individus d'aspect négligé qui pourraient être des peintres. Cet après-midi je suis allé voir l'Arc de Triomphe qui se dresse au bout de l'Avenue des Champs-Elysées et sous lequel se trouve la tombe du Soldat Inconnu.

Il y a trois jours j'ai passé plusieurs heures au musée du Louvre où, entre autres chefs-d'œuvre, j'ai admiré La Joconde (Mona Lisa) de Léonard de Vinci. Mais ce musée contient tant d'objets d'art qu'il faudrait au moins plusieurs jours pour examiner à fond tout ce qu'il y a d'intéressant là-dedans.

Peut-être vous impatientez-vous quand je vous parle d'églises et de musées. Vous allez me demander si je suis monté au haut de la Tour Eiffel. Je vous répondrai que oui. La Tour Eiffel, remarquable édifice en acier, construit pour l'Exposition universelle de 1889, a 300 mètres de haut. Elle est devenue, pour ainsi dire, le symbole de la ville de Paris. Pour y monter on prend l'ascenseur et on paie assez cher. Là-haut, il y a des restaurants et des magasins et la tour supporte une antenne de télévision. Quand j'ai regardé en bas, cela m'a donné le vertige!

Les grands boulevards de Paris sont admirables. Ce sont de larges avenues droites le long desquelles on voit des magasins de tout premier ordre. Grâce à ses boulevards et à ses bâtiments magnifiques Paris est une des plus belles villes du monde.

Lorsqu'on attend un autobus à Paris il n'est pas nécessaire de faire la queue. En arrivant à l'arrêt on détache un petit ticket de priorité qui porte un numéro. Quand l'autobus arrive, le receveur fait montrer les tickets et il laisse monter les voyageurs selon l'ordre de leur arrivée à l'arrêt. Très pratique, n'est-ce pas? De plus, on peut acheter au receveur un carnet de tickets. C'est plus commode et cela revient beaucoup moins cher.

Je voyage souvent par le métro parce que ça va très vite surtout aux heures d'affluence. Souvent je m'amuse à faire de longs parcours pour le seul plaisir de voyager. En regardant les cartes qu'on voit affichées partout dans les stations de métro on peut voir facilement où il faut changer de train et prendre la correspondance. Mais attention! Il est inutile de courir pour attraper les trains au dernier moment. À l'entrée de chaque quai il y a une porte automatique (on appelle ça un portillon) qui se ferme dès qu'un train entre en gare.

Il y a deux jours je me suis rendu au Bois de Boulogne, vaste parc public où l'on peut faire de belles promenades et — si l'on sait ramer — se promener en canot sur le lac. Mais si vous y allez un jour louer un canot, n'oubliez pas de donner un pourboire à celui qui vous aidera à monter en bateau. Autrement il vous dira d'un ton acide: "N'oubliez pas le service, s'il vous plaît." Quand vous serez à Paris vous devriez faire une promenade le long des quais de la Seine pour regarder les étalages des bouquinistes qui y font leur commerce sur le trottoir. On y voit toutes sortes de livres et de bouquins intéressants.

L'Église du Sacré-Cœur, perchée au sommet d'une colline, domine le quartier de Montmartre où se trouvent les fameux établissements de nuit. Dans ce quartier il règne une atmosphère bizarre mais à mon avis tout y est arrangé à l'intention des touristes.

Je quitterai Paris d'aujourd'hui en huit. Je ne saurais vous dire si je resterai quelques jours à Calais mais en tout cas j'espère vous revoir sous peu.

Cordialement à vous,

Robert

(*See notes on the next page. Translation at the end of the book.*)

LEÇON 24

NOTES ON THE TEXT

Peut-être vous impatientez-vous — when **peut-être** precedes the verb either the verb is inverted (as here) or **que** must follow **peut-être** (**peut-être que vous vous impatientez**); **pour ainsi dire** = *so to speak*; **cela m'a donné le vertige** = *that made me giddy*; **le ticket de priorité**, a numbered priority slip obtained at bus stages in Paris; **pour le seul plaisir** = *just for the pleasure of*; **grâce à ses boulevards et à ses bâtiments,** note that à and de must be repeated before every noun to which they refer, e.g. **je parle de mon frère et de ma sœur** = *I speak of my brother and sister*; **à mon avis** = *in my opinion*; **à l'intention de** = *for the benefit of*; **d'aujourd'hui en huit, en quinze** = *a week, fortnight today.*

EXERCISES

I. **Répondez en français aux questions suivantes:**
1. **Qui est Quasimodo?**
2. **Où est enterré le Soldat Inconnu?**
3. **Où se trouve la cathédrale de Notre Dame?**
4. **Quelle peinture célèbre se trouve au Louvre?**
5. **Quelle est la hauteur de la Tour Eiffel?**
6. **Qu'est-ce que c'est qu'un boulevard?**
7. **Que trouve-t-on le long des quais de la Seine?**
8. **Où se trouve la Basilique du Sacré-Cœur?**
9. **Qu'est-ce que c'est que le métro?**
10. **De quoi se sert-on pour ramer?**

II. Translate into English:
1. **Il travaillait depuis six mois à l'usine.**
2. **Venez me voir quand vous serez en ville!**
3. **Voilà deux heures que je vous attends sous la pluie!**
4. **On ne savait jamais s'il arriverait ou non.**
5. **Veuillez me passer le livre qui se trouve à côté du poste de T.S.F.**
6. **Les soldats doivent obéir à leurs officiers.**
7. **Nous devions prendre le train de cinq heures et quart mais hélas! nous l'avons manqué.**
8. **Nous irons visiter le Louvre quand nous serons à Paris.**
9. **Il aurait dû le dire devant le tribunal.**
10. **La guerre éclata il y a douze ans.**
11. **S'il commettait ce crime on le condamnerait à six ans de prison.**
12. **Les petits garçons jouaient aux billes sur le trottoir.**
13. **Il y avait dix ans qu'il habitait Marseille.**
14. **Je viens de lire dans le journal que sa tante est morte.**
15. **Il venait de sortir de l'atelier quand le feu se déclara.**

238

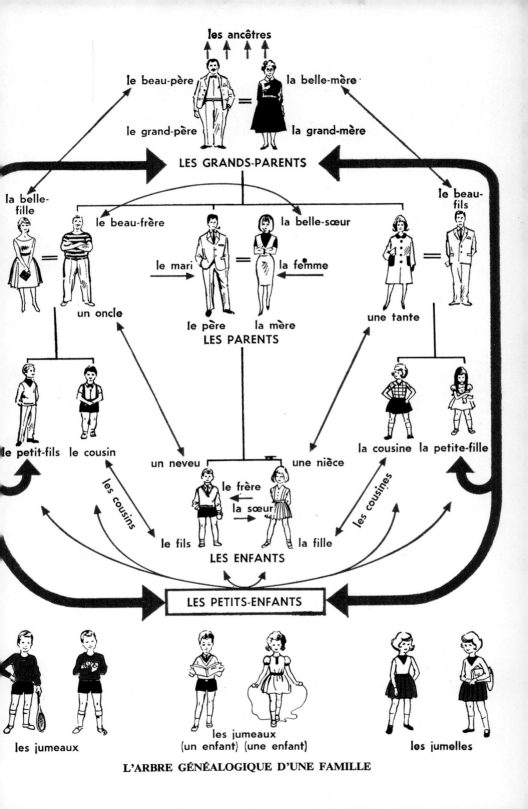

les ancêtres

le beau-père = la belle-mère

le grand-père = la grand-mère

LES GRANDS-PARENTS

la belle-fille

le beau-frère   la belle-sœur

le beau-fils

le mari = la femme

un oncle

le père   la mère
LES PARENTS

une tante

le petit-fils   le cousin

la cousine   la petite-fille

un neveu   une nièce

les cousins

le frère
la sœur

les cousines

le fils   la fille
LES ENFANTS

LES PETITS-ENFANTS

les jumeaux

les jumeaux
(un enfant) (une enfant)

les jumelles

L'ARBRE GÉNÉALOGIQUE D'UNE FAMILLE

le cahier

le calendrier

le carnet

la carte po

le chapitre

CHAPITRE II

le crayon

la colle

le coupe-papier

la c

la cire à cacheter

le dictionnaire

l'encre bleue

un en

la gomme

la lettre

une enveloppe

la feuille de papier

le papier à lettres

le papier buvard

la machine à éc

la marge

la page

le pinceau
à colle

la plume

le plumier

le porte-lett

la règle

la reliure

le stylo

le stylo à b

LA PAPETERIE DU BUREAU ET DE L'ÉCOLE

III. Change the verbs underlined into the perfect tense:

1. **Quelle erreur fait-il ?**
2. **Elle se lave la figure.**
3. **Voilà les lunettes que je cherche partout.**
4. **La somme que vous recevez n'est pas grosse.**
5. **Où sont les valises? Il les emporte.**
6. **Les lettres arrivent à sept heures du matin.**
7. **Quand je leur pose une question ils se taisent.**
8. **Elle se casse la jambe en grimpant sur un arbre.**
9. **Quelles histoires racontez-vous?**
10. **Lisez-vous les vers qu'il compose?**

IV. Translate into French:

1. Kindly put the basket down on the table.
2. He cannot swim in the lake this afternoon because he has to run an errand for his mother.
3. He can play the violin and the clarinet but he cannot play the piano.
4. He knows nothing about it; he ought to be silent.
5. She was to arrive at the port the following morning.
6. He had been working half an hour when the accident happened.
7. If he arrived punctually he would not be scolded.
8. I thought that he would write to me when he received the parcel.
9. You must have a hair-cut. Your hair is too long.
10. I should willingly do so if I had enough money.

V. Translate into French:

Two years ago I spent a month in Paris and I had a good time. When the weather was fine I used to go out to see the sights of the town. I would visit the churches, the museums and even the large stores. When I was tired I used to go into a café and order a cup of coffee or a glass of beer. It was very hot in the streets and I was thirsty. However, as I did not have a great deal of money I could not buy all that I wanted. But who is able to do that? I ought to tell you that everything is very dear in Paris. Sometimes I used to take a walk in the Bois de Boulogne and hire a rowing-boat. Can you row? It is not very difficult. Alas! I do not know whether I shall have enough money to go to France this year.

VI. Describe a visit to a large city.

(*Answers at the end of the book.*)

LEÇON 25

GRAMMAR

USES OF **c'est** AND **il est** TO TRANSLATE *it is*

There are important differences in use between **c'est** = *it is* and **il est** = *it is*.

C'est is used:

(i) when the complement (word which completes the sense of *it is*) is a noun with the article or a pronoun or an adjective standing alone:

C'est un chien = *It is a dog.*   **C'est moi** = *It is I.*
C'est vrai = *It is true.*

(ii) to emphasise a following statement:

C'est à vous que je parle = *It is to you that I am speaking.*
C'est un brave homme que son oncle = *His uncle is a fine fellow (if ever there was).*
C'est un scandale que d'agir ainsi = *It is disgraceful to act like that.*

(iii) to refer to and sum up an idea which precedes it:

Il n'est pas très riche, c'est évident = *He is not very rich, that's evident.*
Vous ne faites pas beaucoup de fautes, c'est vrai = *You do not make many mistakes, it is true.*

(iv) when followed by an adjective + **à** + infinitive:

C'est difficile à faire = *It is difficult to do.*

Il est is used:

(i) when followed by an adjective + **que** (= *that*):

Il est vrai que vous ne faites pas beaucoup de fautes = *It is true that you do not make many mistakes.*
Il est evident qu'il n'est pas riche = *It is obvious that he is not rich.*

(ii) where an adjective is followed by **de** + the infinitive with an object:

Il est difficile de croire cela = *It is difficult to believe that.*
Il est triste de savoir qu'il est malade = *It is sad to know that he is ill.*

(iii) when it refers to a noun already stated or about to be stated — here, of course, *it* = **il** or **elle** to agree with the noun:

Voici la craie; elle est bleue = *Here is the chalk; it is blue.*
Il est intéressant, votre livre? = *Is it interesting, your book?*

(iv) to express the time of day:

Il est trois heures et demie = *It is half past three.*

(v) for most sentences or phrases in parenthesis (i.e. a sentence or phrase inserted by way of a comment in a sentence with which it has no grammatical connection), e.g. **il est vrai** = *it is true*, **n'est‿il pas vrai**= *isn't it true*, **semble-t-il** = *it appears*:

Leur maison, il est vrai, est‿énorme = *Their house, it is true, is huge.*

But note that (*a*) *It appears to me* = **Ce me semble**: **Voilà, ce me semble, une excellente idée** = *That, to my mind, is an excellent idea*; (*b*) *It is a pity* always = **C'est dommage**: **L'enfant a perdu sa balle, c'est dommage** = *The child has lost his ball*; *it's a pity*; (*c*) **N'est-ce pas** is invariable: **Il fait chaud, n'est-ce pas?** = *It is warm, isn't it?*

QUESTIONS

We shall now sum up the different ways of forming questions (Leçon 1).

Any statement can be made interrogative (i.e. into a question) either by placing **est-ce que** in front of it, e.g. **Il fait beau temps** = *It is fine*; **Est-ce qu'il fait beau temps?** = *Is it fine?* or by inverting the verb and a pronoun subject: **Fait‿il beau temps?** = *Is it fine?* Note that:

(*a*) in the third person singular present tense of **-er** verbs (and of the irregular verbs **avoir** and **aller**) and in the third person singular future tense of all verbs **-t-** is inserted between the verb and the subject pronoun:

Mange-t-il une pomme? = *Is he eating an apple?*

A-t-il un rhume de cerveau? = *Has he a cold in the head?*

Ira-t-elle au cinéma ce soir? = *Will she go to the cinema this evening?*

(*b*) in the first person singular present tense the inverted question form is best avoided except in these common forms: **ai-je?** (= *have I?*), **suis-je?**, **dis-je?**, **dois-je?**, **fais-je?**, **puis-je?**, **sais-je?**, **vais-je?**, **vois-je?**

(*c*) when a statement with a noun as subject is changed into inverted question form the noun is followed by a pronoun agreeing with it:

Le chat est‿il noir? = *Is the cat black?*

La chaussée est‿elle large? = *Is the roadway wide?*

INTERROGATIVE PRONOUNS

Questions can also be introduced by interrogative words; some of these such as **quand** = *when* and **pourquoi** = *why* (see p. 19) are simple, but the interrogative pronouns (**qui est-ce**, etc.) require careful study:

who (subject) = **qui** or **qui est-ce qui**:

Qui est‿à la porte? or **Qui est-ce qui est‿à la porte?** = *Who is at the door?*

whom (object) = **qui** or **qui est-ce que**:

Qui voyez-vous? or **Qui est-ce que vous voyez?** = *Whom do you see?*

whom (after a preposition) = **qui**:

Pour qui sont ces souliers? = *For whom are these shoes?*

À qui sont ces livres? = *To whom do these books belong?*

what (pronoun subject) = **qu'est-ce qui**:
  Qu'est-ce qui est sur la table? = *What is on the table?*

what (pronoun object) = **que** or **qu'est-ce que**:
  Que faites-vous? or **Qu'est-ce que vous faites?** = *What are you doing?*

what (after a preposition) = **quoi**:
  Sur quoi met-on la nappe? = *On what does one put the cloth?*
  À quoi sert un stylo? = *What is a fountain-pen used for?*

what (standing alone or followed by a comparative adjective) = **quoi**:
  Cela m'étonne. Quoi? = *That surprises me. What does?*
  Quoi de plus agréable qu'un petit voyage? = *What is more pleasant than a*
Note the expression **à quoi bon** = *what's the use (of)*:   [*little journey?*
  À quoi bon tout ce bruit? = *What's the use of all that noise?*

which or *what* (adjective) = **quel(s), quelle(s)**:
  Quelle heure est-il? = *What time is it?*
  Quel livre est le vôtre? = *Which book is yours?*

which or *which one* (pronoun) = **lequel, laquelle, lesquels, lesquelles**:
  Lequel de ces livres préférez-vous? = *Which of these books do you prefer?*
  Laquelle de ces pages est déchirée? = *Which one of these pages is torn?*
  Auquel de ces contes faites-vous allusion? = *To which of these stories. . . .*

Note that all interrogative words and phrases (except expressions containing **est-ce que**) are always followed by the inverted form of the verb:
  Quand partirez-vous? but **Quand est-ce que vous partirez?**
  Combien en avez-vous? but **Combien est-ce que vous en avez?**

OTHER INSTANCES OF INVERSION
Inversion is also used after quotations and after some adverbial forms when they start a sentence, e.g. **peut-être** = *perhaps*, **aussi** = *so*, **toujours** = *however*, **à peine** = *scarcely*, **encore** = *besides*, **en vain** = *in vain*, etc.:
  "Vous avez tort," dit-il = *"You are wrong," he said.*
  "Quel menteur!" direz-vous = *"What a liar!" you will say.*
  Aussi est-il parti = *So he left.*
  Peut-être avez-vous vu cela = *Perhaps you saw that.*
  À peine fut-elle arrivée. . . . = *Hardly had she arrived. . . .*
  En vain cherchait-il partout = *He looked everywhere in vain.*

VOCABULARY

effroyable [efrwajabl]   *dreadful*
drelin-drelin! [drəlɛ̃-drəlɛ̃]   *ting-a-ling!*
la Sûreté [syrte]   *Criminal Investigation Department*
décrocher [dekrɔʃe]   *to unhook* (receiver)
un appareil [aparɛːj]   *instrument, apparatus*

244

signaler [siɲale]	*to report*	
le meurtre [mœrtr]	*murder*	
la concierge [kɔ̃sjɛrʒ]	*caretaker, concierge*	
un appartement [apartəmɑ̃]	*flat*	
le lieu, les lieux [ljø]	*place, scene*	
raccrocher [rakrɔʃe]	*to hook up* (receiver)	
le grincement [grɛ̃smɑ̃]	*screech, creaking*	**la montre**
le réverbère [revɛrbɛːr]	*street-lamp*	
le policier [pɔlisje]	*policeman, detective*	
le fracas [frakɑ]	*din*	
pénétrer [penetre]	*to go into*	
le cheveu [ʃəvø]	*hair*	
le cadavre [kadɑːvr]	*corpse*	
découvrir (like **ouvrir**) [dekuvriːr]	*to discover*	**la tête chauve**
tout à l'heure [tuta lœːr]	*just now*	
la montre [mɔ̃ːtr]	*watch*	
un intérieur [ɛ̃terjœːr]	*home*	
se passer [sə pɑse]	*to happen, occur*	
par hasard [par azaːr]	*by chance*	
chauve [ʃoːv]	*bald*	**la cicatrice**
le front [frɔ̃]	*forehead*	
la cicatrice [sikatris]	*scar*	
se presser [sə prɛse]	*to hurry, crowd around*	
allonger [alɔ̃ʒe]	*to lengthen*	
le cou [ku]	*neck*	
vider [vide]	*to empty, vacate*	
le sang [sɑ̃]	*blood*	
la pendule [pɑ̃dyl]	*clock*	**la pendule**
le photographe [fɔtɔgraf]	*photographer*	
la photo(graphie) [fɔtɔ(grafi)]	*photograph*	
une empreinte [ɑ̃prɛ̃ːt]	*print, impression*	
digital(e) [diʒital]	*finger* (adj.)	
le, la locataire [lɔkatɛːr]	*tenant*	
la province [prɔvɛ̃ːs]	*province, provinces*	
la veuve [vœːv]	*widow*	**le photographe**
sympathique [sɛ̃patik]	*likeable*	
commettre (like **mettre**) [kɔmɛtr]	*to commit*	
atroce [atrɔs]	*atrocious*	
longuement [lɔ̃gmɑ̃]	*for a long time*	
à quoi bon? [a kwa bɔ̃]	*what is the good of?*	
nier [nje]	*to deny*	
résoudre [rezuːdr]	*to solve*	**une empreinte**

245

UN CRIME EFFROYABLE

Drelin-drelin! Le téléphone sonnait à la Sûreté. D'un geste professionnel l'inspecteur Legros décrocha l'appareil et dit: "Allô, allô." Ce fut un de ses subordonnés qui répondit: "Bonsoir, M. l'Inspecteur. On vient de signaler ce qui pourrait être un meurtre au 35 Boulevard Monceau. La concierge dit avoir trouvé un mort dans un des appartements." "Bon, j'arrive," dit Legros qui comme tous les détectives parlait peu. "Nous nous rendrons sur les lieux tout de suite." En disant cela, il raccrocha. Deux minutes et demie plus tard l'inspecteur Legros, accompagné de quatre de ses meilleurs hommes, montait en voiture. L'auto partit comme un éclair et un quart d'heure plus tard s'arrêta avec un grincement de freins formidable devant un grand édifice où à la lumière d'un réverbère on lisait le numéro 35. Sans dire un mot, les policiers descendirent de voiture comme des automates en claquant les portières avec fracas et pénétrèrent dans la maison.

La concierge, grosse femme aux cheveux gris, vint à la rencontre des cinq policiers. Elle leur raconta avec tous les détails comment elle avait trouvé le cadavre. La pauvre concierge tremblait de tous ses membres mais cela ne l'empêchait pas de parler. L'inspecteur regardait la femme sans mot dire pendant qu'elle lui fournissait des renseignements. "Bon," dit-il enfin. "À quelle heure avez-vous découvert le cadavre?" "Tout à l'heure — c'est-à-dire à onze heures et demie — je me disais justement. . . ." L'inspecteur regarda sa montre. Il était minuit moins cinq. "Comment le mort s'appelle-t-il?" demanda-t-il ensuite. "Il s'appelle M. Duclos," répondit la femme. "Quel âge avait-il?" "Je dirais trente-cinq ans mais il est difficile de le savoir exactement. Mais c'était un homme très gentil.

Il ne loge ici que depuis six mois. Évidemment il n'était pas riche. Son intérieur est assez modeste. Le pauvre homme n'avait pas de femme. Il demeurait seul là-haut. J'ai toujours eu pitié de lui. C'est vraiment dommage." "Qu'elle est bavarde, celle-là," pensa l'inspecteur. "Est-ce qu'il avait souvent des visites?" reprit-il en allumant sa pipe. "Presque pas," répondit la concierge. "Il aimait la solitude; il ne parlait pas beaucoup. Je crois qu'il travaillait en ville. Il était comptable." Il va sans dire que la concierge savait tout ce qui se passait dans la maison. Et elle ajouta: "Justement ce soir vers neuf heures un homme est venu le voir. Par hasard je me trouvais dans l'escalier et j'ai pu le voir. Il est vrai que je ne l'ai pas regardé de près parce que je ne savais pas à ce moment-là qu'il allait tuer M. Duclos (l'inspecteur fronça les sourcils) mais j'ai l'impression qu'il était plutôt petit et chauve. J'ai remarqué cela car il ne portait pas de chapeau. Au front il avait une cicatrice affreuse. Je me suis dit: je ne connais pas ce type-là. Qui peut-il bien être? Et je l'ai regardé monter jusqu'au troisième. Il a frappé à la porte et on l'a fait entrer. Puis je l'ai vu qui descendait l'escalier vers dix heures. Il semblait très pressé." "Cela suffit pour le moment," dit l'inspecteur et il monta au troisième étage. Il y trouva des gens qui se pressaient autour de la porte de l'appartement, allongeant le cou pour voir ce qui se passait là-dedans. D'un mot l'inspecteur fit vider les lieux. La police n'aime pas les curieux.

L'inspecteur passa à l'examen de la pièce. Il s'agissait d'un crime, c'était évident. Le cadavre était étendu par terre au milieu de la chambre. Peut-être y avait-il du sang répandu partout mais je n'en suis pas très sûr. Mais il y avait certainement un revolver sur le tapis. Il y avait aussi par terre une pendule cassée qui marquait huit heures et demie. La pipe de la victime et une lettre déchirée se trouvaient sur la table. Le médecin policier examinait le cadavre et un photographe faisait des photos. On examinait aussi la chambre en vue d'y trouver des empreintes digitales.

L'inspecteur Legros réfléchissait. Il fit venir la concierge: "Quels sont les autres locataires de cette maison?" "Il n'y en a que deux," répondit-elle. "Mlle Lemoine qui est vieille fille demeure seule au premier. En ce moment elle est partie en vacances chez sa sœur qui habite en province. Quant à Mme Mornet, elle est veuve. C'est une personne très sympathique. Elle n'a rien à voir avec ce crime, j'en suis sûre."

Qui donc avait commis ce crime atroce? Est-ce l'homme mystérieux à la cicatrice? Est-ce une des locataires de la maison? Est-ce la concierge elle-même? L'inspecteur y réfléchit longuement mais l'inspecteur n'était pas un détective de roman et — à quoi bon le nier? — il ne put pas résoudre le problème en dix minutes. Quant à moi, dès que je recevrai des renseignements plus amples je les porterai à la connaissance du public.

(*See notes on the next page. Translation at the end of the book.*)

LEÇON 25

NOTES ON THE TEXT

La Sûreté is the French equivalent of Scotland Yard; **venir à la rencontre de** = *to come to meet,* **rencontrer** = *to meet (accidentally)*; **trembler de tous ses membres** = *to tremble in every limb*; **sans mot dire** = *without saying a word*: in some set expressions a noun is used without an article and in an unusual position (cf. **sans coup férir** = *without striking a blow*); **par terre** = *on the ground* (**sur terre** = *in this world*); **il n'y en a que deux** = *there are only two*: when a numeral stands on its own as object **en** precedes the verb (cf. **j'en ai six** = *I have six,* **nous en avons perdu deux** = *we have lost two*); **vieille fille** = *old maid*; **elle n'a rien à voir avec** = *she has nothing to do with, is not implicated in*; **porter à la connaissance de** = *to bring to the notice of.*

EXERCISES

I. Answer in French:
  1. Qu'est-ce qu'on venait de signaler?
  2. Que dit la concierge? Décrivez-la!
  3. Comment l'auto des policiers partit-elle?
  4. À quel étage est-ce que M. Duclos habitait?
  5. Pourquoi examinait on la chambre?

II. Translate into English:
  1. Vous avez fait tout votre possible, c'est vrai.
  2. Il est évident que mon oncle ne veut pas nous aider.
  3. Va-t-il à la campagne cet après-midi? Je crois que oui.
  4. "Soyez le bienvenu!" lui dis-je.
  5. À qui est ce porte-billets bien rempli? À moi.
  6. À quoi faites-vous allusion en parlant ainsi?
  7. Lequel de ces tableaux voulez-vous acheter?
  8. Il n'est pas arrivé à l'heure; aussi suis-je sortie seule.
  9. C'est un mensonge que de dire que je vous ai trompés.
  10. Elle a perdu la bague que sa mère lui avait donnée; c'est dommage.

III. Give (1) the third person plural present tense and (2) third person singular past historic tense of: **craindre, vivre, voir, rire, savoir, mettre, suivre, lire, écrire, naître.**

IV. Replace the nouns underlined by possessive pronouns:
  1. Il a perdu sa balle.
  2. Où est leur maison?
  3. Prête-moi ton stylo!
  4. A-t-il fait ses devoirs?
  5. Nous avons mis nos sandwichs dans le panier.

6. **Voici nos papiers mais il veut voir aussi leurs papiers.**
7. **Voici mon fusil; où est votre fusil?**
8. **J'aime beaucoup mes parents.**
9. **Nous avons donné nos billets à nos amis.**
10. **J'ai trouvé mes gants sur le canapé.**

V. Translate into French:
1. What is a hammer used for?
2. Which apartment did he enter?
3. Has he ever been in prison?
4. His bicycle is broken; that is a pity.
5. He has gone to the stable, hasn't he?
6. It is obvious that he is going to succeed.
7. Which of these bicycles do you want to take?
8. How old are you? I am sixteen.
9. Who saw the postman this morning?
10. What did you find in the well?

VI. Translate into French:

The detective got out of the car and entered the house. He went up the stairs and met the caretaker at the door of the flat. He asked him what had happened. The caretaker was trembling in every limb and it was difficult to understand what he was saying. But our detective was a very patient man: that is why he always succeeded in catching the criminals he was after (**poursuivre**). According to the caretaker M. Duvivier had come home at half past nine and, it appears, had gone to bed about ten o'clock. Half an hour later a shot was heard. The caretaker had gone up at once and had knocked at the door but nobody had opened it. Naturally the caretaker had rung up the police without delay. The detective asked him a few questions then entered the room where the corpse was. The latter was stretched out on the floor. The detective examined all the room carefully in the hope of finding some finger-prints.

VII. Write in the past tense a composition based on the following outline:

Par une nuit obscure un cambrioleur s'introduit dans la maison d'un écrivain — celui-ci est très pauvre — l'écrivain est au lit — il entend quelqu'un qui se remue en bas — il descend et voit le cambrioleur qui est trop étonné pour se sauver — il lui demande ce qu'il cherche — l'homme répond "De l'argent" — l'autre lui dit: "je vous aiderai; moi je n'en trouve pas de jour et vous espérez en trouver la nuit."

(*Answers at the end of the book.*)

LEÇON 26

GRAMMAR

THE VERB AND ITS OBJECT

We are now going to study the differing constructions in French and English followed by verbs which take an object. These lists which follow are not complete but give the most important verbs which you will need.

(i) Some verbs take a preposition in English but not in French:

chercher = *to look for*	**espérer** = *to hope for*
attendre = *to wait for*	**fuir** = *to flee from*
demander = *to ask for*	**payer** = *to pay for*
écouter = *to listen to*	**regarder** = *to look at*

Je cherche mon mouchoir = *I am looking for my handkerchief.*
Il a payé le dîner = *He paid for the dinner.*

(ii) Some verbs take a preposition in French but not in English:

s'apercevoir de = *to perceive*	**manquer de** = *to lack*
s'approcher de = *to approach*	**se servir de** = *to use*
entrer dans = *to enter*	**se méfier de** = *to mistrust*
changer de = *to change* (shirt,	**se souvenir de** = *to remember*
train, opinion, address, etc.)	**sortir de** = *to leave* (= *to come*
jouir de = *to enjoy*	*out of*)

Il entra dans la salle = *He entered the room.*
Elle sortit de la gare = *She left the station.*
Il jouit d'une bonne santé = *He enjoys good health.*

(iii) Some verbs take an indirect object in French, direct in English:

s'attendre à = *to expect*	**plaire à** = *to please*
désobéir à = *to disobey*	**renoncer à** = *to renounce*
dire à = *to tell*	**répondre à** = *to answer*
nuire à = *to harm*	**résister à** = *to resist*
obéir à = *to obey*	**ressembler à** = *to resemble*
ordonner à = *to order*	**succéder à** = *to succeed* (i.e. *to follow*)
pardonner à = *to pardon*	**survivre à** = *to survive*

(Do not confuse **succéder** with **réussir** = *to be successful*.)

Il faut pardonner à ses ennemis = *One must forgive one's enemies.*
Le prince succéda à son père = *The prince succeeded his father.*
Elle lui répondit = *She answered him.*

250

(iv) Many verbs take different prepositions in French, including:

(a) all verbs of *depriving*, *stealing*, etc., which take the dative (à) of the person from whom the thing is stolen, etc.:

acheter quelque chose à quelqu'un = *to buy something from someone*
arracher quelque chose à quelqu'un = *to snatch something from someone*
emprunter quelque chose à quelqu'un = *to borrow something from someone*
ôter quelque chose à quelqu'un = *to take something from someone*
prendre quelque chose à quelqu'un = *to take something from someone*
voler quelque chose à quelqu'un = *to steal something from someone*
cacher quelque chose à quelqu'un = *to hide something from someone*
demander quelque chose à quelqu'un = *to ask someone for something*, or *to ask someone something*

Il lui prit son fusil = *He took his gun from him.*
Il lui vola tout son argent = *He stole all his money from him.*
Elle m'a caché ses larmes = *She hid her tears from me.*

(b) verbs of *taking part in* or *taking interest in* take à:

assister à = *to be present at* **prendre part à** = *to take part in*
jouer à = *to play* (a game) **s'intéresser à** = *to take interest in*
Il assista au concert = *He was present at the concert.*
Elle prit part au travail = *She took part in the work.*
Ils jouaient aux cartes = *They were playing cards.*

(c) many verbs taking **de** which represents various English prepositions:

blâmer de = *to blame for*   **jouer de** = *to play* (musical
dépendre de = *to depend on*   instruments)
se nourrir de = *to live on* **se moquer de** = *to make fun of*
punir de = *to punish for*   **se passer de** = *to do without*
rire de = *to laugh at*   **répondre de** = *to answer for*
vivre de = *to live on*   **triompher de** = *to triumph over*
Cela dépend de vous = *That depends on you.*
Je joue du piano = *I play the piano.*
Il triompha de cette difficulté = *He overcame that difficulty.*

(d) certain verbs (e.g. of *taking*, *reading*, *drinking*) which in English are followed by *out of*, in French by **dans** (= *place out of which*):

J'ai pris la boîte dans un tiroir = *I took the box out of a drawer.*
Elle buvait du café dans un verre = *She was drinking coffee out of a glass.*
Il découpa l'article dans un journal = *He cut the article out of a a paper.*

Note that the same French verb may be followed by different constructions when it is used with different meanings. Learn these constructions:

servir = *to serve*:
  Il lui servit un kilo de beurre = *He served her with a kilo of butter.*
  Elle servait à table = *She was waiting at table.*
servir de = *to serve as*:
  Cela sert d'exemple = *That serves as an example.*
se servir de = *to make use of*:
  Il se sert de son mouchoir = *He uses his handkerchief.*
penser à = *to think of*:
  Je pense à lui = *I am thinking of him.*
penser de = *to have an opinion of*:
  Que penses-tu de cela? = *What do you think of that?*
jouer à = *to play* (a game):
  Il joue au football = *He plays football.*
jouer de = *to play* (an instrument):
  Elle joue du piano = *She plays the piano.*
changer = *to change, exchange, replace*:
  Il changea son argent (le pneu) = *He changed his money (the tyre).*
changer de = *to change* (for something of the same sort):
  Il changea d'avis (de chemise) = *He changed his mind (his shirt).*
  Il changea de train = *He changed (trains).*
manquer de + noun = *to lack*:
  Il manque de courage (d'argent) = *He lacks courage (money).*
manquer de + verb = *to nearly do something*:
  Il a manqué de tomber = *He nearly fell.*
manquer = *to fail*:
  Le coup a manqué = *The plan miscarried.*
manquer = *to run out*:
  Si l'essence manquait. . . . = *If the petrol ran out. . . .*
manquer = *to be insufficient* (with the dative [= **à**] of the person):
  Le temps me manque pour. . . . = *I have not enough time for. . . .*
manquer = *to be lacking* (impersonal verb with **il** as subject):
  Il me manque dix francs = *I am ten francs short.*
manquer à = *to fail in*:
  Il a manqué à son devoir (sa parole) = *He has failed in his duty (his promise).*

It is obvious from the examples already given in this chapter that French and English often use different constructions. Learn these idioms also:

  Je demande de l'argent à mon père = *I ask my father for money.*
  Je lui apprends le désastre = *I tell him of the disaster.*
  Je lui reproche sa conduite = *I reproach him for his conduct.*
  Elle tord le cou à la poule = *She wrings the chicken's neck.*

CONSTRUCTIONS WITH THE INFINITIVE
  (i) The infinitive is used without a linking preposition after these verbs:
   (*a*) **aller, venir** and all verbs of motion — to express purpose;
   (*b*) **aimer, aimer mieux** (= *to prefer*), **préférer, avoir beau** (= *to do something in vain*), **désirer, devoir, espérer, faire, laisser, oser, paraître, sembler, pouvoir, savoir, vouloir**;
   (*c*) verbs of *saying, thinking, believing,* etc., such as — **dire, croire, avouer, déclarer, se rappeler,** etc.;
   (*d*) verbs of *seeing, hearing, feeling,* etc., such as — **voir, regarder, entendre, écouter,** etc.
      Il est allé chercher la bicyclette = *He went to get the bicycle.*
      Il a couru le dire à sa maman = *He ran to tell his mother.*
      Il osa l'attaquer = *He dared to attack him.*
      Il vaut mieux rester = *It is better to remain.*
      Elle a beau crier = *She is shouting in vain.*
      Il déclare l'avoir vu = *He declares that he saw it.*
      Je me rappelle l'avoir fait = *I remember doing it.*
      Je le vois venir = *I see him coming.*
      Elle l'a entendu tomber = *She heard him falling.*
      Voici venir le facteur = *Here is the postman coming* (**voici** = **vois ici**).

  (ii) The infinitive is linked by **à** to these words:
   (*a*) verbs of *beginning* such as — **commencer à, se mettre à, se prendre à**;
   (*b*) verbs of *inviting, compelling,* etc., such as — **inviter à, encourager à, obliger à, forcer à, pousser à, décider à**;
   (*c*) verbs of *taking part* or *interest in,* and of *passing the time in* such as — **s'amuser à, passer son temps (sa vie) à, s'occuper à, travailler à, prendre plaisir à, se devouer à**;
   (*d*) verbs of *learning* and *teaching* such as — **apprendre à, enseigner à**;
   (*e*) various other important verbs including:

aider à = *to help to*	**se décider à** = *to make up one's*
aimer à = *to like to*	**demander à** = *to ask to* [*mind to*
s'accoutumer à = *to get used to*	**se préparer à** = *to prepare to*
s'apprêter à = *to get ready to*	**se résigner à** = *to resign oneself to*
s'attendre à = *to expect to*	**se résoudre à** = *to resolve to*
autoriser à = *to authorise to*	**réussir à** = *to succeed in*
avoir à = *to have to*	**servir à** = *to be useful for doing*
chercher à = *to attempt to*	**tarder à** = *to put off doing*
continuer à = *to continue to*	**venir à** = *to happen to*

Note that **commencer** and **continuer** are often found with **de** not **à** for the sake of euphony if the **à** would otherwise clash with a preceding vowel-sound.

(*f*) certain adjectives such as — **prêt à, le premier à, le seul à, le dernier à, bon à, utile à, agréable à**:

Il commence à pleuvoir = *It is beginning to rain.* (Do not confuse with: **Il commence à pleurer** = *He begins to weep.*)
Je l'ai invité à venir chez moi = *I invited him to come to my house.*
Il passe son temps à rêver = *He spends his time dreaming.*
Elle nous aide à le faire = *She helps us to do it.*
Je demande à entrer = *I ask* (*permission*) *to come in.*
Elle apprend à patiner = *She is learning to skate.*
Il se prépara à sauter = *He prepared to jump.*
Je ne m'attendais pas à tomber = *I was not expecting to fall.*
Il cherche à retrouver son ami = *He is trying to find his friend again.*
Il réussit à le faire = *He succeeded in doing it.*
Il vint à dire. . . . = *He happened to say. . . .*
Nous sommes prêts à partir = *We are ready to go.*
Charles fut le seul à venir = *Charles was the only one to come.*

Note the use of **à** after nouns to show purpose in such phrases as: **une maison à louer** = *a house to let*, **un film à voir** = *a film to see.*

(iii) The infinitive is linked by **de** to these words:
    (*a*) verbs of *finishing* such as — **cesser de, finir de, achever de, s'arrêter de**;
    (*b*) verbs of *trying* such as — **essayer de, tâcher de** (but note **chercher à**);
    (*c*) verbs of *deciding* (when intransitive and not reflexive) such as — **décider de, résoudre de**;
    (*d*) verbs of *requesting* and *ordering*:

        demander à quelqu'un de faire quelque chose = *to ask someone to do something*
        ordonner à quelqu'un de faire quelque chose = *to order someone to do something*
        dire à quelqu'un de faire quelque chose = *to tell someone to do something*
        défendre à quelqu'un de faire quelque chose = *to forbid someone to do something*
    but:
        prier quelqu'un de faire quelque chose = *to beg someone to do something*

    (*e*) various other important verbs including:

empêcher de = *to prevent from*
menacer de = *to threaten to*
promettre de = *to promise to*
refuser de = *to refuse to*
remercier de = *to thank for*
risquer de = *to run the risk of*
se vanter de = *to undertake to*
il s'agit de = *it is a question of*

    (*f*) impersonal expressions containing an adjective:
        Il est facile de le comprendre = *It is easy to understand it.*
        Il est agréable de le voir = *It is pleasant to see it.*

Do not confuse with: [*understand.*

    C'est facile à comprendre = *It* (e.g. *the problem*) *is easy to*
    C'est agréable à voir = *It* (e.g. *some particular sight*) *is pleasant*

(*g*) in this emphatic construction: [*to see.*

    C'est une erreur que de croire cela = *It is an error to believe that.*

(*h*) in general to link nouns with infinitives:

    l'envie de parler = *the desire to speak*
    dans le but de frauder = *with intent to defraud*
    défense de fumer = *smoking forbidden*
    la joie de vivre = *the joy of living*

(iv) The infinitive is linked by **par** to verbs of *beginning* and *finishing* when they mean *to begin by, to finish by*:

    Il commença par se laver = *He began by washing himself.*
    Elle finit par s'endormir = *She ended up by falling asleep.*

(v) The infinitive is preceded by **pour** in these cases:

    (*a*) to denote purpose:

        Il le fait pour plaire à ses amis = *He does it to please his friends.*
        Il travaille pour gagner de l'argent = *He works in order to earn*

    (*b*) after **assez** and **trop**:   [*money.*

        Je n'ai pas assez d'argent pour aller en Allemagne = *I haven't*
                                  enough money to go to Germany.
        Il ne courait pas assez vite pour l'attraper = *He was not running*
                                  quickly enough to catch it.
        Il est trop lâche pour me le dire = *He is too cowardly to tell me.*

    (*c*) when the infinitive is a past infinitive, to show the reason:

        On le fusilla pour avoir trahi ses camarades = *He was shot for*
                                 having betrayed his comrades.

IRREGULAR VERBS

luire [lɥiːr] = *to shine*

past part.: **lui**, past hist.: **je luisis, luis**

je luis	**nous luisons**
tu luis	**vous luisez**
il luit	**ils luisent**

(Like **luire**: **reluire** = *to glisten*.)

nuire [nɥiːr] = *to harm*

past part.: **nui**, past hist.: **je nuisis**

je nuis	**nous nuisons**
tu nuis	**vous nuisez**
il nuit	**ils nuisent**

haïr [aiːr] = *to hate*

past part.: **haï**, past hist.: rarely used

je hais	**nous haïssons**
tu hais	**vous haïssez**
il hait	**ils haïssent**

croître [krwaːtr] = *to grow*

past part.: **crû**, past hist.: **je crûs**

je croîs	**nous croissons**
tu croîs	**vous croissez**
il croît	**ils croissent**

(Like **croître**: **accroître** = *to increase*. Do not confuse **croître** with **croire**.)

255

VOCABULARY

dangereux, -euse [dɑ̃ʒrø, -øːz]	*dangerous*
la naissance [nɛsɑ̃ːs]	*birth*
couramment [kyramɑ̃]	*fluently*
survenir (like **venir**) [syrvəniːr]	*to occur*
tarder à [tarde a]	*to be a long time in*
calmement [kalməmɑ̃]	*calmly*
pas mal de [pɑ mal də]	*quite a few*
une aventure [avɑ̃tyːr]	*adventure*
le navire [naviːr]	*ship*
s'engager dans [sɑ̃gaʒe dɑ̃]	*to join*
une époque [epɔk]	*time, period*
essentiel, -ielle [ɛsɑ̃sjɛl]	*important, essential*
polir [pɔliːr]	*to polish*
le bouton [butɔ̃]	*button*
frotter [frɔte]	*to rub*
un̮ uniforme [ynifɔrm]	*uniform*
reluire [rəlɥiːr]	*to shine* (intrans.)
la courroie [kurwa]	*strap*
la revue [rəvy]	*inspection* (military)
immobile [imɔbil]	*motionless*
le régiment [reʒimɑ̃]	*regiment*
éplucher [eplyʃe]	*to peel*
la vaisselle [vɛsɛl]	*dishes*
démontrer [demɔ̃tre]	*to prove*
clairement [klɛrmɑ̃]	*clearly*
commun(e) [kɔmœ̃]	*common*
s'offrir à [sɔfriːr a]	*to offer to*
lutter [lyte]	*to struggle*
secrètement [səkrɛtmɑ̃]	*secretly*
un̮ oppresseur [ɔprɛsœːr]	*oppressor*
adoptif, -ive [adɔptif, -iːv]	*adopted*
considérer [kɔ̃sidere]	*to consider*
l'Écosse (f.) [ekɔs]	*Scotland*
le château [ʃɑto]	*castle*
le rôle [roːl]	*role, part*
à pied [a pje]	*on foot*
nager [naʒe]	*to swim*
l'eau (f.) [o]	*water*
glacial(e) [glasjal]	*icy*
le plastic [plastik]	*plastic explosive*
le rail [raːj]	*rail*

le bouton

un uniforme

la courroie

la revue

la vaisselle

le château

la machine [maʃin]	*piece of machinery*	
dépendre de [depɑ̃:dr də]	*to rely on*	
sauter en parachute [sote ɑ̃ paraʃyt]	*to jump by parachute*	
plaire à [plɛ:r a]	*to please*	
expérimenté(e) [ɛksperimɑ̃te]	*experienced*	
un ordre [ɔrdr]	*order*	
le colonel [kɔlɔnɛl]	*colonel*	**l'eau** (f.)
renvoyer [rɑ̃vwaje]	*to send back*	
confier [kɔ̃fje]	*to entrust*	
organiser [ɔrganize]	*to organise*	
le groupe [grup]	*group*	
le résistant [rezistɑ̃]	*member of the Resistance*	**le rail**
enseigner [ɑ̃sɛɲe]	*to teach*	
la méthode [metɔd]	*method*	
le sabotage [sabɔta:ʒ]	*sabotage*	
efficace [efikas]	*effective*	
entreprendre [ɑ̃trəprɑ̃:dr]	*to undertake*	
nuire à [nɥi:r a]	*to harm*	**la machine**
le vêtement [vɛtmɑ̃]	*garment*	
le prisonnier [prizɔnje]	*prisoner*	
bonne chance! [bɔn ʃɑ̃:s]	*good luck!*	
le pilote [pilɔt]	*pilot*	
chaleureusement [ʃalœrø:zmɑ̃]	*warmly*	
décoller [dekɔle]	*to take off* (aeroplane)	
survoler [syrvɔle]	*to fly over*	**le colonel**
la Manche [mɑ̃:ʃ]	*English Channel*	
tranquillement [trɑ̃kilmɑ̃]	*peacefully*	
le ronronnement [rɔ̃rɔnmɑ̃]	*purring, humming*	
une explosion [ɛksplozjɔ̃]	*explosion*	
assourdissant(e) [asurdisɑ̃, -ɑ̃t]	*deafening*	
la défense [defɑ̃:s]	*defence*	
descendre [dɛsɑ̃:dr]	*to bring down* (aeroplane)	
se tirer de [sə tire də]	*to get out of*	**le vêtement**
s'apprêter à [saprɛte a]	*to prepare to*	
la lampe [lɑ̃:p]	*lamp*	
doucement [dusmɑ̃]	*gently*	
se balancer [sə balɑ̃se]	*to sway*	
rudement [rydmɑ̃]	*roughly*	
faire mal à [fɛ:r mal a]	*to hurt* (trans.)	
se débarrasser de [sə debarase də]	*to get rid of*	
chuchoter [ʃyʃɔte]	*to whisper*	**le prisonnier**

UNE MISSION DANGEREUSE

John était Anglais de naissance mais il avait passé la plus grande partie de sa vie en France — à Bordeaux où son père était marchand de charbon. Naturellement il parlait couramment le français et tous ceux qui ne connaissaient pas sa famille le prenaient pour un Français. Puis en 1940 survint l'invasion allemande et la situation ne tarda pas à devenir critique. John qui ne manquait pas de courage n'avait pas envie de se laisser prendre par les Allemands. Il ne voulait pas rester à attendre calmement le désastre et il décida de partir. Après pas mal d'aventures il s'embarqua sur un navire marchand et réussit enfin à gagner l'Angleterre.

John s'engagea dans l'armée britannique. À cette époque l'Angleterre s'attendait à une invasion allemande mais dans l'armée John reçut l'impression que l'essentiel pour un bon soldat était de bien polir ses boutons et de bien frotter ses chaussures. Quelquefois le soir il passait des heures à nettoyer son uniforme et à faire reluire ses courroies tandis qu'à la revue du lendemain il devait rester immobile sous la pluie. Au régiment on appelait cela "discipline". John s'ennuyait; il n'était pas venu en Angleterre, se disait-il, pour passer son temps à éplucher des pommes de terre, à laver la vaisselle ni pour travailler au mess des officiers. D'une manière ou d'une autre il put attirer l'attention des autorités militaires sur sa situation malheureuse — ce qui démontre clairement qu'il était un homme peu commun. Il s'offrit à retourner en France lutter secrètement contre les oppresseurs de son pays adoptif.

On considéra longuement son offre et on finit par l'accepter. On l'envoya d'abord en Écosse — dans un château perdu au milieu de la nature. Là, il devait se préparer pour son rôle futur. Il s'exerça à faire de longues promenades à pied, à nager dans l'eau glaciale d'un lac, à grimper sur des arbres. Il apprit aussi à se servir du "plastic" pour détruire les locomotives, les rails, les machines d'usine. On lui apprit tout ce que doit savoir le soldat qui plus tard ne dépendra que de lui-même.

Au bout de quelques semaines John quitta l'Écosse pour se rendre à un aérodrome qui se trouvait au nord de l'Angleterre. Il y apprit à sauter en parachute. D'abord cela ne lui plut guère mais il finit par devenir un parachutiste expérimenté.

Enfin il revint à Londres où il continua de se préparer pour sa tâche. Puis un jour il reçut l'ordre de se présenter à un certain bureau où il eut une entrevue avec un colonel. Celui-ci lui apprit qu'on allait bientôt le renvoyer en France. On lui confiait la mission d'organiser un groupe de résistants et de leur enseigner les méthodes de sabotage les plus efficaces. Il s'agissait, lui dit le colonel, d'une mission très dangereuse. Qu'en pensait-il? John, qui se souvenait de sa famille et de ses amis qui étaient restés là-bas, répondit qu'il était prêt à tout entreprendre pour nuire à l'ennemi. C'était pour cela même qu'il était venu en Angleterre.

Quelques jours plus tard on le pria de se présenter à un certain établissement où on lui fournirait des vêtements français. Si on le faisait prisonnier en France, un habit anglais l'aurait trahi tout de suite. Il fallait penser à tout. On lui donna aussi des cigarettes et des allumettes françaises.

Vint enfin le soir où l'on conduisit John à un aérodrome. Un avion l'attendait sur la piste. L'officier qui l'accompagnait lui souhaita bonne chance et le pilote de l'avion le salua chaleureusement mais ne lui posa pas de questions. L'avion décolla peu de temps après et en un rien de temps on survolait la Manche. John était tranquillement assis à écouter le ronronnement des moteurs et à penser à tout ce qu'il allait faire en France. Tout à coup il y eut une explosion assourdissante. C'était la DCA (défense contre avions). "S'ils nous descendent maintenant . . ." pensait John. Mais le pilote réussit à se tirer d'affaire et vingt minutes plus tard on communiqua à John qu'on s'approchait du point de parachutage et on lui dit de s'apprêter à sauter. Il faut avouer que John avait peur. Mais quand il vit s'allumer la lampe verte il sauta et descendait doucement en se balançant au bout de son parachute. Il entendait l'avion s'éloigner de plus en plus et il se sentait seul. Que la nuit était tranquille! Tout d'un coup il heurta rudement le sol et il se fit mal à la jambe gauche. Mais il n'eut pas le temps d'y penser. Il se débarrassait de son parachute lorsqu'il entendit quelqu'un qui chuchotait dans l'obscurité. "Qui est-ce?" disait la voix. "C'est Marcel," répondit John. "Bon," fit l'autre, "nous vous attendons."

(*See notes on the next page. Translation at the end of the book.*)

NOTES ON THE TEXT

De naissance = *by birth*; **perdu au milieu de la nature** = *lost in the wilds*; **en un rien de temps** = *in no time*; **fit l'autre** = *said the other* (note use of **faire**).

EXERCISES

I. Answer in French:

1. **Est-ce que John était lâche? Que fit-il en Écosse?**
2. **Quand John était soldat, qu'est-ce qu'il devait faire le soir?**
3. **Que veut dire "expérimenté"? Qu'est-ce que c'est que la Manche?**
4. **Quand est-ce que John sauta de l'avion qui le transportait en France?**
5. **Qu'est-ce qu'il entendit quand il se débarrassait de son parachute?**

II. Translate into English:

1. **Il faudra changer de train à Bordeaux.**
2. **Savez-vous jouer de la flûte?**
3. **La semaine dernière on m'a volé ma bicyclette.**
4. **Il était furieux mais il dut obéir aux ordres du colonel.**
5. **Il faut toujours résister à la tentation.**
6. **Pardonnez à vos ennemis; vous ne le regretterez jamais.**
7. **Il se servait d'une scie énorme pour couper l'arbre.**
8. **À quoi pensez-vous à présent? Aux vacances.**
9. **Un manche à balai lui servait de béquille.**
10. **Je n'ose pas accuser le voleur: il pourrait me faire du mal.**
11. **Il vaut mieux accepter ce qu'il offre.**
12. **Je le regardais qui descendait la pente.**
13. **Aidez-moi à réparer le moteur.**
14. **Il s'attendait à voir arriver la voiture.**
15. **Elle lui demanda de faire une commission en ville.**

III. Give (1) first person plural present; (2) third person plural conditional; (3) third person feminine singular perfect; (4) second person plural past historic tenses of: **servir, connaître, recevoir, venir, pouvoir, plaire, apprendre, faire, avoir, lire.**

IV. (i) Give the feminine of these adjectives: **doux, premier, bref, vieux, merveilleux, gros, muet, bon, blanc, inquiet, joyeux, éternel, jaune, fatigué, long, neuf, dernier, vif, fou, nouveau.**

(ii) Give the plural of these nouns: **le bras, le château, le chou, le trou, la croix, l'ouvrier, le nez, le soldat, l'ours, le genou.**

V. Translate into French:

1. Ask your friend for some money; we have none.
2. Last week she broke her arm when she was in the country.
3. He took the paper out of his wallet and gave it to me.
4. He was using a hammer to break the stone.
5. The animal was drinking out of a clear stream.
6. She paid for the ticket and put it on the mantelpiece.
7. "You have no common-sense," he said. "You ought to keep quiet."
8. He disobeyed his father and went to swim in the lake.
9. Forgive your enemies! Do good to them that hate you!
10. It is beginning to rain. It is not necessary to water the lawn.
11. Go upstairs and change your shirt; that one is dirty.
12. He spends his time playing chess.
13. I swear to you that I shall climb to the top of that mountain.
14. A policeman happened to pass: we were in danger of being discovered.
15. It is a question of the country's defence. We cannot refuse to fight.

VI. Translate into French:

He joined the army. Every day he had to polish his buttons and rub up his boots. He used to spend hours cleaning his uniform and his rifle. It is not necessary to say that after some time he got bored with such a life. If you had had to spend every evening peeling potatoes and washing dishes, what would you have said? John decided to return to France to struggle against the oppressors of his country. But how was he to do that? One cannot leave the army as one leaves an ordinary job. He thought about it for a long time. Then he went to get a pen, ink and paper in order to write a letter to his commanding officer. I forgot to tell you that John spoke French fluently as he had lived twenty years in France. After all, his mother was French. When the officer received the letter he sent for John and told him that he did not understand why he was so unhappy. He asked him why he wished to return to France and what he wanted to do there.

VII. Write a composition in the past tense based on this outline:

Un professeur de langues vivantes voyage en autobus pendant la guerre — pour s'amuser en route il lit un roman allemand — le voyageur assis derrière lui remarque cela — descend à l'arrêt suivant et va à la police — au terminus on arrête le professeur qu'on soupçonne d'être un espion — il réussit enfin à convaincre la police qu'il n'est pas Allemand.

(Answers at the end of the book.)

LEÇON 27

GRAMMAR

THE SUBJUNCTIVE MOOD

We have already studied the indicative mood (which states a fact) and the imperative mood (which expresses a command). Various subjunctive forms such as *I were*, *it be*, sometimes occur in English, but they are rare and sound stilted. In French there are still cases where subjunctives must be used.

The French subjunctive can be translated as *may* or *might* but it often becomes indicative in English. But it is always obvious how to translate it, even when the English grammatical construction is different.

The present subjunctive tense of regular verbs is formed by adding the present subjunctive endings -e, -es, -e, -ions, -iez, -ent to the stem of the third person plural present indicative, e.g. **ils donnent**, stem = **donn-**:

donner = *to give*	finir = *to finish*	vendre = *to sell*
que je donne = *that I may*	que je finisse	que je vende
que tu donnes [*give*, etc.	que tu finisses	que tu vendes
qu'il donne	qu'il finisse	qu'il vende
que nous donnions	que nous finissions	que nous vendions
que vous donniez	que vous finissiez	que vous vendiez
qu'ils donnent	qu'ils finissent	qu'ils vendent

Learn carefully these irregular subjunctives in which the stem changes in the first and second persons plural:

être = *to be*	avoir = *to have*	aller = *to go*
que je sois	que j'aie	que j'aille
que tu sois	que tu aies	que tu ailles
qu'il soit	qu'il ait	qu'il aille
que nous soyons	que nous ayons	que nous allions
que vous soyez	que vous ayez	que vous alliez
qu'ils soient	qu'ils aient	qu'ils aillent

valoir = *to be worth*		vouloir = *to wish*	
que je vaille	que nous valions	que je veuille	que nous voulions
que tu vailles	que vous valiez	que tu veuilles	que vous vouliez
qu'il vaille	qu'ils vaillent	qu'il veuille	qu'ils veuillent

262

and these in which the stem remains the same in the plural: **faire, que je fasse**; **pouvoir, que je puisse**; **savoir, que je sache**. Note also: **falloir, qu'il faille**; **pleuvoir, qu'il pleuve**, which occur only impersonally.

All other irregular verbs form their present subjunctives according to the general rule, except that the first and second persons plural have exactly the same form as they do in the imperfect indicative tense, e.g.: **venir: que je vienne**, etc., but note: **nous venions, vous veniez**.

The imperfect subjunctive is formed by taking the second person singular of the past historic, doubling the -s and adding -e for the first person, and other endings for the subsequent persons. These endings are for -er verbs: **-asse, -asses, -ât, -assions, -assiez, -assent**; for -ir and -re verbs: **-isse, -isses, -ît, -issions, -issiez, -issent**; all irregular verbs follow the same rule but sometimes, of course, the endings are: **-usse, -usses, -ût, -ussions, -ussiez, -ussent**:

donner	finir	vendre
que je donnasse	que je finisse	que je vendisse
que tu donnasses	que tu finisses	que tu vendisses
qu'il donnât	qu'il finît	qu'il vendît
que nous donnassions	que nous finissions	que nous vendissions
que vous donnassiez	que vous finissiez	que vous vendissiez
qu'ils donnassent	qu'ils finissent	qu'ils vendissent

boire	venir	voir
que je busse	que je vinsse	que je visse
que tu busses	que tu vinsses	que tu visses
qu'il bût	qu'il vînt	qu'il vît
que nous bussions	que nous vinssions	que nous vissions
que vous bussiez	que vous vinssiez	que vous vissiez
qu'ils bussent	qu'ils vinssent	qu'ils vissent

Two compound past tenses of the subjunctive exist, but they are not often used. The perfect subjunctive is formed with the present subjunctive of **avoir** or **être** and the past participle, e.g.: **que j'aie donné**, etc., **que j'aie fini**, etc., **que j'aie vendu**, etc., **que je sois venu**, etc., **que je me sois levé**, etc.

The pluperfect subjunctive is formed with the imperfect subjunctive of **avoir** or **être** and the past participle, e.g.: **que j'eusse donné**, etc., **que j'eusse fini**, etc., **que j'eusse vendu**, etc., **que je fusse venu**, etc., **que je me fusse levé**, etc.

USES OF THE SUBJUNCTIVE

The subjunctive is used in main clauses in these two ways only:

(i) as an imperative in the third person with **que**:

    Qu'il le fasse tout de suite = *Let him do it at once.*

(ii) to express a wish (without **que**); these are usually set expressions:

Vive le roi! = *Long live the king!*
À Dieu ne plaise que . . . = *God forbid that . . .*
Plût‿au ciel que . . . = *Would to Heaven that . . .*

The subjunctive is used more commonly in noun clauses (i.e. when the whole clause is the object of another verb), in these ways:

(i) after verbs of wishing, requesting, commanding, forbidding, e.g. **vouloir, désirer, demander, dire, ordonner, défendre**, etc.:

Je veux qu'il le fasse = *I want him to do it* (lit. *wish that he do it*).
Il demande qu'on le fasse venir = *He asks that he be sent for.*
Il ordonna qu'on prît la ville = *He ordered the town to be taken* (lit. *that one should take the town*).
Il défendit qu'on‿entrât dans la cave = *He forbade anybody to enter the cellar.*

(ii) after verbs expressing emotion (joy, sorrow, anger, regret, fear, approval, or disapproval), e.g. **être content, regretter, être fâché, craindre**, etc.:

Je suis content qu'il n'ait pas perdu son‿argent = *I am pleased that he has not lost his money.*
Je regrette que vous soyez‿en retard = *I am sorry that you are late.*
J'ai peur qu'il ne perde son‿argent = *I am afraid that he will lose his money.*
J'approuve qu'il se présente comme candidat = *I approve of his standing as a candidate.*

Note that verbs of fearing when used affirmatively require a redundant **ne** in French in the following dependent clause, e.g.:

Je crains qu'il ne vienne = *I am afraid that he will come.*
but: **Je ne crains pas qu'il vienne** = *I am not afraid that he will come.*

(iii) after verbs of trying, striving, preventing, e.g. **tâcher, avoir soin, éviter, empêcher, veiller, prendre garde**, etc.:

Tâchez que votre père vienne = *Try to get your father to come.*
Évitez qu'il ne vous voie = *Avoid his seeing you.*
Prenez garde qu'il ne vous voie = *Take care lest he see you.*
Veillez à ce que le travail se fasse = *See to it that the work is done.*

Note that **éviter** and **prendre garde** also need a redundant **ne** in the dependent clause, which can usually be translated as *lest*.

(iv) after verbs of doubting and denying (this includes verbs of saying and thinking used negatively or in questions):

Je doute qu'il réussisse = *I doubt whether he will succeed.*
Il nie que vous‿ayez raison = *He denies that you are right.*
Croyez-vous qu'il vienne? = *Do you think he will come?*

(v) after impersonal verbs (except those expressing certainty or probability), e.g. **il faut que, il vaut mieux que, il importe que, il est bon que, c'est dommage que, il semble que, il est possible que, il se peut que**:

> **Il faut qu'on le fasse** = *One must do it.*   [*go there.*
> **Il vaut mieux que vous n'y alliez pas** = *It is better that you should not*
> **C'est dommage qu'il soit si vieux** = *It is a pity he is so old.*
> **Il se peut qu'ils ne reviennent pas** = *It is possible that they will not*
> **Il semble qu'il ait raison** = *It appears that he is right.*   [*come back.*
> but: **Il me semble qu'il a raison** = *It seems to me that he is right.*

> Note also that such verbs as **il est évident que, il est vrai que, il est probable que, il paraît que** are followed by the indicative:
> **Il paraît qu'elle est très jeune** = *It appears that she is very young.*
> **Il est probable qu'il viendra** = *It is probable that he will come.*

The subjunctive is also used in relative adjectival clauses:

(i) when the clause qualifies a superlative (**premier, dernier, seul** and **unique** are regarded as superlatives for this purpose):
> **C'est l'homme le plus paresseux que je connaisse** = *He is the laziest man I know.*
> **Voilà le premier sous-marin que j'aie vu** = *That is the first submarine that I have seen.*
> (but the indicative follows **la première fois que, la dernière fois que**).

(ii) when the antecedent is negative:
> **Il n'y a personne qui sache faire cela** = *There is nobody who knows how*
> **Il ne fait rien qui vaille** = *He does nothing of any value.*   [*to do that.*
> **Il n'y en a pas un qui soit rouge** = *There is not one which is red.*

(iii) when the antecedent is indefinite (i.e. indefinite article with the antecedent can be replaced by *any at all* without altering the sense):
> **Montrez-moi un chemin qui conduise à la rivière** = *Show me a path* (i.e. *any path at all*) *which leads to the river.*
> but: **Montrez-moi le chemin qui conduit à la rivière** (i.e. *a definite path*).

SUBJUNCTIVE AFTER CERTAIN CONJUNCTIONS

The subjunctive is used after certain conjunctions including:

quoique = *although*	**de peur que . . . ne** = *for fear that*
bien que = *although*	**de crainte que . . . ne** = *for fear that*
pour que = *in order that*	**à moins que . . . ne** = *unless*
afin que = *in order that*	**pourvu que** = *provided that*
avant que . . . (ne) = *before*	**sans que** = *without*

jusqu'à ce que = *until* **supposé que** = *supposing that*

en attendant que = *until*

de sorte que, de façon que, de manière que which all = *so that* (but only when this expresses purpose, not when it expresses result):

Quoiqu'il soit riche, il est très avare = *Although he is rich he is very miserly.*

Pour que vous arriviez à temps il faut partir tout de suite = *In order that you may arrive in time it is necessary to leave at once.*

Il faut le faire avant qu'il (ne) vienne = *It must be done before he comes.*

Restez ici jusqu'à ce que je revienne = *Remain here until I return.*

Faites votre devoir de façon que le maître en soit content = *Do your exercise in such a way that the master will be pleased with it.*

but: **Il se conduisait bien de sorte que ses parents en étaient très contents** = *He was behaving well so that* (as a result) *his parents were very pleased.*

The subjunctive is also used after **que**, when **que** replaces a second **si** to avoid repetition (**que** is often used to avoid repeating a conjunction):

Si vous faites cela et que votre père l'apprenne . . . = *If you do that and your father hears about it. . . .*

Note these further examples of the subjunctive:

Quoi que vous fassiez . . . = *Whatever you do . . .*

Qui que tu sois . . . = *Whoever you may be . . .*

Quelques efforts que vous fassiez . . . = *Whatever efforts you make . . .*

Quelle que soit votre intention . . . = *Whatever your intention may be . . .*

Si fatigué que vous soyez . . . = *However tired you are . . .*

Quoi qu'il en soit . . . = *However that may be . . .*

SEQUENCE OF TENSES

After a primary (i.e. present or future) tense, the present subjunctive is used in the dependent clause:

Il faut (faudra) qu'il vienne = *It is (will be) necessary for him to come.*

After a historic (i.e. past or conditional) tense, the imperfect subjunctive is used in the dependent clause:

Il fallait qu'il vînt = *It was necessary that he should come.*

Je n'aimerais pas qu'il sortît = *I should not like him to leave.*

A perfect tense can be either primary or historic according to its meaning, and can therefore be followed by a present or past subjunctive, e.g. **Il a défendu** = *He has forbidden* is primary, **Il a défendu** = *He forbade* is historic.

In modern French past subjunctives (especially forms in **-assions, -assiez, -assent**) are avoided and replaced by the present subjunctive:

Il fallait que nous parlions = *It was necessary for us to speak.*

VOCABULARY

affaiblir [afɛbliːr]	*to weaken*	
le réseau [rezo]	*network, system*	
le pont [pɔ̃]	*bridge*	
subir [sybiːr]	*to undergo, suffer*	
les dégâts (m.) [degɑ]	*damage*	
refaire [rəfɛːr]	*to repair*	
l'ampleur (f.) [ɑ̃plœːr]	*fullness, scope*	
endommager [ɑ̃dɔmaʒe]	*to damage*	**le réseau**
la circulation [sirkylasjɔ̃]	*traffic*	
le chômage [ʃomaːʒ]	*unemployment*	
souligner [suliɲe]	*to underline, stress*	
davantage [davɑ̃taːʒ]	*more*	
marquant(e) [markɑ̃, -ɑ̃ːt]	*prominent*	
un‿accroissement [akrwasmɑ̃]	*increase*	
la natalité [natalite]	*birth-rate*	
se dépeupler [sə depœple]	*to become depopulated*	
la puissance [pɥisɑ̃ːs]	*power*	**le pont**
le chiffre [ʃifr]	*figure, number*	
un‿ouvrier [uvrie]	*worker*	
divers(e) [divɛːr(s)]	*various*	
faible [fɛbl]	*weak*	
ailleurs [ajœːr]	*elsewhere*	
exprès [ɛksprɛ]	*on purpose*	
occidental(e) [ɔksidɑ̃tal]	*Western*	
le montant [mɔ̃tɑ̃]	*amount*	
adhérer à [adere a]	*to join*	**un‿ouvrier**
	(party, scheme, etc.)	

la vieillesse [vjɛjɛs]	*old age*	
le salarié [salarje]	*wage-earner*	
convenir de [kɔ̃vniːr də]	*to agree to*	
le siège [sjɛːʒ]	*headquarters*	
la souveraineté [suvrɛnte]	*sovereignty*	
le plan [plɑ̃]	*plane, level*	
riant(e) [rjɑ̃, -ɑ̃t]	*pleasant, rosy*	
un‿événement [evɛnmɑ̃]	*event*	
le pouvoir [puvwaːr]	*power*	**la vieillesse**
s'opposer à [sɔpozea]	*to be opposed to*	
le rapprochement [raprɔʃmɑ̃]	*a coming together, reconciliation*	
susciter [sysite]	*to stir up*	
désigner [deziɲe]	*to point out*	
parmi [parmi]	*among*	

267

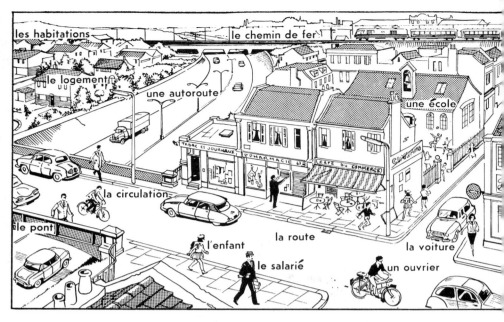

les habitations — le chemin de fer — le logement — une autoroute — une école — la circulation — le pont — l'enfant — la route — la voiture — le salarié — un ouvrier

LA FRANCE AUJOURD'HUI

À la fin de la guerre la France se trouva naturellement dans une situation économique très affaiblie. Une grande partie du pays avait été dévastée et plus d'un million et demi d'habitations avaient été détruites. Le réseau du chemin de fer, les ponts et les routes avaient subi des dégâts considérables. Tout était à refaire. Si l'on ajoute à cela le pillage systématique du pays organisé par l'ennemi on se rendra compte de l'ampleur de la tâche qui se présentait au gouvernement français. Il est vrai que l'aide américaine permit à la France de commencer cet immense travail de reconstruction.

Aujourd'hui, par contre, la France semble fermement engagée sur la voie de la prospérité. Sur une population totale de 45 millions on compte une population active de 20 millions. On a réparé et amélioré les ponts et les routes qui avaient été endommagés pendant la guerre. De plus, on est en train de construire des autoroutes dont cent kilomètres sont à présent ouverts à la circulation. Quant à la construction, on achève plus de 300.000 nouveaux logements par an. La production industrielle et le commerce extérieur augmentent d'année en année et en conséquence le revenu national va croissant à raison de 4,5% par an. Si bien que le chômage n'existe presque pas. Depuis 1958 on lutte contre l'inflation et on a crée "le franc lourd" — autrement dit "le nouveau franc." Selon les calculs des statisticiens il semble qu'une personne sur neuf possède une voiture. On souligne aussi que les achats à crédit vont en augmentant et que les Français voyagent davantage à l'étranger. Il est possible qu'ils commencent à perdre leur esprit de clocher.

Le trait le plus marquant qu'on puisse signaler dans la vie sociale française d'après-guerre, c'est l'accroissement continu de la natalité. Entre les deux guerres on craignait fort que la France n'arrivât à se dépeupler sérieusement et que par la suite elle ne devînt une puissance de troisième ordre. Mais ces derniers temps le chiffre annuel des naissances est de 800.000. Cela va poser naturellement de sérieux problèmes au point de vue du logement et des écoles.

Examinons un moment la question du travail. 25% des ouvriers sont membres des divers syndicats de travail — proportion beaucoup plus faible qu'en Grande-Bretagne. Cela n'étonne pas qu'il y ait en France des troubles industriels comme partout ailleurs dans le monde libre. Mais il est à regretter que certaines organisations politiques qui provoquent exprès des agitations ouvrières soient plus fortes en France qu'en aucun autre pays occidental.

Toute personne qui travaille — quel que soit le montant de son salaire — doit adhérer à la Sécurité sociale qui couvre des risques (pour parler le jargon administratif) tels que la maladie, les accidents du travail et la vieillesse. En outre, tout salarié qui a au moins deux enfants reçoit une allocation familiale. Il semble qu'on soit en train d'établir en France l'État-Providence.

La France est un membre important de la Communauté européenne (plus connue sous le nom de Marché commun). Les six pays qui constituent le Marché commun — France, Allemagne occidentale, Italie, Belgique, Hollande et Luxembourg — signèrent le traité de Rome en 1957. Ils convinrent de travailler en vue de l'abolition totale des tarifs douaniers. On comprendra l'importance d'une telle union en se rappelant que le Marché commun groupe une population de 170 millions. Le siège du Marché commun se trouve à Bruxelles. Certains craignent que cette union n'ait des conséquences politiques incompatibles avec la souveraineté nationale.

Sur le plan économique il y a donc lieu de croire que tout va bien. Mais dans le domaine politique l'avenir est moins riant. On ne trouverait personne qui osât faire des prédictions au sujet d'événements possibles. Le Maroc et la Tunisie avaient obtenu leur indépendance avant que le général de Gaulle ne vînt au pouvoir. À la suite d'une révolte qui dura plus de huit ans, l'Algérie fut déclarée indépendante en juillet 1962. Les Français avaient dû y maintenir une armée de 500.000 hommes et ils avaient subi annuellement plus de 2.000 pertes. En avril 1961 certains généraux qui se trouvaient en Algérie se soulevèrent contre l'autorité du gouvernement central mais leur rébellion échoua misérablement. On voit bien que les problèmes dont le général de Gaulle devait s'occuper étaient assez sérieux.

En 1963 le Général s'opposa à l'entrée de la Grande-Bretagne dans le Marché Commun et préféra chercher un rapprochement avec l'Allemagne; il continuait de susciter des controverses dans son propre pays et à l'étranger. En tout cas, il semblait assez difficile, à ce moment-là, de désigner parmi les politiciens français un homme qui pût le remplacer plus tard à la tête du pays.

(*See notes on the next page. Translation at the end of the book.*)

NOTES ON THE TEXT

L'aide (f.) = *aid, assistance* (**l'aide** (m.) = *assistant*); **par contre** = *on the other hand*; **être engagé sur la voie de** = *to be well on the road to*; **une autoroute** = *motorway*; **va croissant** = *continues to grow*, literally *goes* [*on*] *growing* (distinguish **croître** = *to grow*, from **croire** = *to believe*); **à raison de** = *at the rate of*; **si bien que** = *and so*; **le franc lourd** — the *"heavy"* or *"new"* *franc* is worth a hundred times as much as the old franc; **les achats à crédit** = *hire-purchase*; **un esprit de clocher** = *parochial outlook* (**le clocher** = *church tower, steeple*); **par la suite** = *in the end*; **une puissance** = *power* in the sense of a powerful country, strength, or a power in mathematics, e.g. **les puissances européennes** = *the European powers*, **un poste de haute puissance** = *a high powered* (radio) *set*, x **à la puissance 4** = x^4: **le pouvoir** = *power* in the sense of power to do something, influence, or the authority conferred on someone, e.g. **Ce n'est pas en mon pouvoir** = *It is not in my power*. **Il a pris le pouvoir** = *He assumed power*. **Elle a un pouvoir absolu sur lui** = *She has complete sway over him*; **le syndicat de travail** = *trade union*; **quel(le) que soit** = *whatever, whichever* (note the plural forms **quels, quelles que soient**); **la Sécurité sociale** = *social insurance*, i.e. National Insurance; **en outre** = *moreover*; **une allocation familiale** = *family allowance*; **l'État-Providence** = *Welfare State*; **en vue de** = *with a view to*; **à la suite de** = *following, after*; **son propre pays** = *his own country*, note that **propre**, when it follows the noun it qualifies, = *clean*.

EXERCISES

I. Answer in French:

1. **Comment était la France à la fin de la guerre?**
2. **Comment est la France aujourd'hui du point de vue économique?**
3. **Quelle est la population de la France?**
4. **Qu'est-ce qu'on craignait entre les deux guerres?**
5. **Est-ce qu'il y a en France un système d'allocations familiales?**
6. **Qu'est-ce qu'on entend par "la Communauté européenne"?**
7. **Quels pays font partie de cette organisation?**
8. **Où se trouve le siège du Marché commun?**
9. **Croyez-vous que la vie d'un homme politique soit dure?**
10. **Qu'est-ce qui est nécessaire pour qu'un pays prospère?**

II. Translate into English:

1. **Il semble qu'il ait disparu sans laisser de traces.**
2. **Quoique nous soyons fatigués nous nous mettrons au travail quand même.**
3. **Pour que ma liste soit exacte il faut que je sache qui est absent.**

4. À moins qu'il ne vienne avant trois heures nous ne pourrons pas partir aujourd'hui.
5. Il n'y avait personne qui sût cela.
6. Si vous avez mille francs et que vous vouliez me les prêter, je pourrai acheter tout ce qu'il me faut.
7. C'est la plus belle fleur que j'aie jamais vue.
8. Il est bien évident que vous n'avez rien appris.
9. Je doute qu'elle puisse arriver aujourd'hui.
10. Nous ne serons heureux que lorsque la guerre sera finie.
11. Il pourra arranger les choses de sorte que nos ennemis n'apprennent pas ce qui est arrivé.
12. Cherchez un clou qui ne soit pas rouillé.
13. Il me semble que la plupart des pommes sont pourries.
14. Il vaut mieux que Jean entre le premier.
15. Plût au ciel que le roi eût agi ainsi!

III. Give (1) the third person singular present subjunctive and (2) the first person plural imperfect subjunctive of these verbs: **avoir**, **être**, **porter**, **recevoir**, **savoir**, **répondre**, **pouvoir**, **aller**, **dire**, **faire**, **écrire**, **craindre**, **prendre**, **vouloir**, **partir**.

IV. Note down all the verbs in the subjunctive in the reading text and state briefly which rule for the use of the subjunctive applies in each case.

V. Insert the correct form of the subjunctive in the following sentences:
1. Il semble qu'il (avoir) perdu tout son argent.
2. Pour que nous n' (arriver) pas en retard l'autocar partira à deux heures et quart.
3. Qu'ils (revenir) à la fin de la semaine.
4. Je ne croyais pas qu'il (être) mort.
5. Il demanda qu'on (mettre) le voleur en prison.
6. Elle regrette beaucoup que le travail ne (être) pas fini.
7. Il craignait que l'effort ne l' (épuiser).
8. Il faudra qu'on (surveiller) les enfants toute la journée.
9. C'est dommage que vous (avoir) perdu votre balle.
10. C'est la seule personne que je (reconnaître).

VI. Translate into French:
1. Although he is young he can play the piano.
2. In order that you may understand what I am going to say I shall make a drawing on the blackboard.

3. It is necessary for you to arrive punctually if you do not want to find the door closed.
4. It is a pity that they have no more money.
5. Before they come, clean the sitting-room.
6. It seems to me that you are making a mistake.
7. Bring me a towel which is not dirty.
8. It is possible that they will go to Austria at Easter.
9. Provided that you are rich you can travel over the whole world.
10. See to it that the door is properly shut.

VII. Translate into French:

After the Second World War the economic condition of France was deplorable. The country was very poor because of the pillage organised by the enemy. Besides, the railway network, the roads and the bridges had suffered considerable damage. American help allowed France to begin the work of reconstruction. Today, however, the country is very prosperous. The factories, the roads and the bridges have been repaired and the national income continues to grow. Unemployment is almost non-existent. It is said that one person in nine has a car. Although the country is so rich the political situation is not very good. Sometimes one fears that a civil war will break out. It will be necessary for the government to follow a policy which will be able to unite the country and restore calm to it. Indeed, no country subject to political agitation can hope to remain prosperous for long. In order that the economy may be healthy it is necessary for the workers to live in peace.

VIII. Write a composition in the past tense based on this outline:

Un homme qui est riche est aussi très avare — il a peur des voleurs — il met son argent dans une boîte qu'il enterre dans le jardin — son voisin le voit — le voisin vient pendant la nuit voler l'argent — il met une grosse pierre à la place de la boîte — le lendemain l'avare revient voir si l'argent est toujours là — il découvre le vol — ce qu'il fait.

(*Answers at the end of the book.*)

REVISION SUMMARY OF VERBS

INDICATIVE MOOD

Page
27, 46, 62

First conjugation = **er**   **donn-er**
Second conjugation = **ir**   **fin-ir**
Third conjugation = **re**   **vend-re**

PRESENT TENSE
For example, **je donne** = *I give, am giving, do give.*

donner	finir	vendre
je donne	je finis	je vends
tu donnes	tu finis	tu vends
il donne	il finit	il vend
nous donnons	nous finissons	nous vendons
vous donnez	vous finissez	vous vendez
ils donnent	ils finissent	ils vendent

Verbs ending in **-ger, -cer**:
   je mange
   nous mangeons (e added to keep the g soft)
   je commence
   nous commençons (ç to keep the c soft)

NEGATIVE FORMS

27

donner	finir	vendre
je ne donne pas	je ne finis pas	je ne vends pas
tu ne donnes pas	tu ne finis pas	tu ne vends pas
il ne donne pas	il ne finit pas	il ne vend pas
nous ne donnons pas	nous ne finissons pas	nous ne vendons pas
vous ne donnez pas	vous ne finissez pas	vous ne vendez pas
ils ne donnent pas	ils ne finissent pas	ils ne vendent pas

INTERROGATIVE (QUESTION) FORMS

19, 243

Est-ce que + ordinary statement = question:
   Elle chante.   **Est-ce qu'elle chante?**
With inversion:
   Vous dansez   **Dansez-vous?**
   Est-ce que je danse?   (Inversion form not used with **je**.)
   danses-tu?
   danse-t-il?   Notice **-t-** to avoid the clash of
   dansons-nous?   vowels.
   dansez-vous?
   dansent-ils?   The final **-t** is pronounced in liaison.

ai-je?	**n'ai-je pas?** etc.	**suis-je?**	**ne suis-je pas?** etc.
as-tu?		**es-tu?**	
a-t-il?		**est-il?**	
avons-nous?		**sommes-nous?**	
avez-vous?		**êtes-vous?**	
ont-ils?		**sont-ils?**	

Inversion when the subject is a noun:
L'homme porte un chapeau.
L'homme porte-t-il un chapeau?
L'homme ne porte pas de chapeau.
L'homme ne porte-il pas de chapeau?

The subject is placed at the beginning of the sentence and the proper pronoun introduced so that the subject pronoun and verb can be inverted.

The noun subject and verb are inverted after direct speech:
La vendeuse dit: "Je me suis réveillée à sept heures."
but **"Je me suis réveillée à sept heures," dit la vendeuse.**

REFLEXIVE VERBS
96, 225

se laver = *to wash oneself*

je me lave	**je ne me lave pas**	**nous lavons-nous?**	
tu te laves	**tu ne te laves pas,** etc.	**vous lavez-vous?** etc.	
il se lave			
nous nous lavons			
vous vous lavez		**ne nous lavons-nous pas?**	
ils se lavent		**ne vous lavez-vous pas?**	

Reflexive pronoun as direct object:
Il se rase; elle se lave.

Reflexive pronoun as indirect object (dative):
Il se lave la figure.

Reciprocal use (*one another*):
Ils s'aiment (se is direct object).
Ils se disent des injures (se is indirect object).

As a substitute for the passive:
Cela se comprend = *That is understood.*

Many verbs are reflexive in French but not in English, e.g.:

se battre = *to fight*	**s'ennuyer** = *to be bored*
se tromper = *to be mistaken*	**se fâcher** = *to get angry*
s'écrier = *to exclaim*	

IMPERATIVE FORM:
54

Donne!	*Give!*	**Finis!**	*Finish!*	**Vends!**	*Sell!*
Donnons!	*Let us give!*	**Finissons!**	*Let us finish!*	**Vendons!**	*Let us sell!*
Donnez!	*Give!*	**Finissez!**	*Finish!*	**Vendez!**	*Sell!*

Negative imperatives:

Ne donne pas!	*Don't give!*	**Ne finis pas!**	**Ne vends pas!**
Ne donnons pas!	*Let us not give!*	**Ne finissons pas!**	**Ne vendons pas!**
Ne donnez pas!	*Don't give!*	**Ne finissez pas!**	**Ne vendez pas!**

For an imperative, the pronouns come after the verb:

Montrez-la-moi!   *Give it to me!*
Envoyez-les-leur!   *Send them to them!*

Note: **moi** and **toi** = *for me, to me*; *you, to you*; become **m'** and **t'** before en.

Donnez m'en!   *Give me some!*

The negative imperative has the usual order:

Ne me la montrez pas!
Ne m'en donnez pas!

Reflexive negative:

Lave-toi!   *Wash yourself!*
Lavons-nous   *Let's wash ourselves!*
Lavez-vous!   *Wash yourselves!*
  Wash yourself!
Ne te lave pas!   *Don't wash yourself!*
Ne nous lavons pas   *Let's not wash ourselves!*
Ne vous lavez pas   *Don't wash yourselves!*
  Don't wash yourself!

Avoir and **être** use the subjunctive form:

Sois } *Be ...!*   **Aie** } *Have ...!*
Soyez }   **Ayez** }

VERBS WITH AN IRREGULAR PRESENT TENSE

acheter = *to buy*
j'achète
tu achètes
il achète
nous achetons
vous achetez
ils achètent

aller = *to go*
je vais
tu vas
il va
nous allons
vous allez
ils vont

s'asseoir = *to sit down*
je m'assieds
tu t'assieds
il s'assied
nous nous asseyons
vous vous asseyez
ils s'asseyent

battre = *to beat*
je bats
tu bats
il bat
nous battons
vous battez
ils battent

boire = *to drink*
je bois
tu bois
il boit
nous buvons
vous buvez
ils boivent

conduire = *to conduct*
je conduis
tu conduis
il conduit
nous conduisons
vous conduisez
ils conduisent

connaître = *to know*
je connais
tu connais
il connaît
nous connaissons
vous connaissez
ils connaissent

courir = *to run*
je cours
tu cours
il court
nous courons
vous courez
ils courent

craindre = *to fear*
je crains
tu crains
il craint
nous craignons
vous craignez
ils craignent

275

croire = *to believe*	croître = *to grow*	cueillir = *to gather*
je crois	je croîs	je cueille
tu crois	tu croîs	tu cueilles
il croit	il croît	il cueille
nous croyons	nous croissons	nous cueillons
vous croyez	vous croissez	vous cueillez
ils croient	ils croissent	ils cueillent

cuire = *to cook*	devoir = *to owe*	écrire = *to write*
je cuis	je dois	j'écris
tu cuis	tu dois	tu écris
il cuit	il doit	il écrit
nous cuisons	nous devons	nous écrivons
vous cuisez	vous devez	vous écrivez
ils cuisent	ils doivent	ils écrivent

ennuyer = *to bore*	espérer = *to hope*	essayer = *to try*
j'ennuie	j'espère	j'essaie
tu ennuies	tu espères	tu essaies
il ennuie	il espère	il essaie
nous ennuyons	nous espérons	nous essayons
vous ennuyez	vous espérez	vous essayez
ils ennuient	ils espèrent	ils essaient

faire = *to do, to make*	falloir = *to be necessary*	haïr = *to hate*
je fais		je hais
tu fais		tu hais
il fait	il faut	il hait
nous faisons		nous haïssons
vous faites		vous haïssez
ils font		ils haïssent

jeter = *to throw*	lever = *to lift*	lire = *to read*
je jette	je lève	je lis
tu jettes	tu lèves	tu lis
il jette	il lève	il lit
nous jetons	nous levons	nous lisons
vous jetez	vous levez	vous lisez
ils jettent	ils lèvent	ils lisent

mentir = *to lie*	mettre = *to put*	mourir = *to die*
je mens	je mets	je meurs
tu mens	tu mets	tu meurs
il ment	il met	il meurt
nous mentons	nous mettons	nous mourons
vous mentez	vous mettez	vous mourez
ils mentent	ils mettent	ils meurent

naître = *to be born*	nettoyer = *to clean*	nuire = *to hurt*
je nais	je nettoie	je nuis
tu nais	tu nettoies	tu nuis
il naît	il nettoie	il nuit
nous naissons	nous nettoyons	nous nuisons
vous naissez	vous nettoyez	vous nuisez
ils naissent	ils nettoient	ils nuisent

partir = *to set out,*	payer = *to pay*	plaire = *to please*
je pars [*depart*	je paie	je plais
tu pars	tu paies	tu plais
il part	il paie	il plaît
nous partons	nous payons	nous plaisons
vous partez	vous payez	vous plaisez
ils partent	ils paient	ils plaisent

pouvoir = *to be able*	recevoir = *to receive*	rire = *to laugh*
je peux (puis)	je reçois	je ris
tu peux	tu reçois	tu ris
il peut	il reçoit	il rit
nous pouvons	nous recevons	nous rions
vous pouvez	vous recevez	vous riez
ils peuvent	ils reçoivent	ils rient

savoir = *to know*	suivre = *to follow*	se taire = *to be silent*
je sais	je suis	je me tais
tu sais	tu suis	tu te tais
il sait	il suit	il se tait
nous savons	nous suivons	nous nous taisons
vous savez	vous suivez	vous vous taisez
ils savent	ils suivent	ils se taisent

valoir = *to be worth*	venir = *to come*	vivre = *to live*
je vaux	je viens	je vis
tu vaux	tu viens	tu vis
il vaut	il vient	il vit
nous valons	nous venons	nous vivons
vous valez	vous venez	vous vivez
ils valent	ils viennent	ils vivent

vouloir = *to will*
je veux
tu veux
il veut
nous voulons
vous voulez
ils veulent

Page
78, 88

PERFECT TENSE

This is normally formed with the present tense of **avoir** plus the past participle of the verb in question:

j'ai donné = *I have given, I gave*

(It is the past tense of conversation.)

j'ai donné	ai-je donné
tu as donné	as-tu-donné
il a donné	a-t-il donné
nous avons donné	avons-nous donné
vous avez donné	avez-vous donné
ils ont donné	ont-ils donné

Certain intransitive verbs are conjugated with **être**: 88

arriver	partir	tomber	rester	retourner
entrer	sortir	naître	mourir	(avoir or
aller	venir	monter	descendre	être)

The past participle in these compound tenses agrees with the subject: 224

je suis tombé(e)	nous sommes tombé(e)s
tu es tombé(e)	vous êtes tombé(e)(s)
il est tombé	ils sont tombés
elle est tombée	elles sont tombées

Do not confuse this type of sentence with the past participle used as an adjective:

La tasse est cassée.

Les robes sont déchirées.

NEGATIVE FORMS

88

je n'ai pas fini	n'ai-je pas vendu?
tu n'as pas fini	n'as-tu pas vendu?
il n'a pas fini	n'a-t-il pas vendu?
nous n'avons pas fini	n'avons-nous pas vendu?
vous n'avez pas fini	n'avez vous pas vendu?
ils n'ont pas fini	n'ont-ils pas vendu?

Perfect of reflexive verbs with **être**: 225

se blesser = *to hurt oneself*

je me suis blessé(e)	je ne me suis pas blessé(e)
tu t'es blessé(e)	tu ne t'es pas blessé(e)
il s'est blessé	il ne s'est pas blessé, etc.
elle s'est blessée	
nous nous sommes blessé(e)s	ne nous sommes-nous pas blessé(e)s
vous vous êtes blessé(e)(s)	ne vous êtes-vous pas blessé(e)(s)
ils se sont blessés	ne se sont-ils pas blessés, etc.
elles se sont blessées	

When reflexive verbs are used in compound tenses the past participle must agree like an adjective with the preceding direct object as above: in (1) below the preceding reflexive pronoun is the direct object; in (2) the preceding reflexive pronoun is only the indirect object, hence no agreement.

se laver

Perfect (1)	*Perfect* (2)
je me suis lavé(e)	je me suis lavé les mains
tu t'es lavé(e)	tu t'es lavé les mains
il s'est lavé	il s'est lavé les mains
elle s'est lavée	elle s'est lavé les mains
nous nous sommes lavé(e)s	nous nous sommes lavé les mains
vous vous êtes lavé(e)(s)	vous vous êtes lavé les mains
ils se sont lavés	ils se sont lavé les mains
elles se sont lavées	elles se sont lavé les mains

Irregular past participles:

avoir	j'ai eu	devoir	j'ai dû	lire	j'ai lu
être	j'ai été	pouvoir	j'ai pu	naître	je suis né
savoir	j'ai su	boire	j'ai bu	mourir	je suis mort
faire	j'ai fait	s'asseoir	je me suis assis		

FUTURE TENSE 106

Stems—the infinitive (for regular verbs). Endings—those of **avoir**:

je donnerai	nous donnerons	je finirai, etc.
tu donneras	vous donnerez	je vendrai, etc.
il donnera	ils donneront	je me laverai, etc.

Irregular futures include:

être	je serai, etc.	aller	j'irai
avoir	j'aurai, etc.	devoir	je devrai
savoir	je saurai, etc.	pouvoir	je pourrai
faire	je ferai, etc.	vouloir	je voudrai
venir	je viendrai	s'asseoir	je m'assiérai

The future is used if a future idea is implied:

Quand je serai à Paris, je visiterai le Louvre.

Except after **si**:

S'il fait beau temps, je sortirai.

IMPERFECT TENSE 137

Stem—first person plural of the PRESENT tense minus -ons:

donn-	finiss-	vend-
je donnais	nous donnions	je finissais, etc.
tu donnais	vous donniez	je vendais, etc.
il donnait	ils donnaient	je me lavais, etc.

Only irregular stem: être, ét-, j'étais, etc.

Meaning:

I used to give, finish, sell, wash myself.
I was giving, finishing, selling, washing myself.

Uses:

To express what used to happen (habitual action):
Tous les jours je faisais une promenade.
To express what was happening when something else happened:
Elle pleurait quand je suis entré.
In the *if* clause of conditional sentences to express something contrary to fact:
S'il était ici, il dirait la même chose.

CONDITIONAL TENSE
Page
154

Stem—same as future stem (i.e. the infinitive for regular verbs).

Endings—same as the imperfect:

je donnerais	nous donnerions	je finirais, etc.
tu donnerais	vous donneriez	je vendrais, etc.
il donnerait	ils donneraient	je me laverais, etc.

Meaning:

I should (would) give, finish, sell, wash myself.

Uses:

In the main clause of a conditional sentence:

Si j'avais assez d'argent, j'achèterais ce livre.

In reported speech in past tense to represent the future of direct speech:

Il a dit qu'il ne pourrait pas arriver avant lundi.

In reported speech in past tense to represent the (French) future of direct speech in a clause of time:

Il a dit qu'il le ferait quand il serait en ville.

Tentative statement:

Il serait arrivé à midi.

CONDITIONAL PERFECT
226

Formation—conditional of **avoir** (or **être**) with the past participle.

j'aurais donné, j'aurais fini, j'aurais vendu

but

je me serais levé, je serais tombé, etc.

Meaning:

I should have given, finished, sold.

Je serais arrivé à temps s'il ne m'avait pas retenu.

PAST HISTORIC
190

Stem—infinitive minus ending:

donn- fin- vend-

Endings:

er verbs: -ai, -as, -a, -âmes, -âtes, -èrent

ir, re: -is, -is, -it, -îmes, -îtes, -irent

Certain irregular verbs have -us, -us, -ut, -ûmes, -ûtes, -urent.

donner	finir	vendre	recevoir
je donnai	je finis	je vendis	je reçus
tu donnas	tu finis	tu vendis	tu reçus
il donna	il finit	il vendit	il reçut
nous donnâmes	nous finîmes	nous vendîmes	nous reçûmes
vous donnâtes	vous finîtes	vous vendîtes	vous reçûtes
ils donnèrent	ils finirent	ils vendirent	ils reçurent

Meaning:

I gave, I finished, I sold, I received (i.e. simple past).

Use:

In printed works (not in conversation or letter-writing) to express one completed action in the past.

Irregular forms:

avoir	j'eus	plaire	je plus
être	je fus	pleuvoir	il plut
s'asseoir	je m'assis	pouvoir	je pus
boire	je bus	prendre	je pris
conduire	je conduisis	résoudre	je résolus
courir	je courus	rire	je ris
craindre	je craignis	savoir	je sus
croire	je crus	suivre	je suivis
devoir	je dus	se taire	je me tus
dire	je dis	tenir	je tins
écrire	j'écrivis	venir	je vins
faire	je fis	valoir	je valus
lire	je lus	vivre	je vécus
mettre	je mis	voir	je vis
mourir	je mourus	vouloir	je voulus
naître	je naquis		

PLUPERFECT   172

Formation—imperfect of **avoir** (or **être**) plus the past participle:
> j'avais donné, j'avais fini, j'avais vendu
> but
> je m'étais levé, j'étais tombé, j'étais arrivé, etc.

Meaning:
> *I had given, finished, sold, got up, fallen, arrived, etc.*

PAST ANTERIOR   225

Formation—past historic of **avoir** (or **être**) plus the past participle:
> j'eus donné, j'eus fini, j'eus vendu
> je me fus levé, je fus tombé, etc.

Meaning: same as pluperfect.

Use:
> Used in a clause of time (except after **avant que**) to translate English pluperfect when the verb in the main clause is past historic.
> **Quand tous les invités furent arrivés, on servit le repas.**

FUTURE PERFECT   225

Formation—future of **avoir** (or **être**) plus the past participle.
> j'aurai donné, j'aurai fini, j'aurai vendu
> je me serai levé, je serai tombé, etc.

Meaning:
> *I shall have given, I shall have finished, I shall have sold.*

Use:
> Often appears in a clause of time to translate the English perfect:
> **Quand il sera revenu, je le lui dirai.**
> Sometimes expresses supposition:
> **il sera tombé** = *he must have fallen*

SUBJUNCTIVE MOOD

PRESENT SUBJUNCTIVE

Formation—the stem is the third person of the present indicative plural minus -ent:

donner	finir	vendre
que je donne	que je finisse	que je vende
que tu donnes	que tu finisses	que tu vendes
qu'il donne	qu'il finisse	qu'il vende
que nous donnions	que nous finissions	que nous vendions
que vous donniez	que vous finissiez	que vous vendiez
qu'ils donnent	qu'ils finissent	qu'ils vendent

Irregular:

être	que je sois, soyons	faire	que je fasse
avoir	que j'aie, ayons	pouvoir	que je puisse
aller	que j'aille	vouloir	que je veuille
savoir	que je sache		

IMPERFECT SUBJUNCTIVE

Formation—take the second person singular of the past historic, double the s and add e: this gives the first person singular of the imperfect subjunctive.

donner	finir	vendre
que je donnasse	que je finisse	que je vendisse
que tu donnasses	que tu finisses	que tu vendisses
qu'il donnât	qu'il finît	qu'il vendît
que nous donnassions	que nous finissions	que nous vendissions
que vous donnassiez	que vous finissiez	que vous vendissiez
qu'ils donnassent	qu'ils finnissent	qu'ils vendissent

USES OF THE SUBJUNCTIVE

Main clauses:
Imperative in the third person: **qu'il le fasse**
Wish: **Vive le roi!**

Noun clauses:
After verbs of wishing, commanding, etc.:
Je veux qu'il vienne.
After verbs of emotion:
Je regrette qu'il soit absent.
Je crains qu'il ne soit mort.
After verbs of trying, striving, preventing:
Tâchez qu'il arrive à temps.
Veillez à ce que le travail se fasse.
After verbs of doubting and denying:
Je doute qu'il réussisse.
After impersonal verbs (except of certainty and probability):
Il faut qu'il le dise.
Note: **il me semble** and **il paraît** take the indicative.

Relative clauses:
  After superlative antecedent:
  C'est l'homme le plus paresseux que je connaisse.
  After negative antecedent:
  Il n'y a personne qui veuille le faire.
  After indefinite antecedent:
  Montrez-moi un homme qui ait vu cela.
Adverbial clauses:
  After certain conjunctions: 265
  quoique, bien que, pour que, afin que, jusqu'à ce que, avant que, en attendant que, de peur (crainte) que . . . ne, pourvu que, supposé que.
  and (when expressing purpose) after:
  de sorte que, de façon que, de manière que.
  Quoiqu'il soit riche il n'est pas heureux.
  Pourvu qu'il le fasse tout ira bien.
Other uses:
  After **que** replacing **si.**
  In constructions containing *whatever, whoever, however,* etc.
Sequence of tenses: 266
  Strictly speaking, after a historic tense the imperfect subjunctive should be used. However, in modern French the present subjunctive is generally used instead.

MODAL AUXILIARIES   56, 232

aller (with future meaning): **je vais partir.**
pouvoir = *to be* (physically) *able*: **je peux venir ce soir.**
  Sometimes translates *may* or *might.*
  Il pourrait arriver d'un moment à l'autre.
  He might arrive any minute.
savoir = *to know how to* (often *can* in English):
  Je sais jouer aux échecs.
  Il sait nager.
  Je ne saurais vous le dire.
vouloir = *to wish, to want,* "*will.*"
  Je ne veux pas le faire.
  Il voudrait venir avec nous.
devoir = *must, am to*:
  Je dois partir = *I must go.*
  Il devait arriver à midi = *He was to arrive at midday.*
  J'ai dû le laisser tomber = *I had to drop it* or *I must have dropped it.*
  In the conditional this verb translates *ought*:
  Je devrais partir = *I ought to go.*
  J'aurais dû partir plus tôt = *I should have gone sooner.*
faire = *to cause* (something to be done):
  Je le fais écrire.
  Je lui fais écrire l'exercice.
  Il fait construire une maison.
  Je me suis fait couper les cheveux.
  Note: Object of **faire** is indirect (dative) if the infinitive has an object.

IDIOMATIC TENSE USAGE

venir de = *to have just*:
Used only in the present and imperfect tenses:
Je viens de recevoir un cadeau (*have just*).
Je venais de partir (*had just*).

depuis = *since*:
Used only with the present and the imperfect in the following construction:
Il est ici depuis une demi-heure.
Elle était dans le magasin depuis cinq minutes.

Il y a (avait) or **voici** or **voilà** may be used to express the same idea as **depuis** but with a slightly different construction. Only the present and imperfect tenses are used:
Il y a une demi-heure qu'il est ici.
Voici une demi-heure qu'il est ici.
Il y avait cinq minutes qu'elle était dans le magasin.
Voilà cinq minutes qu'elle était dans le magasin.

Conjunctions of time (except **avant que**):
After **quand, lorsque, aussitôt que, dès que**, etc., the future must be used when future time is implied.
Quand il viendra je le lui dirai.
Il a dit qu'il le ferait quand il viendrait.

Tenses after **si**: 234
After **si** = *whether*, any tense of the indicative is possible.
After **si** = *if*, the future, conditional and present subjunctive are never used. The tenses usually found are:

Present indicative	**S'il vient je serai content.**
Imperfect	**S'il venait je serais content.**
Pluperfect	**S'il était venu, j'aurais été content.**

IMPERSONAL VERBS
254

Impersonal verbs are verbs with the subject *it* which refers to no particular noun.
il pleut, il neige, il tonne, il fait beau temps, il fait chaud, il faut, il vaut mieux, il est nécessaire, il est deux heures et demie, etc.
It is said = **On dit**
Il fait froid, chaud, beau, mauvais, du vent, etc.

VERBS FOLLOWED BY A PREPOSITION PLUS NOUN
250

No preposition in French after: **regarder, chercher, attendre, demander, écouter, payer**, etc.:
Il regarde le tableau.
Il paya le billet.

Many French verbs require **to be** followed by a preposition whereas none is used in English: 251
Il entra dans la salle.
Il se sert d'un stylo pour écrire.
Vous manquez de courage.
Je ne m'attendais pas à cela.
Elle obéit à son père.
Le prince succéda à son père.

Page

Verbs of depriving, stealing, etc., take the dative of the person from   251
whom the thing is taken, stolen, etc.:
> Elle lui arrache le bâton.
> On lui vole les marchandises.
> Il leur cache le livre.

Verbs of taking part or interest take à:
> J'assiste au mariage.
> Nous jouons aux échecs.
> Je m'intéresse à ce qu'il fait.

Many verbs take de: 251, 252
> Cela dépend de vous.
> Je me moque de vos menaces.
> Il vit de fromage et de légumes.
> Elle joue du piano.
> Nous changeons de train.
> Qu'avez-vous fait du (*with the*) journal?

VERBS FOLLOWED BY A PREPOSITION PLUS VERB   253
Verbs with no preposition before following infinitive:
> aimer, désirer, préférer, savoir, devoir, pouvoir, vouloir, oser, sembler, aller, faire, envoyer, etc.

Verbs followed by à:
> (i) beginning: commencer à, se mettre à;
> (ii) inviting, compelling: inviter à, obliger à, forcer à;
> (iii) taking part or interest: s'amuser à, passer son temps à;
> (iv) learning and teaching: apprendre à, enseigner à;
> (v) various others: avoir à, aider à, aimer à, se préparer à, chercher à, se décider à, réussir à, servir à.

Verbs with de: 254
> (i) finishing: cesser de, finir de, s'arrêter de;
> (ii) trying: essayer de, tâcher de;
> (iii) deciding: décider de, résoudre de;
> (iv) ordering: demander, dire, ordonner, prier;
> (v) various others: empêcher de, menacer de, promettre de, refuser de, remercier de, risquer de, se vanter de, il s'agit de;
> (vi) impersonal verbs of form il est plus adjective: il est facile de, il est nécessaire de, etc.
> (vii) between a noun and infinitive: le désir de réussir.

Verbs followed by par: 255
> Verbs of beginning and finishing *by*: il finit par s'endormir.

Verbs followed by pour:
> (i) to show purpose;
> (ii) after assez and trop;
> (iii) with past infinitive to show reason.

VERBS AFTER A PREPOSITION
à, de, par, pour, sans, afin de, avant de are followed by the infinitive:
> sans parler.

après is followed by the perfect infinitive:
> après avoir parlé, après être parti(e).

en is followed by the present participle: en allant.   139

COMMONEST FRENCH IRREGULAR VERBS

Infinitive	Present part.	Past part.	Present tense	Future tense
acquérir	acquérant	acquis	j'acquiers	j'acquerrai
aller*	allant	allé	je vais	j'irai
assaillir	assaillant	assailli	j'assaille	j'assaillirai
s'asseoir	s'asseyant	assis	je m'assieds	je m'assiérai
avoir	ayant	eu	j'ai	j'aurai
battre	battant	battu	je bats	je battrai
boire	buvant	bu	je bois	je boirai
bouillir	bouillant	bouilli	je bous	je bouillirai
conclure	concluant	conclu	je conclus	je conclurai
conduire	conduisant	conduit	je conduis	je conduirai
confire	confisant	confit	je confis	je confirai
connaître	connaissant	connu	je connais	je connaîtrai
coudre	cousant	cousu	je couds	je coudrai
courir	courant	couru	je cours	je courrai
craindre	craignant	craint	je crains	je craindrai
croire	croyant	cru	je crois	je croirai
croître	croissant	crû	je croîs	je croîtrai
cueillir	cueillant	cueilli	je cueille	je cueillerai
dire	disant	dit	je dis	je dirai
dormir	dormant	dormi	je dors	je dormirai
échoir	échéant	échu	il échoit (échet)	il écherra
écrire	écrivant	écrit	j'écris	j'écrirai
envoyer	envoyant	envoyé	j'envoie	j'enverrai
être	étant	été	je suis	je serai
faire	faisant	fait	je fais	je ferai
falloir	—	fallu	il faut	il faudra
fuir	fuyant	fui	je fuis	je fuirai
lire	lisant	lu	je lis	je lirai
maudire	maudissant	maudit	je maudis	je maudirai
mettre	mettant	mis	je mets	je mettrai
moudre	moulant	moulu	je mouds	je moudrai
mourir*	mourant	mort	je meurs	je mourrai
mouvoir	mouvant	mû	je meus	je mouvrai
naître*	naissant	né	je nais	je naîtrai
ouvrir	ouvrant	ouvert	j'ouvre	j'ouvrirai
plaire	plaisant	plu	je plais	je plairai
pleuvoir	pleuvant	plu	il pleut	il pleuvra
pouvoir	pouvant	pu	je peux (puis)	je pourrai
prendre	prenant	pris	je prends	je prendrai
recevoir	recevant	reçu	je reçois	je recevrai
résoudre	résolvant	résolu	je résous	je résoudrai
rire	riant	ri	je ris	je rirai
savoir	sachant	su	je sais	je saurai
suivre	suivant	suivi	je suis	je suivrai
traire	trayant	trait	je trais	je trairai
vaincre	vainquant	vaincu	je vaincs	je vaincrai
valoir	valant	valu	je vaux	je vaudrai
venir*	venant	venu	je viens	je viendrai
vêtir	vêtant	vêtu	je vêts	je vêtirai
vivre	vivant	vécu	je vis	je vivrai
voir	voyant	vu	je vois	je verrai
vouloir	voulant	voulu	je veux	je voudrai

Past historic	*Present subjunctive*	*Other verbs with irregularities*
j'acquis	j'acquière	**acheter,** *present* and *present subjunctive*
j'allai	j'aille	j'achète, tu achètes, il achète, ils
j'assaillis	j'assaille	achètent; *future* j'achèterai, etc., like-
je m'assis	je m'asseye	wise *conditional.*
j'eus	j'aie	**arriver*,** see below.
je battis	je batte	**atteindre,** like CRAINDRE.
je bus	je boive	**céder,** *present* and *present subjunctive,* je
je bouillis	je bouille	cède, tu cèdes, il cède, ils cèdent.
je conclus	je conclue	**couvrir,** like OUVRIR.
je conduisis	je conduise	**descendre*,** see below.
je confis	je confise	**détruire,** like CONDUIRE.
je connus	je connaisse	**devoir,** *past part.* dû, due, dus, dues.
je cousis	je couse	**émouvoir,** *past part.* ému; otherwise like
je courus	je coure	MOUVOIR.
je craignis	je craigne	**employer,** i instead of y before e mute.
je crus	je croie	**entrer*,** see below.
je crûs	je croisse	**exclure,** like CONCLURE.
je cueillis	je cueille	**-ger,** ge before a, o.
je dis	je dise	**haïr,** *present* tense je hais, tu hais, il hait;
je dormis	je dorme	otherwise ï.
il échut	il échoie	**jeter,** *present* and *present subjunctive,* je
j'écrivis	j'écrive	jette, tu jettes, il jette, ils jettent; *future*
j'envoyai	j'envoie	je jetterai, etc.; also *conditional.*
je fus	je sois	**luire,** *past part.* lui; no *past historic* or
je fis	je fasse	*past subjunctive*; otherwise like CON-
il fallut	il faille	DUIRE.
je fuis	je fuie	**médire,** *present* vous médisez; otherwise
je lus	je lise	like DIRE.
je maudis	je maudisse	**mentir,** like DORMIR.
je mis	je mette	**monter*,** see below.
je moulus	je moule	**nuire,** *past part.* nui; otherwise like
je mourus	je meure	CONDUIRE.
je mus	je meuve	**offrir,** like OUVRIR.
je naquis	je naisse	**paraître,** like CONNAÎTRE.
j'ouvris	j'ouvre	**partir*,** like DORMIR, but see below.
je plus	je plaise	**payer,** i or y before e mute.
il plut	il pleuve	**peindre,** like CRAINDRE.
je pus	je puisse	**pourvoir,** *future* je pourvoirai, etc.; *past*
je pris	je prenne	je pourvus, etc.; otherwise like VOIR.
je reçus	je reçoive	**prévoir,** *future* je prévoirai; otherwise like
je résolus	je résolve	VOIR.
je ris	je rie	**rester*,** see below.
je sus	je sache	**sentir,** like DORMIR.
je suivis	je suive	**servir,** like DORMIR.
	je traie	**sortir*,** like DORMIR, but see below.
je vainquis	je vainque	**souffrir,** like OUVRIR.
je valus	je vaille	**suffire,** like CONFIRE.
je vins	je vienne	**taire,** like PLAIRE.
je vêtis	je vête	**tenir,** like VENIR.
je vécus	je vive	**tomber*,** see below.
je vis	je voie	* Compound tenses with être when intransitive.
je voulus	je veuille	

AGREEMENT OF PAST PARTICIPLE

Page
89, 224

When used as an adjective the past participle agrees in gender and number with its noun:

la page déchirée, les pages déchirées.

In compound tenses the past participle agrees with the subject in the case of verbs conjugated with **être**:

elle est arrivée, nous sommes tombés, ils sont morts.

In the case of reflexive verbs in compound tenses, the past participle agrees with the reflexive pronoun only if the latter is DIRECT object:

elle s'est lavée,

but

elle s'est lavé la figure.

In the case of verbs conjugated with **avoir** in the compound tenses, 79, 224 the past participle agrees with the DIRECT object when the latter PRECEDES the verb. The object can precede the verb:

As a personal pronoun: **je les ai vus; il l'a rencontrée.**

Note: **en** is not a direct object: **j'en ai vu.**

As a relative pronoun: **Les balles qu'il a perdues.**

In exclamations and questions: **Quelles femmes avez-vous vues? Quelle surprise il a eue!**

Note: The past participle of an impersonal verb does not agree with a direct object:

Quelle panique il y a eu!

PART III

THE STUDY of basic French grammar has now been completed and it is time to tackle the examination papers themselves. In this part of the book the student is shown by means of examples and hints how to answer the various different types of question in the G.C.E. papers. Idiomatic usage is explored more thoroughly, and the later chapters of this section contain typical examination questions for the student to try on his own.

Model answers are provided to all the passages to be studied, and these can be found in the answer section at the back of the book if not included in the same chapter. Vocabularies are not given in these chapters, and the student is asked to refer to the general vocabulary, which is also at the back of the book, for new words. The coloured revision pages for this part of the book are devoted to a summary of tricky constructions and ways of avoiding the common errors and pitfalls in points of grammar and vocabulary, together with lists of useful idiomatic constructions.

First of all, here are some general hints and advice which should be borne in mind when tackling any of the G.C.E. papers:

1. Read all the instructions carefully. You are usually reminded that spelling, punctuation, writing and style are all taken into account. You may be asked to leave space between paragraphs; if so, remember to do so.

2. Plan your time. If you have three pieces to do in a certain amount of time, do not spend half the time on the first piece. It is essential that you allow yourself time to finish each.

3. Never start a sentence until you are quite sure how the complete sentence is going to end. As far as possible do the questions in the order set.

4. Leave yourself time to re-read all you have written. Put in all accents clearly — never try to deceive by putting vague accents. Make sure that in the French-English paper you do not allow French words to slip in. One often finds **et** for *and*; this must be avoided.

5. If you have to guess, then let your guesses be reasonable ones. They must clearly fit the sense of the passage set. If you are forced to leave a blank you must make this clear. On the other hand take care not to omit words by careless reading. A careful re-reading will ensure that you have not wasted marks in this manner.

LEÇON 28

FRENCH INTO ENGLISH

GENERAL ADVICE

1. Good English is asked for. Word-for-word, literal translations are of little value.

2. Watch carefully for tense changes and get the exact meaning of the tense in your translation. Study the different uses of the imperfect tense:

Comme il entrait dans la chambre il entendit un coup de fusil.	*As he was entering the room he heard a rifle-shot.*
Quand nous étions au bord de la mer nous allions nous baigner quand le temps était beau.	*When we were staying at the sea-side we would go and bathe whenever the weather was fine.*
Si vous le voyiez pendant la journée, je vous saurais bien gré de lui demander de venir me voir demain.	*If you should see him in the course of the day, I should be grateful if you would ask him to come and see me tomorrow.*

Remember that in conversation the perfect tense is used in French. The English may well require the past historic:

Mais oui, je l'ai vu la semaine dernière.	*Yes, of course, I saw him last week.*

3. Beware of words which look alike in the two languages, but which may well have a meaning in French very different from the English:

assister, misérable, la bête, curieux, brave, contempler, remarquer, rester, la monnaie, sensible, la lecture, la place, résumer, ignorer, la cave, prétendre.
(There are more examples on p. 366.)
Look up the meanings of these words in the vocabulary.

4. Pay special attention to past participles in French; they may well be used adjectively. You may need a complete clause to translate a past participle.

Le jeune homme était au désespoir, lorsqu'un vieux monsieur, venu de l'autre bout de l'autobus, s'approcha.	*The young man was in despair, when an elderly gentleman, who had come from the other end of the bus, came up.*
Partis de bonne heure, ils atteignirent, avant midi, le sommet de la montagne.	*Having set out early, they reached the top of the mountain by midday.*

5. Note the construction **ce fut . . . que**:

Ce fut une journée mémorable, que *The day we moved house was a day*
celle où nous déménageâmes. *to be remembered.*

6. Watch for impersonal constructions and those which use **on**:

Il tomba tellement de neige qu'il nous *So much snow fell that we were quite*
était impossible de sortir. *unable to go out.*

Il demanda qu'on lui attachât les *He asked for his hands to be tied in*
mains de manière qu'il les eût croisées *such a way that he would have them*
sur la poitrine. *folded across his chest.*

On était au commencement de l'hiver. *It was the beginning of winter.*

Il m'arrive souvent de le voir quitter *I often see him leaving the house.*
la maison.

On ferait bien de rester ici jusqu'à *It would be as well if we stayed here*
l'arrivée de l'équipe de secours. *until the rescue party arrives.*

7. Remember that some reflexive verbs are followed by **de** (e.g. **s'approcher de,** etc.) which combines with the pronoun **le** to become **en**:

Ils s'en sont approchés. *They went up to it.*

C'est lui qui s'en occupe. *He is the one who looks after it* (*them*).

Elle s'en aperçut au même instant. *At the same time she became aware of it.*

Similarly **en** must be used before the verb with a number which is not followed by a noun:

Il en a trois. *He has three* (*of them*).

Je vais lui en acheter un autre. *I shall buy him another one.*

8. With reflexive verbs (e.g. **se promener,** etc.) do not forget that the auxiliary verb is **être**, which is generally translated by *has* or *had*:

La veille il · s'était promené sans *He had gone for a walk the previous*
manteau et s'était enrhumé. *evening wearing no coat and had caught a cold.*

Ce matin-là ils s'étaient réveillés de *That morning they had awakened*
très bonne heure. *very early.*

9. When translating exclamations, try to find the nearest English equivalent in use, even if it is not a literal translation:

À demain! *Goodbye till tomorrow!*

Au voleur! *Stop, thief!*

Dites donc, Paul! *I say, Paul!*

À Dieu ne plaise! *God forbid!*

Tiens! C'est vous! *Why! It's you!*

Tenez, voici mon porte-monnaie; *Look, here is my purse; go and do*
allez faire des commissions! *some errands!*

Allons, allons donc! *Come, come, no nonsense!*

291

10. To avoid putting a verb at the end of a sentence we may find an inversion in French:

C'était une faute bien grave qu'avait faite Henri.	*Henry had committed a very serious error.*
Sans doute, c'était un objet de grande valeur qu'avaient laissé tomber les voleurs.	*The robbers had, indeed, dropped an article of great value.*

Here are two passages as examples, showing how to apply the rules you have just read; the first is narrative, the second, conversational:

1. FIRST DAYS AT SCHOOL

Au milieu d'un flot d'enfants qui parlaient tous à la fois, je pénétrai dans ce lieu de souffrance. Ma première impression fut toute d'étonnement et de dégoût, devant la laideur des murs barbouillés d'encre, et devant les vieux bancs de bois luisants, usés, tailladés à coups de canif, où l'on sentait que tant d'écoliers avaient souffert. Sans me connaître, ils me tutoyaient, mes nouveaux compagnons, avec des airs protecteurs; moi, je les dévisageais timidement, les trouvant effrontés et, pour la plupart, fort mal tenus.

J'avais douze ans et demi, et j'entrais en troisième; mon professeur particulier avait déclaré que j'étais de force à suivre, si je voulais, bien que mon petit savoir fût très inégal. On composait ce premier jour, en version latine, pour le classement d'entrée, et je me rapelle que mon père m'attendait lui-même assez anxieusement à la sortie de cette séance d'essai. Je lui répondis que j'étais second sur une quinzaine, étonné qu'il parût attacher tant d'importance à une chose qui m'intéressait si peu. Ça m'était bien égal à moi! Navré comme j'étais, en quoi ce détail pouvait-il m'atteindre?

J'avais un calendrier où j'effaçais lentement les jours; vraiment, au début de cette année de collège, j'étais oppressé par la perspective de tant de mois, et de mois interminables comme ils étaient alors, dont il faudrait subir le passage avant d'atteindre seulement ces vacances de Pâques, ce répit de huit jours loin de l'ennui et de la souffrance. (Pierre Loti, *Roman d'un Enfant*)

We shall first of all make a literal translation, paragraph by paragraph, which will be studied closely and improved bit by bit. We shall then make a polished version of the whole piece.

This is our literal translation of the first paragraph:
In the middle of a wave of children who were talking all at the time, I penetrated into this place of suffering. . . .

au milieu = *in the middle of*; but we are not thinking of an exact geometrical spot so we should use *amidst*.

un flot = *a wave, rush* (of water); normally we speak of *a stream* of people.

tous = *all*; but its position is wrong (compare **Ils se dirigeaient tous vers l'entrée** = *They were all making their way towards the entrance*).

à la fois = *at the (same) time*, i.e. *at once.*

pénétrer = *to penetrate into*; the simplest is usually the best so we shall use *entered.*

Amidst a stream of children who were all talking at once, I entered this place of suffering. . . .

Notre Dame de Paris.

My first impression was all of astonishment and of disgust, in front of the ugliness of the walls daubed with ink, and before the old, shining benches of wood, worn, scored by pen-knife cuts, where one felt that so many schoolboys had suffered. . . .

barbouillés = *daubed* or *smeared.*

luisants must refer to **les bancs** and not to *wood*, as it is in the plural.

usés = *worn*; the verb **user** = *to wear out.*

293

tailladés; **la taille** = *stature, figure, waist*; but it also has a meaning connected with cutting; **le tailleur** = *a man who cuts out* [*cloth.*]
l'on = *one.*

My first impression was all of astonishment and disgust, before the ugliness of the walls smeared with ink, and before the old, shining, worn wooden benches, scored by pen-knife cuts, where one felt that so many schoolboys had suffered. . . .

Without knowing me, they used the form 'tu', my new companions, with protecting airs. I looked into their faces timidly, finding them shameless and, for the most part, badly dressed. . . .

connaître = *to know personally; to know* a person or place, not a fact.

protecteurs; **un protecteur** = *patron*, usually a rich person who gave his protection, i.e. patronage.

dévisager = *to stare into the face*; sometimes = *to stare out of countenance.*
effrontés = *cheeky, impudent.*
tenus = *dressed*; compare **tenue de soirée** = *evening dress.*

Without knowing me my new companions used the form 'tu', with patronising looks; I stared at them timidly, finding them shameless and, for the most part very untidy. . . .

Second paragraph:
I was twelve and a half and I was entering into the third; my personal teacher had declared that I was of strength to follow, if I wanted, although my little learning was very unequal. They were composing Latin unseens that day, for the entrance classification, and I remember that my father was waiting for me himself quite anxiously at the exit from this trial sitting. I replied to him that I was second out of fifteen, astonished that he should attach so much importance to a thing which interested me so little. It was all the same to me! Broken-hearted as I was, in what this detail could it reach me? . . .

troisième = *the fourth form* (**sixième** = *the first form* in French schools).
particulier = *private, personal.*
savoir = *knowledge*; it is a noun as well as a verb.
composer = *to sit a written examination*, so this cannot be translated as *composing.*
séance comes from **seoir** = *to sit* (scarcely used but compare **s'asseoir**).
essai comes from **essayer** = *to try.*
second sur une quinzaine = *second out of fifteen* (compare $\frac{12}{20}$ = **douze sur** [**vingt**).
ça m'est égal = *I don't care.*

I was twelve and a half and I was entering into the fourth form; my private teacher had declared that I was strong enough to follow, if I wanted, although my little learning was very uneven. That day they were writing Latin unseens, for the entrance classification, and I remember that my father was waiting for me himself quite anxiously, as we came out of this trial sitting. I told him that I was second out of fifteen or so, astonished that he appeared to attach so much importance to a thing which interested me so little. It was all the same to me. Broken-hearted as I was, in what way could this detail touch me? . . .

Third paragraph:
I had a calendar where I rubbed out slowly the days; really at the beginning of that year of school I was oppressed by the perspective of so many months and interminable months as they were, of which it would be necessary to undergo the passage before reaching only those Easter holidays, this respite of a week far from boredom and suffering. . . .

début = *beginning* (a **débutante** = *a woman starting out in the world*).
collège here = *school* (the words **lycée** and **collège** are almost inter-
subir = *to submit to, endure.*   [changeable).
huit jours = *a week* (*a fortnight* = **quinze jours**).
l'ennui . . . it is unidiomatic to use the article here in English.

I had a calendar in which I slowly rubbed out the days; truly, at the beginning of this school year, I was oppressed by the prospect of so many months, and of interminable months as they were then, whose passage I should have to bear before reaching even those Easter holidays, that respite of one week far from boredom and suffering.

FIRST DAYS AT SCHOOL

Amidst a stream of children all talking at once, I entered this place of suffering. My first impression was one of entire amazement and disgust before the ugliness of the ink-stained walls, the shining old worn wooden forms with their pen-knife carvings, where you felt so many pupils had suffered. Although they did not know me, my new companions addressed me in a familiar and patronising manner. For my part, I looked timidly into their faces, finding them brazen-faced and for the most part extremely untidily dressed.

I was twelve and a half and was going into the fourth form; my private tutor had intimated that I was up to this standard, if I were willing to try, although my small amount of learning was very uneven. That day they were writing Latin unseens to help stream the pupils, and I remember that my father himself was waiting rather anxiously for me as we came out of this trial-test. I told him that I was second out of some fifteen pupils, amazed that he could attach so much importance to something which was of such little interest to me. It really did not matter to me at all. How could such a minor point affect me, heart-broken as I was?

I possessed a calendar in which I slowly marked off the days; and indeed, at the beginning of this year at school, I was weighed down by the prospect of so many months — interminable months as they were at that time — which I should have to go through before reaching even the Easter holidays, and a week's break far from suffering and boredom.

2. PREPARING TO CORNER THE THIEVES

Ce monologue terminé, l'inspecteur se tourna vers Marius et lui demanda en le regardant fixement:

"Aurez-vous peur?"

"De quoi?" dit Marius.

"De ces hommes?"

"Pas plus que de vous!" répliqua rudement Marius qui commençait à remarquer que l'inspecteur ne lui avait pas encore dit "monsieur."

Celui-là regarda Marius plus fixement encore et reprit avec une sorte de solennité:

"Vous parlez là comme un homme brave et comme un homme honnête. Le courage ne craint pas le crime, et l'honnêteté ne craint pas l'autorité."

Marius l'interrompit:

"C'est bon: mais que comptez-vous faire?"

L'inspecteur se borna à lui répondre:

"Les locataires de cette maison-là ont des passe-partout pour rentrer la nuit chez eux. Vous devez en avoir un?"

"Oui," dit Marius.

"L'avez-vous sur vous?"

"Oui."

"Donnez-le-moi!" dit l'inspecteur.

Marius prit sa clef dans son gilet, le remit à l'inspecteur, et ajouta:

"Si vous m'en croyez, vous viendrez en force."

L'inspecteur jeta sur Marius un coup d'œil bizarre; puis il plongea d'un seul mouvement ses deux mains, qui étaient énormes, dans les deux immenses poches de son habit, et en tira deux petits pistolets d'acier. Il les présenta à Marius en disant vivement et d'un ton bref:

"Prenez ceci. Rentrez chez vous. Cachez-vous dans votre chambre. Qu'on vous croie sorti. Ils sont chargés. Chacun de deux balles. Vous observerez. Il y a un trou au mur, vous me l'avez dit. Les gens viendront. Laissez-les aller un peu. Quand vous jugerez la chose à point, et qu'il sera temps de l'arrêter, vous tirerez un coup de pistolet. Pas trop tôt. Le reste me regarde. Un seul coup de pistolet en l'air, au plafond, n'importe où."

Marius prit les pistolets et les cacha dans ses poches.

"Maintenant," poursuivit l'inspecteur, "il n'y a plus une minute à perdre."

Before writing our final version, we shall make a rough, literal one:

This monologue finished, the inspector turned towards Marius and asked him whilst looking hard at him:

"Will you be afraid?"

"Of what?" said Marius.

"Of these men?"

Le Palais des Papes à Avignon.

"No more than of you!" replied Marius sharply, who was beginning to notice that the inspector had not yet said "sir" to him.

Ce monologue . . . = *When he had finished this monologue*; a French past participle often needs to be expanded into a clause, compare: **Le travail fini, ils s'en allèrent** = *When the work was finished, they went off.*

se tourner = *to turn*; compare **se retourner** = *to turn round.*

regarder fixement = *to stare at*; we could say *as he stared hard at him* or simply *staring hard at him.*

aurez-vous peur; this is the future, it may suggest *are you likely to be afraid*; compare **aurez-vous vu mon livre quelque part?** = *Have you by chance* or *Do you happen to have seen my book anywhere?*

rudement = *roughly* or *sharply*; **remarquer** = *to notice* NOT *to remark.*

To address somebody as "sir" is preferable to *to say "sir" to somebody.*

The latter looked harder still at Marius and went on with a sort of solemnity:
"You speak there like a brave man and like an honest man. Courage does not fear crime and honesty does not fear authority."
Marius interrupted him:
"That's good; but what do you count on doing?"
The inspector limited himself to replying:
"The tenants of that house have master keys in order to return to their homes at night. You must have one?"

297

"Yes," said Marius.
"Have you it on you?"
"Yes."
"Give it to me!" said the inspector.
Marius took his key from his waistcoat, gave it to the inspector, and added:
"If you believe me, you will come in strength."

reprendre = *to carry on a conversation.*

un homme brave, un homme honnête = *a brave man, an honest man*; compare
un brave homme, un honnête homme = *a worthy fellow, a sensible, trustworthy man.*

le courage, l'autorité (= *the law*); it would be wrong to use the articles here in English.

c'est bon; some stronger expression must be found than *that's good.*

se borner; compare **une borne** = *a milestone.*

la nuit = *at night*; no preposition is used in French with parts of the day.

en avoir un; there is no need to translate **en** when we have a number.

prit sa clef dans son gilet; compare **Prenez la pomme sur le buffet** = *Take the apple from the sideboard.*

vous m'en croyez; **en** = *about it*; compare **à l'en croire** = *if he is to be believed.*

The inspector cast a strange glance on Marius; then he plunged in a single movement his two hands, which were huge, into the two immense pockets of his jacket, and drew out two small pistols of steel. He gave them to Marius saying sharply and in a brief tone:
"Take this. Go back home. Hide in your room. Let them think you gone out. They are loaded. Each with two bullets. You will observe. There is a hole in the wall, you have told me it. The men will come. Let them carry on a little. When you judge the thing at a head, and that it is time to stop it, you will fire a pistol shot. Not too soon. The rest concerns me. One single shot in the air, in the ceiling, no matter where."
Marius took the pistols and hid them in his pockets.
"Now," went on the inspector, "there is no longer a minute to lose."

en tira; again there is no need to translate the **en**.
bref; the translation of this word needs thought, *brief* will not do.
se cacher = *to hide (oneself)*; **cacher** = *to hide (something).*
qu'on vous croie . . . this idiom with **que** is the third person imperative (command) form, compare: **Qu'il entre!** = *Let him come in!*
charger = *to load* (note: **armer** = *to cock*), **charger de** = *to load with.*
vous observerez = *you will observe* (what is going on), i.e. *keep watch.*

vous me l'avez dit, compare: **Je vous l'ai déjà dit** = *I have already told you.*
quand vous jugerez; note future after **quand,** not required in English.
à point = *at a peak,* compare: **La viande est cuite à point** = *The meat is done to a turn.* **Arriver à point** = *to arrive in the nick of time.*
poursuivre = literally *to pursue,* compare **suivre** = *to follow.*

There are no difficult idioms here, and the aim will be to make the style of the finished piece simple, but as close to the French as possible:

PREPARING TO CORNER THE THIEVES
When he had finished this monologue, the inspector turned towards Marius and asked him, staring hard at him:
"Are you likely to be afraid?"
"Of what?" said Marius.
"Of these men?"
"No more afraid than I am of you!" replied Marius sharply, for he was beginning to notice that the inspector had not yet addressed him as "sir".
The inspector looked at Marius harder than ever and went on, somewhat solemnly:
"You speak like a brave man and like an honest man. Courage is not afraid of crime, and honesty has no fear of the law."
Marius interrupted him:
"That's all very well; but what are you proposing to do?"
The inspector said no more than:
"The tenants of that house have master keys so that they may get in at night. You must have one?"
"Yes," said Marius.
"Have you got it on you?"
"Yes."
"Give it me!" said the inspector.
Marius took the key from his waistcoat, handed it over to the inspector, and added:
"If you take my word for it, you will come in force."
The inspector gave Marius a queer look; in a single movement he plunged his two huge hands into two immense pockets in his jacket, and brought out two small, steel pistols. He handed them to Marius saying briskly and curtly:
"Take these. Go home. Hide in your room. Let them think you have gone out. The pistols are loaded. Two bullets in each. You will keep watch. There is a hole in the wall, you told me so. The men will come. Let them carry on for a while. When you think the right moment has come and it is time to stop the business you will fire one shot only. Not too soon. After that it is my business. One pistol shot in the air, in the ceiling, anywhere.

Le Mont St. Michel, vieux monastère construit sur une île.

Marius took the pistols and hid them in his pockets.
"And now," went on the inspector, "there is not a minute to lose."

EXERCISES

Here are three passages for you to try, with notes to help you. Do not look at the model translations until you have made your own version.

1. HOW A DOG INSPIRED A LOVE OF MUSIC

Gaspard était un petit chien noir, lourd, pas bien de sa personne mais qui possédait deux yeux pleins de vie et de bonne amitié. Je ne sais plus comment il avait été recueilli chez nous, où il passa quelques mois et où je l'aimai tendrement.

Or, un soir, pendant une promenade d'hiver, Gaspard m'avait quitté. On me consola en me disant qu'il rentrerait certainement seul, et je revins à la maison assez courageusement. Mais quand la nuit tomba, mon cœur se serra beaucoup.

Mes parents avaient à dîner ce jour-là un violoniste de talent et on m'avait permis de veiller pour l'entendre. Aux premiers coups de son archet, dès qu'il commença de faire gémir je ne sais quel adagio désolé, ce fut pour moi comme une évocation de routes noires dans les bois, de grande nuit où l'on se sent abandonné et perdu; puis je vis très nettement Gaspard errer sous la pluie, à un carrefour sinistre, et, ne se reconnaissant plus, partir dans une direction inconnue pour ne revenir plus jamais. . . . Alors les larmes me vinrent, et comme on ne s'en apercevait point, le violon continua de lancer dans le silence ses appels tristes.

Ce fut ma première initiation à la musique. Des années passèrent ensuite avant que j'y comprisse de nouveau quelque chose, car les petits morceaux de piano, "remarquable pour mon âge," disait-on, que je commençais à jouer moi-même, n'étaient encore rien qu'un bruit doux et rythmé à mes oreilles.

(Pierre Loti, *Roman d'un Enfant*)

Lourd = *heavy*, but there is a better word to describe a person or animal; **recueillir** = *to gather up, collect*; **serrer** = *to grip*, **se serrer** = *to become tighter*, (of heart) = *to sink*; **un archet** = (*violin*) *bow*; **se reconnaître** = *to make out where one is*; **le carrefour** = *cross-roads*.

2. A HARD LIVING

Il fallait pourtant trouver les moyens de vivre. Son traitement à l'orchestre n'y suffisait plus. Il donna des leçons. Son talent de virtuose, sa bonne réputation, et surtout la protection du prince lui attirèrent une nombreuse clientèle dans la haute bourgeoisie. Tous les matins, depuis neuf heures, il enseignait le piano à des fillettes, souvent plus âgées que lui, qui l'intimidaient par leur coquetterie et qui l'exaspéraient par la niaiserie de leur jeu. Elles étaient, en musique, d'une stupidité parfaite; en revanche, elles possédaient toutes, plus ou moins, un sens aigu du ridicule; et leur regard moqueur ne faisait grâce à Christophe d'aucune de ses maladresses. C'était une torture pour lui. Assis à côté d'elles, sur le bord de la chaise, crevant de colère et n'osant pas bouger, ayant peur du son de sa voix, il s'efforçait de prendre un air sérieux tout en se sentant observé du coin de l'œil; il perdait contenance, craignait d'être ridicule, l'était, et s'emportait jusqu'aux reproches blessants. Il était bien facile à ses élèves de se venger; et elles n'y manquaient point, en l'embarrassant par une certaine façon de le regarder, de lui poser les questions les plus simples, qui le faisaient rougir jusqu'aux yeux; ou bien, elles lui demandaient un petit service — comme d'aller prendre sur un meuble un objet oublié — ce qui était pour lui la plus pénible épreuve. (Romain Rolland, *Jean Christophe*)

Le traitement = *salary*; **la bourgeoisie** = *middle classes*; **leur jeu** = *their silly behaviour*; **en revanche** = *by contrast, on the other hand*; **aigu** = *sharp, keen*; **crever de colère** = literally *to burst with anger*, i.e. *to boil with rage*; **s'emporter** = *to lose one's temper*; **manquer à quelque chose** = *to fail at something*; **poser des questions** = *to ask questions*; **une épreuve** = *test, trial*.

301

3. EATING OUT FOR THE FIRST TIME

Je l'ai dit, nous étions au moment de Pâques. Ces vacances furent marquées par deux faits mémorables. Nous allâmes, un jour, les trois grands, Joseph, Ferdinand et moi, faire avec notre père une promenade à la campagne. En suivant la rue Vercingétorix, on sortait bientôt de Paris. Il suffisait alors de longer le chemin de fer de l'Ouest pour gagner Meudon et les bois.

En arrivant en vue du bois, nous rencontrâmes un sentier gardé par un écriteau sur lequel on pouvait lire: "Passage interdit." Ferdinand, premier de la bande, s'était arrêté, là, devant, comme au pied d'une muraille.

"On ne peut pas aller plus loin," cria-t-il.

Papa souriait, l'air moqueur. Il étendit la main, toucha l'écriteau dont le bois était vermoulu, et, soudain, l'arracha puis le lança très loin, dans une fondrière.

"Voilà," dit-il, en souriant. "Le passage n'est plus interdit. Avancez, mes garçons." Je restais en arrière, troublé jusqu'au fond de l'âme.

L'autre événement fut un repas au restaurant. Nous avions fait des courses tout le jour. Papa dit:

"Rien n'est prêt à la maison. Nous irons manger au restaurant."

"Raymond," dit maman, "c'est la folie."

Et papa:

"On verra bien!"

Le restaurant était presque désert et la salle, peinte en vert, traversée par un énorme tuyau de poêle.

Maman disait:

"Ça me surprend toujours de manger des aliments que je n'ai pas préparés moi-meme."

Nous trouvions tout délicieux et, surtout, de goût étrange.

"C'est un restaurant très chic," murmura Joseph en se rengorgeant.

"Mais non," fit papa. "C'est un restaurant de quatre sous."

Notre grande joie tomba. Maman murmurait:

"Il ne fallait pas le leur dire. Ils ne s'en seraient pas aperçus."

Longer = *to go along beside*; **vermoulu** = *worm-eaten*; **une fondrière** = *a ditch*; **faire des courses** = *to go shopping*; **un tuyau de poêle** = *a pipe from a stove*; **se rengorger** = *to puff oneself up, gorge oneself.*

LEÇON 29

ENGLISH INTO FRENCH

This paper is set to test your ability to translate a simple piece of English accurately into French. This means that your knowledge of (*a*) grammar, (*b*) vocabulary, and (*c*) idiomatic constructions is all being tested at the same time. Here is some helpful practical advice:

1. Read the extract right through very carefully more than once. Even if the passage is divided into paragraphs, it is, none the less, a complete story or conversation.

2. Plan your time. The actual writing of the piece will take only fifteen minutes. It is essential to think it out before writing. Avoid rushing or crossing out. If asked to write in paragraphs, do so.

3. Decide on the main tense (probably past historic or perfect) and stick to it. The type of passage given will help you to decide this.

4. Avoid translating word-for-word; e.g. if you have to translate *ticket-collector* and do not know the correct word, which is **contrôleur**, then the nearest substitute which will not lose many marks is probably **l'employé**; do not use **l'homme qui prend les billets** — this type of word-for-word paraphrase must be avoided.

5. Beware of words which look alike in French and English, but have a very different meaning in each, e.g. **assister,** which does not mean *to assist.*

6. Pay attention to details such as punctuation, accents, hyphens and spelling. Hundreds of candidates each year, who know both verbs perfectly well, write **entendre** when they mean **écouter**, **raconter** when they mean **rencontrer**, or **acheter** when they mean **vendre**. This is careless and is severely penalised.

HOW TO GAIN MARKS

1. Know your irregular verbs, particularly their past historics. It is painful for the examiner to find the same wrong forms each year.

2. Look out for changes in tense. You may well have the present, imperfect, past historic, perfect, future or conditional in the same passage.

3. Look for negatives and be sure to use the appropriate form, e.g. **ne . . . pas, ne . . . que, ne . . . jamais, ne . . . plus, ne . . . personne, ne . . . rien**, etc. Be careful not to add an unnecessary **pas** to one of these other forms.

303

4. Look for common idioms such as **venir de** (e.g. **Il vient de sortir**), **partir en courant, dire en souriant, avoir beau, avoir honte,** etc.

5. Pay careful attention to the passive; try to avoid it as much as possible by using **on** or a reflexive verb, e.g.:

La porte s'ouvrit.	*The door opened.*
On lui demanda.	*He was asked.*
On le fit entrer.	*He was brought in.*

6. Look for commands; remember the irregular imperatives of **avoir, être,** etc.: **ayez la bonté de** (= *have the goodness to*), **soyez raisonnable** (= *be reasonable*), **ne soyez pas désobéissant** (= *don't be disobedient*), **veuillez** (from **vouloir**) **vous asseoir** (= *be so good as to sit down*), **levez-vous** (= *get up*), **ne vous inquiétez pas** (= *don't be anxious*), **souvenez-vous** (= *remember*).

Here are two passages as examples, showing how to apply these rules and hints; the first is conversational, the second pure narrative; sometimes a passage is set in which the verb is in the first person.

A. "Will you come and visit us next year?" said John. "We have a pretty little house and I know you love country life."

"I should very much like to come," answered his new friend. "I shall ask my parents when I return home and I shall write to you at once."

"We generally spend the month of July abroad," continued John, "but we are always at home during August. Father does not go often to the office during these two summer months. He spends hours in the garden, reading or with his painting."

"You are lucky," his friend replied. "We cannot leave London before the end of the summer term. My father is geography master at the grammar school; because of the examinations he has much work to do after the fourteenth of July."

"Two years ago we spent our holidays in Brittany," said John. "Unfortunately, it rained most of the time and we were unable to go bathing, but I loved the scenery, the people and the food. I hope to go back there again in a few years' time."

"My parents have never allowed me to go abroad alone," said his friend. "That is what I really want to do. At school I have always done well in modern languages and I am certain I could make myself understood in France, Germany or Switzerland."

"Perhaps we shall be able to go together one day," said John. "When my parents have met you and your parents, I am sure we shall be able to convince them that we are old enough and sensible enough to travel together without them. I hope so!"

This passage contains a variety of tenses; where someone is actually speaking the appropriate past tense is the perfect tense. For the words which are not actually direct speech you may use either the perfect or the past historic, but, once having decided, you must stick to the same one. We shall translate this passage sentence by sentence, pointing out pitfalls and special grammatical points which you must look out for.

"Will you come and visit us next year?" said John. "We have a pretty little house and I know you love country life."

Will you come = **Voulez-vous venir**; *will you* can be either (*a*) simple future, e.g. *Will you see him tomorrow?* = **Le verrez-vous demain?** or (*b*) it can mean *do you want to, are you willing to*, e.g. **Voulez-vous ouvrir la porte, s'il vous plaît?** = *Will you open the door, please?*

a pretty little house; remember the two agreements — **une jolie, petite. . . .**

I know; be sure to choose the right verb *to know*: **savoir** = *to know* (*a fact* or *how to*), **connaître** = *to know* (*a person* or *place*).

country life, i.e. *the countryside* = **la campagne**; *in the country* = **à la campagne**. (What is the word for *a foreign country*?)

"Voulez-vous venir nous visiter l'année prochaine?" dit Jean. "Nous possédons une jolie, petite maison et je sais que vous aimez la vie à la campagne."

"I should very much like to come," answered his new friend. "I shall ask my parents when I return home and I shall write to you at once."

to want to do something = **vouloir faire** or **aimer faire, quelque chose**; this is a straightforward conditional tense — **je voudrais bien.**

new friend = **nouvel ami** (remember the special forms of **nouveau** and of **vieux** used before a masculine noun beginning with a vowel).

je demanderai à mes parents; look up and revise the list of verbs (p. 251) which take the dative of the person, e.g. **permettre quelque chose à quelqu'un.**

to return home = **rentrer**, or **retourner chez moi.**

"Je voudrais bien venir," répondit son nouvel ami. "Je demanderai à mes parents dès mon retour et je vous écrirai tout de suite."

"We generally spend the month of July abroad," continued John, "but we are always at home during August. Father does not go often to the office during these two summer months. He spends hours in the garden, reading or with his painting."

to spend time = **passer du temps** (*to spend money* = **dépenser**); remember to put the adverb after the verb.

abroad = **à l'étranger** (*to go abroad* = **aller à l'étranger**).

to continue (where this = *to say*, after direct speech) = **reprendre.**

at home = **à la maison** or **chez nous.**

to spend hours doing (*something*) = **passer des heures à** + infinitive.

in the garden = **au jardin** (**dans** usually means *inside* or *into*).

Father = **Papa**; when talking about your father use **papa** or **mon père**.

summer months = **les mois d'été** (*winter months* = **les mois d'hiver**).

with his painting = **à faire de la peinture**.

"**Nous passons généralement le mois de juillet à l'étranger,**" reprit Jean, "**mais nous sommes toujours chez nous pendant le mois d'août. Papa ne va pas souvent au bureau en été. Il passe des heures au jardin à lire ou à faire de la peinture.**"

"*You are lucky,*" *his friend replied.* "*We cannot leave London before the end of the summer term. My father is geography master at the grammar school; because of the examinations he has much work to do after the fourteenth of July.*"

to be lucky = **avoir de la chance**.

to leave (*a town*) = **quitter** (**une ville**).

before = **avant** (for time) or **devant** (for place); which must we use?

the term = **le trimestre**.

a master = **un professeur**; no article is used with trades or professions, compare **Il est médecin** = *He is a doctor*.

geography master = **professeur de géographie**.

because of = **à cause de**.

much = **beaucoup de** + a noun (**il a beaucoup de travail à faire**).

the fourteenth of July = **le quatorze juillet** (do not translate *of*).

"**Vous avez de la chance,**" répondit son ami. "**Nous ne pouvons pas quitter Londres avant la fin du trimestre d'été. Mon père est professeur de géographie au lycée; à cause des examens il a beaucoup de travail à faire à partir du quatorze juillet.**"

"*Two years ago we spent our holidays in Brittany,*" *said John.* "*Unfortunately, it rained most of the time and we were unable to go bathing, but I loved the scenery, the people and the food. I hope to go back there again in a few years' time.*"

two years ago = **il y a deux ans**.

we spent (this must be translated by the perfect tense) = **nous avons passé**.

in Brittany = **en Bretagne** (**en** is seldom followed by an article).

it rained . . . = **il a plu** (past participle of **pleuvoir**); continue to use the perfect tense.

most of the time = **la plupart du temps**.

to go bathing = **aller se baigner**.

I loved = **j'ai aimé** or **j'ai beaucoup admiré, apprécié**.

the scenery, the people, and the food = **le paysage, les habitants et la cuisine** (i.e. *the cooking*); note that the general word for *people* = **les gens**; **le peuple** = *the common masses*.

Carcassonne, ville construite au Moyen Age, a encore ses murailles.

I hope = **j'espère** (be careful to change the accent of **espérer** when the last
-**e** is silent as here).

to go back = **retourner** (*to come back* = **revenir**).

in a few years' time = **dans quelques années (dans** can only be used in this
way of future time).

**"Il y a deux ans nous avons passé nos vacances en Bretagne," dit Jean.
"Malheureusement il a plu la plupart du temps et nous n'avons pas pu aller
nous baigner. Mais j'ai fort apprécié le paysage, les habitants et la cuisine.
J'espère y retourner dans quelques années."**

*"My parents have never allowed me to go abroad alone," said his friend.
"That is what I really want to do. At school I have always done well in modern
languages and I am certain I could make myself understood in France, Germany
or Switzerland."*

to allow someone to do something = **permettre à quelqu'un de faire quelque
chose** (*to allow something* = **permettre quelque chose; ce n'est pas permis** =
that is not allowed).

307

to go abroad = **aller à l'étranger**.

that is what I really want to do = **voilà ce que je voudrais faire**.

to do well in = **être fort(e) en**.

modern languages = **les langues vivantes**.

I am certain I could make myself understood = **je suis certain que** (never omit the **que** in this construction) **je saurais me faire comprendre** (for **savoir** here compare: **Il sait jouer du piano** = *He can play the piano*).

to make oneself understood = **se faire comprendre** (change the **se** to **me** for the first person).

in France = **en France**.

"Mes parents ne m'ont jamais permis d'aller à l'étranger tout seul," dit son ami. **"Voilà ce que je voudrais vraiment faire. À l'école j'ai toujours été fort en langues vivantes et je suis certain que je saurais me faire comprendre en France, en Allemagne ou en Suisse."**

"Perhaps we shall be able to go together one day," said John. "When my parents have met you and your parents, I am sure we shall be able to convince them that we are old enough and sensible enough to travel together without them. I hope so!"

perhaps we = **peut-être que nous**; use this construction to begin a sentence.

we shall be able to go there = **nous pourrons y aller**; remember to put the pronoun **y** directly before the verb it depends on, i.e. **aller** not **pouvoir**.

to meet = **faire la connaissance de** (i.e. *to meet for the first time*, but *to go and meet someone at the station* = **aller à la gare à la rencontre de quelqu'un**) — the action has not yet taken place so we use the future perfect, compare: **J'achèterai une voiture neuve quand j'aurai vendu celle-ci** = *I shall buy a new car when I have sold this one*.

to be old enough to = **être assez âgé pour** + infinitive.

sensible = **sage** or **raisonnable** (not **sensible**, which = *sensitive*).

without them = **sans eux**; the strong form of the pronoun follows a preposition.

I hope so = **je l'espère**, i.e. *I hope it*; *I certainly hope so* = **je l'espère bien**.

"Peut-être que nous pourrons y aller tous les deux un jour," dit Jean. **"Quand mes parents auront fait votre connaissance et celle de vos parents je suis sûr que nous pourrons les convaincre que nous sommes assez âgés et assez sages pour voyager ensemble tous les deux sans eux. Je l'espère bien!"**

Here is the completed final version:

"Voulez-vous venir nous visiter l'année prochaine?" dit Jean. **"Nous possédons une jolie petite maison et je sais que vous aimez la vie à la campagne."**

"Je voudrais bien venir," répondit son nouvel ami. **"Je demanderai à mes parents dès mon retour et je vous écrirai tout de suite."**

"Nous passons généralement le mois de juillet à l'étranger," reprit Jean, "mais nous sommes toujours chez nous pendant le mois d'août. Papa ne va pas souvent au bureau en été. Il passe des heures au jardin à lire ou à faire de la peinture."

"Vous avez de la chance," répondit son ami. "Nous ne pouvons pas quitter Londres avant la fin du trimestre d'été. Mon père est professeur de géographie au lycée; à cause des examens il a beaucoup de travail à faire à partir du quatorze juillet."

"Il y a deux ans nous avons passé nos vacances en Bretagne," dit Jean. "Malheureusement il a plu la plupart du temps et nous n'avons pas pu aller nous baigner. Mais j'ai fort apprécié le paysage, les paysans français et la cuisine. J'espère y retourner dans quelques années."

"Mes parents ne m'ont jamais permis d'aller à l'étranger tout seul," dit son ami. "Voilà ce que je voudrais vraiment faire. À l'école j'ai toujours été fort en langues vivantes et je suis certain que je saurais me faire comprendre en France, en Allemagne ou en Suisse."

"Peut-être que nous pourrons y aller tous les deux un jour," dit Jean. "Quand mes parents auront fait votre connaissance et celle de vos parents je suis sûr que nous pourrons les convaincre que nous sommes assez âgés et assez sages pour voyager ensemble tous les deux sans eux. Je l'espère bien!"

B. The wounded man had been carried to a nearby shop. The shopkeeper was a widow who lived alone in this small shop which was situated in a street at some distance from the centre of the village. She showed no sign of fear and not for a moment did she worry about the danger she was running. The neighbours also were equally courageous. They did all they could to help her look after the sick man. The doctor who was called in decided that an immediate operation was necessary. He carried the soldier into the kitchen and asked the widow to help him. When all was finished he left, saying that he would return the next day. The widow spent the whole night at his bedside. Next day, when the doctor returned, she told him that she would keep the soldier in her house for a few weeks, and that when he was better, she would send a message to the leader of the resistance army. She was sure that the latter would find him clothes, money and food, and obtain a car to take him as far as the frontier.

The wounded man had been carried to a nearby shop. The shopkeeper was a widow who lived alone in this small shop which was situated in a street at some distance from the centre of the village.

the wounded man = **le blessé.**

he had been carried — here it is quite permissible to use the passive; verbs like **demander, dire,** etc., should not be used in the passive.

shop = **la boutique** (*a small shop*; **le magasin** = *a large shop* or *store*).

shopkeeper = **le marchand**; but there is a feminine form — **la marchande.**

widow = **la veuve** (*widower* = **le veuf**).

lived alone, i.e. *was living alone*, so use the imperfect tense; **seul** must be made to agree with **la veuve** — **seule**.

from the centre of the village; **de** + **le** = **du**, i.e. **du centre du village**.

Le blessé avait été porté à une boutique qui se trouvait tout près. La marchande était une veuve qui vivait seule dans cette petite boutique située dans une rue à quelque distance du centre du village.

She showed no sign of fear and not for a moment did she worry about the danger she was running. The neighbours also were equally courageous. They did all they could to help her look after the sick man.

no sign of fear = **aucun signe de peur**; with the negative adjectives **nul** and **aucun** we use **ne** but no **pas**.

did she worry; remember that *did* is not translated in French, compare: **Il ne vint pas** = *He did not come*; **Je ne travaille pas** = *I do not work*.

to worry about = **s'inquiéter de**.

danger she was running; the relative pronoun *that* or *which* = **que** must not be left out in the French.

to do all one can = **faire tout ce qu'on peut**, but here we might use **faire de son mieux** = *to do one's best*.

to look after (a sick person) = **soigner** (compare **chercher** = *to look for*).

the sick man = **le malade** (compare **le blessé** = *the wounded* [*man*]).

Elle ne montra aucun signe de peur et pas un instant ne s'inquiéta du danger qu'elle courait. Les voisins, aussi, étaient également courageux. Ils firent de leur mieux pour l'aider à soigner le malade.

The doctor who was called in decided that an immediate operation was necessary. He carried the soldier into the kitchen and asked the widow to help him. When all was finished he left, saying that he would return the next day. The widow spent the whole night at his bedside.

to call in = **appeler**; use **on** instead of the passive; **le médecin** is not the subject of the first clause so we use **que**, not **qui**.

an immediate operation . . . ; the simple construction *it was necessary to operate* . . . is preferable here, i.e. **il fallait l'opérer**.

he asked the widow to help him; remember that the construction is **demander à quelqu'un de faire quelque chose**.

all = **tout** (the masculine singular form is used in this way).

he left = **il partit** or **il s'en alla** (we could not use **il quitta** here).

saying = present participle — **en disant**.

he would come back = **il reviendrait** (**retournerait** = *would go back*).

bedside — it is better to use the simple phrase **près de son lit** here.

Le médecin qu'on avait appelé, décida qu'il fallait l'opérer sur-le-champ. Il

porta le soldat dans la cuisine et demanda à la veuve de l'aider à faire l'opération. Quand tout était terminé il s'en alla, en disant qu'il reviendrait le lendemain matin. La veuve passa la nuit tout entière près de son lit.

Next day, when the doctor returned, she told him that she would keep the soldier in her house for a few weeks, and that when he was better, she would send a message to the leader of the resistance army. She was sure that the former would find him clothes, money and food, and obtain a car to take him as far as the frontier.

to return = **revenir** (like **venir**).

she told him = **elle lui dit**; remember it is **dire quelque chose à quelqu'un.**

to keep = **garder.**

for a few weeks; for duration of time we use **pendant.**

she would send; this must be the conditional tense of **envoyer.**

sure must agree with **elle** — **sûre.**

the former = **celui-là** (*the latter* = **celui-ci**).

would find him clothes, i.e. *would find clothes for him* = **lui.**

clothes, money, etc.; we must use the partitive **des vêtements, de l'argent**, etc. (not **monnaie** which = *coins* specifically, or *change*).

to take him; beware, this really means *to get him taken* = **le faire conduire, transporter** (**prendre quelqu'un** = *to catch, capture* prisoner, etc.).

Le lendemain matin, quand le médecin revint, elle lui dit qu'elle garderait le soldat chez elle pendant quelques semaines, et que, quand il irait mieux, elle enverrait un message au chef de la Résistance. Elle était sûre que celui-ci lui trouverait des vêtements, de l'argent et de la nourriture, et qu'il trouverait une voiture pour le faire transporter jusqu'à la frontière.

Here is the completed final version:

Le blessé avait été porté à une boutique qui se trouvait tout près. La marchande était une veuve qui vivait seule dans cette petite boutique située dans une rue à quelque distance du centre du village. Elle ne montra aucun signe de peur et pas un instant ne s'inquiéta du danger qu'elle courait. Les voisins, aussi, étaient également courageux. Ils firent de leur mieux pour l'aider à soigner le malade. Le médecin qu'on avait appelé, décida qu'il fallait l'opérer sur-le-champ. Il porta le soldat dans la cuisine et demanda à la veuve de l'aider à faire l'opération. Quand tout était terminé il s'en alla, en disant qu'il reviendrait le lendemain matin. La veuve passa la nuit tout entière près de son lit. Le lendemain matin, quand le médecin revint, elle lui dit qu'elle garderait le soldat chez elle pendant quelques semaines, et que, quand il irait mieux, elle enverrait un message au chef de la Résistance. Elle était sûre que celui-ci lui trouverait des vêtements, de l'argent et de la nourriture, et qu'il trouverait une voiture pour le faire transporter jusqu'à la frontière.

Les cônes des deux volcans du Puy de Dôme sont surmontés l'un par une église et l'autre par une statue de la Vierge Marie.

EXERCISES

Here are six passages for you to try; there are notes with each one, to help you. Do not look at the model versions until you have made your own. The first should be put into the past historic tense.

1. The following morning Henry got up earlier than usual. When he had washed and dressed, he went into his mother's bedroom. She was still very weak after her illness. Fortunately, her sister, Madame Villeneuve, had been able to delay her departure, and had promised Henry that she would remain until the arrival of the daily help.

Henry told his mother not to worry, kissed her and said goodbye. He had barely half an hour left and he ate his breakfast hurriedly. He was on the point of leaving when the postman knocked at the door. Henry took the letters, glancing at them quickly to see if there was one for him. In fact, there were two — one from Germany — this was probably from his elder brother George, who was doing his military service abroad — the other was evidently from his new employer.

Without waiting to open them, Henry put them in his pocket and left the others on the dining-room table. As he was making his way to the station, he heard the town hall clock strike eight o'clock. There were few people in the street at this early hour. Henry stopped at the corner of the street and bought a newspaper, then, hastening a little, he crossed the road and arrived, five minutes later, before the large entrance.

At the ticket-office he asked for a return ticket. At the gate the ticket-collector gave him a pleasant smile and told him that the train was already waiting at platform six, and would depart in four minutes. Henry found a second-class compartment, chose a seat in the corner and sat down. Here he was, at last, on his way to London to begin his new job.

To wash and dress = **faire sa toilette**; *to be weak* = **être faible**; *to delay one's departure* = **retarder son départ**; *to promise someone something* = **promettre quelque chose à quelqu'un**; *to kiss somebody* = **embrasser quelqu'un**; *to eat hurriedly* = **manger à la hâte**; *to glance at* = **jeter un coup d'œil à**; *to do one's military service* = **faire son service militaire**; *the town hall* = **l'hôtel de ville**; *the ticket-office* = **le guichet**; *to hasten* = **se hâter**; *the daily help* = **la femme de ménage**.

The second is personal and needs the perfect tense.
2. When I arrived home, mother seemed worried. For a few moments she said nothing, then at last, after putting my meal on the table, she turned to me and said:

"I have bad news for you. Your father fell ill at the office today and they sent him to hospital. Hurry up and eat; we must take the bus at the corner of the road at half-past seven and go and visit him."

She had just finished saying this when there was a ring at the door. Mother went to open it but returned almost at once, followed by Uncle Thomas, father's brother. He had obviously come to offer to help us.

"My car is at the door," he said. "I have already phoned the hospital. Your father is not too ill to receive visitors. We ought to take a few of his belongings and some books. Perhaps he will want to read in a few days. Come along, Charles! You need not look so sad. All will be well again soon. Help your mother to put on her coat. We shall leave at once."

After putting — use **après** with the past infinitive; *to turn to* = **se tourner vers**; *to fall ill* = **tomber malade**; *to make haste to do something* = **se dépêcher de** + the infinitive; *we must* — take care with the tense; *went to open it* — leave out *it* in your translation; *too ill to* = **trop malade pour** + the infinitive; *we ought* — conditional of **devoir**; *to look sad* = **avoir l'air triste**; *soon* (i.e. *shortly*) = **avant peu**; *to help someone to do something* = **aider quelqu'un à faire quelque chose**.

The third passage is a first person narrative, but less conversational in style and might well be written in the past historic tense.
3. I hastily left my little shelter and, when I found myself in the open air again, I had the strength to wipe my red, damp brow. For a moment I leaned against a tree and shortly afterwards the surgeon came and bandaged my forehead.

313

Great, cold drops of rain were falling on my head and seemed to be doing me some good.

"I am tired of the war," I said to the doctor — at least I thought it was the doctor.

"And so am I," said a deep voice which I seemed to recognize.

I raised the bandage from my eyes and I saw, not the doctor, but the general. He was alone, standing in front of me, looking very sad. His great boots were sunk in the mud, his coat torn, the rain was dripping from his hat. He stared at me and said:

"I have seen you somewhere, haven't I?" These words made me realize that I had aged more in looks than in years.

"I have seen you many times, without being seen myself," I replied.

"Do you want to be promoted?"

I said: "It is too late."

He folded his arms for a moment without replying, then said:

"You are right. In a few days we shall probably both be dead."

Hastily = **à la hâte**; *in the open air* = **en plein air, au grand air**; *came and bandaged* — translate *came to bandage*; *to do good* = **faire du bien**; *tired of* = **las de** (not **fatigué**); *I thought it was . . .* — translate *I thought (myself) to be talking to the doctor*; *not the doctor* = **non pas le docteur**; *to drip (trickle)* = **ruisseler**; *to stare at* = **considérer**; *haven't I* — remember the special French idiom for phrases of this nature; *in looks* = **de visage**; *to be promoted* — use *promotion* = **l'avancement** (m.); *we shall* = **vous et moi, nous serons**.

4. On arriving at the school, I went into the recreation room and sat down at a table some distance from the boys. I heard them laughing and talking; I saw, as if in a dream, the smiling face of Dupré, and little Berger's, and Lambert busy suggesting to Fauriat that if it snowed on Thursday they would be able to organize a snowball fight between the third and fourth forms. Suddenly I stood up and walked around the room. I had to find a means of reaching my brother. How was I to do it? I could no longer remain in that school where I was ashamed and too unhappy to work. Then I had an idea. "I shall go away," I thought. "When I arrive in Paris I shall look for my brother's flat. I shall tell him. . . ." A stern voice interrupted my thoughts. "Sir," the Headmaster was saying, "take your books and follow me."

On arriving = **en** + the present participle; *some distance from* = **à quelque distance de**; *laughing and talking* — use the infinitives; *as if* = **comme**; *Berger's* = **celui de Berger**; *to be busy doing something* = **être en train de faire quelque chose**; *if it snowed* — imperfect tense; *on Thursday* = **jeudi**; *I had to find* = **il me fallait** + the infinitive; *I could* — be careful which tense you use; *too unhappy to* = **trop malheureux pour** + the infinitive; *when I arrive* — be careful of the tense of the verb; *follow (me)* = **moi**.

5. The boy turned back and soon found himself in the neighbourhood of the station. He had been walking for two hours; he was beginning to feel hungry and thought longingly of his bed at home. "What has become of Jacques?" he wondered.

Suddenly, he saw the café where they had had breakfast that morning. He went in and settled himself at a table near the window. "I ought to wait here," he thought. "I shall be sheltered from the rain and able to see Jacques approaching from the direction of the town."

He had just asked the waiter for a cup of coffee when he thought he recognized his friend running out of the baker's shop opposite. But he was mistaken: it was only a stranger carrying a loaf under his arm.

For two hours — use **depuis**, and take care with the tense of the verb; *to begin to* = **commencer**; *to be hungry* = **avoir faim**; *to become of* = **devenir** (= *to become*); *to wonder* = **se demander**, take care with the word order; *to go in* = **entrer**; *near* = **près de**; *I ought* — use the conditional of **devoir**; *to be sheltered from* = **être à l'abri de**; *and able* — use the future of **pouvoir**; *approaching from* — use **venir de**; *to ask someone for something* = **demander quelque chose à quelqu'un**; *to run out of* = **sortir en courant de**; *carrying* = **qui portait**.

6. When we had finished eating, I helped Eliane to wash up. Then we were so tired that we went to bed and slept soundly until the next morning. For breakfast we had only a small roll with a large cup of coffee, and then we hurried out to meet my father who was to leave his office at half-past eleven.

He arrived a little late at eleven-forty, saying that a difficult customer had come in at the last moment and he had not been able to get away. We all got into Eliane's little car and were soon speeding towards St. Lazare station to catch the twelve o'clock train.

We found an empty second-class compartment. My father sank into a corner seat and closed his eyes, exhausted. We had been there only a short time when we were joined by an old man and a little boy, whom I had noticed at the ticket office, busy searching their pockets to find enough money for the journey. They told us they were going to Le Havre to meet the boy's father returning from America.

Eating — use the infinitive; *to help someone to do something* = **aider quelqu'un à faire quelque chose**; *we had* — use **prendre**; *out to meet* = **pour aller attendre**; *to leave his office* = **quitter le bureau**; *to get into* = **monter dans**; *to speed towards* = **filer vers**; *to sink into* = **se laisser tomber dans**; *his eyes* — use the definite article; *we had been there only a short time* — use a construction with **depuis**; *we were joined* — alter this so that you use the active, not the passive form of **joindre**; *the ticket office* = **le guichet**; *busy searching* — use **en train de** + the infinitive; *returning from* — use **revenir de**.

LEÇON 30

COMPOSITION

The essay or free composition is a very important part of the examination. Different types of essay are set by the different examining Boards, but the essentials are the same in each. You are usually required to write between 150 and 200 words — seldom more — either on a title given, or in the form of a letter, or a story on a theme depicted in a set of pictures, or the continuation of a story already begun in the English-French translation. You are normally asked to write this in past tenses — often you are told to avoid the past historic. You will, however, still use the imperfect tense for the descriptive parts, for the background of the story, and to describe feelings as opposed to actions; you may even need to use the present tense — especially if you bring in some conversation.

1. The length of your composition is most important; no marks are given for writing more than you are asked to. You may be asked to state the number of words you have written; if so, do so reasonably accurately. Do not state about 150 if you have written 250 words.

2. Plan your time; you will probably have about forty to forty-five minutes in which to write your composition. If you are given a set of pictures, do not spend 100 words on the first picture.

3. Read all the instructions carefully; sometimes you are asked to tell the story as if you are one of the persons involved, i.e. in the first person. If so, be sure to use first person verb-endings.

4. Do not attempt to prepare a composition which you intend to use, whatever the title or type of subject set. The story or letter should be quite simple, must be in your own words, be accurate, and should have a beginning, a middle and an end. Do not break off abruptly.

5. If possible use the perfect tense as the main tense, i.e. to denote every step forward in the narrative. Check this carefully; consider:

> *On opening the suitcase he was astonished to find inside a bundle of notes.* **En ouvrant la valise il s'est étonné d'y trouver un paquet de billets de banque.**

We use the perfect tense here to translate *he was astonished* because although this is a state or feeling, it is here the result of a specific action and constitutes one distinct step in the narrative.

6. Remember that all reflexive verbs are conjugated with **être** in the perfect tense, and that the rule for the agreement of the past participles of such

verbs is the same as for verbs which take **avoir** (see page 225).

Here are five examples of different types of composition as might be set by the various examination Boards. Study them carefully, paying special attention to the tenses used.

A. A story in the present tense is read out in English; candidates are also given a short summary in French. They are then asked to tell the story in French using the past tense, but changing it into the first person.

Summary: **Fin des vacances — faire une promenade à bicyclette — aller pêcher — s'arrêter — manger une glace — bicyclette volée — poursuite — retrouver la bicyclette.**

UNE AVENTURE À LA CAMPAGNE

C'était le dernier jour des vacances. Mon frère et moi voulions faire quelque chose d'intéressant pour célébrer nos derniers moments de liberté avant la rentrée au lycée. Comme il faisait beau nous avons décidé de partir faire une belle promenade à bicyclette. Dans un panier nous avons mis des sandwichs, des fruits de toutes sortes et un thermos de thé. Le sac au dos, nous sommes partis, après avoir promis à maman de rentrer avant la tombée de la nuit. Bientôt nous étions sur la route vers la campagne. Nous espérions arriver au bord d'une belle petite rivière où nous pourrions nous amuser à pêcher à la ligne, ou peut-être à nous baigner, car il faisait très chaud. Dans un petit village nous nous sommes arrêtés un instant pour acheter une glace. En sortant du magasin, imaginez notre horreur de trouver que la bicyclette de mon frère ne se trouvait plus à l'endroit où nous l'avions laissée. Au loin nous voyions un jeune homme qui s'éloignait à toute vitesse. Je me suis décidé vite; j'ai crié à mon frère de rester là et je suis parti le plus vite possible à la poursuite du voleur. Peu à peu je me suis rapproché de lui. À la fin il a laissé tomber la bicyclette et s'est sauvé à travers les champs. Moi aussi, je suis descendu et courant à toutes jambes j'ai réussi à l'attraper.

Pendant quelques moments nous nous sommes battus. La lutte était courte. Je l'ai conduit au village où un agent de police l'a emmené au commissariat de police. Mon frère a été très content de retrouver sa bicyclette et nous nous sommes remis en route.

Mon frère et moi = **nous**, therefore **voulions**; **il faisait beau** — imperfect because this is a description; **nous avons mis** (past participle of **mettre**); **le sac au dos** = *with bags on our backs* (not **sur le dos** — it is not necessary to use the possessive pronoun here in French, nor the plural); **nous pourrions** (conditional — *we should be able to*) **nous amuser à** + infinitive; **en sortant** = *as we came out*; **je suis parti** — **partir** is one of the twelve verbs which take **être**;

laisser tomber = *to drop*; **moi aussi** = *I also*; **réussir à** + infinitive = *to succeed in*; **nous nous sommes battus** — note the agreement; **conduire quelqu'un à** = *to take someone to*. Note the accents, especially on such words as: **rivière, bientôt, réussir, peut-être, s'arrêter, décider.**

Les sports d'hiver sur les montagnes couvertes de neige près de Chamonix.

B. This is a similar type of composition. A story is read out in the third person in English; while it is read, candidates have a summary in French to look at. The summary is then taken away and candidates are asked to retell the story in French.

Summary: **Monsieur Dupré — se coucher tôt — chats sur le toit — prendre un soulier — vagabond trouver — bonne idée — miaulement — l'autre soulier.**

318

LE VAGABOND ACCEPTE UN DON DU CIEL

Monsieur Dupré était bien fatigué après avoir travaillé toute la soirée au jardin. Il s'est couché de bonne heure et bientôt il s'est endormi. Vers minuit il a été réveillé par le miaulement de deux chats sur le toit d'une maison voisine. Exaspéré, il a ouvert la fenêtre de sa chambre à coucher et a jeté un de ses souliers, pensant faire taire les chats. Par hasard, un vagabond, dont les vêtements étaient déchirés et qui portait des souliers tout troués, descendait la rue juste au moment où le soulier est tombé sur le trottoir. Il a ramassé le soulier et l'a examiné avec soin. Celui-ci lui semblait un véritable don du ciel. Mais il lui en fallait deux! Que faire pour en avoir l'autre? Levant les yeux il a vu la fenêtre ouverte et soudain il a eu une idée. Il a commencé à miauler comme un chat. La ruse a bien réussi! Au bout de trois minutes la fenêtre s'est ouverte de nouveau et un deuxième soulier n'a pas tardé à tomber à ses pieds. Il l'a ramassé vite et s'en est allé tout heureux. Aide-toi, le ciel t'aidera!

Après avoir + part participle — après is always followed by the past infinitive; il s'est couché (reflexive verbs are conjugated with être); il a jeté (only one -t- in the past participle); il a été réveillé — this is the passive form; il lui en fallait deux = *he needed two (of them)*; les vêtements déchirés — note agreement; des souliers tout troués — tout is an adverb here, therefore no agreement; la fenêtre s'est ouverte — remember the agreement; faire taire = *to silence*. Note the spelling of: fatigué, miauler, ramasser, minuit, la soirée, un don, par hasard; and the accents on: deuxième, exaspéré, fenêtre, vêtement, idée. There is no accent on descendait!

C. We are going to study the structure and syntax of this next essay in more detail. In this case the candidates are merely given the outline of the story in French: Votre sœur et vous désirez faire un cadeau à votre mère. Vous voulez gagner vous-mêmes l'argent nécessaire pour acheter le cadeau. Décrivez ce que vous faites et comment vous dépensez l'argent.

COMMENT NOUS AVONS PU ACHETER
UN BEAU CADEAU

On était au mois d'avril et nous avions quinze jours de vacances. L'anniversaire de maman s'approchait. Nous voulions, ma sœur et moi, lui donner un beau cadeau. Nous tenions à gagner nous-mêmes l'argent nécessaire pour acheter quelque chose de très joli. Jeanette a décidé, donc, de chercher du travail. Elle a lu toutes les annonces dans le journal du soir. Elle a eu de la chance car, justement, on demandait dans un des grands magasins des demoiselles pour aider les vendeuses pendant les "Soldes du printemps." Jeanette a trouvé le travail intéressant mais assez fatigant. Elle n'a pas l'habitude de rester debout toute la journée. Elle a trouvé aussi que les clients sont quelquefois bien difficiles!

Pour moi c'était bien différent. Je suis allé travailler dans une ferme située à une vingtaine de kilomètres de chez nous. J'ai aidé le fermier avec tout le travail de la ferme — j'ai donné à manger aux animaux, j'ai nettoyé l'écurie et l'étable, j'ai même aidé à planter des milliers de choux. Le samedi je suis allé au marché où le fermier vend tous ses légumes et ses volailles. C'était un travail dur et souvent pénible, mais j'adore la vie en plein air. À la fin des vacances nous avions gagné assez d'argent pour pouvoir aller chez le bijoutier où nous avons acheté une jolie montre-bracelet. Maman a été bien contente, le jour de son anniversaire, de trouver sur la table ce cadeau inespéré.

You will see that we have used simple vocabulary and have a definite beginning — **on était au mois d'avril** — we do not plunge straight into the middle of the story. We use the imperfect (descriptive tense) to give the background, e.g. **nous avions . . . , s'approchait . . . , nous voulions . . .** (none of these is an action); we have used the perfect for actions, e.g. **Jeanette a décidé . . . , elle a lu . . . , a trouvé . . . , je suis allé . . . , j'ai aidé . . . , j'ai donné à manger** (= *I fed*). Note the use of the simple idiom **tenir à** = *to be keen to* (do something), and the use of the typical French constructions **on était au mois d'avril . . . ,** and **on demandait. . . .** Prepositions are followed by the infinitive: **nous tenions à gagner . . . , j'ai aidé à planter. . . .** We finish with the perfect tense (this, not the imperfect, is the correct tense here) to show a feeling of pleasure at a particular event which constitutes part of the action: **Maman a été bien contente le jour de. . . .**

Note these useful expressions: **avoir de la chance** = *to be lucky*; **justement** = *as it so happened*; **en plein air** = *in the open air*; **toute la journée** = *all day long*; **assez fatigant** (no -u- in the present participle) = *quite tiring*; **au bout de** = *at the end of*; **trouver quelqu'un difficile** = *to find someone hard to please*.

We have remembered the question of agreement: **quelque chose de joli** (masculine); **un cadeau inespéré** (= *unhoped for*); **toutes les annonces** (feminine); **le travail intéressant**; **debout**, unlike **assis**, does not change to show agreement; **Jeanette a décidé . . .** not conjugated with **être** and there is no preceding direct object so no agreement here.

We have placed the correct accents on: **nous-mêmes, différent, pénible, nécessaire, kilomètres, la journée, très, écurie, étable, marché.**

D. For this composition candidates are given only the title:

UNE VISITE AU ZOO

Un jour les parents de Jacques Devraine ont consenti à accompagner leur fils au zoo. De tous les animaux Jacques préférait les singes, et, enchanté, il les regardait pendant qu'ils s'amusaient à manger et à jouer dans leur cage.

Quand Monsieur et Madame Devraine ont décidé de quitter les singes pour aller voir les lions, le petit garçon les a priés d'y rester plus longtemps.

"Je t'en prie, maman — je n'aime pas les lions; ils me font peur. Moi, je voudrais rester ici s'il te plaît."

Saisissant le bras de son fils, Monsieur Devraine a répondu:

"Ne sois pas désobéissant, mon petit. Tu dois nous suivre, ta mère et moi."

Donc, Jacques les a suivis, mais il a gardé un air pensif et il a dit:

"Papa, papa, puis-je retourner aux singes pour . . . ?"

"Henri, regarde!" a crié Madame Devraine. "On donne à manger aux lions. Qu'ils sont féroces quand ils voient les morceaux de viande. . . ."

"Maman, papa . . . ?" a-t-il crié désespérément, mais ils ne l'ont pas entendu. Enfin, après que ses parents, causant et riant, avaient continué leur tour, il s'est sauvé et s'est dirigé de nouveau vers la cage des singes.

Un peu plus tard, pendant qu'ils regardaient deux ours amusants, Monsieur et Madame Devraine se sont aperçus que Jacques avait disparu. Ils l'ont cherché partout, et voyant beaucoup de monde près d'une cage ils s'en sont approchés et, horrifiés, ils ont vu leur fils qui jouait heureusement avec ses amis, les singes! Comment avait-il jamais pu y entrer?

You will see that this essay is varied and interesting because of its alternate use of action and conversation, and the fact that it contains several characters. Note the use of the past participle in French to replace what might be a whole clause in English, e.g. **horrifiés, ils ont vu** . . . = *they were horrified to see*; and of the second person singular of the verb which denotes close relationship, e.g. the imperative form: **Ne sois pas désobéissant!** Note the perfect tense of some reflexive verbs (conjugated with **être**): **il s'est sauvé . . . , il s'est dirigé . . . , ils se sont aperçus.** = *they realised*; and the use of present participles: **causant, riant, saisissant, voyant. Devoir** is followed by the infinitive: **tu dois nous suivre.**

We have remembered the agreement of the past participle: **ils les a priés** (**prier**, unlike **demander**, takes a direct object), **ils s'en sont approchés, Jacques avait disparu** (no agreement necessary), **Jacques les a suivis.**

Note the accents on: **préférait, féroces, désespérément, décidé, après.**

E. For this composition the candidates are given a set of pictures and asked to describe the story portrayed in them. Do not try to describe every picture in detail — you will never finish. Indeed, it is probably best to study the pictures carefully first, then put them aside and write the story.

The pictures show a group of children happy with a snowman. Their comrades come and knock it over. A fight results. The little dog is nearly killed but is saved by one of the opponents. They build a new snowman together and all ends well.

321

Let us first make a list of useful words and expressions which we know: **le bonhomme de neige** = *the snowman*; **être en train de** = *to be in the act of*; **essayer de détruire** = *to try to destroy*; **un combat** = *a fight*; **avoir lieu** = *to take place*; **traverser la rue** = *to cross the street*; **s'approcher vite** = *to come rapidly closer*; **filer à toute vitesse** = *to spin along at top speed*; **être en danger** = *to be in danger*; **remarquer l'absence** = *to notice the absence*; **sauver la vie à quelqu'un** = *to save someone's life*; **tout est bien qui finit bien** = *all's well that ends well*.

LE BONHOMME DE NEIGE

Il avait neigé toute la nuit. Le lendemain matin la terre était couverte d'une belle nappe de neige blanche. Henri et sa sœur Marie sont sortis. Dans un champ qui bordait la route ils se sont amusés à faire un bonhomme de neige. Leur petit chien Médor les a accompagnés et il a été très content de rester là à les regarder entasser la neige. Le travail était presque terminé quand une bande de gamins est arrivée. Deux d'entre eux se sont mis à renverser le bonhomme. Henri et sa sœur n'ont pas été bien contents de voir le pauvre bonhomme perdre sa tête! Ils se sont disputés avec les méchants enfants dont l'un a essayé de prendre la pelle qu'Henri tenait toujours à la main. C'était bientôt une véritable lutte. Tout à coup les enfants ont remarqué que Médor était parti. Ils l'ont vu traverser la route et à leur grande surprise il ne faisait aucune attention à une grosse voiture qui s'avançait à toute vitesse. Celui qui était en train de saisir la pelle l'a laissée tomber par terre et s'est précipité vers l'animal qui était en grand danger d'être renversé par l'automobile. Heureusement l'enfant a pu atteindre le chien et l'a conduit sain et sauf vers le petit groupe. On a vite oublié la dispute et tout le monde s'est réuni pour faire un bonhomme magnifique, On lui a mis un chapeau sur la tête, une pipe à la bouche. Médor a été très content de voir les enfants si gais, si joyeux. Aux éclats de rire il a ajouté des aboiements de plaisir. De sa façon à lui il disait, sans doute, employant le langage des chiens, "Tout est bien qui finit bien."

EXERCISES

Here are six essays for you to try on your own:

1. **Une excursion à Londres.** Tell in about 150 words the story suggested in the set of pictures. Do not attempt to describe each picture, but, if you wish imagine yourself as one of the characters. Do not use the past historic tense.

2. Write a letter in French to your correspondent in France telling him how you spent your summer holidays. When you begin a letter you should use one of these forms: **mon cher papa, ma chère maman, cher oncle, chère tante, mon cher Charles, ma chère Anne**, etc. When you end a letter you should use one of these forms: to friends — **meilleurs sentiments, je vous serre cordialement la main, recevez toutes mes amitiés**; to parents or relatives — **bien à toi,**

je t'embrasse affectueusement, affectueusement à toi; to intimate friends — **bien à toi, reçois mon affectueuse amitié**; *kind regards to* = **bien des choses de ma part à**. . . .

Here are some useful phrases: **au bord de la mer** = *by the seaside*; **faire ses valises** = *to pack one's cases*; **faire de la vitesse** = *to speed*; **mettre du temps à** = *to take time doing something*; **à mi-chemin** = *half-way*; **aller à la pêche** = *to go fishing*; **avoir une panne** = *to have a motor breakdown*.

3. Continue, in your own words, the story about Henri, begun on p. 312 in the English-French chapter (Chapter 29). (The continuation of the English-French translation is frequently set in "O" level papers as composition.)

Here are some useful phrases and vocabulary: **la portière** = *carriage-door*; **s'asseoir en face de** = *to sit opposite*; **engager la conversation à** = *to start a conversation with*; **un nouvel emploi** = *a new job*; **avoir l'occasion de** = *to have the opportunity to*; **la station de métro** = *the tube* (*underground*) *station*.

4. Write about 200 words in French in the past tense, but avoiding the use of the past historic, making use of this summary:

Deux enfants — bonnes intentions — parents sortis — faire le café — renverser deux paquets — mauvais goût du café.

Here are some useful phrases and vocabulary: **à l'égard de** = *with regard to*; **bouillir** = *to boil*; **moudre** = *to grind*; **quel gâchis!** = *what a mess!* **le carrelage** = *tile-floor*; **le mélange** = *mixture*; **se répandre dans** = *to spread through*; **faire le ménage** = *to do the housework*.

5. Write in French not more than 200 words on this subject: **Pierre fait l'école buissonnière** (= *plays truant from school*); **le lendemain il essaie d'expliquer son absence au professeur; le professeur ne le croit pas et le punit.**

Here are some phrases and vocabulary you might need: **détester les mathématiques** = *to hate mathematics*; **passer la journée en ville** = *to spend the day in town*; **trouver des excuses** = *to find excuses*; **avoir l'air mécontent** = *to appear dissatisfied*; **poser une question** = *to ask a question*; **refuser de croire** = *to refuse to believe*; **demander une lettre de ses parents** = *to ask for a letter from his parents*; **rougir de honte** = *to blush with shame*; **avoir l'air coupable** = *to look guilty*; **être reconnu par des amis** = *to be recognized by some friends*; **une heure de retenue** = *one hour's detention*; **une punition bien méritée** = *a well-deserved punishment*; **professeur sévère** = *strict master*; **avoir la réputation** = *to have the reputation*; **empêcher les autres** = *to prevent* (*discourage*) *the others*; **être très paresseux** = *to be very lazy*; **ne pas faire ses devoirs** = *to shirk one's homework*; **donner zéro sur vingt** = *to give nought out of twenty*.

6. Write an essay of about 150 words on this subject: **Une aventure à la campagne.** Here is some useful vocabulary: **il y avait une fois** = *once upon a time*; **le pré** = *field, meadow*; **faire une promenade** = *to go for a walk*; **se sauver** = *to run away*; **grimper dans un arbre** = *to climb a tree*.

LEÇON 31

COMPREHENSION

Many examination boards test your ability to understand and answer questions on a passage of French without having first translated it. Some expect you to give your answers in French, others are quite satisfied if you can answer the questions in English. Whichever they ask you to do, however, there are some sensible rules you must follow:

1. Read the instructions very carefully and answer in the language required.
2. Your answers must be concise and contain no irrelevant details, but they should be complete sentences. Be sure not to say the same thing twice in answer to different questions.
3. The questions are not always set in the strict order of the events in the passage, so it is essential that you read all the questions before you begin to answer any of them.
4. Wherever possible, follow the sequence of tense used in the passage.
5. All your replies should be of a nature to show that you have understood the main outline and the more important details, and that you have a clear idea of the sense of the whole passage.
6. Spelling, punctuation and handwriting are just as important in the comprehension question as in other questions.

Here are two examples which we have done for you, following these rules. The first example requires answers in English, the second in French.

A. Candidates are asked to read an extract and then answer in English briefly and to the point the questions which follow:

Il était une fois un homme qui avait une cervelle d'or; oui, une cervelle toute en or. Lorsqu'il vint au monde, les médecins pensaient que cet enfant ne vivrait pas, tant sa tête était lourde et son crâne démesuré. Il vécut cependant et grandit au soleil comme un beau plant d'olivier; seulement sa grosse tête l'entraînait toujours, et c'était pitié de le voir se cogner à tous les meubles en marchant. . . . Il tombait souvent. Un jour, il roula du haut d'un perron et vint donner du front contre un degré de marbre, où son crâne sonna comme un lingot. On le crut mort; mais, en le relevant, on ne lui trouva qu'une légère blessure, avec deux ou trois gouttelettes d'or caillées dans ses cheveux blonds. C'est ainsi que ses parents apprirent que l'enfant avait une cervelle en or.

La chose fut tenue secrète; le pauvre petit lui-même ne se douta de rien. De

temps en temps, il demandait pourquoi on ne le laissait plus courir devant la porte avec les garçonnets de la rue.

"On vous volerait, mon beau trésor!" lui répondit sa mère.

Alors le petit avait grand'peur d'être volé; il retournait jouer tout seul, sans rien dire, et se traînait lourdement d'une salle à l'autre. . . . À dix-huit ans seulement, ses parents lui révélèrent le don monstrueux qu'il tenait du destin; et, comme ils l'avaient élevé et nourri jusque-là, ils lui demandèrent en retour un peu de son or. L'enfant n'hésita pas; sur l'heure même, il s'arracha du crâne un morceau d'or massif, un morceau gros comme une noix, qu'il jeta fièrement sur les genoux de sa mère. . . . Puis, tout ébloui des richesses qu'il portait dans sa tête, fou de désirs, ivre de sa puissance, il quitta la maison paternelle et s'en alla par le monde en gaspillant son trésor.

Answer concisely, in English, the questions below, taking care to include all the relevant details.

1. Why did the doctors say the child would not live?
2. What did his deformity make him do all the time?
3. What happened on one special occasion?
4. What question did the boy ask his parents, and how did they answer him?
5. How old was he when the secret was told him, and what did his parents ask him to give them? What excuses did they have for making this request?
6. What did he do when he left home and what were his feelings?

You will probably find that there are several words you do not know, but before we resort to the vocabulary, let us see if we can work some of them out for ourselves:

la cervelle = la substance du cerveau = *brain matter.*

démesuré = qui excède la mesure ordinaire = *unusually big.*

entraîner (compare le traîneau = *sledge*) = *to drag.*

cailler (faire cailler du lait = *to curdle milk*) = *to clot, coagulate.*

le don (compare donner = *to give*) = *gift.*

1. Why did the doctors say the child would not live?

The answer to this question is found in the words "**tant sa tête était lourde et son crâne démesuré. . . .**" We must be careful to show that we distinguish between **la tête** and **le crâne**, and we must remember to use a complete sentence:

The doctors said the child would not live because his head was so heavy and his skull of such huge proportions.

2. What did his deformity make him do all the time?

Sa tête l'entraînait (compare: **La locomotive entraîne le train**) and as a result of this one could see him **se cogner (cogner = frapper** or **heurter) à tous les meubles**:

His head dragged him down and made him bump into the furniture as he walked.

3. What happened on one special occasion?

The special occasion is **un jour** when **il roula du haut d'un perron**; the special thing that happened on this occasion — **il vint donner du front contre** (compare **donner de la tête contre** = *to run one's head into*) **un degré de marbre; son crâne sonna comme un lingot** (you can guess this word from ingot):

One day he rolled from the top of a flight of steps; his head, striking the marble step, resounded like a gold ingot.

4. What question did the boy ask his parents, and how did they answer him?

The question is introduced by **il demanda**; remember that the French construction with **on** is often translated into English by the passive:

He asked why he was not allowed to play any more in the street with the other small boys. He was told that he would be stolen.

5. How old was he when the secret was told him, and what did his parents ask him to give them? What excuses did they have for making this request?

The answer to this is introduced by **À dix-huit ans seulement . . .** :

He was eighteen when the secret was told him. His parents asked him to give them some of this gold, on the grounds that they had brought him up and fed him.

6. What did he do when he left home and what were his feelings?

He left home = **il quitta la maison paternelle**; what he did was **s'en alla par le monde en gaspillant son tresor**. His feelings are expressed in the first part of the same sentence:

He went around wasting his wealth. He was dazzled by the wealth in his head, mad with ambition and drunk with his own power.

B. **Fatigué d'en avoir tant dit, le berger s'assit, et le patron reprit la parole:**

"**Oui, monsieur, c'est ce pauvre vieux qui est venu nous prévenir. Il était presque fou de peur; et, de l'affaire, sa cervelle en est restée détraquée. Le fait est qu'il y avait de quoi. . . . Figurez-vous six cents cadavres en tas sur le sable, pêle-mêle avec les éclats de bois et les lambeaux de toile. . . . Pauvre 'Sémillante!' . . . la mer l'avait broyée du coup, et si bien mise en miettes que dans tous ses débris le berger Palombo n'a trouvé qu'à peine de quoi faire une palissade autour de sa hutte. . . . Quant aux hommes, presque tous défigurés, mutilés affreusement . . . c'était pitié de les voir accrochés les uns aux autres,** par grappes. . . . Nous trouvâmes le capitaine en grand costume; dans un coin, entre deux roches, un petit mousse, les yeux ouverts . . . on aurait cru qu'il vivait encore; mais non! Il était dit que pas un n'en échapperait. . . ."

Ici le patron s'interrompit: "Attention, Nardi!" cria-t-il, "le feu s'éteint."

Nardi jeta sur la braise deux ou trois morceaux de planches goudronnées qui s'enflammèrent, et Lionetti continua:

"Ce qu'il y avait de plus triste dans cette histoire, le voici. . . . Trois semaines avant le naufrage, une petite corvette, qui allait en Crimée comme la 'Sémillante,' avait fait naufrage de la même façon, presque au même endroit; seulement, cette fois-là, nous étions parvenus à sauver l'équipage et vingt soldats qui se trouvaient à bord. On les emmena à Bonifacio et nous les gardâmes pendant deux jours avec nous. . . . Une fois bien secs et remis sur pied, ils retournèrent à Toulon, où, quelque temps après, on les embarqua de nouveau pour la Crimée. . . . Devinez sur quel navire! . . . Sur la 'Sémillante,' monsieur. . . . Nous les avons trouvés tous, tous les vingt, couchés parmi les morts, à la place où nous sommes. . . . Je relevai moi-même un joli brigadier que j'avais couché à la maison et qui nous avait fait rire tout le temps avec ses histoires. . . ."

Là-dessus, le brave Lionetti, tout ému, secoua les cendres de sa pipe et se roula dans son manteau en me souhaitant la bonne nuit. . . . Pendant quelque temps encore, les matelots causèrent entre eux à demi-voix. . . . Puis, l'une après l'autre, les pipes s'éteignirent. . . . On ne parla plus. . . . Le vieux berger s'en alla. . . .

Répondez en français à ces questions; pour chaque réponse employez une phrase entière.

1. Pourquoi y avait-il de quoi rendre fou le vieux berger?
2. Où le vieux berger Palombo a-t-il essayé de faire une palissade?
3. Pourquoi était-il pitié de voir les hommes?
4. Comment le capitaine était-il habillé?
5. Où a-t-on trouvé le petit mousse? Comment était-il?
6. Pourquoi le petit mousse avait-il péri comme les autres?
7. Qu'est-ce qui s'est enflammé?
8. Quel navire avait fait naufrage de la même façon? Quand?
9. Combien de soldats avait-on pu sauver?
10. Où les soldats sont-ils retournés quand ils étaient bien secs?
11. Sur quel bateau sont-ils partis en Crimée la seconde fois?
12. Où a-t-on trouvé les vingt soldats?
13. Comment le brigadier avait-il fait rire le patron?
14. Nommez deux choses qu'a faites le brave Lionetti avant de se rouler dans son manteau.

When you first read the passage through, you will probably find that there are some parts you cannot understand, and several words that you don't know and will have to guess; but if you look at the questions carefully you will see that most of them can be answered quite easily from the parts of the passage that you do understand. Be sure to read the passage through several times as a whole; if you keep the beginning in mind you may find it will help you to understand something at the end and vice versa. For example, the first time you come to the proper name **"Sémillante,"** you may not know what it

Dans une rue de Paris une danse basque.

refers to, but later in the passage you will find the words **Devinez sur quel navire!** ... **Sur la "Sémillante"** ... so you will know that the **"Sémillante"** is a ship. This may help you to realize, if you do not know the word **naufrage**, that the passage concerns a *shipwreck*, that the *six hundred bodies in heaps on the sand* (**six cents cadavres en tas sur le sable**) were the crew and passengers of the shipwrecked vessel and that **le capitaine** refers to the captain of the ship. You can also guess the meaning of **un petit mousse** if you realize that the author is talking of the finding of the ship's crew, that **un petit** must refer to a child and that the only child normally found amongst a ship's crew is a *cabin-boy*.

If you read the passage over and over, you will find that you can work out much of the sense of it in this way. When you look at the questions you will find that many of them can be answered by adapting the actual French of the passage, but remember always to write the answer as a complete sentence.

1. **Pourquoi y avait-il de quoi rendre fou le vieux berger?**
We can answer the **pourquoi** with **parce que** and use the actual words of the question itself here; the reason is found in the passage:
Il y avait de quoi rendre fou le vieux berger parce qu'il y avait six cents cadavres en tas sur le sable.

2. **Où le vieux berger Palombo a-t-il essayé de faire une palissade?**
The answer to this can be found quite easily in the passage:
Le vieux berger a essayé de faire une palissade autour de sa hutte.

3. **Pourquoi était-il pitié de voir les hommes?**
The answer to this is also in the passage, but we must look for it a little more carefully; it is not the fact that they are piled up, *clinging to each other* (**accrochés les uns aux autres**) which is **pitié de voir**, but the fact that they are **défigurés** and **mutilés**:
Il était pitié de voir les hommes parce qu'ils étaient tous défigurés.

4. **Comment le capitaine était-il habillé?**
Comment requires a plain statement of fact in answer to it, without any introductory word; this can be taken from the passage (it doesn't matter if you don't know exactly what **en grand costume** means):
Le capitaine était en grand costume.

5. **Où a-t-on trouvé le petit mousse? Comment était-il?**
Comment = *How was he?* The complete answer is in the passage:
On a trouvé le petit mousse dans un coin, entre deux roches. Il avait les yeux ouverts.

6. **Pourquoi le petit mousse avait-il péri comme les autres?**
If you read the text carefully you will find an answer for this (**pas un** = *not a single one*):
Le petit mousse avait péri comme les autres parce qu'il était dit que pas un n'en échapperait.

7. **Qu'est-ce qui s'est enflammé?**
Qu'est-ce qui = *what*; this means that the answer must begin with a noun, we may add a time clause to show that we have understood the context here:
Les morceaux de planches goudronnées se sont enflammés quand Nardi les a jetés sur la braise.

8. **Quel navire avait fait naufrage de la même façon? Quand?**

You can answer this from the passage in either two sentences or one. Remember that **corvette** is feminine:

Une petite corvette avait fait naufrage de la même façon. Elle avait fait naufrage trois semaines avant.

9. **Combien de soldats avait-ou pu sauver?**

The answer to **combien** is likely to be a number, which you will find in the passage; remember to change the wording in the passage (**nous étions parvenus à sauver**) to answer the question **avait-on**:

On avait pu sauver vingt soldats.

10. **Où les soldats sont-ils retournés quand ils étaient bien secs?**

All we have to do here is to change the past historic tense of the passage to the perfect tense of the question:

Quand ils étaient bien secs les soldats sont retournés à Toulon.

11. **Sur quel bateau sont-ils partis en Crimée la seconde fois?**

Again we must follow the tense of the question; we can use the idiom **partir en** which we take from the question:

Ils sont partis en Crimée la seconde fois sur la "Sémillante."

12. **Où a-t-on trouvé les vingt soldats?**

À la place où nous sommes in the passage must become third person in the answer, so **nous** must be changed to **les hommes**:

On a trouvé les vingt soldats couchés parmi les morts à la place où étaient les hommes qui écoutaient l'histoire.

13. **Comment le brigadier avait-il fait rire le patron?**

Here the answer is obtained from the sentence containing . . . **qui nous avait fait rire. . . .** As long as we are clear that it is **le patron** who is telling the story all we have to do is to change the first person pronoun **nous** into le **patron** as in the question itself:

Le brigadier avait fait rire le patron en racontant des histoires amusantes.

14. **Nommez deux choses qu'a fait le brave Lionetti avant de se rouler dans son manteau.**

The first part of the answer is in the question — so we can start with **Avant de. . . .** We must just remember to change the tense of the passage into the tense used in the question and change the **me** to **lui**:

Avant de se rouler dans son manteau le brave Lionetti a secoué les cendres de sa pipe et lui a souhaité la bonne nuit.

EXERCISES

Here are six comprehension passages for you to try on your own. If you remember that the last part of the question can frequently form the first part of the answer, you will feel more confident in answering the questions, especially when you must answer in French. Look at the questions on passages A and B and you will find that they have nearly all been answered in this way.

I. Read this passage carefully, then answer in English the questions which follow, taking care to include all relevant detail:

THE UNPOSTED LETTER

Ne regardant pas où il allait, Eugène s'était engagé par hasard dans ce dédale de petites rues qui sont derrière le carrefour Buci, et dans lesquelles une voiture passe à peine. Au moment où il allait revenir sur ses pas, une femme, enveloppée dans un mauvais peignoir, la tête nue, les cheveux en désordre, pâle et défaite, sortit d'une vieille maison. Elle semblait tellement faible, qu'elle pouvait à peine marcher; ses genoux fléchissaient; elle s'appuyait sur les murailles, et paraissait vouloir se diriger vers une porte voisine, où se trouvait une boîte aux lettres, pour y jeter un billet qu'elle tenait à la main. Surpris et effrayé, Eugène s'approcha d'elle, et lui demanda où elle allait, ce qu'elle cherchait, et s'il pouvait l'aider. En même temps il étendit le bras pour la soutenir, car elle était près de tomber sur la borne. Mais, sans lui répondre, elle recula avec une sorte de crainte et de fierté. Elle posa son billet sur une borne, montra du doigt la boîte, et paraissant rassembler toutes ses forces: "Là!" dit-elle seulement; puis, continuant à se traîner aux murs, elle regagna sa maison. Eugène essaya en vain de l'obliger à prendre son bras et de renouveler ses questions. Elle rentra lentement dans l'allée sombre et étroite dont elle était sortie.

Eugène avait ramassé la lettre; il fit d'abord quelques pas pour la mettre à la poste, mais il s'arrêta bientôt. Cette étrange rencontre l'avait si fort troublé, et il se sentait frappé d'une sorte d'horreur mêlée d'une compassion si vive, que, avant de prendre le temps de la réflexion, il rompit le cachet presque involontairement. Il lui semblait odieux et impossible de ne pas chercher, n'importe par quel moyen, à pénétrer un tel mystère. Évidemment, cette femme était mourante; était-ce de maladie ou de faim? Ce devait être, en tout cas, de misère. Eugène ouvrit la lettre; elle portait sur l'adresse: "À monsieur le baron de . . .", et il commença à lire les mots qui suivaient.

1. Where was the medley of streets into which Eugène turned? What made him turn that way?

2. What was he about to do when he saw the lady?
3. Give three phrases to describe her appearance.
4. Where did she seem to be going and how was she walking?
5. What questions did Eugène ask her?
6. What was her reaction to the questions?
7. What did she say and how did she make her way back to her house?
8. What did Eugène offer to do?
9. What reasons are given for explaining why Eugène broke the seal of the letter?
10. What conclusions did he come to about the lady?

II. Lisez le passage qui suit; répondez en français aux questions, employant pour chaque réponse une phrase complète:

A DEAF-MUTE CHILD

Madame des Arcis parlait par signes à l'enfant et savait seule se faire comprendre. Les autres personnes de la maison, le chevalier lui-même, semblaient étrangers à Camille. La mère de Mme des Arcis, femme d'un esprit assez vulgaire, ne venait guère à Chardonneux (ainsi se nommait la terre du chevalier) que pour déplorer le malheur arrivé à son gendre et a sa chère Cécile. Croyant faire preuve de sensibilité, elle s'apitoyait sans relâche sur le triste sort de cette pauvre enfant, et il lui échappa de dire un jour: "Mieux eût valu pour elle ne pas être née."

"Qu'auriez-vous donc fait si j'étais ainsi?" répliqua Cécile presque avec l'accent de la colère.

L'oncle Giraud, le maître maçon, ne trouvait pas grand mal à ce que sa petite-nièce fût muette: "J'ai eu," disait-il, "une femme si bavarde, que je regarde toute chose au monde, n'importe laquelle préférable. Cette petite-là est sûre d'avance de ne jamais tenir de mauvais propos, ni d'en écouter, de ne pas impatienter toute une maison en chantant de vieux airs d'opéra, qui sont tous pareils; elle ne sera pas querelleuse, elle ne dira pas d'injures aux servantes, comme ma femme n'y manquait jamais; elle ne s'éveillera pas si son mari tousse, ou bien s'il se lève plus tôt qu'elle pour surveiller ses ouvriers; elle ne rêvera pas tout haut, elle sera discrète; elle y verra clair, les sourds ont de bons yeux; elle pourra régler, quand elle ne ferait que compter sur ses doigts, et payer, si elle a de l'argent; elle saura d'elle-même une chose très bonne qui ne s'apprend d'ordinaire que difficilement, c'est qu'il vaut mieux faire que dire. . . ."

1. Comment Madame des Arcis se faisait-elle comprendre à sa fille?
2. Qu'est-ce que la mère de Madame des Arcis a dit qui a rendu sa fille bien fâchée?
3. Quel était le métier de l'oncle Giraud?

4. Qu'est-ce que l'oncle Giraud accusait sa femme d'avoir fait?
5. Comment savons-nous que l'oncle Giraud n'aimait pas les vieux airs d'opéra?
6. Nommez deux choses que l'oncle Giraud croyait pouvoir éveiller une femme quand elle dormait?
7. Comment la petite pourrait-elle apprendre un jour à régler?
8. Quelle était la chose qui, d'après l'oncle Giraud, était difficile à apprendre?

III. Read the passage; without translating, answer in English the questions which follow:

CHILDHOOD MEMORIES OF A JOURNEY ON THE RHÔNE

Il me semble que c'est hier, ce voyage sur le Rhône. Je vois encore le bateau, ses passagers, son équipage; j'entends le bruit des roues et le sifflet de la machine.

La traversée dura trois jours. Je passai ces trois jours sur le pont, descendant au salon juste pour manger et dormir. Le reste du temps, j'allais me mettre à la pointe extrême du navire, près de l'ancre. Il y avait là une grosse cloche qu'on sonnait en entrant dans les villes; je m'asseyais à côté de cette cloche, parmi des tas de cordes; je posais la cage du perroquet entre mes jambes et je regardais. Le Rhône était si large qu'on voyait à peine ses rives. Moi, je l'aurais voulu encore plus large, et qu'il se fût appelé — la mer! Le ciel riait, l'onde était verte. Parfois, le bateau longeait quelque île bien touffue, couverte de joncs et de saules. "Oh, une île déserte," me disais-je dans moi-même; et je la dévorais des yeux.

Vers la fin du troisième jour, je crus que nous allions avoir un orage. Le ciel s'était assombri subitement; un brouillard épais dansait sur le fleuve; à l'avant du navire on avait allumé une grosse lanterne, et, ma foi, en présence de tous ces symptômes, je commençais à être ému. À ce moment, quelqu'un dit près de moi: "Voilà Lyon!"

1. What impressions of the boat does the author still recall?
2. Where did he spend most of his time during the journey?
3. What happened when the boat passed through towns?
4. What article of luggage did the child keep with him?
5. Where would he have preferred to be?
6. What was the weather like during the first two days? What colour was the Rhône?
7. What did the child imagine when they passed the river islands?
8. What were the symptoms of a change in the weather?
9. What precaution was taken on the boat?
10. How did the child feel in the face of all this?

Le port de Marseille avec ses barques de pêche.

IV. Read the passage through and, without translating, answer the questions which follow:

A GIRL LEAVES BOARDING SCHOOL TO BEGIN
HER LIFE IN PARIS

Je me rappelle les quatre tilleuls dans la cour d'une pension de province, leur parfum et le sourire de mon père sur le quai de la gare, il y a trois ans, à ma sortie de pension, ce sourire gêné parce que j'avais des nattes et une vilaine robe presque noire. Et dans la voiture, son explosion de joie, subite, triomphante, parce que j'avais ses yeux, sa bouche, et que j'allais être pour lui le plus cher, le plus merveilleux des jouets. Je ne connaissais rien: il allait me montrer Paris, le luxe, la vie facile. Je crois bien que la plupart de mes plaisirs d'alors, je les dus à l'argent: le plaisir d'aller vite en voiture, d'avoir une robe neuve, d'acheter des disques, des livres, des fleurs. Je n'ai pas honte encore de ces plaisirs faciles, je ne puis d'ailleurs les appeler faciles que parce que j'ai entendu dire qu'ils l'étaient. Le goût du plaisir, du bonheur représente le seul

335

côté cohérent de mon caractère. Peut-être n'ai-je pas assez lu? En pension, on ne lit pas, sinon des œuvres édifiantes. À Paris, je n'eus pas le temps de lire: en sortant de mon cours, des amis m'entraînaient dans des cinémas; je ne connaissais pas le nom des acteurs, cela les étonnait. Ou à des terrasses de café au soleil, je savourais le plaisir d'être mêlée à la foule et de boire. Le soir, je vieillissais; nous sortions avec mon père dans des soirées où je n'aurais pas dû être, soirées assez mélangées où je m'amusais, où j'amusais aussi par mon âge.

(Françoise Sagan, *Bonjour Tristesse*)

Answer in French:

1. Où la jeune fille avait-elle passé les plus jeunes années de sa vie?
2. Pourquoi son père a-t-il été gêné sur le quai de la gare?
3. Comment a-t-il changé dans la voiture? Pourquoi?
4. Est-ce que la jeune fille appartenait à une famille riche ou pauvre?
5. Quelles sortes de choses lui faisaient plaisir?
6. Quel était le trait le plus important de son caractère?
7. Quelles sortes de livres lisait-elle à l'école? Et à Paris?
8. Pourquoi ses amis parisiens étaient-ils surpris?
9. Comment passait-elle ses journées à Paris?

Answer in English:

10. What does the girl remember about the school?
11. What was her father's reaction when he met her at the station? Why?
12. Why did his attitude change later? How did he look upon his daughter?
13. What kind of background did the girl belong to in Paris?
14. What is the most outstanding feature of her character?
15. How did she spend her time during the day?
16. With whom did she go out in the evening? Why was this unsuitable? What effect did she produce?

V. Read the passage. Answer the questions which follow; numbers 1-10 should be answered in French, numbers 11-20 in English. Do not translate the passage:

A FAITHFUL SERVANT FROM CHILDHOOD TIMES IS FOUND AGAIN

Après l'enterrement de sa tante, au cimetière, Jeanne, brisée de fatigue et de tristesse, s'affaissait et tombait par terre. Une forte paysanne la saisit dans ses bras et l'emporta comme elle eût fait d'un petit enfant.

En rentrant au château, Jeanne qui venait de passer cinq nuits au chevet de sa tante mourante, se laissa mettre au lit sans résistance par cette campagnarde inconnue qui la maniait avec douceur et autorité; et elle tomba dans un sommeil d'épuisement, accablée de fatigue et de souffrance.

Elle s'éveilla vers le milieu de la nuit. Une veilleuse brûlait sur la cheminée. Une femme dormait dans un fauteuil. Qui était cette femme? Elle ne la reconnaissait pas et elle cherchait, s'étant penchée au bord de sa couche, pour bien distinguer ses traits sous la lueur tremblotante de la mèche flottant sur l'huile dans un verre de cuisine.

Il lui semblait pourtant qu'elle avait vu cette figure. Mais quand? Mais où? La femme dormait paisiblement, la tête inclinée sur l'épaule, le bonnet par terre. Elle pouvait avoir quarante ou quarante-cinq ans. Certes elle avait vu ce visage! Était-ce autrefois? Était-ce récemment? Elle n'en savait rien.

Elle se leva doucement pour regarder de plus près la dormeuse, et elle s'approcha sur la pointe des pieds. C'était la femme qui l'avait relevée au cimetière, puis l'avait couchée. Mais l'avait-elle rencontrée ailleurs. à une autre époque de sa vie?

La femme souleva sa paupière, aperçut Jeanne et se dressa brusquement. L'inconnue grommela: "Comment! Vous voilà debout! Vous allez attraper du mal à cette heure-ci. Voulez-vous bien vous recoucher!"

Jeanne demanda: "Qui êtes vous?"

Mais la femme, ouvrant les bras, la saisit, l'enleva de nouveau, et la reporta sur son lit avec la force d'un homme. Et comme elle la reposait doucement sur ses draps, elle se mit à pleurer en l'embrassant sur les joues, sur les yeux, lui trempant la figure de ses larmes, et balbutiant: "Ma pauvre maîtresse, Mlle Jeanne, vous ne me reconnaissez donc pas?" Et Jeanne s'écria: "Rosalie, ma fille." Et, lui jetant les deux bras au cou, elle l'étreignit en la baisant: et elles sanglotaient toutes les deux.

1. Pourquoi Jeanne était-elle triste?
2. Qui l'a emportée quand elle s'est affaissée?
3. Comment savez-vous que la femme était très forte?
4. Quand Jeanne s'est réveillée qui est-ce qui se trouvait dans la chambre?
5. Où se trouvait la mèche dont la lueur tremblotait?
6. Comment était la femme endormie?
7. Comment Jeanne s'est-elle approchée de la dormeuse?
8. Qu'est-ce que la femme lui a ordonné de faire?
9. Comment s'appelait la servante?
10. Qu'est-ce que les deux femmes ont fini par faire?
11. Why was Jeanne so tired?
12. How did the stranger handle her when she put her to bed?
13. How old did Jeanne think the stranger to be?
14. What time was it when Jeanne woke up?
15. Where did Jeanne think she had seen her before?
16. What did the stranger do when she saw Jeanne near her armchair?
17. How did the stranger show her affection?
18. Where was Jeanne at the beginning of this story?
19. What made the stranger cry?
20. How did Jeanne try to make out who she was?

VI. Read through the poem, which is not to be translated, and answer, as concisely as possible, the questions which follow:

LISE

J'avais douze ans; elle en avait bien seize.
Elle était grande, et, moi, j'étais petit.
Pour lui parler le soir plus à mon aise,
Moi, j'attendais que sa mère sortît;
Puis je venais m'asseoir près de sa chaise
Pour lui parler le soir plus à mon aise.

Dieu l'avait faite ange, fée et princesse.
Comme elle était bien plus grande que moi,
Je lui faisais des questions sans cesse
Pour le plaisir de lui dire: Pourquoi?
Et par moments elle évitait, craintive,
Mon œil rêveur qui la rendait pensive.

Puis j'étalais mon savoir enfantin,
Mes jeux, la balle et la toupie agile;
J'étais tout fier d'apprendre le latin;
Je lui montrais mon Phèdre et mon Virgile;
Je bravais tout; rien ne me faisait mal;
Je lui disais: Mon père est général.

Elle disait de moi: C'est un enfant!
Je l'appelais mademoiselle Lise,
Pour lui traduire un psaume, bien souvent,
Je me penchais sur son livre à l'église;
Si bien qu'un jour, vous le vîtes, Mon Dieu!
Sa joue en fleur toucher ma lèvre en feu.

(Victor Hugo)

Answer in English:
1. What is the main theme of this poem?
2. When did the poet visit Lise? Why?
3. To what does he compare the girl?
4. How does he show recognition of her superiority in years?
5. What shows that Lise is aware of his feelings?
6. In what ways does the boy show off before the girl?
7. What did he often do in church?

LEÇON 32

DICTATION

A short dictation test forms part of the "O" level examination; it is usually given immediately before the rest of the written paper. The passage, which is normally untitled, is read out three or four times in all (different examination boards have a slightly different procedure), and any proper names are written on a blackboard or spelt out. Punctuation and paragraphing are given in French. Here are the French words for punctuation and some phrases you may need to understand:

.   (le) **point** = *full stop*
.   , (la) **virgule** = *comma*
;   (le) **point-virgule** = *semi-colon*
:   (les) **deux points** = *colon*
?   (le) **point d'interrogation** = *question mark*
!   (le) **point d'exclamation** = *exclamation mark*
"   (les) **guillemets** (m.) = *inverted commas*
—   (le) **tiret** = *dash*
-   (le) **trait d'union** = *hyphen*
((la) **parenthèse** = *bracket*
'   (une) **apostrophe** = *apostrophe*
    à la ligne = *new paragraph*
    ouvrez les guillemets = *open inverted commas*
    fermez les guillemets = *close inverted commas*

The passage is read through first as a whole to enable the candidates to get a good idea of the subject and general sense of the passage. During this first reading the candidates are not allowed to write anything down, but should listen very carefully and try to get a picture of the characters or situation involved. Notice whether the passage is conversational, narrative or descriptive, and whether the sentences are about one person or a group of people.

The passage is then read at dictation speed in small groups of words; each group is read twice — when the whole passage has been written down, it is read again once and the candidates are then given five minutes in which to look over and revise what they have written.

LEÇON 32

GENERAL ADVICE ON THE DICTATION PAPER

There are in the French language many sounds that are spelt differently but pronounced the same, but remember that you can distinguish between these usually in dictation if you have grasped the meaning of the passage. It is, however, quite possible that you will hear an unfamiliar word or so in the passage. If this happens, do not panic, but listen very carefully when the word is read next time; it may turn out to be quite familiar. If it is still unfamiliar, you can only guess the French spelling from your knowledge of French pronunciation.

Most mistakes in dictation, however, arise not from unfamiliar words but from carelessness and can be avoided if you observe these rules:

1. Notice, from the sense of the passage, numbers and genders of nouns and be sure that the articles and adjectives agree with them.
2. Distinguish between the singular and the plural of third person verbs; i.e. do not write **il était** for **ils étaient** — here you can tell from the liaison which to write; do not write **elle donne** for **elles donnent** — here you must tell from the sense.
3. Remember to make past participles agree with the subject or preceding direct object where necessary, according to the rules on page 88.
4. Distinguish between parts of the verb which sound the same but have different endings, e.g. **donnait, donnaient; donner, donné(es)**.
5. Distinguish between the sounds -**ant** [ɑ̃] and -**ont** [ɔ̃], and remember the silent -**ent** ending of the third person plural in the present, imperfect, past historic and conditional tenses.
6. Remember the silent -**e**- and the cedilla in e.g. **mangeant, agaçant**.
7. Remember that in liaison **s** sounds like **z**, **d** like **t**, e.g. **quand‿elle** [kɑ̃tɛl].
8. Don't forget the accents!

Here are some dictation passages; the diagonal strokes divide them up into sense groups to show how they would be read out. The liaisons marked are the only ones which would be made. Read these passages out loud in their sense groups and notice where there are silent letters, word endings and agreements, which cannot be heard in dictation.

1. **Il était six‿heures du soir. / On vint m'avertir, / un moment après mon retour / au collège, / qu'une dame demandait / à me voir. / J'allai tout de suite / au parloir. / Dieux! / quelle apparition surprenante! / J'y trouvai Manon. / C'était‿elle, / mais plus‿aimable / et plus brillante / que je ne l'avais jamais vue. / Elle était dans sa dix-huitième année. / Ses charmes / dépassaient tout ce que / l'on peut décrire. / Elle avait‿un‿air / si fin, / si doux, / si engageant. / Toute sa figure / me parut‿un‿enchantement. /**

Un marché de volaille avec des dindons bien en évidence.

Je demeurai / interdit à sa vue, / et, ne pouvant deviner / quel était le but / de cette visite, / j'attendis, / les yeux baissés / et avec tremblement. / Elle était aussi embarrassée que moi / et, voyant / que mon silence continuait, / elle mit la main / devant ses yeux, / pour cacher quelques larmes. / Puis, elle me demanda / pourquoi je l'avais laissée / deux ans / sans aucune nouvelle. / Sans oser l'envisager directement, / je commençai plusieurs fois / une réponse, / que je n'eus pas la force d'achever.

2. Monsieur et Madame Taton / avaient quatre filles. / L'aînée, Odette, / âgée alors de vingt-six ans, /avait épousé un riche exportateur. / Je ne la vis / que pendant les vacances / de son mari. / Elle était grande, / blonde et très élégante. / Pour les nombreuses réceptions / auxquelles elle assistait, / elle faisait faire / beaucoup de toilettes / dont elle envoyait les restes / à sa sœur. /

Laure était grande, / avec le teint de Monsieur Octave. / Elle portait un gros chignon / qu'ornait un ruban de velours. / Elle travaillait /de la façon la plus surprenante / pour cette époque / où les seules femmes / qui travaillaient au dehors /étaient les bonnes, / les cuisinières, / les postières, / les ouvrières, / les institutrices / et les professeurs. /

Le Pont du Gard, vieux pont-aqueduc des Romains.

3. Christophe prolongea son voyage encore / de trois ou quatre jours. / Il n'était pas pressé. / Ce ne fut / que dans le wagon, / sur le chemin du retour, / qu'il se remit à penser / à Sabine. / Ils ne s'étaient pas écrit, / mais il savait / qu'elle l'attendait / et qu'il allait bientôt / la revoir. / Il était six heures et demie / quand il rentra / dans la maison. / Personne n'était encore levé / et les fenêtres de Sabine / étaient fermées. / Il avait faim / mais en cherchant dans le buffet / il craignait /d'éveiller Louise. / Il monta donc / tout de suite / à sa chambre, / sur la pointe des pieds. / Sa toilette faite, / il entendit des pas / dans la cour; / se penchant par la fenêtre / il vit Rosa / qui, la première levée / comme d'habitude, / commençait à balayer. / Il l'appela à mi-voix. / "Rosa," dit-il joyeusement, / "donne-moi à manger, / ou je te mange! / Je meurs de faim!" / Rosa sourit / et lui dit de descendre / dans la cuisine / du rez-de-chaussée; / là elle lui versa / un bol de lait / et lui fit manger / des tartines de beurre / et de confiture. /

(Romain Rolland, *Jean Christophe*)

LEÇON 33

CONVERSATION

All examination boards set an oral French examination for "O" level which is held by an outside examiner. This usually comprises a passage of French which the candidate has to read aloud and which tests his pronunciation, and some general conversation in French which tests his ability to understand and make himself understood in spoken French. The examiner questions the candidate on familiar, everyday topics — his home and family, his school and town, hobbies, ambitions, holidays and any travelling abroad that he has done. Some examiners give candidates a picture to study and then ask for a description of the picture in French.

Here are some questions and answers on typical subjects, though you must be ready to answer questions on almost anything. You can gain valuable practice by reading these answers aloud.

YOURSELF AND YOUR FAMILY

1. **Comment vous appelez-vous? Je m'appelle. . . .**
2. **Où demeurez-vous? Je demeure à Londres / dans une ville / à la campagne.**
3. **Depuis combien de temps étudiez-vous le français? J'étudie le français depuis cinq ans.**
4. **Où êtes-vous né? Je suis né à Londres.**
5. **En quelle année êtes-vous né? Je suis né en dix-neuf cent quarante-neuf / cinquante, etc. Quel âge avez-vous? J'ai quinze / seize / ans, etc.**
6. **Combien de personnes y a-t-il dans votre famille? Dans ma famille il y a cinq personnes, mon père, ma mère, mes deux sœurs et moi.**
7. **Combien de frères avez-vous? J'en ai un. Comment s'appelle-t-il? Il s'appelle Charles.**
8. **Habitez-vous une maison ou un appartement? J'habite une maison. Combien de pièces y a-t-il dans votre maison? Il y en a huit.**
9. **Êtes-vous jamais allé en France? Je suis allé en France une fois. Quand? J'y suis allé en dix-neuf cent soixante-deux. Où? Je suis allé à Paris. Comment y êtes-vous allé? J'ai fait la traversée de la Manche par paquebot.**
10. **Comment avez-vous trouvé les Français? J'ai trouvé les Français très sympathiques / différents / charmants.**

343

LEÇON 33

1. Sur quoi cette salle donne-t-elle? Cette salle donne sur le jardin / sur la rue.
2. Qu'est-ce que vous voyez là-bas, dans la rue? Je vois la circulation.
3. Savez-vous conduire une auto? Oui, je sais conduire une auto et j'ai déjà mon permis de conduire.
4. Dans quel pays faut-il conduire à droite? Dans tous les pays sauf en Suède et en Angleterre il faut conduire à droite.
5. Combien de repas par jour les Français prennent-ils d'habitude? D'habitude les Français ne prennent que trois repas par jour.
6. Où faut-il aller en France pour acheter des timbres-poste? En France on peut acheter des timbres-poste dans un bureau de tabac ou dans un bureau de poste.
7. Quels sont les deux sports essentiellement français? La pêche et le cyclisme sont les deux sports les plus populaires en France.
8. À quelle heure les classes commencent-elles en France? Souvent en France les classes commencent à huit heures du matin.
9. Où les Français aiment-ils passer les vacances d'été? Les Français aiment passer les vacances sur la côte d'Azur.
10. La France est-elle une monarchie ou une république? La France est une république.

YOURSELF AND YOUR HABITS

1. À quelle heure vous levez-vous le matin? Le matin je me lève de bonne heure — avant sept heures.
2. Que portez-vous à la maison le matin avant de vous habiller? Le matin avant de m'habiller je porte une robe de chambre.
3. Que portez-vous quand il fait bien froid? Quand il fait bien froid je porte un pardessus et des gants.
4. Que portez-vous dans un porte-monnaie? Dans mon porte-monnaie je porte mon argent de poche.
5. Comment saluez-vous un ami dans la rue? Je lève mon chapeau; je me découvre.
6. Que portez-vous souvent au lieu d'un gilet? Souvent au lieu de porter un gilet je mets un chandail.
7. Qui faites-vous venir quand vous êtes malade? Quand je suis malade je fais venir le médecin.
8. Que faites-vous ordinairement pendant les vacances d'été? Généralement je passe les vacances d'été au bord de la mer.
9. Quel est votre passe-temps favori? Mon passe-temps favori est la natation.
10. Quel métier allez-vous suivre quand vous quitterez l'école? Quand je quitterai l'école j'espère devenir ingénieur / j'irai à l'université suivre des cours de médecine.

TRAFFIC AND TRAVELLING

1. **Qui est-ce qui dirige la circulation à un carrefour? C'est l'agent de police qui dirige les voitures à l'aide d'un bâton.**

2. **Où devez-vous traverser la chaussée? Je dois traverser à un passage clouté avec les autres piétons.**

3. **Comment s'appelle le chemin de fer souterrain à Paris? Le chemin de fer souterrain s'appelle le Métro; il est très commode parce qu'il va beaucoup plus vite que l'autobus.**

4. **Avez-vous une bicyclette? Oui, j'ai une bicyclette neuve et je fais du cyclisme.**

TIME AND WEATHER

1. **Qu'est-ce que vous faites quand il fait beau? Je fais une promenade avec mon chien ou à bicyclette, ou je travaille dans le jardin.**

2. **Qu'est-ce que vous faites quand le temps est mauvais? Quelquefois, s'il y a un bon film, je vais au cinéma avec mes camarades ou je reste à la maison et je joue aux cartes.**

3. **Qu'est-ce qu'il vous faut, s'il vient à pleuvoir? Il me faut un parapluie, surtout les jours où j'ai oublié mon imperméable.**

4. **À quelle heure prenez-vous généralement vos repas? Je prends mon petit déjeuner à huit heures et demie et mon déjeuner à une heure; quelquefois je prends le goûter à cinq heures, quand je reviens de l'école, mais plus souvent je dîne avec mes parents à sept heures.**

DESCRIBING A PICTURE

If you are given a picture to describe, do not go into great detail. Whether the picture is a landscape, a street scene, a picture of people or action, pick out the main features. If you find it necessary to give their position in the picture, these expressions should help you:

au premier plan = *in the foreground*   **au fond** = *in the background*
à l'angle de l'image=*in the corner of the picture* **le paysage**=*in the landscape*

On the following pages are three pictures as examples. In the first picture a set of questions and suitable answers are given. Study the questions and answers carefully. Some of the pictures given may well be in colour, so learn the names of simple colours.

In pictures 2 and 3 you are shown how to describe without being prompted by. questions. Note also that the descriptions are best made *impersonally*— not using **je** but **on** or **nous**. Although most descriptions are likely to require the present tense, you should not restrict yourself. It is still possible to use the future or the perfect (e.g. **la neige a été entassée**).

If you study these examples you will see that the sequence is reasonably logical. Continue on one line of thought—and expand your sentences (e.g. **à droite on aperçoit un hôtel dont les fenêtres s'ouvrent sur des balcons**).

PORT DE PÊCHE ET STATION BALNÉAIRE

1. **Où se trouve-t-on ici, et en quelle saison sommes-nous?**
   Ici on se trouve au bord de la mer et nous sommes en été.

2. **Qui sont les gens que vous voyez?**
   Ce sont les touristes et les baigneurs qui sont venus se détendre sur cette belle plage.

3. **Comment savez-vous que cette station balnéaire est également un petit port de pêche?**
   Nous voyons les barques sur la grève et les vieux pêcheurs assis sur le mur.

4. **Que font ceux-ci?**
   Ils se reposent; ils parlent de leurs prises. Le jeune pêcheur, assis à côté de son fils, regarde du côté des baigneurs.

5. **Comment est la mer?**
   Sur les bords l'eau est d'un bleu clair. La mer est douce aujourd'hui, il n'y a pas de vent.

6. **Où se trouve l'hôtel principal?**
   L'hôtel principal est situé sur la colline d'où il domine la baie.

7. **Cette petite ville, quand retrouvera-t-elle son calme habituel?**
   Quand les vacances seront terminées cette petite ville reprendra sa tranquillité.

8. **Pourquoi les enfants aiment-ils la plage?**
   Les enfants aiment se baigner et jouer (sur le sable).

346

À LA TERRASSE DU CAFÉ

Nous sommes à la terrasse d'un café-restaurant. C'est l'été, il fait chaud et pour protéger les clients contre les rayons du soleil il y a des parasols multi-colores. On voit qu'il y a une circulation intense — autobus, voitures privées, taxis — qui passent tous rapidement.

Les tables ne sont pas toutes occupées — il doit être encore assez tôt — car à midi et demi chacun quitte son travail pour aller manger.

À l'entrée, un garcon de café surveille l'arrivée des clients. Un autre garcon sert à manger à des gens qui sont déjà installés. À droite, deux dames sont assises; devant elles sur la nappe blanche on aperçoit une bouteille de bon vin et des verres. À gauche, un couple est en train de manger; le monsieur porte des lunettes.

Sur les tables libres les couverts sont mis. À la sortie des bureaux d'autres personnes viendront prendre leur repas. Sur une des tables il y a des petits pains, sur une autre un journal et des bouteilles. Les chaises sont de style moderne et sont placées autour des tables. Plus près de la chaussée on voit des fauteuils de paille. Ils ont l'air très confortables. C'est là qu'il faut se mettre pour prendre l'apéritif qui précède un bon repas.

PAYSAGE D'HIVER À LA MONTAGNE

Nous voici dans un village montagnard en pleine saison de sports d'hiver. Dans la rue principale du village nous voyons des skieurs. Ils sont tous chaussés de grosses chaussures de ski. Hommes et femmes sont vêtus de leurs pantalons et de leurs blousons. Sur leurs épaules ils portent leurs skis et leurs bâtons dont ils vont se servir pour faire des prouesses sur les pistes.

De chaque côté de la rue la neige a été entassée. À la suite d'une forte chute de neige il faut faire cela pour permettre aux gens de circuler plus facilement. On voit des maisons et des magasins dont les toits sont couverts de neige. Dans la rue aucune voiture ne circule.

À droite on aperçoit un hôtel dont les fenêtres s'ouvrent sur des balcons. Plus près, à l'angle de l'image, il y a un magasin où l'on vend toutes sortes de souvenirs. Au fond, sur les pentes boisées de la montagne, on voit la neige qui brille au soleil.

LEÇON 34

THE EXAMINATION

This chapter takes the form of a specimen examination paper such as might be set by any of the examination boards. It consists of five parts: two French passages to be translated into English, one English passage to be translated into French, a composition and a passage for comprehension. This is slightly more than is set in the average G.C.E. paper, so we are allowing three hours, half an hour longer than the time allowed by most boards.

When you think that you have learned and understood everything in Parts I and II of this book, and when you have tried most of the exercises in the earlier chapters of this third part, you should find it quite possible to tackle this specimen paper.

IMPORTANT POINTS TO REMEMBER

Immediately before you start the paper re-read all the hints and advice in the introduction to the third part and at the beginnings of Lessons 28 to 32. Remember also to read the whole paper right through once before you begin, and if there is a question which you find more difficult than the rest, leave it until the end and do your best questions first.

DOING THE PAPER

Choose a quiet room and a time when you are not likely to be interrupted, and behave exactly as though you were doing a real examination. Provide yourself before you start with everything you may need in the way of pens, pencils, blotting-paper, etc. Remember that you are not allowed to refer to any books or notes in a real examination, so when you try this paper you must resist the temptation to refer back to earlier lessons or to look up words you don't know or have forgotten in the vocabulary. Time yourself strictly and stop writing immediately the three hours is up, whether you have finished the paper or not.

CORRECTING THE PAPER

Afterwards go over your paper carefully, comparing it with the model versions at the back of the book. Learn anything which you got wrong, or which is new, and make sure that you know any new vocabulary. If you did not manage to finish the paper in the time, finish it, and practise writing

349

questions of the type you find most difficult. You may find, for example, that you dawdle over the composition; if so, set yourself composition subjects and practise writing 150 to 200 words in half an hour.

SPECIMEN EXAMINATION PAPER
(Time allowed: three hours.)

1. Translate into English:

(*a*) **Je courus quelque temps comme une chèvre blessée. Je me sentais perdu. Où trouver de l'argent? Comment m'en aller? Comment rejoindre mon frère?**

Enfin, accablé, épuisé de fatigue et de douleur, je me laissai tomber dans la neige au pied d'un chataîgnier. Je serais resté là jusqu'au lendemain peut-être, pleurant et n'ayant pas la force de penser quand tout à coup, bien loin, j'entendis sonner une cloche. C'était celle du collège. J'avais tout oublié; cette cloche me rappela à la vie; il me fallait rentrer et surveiller la récréation des élèves dans la salle. . . . En pensant à la salle, une idée subite me vint. Sur-le-champ mes larmes s'arrêtèrent; je me sentis plus fort, plus calme. Je me levai, et, de ce pas délibéré de l'homme qui vient de prendre une irrévocable décision, je repris le chemin de Sarlande.

Si vous voulez en savoir davantage sur cette décision importante, suivez-moi à travers cette plaine blanche, dans les rues sombres et boueuses de la ville, sous le porche du collège, et dans la salle de récréation des élèves. Et lisez pardessus mon épaule la lettre que je suis en train d'écrire à mon frère:

"Pardonne-moi, mon bien-aimé Roger, la douleur que je viens de te causer. Quand tu recevras cette lettre, ton pauvre Dédé sera mort. . . ."

(*b*) **Pendant un demi-siècle, les bourgeoises de Pont-l'Evêque envièrent à Mme Aubain sa servante Félicité. Pour cent francs par an, elle faisait la cuisine et le ménage, cousait, lavait, repassait, savait brider un cheval, engraisser les volailles, battre le beurre, et resta fidèle à sa maîtresse — qui, cependant, n'était pas une personne agréable.**

Elle avait épousé un beau garçon sans fortune, mort au commencement de 1809, en lui laissant deux enfants très jeunes avec une quantité de dettes. Alors elle vendit ses meubles, quitta sa maison de Saint-Melaine pour en habiter une plus modeste située dans une ruelle aboutissant à la rivière.

Elle se levait dès l'aube, pour ne pas manquer la messe, et travaillait jusqu'au soir sans interruption. Son visage était maigre et sa voix aiguë. À vingt-cinq ans, on lui en aurait donné quarante. Dès la cinquantaine, elle ne marqua plus aucun âge — et, toujours silencieuse, la taille droite et les gestes mesurés, elle semblait une femme en bois, fonctionnant d'une manière automatique.

350

Les vendangeurs récoltent les raisins pour le vin.

2. Translate into French:

As soon as he had received his change, George left the café and found a bench near by on the boulevard. There he took out from his pocket the money he had left and counted it. He would have to economize until the end of the month, he thought. Before continuing on his way, he stayed there several minutes, gazing straight in front of him, but seeing nothing, not even the crowd hurrying along the pavement, nor the cars, taxis and buses taking men more fortunate than he back to the soup which their devoted and affectionate wives had prepared at home. He wondered, for the twentieth time, what he was going to do. Where would he sleep? He knew no one in that town who could give him a bed for the night. If he went to a hotel he would not have enough money to pay for his next meal.

Suddenly, he started. He thought he recognized the back of a young man who was about to enter the café George had just left. Yes, it was indeed Bonvier, the man who had worked with him in the post office a few years ago and who had once borrowed from him five hundred francs which he had never returned. George got up quickly and followed his former colleague to the table where he had ordered a glass of beer.

351

3. Comprehension: read the French passage and answer the questions which follow in English. Do not translate the passage.

A LITTLE GIRL'S RISK TO SATISFY HER CURIOSITY

Les jours suivants, les garçons d'en face refusèrent toujours de me révéler à quoi ils jouaient.

"Viens le voir," me dit le blond.

Je pris au mot son invitation. J'aurais pu descendre dans la petite rue et remonter à l'arrière de la pharmacie par une petite porte. Mais l'aurais eu peur de rencontrer des grandes personnes dans cette maison inconnue. Dans un coin du grenier, derrière une malle, je trouvai une planche à repasser. Je l'enfilai par la fenêtre. Le blond l'assujettit à la sienne.

"Ça tient fort," dit-il.

Je m'engageai sur la planche, à quatre pattes. J'avançai centimètre par centimètre. J'étais à la hauteur d'un troisième étage. Quand j'arrivai au milieu, je ne pus m'empêcher de voir, en bas, le pavé de la ruelle. Autour de moi je sentis vaciller les murs. Au-dessous, pendaient des chemises d'hommes, fendues sur les côtés. Elles laissaient échapper des gouttes d'eau dont la vue me glaçait. Tout basculait. Le ciel et la ruelle allaient se mélanger. J'enfonçai mes ongles dans la planche pour que le ciel restât en haut, la ruelle en bas.

"Elle a la frousse!" chuchota le blond aux deux autres. Cette remarque me stimula. Comme une louve indignée, je me mis à ramper. J'arrivai de l'autre côté, j'enjambai la fenêtre. Je sautai triomphalement sur le plancher.

1. What was the little girl curious about?
2. What was the easiest means of reaching the boys? Why did she not take this way?
3. What did she use to make a bridge?
4. How did she cross? How high was she?
5. What happened when she was half-way across?
6. What did she see down below?
7. How did she attempt to put things right?
8. What spurred her on to reach the other side?

4. Composition: write about 250 words in French based on this outline:

Michel — jeune citadin — passer ses vacances à la campagne — la vie en plein air — couper le blé — traire les vaches — fatigué — fier.

ALPHABETICAL LIST OF SPECIAL DIFFICULTIES

ACTIONS AS OPPOSED TO STATES

s'asseoir = *to sit down*
    Il s'assit dans un fauteuil et commença à lire le journal.
    He sat down in an armchair and began to read the paper.
    En été il s'asseyait souvent devant la porte de sa maison.
    In summer he often used to sit in front of the door of his house.
    Note: **asseoir** is an active verb and means *to give a seat to.*
être assis = *to be seated* or *sitting down*
    Il était assis devant la cheminée.
    He was sitting in front of the fireplace.
se coucher = *to lie down* or *to go to bed*
    Il s'est couché de bonne heure ce soir.
    He went to bed early this evening.
être couché = *to be lying down*
s'étonner = *to be astonished*
    Il s'étonna, en ouvrant la porte, de voir son chien couché au coin de la chambre.
    On opening the door he was astonished to find his dog lying down in the corner of the room.
se lever = *to get up*
    Il s'est levé ce matin dès l'aube.
    This morning he got up at dawn.
être levé = *to be up*
    Quand j'y suis arrivé Robert était déjà levé depuis une heure.
    When I got there Robert had already been up for an hour.
s'endormir = *to fall asleep*
    Il était tellement fatigué qu'en se couchant il s'est endormi tout de suite.
    He was so tired that he fell asleep immediately on going to bed.
être endormi = *to be asleep*
être pressé = *to be in a hurry*
    Nous ne pouvons pas rester, nous sommes vraiment pressés.
    We can't stop, we are in a great hurry.
se presser = *to hurry*
    Les voyageurs se sont pressés pour arriver avant la tombée de la nuit.
    The travellers hurried to arrive before nightfall.
Note also:

être accoudé = *to be leaning*	**être agenouillé** = *to be kneeling*
être accroupi = *to be squatting*	**être pendu** = *to be hanging*
être étendu = *to be stretched out*	**être debout** = *to be standing*
être tapi = *to be crouching*	**être cramponné** = *to be clinging*

age.
Il a trente ans.
Je suis plus âgé que lui.
Quel âge avez-vous?

AGREEMENT OF PAST PARTICIPLE
1. **Ils se sont rappelé les bons repas qu'ils mangeaient à la maison.** No agreement as se = *to themselves.* Direct object **les bons repas** comes AFTER the past participle.
2. **Ils ont laissé dans le compartiment les beaux cadeaux qu'ils avaient achetés.** Agreement with preceding direct object.
3. **Ils se sont élancés hors de la maison terrifiés de ce qu'ils avaient vu.** Agreement with se = *themselves.*
4. **Mes beaux gants, que sont-ils devenus, s'est-elle écriée.**

AGREEMENT OF SUBJECT AND VERB
1. *My brother and I = we.* **Mon frère et moi avons** (not **ont**) **quitté la maison de bonne heure.**
2. **Étant arrivés au sommet de la colline nous nous sommes reposés un instant** (arrivés must agree with **nous**).
3. **Elles et leurs amis** (= **ils**) **sont partis sans plus attendre.**

all.
1. *All of us* = **Nous tous.**
   All of us know that he was born in France.
   Nous savons tous qu'il est né en France.
2. *All that* = **Tout ce qui** or **tout ce que** or **tout ce dont.**
   We know all that has happened to you.
   Nous savons tout ce qui vous est arrivé.
   All that you can see there belongs to the Baron.
   Tout ce que vous voyez là appartient à Monsieur le Baron.
   You will find all you need on the table.
   Tout ce dont vous avez besoin se trouve sur la table.
3. *All who* = **Tous ceux qui** or **tous ceux que.**
   All who come won't be disappointed.
   Tous ceux qui viendront ne seront pas déçus.
   All who were taken prisoner by the Germans were sent to Germany.
   Tous ceux que les Allemands ont fait prisonniers ont été envoyés en Allemagne.
4. *Nothing at all* = **Rien du tout.**
   Not at all = **Pas du tout.**
5. *All* as a noun = **Le tout.**
   He risked all by lending him the money.
   Il a risqué le tout en lui prêtant l'argent.

an, année.
After a number, use **an**, e.g.:
In a vingt ans.
Il y a trois ans je suis allé à Paris.
But,
Il y a quelques années je suis allé à Paris.
Bien des années après. . . .

any and *anyone.*

1. *I don't know if there is enough change to give you any coins of a hundred francs.*
   Je ne sais pas s'il y a assez de monnaie pour vous donner des pièces de cent francs.
2. *I don't know if anyone got into the house whilst I was away, but several articles are missing.*
   Je ne sais pas si quelqu'un est entré dans la maison pendant mon absence, mais il y manque quelques articles.
3. *Anyone could have done it. We shall never find the culprit.*
   N'importe qui aurait pu le faire. On ne découvrira jamais le coupable.
4. *I do not know whether there is any chance of getting tickets for the theatre now.*
   Je ne sais pas s'il y a maintenant quelque possibilité de trouver des places au théâtre.

après with an infinitive.
   Use the perfect infinitive:
   After reaching the main road = Après avoir gagné la grand'route.
   After stopping for a moment = Après s'être arrêté(s) un moment.

as.

1. *As quickly as possible* = Aussi vite que possible or Le plus vite possible.
2. *In a negative comparison* = si.
   He is not as silly as you would have thought.
   Il n'est pas si bête que vous ne l'auriez cru.
3. *As I went further on the road became more difficult.*
   À mesure que j'avançais la route devenait plus difficile.
4. *As you can see I am not short of provisions.*
   Comme vous le voyez je ne manque pas de provisions.
5. *They are as alike as twins* = Ils se ressemblent comme des jumeaux.
6. *As though nothing has happened* = Comme si de rien n'était.
7. *As meaning since you are:*
   As a true Christian you cannot . . . = En vrai chrétien vous ne pouvez pas. . . .
8. *As much, as many (as)* = autant (que).

bien: different ways of using and translating this adverb.

1. Il n'a pas bien compris la question.
   He did not understand the question properly.
   (Note the position of **bien** in a perfect tense.)
2. Bien sûr que non = *most certainly not.*
3. Nous avons bien reçu le paquet que vous nous avez envoyé.
   We duly received the parcel you sent us.
4. Vous êtes très bien là devant ce beau feu.
   You are very comfortable there in front of this lovely fire!
5. Je l'espère bien = *I certainly hope so.*
6. Qu'est-ce qu'on pourrait bien faire? = *What on earth could we do?*
7. On était bien une douzaine de personnes = *There were quite a dozen people.*
8. C'est bien de lui = *That's just like him.*
9. Je prendrais bien une tasse de thé = *I could certainly do with a cup of tea.*
10. Il a bien cinquante ans = *He is fifty years old at least.*

by.
 by bicycle = à bicyclette
 by horse = à cheval
 by car = en auto
 by train = par le train, par le chemin de fer
 by plane = en avion

carry. With things use the verbs **porter, apporter, emporter.**
 1. **C'est Robert qui va porter la valise. Il est plus fort que sa sœur.**
    Robert will carry the case. He is stronger than his sister.
 2. **Ramassez les cahiers s'il vous plaît et apportez-les ici.**
    Collect the exercise books, please, and bring them here.
 3. **Le vent a emporté le ballon qui est tombé dans la rivière.**
    The wind carried off the balloon which fell into the river.

colour.
 De quelle couleur est votre robe?
 Ma robe est verte.

DATE
 Le premier (deux, trois) mai, mil neuf cent (dix-neuf cent) soixante-cinq.
 The first (second, third) of May, 1965.
 Le lundi deux janvier
 En (l'an) dix-huit cents = *In (the year)* 1800.

DATIVE OF THE PERSON AFTER CERTAIN VERBS
 1. **J'ai demandé au concierge d'aller ouvrir la porte.**
 2. **Le professeur ne voulait permettre à Gaspard de rester dans la cour.**
 3. **Il a fait de son mieux pour persuader à ses parents de le laisser partir seul.**
 4. **L'agent a dit à Robert de se présenter le lendemain à la gendarmerie.**

DAYS
 lundi, mardi, mercredi, jeudi, vendredi, samedi, dimanche (all masculine)
 on Monday = **lundi**
 last Monday = **lundi dernier**
 next Monday = **lundi prochain**
 on Mondays = **le lundi**
 the day after = **le jour suivant, le lendemain**

demi.
 un demi = *a half*
 une heure et demie (to agree with **heure**), but **une demi-heure.**

dernier and **prochain** — position.
 1. **Samedi dernier il a accompagné le fermier au marché.**
 2. **Il va toujours voir sa vieille mère le dernier samedi du mois.**
 3. **La semaine prochaine nous pensons aller passer une journée à Londres.**
 4. **Nous devrons descendre à la prochaine station de métro.**

en and **y.**
 (*a*) **Il s'est approché de la barrière.**
    He went up to the gate.

Il s'en est approché.
He went up to it.

(b) **Elle s'en souvient.**
She remembers it.

(c) **Il s'en vante.**
He boasts about it.

(d) **Vous devriez en avoir honte.**
You ought to be ashamed of it.

(e) **J'ai reçu une lettre de mon ami. Je n'y ai pas répondu.**
I have received a letter from my friend. I haven't answered it.

entendre parler or **dire** = *to hear.*
Avez-vous entendu parler de l'homme qui a épousé une femme muette?
Avez-vous entendu dire qu'il y a un homme avec une femme muette?

faire.

1. **Je voudrais me faire couper les cheveux.**
I should like to get my hair cut.

2. **Il va se faire faire un costume tout neuf.**
He is going to have a new suit made for himself.

3. **Faites asseoir le monsieur, s'il vous plaît.**
Let the gentleman be seated, please.

4. **Faites entrer le monsieur.**
Show the gentleman in.

5. **Il fallait faire venir immédiatement les pompiers.**
We had to send for the firemen at once.

6. **Il a réussi à faire marcher le moteur.**
He succeeded in getting the engine to start.

7. **Il s'est fait mal en allumant le feu.**
He hurt himself lighting the fire.

8. **Je m'excuse de vous avoir fait attendre si longtemps.**
I am sorry I kept you waiting so long.

9. **Le gérant a demandé au petit chasseur de faire monter mes bagages.**
The manager asked the bell-boy to take my luggage upstairs.

10. **Il ne pouvait pas réussir à se faire comprendre.**
He could not succeed in making himself understood.

11. **Elle a fait courir le bruit qu'on avait trouvé un noyé sur la plage.**
She spread the rumour that a drowned man had been found on the beach.

12. **Il m'a fallu une demi-heure pour faire bouillir l'eau.**
It took me half an hour to get the water to boil.

13. **Il a fait avertir tous ses camarades que les Allemands se trouvaient dans le voisinage.**
He sent to warn all his friends that the Germans were in the neighbourhood.

14. **Elle a fait remarquer à son mari que la vaisselle n'était pas propre.**
She pointed out to her husband that the crockery was not clean.

first.
I saw him first = **C'est moi qui l'ai vu le premier.**
She was always the first to wake up = **C'était elle qui s'éveillait toujours la première.**
It was the first time that . . . = **C'était la première fois que. . . .**

go and with another verb.
Let's go and see = **Allons voir.**

I have no time to go and visit him = **Je n'ai pas le temps d'aller le visiter.**
home.
She went home = **Elle est rentrée à la maison (chez elle).**
They all left their homes = **Ils sortirent tous de chez eux.**

Il y a
(a) **Il y avait un œuf dans le nid.**
   There was an egg in the nest.
(b) **Il devrait y avoir de la place pour nous deux.**
   There ought to be room for the two of us.
(c) **"Il y a eu un accident terrible," a-t-il répondu.**
   "There has been a terrible accident," he replied.
(d) **Il y aura toujours assez de temps pour gagner le sommet.**
   There will be plenty of time to reach the top.
(e) In these expressions **il** is always singular, though the correspond-
   ing English may be *are*:
   Il y avait plus de dix mille hommes sur la place.
   There were more than ten thousand men in the square.

IMPERATIVE
Note position of the pronoun:
(a) **Asseyez-vous, donc.**
   Do sit down.
(b) **Mais tais-toi, donc.**
   Do be quiet.
(c) **Ne vous en inquiètez pas.**
   Don't worry about it.
(d) **Allons-nous-en tout de suite.**
   Let's get off at once.

IMPERFECT TENSE
1. Two actions — one interrupts the other:
   Quand je suis entré dans la salle il travaillait devant sa table.
   When I entered the room he was working at his table.
2. To be in the habit of = *would.*
   Quand il était à la campagne il se levait toujours de très bonne heure.
   When he was in the country he would always get up very early.
3. To keep on doing something:
   Élle se levait à chaque instant pour aller à la cuisine vérifier si tout marchait bien.
   She kept getting up all the time to go and see if everything was all right in the kitchen.
4. With **depuis** = *had been*:
   Il travaillait déjà depuis quatre heures quand je suis arrivé.
   He had already been working for four hours when I arrived.
5. Imperfect of **devoir** = *was to* or *should have.*
   Le train devait partir à huit heures.
   The train was due to leave at eight o'clock.
6. The imperfect of **falloir** can mean *should have.*
   Il fallait voir combien il faisait de la vitesse.
   You should have seen how fast he was travelling.

7. In dramatic situations after si the imperfect can mean *should have*:
   J'étais raide de peur mais je savais que si je bougeais j'étais mort.
   I was stiff with fear, but I knew that if I moved I would have been killed.
8. **À mesure que** + imperfect = *to keep getting.*
   À mesure que nous nous éloignions de la côte, la forêt devenait plus épaisse.
   Gradually as we left the coast, the forest kept getting denser.

it is.
   C'est + noun or pronoun:
      C'est Georges.   **C'est lui.**
   Ce sont + plural noun or pronoun:
      Ce sont les soldats.   **Ce sont eux.**
   But
   Il (elle) est + adjective:
      Il (elle) est jeune
   Ils (elles) sont + adjective:
      Ils (elles) sont pauvres
   when referring to a noun with a gender.

   C'est vrai.
   Il est vrai que. . . .
   C'est facile à faire. (C'est . . . à. . . .)
   Il est facile de faire cela. (Il est . . . de. . . .)

   Ce with **être**, otherwise **ça.**
   Ça ne vaut pas la peine.

   La route, il est vrai, est très longue.
   Il est huit heures.

just, in the expression *to have just* (*done something*).
   Someone has just hidden behind the hedge.
   Quelqu'un vient de se cacher derrière la haie.

late.
   1. *We must go home. It is late and mother will be wondering what has happened.*
      Il faut rentrer. Il est tard — Maman se demandera ce qui s'est passé.
   2. *We must hurry — we are going to arrive at school late.*
      Il faut nous dépêcher — nous allons arriver à l'école en retard.
little.
   a little boy = **un petit garçon**
   a little butter = **un peu de beurre**
   little liked = **peu aimé**

MONTHS
   janvier, février, mars, avril, mai, juin, juillet, août, septembre, octobre, novembre, décembre.
   in January = **en janvier, au mois de janvier**

MOVEMENT
Notice the following verb constructions:
   (a) *Come and see me tomorrow.*
      Venez me voir demain.

(b) *Go and tell him what has happened.*
Allez lui dire ce qui est arrivé.
(c) *Go up and see if grandfather is asleep.*
Montez voir si grandpère est endormi.

NEGATIVES

1. *Nor did I succeed in saving him.*
Moi non plus, je n'ai pu réussir à le sauver.
2. Note the position of **personne** in a perfect tense.
Nous avons cherché partout, mais nous n'avons vu personne.
We looked everywhere but we saw no one.
3. **Je ne le vois nulle part** = *I can't see him anywhere.*
4. **Mais à aucun prix je ne voulais risquer un coup d'œil.**
Not at any cost did I want to risk a glance.
5. Note the use of the negative infinitive in public notices.
Ne pas toucher or **Prière de ne pas toucher** = *Please do not touch.*
Ne pas marcher sur la pelouse = *Please do not walk on the lawn.*
Ne pas répondre à plus de quatre questions.
Do not answer more than four questions.
6. *Not only* = **Non seulement** (no inversion).
Non seulement il avait les poches pleines de pommes, mais il en avait rempli aussi son sac.
Not only did he have his pockets full of apples, but he had filled his bag with them as well.
7. Note **ne que** + **plus, jamais** or **guère.**
Il ne m'en reste plus que la moitié = *I have only half of them left.*
Je ne bois jamais que de l'eau = *I never drink anything but water.*
8. **N'importe** = *No matter.*

The following are not negative despite the **ne.**

9. **Je crains que vous ne preniez froid** = *I am afraid that you will catch cold.*
10. **Peu s'en fallut que la voiture ne fût complètement détruite.**
The car came near to being completely destroyed.
11. **Restez ici sans bouger à moins qu'on ne vous appelle.**
Stay here without moving unless you are called.
12. **Il est beaucoup plus âgé que je ne le croyais.**
He is much older than I thought.
13. **Il y a longtemps que je ne les ai vus** = *It's a long time since I saw them.*
14. **J'ai plus qu'il ne m'en faut** = *I have more than I need.*

next.
Suivant = *next* when future time is NOT implied.
On the following Saturday = **Le samedi suivant.**
Next Saturday I shall go to market with the farmer.
Samedi prochain j'irai au marché avec le fermier.

nouveau, neuf.
1. **Nous avons un nouveau camarade dans la classe aujourd'hui.**
2. **Son père vient de lui acheter une bicyclette toute neuve** (*brand new*).

Once upon a time. . . .
1. *Once upon a time there was a man who set out to climb a mountain.*
   Il y avait une fois un homme qui est parti pour faire l'ascension d'une montagne (or il était une fois . . .).
2. *Once upon a time a lonely traveller lost his way.*
   Il y avait une fois un voyageur solitaire qui s'est égaré.

PAST PARTICIPLES DOING THE WORK OF A CLAUSE
1. **Partis de bon matin, ils ont pu arriver avant midi en pleine montagne.**
   Having set out (or as they had set out) very early they were able to reach the heart of the mountains before midday.
2. **Étendus sur la falaise, ils regardaient dans le nid pour voir combien d'œufs s'y trouvaient.**
   Lying down over the cliff they were looking into the nest to see how many eggs it contained.
3. **Arrivés à la gare, les élèves se sont étonnés de trouver que le train partait déjà.**
   Having reached the station the pupils were amazed to find that the train was already leaving.
4. **Très surpris, l'enfant s'est retourné pour essayer de trouver d'òu venait le bruit.**
   Thoroughly amazed the child turned round to try to find out where the noise was coming from.
5. **Très fatigués de leur long voyage, les élèves se sont reposés à l'ombre d'un arbre.**
   Thoroughly tired by their long journey the pupils rested under the shade of a tree.

personne.
Il y a trois personnes dans la maison.
Nous ne voyons personne (*nobody*).
Qui est là? Personne (*nobody*).

peut-être.
"*Perhaps it is a thief,*" *he said.*
Peut-être est-ce un voleur, dit-il or Peut-être que c'est un voleur or C'est peut-être un voleur.

plus.
J'en ai plus que vous.
J'ai plus de trois chapeaux (plus de with numbers).

PREPOSITIONS
Each example should be studied carefully.
1. *I ran* out *of the house* = Je me suis élancé *hors* de la maison.
2. *He climbed* into *a tree to hide* = Il est monté *dans* un arbre pour se cacher.
3. *He went* on *his way without a word* = Il continua son chemin sans rien dire.
4. On *a fine summer's day he set off early to go to the seaside.*
   Par un beau jour d'été il se mit en route de bonne heure pour aller au bord de la mer.

5. In *which direction are you going?* = *De* quel côté allez-vous?
6. *He works* on *a farm* = Il travaille *dans* une ferme.
7. About *two o'clock* = *Vers* les deux heures.
  About *two o'clock* in *the afternoon* = Vers deux heures *de* l'après-midi.
8. *He loved to go walking* in *the rain* = Il aimait se promener *sous* la pluie.
9. Under *the shelter of the tent he was trying to light the stove.*
  A l'abri de la tente il essayait de faire marcher le réchaud.
10. *One day* in *the month of May* = Un jour *au* mois de mai.
11. With *his rucksack* on *his back, his rope on his shoulder he set off for the mountain.*
  Le sac au dos, sa corde à l'épaule, il partit pour la montagne.
12. *He went to his lessons carrying a brief-case full of exercise books.*
  Il allait *en* classe portant une serviette chargée de cahiers.
13. *He has fallen* down *the stairs* = Il est tombé *en bas* de l'escalier.
14. *He was sitting* at *his table correcting the homework.*
  Il était assis *devant* sa table à corriger les devoirs.
15. *They were everywhere* — in *hundreds, in thousands.*
  Ils étaient partout — *par* centaines, par milliers.
16. *I drove gently* towards *him* = Je roulai doucement *à* sa rencontre.
17. On *behalf of all my friends I extend a warm welcome to you.*
  De la part de tous mes amis je vous souhaite la bienvenue.
18. *He used to pass the baker's shop every day* on *his way to the office.*
  Tous les jours, *en* route à son bureau il passait devant la boulangerie.
19. *He went and picked something up* from *the table.*
  Il est allé ramasser quelque chose *sur* la table.
20. But *for me he would have fallen* over *a precipice.*
  Sans moi, il serait tombé *dans* un précipice.
21. *He drank out of a glass* = Il a bu *dans* un verre.
22. *For the first time* in *my life* = Pour la premiere fois *de* ma vie.
23. *He could see* by *his dress* = Il a pu voir *à* son veston.

propre — position.
  1. Je l'ai fait de mes propres mains = *I did it with my own hands.*
  2. Il ne faut pas y toucher. Tu n'as pas les mains propres.
    You must not touch it. Your hands are not clean.

QUESTIONS

  1. *Are you John?* = Êtes-vous Jean? Est-ce que vous êtes Jean?
  2. *Has he answered my letter?* = A-t-il répondu à ma lettre?
  3. *Has Monsieur Bonnard answered my letter?*
    Monsieur Bonnard a-t-il répondu à ma lettre?
  4. *Why hasn't Monsieur Bonnard answered my letter?*
    Pourquoi monsieur Bonnard n'a-t-il pas répondu à ma lettre?
  5. *What of that?* = Et alors?
  6. *What has become of him?* = Qu'est-il devenu?
    What has become of my gloves? = Mes gants, que sont-ils devenus?
  7. *Which of* = lequel, laquelle, etc.
    Which of these hats is yours? = Lequel de ces chapeaux est le vôtre?
  8. *Whose son are you? Whose book is this?* (**Dont** cannot be used in a question.)
    De qui êtes-vous le fils? À qui est ce livre?

9. *When will you come and see me again?* (**Lorsque** cannot be used in a question.)
   Quand reviendrez-vous me voir?
10. *Would the master like to be served now?*
    Monsieur, veut-il que je le serve maintenant?

Questions may be formed merely by using a question mark.
1. **Vous comptez rester longtemps, Monsieur?**
   Do you expect to remain here for a long time, sir?
2. **Et vous?** = *And what about you?*
   Et mes affaires? Je peux les laisser ici?
   And what about my things? Can I leave them here?
3. **S'il venait à pleuvoir?** = *And what if it happened to rain?*
4. **Il songeait où les cacher?** = *He was thinking — where can I hide them?*
5. **Vous ne vous êtes pas fait mal, Monsieur?**
   You haven't hurt yourself have you, sir?
6. **Que faire? s'est-il dit** = *What can I do? he said to himself.*
7. **S'il avait manqué le train?** = *And what if he had missed the train?*
8. **Il n'y a donc personne ici qui parle français?**
   Isn't there anyone here who speaks French?
9. **Monsieur désire?** = *What would you like, sir?*

SEASONS
en été, en automne, en hiver, but **au printemps.**

SEQUENCE OF TENSE
1. **Quand nous sommes arrivés à la maison nous avons trouvé que le pauvre vieillard était tombé en bas de l'escalier.** (Not **est tombé**: the latter action took place before the first.)
2. **Quand nous avons ouvert le coffre-fort nous avons découvert que le voleur avait tout vidé.** (Not **a vidé**.)
3. **Quand nous sommes arrivés à notre destination le train avait déjà deux heures de retard.**
4. **Deux jours plus tard nous avons reçu le courrier qui était arrivé après notre départ.**

so.
(*a*) In front of adjectives = **si.**
   si grand, si petit, si important.
(*b*) Meaning *therefore* = **donc.**
   Donc, nous sommes arrivés en retard.
   So we arrived late.
(*c*) Meaning *in order that* = **Pour que.**
   Pour que vous puissiez comprendre . . . je vais vous expliquer.
   So that you may understand . . . I am going to explain.

some and *some of.*
1. *Some people like getting up early.*
   Il y a des gens qui aiment se lever de bon matin.
2. *Some time this morning we shall see the postman arrive.*
   Dans la matinée nous verrons arriver le facteur.
3. *Some of the pupils have forgotten to bring their exercise books.*
   Quelques-uns des élèves ont oublié d'apporter leurs cahiers.

4. *Some of the apples in the basket were rotten.*
   Quelques-unes des pommes dans le panier étaient pourries.
5. *Some ten years ago* = **Il y a environ dix ans.**
6. *Do you want some paper? No thanks, I have some.*
   Voulez-vous du papier à lettre? Merci, j'en ai.
7. *Something* = **quelque chose.**
   Note: *something difficult* = **quelque chose de difficile.**

take.
Distinguish carefully the various ways of translating this verb.
1. *I should have taken him to be older.*
   Je l'aurais cru plus âgé.
2. *He has taken his dog for a walk.*
   Il est allé promener son chien.
3. *The ambulance had to be sent for to take the wounded man to hospital.*
   Il fallait faire venir l'ambulance pour emmener le blessé à l'hôpital.
4. *How long did you take to come from Marseilles to Paris?*
   Combien de temps avez-vous mis pour venir de Marseille jusqu'à Paris?
5. *Will you take our visitor as far as the end of the road?*
   Voulez-vous conduire notre visiteur jusqu'au bout de la rue?
6. *Without too much difficulty he took the first prize.*
   Sans trop de difficulté il a remporté le premier prix.
7. *On seeing the Queen they all took their caps off and bowed.*
   En voyant la reine ils ont tous enlevé la casquette et se sont inclinés.
8. *In England we usually take four meals a day.*
   En Angleterre on fait ordinairement quatre repas par jour.
9. *Early in the war he was taken prisoner and remained four years in Germany.*
   Pendant la première partie de la guerre il a été fait prisonnier et il est resté quatre ans en Allemagne.
10. *Taking all in all* = **A tout prendre.**
11. *We took off the wallpaper and underneath we found a hiding place in which there was a fine portrait.*
    Nous avons enlevé le papier peint et dessous nous avons découvert une cachette dans laquelle se trouvait un beau portrait.
12. *Father took the portrait to an art dealer and sold it to him for a large sum.*
    Papa a emporté le tableau chez un antiquaire et il le lui a vendu moyennant une grosse somme d'argent.
13. *I shall be unable to attend the meeting as I took cold yesterday in the fog.*
    Je ne pourrai assister à la réunion car je me suis enrhumé hier à cause du brouillard.
14. *I received a letter from mother telling me that father had been taken ill.*
    J'ai reçu une lettre de maman me disant que papa était tombé malade.
15. *I was unable to take my eyes off the newcomer, so handsome was he.*
    Je ne pouvais pas détourner les yeux du nouveau-venu tellement il était beau.

time.
What is the time? = **Quelle heure est-il?**
He has no time to . . . = **Il n'a pas le temps de. . . .**
He did it four times = **Il l'a fait quatre fois.**

veille and vieille.
La veille, il avait été au théâtre = *The night before, he had been to the theatre.*
La vieille (femme) restait toujours au bord du trottoir.
The old lady was still standing on the edge of the pavement.

WEATHER
Il fait beau (mauvais, chaud, froid).
Il fait beau temps.
Le temps est beau.
Il fait du vent.

what.
1. *I don't know what he is doing.*
 Je ne sais pas ce qu'il fait.

2. *What are you thinking of?*
 A quoi pensez-vous?

3. *What are you talking about?*
 De quoi parlez-vous?

4. *What makes you think that he will not come?*
 Qu'est-ce qui vous fait penser qu'il ne viendra pas?

5. *What is happening?*
 Qu'est-ce qui se passe?

6. *What is making him so unhappy?*
 Qu'est-ce qui le rend si malheureux?

7. *What is there to eat?*
 Qu'est-ce qu'il y a à manger?

8. *What day is it today?*
 Quel jour sommes-nous aujourd'hui?

9. *What news have you for us today?*
 Quelles nouvelles avez-vous à nous donner ce matin?

10. *What time is it, please?*
 Quelle heure est-il, s'il vous plaît?

11. *What time do you make it by your watch?*
 Quelle heure avez-vous à votre montre?

12. *Anything new?*
 Quoi de nouveau?

while.
While you are doing that . . . = Pendant que vous faisiez ça. . . .
He was reading the paper while eating his breakfast.
Tout en mangeant son petit dejeuner il lisait le journal.

WORDS WHICH LOOK ALIKE IN ENGLISH AND FRENCH

assister à = *to be present at*
to assist = **aider**

agréable = *pleasant*
agreeable = **raisonnable.** *If you are agreeable* = **Si vous êtes d'accord**

avertir = *to warn*
to avert = **éviter**

ancien = *former*, e.g. **un ancien élève** = *a former pupil*
ancient = **vieux,** or **ancien** (used after the noun)

brave = *worthy*
brave = **courageux**

content = *pleased*
to be content with something = **se contenter de**

la cave = *the cellar*
the cave = **la caverne**

la chance = *luck*
chance = **le hasard; par hasard** = *by chance*

commander = *to order* (e.g. in a shop)
to command = **ordonner**

la cloche = *the bell* (a large one)
the clock = **l'horloge** (a large church clock)

la déception = *disappointment*
deception = **la duplicité**

demander = *to ask*
to demand = **exiger**

la figure = *the face*
the figure = **la taille**

large = *broad, wide*
large = **grand**

la librairie = *the bookshop*
the library = **la bibliothèque**

366

BUT WHICH NEED SPECIAL CARE IN TRANSLATION

la monnaie = *change*
money = **l'argent**

une occasion = *opportunity, bargain*
occasion = **la fois**

passer un examen = *to take an exam*
to pass an exam. = **réussir dans un examen**

la place = *the square* (**la place du marché**). **La place** also = *a seat* (in a train)
a place = **un endroit**

la peine = *effort, trouble, difficulty*
a pain = **une douleur**

prétendre = *to claim*
to pretend = **faire semblant de**

sage = *good, well-behaved*
sage = **prudent**

succéder = *to come after*
to succeed = **réussir**

sensible = *sensitive*
sensible = **raisonnable**

supporter = *to tolerate*
to support = **soutenir**

traîner = *to drag*
to train (animals) = **dresser**

rare = *scanty, few* (of hair = *thin*)
rare = **précieux, exquis, impayable**

unique = *only, single,* as well as *unique*

travailler = *to work*
to travel = **voyager**

labourer = *to plough*
to labour = **travailler**

troubler = *to disturb* (usually of water)
to trouble = **gêner, déranger**

MISCELLANEOUS SENTENCES

1. **Professeur d'histoire au Lycée de Rouen, il n'avait pas l'habitude, comme les autres, de fréquenter les cabarets le soir.**
   He was history-master at the Lycée of Rouen and was not in the habit, as were the others, of spending his evenings in low taverns.
2. **Il était sûr de n'avoir pas dormi, de s'être assoupi tout au plus.**
   He was sure he had not been sleeping, at the very most to have been dozing.
3. **Le domestique n'avait aucune envie de se déranger, et ne fit pas un seul effort pour aller ouvrir la porte.**
   The servant had no wish to be disturbed at all, and made no effort at all to go and open the door.
4. **Ils ouvrirent de grands yeux en voyant un jeune homme traverser la place pour sortir de la ville.**   [*leave the town.*
   They opened their eyes wide on seeing a young man crossing the square to
5. **Elle se tourna vers Henri et lui chatouilla la joue.**
   She turned to Henry and tickled his cheek.
6. **En entendant le coup de pistolet, Robert, qui tenait l'ouvrage de sa grand' mère à la main, poussa un cri et lâcha tout.**
   On hearing the pistol shot, Robert, who was holding his grandmother's work in his hand, shouted and let everything fall.
7. **Il était peu aimé de ses ouvriers.** *His workmen had little love for him.*
8. **Il vivait en reclus dans un chalet au bord du lac.**
   He lived as a recluse in a chalet at the edge of the lake.
9. **Il y avait deux autres personnes dans le compartiment, un homme et une femme, qui avaient lu pendant tout le voyage, en levant parfois la tête pour échanger quelques phrases.**
   There were two other people in the compartment, a man and a woman, who had been reading for the whole of the journey, sometimes looking up to exchange a few remarks.
10. **L'un d'eux courut d'abord à Daniel et, le trouvant essoufflé, mais sain et sauf, revint vers Denise, qui s'était assise, tremblante et muette, sur le bord de la route.**
    One of them ran first to Daniel and, finding him breathless but unharmed, came back towards Denise who had sat down, trembling and silent, at the side of the road.
11. **Ils se sont trompés de maison, tellement il faisait noir.**
    It was so dark they went to the wrong house.
12. **À quoi bon refuser? On a beau dire ils sont plus forts que nous.**
    What is the good of refusing? Whatever you say they are stronger than we are.
13. **La foire se tient tous les ans dans le quartier très ancien de la ville.**
    The fair takes place each year in the ancient part of the town.
14. **Pendant que nous étions assis là nous avons entendu aboyer un chien.**
    While we were sitting there we heard a dog barking.
15. **Il descendit du train et il était sur le point d'appeler un porteur quand il reconnut son cousin qui était venu à sa rencontre.**
    He got out of the train and was just about to call a porter when he recognised his cousin who had come to meet him.
16. **"Je suis content que vous soyez venu," dit-elle. "J'espère que nous deviendrons de bons amis."**
    "I am glad you have come," she said. "I hope we shall become good friends."

368

TRANSLATION OF THE TEXTS

LEÇON 1: A CONVERSATION IN THE KITCHEN

Here is a part of a house. It is the house of the Girard family. There are several rooms: a kitchen, a sitting-room, a dining-room. The kitchen is small: in the kitchen there are an electric stove, a sink, a small table, a refrigerator, a cupboard and a set of shelves. The dining-room is spacious: it has a large table and six chairs; on the floor there is a beautiful carpet; against the wall there is a sideboard. The sitting-room is very big: it has a fine fire-place, a settee, and two armchairs.

Mr. Girard has a wife and three children (a son and two daughters). The two girls are very pretty, but they are often naughty. Is the little boy always well-behaved?

Here is the Girard family in the kitchen one evening. Suzanne says: "You are naughty, Josette." Mother and father say: "Yes, Josette is naughty and Suzanne is also naughty; they are naughty even when there is a good programme on the television." Josette says: "I am naughty because the programme is awful. They are often awful. Mother and father, are you sure that Jacques is always good, even when you are busy in the garden?" Jacques says: "I am very good when mother and father are away." Mother and father say: "Yes, we are sure that he is good when we have a lot of work in the garden. Suzanne, do you also say that Jacques is good? Girls often have a lot of affection for a brother; are you an exception?" Suzanne and Josette say together: "We say that he is often naughty and we are often well-behaved. There!"

Poor girls: Suzanne is so pretty in a little red and blue dress; Josette is so smart in a little green two-piece — and Jacques is so good, in spite of a dirty face.

After the conversation the parents and the children are happy. Is the programme on the television interesting?

LEÇON 2: ON THE LANDING

Here is another part of the Girard family's house: it is the first floor. There are once again several rooms: three bedrooms, a bathroom, a lavatory and a boxroom. One goes up the stairs and one arrives on the landing where one sees six doors; one enters the first bedroom and one sees a large bed, a fine carpet, an oak wardrobe and a dressing-table. In the second room there are two small beds for the little girls, a small chest of drawers, a small wardrobe and a lot of toys. One does not go into Jacques' room because it is untidy: there are too many toys and comics. In the bathroom there is naturally a bath, and a wash-basin in which Mrs. Girard washes (ten times a day) the dirty face of . . . whom?

A little scene in Suzanne and Josette's bedroom:

Josette: "I cannot see the doll! Can you see the doll, Suzanne? It is Jacques who takes the toys and leaves everything under the comics."

Suzanne: "Yes, he is as naughty as a monkey. He has a lot of toys but he is not happy when he is not with us. He likes to play with the doll in spite of mother's threats. . . ." (Jacques is hidden behind the bathroom door. Mr. and Mrs. Girard go upstairs, see the two girls immediately and look for the little boy. They find poor Jacques, they scold the poor boy.)

Mr. Girard: "Suzanne and Josette, why are you shouting so loudly? Is Jacques being naughty? Jacques, why are you always playing with Suzanne and Josette's toys? I am angry and I spank little boys who are not well-behaved. Why do you not take a book? Mother and I take an interesting book when we do not have too much work; Josette and Suzanne also take a book. . . ." A large book is given to the boy, two attractive books to the girls; Mrs. Girard picks up a novel and poor father goes back into the garden where he is working.

LEÇON 3: IN THE GARDEN

Behind the Girard family's house there is a beautiful garden: in the garden Mr. Girard grows potatoes, cabbages, carrots, turnips and spinach. The children do not play near the vegetables, they play on the lawn close to the apple-tree, but far from the window of course. Around the garden there is a wooden fence: so the children do not go into the neighbours' gardens and the dogs of the neighbourhood do not come into the Girards' garden. Between the lawn and the vegetable garden there is a narrow path; at the end, a heap of grass and dead leaves.

One fine afternoon in summer, the children come out of the house and go into the garden to play with a ball on the lawn. Josette says: "Jacques come with me. Suzanne, go to the edge of the lawn. We are going to throw the ball to Suzanne," she says to Jacques. The little boy's younger sister is vexed; she pulls a long face because she has two opponents. However she goes to the bottom of the garden and says: "Jacques and Josette, throw the ball now, I am ready."

The little game continues for a few minutes without quarrels, but soon Suzanne is tired. "What time is it?" she asks. "It is half-past two," says Josette. "It is a quarter to three," says Jacques. Without doubt a quarrel is going to start — but Mrs. Girard comes into the garden; she says: "It is five minutes past three." "So late!" shouts Suzanne. "I usually do some sewing before tea." "That is not true," says Josette, "we do some sewing when the weather is bad. If you hate the game, Jacques and I will play together. Are you going to work in the house?" Suzanne says nothing, she goes with her mother into the sitting-room to look for some cotton.

At a quarter past three Josette and Jacques are also tired: the little girl's cheeks are red, the little boy's legs are dirty; and (here is the secret) the little dressmaker's frock is torn.

LEÇON 4: TEA IN THE SITTING-ROOM

The Girard family are in the sitting-room: it is half-past four and each member of the family is having his tea. They are not sitting at the table because tea is not an important meal; they eat a lot at lunchtime, around midday or half-past twelve, and also around seven o'clock — even the children are not often hungry four hours after their lunch. On the table there is a long loaf of bread, slices of bread, a jar of jam, some butter, two bars of chocolate, some apples, six cups on saucers, sugar and a teapot. There is nothing covering the teapot: the tea becomes cold very quickly, but that is of no importance when the weather is hot.

Mr. Girard takes off his shoes, puts on his slippers and asks: "Where is my coffee?" "There is no coffee," replies his wife, "we are going to have tea for a change." (She gives a cup of tea to her husband.) "Where is the milk?" he asks. "Oh, I am absent-minded today," says Mrs. Girard. "Jacques, go and fetch the milk out of the kitchen! . . ." A minute later Jacques arrives with a bottle of milk and explains that the cream-jug is broken. He gives the bottle to his father. Alas, Mr. Girard is also absent-minded, for he is reading the daily paper: he spills some milk on his trousers. In spite of his anger he says nothing; he puts the bottle on the table, takes a serviette and finishes the article that he is reading in his paper.

Mrs. Girard scolds her children because they are reading their comics insteady of eating: Jacques is sitting on the carpet and his cup is on the floor, Josette is sitting on a chair near the French-window. Suzanne is standing near the fire-place and a good way from the table because she does not like tea and does not pick up her cup. She says to her mother: "I prefer lemonade. Tea stains my frocks if I knock my cup over."

In spite of everything they finish their tea before five o'clock: the children take away their cups. "Wash your cups," shouts Mrs. Girard. "Your father is tired and as for me, I am reading my detective story."

LEÇON 5: AN EVENING WITH VISITORS

In the evening, after tea, the Girards usually stay at home; they keep on the clothes that they wear during the day. What clothes do they wear? Look at Mr. Girard: he wears a white shirt, a blue tie, a woollen sweater, trousers,

371

a pair of socks and black shoes or red slippers. His son does not yet wear long trousers, he prefers shorts. Mrs. Girard, like her daughters, wears a pretty green, white, or yellow frock and a pair of high-heeled shoes. They are well-dressed — but little Jacques' hair is untidy, whilst his sisters have a neat hair style. They already imitate models.

However, one evening the parents want to play bridge; they invite some neighbours, Mr. and Mrs. Larivière. The children have to go to bed at a quarter past seven in spite of their objections. ("Why must we go to bed now? Can we stay downstairs until eight o'clock? We are always good when there are visitors!") These objections end when their father says sternly: "Go to bed now. You know that you can read your books and comics."

At half-past seven, in the sitting-room: "Take this chair, sir," says Mr. Girard. "Mrs. Larivière can take this armchair, near the window. Now, dear," he says to his wife, "we must find the cards! Are they in the desk?" "Yes, I can find the packs of cards without difficulty," she says. Five minutes later she comes back and says: "We must count these cards, I do not want to play with fifty cards. One, two, three. . . ." "Can you count up to fifty?" he asks in a mocking voice. "You must not talk when I am counting. Oh bother! This card is dirty. Darling, fetch the pack of cards that we leave upstairs; they are clean." He goes upstairs, and his wife starts a conversation: "Do you know Mrs. Lucas? Well, she knows. . . ."

LEÇON 6: A GAME OF CARDS

In a pack of cards there are fifty-two different cards. Twenty-six of these cards are red, the others are black — but there are four colours (suits) in all! Can you find the solution to this puzzle? Well, there are thirteen hearts, thirteen diamonds, thirteen clubs and thirteen spades. The clubs are black, the spades are also black, but they are different suits! In each suit there are nine ordinary cards, that is to say two to ten; after the ten we find the jack, queen, king and ace, that is to say the picture-cards, because three of these cards show the face of a young man, a queen and a king.

It is the twenty-fifth of April . . . it is eight o'clock in the evening. What is Mr. Girard doing? He is looking for the pack of cards; after five minutes he finds it, he takes it into the sitting-room and puts it on the card-table. "We can now begin to play. Cut the cards!" His neighbour, Mr. Larivière, cuts an ace. . . . "Here are the green cards," he says to Mrs. Larivière. "Shuffle them, please." She shuffles them well. Mrs. Girard cuts them once again, and Mr. Larivière deals them. They play patiently for a quarter of an hour, attentively, without chatting. (It must be admitted, they do not often play like that!) There are only brief comments, questions, bids and of course sighs. "We lose the first game," says Mr. Girard. "I always lose on Fridays!" "Why do you lose especially on Fridays?" asks his wife, who laughs gleefully when he betrays his little weakness (he is superstitious). "Yes, you lose," says Mr. Larivière, "I am writing the number of points on my sheet of paper. You write it too," he adds, when he sees that his wife is not writing anything. The two women laugh, they do not write anything, they forget the game for a few moments. Finally Mrs. Girard innocently asks, "Why do men always look for an excuse when they lose?"

LEÇON 7: AT THE CINEMA

Mr. and Mrs. Girard are quite content to stay at home in the evening because the weather is bad. It is winter: it is not snowing, but it is very cold, it is windy. The clouds are so black that it is doubtless going to rain before dawn. In winter the Girards do not often go out after tea; they entertain friends two or three times a week. Mrs. Girard entertains so many friends instead of going out herself because she often suffers from chest-colds. The doctor says that she must never go out after night-fall when the weather is not fine and warm. In summer and in spring she suffers less when the atmosphere is not so damp. Mrs. Girard does not fear mild evenings and in summer she often goes for a walk after dinner; she is not lying when she says that she prefers the country to the theatre or cinema.

Generally she goes out alone through the garden gate, crosses the meadows and follows a little path that leads to the river. She usually returns home before ten o'clock; she does not want to stay out when it is dark because she is afraid of the dark. Besides she is often hungry and thirsty after a pleasant walk, so she eats some biscuits and drinks some chocolate before going to bed. If he is not too busy Mr. Girard serves this little supper while his wife goes to look at the children sleeping.

However, one week in the month of February there is a detective film at the local cinema. Mrs. Girard wants to see it, but her husband who likes comfort by the fireside objects: "I am afraid of the influenza germs that one can catch in cinemas at this time of the year. And as for yourself, my dear, are you not afraid of the cold when you go out?" Mrs. Girard replies: "I never go out in winter, I stay at home all day. Anyway you can take us by car and so we need not be afraid of bad weather." Mrs. Girard wins.

At the entrance to the cinema Mr. Girard buys the tickets at the box-office, two seats in the balcony. The usherette takes them to their seats, with the help of her torch. Mr. Girard gives this young woman a fifty centimes tip, for in French cinemas usherettes do not receive any wages. If one forgets to give a tip, the usherette asks for it, often in an aggressive voice! It is twenty to nine, but on the screen there are only advertisements, for in France the cinemas start their last showing quite late, around say a quarter to nine.

Here at last is a documentary about cathedrals in France. Mr. Girard is studying architecture and he very much enjoys this film which puts him in a good mood. During the interval they go to the foyer where Mr. Girard buys his wife a glass of her favourite liqueur. The interval lasts twenty minutes, so he has time to smoke a cigarette. People cannot smoke during the show for on the walls of the cinema one can see the words "No Smoking."

After the interval Mr. and Mrs. Girard return to their seats. The main film begins at half-past nine and holds everybody's attention. There are a thousand dramatic incidents, several murders, thefts, pursuits, a brawl, and a scene where the hero saves the beautiful lady (the victim!) at the last minute.

At the end of the show the satisfied audience make their way quickly towards the exit in order to leave the cinema immediately — they do not have to sing their national anthem! Mr. Girard puts on his coat again and his wife carefully adjusts her fur coat, for it is very cold outside.

It is now nearly midnight and frost covers the roadway and the pavements. When they are nicely settled in the car (a lovely blue Citroën), Mrs. Girard says: "Drive slowly, dear. I am afraid of the slippery roads." He drives carefully of course and a few minutes later they arrive home safe and sound. But what is this mystery? . . . The front door is open, the house is all lit up!

LEÇON 8: AT THE MARKET

Two or three times a week, instead of going to the shops to do their shopping, people go to the market. The market is in the open air or in covered halls. A lot of tradesmen have stalls at the market and farmers and country-people come from the neighbouring villages too to bring their vegetables, fruit, eggs, etcetera. When the weather is fine, there are a lot of people at the market and the tradesmen sell their goods quickly, but when it is raining they often have to lower their prices to attract buyers.

Mrs. Girard does not often go the market with her children because, when she is not looking, they run all over the place or absent-mindedly follow people doing their shopping. If she scolds Jacques, he replies: "I am following you, mother, but I want to look at all the interesting things on the stalls. In any case I run quickly if I lose you, because I do not like being all alone in the middle of this crowd of people."

Last Sunday it was market-day in the town. Mrs. Girard went to church alone early and then, like a lot of other housewives, she went to the market which is always to be found in the square in front of the church. That morning, she bought some spinach, some pears and a melon for the midday meal. "How much is the spinach?" she asked. "One franc fifty centimes a kilogramme, madam." And the old peasant woman weighed a kilogramme of spinach on her scales. Mrs. Girard put it into her basket. Then she saw some beautiful melons.

"How much is this melon, sir?" "Two francs, lady," replied the tradesman.

"Oh! but it is still green, that is too dear," suggested Mrs. Girard. "It is a melon from the Charente, guaranteed," replied the tradesman, who wanted at all costs to defend his goods. "No, thank you, I do not like green melons," was Mrs. Girard's reply. She went all over the market and finally found a fine golden melon . . . not so dear as the green melon and just as big!

Then Mrs. Girard saw several fishmongers who called out to her; in spite of the reasonable prices she did not buy anything, because her family does not often eat fish, especially on Sundays — the children prefer beef or chicken. . . . Fortunately for her, her conversation with the fishmongers did not take long: suddenly, in one corner of the market a man beat a drum and the crowd filled with curiosity surrounded his stall.

"Ladies and gentlemen," he said, "I offer you a sensational product, at a sensational price. Come forward, come closer! A few drops of this liquid in your washing-up water and all your plates, all your cutlery, all your glasses are clean in the twinkling of an eye. And you, sir, you can wash your car in five minutes with this marvellous liquid. As a special offer, I give you not one bottle, but two bottles for the price of one! I do not ask for three francs, no, two francs sixty-five centimes."

Mrs. Girard, who is thrifty, listened to this sales talk with interest, but she smiled. She is not easy to take in and she left this stall also without buying anything. To finish her shopping she finally bought half a dozen eggs and also a bunch of carnations (which will adorn the sideboard in the dining-room).

She left the market at about a quarter past twelve to return home. In the main street which she had to follow, she noticed that the café terraces were already full of people, for it is Sunday and people are not working, except for the poor tradesmen. Finally, Mrs. Girard reached the avenue where she lives and from a distance she saw her children at the windows of their rooms. She is always rather anxious when she goes out without the children, because one knows that they take advantage of their freedom! You must not forget the evening that Mr. and Mrs. Girard spent at the cinema . . . but, dear reader, what was it that the children did that evening? It is a secret which I am going to keep — you yourself must find the solution to this problem. . . .

LEÇON 9: A SAD JOURNEY

Two weeks ago an old aunt of Mrs. Girard's (her father's eldest sister) died. That morning, at half-past ten, the telegraph boy rang at the door; he gave a blue slip of paper to Mrs. Girard. She was afraid, because this blue slip of paper is a telegram and people are almost always afraid when they receive a piece of news in this way. The postman delivers letters and parcels every morning, but telegrams have to be delivered more quickly. A special messenger brings them at any hour of the day.

When Mrs. Girard read the sad news written on the blue paper, she decided to go to her uncle's for the funeral. Unfortunately her husband cannot take her by car, for he needs the car to go to work. What is she going to do? She must make the journey by train.

She went immediately to the station to look at the train time-table. The departure and arrival times are written up on large notices inside the station. People can also ask for them at the enquiry office. Mrs. Girard finally found a suitable train, then went back home in order to pack her small case. . . . She was not able to take the children whom one of her friends looked after for the three days of her absence.

The moment of departure arrived. Mrs. Girard put on a grey coat and a black hat as a sign of mourning. The taxi arrived, she got into it and soon she got out in front of the station. She bought a return ticket at the ticket-office. She had to wait because the train arrived late. In order to while away the time she bought a magazine at the bookstall and went into the waiting room. All round this room there are benches and on the walls pictures of the picturesque corners of France which one can go to by train.

At last at half-past twelve the station loudspeaker announced Mrs. Girard's train. She went quickly out on to the platform and showed her ticket to the ticket-collector who punched it. At first she could not find her train. The loudspeaker repeated: "Attention, attention! Passengers for X . . . Y . . . Z, all aboard, please, on platform three." In order to reach this platform you must take the subway, because you must never cross the track; even if you look at all the tracks before crossing, the express trains pass through so quickly that you are never out of danger.

In order to be sure of catching the train, Mrs. Girard gave a tip to a porter who carried her case and took her straight to a second class compartment. She climbed in immediately (. . . it is necessary to say "climbed in" for the platform is low and you must climb up three steps in order to reach the level of the compartments). The porter closed the carriage-door and at twenty-seven minutes to one the stationmaster blew his whistle. The powerful engine slowly began to pull the four coaches; the train passed a diesel train and a goods train, crossed a level-crossing, and within a minute left the station. Two kilometres further on it entered a tunnel.

Poor Mrs. Girard does not like tunnels because it is dark and the smoke from the engine gets in through the windows. Of course she prefers to admire the countryside where she has never lived (. . . she was born in an industrial town in the centre of France); she likes to look at the cows in the meadows, the river that they cross on a viaduct, and the dark woods on the horizon.

After two and a half hours her train arrived at its destination: there were a lot of stops because a local train must serve all the small towns and villages in the region. Tired and sad, Mrs. Girard left the station to look for a motor-coach.

LEÇON 10: MRS. GIRARD'S NAME-DAY

In France you wish many happy returns on birthdays, but you do this especially on name-days. What is a name-day? Well, almost every Christian name is also the name of a saint (or of a female saint). You must celebrate a name-day on the day when you find the name of this saint on the calendar, because, each day of the year, the church celebrates a saint (who is called "the saint of the day"). Thus St. Michael's day is the twenty-ninth of September: on that day all boys who are called Michael receive best wishes and presents from their parents and friends. In a florist's window there is often a little card which says which name-day one must celebrate.

Mrs. Girard is called Anne-Marie: her name-day is celebrated on the twenty-sixth of July. On the morning of that day the children got up early and went secretly to pick a bunch of flowers in the garden. Jacques even trampled on the flower-beds, but since it is mother's name-day his father did not scold him!

Josette tied a pretty ribbon around the bunch, and then the three children went into the dining-room and called out. "Mother, I wish you many happy returns!" Mrs. Girard pretended to be surprised and kissed the children. Then Mr. Girard came in and said to his wife: "Many happy returns, dear." He have her a small parcel which she opened right away. "Oh, but you are too kind, René! What lovely gloves! What a pretty colour! They go well with my blue coat."

But Mr. Girard (what an exemplary husband!) has another surprise for his wife. "You do the cooking every day," he said, "but this evening we are going to dine at the Trout Restaurant."

They arrived there at about eight o'clock. Since it is warm at this time in the month of July, they were able to stay outside in the beautiful garden, seated near the river. Mrs. Girard was delighted to see two swans on the water . . . she likes to watch these graceful birds which never seem to get themselves dirty. "It is nice and cool here," she said, "whereas in town it is nearly always too hot."

After a few moments a waiter came to give them a menu and to lay two places on the white cloth. "You choose, dear," said Mr. Girard. "I do not want any soup," she said. "Let us have a tomato salad to begin with, and then blue trout, since it is the speciality of this restaurant. As the main dish, let us have pigeon with green peas. And my favourite dessert, rum-baba. You do agree, dear, don't you?" asked Mrs. Girard, in a persuasive voice.

Her husband agreed (he always approves of his wive's choice — on the twenty-sixth of July at least!), but he reserved for himself the choice of wines and asked for the list. The wine-waiter brought it himself. After careful deliberation Mr. Girard finally ordered a carafe of rosé wine which the waiter served on a handsome silver tray.

That evening, there were a lot of people at the restaurant, for many towns-people agree with Mrs. Girard's opinion: namely, that it is too hot and too sultry in town, and after a day spent in an office or a shop they go to the Trout to be in the open air for a while, by the water. Not all of them ordered a meal for it is quite expensive and it is not everybody's name-day! They merely had a glass of beer or of really cold lemonade.

Mr. and Mrs. Girard ate their celebration dinner unhurriedly; after the dessert they drank a cup of black coffee, then Mr. Girard asked for the bill. The waiter was not able to bring it right away, but when he arrived at their table five minutes later he apologized so politely that Mr. Girard gave him a generous tip nevertheless. Then his wife and he went for a walk along the little road which runs along by the river and admired the setting sun reflected in the water. The profound peace of evening descended upon all nature and soon they had to return home.

LEÇON 11: THE PRIZE-GIVING

One evening, at the beginning of summer, Mr. Girard and his wife held the following conversation. "The summer holidays will soon be here, dear! Have you thought about them? What shall we do this year?" "Yes, I have thought about them," replied Mrs. Girard, "perhaps we shall go to a small Normandy seaside resort, like last year." "But the hotels put up their prices in spring, you know. And during the winter we incurred a great deal of expense: we bought a new carpet for the sitting-room and a refrigerator. When we buy such things, we cannot save much money. I hope at least that we shall have enough saved for a simple holiday, because I always try to economize as much as possible. We shall not be able to stay at a hotel for more than about ten days." "Oh! No indeed then! I like long holidays. And it is also better for the children. . . . I have an idea. I shall write to Uncle Julian to ask if he will be able to entertain us in his chalet. What do you think about that? His children are married and now he has a lot of room." "Indeed yes, that should be possible, if your uncle agrees. We shall perhaps be able to spend a month there. The children will breathe the pure mountain air and they will have a good time, just as good as they would at the seaside, I am sure. Besides, Uncle Julian is getting old and I shall help him with his work. That will be a change for me from the office," said Mr. Girard.

The day after this conversation, Mrs. Girard wrote to her uncle who owns a cheesemonger's chalet in the Jura mountains. The Jura is a chain of mountains, in the east, between France and Switzerland. It is a very picturesque region of pastures, rocks and coniferous woods. Before the end of the week an affirmative answer arrived. Uncle Julian wrote that he would be very pleased to see his nephews and nieces again. His wife, Aunt Louise, would prepare their rooms for the end of July. Mr. Girard has only a month's holiday. The children, like all schoolchildren, have two and a half months' holiday in the summer. (It is very long, at times, Mrs. Girard says to herself!) But now everything is settled, they will spend the month of August together in the mountains.

However, before the long holidays there was an important event for the two girls. At the end of the third term of the school year, there was the prize-giving at the school which Suzanne and Josette attend. On that day, all the girls came to school dressed in their best dresses. At eleven o'clock exactly they assembled, supervised by the mistresses, and sat down on the benches in the big court-yard. At the end of the yard, on a platform covered with a red carpet, they recognized the mayor and the headmistress. And what is there on the long wooden table on the front of the stage? Obviously, a lot of books — they are the prize books.

In the meantime the parents and brothers of the pupils arrived and sat down on chairs behind the girls. So everything is ready and the annual ceremony is about to begin. After a song sung by the members of the choir, the headmistress began to read out the long list of pupils who won prizes for their hard work and good conduct. Each girl got up from her bench and went to receive a handsome bound book from the mayor. Suzanne had the first prize for arithmetic and the second form-prize. Josette had only the second prize for singing and a certificate of merit for drawing, but she was nevertheless very pleased and smiled to her parents from a distance.

Before the end of the ceremony the mayor made a short speech to congratulate all the pupils on their success in the course of the past year and to encourage them to keep up their efforts. Then the choir sang a second time and the headmistress thanked the mayor and parents. She added: "I hope that you will enjoy your holidays. Next term will begin on the fifteenth of September and you will all return rested and ready to resume work."

Like all their friends, Suzanne and Josette left the school at half-past twelve with their parents. They always prefer to forget the headmistress's last words. Three cheers for the holidays!

LEÇON 12: ON HOLIDAY

The Girard family arrived at Uncle Julian's chalet on the second of August, at about half-past three in the afternoon. They settled down there very quickly. In the mountains, at Aunt Louise's, the children are never homesick, because she spoils them. Provided that they keep quiet during meals and at night Aunt Louise almost never scolds them. She believes that children need to exercise their lungs and their limbs! She delights in seeing them play; she is a good, tender-hearted woman — she and her husband believe that children are worth their weight in gold!

Saturday, the ninth of August: the Girards have already spent a week at their uncle's house. Mr. Girard especially loves to go on excursions in the surrounding country and the children have been several times with him to explore the picturesque spots of the region. So, last Tuesday, he took them into the woods to look for mushrooms of all kinds and colours, for in France there are many varieties of edible mushrooms. People are not afraid to pick them in large quantities because they easily recognize the poisonous kinds. They did not find many that day — but, after an hour's searching Jacques suddenly bent down and picked up something. Suzanne, a few steps behind him, cried: "What have you found?" "Come and see, sister!" the rascal replied. "It is not a mushroom, I am sure." Mr. Girard turned round, laughed and said: "That is a frog, you know very well, Jacques." Poor Josette came up to them too and looked at it closely. "Oh, I am afraid of it," she said. "Throw it away quickly, Jacques." But he teasingly pretended to throw the frog at his sister who ran away as fast as her legs could carry her. "Behave, you scamp," shouted Mr. Girard, "if you throw it at her, you will regret your prank." Jacques let go of his "missile" and shouted: "Come back, Josette, don't be afraid! Let us play wolf, since it is not worth the trouble of looking for mushrooms today. You will be the wolf, father. Let's start singing: 'Let us go for a walk through the wood while the wolf is not there. Wolf, are you there? What are you doing? Can you hear?' " "I am putting on my shirt," replied the "wolf" and the children continued to sing, at a little distance from him, until the "wolf" said: "I am putting on my hat and am coming to eat you." Then the children ran away behind the trees and bushes, but Mr. Girard finally caught them. "Next time it is I who shall be the wolf," said Jacques. "It will not be you," insisted Josette. "Be quiet," interrupted their father, "you will be it in turns; but do be patient."

At four o'clock they returned to the chalet with very few mushrooms but with a hearty appetite. On the way they came to the top of a meadow. Suzanne ran in front and suddenly she exclaimed: "What is that, father, that wooden scaffolding that I can see down there?" "Well, the meadow slopes down and the scaffolding you can see is a ski-jump. This winter, when there is a lot of snow, the village people will go skiing, and perhaps tourists will come too for the winter sports. Your uncle told me there are a few good ski-runs in the vicinity. Agile skiers go to the top of the slope, come down it at top speed, and when they get to the bottom they jump from the spring-board." "Father," said Suzanne, "let us come back too this winter to do some skiing " "Perhaps, in a year or two," Mr. Girard promised. "For the moment let's return quickly to the chalet. It is nearly five o'clock. The country-people and the farmers will soon be bringing their milk to Uncle Julian's and we shall miss tea. Hurry up, children."

Fortunately they arrived in time for the good tea of bread, butter and honey that Aunt Louise and Mrs. Girard had prepared for them. As usual the daily question is asked: "What are we going to do tomorrow, mother?" "Do not be so impatient, children. You are going to spend a whole month in the mountains, do not tire yourselves out the very first week! Go to bed early, because father and I want to go down to the village. Uncle Julian has told me that there are some friends who have invited us to spend an evening at their house. Jacques, do not eat too quickly! Pick up all the crumbs!"

LEÇON 13: SCHOOL

I am no longer young, alas! but I very well remember my schooldays. How sad was the life of a schoolboy! At least, that is what I thought at the time; and today, after so many years, I do not dare to say whether the impressions which I retain of my childhood are accurate or not. In any case, I very well remember that every day, except Sunday, you had to get up early, dress, wash as quickly as possible, swallow a cup of coffee and leave the house in great haste in order not to be late for school.

Arriving at the lycée you entered the playground, greeted your friends, chatted with them but, at a certain moment the bell rang and all the pupils filed into class.

That is when the trouble started. You had to pay attention all the time even if the lesson was not very interesting. But I have a feeling that during the history lesson, for example, while the master was droning on about the glorious exploits of the Emperor Napoleon, there were some pupils who were thinking of what they were going to do in the holiday. Maybe I am wrong.

What a number of subjects to study! In the syllabus there were mathematics, Greek, Latin, English, German, etc. I have neither the time nor the intention of giving a full list of them. It is obvious that you have to possess a good memory to learn so many things and get "excellent" in your reports. At the risk of appearing somewhat immodest I can say that I always had a good mark in English. But I didn't like mathematics; I always found it so difficult. In the evenings my father used to help me to do my homework and I would listen to him without understanding anything. One day the teacher said to me jokingly, "Your father is beginning to make some progress."

From morning to night we worked like slaves. We did sums and problems. We studied modern languages — but, when I was young, the teachers had no gramophones. Sometimes we used to take down notes in our exercise-books or else we took dictation from the master. Very often we read aloud from a text-book. I must confess that, for my part, I found English pronunciation very difficult. I sincerely hope that it isn't English that they speak in Heaven! After working hard all day, we had to do homework in the evening. What a wretched life!

What shall I say about the teachers? They were almost always in a bad mood. They used to ask so many difficult questions. From time to time they uttered insults which we endured in silence. One of our masters, in particular, was a real terror. He used to stride up and down with a big book in his hand. When a pupil said something silly or did not answer a question quickly enough, this master used to get angry and wave his book about like a sword. We trembled with fright for we thought that he was going to strike our unfortunate comrade.

As for the headmaster, let's not speak of him — he was a regular tyrant. But, fortunately, we saw him only very rarely when he wandered in the corridors in search of a victim. We were sure that he was generally too busy in his office to worry about us.

In our class (I was then fourteen and was in the third form) there was a badly-behaved pupil named François. Very often he was late for school and the master gave him a dressing-down. François offered wretched excuses and the master was not very pleased. Instead of applying himself to his studies this same François wasted his time and annoyed the master. On occasion he took advantage of the moment when the master was writing on the blackboard to kick his neighbour, Victor.

The latter was a well-behaved pupil who never did anybody any harm but he did not put up meekly with François' attacks. Often he tried to defend himself. Unfortunately, at that moment the master would turn round and see Victor, with raised fist, in the act of striking the mighty François. The master would flare up with anger. "What are you doing there?" he would shout, "I am going to give you a punishment. Write out two hundred times the sentence: 'I must keep still in class.' You will give me your lines tomorrow morning without fail. Otherwise. . . ." He never used to finish the sentence. Unhappy Victor! It is not always the guilty who suffer.

LEÇON 14: DEPARTMENT STORES

In almost every town there is a department store. If the town is large enough there are even several of them. These stores are huge establishments where you can buy all sorts of goods. People who are rich and those who prefer exclusive articles of the highest quality do not, as a rule, make their purchases in the large stores. In the department stores everything is arranged for the convenience and comfort of the customers. You generally find in them a restaurant, a hairdressing saloon and fitting rooms. You can even watch a mannequin parade if you are interested.

Today we are going to have a little walk around town. We shall look round such a shop and perhaps we shall buy something in it. Let us catch the bus at the corner of the street over there. . . . Not that one — it is packed — the next one . . . there we are!

Half an hour later we are on the pavement in front of the windows of a large store — a vast building situated in one of the main streets of the town. We remain a few moments admiring the latest-style frocks displayed in the window or, if we do not care much for frocks, perhaps it is the fishing or sports equipment which attract our attention. But everything is quite dear and today of all days we cannot afford to buy those things. We make our way towards the entrance but first of all we must pass a man standing on a chair or a packing-case. He is waving his arms about and appears to be making a speech. Let us stop for a moment to listen to him. . . . Outside the large stores you often see counters set up on the pavement behind which salesmen reel off the virtues of the miraculous products which they are offering to the public. If you have the necessary time you can obtain a little inexpensive amusement by watching the wonderful demonstrations carried out by these enthusiastic salesmen. Naturally, you do not have to believe everything they say. . . .

Here we are at last in the shop. Good heavens, what a crowd on the ground floor! What heat! People jostle and elbow one another. On all sides innumerable counters are to be seen where goods of every sort are displayed. For example, in the stationery department writing paper, pencils of every colour and ball-point pens are on sale whilst in the toilet goods department there is scented soap, toothpaste, boxes of face powder, brushes, etc. But let us take the lift up to the first floor. There we find the furniture department and that of radio and television. We walk round a little and our curiosity is soon satisfied. We need a new television set but, as I have already said, we are short of money. I rather think that we are not genuine customers. Never mind! To go up to the second floor let us take the escalator. This is the book department — novels, dictionaries, maps. Wait a moment. I am going to buy that pamphlet, the one you see right at the back.

Right at the top of the building are the restaurant and the accounts department where the typists and accountants work. As for the manager, he is rarely to be seen; he is too important to waste his time chatting with the customers.

As we go down the stairs we read on a notice: "Goods delivered." In the town and suburbs deliveries are made every day, even twice a day, but in the neighbouring villages goods are delivered only once or twice a week.

There are certainly many people in this shop today but, compared with sale-time, it is nothing at all. Right from the early hours of the morning the women queue up at the door of the shop. When it opens, they rush headlong like an army of Amazons to fight for the best bargains. Unfortunate the man who is incautious enough to be in their path!

In certain shops discordant music is broadcast by loudspeakers placed at strategic points in the store. From time to time the music gives way to a voice making advertising announcements. Fortunately, that is not the case in this shop. . . . But look at the time. It is getting late. Let us get out of here past the information desk. Indeed, it has not been a very expensive day for us and just now we sampled some wine — for nothing!

LEÇON 15: MY NEIGHBOUR

The name of my neighbour is Mr. Durand. He is a very talkative man and unfortunately from time to time he happens to catch sight of me when I am quietly working in my garden. I assure you that I do everything in my power to avoid him but my neighbour brings all my efforts to nought.

"Hello," he says to me, "how are you?" As a rule I have no inclination at all to speak to him and I should prefer to finish my work. But one must be polite, of course — and, after all, he is my neighbour. . . . Without giving me time to reply to his greeting, this confounded chatterbox asks me: "Have you read today's paper?" I know very well that he does not expect an answer from me and I hold my tongue. "Didn't you see that. . . ."

He is in his stride now and he begins to relate everything that there is in the paper. But that is not all; he adds comments of his own. He reviews all the members of the present government. Then he tells me quite seriously that if he, Durand, were prime minister he would arrange things very differently. "If I were prime minister . . ." that is what he always says. Just imagine, Durand prime minister! That would be funny. I can not imagine why he likes to make such absurd suppositions. A trader in a small way, about fifty years old, he is narrow-minded. He knows quite a lot as far as foodstuffs are concerned, I agree; but when it comes to politics he is very ignorant.

But I beg your pardon, dear reader; I have just digressed and interrupted Mr. Durand's fine speech. "It's nothing but a scandal," he says, speaking about something or other. "If I were prime minister, I should soon put a stop to such abuses. I should dismiss on the spot all those corrupt officials who think only of getting rich. I should not allow them to fool the good citizens who have to work from morning to night. I should throw them all into prison. Besides, did you read how much that is going to cost?" Frankly, no. I haven't the least idea because I don't even know what it is all about. I was getting bored and was almost dropping off to sleep.

"It's going to cost a lot of money," he continues, evidently without noticing my drowsiness. "And who is going to find such a sum? We taxpayers — poor fools that we are. Ten years ago I wanted to go off to America. But it's the wife. You know what women are! She wouldn't go. If we had emigrated then we should be rich today and perhaps in a country where merit triumphs over all obstacles I should be at least a senator by now. Whereas in this country taxes go up almost daily. It's the government which is wildly squandering our money. If I were a minister I should put an end to it. In the old days things were better: one was well-off. But nowadays. . . . I don't know what is going to become of us. And our foreign policy, it's disgraceful. I have just read in the paper that war is going to break out any day. If our politicians were more intelligent and more prudent we should not be in such a sorry plight at present." My neighbour never tires of talking about the disasters which threaten us. "The future is gloomy," he continues, "but *I* always say that one must look on the bright side of things. There are some people who take a gloomy view of everything. You know some of them, doubtless. And the young people. What would our grandfathers say if they were alive today? They would think that the world has gone mad. . . . All these young men who smoke, dance, drink too much wine and who don't like working. You would think as well that they never wash — and hair down to here! It's abominable. I've hardly the heart to go on living. Besides, I hear that next week. . . ."

Whilst he is speaking I remain standing, leaning on my spade, near the fence. From time to time I say "yes" or "no" according to circumstances. I only hope that I don't say "yes" when I ought to say "no." It is so easy to make a mistake.

Suddenly a shrill cry is heard. "Louis, where are you? What are you doing? Come here." "Excuse me, sir, I must leave you," says my neighbour in a tone which seems to me rather forlorn. "It's my wife calling me. I must go in right away. Goodbye. . . ." And he slowly makes his way towards the house. Indeed, my neighbour gets on my nerves sometimes when he prevents me from working but I have some acquaintance with his wife and . . . I am sorry for my unhappy neighbour.

LEÇON 16: FRANCE

France extends from Belgium in the north as far as Spain in the south — about 900 kilometres. In the east she borders on Germany, Switzerland and Italy. As on the west she faces England and, across the Atlantic, America, France is very favourably placed from a commercial point of view. If a railway map is consulted it will be seen that all the western ports are directly linked with Paris, from which railways run to all the capitals of Europe. Besides, of all the countries on the Continent only France and Spain border on both the Atlantic Ocean and the Mediterranean. It can be said, therefore, that France is both a northern country and a Mediterranean country. As might be expected, she offers a great variety of climate and scenery. The climate of Normandy, for example, is hardly different from that of the south of England whilst Provence (in the south-east of France) enjoys a Mediterranean climate. Everybody has heard of Cannes, Nice and other bathing resorts where wealthy foreigners relax in the sun.

From the military point of view, the frontiers of France are protected in the south and in the east by the Pyrenees, the Alps, the Vosges and the Ardennes. But in the atomic age one wonders whether mountains are still valuable as a defence. It was right in the north, across the plains of the Low Countries, that invaders entered France in times past. Frenchmen will not forget the invasions of 1870, 1914 and 1940.

France has forty-five million inhabitants; Great Britain has fifty million. In comparison with the United States, Russia and China, England and France are small countries. The area of France is 551,000 sq. km.; that of the United Kingdom 245,000 sq. km.

Fifty-six per cent of the French population lives in towns. For Great Britain the propoition is 80 per cent. It can be said, then, that a large part (almost half) of the French population is rural whilst in England the opposite is the case. In France there are not many large cities: there are only eight which have more than 200,000 inhabitants. After Paris which, with its suburbs, has almost five million inhabitants the most important cities are Marseilles, Lyons, Bordeaux, Lille, Saint-Étienne, Nantes, Nice, Toulouse, Strasbourg and Le Havre. Because of this economic balance between industry and agriculture France is not obliged to import large quantities of agricultural products to feed herself.

From the industrial point of view France is not self-sufficient. She produces only three-quarters of the coal necessary for her industry and consequently has to import some fifteen million tons of coal a year. Nevertheless, it must be noted that hydro-electric power (sometimes called "white coal" which France has in abundance) makes up to a certain extent for the lack of coal. The majority of the steelworks as well as the chief cotton and wool mills are in the north but Lyons is the most important centre for silk. The motor industry must also be mentioned, the centre of which is Paris. The Citroën, Renault, Peugeot, etc. makes are known throughout the world.

As for agriculture, it can be said that France grows enough wheat, potatoes and sugar-beet to supply her needs. Cattle-raising is important in Normandy and other regions of France. Everybody is acquainted with the famous French cheeses such as Camembert, Brie and Roquefort. Tobacco is also grown and the French, it appears, prefer the home-grown product to tobacco imported from the United States. Every man to his taste.

Where wine is concerned France has no rival. Everyone knows the wines of Champagne, Bordeaux and Burgundy, prized by epicures throughout the world. But one is allowed to think that Englishmen would prefer their beer even if wine were sold at a very low price.

To end this economic sketch we shall point out that the tourist trade represents a large income for France. The balmy climate, the great variety of the scenery and French cooking certainly have something to do with it.

386

LEÇON 17: A RUN IN THE CAR

One day my friend, Mr. Leblanc, asked me if I would like to go with him for a short run in the car. As the weather was fine I accepted his offer with pleasure. Mr. Leblanc has a fine car. We left his house about ten o'clock in the morning and went straight to a filling-station where we filled up with petrol. After cleaning the windscreen we started off.

We had soon left the town and were running on the main road at a great speed. My friend was talking all the time and seemed to be paying no attention to the road. I was already beginning to repent of having accepted his invitation. We were going along in the middle of the road which was several metres wide and from time to time Mr. Leblanc would turn his head to draw my attention to something on the right or the left. "Do you see that hill over there? It is two hundred metres high," or "That lake at the side of the wood is fifty metres deep. That barn was struck by lightning six months ago" . . . and so on. It was doubtless because of this that the drivers coming in the opposite direction kept on hooting furiously. But Mr. Leblanc did not worry about that. Indeed he was saying: "Those people are making a lot of noise and are going far too fast. That's not the way to drive."

From time to time we flashed past traffic signs — "Caution," "Work in progress," "Level-crossing" — but we did not slow up. I can understand now the feelings of the pilot who, as a result of engine trouble, prepares to leave his doomed aircraft.

I had told my wife, before setting out, that I should be returning in the evening about six o'clock. I did not foresee at the time the dangers which I was going to face in the course of the day. "We have plenty of time," I say at last to my friend who seems determined to kill me. "It's the first time that I have come this way and I should like to have a chance to look around." "We must push on." he replies. "I should like to get to Moulins before twelve. Besides, the scenery around here is not very good. It's not worth wasting time." I glanced furtively at the speedometer. We were doing a hundred kilometres per hour. Good Heavens!

I had just remembered that Mr. Leblanc had obtained his driving licence only six months previously. The situation was becoming critical. Besides, the sky was now overcast and a fine drizzle was beginning to fall. If our car skidded we were in danger of crashing into a tree or a telegraph pole. Instead of being home at 6 p.m. I should be in hospital — if I were lucky. I decided to teach my friend a lesson and to do something right away.

Five minutes elapse. Suddenly I ask with an air of innocence: "Can you smell anything? It seems to me there's something wrong." My companion sniffs. "Indeed," he answers, "there's a smell of burning. I'll stop right away." "Not here," I say to him, "a little further on." We were entering a small town and the roadway was not very wide. After turning into a narrow street marked "One-way traffic" we stop right in front of a "No parking" sign. My friend immediately gets out of the car and begins to inspect tyres, wheels, headlamps. He carefully examines the engine. I was calm: I knew very well what the matter was. Unknown to him, I had pulled on the handbrake. Don't ask me now how I did it. I am not going to tell you. Mr. Leblanc was unable to discover the cause of the smoke which we had seen before stopping. At last, I too had got out of the car and was helping my friend in his task. "Come," I say to him in the end, "let's go on. Drive carefully. Don't go too fast and everything will be all right."

No sooner said than done. We started off again — rather abruptly perhaps and suddenly — crash! Another car which was about to overtake us had collided violently with us. "Blithering idiot!" cries the other driver quickly getting out of his car. "Are you blind? . . ." That man seemed to me to be angry with us and as I am a peaceloving individual I left my friend arguing with the stranger. I came back by train — safe and sound. I am no hero: I just want to die in my bed.

LEÇON 18: THE FARM

Last year I went and spent a few weeks with a farmer who is a friend of my father's. His farm which is a few kilometres from our town is not very large. It consists of a house in which the farmer lives with his family, of a stable, a cowshed and a pigsty. In the cowshed they keep the cows, in the stable the horses and in the pigsty the pigs. There is nothing unusual about that, is there? The hay and the corn are stored in barns. There is also an open shed in which the carts and cars are put. Near the shed is a store where the firewood is kept.

During my stay I noticed that the farmer's life is quite a hard one. He must get up early, often before dawn, in order to go and milk the cows. When it is fine he works the whole day long in the fields. Sometimes he has hardly time to come back to the house for his meals. They are brought to him at the place where he is working. He works in the sun and in the rain. He ploughs the land, sows the seed, watches over its growth and later reaps the harvest. There are a thousand tasks for him to do. He continually repairs the fences destroyed by the wind and the cattle; he fills up forms, dozens of which he receives each month. Every week he goes to market to sell his animals or buy others. True enough, he takes advantage of the opportunity to have a little chat with his friends in town and to have a little drink with them in the café. When his animals fall ill he sends for the vet. Naturally, he dreads diseases which might cause the death of hundreds of his cattle. As I spent only three weeks on the farm obviously I was not able to watch all the work that is done in the course of a year. But I saw enough to be convinced that the farmer's life is very arduous.

The farmer I am speaking of grows wheat, barley and oats as well as potatoes, turnips and other vegetables. He has also an orchard in which fruit-trees are to be seen — apple-, pear-, and cherry-trees. We all like fine red apples and juicy pears, don't we? But, unfortunately, when I am in the country and am surrounded by trees bearing fine fruit I don't feel like eating anything. That's a curious thing.

Naturally, the farmer would not be able to do all the work which I have just described on his own. He is assisted by a few farm-labourers. The latter, as there are not very many of them, live in the same house as he and dine at the same table: they all live as one family.

As for the farmer's wife, she looks after the hens, ducks and geese, that is to say, all the poultry in the farmyard — and all the housework. The farmer's wife must be a strong woman to stand the rigours of such a life. I sometimes wonder what our young town women would do if they were obliged to lead a life like that.

Nowadays the tractor is beginning to replace animals for agricultural work. However, in France they still use oxen to pull the plough or the harrow. Besides, the women work in the fields as much as the men, a thing which might surprise foreign tourists motoring through the country. These lusty, wrinkled, sun-tanned peasant women are part, so to speak, of the French scene.

The hay-making season is a period of feverish activity. They work in the fields from morning to night and the farmer anxiously scans the sky. He is afraid of rain which might spoil everything and cause him considerable loss. As for the hay which must be left in the open, it is made into ricks. What a lovely smell a field has when they have just cut the grass!

Sitting in the evening at the fireside, the farmer would tell me sometimes of the misfortunes which threaten him from time to time and which must always be expected. He would tell me of the gales which blow down the trees and devastate the fields. Of the frosts which kill the plants and of the insect pests which devour everything. Indeed, his life is a continual struggle against Nature.

My stay at the farm did me the world of good. The food there was wholesome and plentiful. Ham, butter, cheese tasted delicious. And I had all I could eat! I enjoyed myself the whole day long. In the morning it was impossible to lie in bed. One was awakened at dawn by the joyous singing of the birds. In the yard the cows could be heard lowing, the horses neighing and the dogs barking. It was, in short, a real pastoral symphony.

LEÇON 19: THE DELIGHTS OF CAMPING

"What joy to find oneself at dawn in the midst of awakening Nature! The rising sun gilds the heavens with its magic rays. The birds salute the dawn with their joyous warbling. . . ." Mr. Leclerc heaved a sigh and put down his book — *Camping for Everybody*. He meditated for a few moments after which he addressed his wife who was sitting opposite him. "I say, do you like camping? I feel like going and spending a few days in the country on the bank of a river which I know. As you know, I have three days' leave and it would be a pity to stay at home. What do you say? Will you come with me?"

To tell the truth, Mrs. Leclerc, a very practical woman, was not very keen on camping but as she wanted to please her husband she agreed to go away with him. Two hours later, after jumbling into the boot of the car tent, ropes, pegs, cooking utensils — in short, everything enabling one to live comfortably in the middle of the fields far from all civilization — they set out.

When they had been driving for ten minutes Mrs. Leclerc informed her husband that she had forgotten to disconnect the electric fire. So they turned round and came back to the house. When everything was finally arranged to Madame's satisfaction, they set out again. They drove for two hours on the main road and Mr. Leclerc paid no attention at all to several hitch-hikers desperately waving their hands. Arriving finally at the place where they reckoned on spending three delightful days, they stopped and got out of the car. "This is the place," said Mr. Leclerc to his wife, "where we must leave the car but we shall have to cross three fields to reach the river bank. We have to carry everything there!" On hearing these words, Mrs. Leclerc frowned but said nothing. One hour later, after crossing and recrossing the fields three times, they had at last managed to get all the equipment to the river bank. "Come on," panted Mr. Leclerc, "we must now get the tent up." He took the mallet and aimed some furious blows at the tent-pegs. More than once he nearly crushed his thumb. However, after a great deal of effort and not without a few mild oaths which we shall say nothing about, he succeeded in pitching the tent. Meanwhile, his wife who, like nearly all women, understood nothing about things like that, had seated herself on a tree-trunk, thinking that she would rather be at home where it was warmer. Mr. Leclerc crawled into the tent and Madame followed her husband on all fours — a rather undignified posture for a middle-aged lady.

There was precious little room in that tent and Mrs. Leclerc finding it impossible to be of any help to her husband came out again immediately, leaving him to get on as best he could on his own — which did not worry him unduly. But she did not stay outside for long. It was getting dark and it was chilly. Besides, an unpleasant wind was getting up and it flapped the canvas and the ropes. She quickly got back into the tent. After chatting for half an hour our two campers fell asleep. But the wind was blowing ever more strongly and great drops of rain began to fall on the tent, making a terrific noise. Impossible to sleep under such conditions. "I am horribly cold," moaned Mrs. Leclerc, "and I hope that you put the tent up properly. Otherwise. . . ." "Don't worry," replied her husband in an abrupt tone. "You are always expecting some calamity. In the country it is not the same as home, you know. Do try to sleep. *I* am tired." "That's not my fault, all the same," continued Mrs. Leclerc who, like all women, wanted to have the last word — even in the middle of the night. "Besides, I find the ground is very hard." In the end they went to sleep again.

A few hours elapsed. Outside it was pouring with rain and occasionally a few drops would fall on the sleepers. That finally woke them up again. "Heavens above!" exclaimed Mrs. Leclerc, "I am soaked to the skin. I am not staying here any longer. Let's go and spend the rest of the night in the car." And that's what they did in spite of Mr. Leclerc's protests. For, to make a pig-headed woman see reason is next to impossible.

Up to now Mr. Leclerc has not been able to know the true delights of camping for, first thing next morning, he and his wife came back home, each of them with a cold.

LEÇON 20: END OF THE THIRD REPUBLIC

On September 1st 1939 the Germans, who had just signed a non-aggression pact with Russia, invaded Poland — an act which caused the Second World War. On September 3rd Great Britain and France declared war on the Third Reich after asking the aggressors in vain to withdraw from Polish territory. This conflict was to last almost six years — till the defeat of Germany in 1945. The heroic resistance of Poland lasted only a few months and the Allies who lacked modern armaments did not dare to attack the enemy. It is true that the French won a few square kilometres of German territory but when Poland was defeated they made haste to get back to the Maginot Line — a vast system of fortifications protecting the French frontier.

During the winter of 1939 there was hardly any military activity. The Germans took advantage of this to engage in propaganda in the hope of demoralizing their adversaries. In this they succeeded to a certain extent. The French had not forgotten the horrors and losses of the 1914 war. In the month of April of the following year (1940) Hitler seized Denmark and Norway; once again the Allies were not able to prevent the attack. But it was on May 10th 1940 that the war started in earnest in the West: the German troops crossed the frontiers of Holland, Belgium and Luxembourg— neutral countries who had hoped to remain outside the conflict. It was the beginning of the "blitzkrieg" which was to crush France in less than two months. On May 27th the Belgians, utterly exhausted, surrendered. The British who were fighting at the side of the Belgians had to beat a retreat and make for the port of Dunkirk where, thanks to the efforts of the rearguard and the Royal Navy, they were able to embark and return to England.

Meanwhile, the French government had abandoned Paris and had established itself at Bordeaux. The roads were choked with refugees fleeing before the enemy and the German planes were spreading panic and death everywhere. On June 14th the Germans entered Paris which had been declared an open city in order to spare it the fate of Warsaw and so many other towns. The loss of the capital — which the Germans had been unable to take during the Great War — demoralized the French Army completely. Reynaud, the prime minister, made way for Marshal Pétain, a hero of the First World War. But Petain was really too old (he had already turned eighty) to guide France in such a crisis. He asked the Germans for an armistice which was signed on June 22nd at Compiègne in the railway coach in which the Germans had signed that of 1918. According to the terms of this armistice the victors allowed France to keep her colonial empire and her fleet and to maintain an army of a hundred thousand men. But the country was divided into two zones and the Germans occupied the northern one which, moreover, included all the Atlantic coast.

A French officer who did not wish to give up the struggle against the enemies of his country took refuge in England where he became the leader of all Frenchmen who had been able to reach the United Kingdom. General de Gaulle called his army "Free France" and adopted as his emblem the Cross of Lorraine.

At the beginning of the occupation the Germans were quite polite and correct in order not to arouse the hostility of the population. But the vanquished, once they had recovered from the first shock of their country's disaster, clearly understood the fate which awaited them. The Germans began to send to Germany all those who were in a fit state to work. Right from the start of the occupation the Jews were deprived of the greater part of their civil rights and forced to wear distinguishing marks. Eventually food became scarce for Hitler had said that if all Europe were destined to starve to death the Germans would be the last to suffer such a fate. The German authorities issued valueless bank-notes thanks to which the army of occupation could buy very cheaply all that remained in the shops. In this way the pillage of the country was "legalized."

A certain number of Frenchmen led astray by ambition and the desire to get rich agreed to collaborate with their new masters but, in general, the vanquished remained faithful to their traditions of liberty and independence. Thus was born the Resistance which with the help of the British and the Free French was to sabotage the railways, the ports and the factories used by the Germans. . . . The Third Republic was dead but France lived on.

392

LEÇON 21: AT THE OFFICE

Mr. Duval lived on the outskirts of Paris. As he had no car, he used to take the train every morning to go into the city where he worked in an office. He used to leave the house at half past seven and arrive at the station at a quarter to eight. The train came in at ten to eight. As a rule everything went well, Mr. Duval caught his train and arrived at the office on time. But last Monday everything went wrong. For a start, Mr. Duval got up late: he had not heard the alarm or the latter had not rung. There is no means of knowing exactly. In any case, he had to hurry his breakfast. Whilst he was eating, his wife — a very pleasant woman but a trifle talkative — told him that he could do a few errands for her in town. Mr. Duval listened to her patiently, seized his overcoat, tucked his brief-case under his arm and rushed out of the house — after kissing his wife, of course.

His little dog went out with him and followed him along the road, barking with delight. Notwithstanding, Mr. Duval continued on his way without bothering about the dog. But suddenly the idea struck him that his wife would not be very pleased if anything happened to the dog. He turned back and took the animal home. The trains leave on time; the upshot was that he missed his train and had to wait for the next. What a crowd there was on the platform that morning! Mr. Duval bought a paper and began to read. After a quarter of an hour the train came into the station and Mr. Duval found a seat in a smoking compartment. He wasn't at all pleased.

He eventually arrived at the office but he was at least half an hour late and everybody was beginning to get worried about him because they knew that Mr. Duval was a conscientious and punctual employee.

He entered the office then. In the main office there were typists typing letters and a young man filing papers and sticking stamps on envelopes. Everybody was working assiduously — and in silence. That is what surprised Mr. Duval who knew very well that the typists were in the habit of chattering all day. He entered saying: "Good morning." The reply to his greeting was rather dry and they did not look up at him. "Ho! Ho!" thought Mr. Duval, "that's not a good sign." He hung his overcoat and his hat on a nail, slipped between the desks to reach his own where he set to work. He was about to open a ledger all covered in dust — Mr. Duval was a book-keeper — when the office-boy approached him and informed him that the boss wanted to speak to him immediately. The boss, whose name was Mr. Ledoux, was a fierce man and a big black moustache adorned his ogre-like face. Besides, he smoked a pipe which filled all the room with a cloud of smoke.

Mustering all his courage, Mr. Duval knocked at the door of the director's private office and entered. Immediately he began to cough frightfully. Never was a man so unfortunate. "Ah! Good morning," said the boss in an ironic tone. "They told me that you were late. Does this happen often?" "Once every five years," thought Mr. Duval, but he took good care not to say it aloud. "I wanted to open the safe," continued the boss, "but you have the keys." That was true. As Mr. Duval enjoyed the confidence of his superiors he had the right to carry the key of the safe in which the important books and documents were kept. In Mr. Duval's absence no work had been possible. What a nuisance! Poor Mr. Duval, terribly confused, began to search in his pockets but he found nothing in them. Good Heavens! He had changed his suit the night before and the keys were still in the pocket of his grey suit and the latter was at home. What was he to do? "I am very sorry, sir, but. . . ." "Give me them right away," curtly said Mr. Ledoux who was not listening and was examining some letters which he had in front of him. "But, sir," stammered Mr. Duval very confused and blushing with shame, "I have forgotten them." "What?" roared the other. Mr. Duval remained silent. Fortunately the telephone rang bringing the interview to a close and the boss gestured impatiently to Mr. Duval to withdraw. The latter heaved a sigh of relief and went out.

He thought for a moment and then went to find one of the clerks who was a motor-cyclist. The latter set off on his motor-cycle to get the keys and returned with them in twenty minutes. . . . I am sure that his whole life through Mr. Duval will never forget the day when he left his keys at home. What a misfortune for such a man!

LEÇON 22: TRAVELLING

The Trotters were English and they liked travelling. Mr. Trotter was a well-educated man whilst his wife was not at all like the women whom I have described up to now. She was the most likeable woman in the world and she was not more talkative than any other. Two years ago they decided to go and spend their summer holidays in Switzerland. What more pleasant than a short stay abroad? They went one fine morning to the railway terminus and caught the train for Dover, where there was a queue. After a quarter of an hour the queue began to move forward but more slowly than a tortoise. It was the inspection of passports. They emerged from this ordeal without difficulty and went at last on to the boat. "First class on the right, second class on the left," a sailor was shouting near the gangway and he was preventing those who had second-class tickets from entering the first-class saloon. He seemed to consider it a matter of the greatest importance.

Three-quarters of an hour later the ship left the harbour. Mr. and Mrs. Trotter went and settled themselves comfortably in armchairs but almost immediately the loudspeakers dotted about everywhere on board began to thunder. An announcement was made in good English and bad French to the effect that landing-cards must be obtained immediately and that for this purpose it was necessary to call at the ship's office. Mr. Trotter got up and made his way there. As he was waiting he watched at his leisure the white cliffs of England gradually fading into the distance.

There were a lot of people on board — more people than Mr. Trotter had ever seen in such a restricted space. There were young people and old people, Englishmen and foreigners, nuns and women who looked anything but. Mr. Trotter easily recognized the foreigners because, in general, their complexion was darker than that of his compatriots and many of them seemed to be dressed for mountain-climbing. There were several of them who gave the impression that they were in love. To pass the time, Mr. and Mrs. Trotter went to have something to drink but they had to queue because there were so many people buying cigarettes and spirits — goods which are much cheaper on the high seas than ashore. Already the French coast could be seen in the distance. Everybody was bustling about asking the sailors: "Which way are we going to get off?" The sailors didn't know and merely answered: "That depends." Small queues started to form everywhere.

Twenty minutes later the ship was alongside. The gangways were placed in position but nobody disembarked. Suddenly, an army of men dressed in blue rushed aboard shouting: "Porter." One of these porters seized Mr. Trotter's suitcases in spite of the protests of the latter who wouldn't let go and kept on repeating unceasingly: "No, thanks. No, thanks." But probably that porter didn't understand French very well for he disappeared with the cases after saying: "Thirty-four." That was his number.

They got off at last but it took time. "Anything to declare?" asked the customs officers who didn't appear to be in much of a hurry. Mr. Trotter found these formalities as tedious in France as in England. But nobody aroused the suspicions of the customs officers and all made their way at full speed towards the train. You would have said it was an army in retreat. One had to choose between three trains and not a railwayman in sight. . . . Comfortably settled in train number two marked "Bâle," Mr. and Mrs. Trotter looked at one another with satisfaction. By a miracle their cases were in the rack above their heads. But the departure of the train was delayed. Mr. Trotter had noticed that in France the locomotives were bigger than in England. The second-class seats were harder than those in the English trains and the coaches were made of steel. Because of that you hear more noise than in England.

At last the train started off and soon it was careering at a dizzy speed. Mr. Trotter wondered whether the engine-driver was in a hurry to get home for some urgent family reason. But the hours passed slowly all the same.

It was one o'clock in the morning and all the passengers were sleeping. Suddenly an infernal din shattered the calm of the night. (When I say "calm," I mean by that, that kind of monotonous rumbling peculiar to trains.) It was the ticket-inspector who was opening the door and shouting: "Tickets, please!" One o'clock in the morning is the ticket-inspectors' favourite hour. Half asleep, Mr. Trotter looked in his wallet for the tickets. . . .

LEÇON 23: CONVERSATION IN THE CAFÉ

Two young ladies who had known each other since childhood had arranged to meet at three o'clock in the Café Royal opposite the town-hall. They met there at the hour agreed upon and after looking at the menu they ordered two coffees with cream. When the waiter had brought the cups of coffee the two young ladies, who had many things to tell each other, began to chat. The conversation turned to young men — which is not surprising when it is two young ladies who are speaking to one another. But that day they were speaking neither of the beauty nor the virtues of those gentlemen but of their faults.

"I have a friend," Mlle. Lucienne was saying, "who is so mean that he goes to bed early in the evening in order to save electricity. I am convinced that, when he walks, he takes great strides in order not to wear out the soles of his shoes. One day I went out with him for a walk. We intended to visit a park which is not very far from my house. As he came out of the house he asked me if I could give him a light for a cigarette which he had obtained from a friend. I offered him a match which I had found at the bottom of my handbag. Full of excuses he explained to me that he couldn't offer me a cigarette because he had no more left. As we were passing a paper-stall he asked me to buy a newspaper because there was an article in it which he wanted to read. I complied unwillingly. Immediately he took possession of the paper which I didn't see again. Then we made our way towards the bus-stop in order to wait for the bus. It arrived at last and we got in. The conductor approached us and my friend began to rummage in his pockets. 'What a nuisance!' he said at last, 'I changed my suit and I have left my money at home. Could you pay for the tickets?' Fortunately I had in my bag a few francs that my father had given me the previous day and I paid for the tickets. My friend took them and examined them carefully. He explained to me that I could have taken cheaper tickets and then we would have got off at such and such a place to do the rest of the journey on foot. At last we got off the bus and entered the park. There we saw a shady-looking individual. This man was collecting for Chinese children. Now, Julien — that's my friend's name — is tender-hearted, it must be admitted. He is a sensitive soul. Taking pity on the little Chinese orphans, Julien gave the man a Russian coin. As for the gentleman, you can imagine the look on his face!"

"What you are telling me is very interesting," replied Yolande, "but I am going to tell you about Lucien. He was not mean but he had another fault: he always said the wrong thing at the wrong time. One day I was with him at the house of my old aunt. Now, my aunt is quite rich and she has no other niece but me. But she doesn't like anything that is modern — neither houses, furniture, books nor music. I had warned my friend Lucien about this and I had advised him not to say anything one shouldn't say to a fussy old aunt. Well, we were sitting down having tea. I was admiring my aunt's beautiful china. 'What do you think of it?' I said, addressing my friend. 'It's not exactly the latest fashion,' he replied. I looked daggers at him and gave him a kick under the table. Such things are not said. I noticed at once that my aunt was angry but she was too polite to argue with Lucien. Later, we were speaking about the drawing-room and the furniture. My aunt was in raptures in front of an old oak sideboard. 'I like furniture of a simpler style,' said Lucien. I was beside myself. I could see my future wealth evaporating before my eyes like the dew at sunrise. Consequently I judged it prudent to cut short our visit especially when Lucien began to expound political ideas which my aunt has always loathed. Naturally I am not telling you all the rude things that Lucien said that day. I am too ashamed. In any case I have not wished to see him since. After all, you must not hurt the feelings of a rich old aunt. It isn't done."

The two young ladies looked at the time by the clock of the town-hall opposite. It was getting late. As soon as they had paid the bill (not forgetting to give the waiter a tip) they left the café, said goodbye to one another and each went home.

LEÇON 24: A LETTER FROM PARIS

Dear Charles,

As it is quite a long time since I saw you I do not remember if I told you that I was going to spend a fortnight in Paris. Well, I have already been in the City of Light for a week. I arrived last Monday and I have found accommodation at the house of one of my friends at Bécon-les-Bruyères. I was lucky for I would not have been able to afford a hotel. At Paris everything is quite dear.

I go out every day to see the sights of the city. Yesterday I admired Notre Dame, the great Gothic cathedral built on an island in the middle of the Seine. That made me think of Victor Hugo's famous novel in which he tells the story of the hunchback Quasimodo and the latter's love for the beautiful Esmeralda. I also visited the Hôtel des Invalides where Napoleon's tomb is to be found and the Panthéon where many famous Frenchmen are buried.

Today I took a stroll in the Latin Quarter — one of the oldest districts of Paris. That is where the University of Paris is, known by the name of the Sorbonne. One often sees there also shabby-looking individuals who might be painters. This afternoon I went to see the Arc de Triomphe which stands at the end of the Avenue des Champs-Elysées and beneath which is the tomb of the Unknown Soldier.

Three days ago I spent several hours in the Louvre museum where among other masterpieces I admired the Mona Lisa by Leonardo da Vinci. But that museum contains so many art treasures that you would need at least several days to examine thoroughly everything of interest in it.

Perhaps you are getting impatient while I am telling you about churches and museums. You are going to ask me if I have been to the top of the Eiffel Tower. My answer to you will be "yes." The Eiffel Tower, a remarkable steel structure built for the World Exhibition of 1889 is 300 metres high. It has become, so to speak, the symbol of the city of Paris. To go up it you take the lift and you pay quite a lot. Up there are restaurants and shops and the tower supports a television aerial. When I looked down it made me quite dizzy!

The great Paris boulevards are wonderful. They are wide, straight avenues all along which you see first-class shops. Thanks to its boulevards and magnificent buildings Paris is one of the most beautiful cities in the world.

When you are waiting for a bus in Paris it is not necessary to queue up. On arriving at the bus-stop you tear off a little priority ticket which bears a number. When the bus arrives the conductor makes people show their tickets and he lets the passengers get in according to the order of their arrival at the stop. Very practical, isn't it? Besides, you can buy a book of tickets from the conductor. It is more convenient and it comes out much cheaper like that.

I often travel by Underground because it is very quick especially at the rush hour. Often I amuse myself by making long trips just for the pleasure of travelling. By looking at the maps which you see posted up everywhere in the Underground stations you can easily see where you must change and catch a connection. But beware! It is useless to run to catch the trains at the last moment. At the entrance to every platform is an automatic door (it is called a "portillon") which closes as soon as a train enters the station.

Two days ago I went to the Bois de Boulogne — a huge public park where you can go for some fine walks and, if you can row, take a trip on the lake in a rowing-boat. But if you go there some day to hire a boat do not forget to give a tip to the man who helps you to get into the boat. Otherwise he will say to you in a biting tone: "Don't forget the service, please." When you are in Paris you ought to take a walk along the embankments of the Seine to have a look at the displays of the second-hand booksellers who trade there on the pavement. You can see all sorts of books and interesting old volumes there.

The church of the Sacred Heart, perched on the top of a hill, overlooks the Montmartre district where the famous nightclubs are to be found. A quaint atmosphere pervades this quarter but, in my opinion, everything there is arranged for the benefit of tourists.

I shall leave Paris a week today. I cannot tell you whether I shall stay a few days in Calais but in any case I hope to see you very soon.

Sincerely yours,
Robert

LEÇON 25: A DREADFUL CRIME

Ting-a-ling! The telephone was ringing in the Sûreté. With a professional flourish Inspector Legros took off the receiver and said: "Hello! hello!" It was one of his subordinates who answered: "Good evening, Inspector. A report has just been made of what might be a murder at 35, Boulevard Monceau. The concierge says that she found a dead man in one of the flats." "Good, I'll come right away," said Legros who like all detectives did not speak much. "We shall go to the spot immediately." So saying, he rang off. Two and a half minutes later Inspector Legros accompanied by four of his best men was getting into a car. The car shot away at lightning speed and a quarter of an hour later stopped with a terrific screech of brakes in front of a great building on which by the light of the street-lamp could be read the number 35. Without saying a word the policemen alighted like automatons slamming the doors with a great din and went into the house.

The concierge, a fat woman with grey hair, came to meet the five policemen. She told them with all the details how she had found the corpse. The poor concierge was trembling in every limb but that did not prevent her from talking. The inspector looked at the woman without saying a word whilst she was giving him information. "Good," he said at last. "At what time did you discover the corpse?" "Just now — that is to say, at half past eleven — as it happened I was saying to myself. . . ." The inspector looked at his watch. It was five minutes to midnight. "What is the dead man's name?" he asked next. "His name is Mr. Duclos," the woman replied. "How old was he?" "I should say thirty-five but it is difficult to know exactly. But he was a very nice man. He has been living here only six months. Obviously he was not rich. His flat is quite modest. The poor man had no wife. He lived alone up there. I have always been sorry for him. It really is a pity." "How talkative that woman is," thought the inspector. "Did he often have visitors?" he continued, lighting up his pipe. "Hardly any," answered the concierge. "He liked to be alone; he didn't have much to say. I think he worked in the city. He was a book-keeper." Needless to say, the concierge knew everything that took place in the house. And she added: "This very evening about nine o'clock a man came to see him. I happened to be on the stairs and I was able to see him. It is true that I didn't look at him closely because I didn't know at that time that he was going to kill Mr. Duclos (the inspector frowned) but my impression is that he was rather small and bald. I noticed that because he wasn't wearing a hat. On his forehead he had a frightful scar.

I said to myself: 'I don't know that fellow. Who can he be?' And I watched him go up to the third floor. He knocked at the door and was let in. Then I saw him coming down the stairs about ten o'clock. He seemed to be in a great hurry." "That will do for the moment," said the inspector and he went up to the third floor. There he found people crowding around the door of the flat, craning their necks to see what was going on inside. With a word the inspector sent them packing. The police do not like inquisitive people.

The inspector went on to examine the room. They were dealing with a crime, that was obvious. The corpse was stretched out on the floor in the middle of the room. Perhaps there was blood spattered all over the place but I am not very sure about that. But there certainly was a revolver on the carpet. On the floor there was also a broken clock showing half past eight. The victim's pipe and a torn-up letter were on the table. The police doctor was examining the corpse and a photographer was taking photographs. The room was being examined too, with a view to finding finger-prints.

Inspector Legros was thinking. He sent for the concierge: "Who are the other tenants of this house?" "There are only two," she replied. "Mlle Lemoine who is an old maid lives alone on the first floor. At the moment she is away on holiday at the house of her sister who lives in the provinces. As for Mrs. Mornet, she is a widow. She is a very pleasant person. She has nothing to do with the crime, I am sure."

Who then had committed this atrocious crime? Was it the mysterious man with the scar? Was it one of the tenants in the house? Was it the concierge herself? The inspector thought about it for a long time but the inspector was not the sort of detective you find in novels and — what's the use of denying it? — he could not solve the problem in ten minutes. As for myself, as soon as I receive fuller information I shall bring it to the notice of the public.

LEÇON 26: A DANGEROUS MISSION

John was English by birth but he had passed the greater part of his life in France — at Bordeaux where his father was a coal merchant. Naturally he spoke French fluently and all who did not know his family took him for a Frenchman. Then in 1940 came the German invasion and the situation soon became critical. John, who was not lacking in courage, did not feel like allowing himself to be captured by the Germans. He did not wish to remain calmly awaiting disaster and he decided to leave. After quite a few adventures he embarked in a merchant vessel and finally succeeded in reaching England.

John joined the British Army. At that time England was expecting a German invasion but in the army John gained the impression that the main thing for a good soldier was to polish his buttons well and to shine his boots well. Sometimes in the evening he spent hours cleaning his uniform and shining up his straps whilst at the inspection on the following day he had to stand motionless in the rain. In the army they called that "discipline." John became bored; he had not come to England, he said to himself, to spend his time peeling potatoes, washing dishes or to work in the officers' mess. Somehow or other he was able to draw the attention of the military authorities to this unfortunate position — which clearly shows that he was no ordinary man. He offered to go back to France to wage a secret struggle against the oppressors of his adopted country.

His offer was given lengthy consideration and in the end it was accepted. He was sent first to Scotland — to a manor lost in the wilds. There he was to prepare himself for his future role. He practised walking for long distances, swimming in the icy waters of a loch and climbing trees. He learned also to use plastic explosive to destroy locomotives, rails, factory machinery. They taught him everything that a soldier must know who later on will have to rely only on himself.

After a few weeks John left Scotland to go to an aerodrome which was in the north of England. There he learned to jump by parachute. At first he did not like it very much but in the end he became an experienced parachutist.

Eventually he returned to London where he continued to prepare himself for his task. Then one day he received the order to present himself at a certain office where he had an interview with a colonel. The latter told him that they were soon going to send him back to France. He was being entrusted with organizing a group of members of the Resistance and teaching them the most effective methods of sabotage. It was a question, the colonel told him, of a very dangerous mission. What did he think of it? John who remembered his family and his friends who had remained over there replied that he was ready to undertake anything to harm the enemy. It was for that very reason that he had come to England.

A few days later he was requested to present himself at a certain establishment where he would be given French clothes. If he were captured in France an English suit would have betrayed him at once. One had to think of everything. He was also given French cigarettes and matches.

At last the evening came when John was taken to an aerodrome. An aeroplane was waiting for him on the runway. The officer with him wished him good luck and the pilot of the aeroplane greeted him warmly but asked him no questions. The plane took off shortly afterwards and in no time they were flying over the English Channel. John was sitting quietly listening to the drone of the engines and thinking of what he was going to do in France. Suddenly there was a deafening explosion. It was the anti-aircraft fire. "If we are brought down now . . ." thought John. But the pilot managed to get out of this difficult position and twenty minutes later John was informed that they were approaching the dropping point and he was told to get ready to jump. It must be said that John was afraid. But when he saw the green light come on he jumped and he was falling gently as he swayed on the end of his parachute. He heard the aeroplane getting further and further away and he felt alone. How quiet the night was! Suddenly he hit the ground roughly and hurt his left leg. But he had no time to think of it. He was freeing himself from his parachute when he heard someone whispering in the darkness. "Who is it?" asked the voice. "It is Marcel," replied John. "Good," said the other, "we are expecting you."

LEÇON 27: FRANCE TODAY

At the end of the war France naturally found herself in a very weak economic position. A great part of the country had been devastated and more than a million and a half dwellings had been destroyed. The railway network, the bridges and the roads had suffered serious damage. Everything had to be repaired. If to that is added the systematic plundering of the country by the enemy, the magnitude of the task facing the French Government will be realized. It is true that American help allowed France to begin on this immense work of reconstruction.

Today, on the other hand, France seems well upon the road to prosperity. Of a total population of 45 million the working population is estimated at 20 million. The bridges and roads which had been damaged during the war have been repaired and improved. Besides, motorways, of which 100 km. are at present open to traffic, are in the process of construction. As for building, more than 300,000 new dwellings a year are completed. Industrial production and foreign trade increase every year and, as a result, the national income continues to grow at the rate of 4·5 per cent per annum. So that unemployment is practically non-existent. Since 1958 a struggle has been carried on against inflation and the "heavy franc" or — in other words — the "new franc" has been created. According to the calculations of the statisticians it appears that one person in nine has a car. It is also stressed that hire-purchase continues to increase and that the French are travelling abroad more. It is possible that they are beginning to lose their parochial outlook.

The most marked feature which can be pointed out in the post-war social life of France is the continued increase in the birth-rate. Between the two wars there was grave fear that France might suffer serious depopulation and that in the end she might become a third-class power. But in recent times the annual figure for births is 800,000. That is naturally going to raise serious problems from the point of view of housing and schools.

Let us examine for a moment the labour question. Twenty-five per cent of the workers are members of the various trade unions — a proportion much smaller than in Great Britain. It is not surprising that in France there is industrial unrest as everywhere else in the free world. But it is to be regretted

402

that certain political organizations which purposely provoke labour unrest are stronger in France than in any other Western country.

Every employed person — whatever may be the amount of his salary — must belong to the national social insurance scheme which covers risks (to use administrative jargon) such as illness, industrial accidents and old age. Moreover, every wage-earner who has at least two children receives a family allowance. It seems that they are in the process of setting up the Welfare State in France.

France is an important member of the European Community (better known by the name of the Common Market). The six countries which make up the Common Market — France, Western Germany, Italy, Belgium, Holland and Luxembourg — signed the Treaty of Rome in 1957. They agreed to work for the total abolition of customs dues. The importance of such a union will be understood when it is remembered that the Common Market has a combined population of 170 million. The headquarters of the Common Market are at Brussels. Certain people fear that this union may have political consequences incompatible with national sovereignty.

On the economic plane there is reason, therefore, to believe that all is well. But in the political sphere the future is less rosy. Nobody would be found who would dare to make any forecasts about possible events. Morocco and Tunisia had obtained their independence before General de Gaulle came to power. Following a revolt which lasted more than eight years, Algeria was declared independent in July, 1962. The French had had to keep an army of 500,000 men there and had suffered more than 2,000 casualties per year. In April, 1961, certain generals who were in Algeria revolted against the authority of the central government but their rebellion failed miserably. It can be seen that the problems with which General de Gaulle had to deal were quite serious.

In 1963 the General opposed Great Britain's entry into the Common Market and preferred to seek a reconciliation with Germany; he continued to give rise to controversy in his own country and abroad. In any case, it seemed a matter of some difficulty at that time to point out among the French politicians a man who would be able to replace him later at the head of the state.

ANSWERS TO EXERCISES

Note that (*a*) in exercises containing second person verbs, pronouns, possessive adjectives, etc., the singular or plural forms are equally correct but both are not always given, e.g.: *You are right* = **Tu as raison** OR **Vous avez raison**; (*b*) where a verb-table forms the answer to a question the third person feminine forms are not given, unless they differ from the masculine forms; (*c*) where a French composition or description is set as one of the exercises and there is no one correct version, you should check your own work as thoroughly as possible using the index, the grammar sections in each chapter, the grammar summaries and the vocabularies at the end of the book.

LEÇON 1:

I. 1. **Elle est dans la cuisine.**
2. **Il est dans la salle à manger, contre le mur.**
3. **La famille Girard est dans la cuisine.**
4. **Les petites filles sont dans la cuisine, à la table.**
5. **La cheminée est dans le salon.**
6. **Les‿enfants sont méchantes même quand‿il y a un bon programme à la télévision.**
7. **Dans le salon il y a une cheminée, un canapé, et deux fauteuils.**
8. **Il y a deux fauteuils dans le salon.**
9. **Suzanne dit que Josette est méchante.**
10. **Maman et papa disent que Suzanne est méchante aussi.**
11. **Jacques dit qu'il est très sage quand maman et papa sont‿absents.**
12. **. . . parce qu'elle n'a pas beaucoup d'affection pour Jacques.**
13. **Ils sont contents après la conversation.**
14. **Il y a deux petites filles.**
15. **Oui, je suis sage.**
16. **Le beau tapis est dans la salle à manger.**
17. **La cheminée est belle.**
18. **Suzanne est jolie et Josette est coquette.**
19. **Le salon est très grand.**
20. **Elle est méchante quand le programme est‿affreux.**

II. 1. **dites**: *Do you say that the boy is naughty?*
  2. **Avez**: *Have you got several cupboards in the kitchen?*

3. **disent**: *Suzanne and Jacques do not say that Josette is good.*
4. **sommes**: *We are not always happy.*
5. **sont**: *Are the little girls often naughty?*
6. **Ont**: *Have they many carpets in the dining-room?*
7. **Êtes**: *Are you busy in the garden?*
8. **sont**: *Where are the sink and the stove?*
9. **suis**: *"I am not very small," says Suzanne.*
10. **y a**: *There is a chair in the sitting-room.*

III. 1. **Malgré un visage sale.**
2. **Beaucoup de travail.**
3. **Une belle cheminée.**
4. **Plusieurs pièces.**
5. **Même quand il y a.**
6. **La maison de la famille Girard.**
7. **Sur le plancher.**
8. **Un beau tapis.**
9. **Oui, nous sommes sûrs.**
10. **Dans un deux-pièces vert.**
11. **Mais elles sont souvent méchantes.**
12. **Parce que le programme est affreux.**
13. **Quand nous avons beaucoup de travail.**
14. **Es-tu une exception?**
15. **Un bon programme à la télévision.**

IV.
la cuisine . . . petite
une petite table
une grande table
la salon . . . grand
les petites filles . . . jolies . . . méchantes

une cuisinière électrique
la salle à manger . . . spacieuse
un beau tapis
une belle cheminée
le petit garçon . . . sage, tu . . . méchante, Josette

Suzanne . . . méchante
un bon programme
le programme . . . affreux
Maman et papa . . . sûrs
vous . . . occupés
nous . . . sûrs
il . . . méchant
les pauvres petites filles
une petite robe rouge et bleue
un petit deux-pièces vert
les parents et les enfants . . . contents

elles . . . méchantes
je . . . méchante
les programmes . . . affreux
Jacques . . . sage
maman et papa . . . absents
il . . . sage
nous . . . sages
Suzanne . . . jolie
Josette . . . coquette
un visage sale
le programme . . . intéressant

French adjectives may vary in form to agree in number and gender with the nouns or pronouns they describe; thus **petit** when it describes the feminine noun **cuisine** takes the feminine ending **-e**, and when it describes a plural noun, e.g. **filles**, it takes in addition the plural ending **-s**.

405

V. Words that are the same in French and in English: **conversation, table, buffet, papa, programme, télévision, absent, affection, exception, robe, coquette, visage, content.**

A **fiancé** is masculine and a **fiancée** is feminine.

LEÇON 2:

I. 1. **On voit six portes sur le palier.**
2. **On voit un grand lit dans la première chambre.**
3. **On voit deux petits lits dans la seconde chambre.**
4. **On voit beaucoup de jouets et d'illustrés sur le plancher.**
5. **On n'entre pas dans la chambre de Jacques parce qu'elle n'est pas en bon ordre.**
6. **Mme Girard lave le visage de Jacques.**
7. **Les petites filles crient très fort.**
8. **Non, elle cherche la poupée.**
9. **Elle est fâchée parce qu'elle ne voit pas la poupée.**
10. **Il y a une poupée dans la chambre.**
11. **Jacques est méchant comme un singe.**
12. **Jacques aime jouer avec la poupée.**
13. **Non, il ne travaille pas dans le jardin.**
14. **Il est caché derrière la porte de la salle de bain.**
15. **M. et Mme Girard montent l'escalier.**
16. **Il dit: "Suzanne et Josette, pourquoi criez-vous si fort?"**
17. **Il fouette les méchants garçons.**
18. **Ils prennent un livre quand ils n'ont pas trop de travail.**
19. **On donne un grand livre à Jacques.**
20. **Il travaille dans le jardin.**

II. 1. *Where can one see six doors?*
2. *Where can one see a big bed?*
3. *Where can one see two small beds?*
4. *What can one see in Jacques' bedroom?*
5. *Why does one not go into the room?*
6. *Whose face does Mrs. Girard wash?*
7. *In what way do the little girls shout?*
8. *Is Josette looking for a chair?*
9. *Why is she angry?*
10. *How many dolls are there in the room?*
11. *Who is as naughty as a monkey?*
12. *Who likes to play with the doll?*
13. *Does Jacques work in the garden?*
14. *Where is he hidden?*

15. *Who climbs the stairs?*
16. *What does Mr. Girard say?*
17. *Which boys does he whip?*
18. *When do the parents take a book?*
19. *What is given to Jacques?*
20. *Mr. Girard is working: where?*

III. 1. Je donne un livre au garçon.
 2. Je donne deux grands livres aux enfants.
 3. Nous donnons un petit livre aux fillettes.
 4. Nous donnons les beaux jouets aux enfants.
 5. Nous donnons la poupée rouge à une petite fille sage.

IV. 1. belles
 2. bleus
 3. méchantes
 4. contentes
 5. fâchés
 6. blanche
 7. petite
 8. intéressants
 9. beaux, grande
 10. grands

V. 1. M. et Mme Girard travaillent dans le jardin.
 2. Nous ne disons pas qu'il est méchant.
 3. Les garçons laissent tout sous les illustrés.
 4. Ils prennent un livre quand ils n'ont pas trop de travail.
 5. Êtes-vous toujours occupé dans le jardin?
 6. Grondez-vous souvent les enfants?
 7. Ils voient les chaises dans la chambre.
 8. Nous montons l'escalier et nous arrivons sur le palier.
 9. On voit que la baignoire est dans la salle de bain.
 10. Que prends-tu quand tu n'as pas trop de travail?

VI. 1. derrière
 2. sur
 3. sous
 4. dans
 5. de, de
 6. malgré
 7. avec
 8. dans
 9. sur
 10. contre

LEÇON 3:

I. 1. Il est trois heures dix; à trois heures dix.
 2. Il est onze heures moins le quart; à onze heures moins le quart.
 3. Il est neuf heures et demie; à neuf heures et demie.
 4. Il est midi (or minuit) moins vingt; à midi moins vingt.
 5. Il est huit heures et quart; à huit heures et quart.
 6. Entre deux heures et quatre heures.
 7. Peu après minuit et demi.

      8. Avant onze heures moins vingt-cinq.

      9. Il n'est pas minuit moins cinq.

    10. Il n'est pas deux heures treize.

II. 1. Du fil; du bois; du travail; du pain.

     2. De la couture; de la confiture.

     3. De l'herbe; de l'eau.

     4. Des légumes; des feuilles; des chiens; des ballons.

     5. Suzanne n'a pas de fil.

     6. Mme Girard n'a pas de légumes.

     7. Au fond du jardin; les jouets du garçon.

     8. Au bord de la pelouse; la robe de la petite fille.

     9. Les jouets des enfants; les feuilles des légumes.

    10. Des feuilles, du bois et de l'herbe.

III. 1. Le jardin de la famille Girard est beau.

     2. Le sentier est étroit.

     3. Les feuilles sont mortes.

     4. Les joues de la petite fille sont rouges.

     5. Elle est déchirée.

     6. Ils sont dans le potager (or le jardin).

     7. Il est derrière la maison.

     8. Il est entre la pelouse et le potager.

     9. Le fil est dans le salon.

    10. Je suis à la maison (or dans le jardin, etc.).

    11. Il cultive des pommes de terre, des choux, des carottes, des navets et des épinards.

    12. Ils quittent la maison.

    13. Ils lancent un ballon à Suzanne.

    14. Quand il fait mauvais elles font de la couture.

    15. Elle cherche du fil.

    16. M. Girard cultive des légumes.

    17. Suzanne est la sœur cadette.

    18. Jacques est le frère de Josette.

    19. Mme Girard est la mère du garçon.

    20. Suzanne est la petite couturière.

IV.   Answers here will vary. Use the clocks on page 37 to help you to check your answers to this question.

V. 1. Des choux, des navets et des épinards.

    2. Près du pommier . . . loin de la fenêtre.

    3. Les chiens du voisinage ne viennent pas dans le jardin des Girard.

4. **Une belle après-midi d'été.**
5. **La sœur cadette du petit garçon est fâchée.**
6. **La robe de la petite couturière est déchirée.**
7. **Elle fait la grimace parce qu'elle a deux adversaires.**

VI.
1. **Il est midi (ou minuit) moins vingt.**
2. **Il est une heure moins le quart.**
3. **Il est sept heures moins dix.**
4. **Il est six heures.**
5. **Il est quatre heures cinq.**
6. **Il est une heure et quart.**
7. **Il est deux heures vingt-cinq.**
8. **Il est huit heures et demie.**

LEÇON 4:

I.
1. **son goûter**
2. **leur déjeuner**
3. **ses souliers**
4. **mon café**
5. **son mari**
6. **sa tasse**
7. **sa tasse**
8. **mes robes**
9. **votre** (or **ton**) **père**
10. **sa mère**
11. **son père**
12. **son pantalon**
13. **sa colère**
14. **ses enfants**
15. **leurs illustrés**
16. **ma tasse**
17. **leur thé**
18. **vos** (or **tes**) **tasses**
19. **leurs tasses**
20. **mon roman**

II. **entre; avec; Malgré; À; dans; pour; près; sans; au lieu d(e); dans; derrière; de; de; de.**

Jacques plays in the garden between two o'clock and four o'clock with his sisters. In spite of the threats of their mother they eat some apples. At ten past four, Mrs. Girard comes into the kitchen-garden to look for some spinach. She sees Jacques near the apple-tree. The little boy is eating an apple without noticing his mother. She scolds Jacques, but instead of being penitent the naughty boy says that his sisters are in the house and that they also are eating apples. Five minutes later Mrs. Girard finds Suzanne and Josette behind the door of the dining-room: but now they are not eating apples, they are eating Jacques' bar of chocolate.

III.
1. **Punissent-ils leurs enfants** (or **Est-ce qu'ils punissent . . .**)?
2. **Vous punissez vos enfants** (or **Tu punis tes enfants**).
3. **Punit-il ses enfants** (or **Est-ce qu'il punit . . .**)?
4. **Nous punissons nos enfants.**
5. **Je ne punis pas toujours mes enfants.**
6. **Suzanne et Josette punissent Jacques.**

IV. 1. **Oui, il est dans le salon quand il lit le journal.**
  2. **Oui, il trouve le pot à crème.**
  3. **Oui, elle donne une tasse de thé à son mari.**
  4. **Elle est dans le salon.**
  5. **Elles sont sur la table.**
  6. **Elle est debout près de la cheminée et loin de la table.**
  7. **Il ôte ses souliers.**
  8. **Il met ses pantoufles.**
  9. **Il va chercher le pot à crème.**
  10. **Il explique qu'il est cassé.**
  11. **Il lit le quotidien.**
  12. **Il renverse du lait sur son pantalon.**
  13. **Il met la bouteille sur la table.**
  14. **Il prend une serviette.**
  15. **Ils finissent le goûter avant cinq heures.**
  16. **Ils emportent leurs tasses.**
  17. **Jacques arrive avec une bouteille de lait.**
  18. **Josette est assise sur une chaise près de la porte-fenêtre.**
  19. **M. Girard est fatigué.**
  20. **Mme Girard lit un roman policier au lieu de laver les tasses.**

V. 1. **À l'heure du déjeuner; vers midi; midi et demi.**
  2. **Même les enfants ne sont pas souvent affamés.**
  3. **Des tranches de pain, un pot de confiture et du beurre.**
  4. **Il n'y a rien sur la théière, le thé devient très vite froid.**
  5. **Il n'y a pas de café — nous allons prendre du thé pour changer.**
  6. **Malgré sa colère, il ne dit rien.**
  7. **Il finit l'article qu'il lit dans son journal.**
  8. **Suzanne est debout près de la cheminée et loin de la table.**
  9. **Le thé tache mes robes si je renverse ma tasse.**
  10. **Malgré tout, ils finissent leur goûter avant cinq heures.**

VI. 1. **J'ôte mes souliers et mets mes pantoufles.**
  2. **Je finis l'article que je lis et prends ma serviette.**
  3. **Je suis assis(e) sur le tapis et ma tasse est sur le plancher.**
  4. **Je suis debout parce que je n'aime pas mon thé.**
  5. **Je suis assis(e) sur ma chaise près de mon père.**

LEÇON 5:

I. 1. **Ce soir; ce chandail; ce jeu de cartes; ce bureau.**
  2. **Cette laine; cette paire; cette voix; cette coiffure.**
  3. **Ces vêtements; ces chaussettes; ces chemises; ces cravates.**

4. Cet escalier; cet escalier; ce pantalon; cette carte.
5. Ce jardin; ces fleurs; ce pommier; cette armoire (or ce placard).
6. Ils doivent; je peux; il veut; il connaît.
7. Je sais; nous devons; ils veulent; il doit.
8. Je dois; ils savent; nous connaissons; vous voulez (or tu veux).
9. Peut-il? Voulez-vous (or veux-tu)? Faut-il? Doit-il?
10. Savons-nous? Veut-il? Savez-vous (or sais-tu)? Peuvent-ils?

II. 1. **blanc**: *Milk is white.*
2. **verte**: *Grass is green.*
3. **bleu**: *The sky is blue.*
4. **brun**: *Chocolate is brown.*
5. **blanche**: *My cup is white.*
6. **jaune** (etc.): *A carrot is not yellow.*
7. **noir** (etc.): *A cabbage is not black.*
8. **rouge** (etc.): *My dog is not red.*
9. **verte** (etc.): *The door of our sitting-room is not green.*
10. **jaune** (etc.): *My tie is not yellow.*

III. 1. Il est blanc.
2. Elle est verte.
3. Il est bleu.
4. Il est brun.
5. Elle est blanche.
6. Non, elles ne sont pas noires.
7. Non, un chou n'est pas bleu.
8. Non, il n'est pas noir.
9. Non, elle n'est pas blanche.
10. Non, elle n'est pas verte.

IV. 1. Il va en haut.
2. Sais-tu compter?
3. Vous pouvez lire.
4. Pouvons-nous rester en bas?
5. Les parents veulent jouer.
6. Je peux trouver les jeux de cartes.
7. Il faut compter ces cartes.
8. Tu ne dois pas parler.
9. Je ne veux pas jouer.
10. Connaissez-vous Mme Lucas?

V. 1. Non, ils sont en désordre.
2. Le soir ils restent généralement à la maison.
3. Elle laisse un jeu de cartes en haut.
4. Il porte une chemise blanche, une cravate bleue, un chandail de laine, un pantalon, une paire de chaussettes et des souliers noirs ou des pantoufles rouges.
5. Ils doivent aller au lit à sept heures et quart.
6. Ils disent: "Pouvons-nous rester en bas jusqu'à huit heures?"
7. M. Girard porte une chemise blanche.
8. Les enfants doivent aller au lit à sept heures et quart.
9. Elles sont rouges, bleues ou vertes.
10. Elles sont brunes.

VI. 1. Dans notre salle à manger il y a un grand tapis vert; ce tapis est très beau. Les‿enfants jouent sur ce beau tapis quand‿ils ne veulent pas jouer dans le jardin.

2. Dans notre jardin il y a une belle pelouse verte; cette pelouse est très belle quand l'herbe est verte. Les‿enfants jouent sur cette pelouse, mais‿ils ne peuvent pas jouer dans le potager.

3. Dans notre potager il y a beaucoup de beaux légumes verts; papa cultive ces légumes, quand‿il n'est pas trop fatigué (or occupé)! Il dit que nous ne devons pas jouer près de ces légumes. Oui, il ne faut pas faire cela, parce que les légumes qu'on cultive dans les petits potagers sont très bons.

1. *In our dining-room there is a large green carpet; this carpet is very beautiful. The children play on this beautiful carpet when they do not want to play in the garden.*

2. *In our garden there is a beautiful green lawn; this lawn is very beautiful when the grass is green. The children play on this lawn, but they cannot play in the kitchen-garden.*

3. *In our kitchen-garden there are many fine green vegetables; father cultivates these vegetables, when he is not too tired* (or *busy*)! *He says that we must not play near these vegetables. Yes, people must not do that, because vegetables which are grown in small kitchen-gardens are very good.*

VII. There are at least two different ways of getting to the garage. Here is one way:

Tournez à gauche! Attention! Tournez à droite! Prenez le premier tournant à gauche! Attention aux piétons! Prenez le premier tournant à droite! Attention aux piétons! Allez tout droit! Tournez à droite! Tournez à gauche! Prenez le premier tournant à gauche! Allez tout droit! Attention! Arrêtez-vous!

LEÇON 6:

I. 1. Vendez-vous votre maison (or Vends-tu ta maison)?

2. M. et Mme Girard vendent leur maison.

3. M. Girard dit: Jacques, vends tes jouets!

4. Vend-il cette maison (or Est-ce qu'il vend cette maison)?

5. Pourquoi vendent-ils leurs pommes de terre?

6. Jacques vend ses jouets.

7. Je vends mes légumes.

8. Vendez-vous vos pommes (or Vends-tu tes pommes)?

9. Josette vend sa poupée.

10. Nous vendons nos carottes.

II. 1. maintenant   5. souvent   9. innocemment   13. prudemment
   2. encore une fois   6. seulement   10. toujours   14. constamment
   3. patiemment   7. naturellement   11. bien   15. évidemment
   4. attentivement   8. joyeusement   12. surtout   16. violemment

III. 1. *Who knows Mr. and Mrs. Larivière?* **Mme Girard les connaît.**
   2. *Who reads the books and comics?* **Jacques et ses sœurs les lisent.**
   3. *Who takes the armchair near the window?* **Mme Aubert le prend.**
   4. *"Who is looking for me?" asks Jacques.* **"Josette te cherche," dit son père.**
   5. *"Who is looking for us?" they ask.* **"Vos parents vous cherchent," dit le voisin.**
   6. *Where are you putting the cards?* **Je les mets sur la table.**
   7. *Who scolds you now?* **Maman nous gronde maintenant.**
   8. *Do you know Mrs. Lucas?* **Non, je ne la connais pas.**
   9. *Are you looking for the broken toy?* **Non, je ne le cherche pas.**
   10. *Is mother looking for us?* **Oui, elle nous cherche.**

IV. 1. **Donnez-les aux garçons!**   9. **Le vingt et un mars.**
   2. **Ne les donnez pas aux petites filles!**   10. **Le six décembre.**
   3. **Mettez-le sur le plancher!**   11. **Le trente mai.**
   4. **Ne le mets pas sur la table!**   12. **Le quatorze juillet.**
   5. **Grondez-les (or Gronde-les)!**   13. **Le vingt-sept août.**
   6. **Ne nous gronde(z) pas!**   14. **Le seize février.**
   7. **Voici une tasse: mets-la sur la table!**   15. **Le quinze juin.**
   8. **Ne la mettez pas sur le tapis!**   16. **Le premier avril.**

V. 1. **Ils jouent patiemment, attentivement, sans bavarder.**
   2. **Elle rit joyeusement.**
   3. **Il est superstitieux.**
   4. **Elle le demande innocemment.**
   5. **Il les porte au salon.**
   6. **Il les met sur la table de jeu.**
   7. **Il dit: "Voici les cartes vertes, mêlez-les, s'il vous plait."**
   8. **Il faut écrire le nombre de points.**
   9. **Mme Larivière les mélange.**
   10. **M. Larivière les distribue.**
   11. **Ils sont rouges.**
   12. **Ils sont noirs.**
   13. **Non, ils ne sont pas verts, ils sont noirs.**
   14. **Non, ils ne sont pas bleus, ils sont rouges.**
   15. **Il y en a cinquante-deux.**
   16. **Il y en a treize.**

17. **Il y en a seize.**
18. **J'en ai deux.**
19. **J'en ai . . .** (answers here will vary).
20. **Oui, je joue au bridge** (or **Non, je ne joue pas au bridge**).

VI. 1. **Parce que trois de ces cartes montrent la figure.**
    2. **Quand il voit que sa femme n'écrit rien.**
    3. **"Voici les cartes vertes," dit-il à Mme Larivière.**
    4. **Pouvez-vous trouver la solution de cette énigme?**
    5. **Au bout de cinq minutes il le trouve.**

VII. 1. **M. Girard est-il superstitieux?**
    2. **Les enfants de Mme Girard sont-ils souvent très méchants?**
    3. **M. Girard trahit-il sa petite faiblesse?**
    4. **Les sœurs de Jacques jouent-elles dans le jardin?**
    5. **Le garçon donne-t-il une tasse de thé à son père?**

LEÇON 7:

I. 1. **Il y a plusieurs assassinats, des vols, des poursuites, une bagarre, et une scène où le héros sauve la belle dame.**
    2. **Il la conduit avec précaution.**
    3. **Elle le demande souvent d'un ton agressif.**
    4. **Le petit sentier conduit à la rivière.**
    5. **Il prend deux billets, deux places de balcon.**
    6. **On voit les mots "Défense de fumer."**
    7. **Une ouvreuse les conduit à leurs fauteuils.**
    8. **Le héros la sauve à la dernière minute.**
    9. **Il est blanc.**
    10. **Ils sont verts.**
    11. **Elle en reçoit cinquante.**
    12. **Il y en a mille.**
    13. **. . . parce qu'elle a souvent faim après une promenade agréable.**
    14. **. . . parce qu'il aime le confort au coin du feu.**
    15. **Elle l'ajuste parce qu'il fait très froid dehors.**

II. 1. | **j'aperçois** | **nous apercevons** | 4. | **je souffre** | **nous souffrons** |
|---|---|---|---|---|
| **tu aperçois** | **vous apercevez** | | **tu souffres** | **vous souffrez** |
| **il aperçoit** | **ils aperçoivent** | | **il souffre** | **ils souffrent** |

    2. | **je peins** | **nous peignons** | 5. | **je réduis** | **nous réduisons** |
|---|---|---|---|---|
| **tu peins** | **vous peignez** | | **tu réduis** | **vous réduisez** |
| **il peint** | **ils peignent** | | **il réduit** | **ils réduisent** |

    3. | **je pars** | **nous partons** | 6. | **je joins** | **nous joignons** |
|---|---|---|---|---|
| **tu pars** | **vous partez** | | **tu joins** | **vous joignez** |
| **il part** | **ils partent** | | **il joint** | **ils joignent** |

III. 1. J'ai faim mais je n'ai pas soif.
   2. Il a raison, mais sa sœur a tort.
   3. Avez-vous faim et soif? Vos amis ont-ils faim aussi?
   4. Ils n'ont pas froid dans le cinéma, malgré le temps.
   5. Quand il pleut vous ne pouvez (or tu ne peux) pas aller au cinéma.
   6. Quand il fait du brouillard nous ne pouvons pas voir où nous conduisons.
   7. Quand il ne fait pas froid, ils ne portent pas de manteau.
   8. Ils aiment le premier film mais ils n'aiment pas le deuxième film.
   9. N'avez-vous pas froid dans le salon quand il n'y a pas de feu?
   10. Pourquoi fait-il chaud dans la cuisine et froid dans la salle à manger?

IV. continue, donne, jouent, gagne, ramasse, crie, ai, vois, entend, est, exprimer, dit, crains, est, mens, offre, rient, rit, craint, craint, perdre, reprennent, sont, jouent, ouvrir, parle, dit, ai, pouvons, peut, rester, sent.

V. *The game of bridge continues. This time Mrs. Larivière deals the cards. After the bids, they play quickly. Mr. Girard wins the first trick, the second trick, the third trick . . . eleven tricks, and just as he is picking up the twelfth trick Mrs. Girard exclaims, "I haven't any more cards, I see the queen of hearts on the carpet near the fireplace." Her husband hears these words and is on the point of expressing his resentment when she says, "Have no fear, my dear. It's a little joke. I am lying. I apologize to you." The guests laugh heartily; Mr. Girard laughs too. He is not afraid of his wife's jokes, he is no longer afraid of losing his thirteen tricks. They resume the game; all four are happy. They play for an hour almost without opening their mouths. Mr. Girard speaks first; he says, "I am thirsty. We can go into the dining-room and drink some hot coffee. We cannot stay here, this sitting-room smells of tobacco."*
      La partie de bridge continue. Cette fois Mme Larivière donne les cartes. Après les annonces, nous jouons vite. Je gagne le premier pli, le deuxième pli, le troisième pli . . . onze plis, et au moment où je ramasse le douzième pli ma femme crie, "Je n'ai plus de cartes, je vois la dame de cœur sur le tapis près de la cheminée." J'entends ses mots et je suis sur le point d'exprimer mon dépit quand elle dit: "Ne crains rien, mon chéri. C'est une petite plaisanterie. Je mens. Je t'offre mes excuses." Les invités rient de bon cœur; je ris aussi. Je ne crains pas les plaisanteries de ma femme, je ne crains plus de perdre mes treize plis. Nous reprenons la partie; nous sommes heureux tous quatre. Nous jouons pendant une heure presque sans ouvrir la bouche. Je parle le premier; je dis: "J'ai soif. . . ." (The rest of the passage is the same as the original version.)

VI. 1.
Huit‿heures	Neuf‿heures moins vingt-cinq
Huit‿heures cinq	Neuf‿heures moins vingt
Huit‿heures dix	Neuf‿heures moins le quart
Huit‿heures et quart	Neuf‿heures moins dix
Huit‿heures vingt	Neuf‿heures moins cinq
Huit‿heures vingt-cinq	Neuf‿heures
Huit‿heures et demie	

   2. La douzième page, la treizième page, la quatorzième page, la quinzième page, la seizième page, la dix-septième page, la dix-huitième page, la dix-neuvième page, là vingtième page, la vingt‿et unième page, la vingt-deuxième page, la vingt-troisième page, la vingt-quatrième page, la vingt-cinquième page, la vingt-sixième page, la vingt-septième page, la vingt-huitième page, la vingt-neuvième page, la trentième page.

   3. Check your list in the vocabulary at the end of the book and look up Leçon 3 for any words which you may have forgotten.

   4. Here are some examples, note the agreement of the colour adjectives:

les‿yeux bleus	la pomme de terre brune
la carte blanche	le chien brun
l'herbe verte	la chambre rouge
le visage jaune	le mur blanc
le singe noir	le ballon rouge

   5. Check this exercise carefully and learn your corrections.

LEÇON 8:

I. 1. Il est doré.
   2. Elles sont remplies de monde.
   3. Elle est‿économe et difficile à duper.
   4. Ils courent partout.
   5. Elle l'écoute dans‿un coin du marché.
   6. On les voit sur les trottoirs dans la grand'rue.
   7. Le dimanche ils‿aiment manger du bœuf ou du poulet.
   8. Il dit: "Approchez, venez plus près!" (etc.).
   9. Plusieurs marchands de poisson l'ont‿appelée.
  10. Une vieille paysanne les‿a pesés.
  11. Mme Girard les‿a mis dans le panier.
  12. Ils sont verts.
  13. Elle en‿a acheté une demi-douzaine.
  14. On peut la laver en cinq minutes.
  15. Elle l'a acheté pour orner le buffet de la salle à manger.
  16. Elle n'aime pas‿y aller avec les‿enfants parce qu'ils courent partout.
  17. Ils‿y vont parce qu'ils ne travaillent pas le dimanche.
  18. Elle l'a quitté vers midi et quart.

19. **On_y va généralement à onze heures.** (Answers here will vary.)
20. **J'ai commencé à y répondre à midi.** (Answers here will vary.)

II. Correct your own account as much as you can by checking the grammar in the grammar pages and the verb-tables and checking the vocabulary at the end of the book.

III.

lire	écrire	mettre	être	avoir	pouvoir
j'ai lu	**j'ai écrit**	**j'ai mis**	**j'ai été**	**j'ai eu**	**j'ai pu**
tu as lu	etc.	etc.	etc.	etc.	etc.
il a lu					
nous_avons lu					
vous_avez lu					
ils_ont lu					

IV.
1. **tous les garçons**
2. **tout le gâteau**
3. **toutes les poires**
4. **tous les paniers**
5. **tous les gens**
6. **tout le melon**
7. **toute la foule**
8. **toute la semaine**
9. **tous les marchands**
10. **toutes les paysannes**

V.
1. **Je ne peux pas trouver les légumes (qu'elle a achetés).**
2. **Ne peux-tu pas trouver les provisions (que j'ai achetées)?**
3. **Il ne peut pas trouver les pommes (que vous_avez pesées).**
4. **Ne pouvons-nous pas manger les melons dorés (que maman a trouvés)?**
5. **"Quelles poires avez-vous mises sur l'étalage aujourd'hui?" demande sa femme.**
6. **Les marchandises (que les paysans ont vendues au marché), je ne les_ai pas trouvées trop sales.**
7. **L'auto (que votre père a achetée la semaine dernière), je l'ai vue pour la première fois devant votre maison.**
8. **"Combien de poulets avez-vous vendus cette semaine?" a-t-elle demandé.**
9. **Elle les_a achetés au marché (qu'il y a eu dimanche).**
10. **La poupée (que Jacques a cassée) n'a pas de jolies robes.**

1. *I cannot find the vegetables which she bought.*
2. *Can you not find the provisions which I bought?*
3. *He cannot find the apples which you weighed.*
4. *Can we not eat the golden melons which mother found?*
5. *"Which pears have you put on the stall today?" asks his wife.*

6. *I did not find the goods which the country people sold at the market too dirty.*
7. *I have seen for the first time the car which your father bought last week in front of your house.*
8. *"How many chickens have you sold this week?" she asked.*
9. *She bought them at the market which took place on Sunday.*
10. *The doll which Jacques broke has no pretty dresses.*

LEÇON 9:

I. 1. Elle est triste.
2. Elle a décidé d'aller chez son oncle.
3. Elle l'a pris au guichet.
4. Elle a trouvé l'heure d'un train convenable.
5. Avant le départ du train il donne un coup de sifflet.
6. Le garçon télégraphiste ou un messager spécial les apporte.
7. En Angleterre ils sont blancs.
8. Elle a mis un chapeau noir en signe de deuil.
9. ... quand on veut prendre un train convenable.
10. Il a duré deux heures et demie.

Here are examples of the sort of question you may ask:

11. Comment est Mme Girard quand elle quitte la gare à sa destination?
12. Où les enfants restent-ils pendant son absence?
13. Mme Girard, que donne-t-elle au porteur qui la conduit au train?
14. Qui donne un coup de sifflet à l'heure de départ du train?
15. Qu'est-ce qu'il faut faire si le train est en retard?
16. Pourquoi Mme Girard n'aime-t-elle pas les tunnels?
17. Combien de valises un porteur peut-il porter?
18. Quels mots sont inscrits sur les grandes affiches?
19. Quelle couleur doit-on mettre en signe de deuil?
20. De quelle couleur sont les vaches dans les prés?

Here are the answers:

11. Elle est fatiguée et triste.
12. Ils restent chez une amie de leur mère.
13. Elle lui donne un pourboire.
14. Le chef de gare en donne un.
15. Il faut attendre dans la salle d'attente.
16. Elle ne les aime pas parce qu'il fait noir et la fumée de la locomotive entre par les fenêtres.
17. Il peut en porter trois ou quatre.
18. Les heures de départ et d'arrivée y sont inscrites.
19. On doit mettre des vêtements noirs.
20. Les vaches dans les prés sont noires, brunes ou blanches.

II.

j'ai sonné	j'ai emmené	j'ai gardé
tu as sonné	tu as emmené	tu as gardé
il a sonné	il a emmené	il a gardé
nous avons sonné	nous avons emmené	nous avons gardé
vous avez sonné	vous avez emmené	vous avez gardé
ils ont sonné	ils ont emmené	ils ont gardé

j'ai eu	j'ai demandé	j'ai distribué
tu as eu	tu as demandé	tu as distribué
il a eu	il a demandé	il a distribué
nous avons eu	nous avons demandé	nous avons distribué
vous avez eu	vous avez demandé	vous avez distribué
ils ont eu	ils ont demandé	ils ont distribué

je suis parti(e)	je suis tombé(e)	je suis revenu(e)
tu es parti(e)	tu es tombé(e)	tu es revenu(e)
il est parti	il est tombé	il est revenu
elle est partie	elle est tombée	elle est revenue
nous sommes parti(e)s	nous sommes tombé(e)s	nous sommes revenu(e)s
vous êtes parti(e)(s)	vous êtes tombé(e)(s)	vous êtes revenu(e)(s)
ils sont partis	ils sont tombés	ils sont revenus
elles sont parties	elles sont tombées	elles sont revenues

je suis resté(e)	elle est restée	vous êtes resté(e)(s)
tu es resté(e)	nous sommes resté(e)s	ils sont restés
il est resté		elles sont restées

III.
1. Il y a deux semaines.
2. Elle a eu peur.
3. Chez son oncle.
4. Pour faire sa petite valise.
5. Elle a dû attendre.
6. Où on peut aller par le train.
7. En un minute.
8. Où elle n'a jamais vécu.
9. Au bout de deux heures et demie.
10. Toutes les petites villes et tous les villages.
11. La sœur aînée de son père.
12. À n'importe quelle heure de la journée.
13. Il a besoin de la voiture.
14. Elle est montée dedans.
15. Pour passer le temps.
16. Pour être sûr d'attraper le train.
17. Par les fenêtres.
18. À l'horizon.
19. Il y a eu beaucoup d'arrêts.
20. Pour chercher un car.

IV. 1. Ne les avez-vous (or as-tu) pas emmené(e)s chez leur oncle?
2. Les renseignements qu'elle a demandés sont sur l'affiche.
3. Les télégrammes que le messager spécial a distribués sont sur la table.

4. Pourquoi n'a-t-il pas gardé les billets que vous avez donnés à sa femme?
5. Ils n'ont pas encore mangé toutes les poires qu'elle a achetées il y a une semaine.

V. 1. Elle est arrivée avec son frère à six heures et demie du soir.
2. Ils sont entrés dans la gare à trois heures moins le quart.
3. Nous ne sommes pas resté(e)s sur le quai jusqu'à huit heures moins cinq.
4. Pourquoi la vieille dame est-elle tombée sur la voie?
5. Ils sont allés au bureau de renseignements à midi et quart.
6. N'est-elle pas partie avant l'arrivée du taxi?
7. Nous sommes sorti(e)s de la maison à onze heures moins vingt-cinq.
8. Il a sorti son billet pour le montrer au contrôleur.
9. Le porteur a descendu toutes les valises, parce qu'elle est fatiguée.
10. Ils quittent la gare parce qu'il n'y a pas de train avant midi.

VI. Quand j'ai lu la triste nouvelle écrite sur le papier bleu, j'ai décidé d'aller chez mon oncle pour l'enterrement. Malheureusement mon mari ne peut pas me conduire en auto, car il a besoin de la voiture pour aller à son travail. Que vais-je faire? Je dois faire le voyage par le chemin de fer.

Aussitôt je suis allée à la gare pour regarder l'horaire des trains. Les heures de départ et d'arrivée sont inscrites sur de grandes affiches à l'intérieur de la gare. On peut aussi les demander au bureau de renseignements. J'ai enfin trouvé un train convenable, puis je suis rentrée à la maison pour faire ma petite valise. . . . Je n'ai pas pu emmener les enfants qu'une de mes amies a gardés pendant les trois jours de mon absence.

Le moment du départ est arrivé. J'ai mis un manteau gris et un chapeau noir en signe de deuil. Le taxi est arrivé, je suis montée dedans et bientôt je suis descendue devant la gare. J'ai pris un billet aller et retour au guichet. J'ai dû attendre parce que le train est arrivé en retard. Pour passer le temps j'ai acheté une revue au kiosque et suis allée dans la salle d'attente.

LEÇON 10:

I. 1. Il s'est excusé poliment.
2. Ils se rendent à la Truite.
3. Il lui a donné le menu.
4. Il lui a dit: "Choisis, chérie."
5. Elle lui a répondu: "Je ne veux pas de potage."
6. On lui donne généralement un pourboire.
7. Oui, il lui a donné un pourboire généreux.

8. . . . parce qu'il s'est excusé très poliment.
9. Le sommelier l'a apportée. Le garçon l'a apportée.
10. Ils sont blancs. Oui, il y en a.
11. Ils y sont arrivés vers huit heures.
12. Elle a choisi le baba au rhum.
13. . . . parce que c'est son dessert favori.
14. Il y en a deux.
15. Ils se sont promenés près de la rivière.
16. Il a fait beau et chaud.
17. C'est le vingt-six juillet.
18. Il l'a apporté sur un beau plateau d'argent.
19. Non, ils ne s'en sont pas contentés, ils ont commandé une carafe de vin rosé.
20. . . . parce que c'est la fête de Mme Girard.

II. je me suis contenté(e)   je me suis rendu(e)
     tu t'es contenté(e)   tu t'es rendu(e)
     il s'est contenté   il s'est rendu
     elle s'est contentée   elle s'est rendue
     nous nous sommes contenté(e)s   nous nous sommes rendu(e)s
     vous vous êtes contenté(e)(s)   vous vous êtes rendu(e)(s)
     ils se sont contentés   ils se sont rendus
     elles se sont contentées   elles se sont rendues

     je me suis fatigué(e)   je me suis souvenu(e)
     tu t'es fatigué(e)   tu t'es souvenu(e)
     il s'est fatigué   il s'est souvenu
     elle s'est fatiguée   elle s'est souvenue
     nous nous sommes fatigué(e)s   nous nous sommes souvenu(e)s
     vous vous êtes fatigué(e)(s)   vous vous êtes souvenu(e)(s)
     ils se sont fatigués   ils se sont souvenus
     elles se sont fatiguées   elles se sont souvenues

     je me suis sali(e)   nous nous sommes sali(e)s
     tu t'es sali(e)   vous vous êtes sali(e)(s)
     il s'est sali   ils se sont salis
     elle s'est salie   elles se sont salies

III. 1. Je n'ai pas donné de pourboire au garçon parce qu'il ne nous a pas servis.
     2. Je ne lui ai pas donné de pourboire parce que je n'ai pas assez d'argent.

421

3. Je ne le lui ai pas donné parce que le vin n'est pas frais.

4. Il apporte le vin aux Girard; il ne leur apporte pas un verre de bière.

5. Pourquoi ne le leur apporte-t-il pas tout de suite?

6. Le sommelier l'apporte-t-il aux Girard quand ils entrent?

7. Vous m'avez (or tu m'as) vu(e), mais vous ne les avez pas (or tu ne les as pas) vu(e)s.

8. Vous êtes allé(e)(s) (or tu es allé(e)) à la gare, mais je n'y suis pas allé(e).

9. Vous avez (or tu as) bu beaucoup de vin rouge, mais je n'en ai pas bu.

10. Mon ami nous les a donné(e)s, vous ne nous les avez pas vendu(e)s.

11. Je ne lui ai pas donné ce cadeau; sa tante le lui a envoyé.

12. La tasse est-elle sur la table? Oui, Jacques l'y a mise il y a dix minutes.

13. Elle leur en a donné quand ils sont rentrés du restaurant.

14. Ils se salissent toujours quand ils jouent ensemble près de l'eau.

15. Ils s'embrassent toujours, même quand ils se voient dans la rue.

IV.   Check your sentences as carefully as you can using the grammar and vocabulary sections of the book.

V.   Here are some ways of turning the remaining four examples in Exercise IV into questions. Check the expressions of time in your own questions using the grammar section in Leçon 3.

Est-ce que je me suis habillé(e) à onze heures?

Me suis-je lavé(e) à neuf heures moins le quart?

Est-ce que j'ai pris mon petit déjeuner à minuit moins vingt?

Est-ce que je suis allé(e) en ville à quatre heures dix?

LEÇON 11:

I. 1. Ils sont beaux et reliés.

2. Ils ne pourront pas les passer dans un hôtel au bord de la mer.

3. Elle lui écrit une lettre pour demander s'il pourra les recevoir.

4. Il lui répond qu'il pourra les recevoir.

5. Non, il va en avoir seulement un mois.

6. ... parce qu'ils ont fait de grandes dépenses pendant l'hiver.

7. Elles sont généralement blanches.

8. Elles se sont rassemblées à onze heures précises.

9. Elles y sont rentrées à midi et demi.

10. La distribution des prix a eu lieu avant les grandes vacances.

11. Il fait beau et chaud.

12. Tante Louise va les préparer.

13. Il les a félicitées de leur succès au cours de l'année passée.

14. Elle en a reçu deux.

15. ... parce que ses enfants sont mariés maintenant.

II.

je commencerai	je ferai	je courrai	je voudrai
tu commenceras	tu feras	tu courras	tu voudras
il commencera	il fera	il courra	il voudra
nous commencerons	nous ferons	nous courrons	nous voudrons
vous commencerez	vous ferez	vous courrez	vous voudrez
ils commenceront	ils feront	ils courront	ils voudront

je viendrai	je devrai	je recevrai	je vendrai
tu viendras	tu devras	tu recevras	tu vendras
il viendra	il devra	il recevra	il vendra
nous viendrons	nous devrons	nous recevrons	nous vendrons
vous viendrez	vous devrez	vous recevrez	vous vendrez
ils viendront	ils devront	ils recevront	ils vendront

je verrai	nous verrons	je saurai	nous saurons
tu verras	vous verrez	tu sauras	vous saurez
il verra	ils verront	il saura	ils sauront

III.
1. Plus d'une dizaine de jours.
2. Qu'en penses-tu?
3. Cela pourra se faire.
4. Les grandes vacances seront bientôt là.
5. Y as-tu pensé?
6. Peut-être irons-nous sur une petite plage de Normandie.
7. Nous avons fait pendant l'hiver de grandes dépenses.
8. Cela me changera du bureau.
9. L'école que fréquentent Suzanne et Josette.
10. La directrice s'est mise à lire la longue liste.
11. J'espère que vous passerez de bonnes vacances.
12. La rentrée aura lieu le quinze septembre.
13. J'en suis sûr.
14. L'oncle Julien se fait vieux.
15. Habillées de leur robe de fête.

IV.
1. Nous cueillerons des fleurs dans les bois.
2. Nous allons partir dans une demi-heure, à huit heures moins le quart.
3. Je m'essuierai les mains dans la salle de bain.
4. Il espérera sans doute que vous mettrez (or tu mettras) de l'argent de côté.
5. Ils jettent toujours leurs chapeaux sur le canapé.
6. À la fin de la semaine elle achète beaucoup de légumes.
7. Je me lève à sept heures et demie quand je dois aller au bureau.
8. Je m'assiérai derrière les élèves s'il y a assez de place.

9. **Quand il arrivera ce soir je préparerai son repas de soir.**
10. **Ils croient que vous buvez** (or **tu bois**) **trop de thé après vos** (or **tes**) **repas.**

V.   Here are additional examples which should help you to check your own work.

Je prendrai du café pour mon petit déjeuner à huit heures moins cinq.

Je sortirai de la maison à huit heures vingt pour prendre l'autobus.

À l'école (or **au bureau**) **je travaillerai jusqu'à midi et demi.**

À une heure moins le quart nous irons, mes amis et moi, au restaurant pour le déjeuner.

Nous nous promènerons dans les bois pendant une demi-heure jusqu'à deux heures.

Nous jouerons au tennis à quatre heures.

Je prendrai mon repas du soir à six heures moins le quart.

J'aiderai à ma mère à faire la vaisselle à six heures vingt-cinq.

À sept heures moins dix j'irai au cinéma voir un film policier.

Mon ami et moi, nous boirons une tasse de café à neuf heures et quart.

Je rentrai chez moi à bicyclette vers dix heures.

À onze heures moins vingt je me laverai la figure et les mains et je m'essuierai avec ma serviette avant d'aller au lit.

Je m'endormirai vers onze heures.

VI. 1. **Je ne le leur donnerai pas demain.**
2. **Ne les finiront-ils pas avant huit heures moins le quart?**
3. **Ils sont allés dans la cour et y ont vu le maire et sa femme.**
4. **Il a cueilli des fleurs mais il ne leur en donnera pas.**
5. **Ne nous les donneront-ils pas après les vacances?**

LEÇON 12:

I. 1. **Ils en font sur les pentes.**
2. **Il a fait semblant de lui lancer son projectile, une grenouille.**
3. **Elle veut y revenir pour faire du ski.**
4. **Elles sont vertes.**
5. **Ils y sont arrivés vers trois heures et demie de l'après-midi.**
6. **Ils se sont sauvés derrière les arbres et les buissons.**
7. **Elle va y passer quatre semaines.**
8. **Tante Louise et Mme Girard ont préparé leur goûter.**
9. **Oui, j'y en ai fait** (or **Non, je n'y en ai jamais fait**).
10. **Oui, elles sont comestibles** (or **Oui, elles le sont**). **On les mange en France.**

II. 1. Le deux août, vers trois heures et demie de l'après-midi.

2. Pourvu qu'ils se taisent au cours des repas et pendant la nuit.

3. Josette aussi s'est approchée d'eux et l'a regardée de près.

4. Ça ne vaut pas la peine de chercher des champignons aujourd'hui.

5. Les enfants ont continué à chanter, à quelque distance de lui.

6. La prochaine fois c'est moi qui serai le loup.

7. Ils n'en ont pas beaucoup trouvé ce jour-là.

III. 1. Sans moi.

2. Pour elles.

3. Près de nous.

4. Y or dessus.

5. Malgré elles.

6. Contre eux.

7. Je pense à lui.

8. C'est moi qui les aidés.

9. C'est vous qu'ils ont invités.

10. C'est lui qu'ils ont écouté.

11. C'est elle qui les a trouvés.

12. C'est nous que tu as entendus.

13. C'est vous qui les avez mangés.

14. Ce sont eux qu'il a attrapés ici.

15. Ce sont elles qui les ont cueillies.

16. Mon ami et moi y sommes allés avec mon père.

17. Son ami(e) et lui n'y sont pas arrivés en retard.

18. Eux et nous sommes arrivés ensemble avant la fin du premier film.

19. Je crois que tu as raison mais ils croiront que tu as tort.

20. Donnez-moi du pain et du miel, s'il vous plaît.

21. Donnez-le-leur!

22. Donnez-moi cette tasse!

23. Ne me les donnez pas!

24. Lave-toi dans la salle de bain!

25. Ne le leur donnons pas!

26. Lavons-nous dans la rivière!

27. Soyons sages!

28. Ne soyez pas impatient(s)!

29. Donnes-en à ton frère!

30. N'ayons pas peur!

LEÇON 13:

I. 1. Selon l'auteur la vie d'un lycéen était très triste.

2. Quand on arrivait au lycée on entrait dans la cour et saluait ses amis.

3. Il brandissait son livre comme une épée.

4. Non, ils étaient généralement de mauvaise humeur.

5. Le mauvais élève s'appelait François.

II. 1. *I have only two books and I have no pen.*

2. *He says nothing to the teacher because he is guilty.*

3. *He did not go to market on Mondays; he remained at home.*

4. *I used to leave the house early so as not to be late.*

5. *The pupil was busy copying out his exercise again.*

6. *The naughty boy was hiding a mouse in his desk.*

7. *My father had a big stick in his hand.*

8. *When we left it was raining.*

9. *I know that she saw nobody in the street.*
10. *He always asks me the same question. How boring it is!*

III. 1. Je ne la voyais jamais dans la rue.
    2. Cet après-midi nous y allons.
    3. Nous en avons vu six dans la boîte.
    4. Donnez-lui les cahiers.
    5. Ils leur ont dit la vérité.
    6. Ne lui parlez pas.
    7. Il faut en profiter pour étudier l'anglais.
    8. Combien en avez-vous dans votre poche?

IV.   Tous les jours Mme Dubois se levait de bonne heure, se lavait dans la salle de bain et descendait à la cuisine préparer son petit déjeuner. Le matin elle ne mangeait pas beaucoup. Après le petit déjeuner elle lavait la vaisselle et faisait le ménage. Vers dix heures et quart elle sortait pour aller en ville faire des emplettes. Elle prenait l'autobus au coin de la rue et descendait près de la gare. Elle allait droit au marché où elle achetait des légumes, des fruits et des œufs. Elle revenait chez elle à onze heures et quart et commençait à préparer le repas de midi.

V. 1. Pendant les vacances nous allions au bord de la mer.
    2. Je ne suis pas coupable. Je n'ai jamais fait de mal à personne.
    3. De temps en temps il écrivait un mot au tableau noir.
    4. Tous les jours en classe nous lisions à haute voix.
    5. Je vais vous poser une question très facile.
    6. Mon ami pensait aux vacances quand le professeur est entré.
    7. En ce temps-là nous étudions l'anglais et l'allemand.
    8. Arrivés à l'école à huit heures et demie, nous entrions dans la cour.
    9. Après avoir fini son travail l'homme se lavait et retournait chez lui.
    10. Le professeur grondait les élèves quand ils disaient des bêtises.

LEÇON 14:

I. 1. Il y a trois grands magasins dans notre ville.
    2. "Bondé" veut dire "rempli de gens." Le salle était bondée.
    3. À la devanture d'un magasin on voit souvent des mannequins.
    4. Celui qui fait un discours s'appelle un orateur.
    5. Non, les gens polis ne se bousculent jamais.
    6. Dans un grand magasin on peut voir des habits, des robes, des manteaux, des meubles, des livres, etc.
    7. On prend l'ascenseur pour monter au troisième.
    8. Le restaurant se trouve tout en haut du bâtiment.

9. Non, le gérant ne vend pas les marchandises; il travaille dans son bureau.
10. Non, je n'aime pas faire des réclamations dans un magasin.

II. 1. *I have read these books but I have not read those.*
2. *Here are two dresses: this one is red, that one is blue.*
3. *That pupil is the one to whom I spoke in the playground.*
4. *Which flowers are the prettiest? These.*
5. *The man you are speaking about is a good-for-nothing.*
6. *She who is sitting in the armchair is James' aunt.*
7. *You can see the father and the uncle there; the latter is older than the former.*
8. *Which fountain-pen do you prefer? This one.*
9. *John's suit is blue, Andrew's is grey.*
10. *Those who work well make progress.*

III. 1. Il ne pleuvait plus quand je suis sorti.
2. Je n'ai vu personne dans la rue quand je suis arrivé.
3. Aujourd'hui ils n'ont rien fait d'amusant.
4. Il promet de ne rien dire.
5. Je n'avais que vingt francs dans ma poche.
6. Au lieu de répondre il a commencé à pleurer.
7. Après avoir regardé sa montre, il est sorti du magasin.
8. Il écrivait quelques mots au tableau noir.
9. C'est un mauvais père: il ne se soucie pas de ses enfants.
10. Il ne voulait pas répondre à la question.

IV. 1. Il en a fait un à l'assemblée.
2. Cet après-midi j'y ai assisté.
3. Montrez-lui votre nouveau stylo.
4. Nous en avons vu une sur le trottoir.
5. Le vendeur leur donne les paquets.

V. 1. Nous voyons beaucoup de monde au rez-de-chaussée.
2. Le rayon des meubles est au deuxième étage.
3. Je vais acheter le dictionnaire que je vois sur le comptoir.
4. Il va en ville deux fois par jour.
5. J'y serai à sept heures et demie sans faute.
6. Les jeunes femmes font la queue à la porte.
7. De temps en temps je vois un de mes amis en ville.
8. Montrez-moi l'article en question, s'il vous plaît.
9. Sur le trottoir on se bouscule et se coudoie.
10. Je n'ai pas les moyens d'acheter un poste de télévision comme je suis à court d'argent.

LEÇON 15:

I. 1. Il s'appelle M. Durand.
   2. Il est très bavard.
   3. Oui, j'aime beaucoup lire le journal.
   4. Il a mauvaise opinion des membres du gouvernement.
   5. S'il était premier ministre, il mettrait fin aux abus.
   6. Il était un petit commerçant.
   7. Oui, j'en connais plusieurs.
   8. Si j'étais millionnaire, je donnerais de l'argent aux pauvres.
   9. Oui, j'en connais. "Bavard" veut dire "loquace, qui parle beaucoup."
   10. Oui, si j'avais assez d'argent, j'irais en France.

II. 1. *If it rains tomorrow, I shall not go to town.*
   2. *Even if she were rich, she would not be happy.*
   3. *The train which has just entered the station is not the one we are waiting for.*
   4. *I should not answer him if he asked me a question.*
   5. *If it poured with rain, she would not go out.*
   6. *I ought to do my homework but I must go to town.*
   7. *The table which is at the back of the room is made of oak.*
   8. *The room in which there were two large beds was at the end of the corridor.*
   9. *The man we have just left is a merchant.*
   10. *Last night my neighbour attended a concert in town.*

III. 1. Je l'ai aperçu qui travaillait dans son jardin.
   2. Nous en avons perdu cinq.
   3. J'y vais tous les matins.
   4. Qu'en pensez-vous?
   5. Il les garde dans un album.

IV. 1. Il appelle, ils appellent; il jette, ils jettent; il se plaît, ils se plaisent; il aperçoit, ils aperçoivent; il souffre, ils souffrent; il doit, ils doivent.
   2. J'étais, nous étions; je me taisais, nous nous taisions; je jetais, nous jetions; tu sauras, vous sauriez; tu iras, vous irez; tu tiendras, vous tiendrez.
   3. Tu voudrais, vous voudriez; tu t'assiérais, vous vous assiériez; elle a pu, elles ont pu; elle est tombée, elles sont tombées.

V. 1. Je voudrais aller au théâtre ce soir.
   2. Que feriez-vous si vous aviez beaucoup d'argent?
   3. Il a dit qu'il viendrait quand il serait en ville.
   4. Nous devrions faire toujours notre devoir.

5. **Elle ne savait pas s'il irait en France.**
6. **Pourriez-vous me rendre ce service?**
7. **Que dirait-il, si je le trompais?**
8. **Elle chercherait partout qu'elle ne le trouverait pas.**
9. **S'il arrivait en retard, que dirait le maître?**
10. **Il voulait savoir s'ils arriveraient à temps.**

VI. 1. **De temps en temps il me voit dans le jardin.**
2. **Je n'ai pas envie de vous parler aujourd'hui.**
3. **Sans me laisser le temps de répondre, il s'est fâché.**
4. **Je ne sais pas ce que je ferais sans vous.**
5. **Ils viennent d'apprendre que le premier ministre arrivera bientôt.**
6. **Le livre que je viens de trouver est rouge.**
7. **Ils doivent travailler du matin au soir. Quel dommage!**
8. **Il est entré dans la maison et il a trouvé que son oncle venait de partir.**
9. **Je ne sais même pas ce dont il s'agit.**
10. **Ils devraient être polis même s'ils sont riches.**

LEÇON 16:

I. 1. **La Belgique se trouve au nord de la France.**
2. **L'Espagne se trouve au sud.**
3. **La superficie de la France est de 551.000 kilomètres carrés.**
4. **56% de la population française habite des villes.**
5. **Non, la France ne produit que les trois quarts du charbon dont elle a besoin.**
6. **L'énergie hydro-électrique compense dans une certaine mesure le manque de charbon.**
7. **Les filatures principales se trouvent au nord.**
8. **La France est célèbre pour son vin.**
9. **Non, on préfère le café.**
10. **Cela dépend. Je ne sais pas si j'aurai assez d'argent.**

II. 1. *Brussels is 270 km. from Paris as the crow flies.*
2. *The sum lost was a thousand francs.*
3. *After waiting ten minutes he went away.*
4. *I wonder whether they are able to do that.*
5. *What would I not do for my mother?*
6. *The inn is some two hundred metres from the square.*
7. *I must buy a dozen fresh eggs.*
8. *She has gone to spend a fortnight at the seaside.*
9. *If I am not mistaken, he died in 1958.*
10. *In Belgium instead of saying "soixante-dix" they say "septante."*

III. 1. Quinze, vingt et un, quatre-vingt-un, cent un, deux cent un, soixante-quinze, quatre-vingt-seize, quatre-vingts, quatre-vingt-sept, trois cent quatre-vingt-quatre, trente-neuf, quarante-deux, cinquante et un, soixante-huit, quatre-vingt-onze, deux mille cinq cent cinquante-cinq, quatre cent soixante-douze, neuf cent quatre-vingt-onze.

2. Le premier avril, dix-neuf cent vingt; le trente octobre dix-neuf cent soixante; le quatorze juillet dix-sept cent quatre-vingt-neuf; le quatre août dix-neuf cent quatorze; le trois septembre dix-neuf cent trente-neuf.

3. Un demi, deux tiers, trois quarts, cinq sixièmes, huit neuvièmes, neuf dixièmes, onze douzièmes, treize quatorzièmes, quinze seizièmes, vingt vingt et unièmes.

IV. 1. Une vingtaine d'hommes.
2. Une cinquantaine de villes.
3. Une douzaine de plumes.
4. Une centaine de soldats.
5. Des milliers de livres.
6. Il a passé la cinquantaine.

V. 1. Si j'avais mille livres, je serais riche.
2. Qui le croirait s'il disait cela?
3. Que ne ferais-je pour elle?
4. S'il pleuvait à verse, je resterais à la maison.
5. Est-ce qu'on pourrait le faire en deux heures?
6. S'il remontait la rue, je le verrais tout de suite.
7. Si j'en avais assez, j'en enverrais un paquet à mon ami.
8. Il aurait tort s'il disait cela.
9. Si elle faisait attention, elle poserait des questions.
10. On aurait dit qu'il était fou.

VI. 1. En France on cultive le blé, les pommes de terre, les betteraves à sucre et le tabac.
2. Il faut mentionner aussi l'industrie automobile.
3. En Angleterre quatre-vingts pour cent de la population habite des villes.
4. Où les étrangers riches passent-ils leurs vacances?
5. Si j'ai assez d'argent, j'irai en France l'année prochaine.
6. La superficie du pays est de cinq cent cinquante et un mille kilomètres carrés.
7. Je me demande où il était la semaine dernière.
8. Si l'on va en Espagne on traverse la frontière française à Hendaye.
9. À cause du temps il n'est pas allé hier chez sa tante.
10. On boit le café en France mais je connais des Français qui aiment le thé.

ANSWERS TO EXERCISES

LEÇON 17:

I. 1. Il avait une belle voiture.
   2. Vous avez quitté la maison vers dix heures du matin.
   3. Elle avait deux cents mètres de haut.
   4. Ils donnaient de furieux coups de klaxon parce que vous rouliez au beau milieu de la route.
   5. En approchant d'un passage à niveau on devrait ralentir.
   6. Vous lui aviez dit que vous rentreriez vers six heures du soir.
   7. Au contraire, c'est très désagréable et souvent dangereux.
   8. Le contraire de "large" est "étroit."
   9. Vous avez serré le frein à main.
   10. Non, il était furieux.

II. 1. *He had gone to get a plank three metres long.*
   2. *What are the dimensions of this room?*
   3. *This room is eight metres long, six metres wide and four metres high.*
   4. *There is a wall six feet high.*
   5. *The little boy who had fallen in the water was six years old.*
   6. *Alas! We had lost our way in the wood.*
   7. *What had he done to deserve such a severe punishment?*
   8. *We had started out without thinking of what might happen.*
   9. *Had you noticed that the poor woman was weeping?*
   10. *What would you have said if you had seen someone driving like a madman?*

III. 1. J'étais allé(e); j'avais eu; j'avais connu; j'avais dû; j'avais dit; j'avais écrit; j'avais été; j'avais fait; je m'étais levé(e); j'avais lu; j'étais né(e); j'étais parti(e); j'avais pu; j'avais pris; j'avais ri; j'avais su; j'étais tombé(e); j'étais venu(e); j'avais vu; j'avais voulu.
   2. Elles étaient allées; elles avaient eu; elles avaient connu; elles avaient dû; elles avaient dit; elles avaient écrit; elles avaient été; elles avaient fait; elles s'étaient levées; elles avaient lu; elles étaient nées; elles étaient parties; elles avaient pu; elles avaient pris; elles avaient ri; elles avaient su; elles étaient tombées; elles étaient venues; elles avaient vu; elles avaient voulu.

IV. 1. Elle ne l'a pas vu.
   2. Tous les jours j'allais chez lui.
   3. Il le lui a donné.
   4. Nous y en avons mis une vingtaine.
   5. Donnez-le-moi tout de suite. Ne le laissez pas tomber.

431

V. 1. Mon_ami conduisait_une voiture rouge.
    2. Nous_avons_assez de pommes, merci.
    3. J'ai dit au garçon boucher d'apporter la viande avant midi.
    4. L'auto filait_à toute vitesse.
    5. Sa figure était couverte d'encre.

VI. 1. Cette salle a vingt-cinq pieds de long.
    2. Le lac a cinq mètres de profondeur.
    3. La planche a trois centimètres d'épaisseur.
    4. Il était_arrivé trop tard.
    5. La salle à manger a quarante mètres sur vingt mètres.
    6. Au bout du parc il y a un mur haut de huit pieds.
    7. Sa boîte n'a que dix centimètres de long.
    8. Elle n'avait pas fini le travail.
    9. Il s'était_assis pour se reposer.
   10. Ils_avaient donné de l'argent aux_enfants.

VII. 1. En_été il est_agréable de faire une promenade en_auto.
    2. On doit s'arrêter (stopper) quand_on voit les feux rouges.
    3. Où est votre permis de conduite? Voilà un_agent qui arrive.
    4. Vers dix_heures la pluie a commencé à tomber.
    5. Je commençais à me fâcher car nous_allions trop vite.
    6. Ce n'est pas la peine de sortir ce soir; restons à la maison.
    7. Dix minutes se sont_écoulées. Tout_à coup il a dit: "Ça sent le brûlé."

LEÇON 18:

I. 1. À l'étable on trouve les vaches.
    2. On laboure la terre avec la charrue.
    3. Il y va vendre ses bêtes.
    4. Quand_un_animal est malade, on fait venir le vétérinaire.
    5. Le fermier cultive le blé, l'avoine et l'orge.
    6. Ce sont les valets de ferme qui aident le fermier.
    7. Une besogne est_une tâche.
    8. Il va d'abord au marché. Après, il bavarde avec ses_amis.
    9. Il craint la pluie parce qu'elle peut lui causer des pertes.
   10. Après l'avoir coupé, on met le blé dans les granges.

II. 1. *I do not know what has become of them.*
    2. *The farmer he is speaking about is a rich man.*
    3. *The fountain-pen with which he is writing at the moment belongs to me.*
    4. *The principles for which he is fighting are excellent.*
    5. *He doesn't go there any more. That's a strange thing.*

6. *It's enough to drive you mad.*
7. *The events to which you refer took place last year.*
8. *You who are complaining all the time do not work hard enough.*
9. *My neighbour's son who has just taken his examination is a lazy pupil.*
10. *Those present, among whom were a few enemy agents, were behaving in a disorderly manner.*

III. 1. **Ils reçoivent; ils disent; ils prennent; ils vainquent; ils naissent; ils lisent; ils mettent; ils font; ils sèment; ils peuvent.**
   2. **Nous devrons; nous courrons; nous cueillerons; nous enverrons; nous mourrons; nous ferons; nous saurons; nous ouvrirons; nous serons; nous irons.**
   3. **Je viendrais; je verrais; je boirais; j'irais; j'aurais.**
   4. **Lu; venu; dû; écrit; vu; pu; voulu; fait; mis; pris.**

IV. 1. **La ferme à laquelle (or où) je passe mes vacances n'est pas grande.**
   2. **Il a soupé à neuf heures, après quoi il s'est couché.**
   3. **La femme pour le fils de qui (or duquel) il a fait tant de sacrifices l'estime beaucoup.**
   4. **Le marchand dont la femme est si méchante n'est pas heureux.**
   5. **Les élèves à qui j'avais donné des conseils m'ont fait un petit cadeau.**

V. 1. **Cette grange fait partie de la ferme que vous voyez là-bas.**
   2. **Le fermier dont je parle est un homme très laborieux.**
   3. **De nos jours le tracteur commence à remplacer les bœufs.**
   4. **Ils travaillent du matin au soir à couper le blé.**
   5. **Il ne peut pas faire tout cela à lui seul. C'est impossible.**
   6. **Il redoute le mauvais temps qui lui cause des pertes considérables.**
   7. **Il faut se lever de bonne heure, ce que je déteste.**
   8. **Dans son jardin potager il cultive des pommes de terre, des carottes et des navets.**
   9. **Chaque semaine je vais au marché vendre mes vaches ou acheter ce dont j'ai besoin.**
   10. **Dans la ferme on entend les vaches qui meuglent, les chevaux qui hennissent et les chiens qui aboient.**

LEÇON 19:

I. 1. **Il avait envie de faire du camping.**
   2. **Elle y consentit parce qu'elle voulait faire plaisir à son mari.**
   3. **Dans le coffre de l'auto ils mirent la tente, les cordes, les piquets, le maillet et les ustensiles de cuisine.**

4. Non, elle ne l'aida pas à dresser la tente.
5. Il pleuvait pendant la nuit.
6. Les gouttes de pluie qui tombaient les réveillèrent.
7. Elle dit: "Je ne reste plus ici."
8. Elle voulait y retourner parce qu'elle était trempée jusqu'aux os.
9. Pas du tout. Il fit des protestations.
10. Le lendemain matin ils revinrent à la maison.

II. 1. *It was pouring with rain when they set out.*
2. *It is impossible to know whether he is dead or not.*
3. *Arriving at the village, they got out at the inn.*
4. *A shot rang out in the forest.*
5. *He was fifty when he went to Paris.*
6. *As he was tired, he fell asleep immediately.*
7. *A misfortune came and upset our peaceful existence.*
8. *He made too many mistakes in his exercise.*
9. *It is sometimes pleasant to pass the night in a tent.*
10. *One day a letter arrived which made my friend sad.*

III. 1. Il alla; il fut; il prit; il monta; il répondit; il fit; il eut; il reçut; il dut; il conduisit; il rougit; il attendit; il vint; il mit; il ouvrit.
2. Nous allâmes; nous fûmes; nous prîmes; nous montâmes; nous répondîmes; nous fîmes; nous eûmes; nous reçûmes; nous dûmes; nous conduisîmes; nous rougîmes; nous attendîmes; nous vînmes; nous mîmes; nous ouvrîmes.
3. Ils allèrent; ils furent; ils prirent; ils montèrent; ils répondirent; ils firent; ils eurent; ils reçurent; ils durent; ils conduisirent; ils rougirent; ils attendirent; ils vinrent; ils mirent; ils ouvrirent.

IV. En ce temps-là Jean était assez jeune; je crois qu'il avait huit ans. Son père travaillait dans un bureau qui se trouvait de l'autre côté de la ville. Un jour que son père était sorti, un étranger se présenta à la porte et demanda d'un ton brusque si c'était bien là que demeurait M. Lekeux. Jean répondit que oui. Alors l'inconnu demanda s'il était visible. Jean dit que non et expliqua que son père était en ville. L'inconnu dit qu'il attendrait son retour et il pénétra dans la maison sans plus de façons. Jean qui était tout petit avait peur de cet homme énorme. Celui-ci sortit de sa poche un paquet de cigarettes, frotta une allumette et alluma une cigarette. Puis, il se mit à examiner la pièce. Jean se demandait s'il allait voler quelque chose.

V. 1. **Il est trois heures et demie.**   6. **Il est six heures et quart.**
   2. **À quatre heures moins le quart.**   7. **Il est neuf heures vingt.**
   3. **À minuit et demi.**   8. **Il faut le faire.**
   4. **À huit heures du soir.**   9. **Il fait du vent.**
   5. **À sept heures du matin.**   10. **De quoi s'agit-il?**

VI. 1. **"Je suis trempé jusqu'aux os," dit le campeur.**
   2. **À vrai dire, je ne suis pas un enthousiaste du camping.**
   3. **Il faisait du vent et il pleuvait à verse quand ils arrivèrent au village.**
   4. **Ce disant, il claqua la porte et sortit de la maison.**
   5. **La nuit tombait quand ils descendirent à l'hôtel.**
   6. **Elle s'introduisit vite sous la tente parce qu'il faisait froid dehors.**
   7. **Ils étaient tous les deux très fatigués et ils s'endormirent bientôt.**
   8. **Il consentit à travailler au jardin jusqu'à cinq heures.**
   9. **Il sortit une boîte d'allumettes de sa poche et frotta une allumette.**
   10. **Il s'agit d'arriver à la maison avant le retour de mon père.**

LEÇON 20:

I. 1. **La Seconde Guerre mondiale éclata le premier septembre 1939.**
   2. **Pendant l'hiver de 1939 les Allemands se livrèrent à la propagande.**
   3. **Ils n'avaient pas oublié les horreurs et les pertes de la guerre de 1914.**
   4. **Les Allemands mirent moins de deux mois à écraser la France.**
   5. **On signa l'armistice dans la forêt de Compiègne.**

II. 1. *On Fridays I generally go to the market.*
   2. *He murders French when he speaks it* (literally *He speaks French like a Spanish cow*).
   3. *Translate this piece into Italian.*
   4. *They cut off his head because he had fought against the king.*
   5. *How much are these apples? One franc a kilo.*
   6. *Captain Dupont arrived in Germany on the seventh of May.*
   7. *Nowadays nylon is used in numerous industries*
   8. *He fell in love with fair Isabel.*
   9. *Take care! I am at the end of my patience.*
   10. *When he was in Switzerland he wrote a few letters to us.*

III. 1. **Il envahit, ils envahirent; il demanda, ils demandèrent; il protégea, ils protégèrent; il commença, ils commencèrent; il naquit, ils naquirent; il appela, ils appelèrent; il put, ils purent; il voulut, ils voulurent; il écrivit, ils écrivirent; il fuit, ils fuirent; il fut, ils furent; il eut, ils eurent.**

2. Je serais, nous serions; je viendrais, nous viendrions; je jetterais, nous jetterions; j'écrirais, nous écririons; je ferais, nous ferions; je pourrais, nous pourrions; j'appellerais, nous appellerions; je tiendrais, nous tiendrions; je saurais, nous saurions; je m'assiérais, nous nous assiérions.

3. Tu avais dit, vous aviez dit; tu avais couru, vous aviez couru; tu t'étais levé(e), vous vous étiez levé(e)(s); tu étais arrivé(e), vous étiez arrivé(e)(s); tu avais mis, vous aviez mis; tu avais pris, vous aviez pris; tu avais pu, vous aviez pu; tu étais descendu(e), vous étiez descendu(e)(s); tu avais couvert, vous aviez couvert; tu étais monté(e), vous étiez monté(e)(s).

IV. Ce jour-là il ne faisait pas beau temps. Soudain il commença à pleuvoir à verse. Pierre se dépêcha pour arriver à la maison car il voulait parler avec son frère. Quand il rentra il trouva que celui-ci était sorti faire une commission pour leur maman. Jean (c'était son frère) revint peu de temps après. Pierre lui parla du vieux matelot qu'il avait rencontré au port et il lui répéta tout ce que le vieillard lui avait raconté. Pierre expliqua aussi qu'il n'avait pas pu trouver le jeune homme qu'ils avaient rencontré la veille. Son frère l'écouta avec intérêt mais il ne dit rien. Cinq minutes plus tard les deux frères quittèrent (or quittaient) la maison à l'insu de leur mère qui travaillait dans la cuisine.

V. 1. Je parle français et à présent j'étudie l'allemand.
2. On dit que l'Allemagne est devenue un pays riche.
3. Levez la main si vous savez ce que ce mot veut dire.
4. Il s'est foulé le pied en jouant au tennis.
5. Le jeudi nous allons toujours au théâtre.
6. Au printemps il fait souvent beau temps. C'est pourquoi j'aime le printemps.
7. Le roi Edouard VII naquit en 1841.
8. Demain je partirai pour l'Espagne où il fait toujours chaud en été.
9. Après le déjeuner il fit une promenade à la campagne.
10. Le cuivre est un métal rougeâtre, n'est-ce pas?

VI. Le premier septembre les Allemands attaquèrent la Pologne. Le trois septembre la Grande-Bretagne et la France déclarèrent la guerre à l'Allemagne. Ainsi commença la Seconde Guerre mondiale. La résistance de la Pologne ne dura pas longtemps et les Allemands occupèrent bientôt tout le pays. Le dix mai 1940, Hitler attaqua à l'ouest. Les troupes allemandes franchirent les frontières de la Hollande et de la Belgique. Les armées alliées ne purent pas arrêter

436

les Allemands et les Belges se rendirent. Par conséquent, l'armée britannique dut se retirer vers Dunkerque où, grâce à la flotte anglaise, elle put s'embarquer et rentrer en Angleterre.

LEÇON 21:

I. 1. Il prenait le train tous les matins pour aller au bureau.
    2. Il travaillait en ville.
    3. Lundi dernier tout alla de travers.
    4. Les dactylos tapent des lettres à la machine.
    5. Il l'accrocha à un clou.
    6. Le garçon de bureau lui dit que le chef voulait lui parler tout de suite.
    7. C'était un homme féroce qui portait de grandes moustaches noires.
    8. M. Duval avait oublié les clefs du coffre-fort.
    9. Il toussait parce que le chef fumait une pipe qui répandait un nuage de fumée.
    10. Le téléphone sonna, ce qui mit fin à l'entrevue.

II. 1. *We have no money. It's a pity.*
     2. *On that day there were only young men in the swimming-pool.*
     3. *He had lost everything — house, furniture and money.*
     4. *The young man wanted to be a soldier but his father was against it.*
     5. *The burglar carried neither revolver nor knife.*
     6. *He was so pleased that he threw his hat in the air.*
     7. *As he was a foreigner everybody mistrusted him.*
     8. *The majority of the workers were Italians.*
     9. *On arriving at the workshop she set to work.*
     10. *Suddenly the swimmer shouted: "Help!" and disappeared beneath the water.*

III. Il but, ils burent; il conduisit, ils conduisirent; il dit, ils dirent; il fut, ils furent; il lut, ils lurent; il porta, ils portèrent; il put, ils purent; il sut, ils surent; il suivit, ils suivirent; il vint, ils vinrent.

IV. 1. Ils ont déjà fait la leur.
     2. Avez-vous vu la nôtre?
     3. Prêtez-moi votre crayon; j'ai perdu le mien.
     4. Voici ma bicyclette. Où est la vôtre?
     5. La mienne est sur la commode.
     6. Il a pris le sien et il est sorti.
     7. Elle est arrivée avec les siens.
     8. Les enfants ont perdu la leur.
     9. Il a rencontré les vôtres.
     10. Tu as cassé le tien.

V. 1. Il a fait beaucoup de fautes.
2. Hélas! Nous n'avons pas d'argent.
3. Il y avait beaucoup de monde dans la rue.
4. J'ai soif; j'ai envie de boire quelque chose.
5. Il jeta son chapeau en l'air. Quel imbécile!
6. Il répondit qu'il n'était pas Français.
7. "Vous avez tort," dit le professeur et le professeur a toujours raison.
8. Tous les mercredis il va au marché.
9. Il mangeait des petits pois.
10. Combien de livres avez-vous?

VI. Il se leva tard et déjeuna à la hâte. Il embrassa sa femme, saisit son chapeau et son parapluie et sortit de la maison. Il dut se dépêcher pour ne pas manquer son train qui partait à huit heures et demie. Le train entra en gare au moment où il achetait son billet. Il montra son billet au contrôleur et se précipita vers un compartiment. Ce matin-là il y avait beaucoup de monde sur le quai et il n'était pas facile de trouver une place. Il y réussit cependant.

LEÇON 22:

I. 1. Ils décidèrent d'aller passer leurs vacances en Suisse.
2. Ils se rendirent à la gare terminus.
3. Ils s'embarquèrent à Douvres.
4. On achetait des cigarettes à bord parce qu'elles coûtent beaucoup moins cher en haute mer qu'à terre.
5. Il s'empara des valises de M. Trotter. Les douaniers examinent les bagages.
6. On contrôle les passeports à la frontière.
7. La foule de voyageurs ressemblait à une armée en déroute.
8. On met les valises dans le filet.

II. 1. *At the circus we saw the biggest woman in the world.*
2. *He is much older than his brother.*
3. *The town in which I live is a little bigger than Rennes.*
4. *She is less intelligent than her elder sister.*
5. *The pupil has made more mistakes than he says.*
6. *As we advanced the forest became thicker and thicker.*
7. *It is less cold here than outside.*
8. *The more we work the more money we earn.*
9. *We haven't the slightest chance of getting to the summit.*
10. *I am told that since the snows last month the state of the road is worse than ever.*

11. *Don't shout so loud. They might hear you.*
12. *The train was going faster and faster.*
13. *You will have to get up earlier.*
14. *She was wearing new shoes and she was very proud of them* (or *about it*).
15. *There is nothing worse than a woman* [*who is*] *at one and the same time hard-working and stupid.*

III. **Secrète, actuelle, grosse, dernière, polie, jeune, fatiguée, vive, malheureuse, inquiète, bonne, douce, publique, folle, nouvelle, favorite, brève, vieille, longue, fraîche.**

IV. **Plus grand, le plus grand; meilleur, le meilleur; plus mauvais (or pire), le plus mauvais (or le pire); plus haut, le plus haut; plus petit (or moindre), le plus petit (or le moindre).**

   Moins, le moins; plus vite, le plus vite; mieux, le mieux; pis, le pis; plus, le plus.

V. 1. **Je me dirigeai, ils se dirigèrent; je bus, ils burent; je commençai, ils commencèrent; je fis, ils firent; j'ouvris, ils ouvrirent; je vins, ils vinrent; je voulus, ils voulurent; je dis, ils dirent; j'écrivis, ils écrivirent; je tins, ils tinrent.**
   2. **Je me dirigeais, ils se dirigeaient; je buvais, ils buvaient; je commençais, ils commençaient; je faisais, ils faisaient; j'ouvrais, ils ouvraient; je venais, ils venaient; je voulais, ils voulaient; je disais, ils disaient; j'écrivais, ils écrivaient; je tenais, ils tenaient.**

VI. 1. **Elle est plus âgée que son frère.**
   2. **J'ai moins d'argent que vous.**
   3. **Courez plus vite! Nous sommes déjà en retard.**
   4. **C'est l'homme le plus riche du monde.**
   5. **Ce marchand est plus riche que vous ne croyez.**
   6. **Celui-ci n'est pas si riche que vous croyez.**
   7. **Plus il lit, plus il sait.**
   8. **Il rencontra son vieil ami dans la rue.**
   9. **Ce vieillard est aussi intelligent que son fils.**
   10. **Cette vieille bicyclette est plus lourde que la mienne.**

VII. **Comme ils avaient décidé d'aller passer leurs vacances à l'étranger, ils se rendirent un jour à la gare terminus et prirent le train de Douvres. Quelle foule il y avait sur le quai! Cependant ils trouvèrent des places dans le train et bientôt ils étaient confortablement assis dans un** compartiment. Mais il y faisait très chaud. Le train mit deux heures environ à arriver au port. Ils descendirent du train et firent la queue pendant dix minutes. Après le contrôle des passeports ils purent monter sur le bateau. Il est agréable de traverser la Manche quand il fait beau temps et que la mer est calme. Ce jour-là il faisait chaud et il n'y avait pas de vent. La traversée dura moins de deux heures. Ils dirent plus tard qu'ils n'avaient jamais passé de journée plus agréable.

LEÇON 23:

I. 1. Elles se connaissaient depuis l'enfance.
   2. Elles parlaient de leurs amis.
   3. L'ami de Lucienne était avare.
   4. Un autobus s'arrête à un arrêt d'autobus.
   5. Ils y avaient rencontré un homme de mauvaise mine.
   6. Lucien parlait mal à propos et il était très impoli.
   7. Elle n'aimait pas les choses modernes.
   8. Elle était fâchée parce que Lucien disait des choses désobligeantes.
   9. Yolande était furieuse parce que son ami se montrait si impoli.
   10. Il est trois heures et demie (etc.) à ma montre.

II. 1. *What books did you buy this morning?*
   2. *She pulled a handkerchief out of her pocket.*
   3. *The nun whom I had seen once at my aunt's died last month.*
   4. *We saw her coming out of the station.*
   5. *When I told them that it was already half-past twelve [p.m.], they hurried.*
   6. *She arrived in Paris two months ago.*
   7. *I remember that John was always bored when they told him stories.*
   8. *As soon as the train had left she returned home.*
   9. *You are mistaken, sir, my name is not Durand.*
   10. *If I had not missed the six o'clock train I should have arrived sooner.*
   11. *You can see he is cheating: there are the cards which he played.*
   12. *She went mad and cut her throat.*
   13. *The letter which I received this morning comes from Berlin.*
   14. *Where are your lady friends? We saw them on the beach.*
   15. *It is said that during the war he was working in Switzerland.*

III. 1. Elle se sera dépêchée; elle aura vu; elle sera venue; elle aura dit; elle sera montée; elle aura conduit; elle aura écrit; elle sera arrivée; elle aura fait; elle aura lu.
   2. Elle se serait dépêchée; elle aurait vu; elle serait venue; elle aurait dit; elle serait montée; elle aurait conduit; elle aurait écrit; elle serait arrivée; elle aurait fait; elle aurait lu.

3. Elle se fut dépêchée; elle eut vu; elle fut venue; elle eut dit; elle fut montée; elle eut conduit; elle eut écrit; elle fut arrivée; elle eut fait; elle eut lu.

IV. 1. Oui, j'en ai une.
2. Donnez-la-lui.
3. Il m'en a donné un.
4. Il y en a un sur le toit.
5. Il va nous la dire.

6. Hier soir nous y sommes allés.
7. Ne le lui envoyez pas.
8. Qui veut y aller avec lui?
9. Elle nous l'avait montré.
10. Nous n'y en avons pas vu.

V. 1. Elle s'est précipitée vers la porte pour voir la voiture.
2. Nous nous sommes rasés ce matin avant de partir.
3. Il s'est cassé la jambe quand il était en Suisse.
4. On dit qu'il fera beau en juillet.
5. La planche que j'ai apportée a trois mètres de long.
6. Nous sommes fatigués et nous ne voulons pas jouer aux cartes.
7. Je m'ennuie toujours quand je vais chez mon oncle.
8. Vous vous trompez. Ma sœur est plus âgée que moi.
9. Je me souviens de la maison où je suis né.
10. Quand elle eut préparé le déjeuner nous nous mîmes à table.

VI. Nous sommes entrés dans le café et nous nous sommes assis à une table près de la fenêtre. Le garçon s'est présenté et nous avons commandé deux tasses de café. Le garçon les a apportées et il les a mises sur la table. Il nous a demandé si nous voulions jouer aux cartes. Nous lui avons dit que non. Nous avons commencé à causer et j'ai raconté une histoire que j'avais lue quelques jours auparavant. Mon ami a ri et, lui aussi, il a commencé à raconter des histoires. Nous nous amusions bien. Cependant, comme il se faisait tard, nous avons demandé l'addition, nous avons donné un pourboire au garçon et nous avons quitté le café. Nous avons pris l'autobus au coin de la rue.

LEÇON 24:

I. 1. Quasimodo est le bossu qui figure dans le célèbre roman de Victor Hugo, "Notre Dame de Paris".
2. Le Soldat Inconnu est enterré sous l'Arc de Triomphe.
3. La cathédrale de Notre Dame se trouve dans l'île de la Cité.
4. La Joconde est le portrait célèbre qui se trouve au musée du Louvre.
5. La Tour Eiffel a trois cents mètres de haut.
6. Un boulevard est une large avenue.

7. Le long des quais de la Seine on trouve les étalages des bouquinistes.
8. La Basilique du Sacré-Cœur se trouve au sommet d'une colline.
9. Le métro est le chemin de fer souterrain de Paris.
10. Pour ramer on se sert d'avirons.

II.
1. *He had been working for six months at the factory.*
2. *Come to see me when you are in town.*
3. *Two hours I have been waiting for you in the rain!*
4. *One never knew whether he would arrive or not.*
5. *Kindly pass me the book which is at the side of the radio set.*
6. *Soldiers must obey their officers.*
7. *We were to catch the quarter past five train but, alas, we missed it.*
8. *We shall go and visit the Louvre when we are in Paris.*
9. *He ought to have said it in court.*
10. *War broke out twelve years ago.*
11. *If he committed that crime he would be sentenced to six years in prison.*
12. *The boys were playing marbles on the pavement.*
13. *He had been living in Marseilles for ten years.*
14. *I have just read in the paper that his aunt has died.*
15. *He had just left the workshop when fire broke out.*

III.
1. Quelle erreur a-t-il faite?
2. Elle s'est lavé la figure.
3. Voilà les lunettes que j'ai cherchées partout.
4. La somme que vous avez reçue n'est pas grosse.
5. Où sont les valises? Il les a emportées.
6. Les lettres sont arrivées à sept heures du matin.
7. Quand je leur ai posé une question ils se sont tus.
8. Elle s'est cassé la jambe en grimpant sur un arbre.
9. Quelles histoires avez-vous racontées?
10. Avez-vous lu les vers qu'il a composés?

IV.
1. Veuillez poser le panier sur la table.
2. Il ne peut pas nager dans le lac cet après-midi parce qu'il doit faire une commission pour sa mère.
3. Il sait jouer du violon et de la clarinette mais il ne sait pas jouer du piano.
4. Il n'en sait rien; il devrait se taire.
5. Elle devait arriver au port le lendemain matin.
6. Il travaillait depuis une demi-heure quand l'accident arriva.
7. S'il arrivait à l'heure on ne le gronderait pas.

8. Je croyais qu'il m'écrirait quand il recevrait le colis.
9. Vous devez vous faire couper les cheveux. Vos cheveux sont trop longs.
10. Je le ferais volontiers si j'avais assez d'argent.

V. Il y a deux ans j'ai passé un mois à Paris et je me suis bien amusé. Quand il faisait beau je sortais visiter les monuments de la ville. Je visitais les églises, les musées et même les grands magasins. Quand j'étais fatigué j'entrais dans un café commander une tasse de café ou un verre de bière. Il faisait très chaud dans les rues et j'avais soif. Cependant, comme je n'avais pas beaucoup d'argent je ne pouvais pas acheter tout ce que je désirais. Mais qui peut faire cela? Je devrais vous dire que tout est cher à Paris. Quelquefois je me promenais au Bois de Boulogne et je louais un canot. Savez-vous ramer? Ce n'est pas très difficile. Hélas! Je ne sais pas si j'aurai assez d'argent pour aller en France cette année.

LEÇON 25:

I. 1. On venait de signaler un crime.
2. Elle dit avoir trouvé un cadavre dans un des appartements. C'était une grosse femme aux cheveux gris.
3. Elle partit comme un éclair.
4. Il habitait au troisième étage.
5. On examinait la chambre en vue d'y trouver des empreintes digitales.

II. 1. *You have done all you can, it is true.*
2. *It is obvious that my uncle does not want to help us.*
3. *Is he going into the country this afternoon? I think so.*
4. *"Welcome!" I said to him.*
5. *Whose is this well-filled wallet? Mine.*
6. *To what are you referring when you speak thus?*
7. *Which of these pictures do you wish to buy?*
8. *He did not arrive punctually; so I went out alone.*
9. *It is a lie to say that I deceived you.*
10. *She lost the ring which her mother had given her; it is a pity.*

III. 1. Ils craignent; ils vivent; ils voient; ils rient; ils savent; ils mettent; ils suivent; ils lisent; ils écrivent; ils naissent.
2. Il craignit; il vécut; il vit; il rit; il sut; il mit; il suivit; il lut; il écrivit; il naquit.

443

IV. 1. **Il a perdu la sienne.**
    2. **Où est la leur?**
    3. **Prête-moi le tien.**
    4. **A-t-il fait les siens?**
    5. **Nous avons mis les nôtres dans le panier.**
    6. **Voici les nôtres mais il veut voir aussi les leurs.**
    7. **Voici mon fusil; où est le vôtre?**
    8. **J'aime beaucoup les miens.**
    9. **Nous avons donné les nôtres à nos amis.**
    10. **J'ai trouvé les miens sur le canapé.**

V. 1. **À quoi sert un marteau?**
    2. **Dans quel appartement est-il entré?**
    3. **A-t-il jamais été en prison?**
    4. **Sa bicyclette est cassée; c'est dommage.**
    5. **Il est allé à l'écurie, n'est-ce pas?**
    6. **Il est évident qu'il va réussir.**
    7. **Laquelle de ces bicyclettes voulez-vous prendre?**
    8. **Quel âge avez-vous? J'ai seize ans.**
    9. **Qui a vu le facteur ce matin?**
    10. **Qu'est-ce que vous avez trouvé dans le puits?**

VI.   **Le détective descendit de voiture et entra dans la maison. Il monta l'escalier et rencontra le concierge à la porte de l'appartement. Il lui demanda ce qui était arrivé. Le concierge tremblait de tous ses membres et il était difficile de comprendre ce qu'il disait. Mais notre détective était un homme très patient: c'est pourquoi il réussissait toujours à prendre les criminels qu'il poursuivait. Selon le concierge M. Duvivier était rentré à neuf heures et demie et il s'était couché, paraît-il, vers dix heures. Une demi-heure plus tard on entendit un coup de revolver. Le concierge était monté tout de suite et il avait frappé à la porte. Mais personne ne l'avait ouverte. Naturellement le concierge avait téléphoné sans tarder à la police. Le policier lui posa quelques questions et puis il entra dans la pièce où se trouvait le cadavre. Celui-ci était étendu par terre. Le détective examina toute la pièce avec soin dans l'espoir d'y trouver des empreintes digitales.**

LEÇON 26:

I. 1. **Non, au contraire il était très courageux. Il apprit à se servir du plastic.**
    2. **Le soir il devait polir ses boutons et faire reluire ses chaussures.**
    3. **"Expérimenté" veut dire "instruit par l'expérience." La Manche est le bras de mer qui sépare l'Angleterre et la France.**

4. Il sauta quand il vit s'allumer la lampe verte.

5. Quand il se débarrassait de son parachute il entendit une voix qui chuchotait dans l'obscurité.

II. 1. *You [one] will have to change at Bordeaux.*
  2. *Can you play the flute?*
  3. *Last week my bicycle was stolen from me.*
  4. *He was furious but he had to obey the colonel's orders.*
  5. *Temptation must always be resisted.*
  6. *Forgive your enemies; you will never regret it.*
  7. *He was using an enormous saw to cut the tree.*
  8. *What are you thinking of at the moment? Of the holidays.*
  9. *A broomstick served him as a crutch.*
  10. *I do not dare to accuse the thief: he might harm me.*
  11. *It is better to accept what he offers.*
  12. *I was watching him coming down the slope.*
  13. *Help me to repair the engine.*
  14. *He expected to see the car arrive.*
  15. *She asked him to do an errand in town.*

III. 1. Nous servons; nous connaissons; nous recevons; nous venons; nous pouvons; nous plaisons; nous apprenons; nous faisons; nous avons; nous lisons.

  2. Ils serviraient; ils connaîtraient; ils recevraient; ils viendraient; ils pourraient; ils plairaient; ils apprendraient; ils feraient; ils auraient; ils liraient.

  3. Elle a servi; elle a connu; elle a reçu; elle est venue; elle a pu; elle a plu; elle a appris; elle a fait; elle a eu; elle a lu.

  4. Vous servîtes; vous connûtes; vous reçûtes; vous vîntes; vous pûtes; vous plûtes; vous apprîtes; vous fîtes; vous eûtes; vous lûtes.

IV. 1. Douce, première, brève, vieille, merveilleuse, grosse, muette, bonne, blanche, inquiète, joyeuse, éternelle, jaune, fatiguée, longue, neuve, dernière, vive, folle, nouvelle.

  2. Les bras, les châteaux, les choux, les trous, les croix, les ouvriers, les nez, les soldats, les ours, les genoux.

V. 1. Demandez de l'argent à votre ami; nous n'en avons pas.

  2. La semaine dernière elle s'est cassé le bras quand elle était à la campagne.

  3. Il sortit le papier de son portefeuille et il me le donna.

  4. Il se servait d'un marteau pour casser la pierre.

445

5. L'animal buvait dans un ruisseau clair.
6. Elle paya le billet et le mit sur la cheminée.
7. "Vous manquez de sens commun," dit-il, "vous devriez vous taire."
8. Il désobéit à son père et il alla nager dans le lac.
9. Pardonnez à vos ennemis! Faites du bien à ceux qui vous haïssent!
10. Il commence à pleuvoir. Il n'est pas nécessaire d'arroser la pelouse.
11. Montez changer de chemise; celle-là est sale.
12. Il passe son temps à jouer aux échecs.
13. Je vous jure que je grimperai jusqu'au sommet de cette montagne.
14. Un agent vint à passer: nous étions en danger d'être découverts.
15. Il s'agit de la défense du pays. Nous ne pouvons pas refuser de nous battre.

VI. Il s'engagea dans l'armée. Tous les jours il devait polir ses boutons et frotter ses souliers. Il passait des heures à nettoyer son uniforme et son fusil. Il n'est pas nécessaire de dire qu'au bout de quelque temps il s'ennuya d'une telle vie. Si vous aviez dû passer toutes les soirées à éplucher des pommes de terre et à laver la vaisselle, qu'auriez-vous dit? John décida de retourner en France lutter contre les oppresseurs de son pays. Mais comment allait-il faire cela? On ne peut pas quitter l'armée comme on quitte un emploi ordinaire. Il y réfléchit longuement. Puis il alla chercher une plume, de l'encre et du papier pour écrire une lettre au commandant. J'ai oublié de vous dire que John parlait couramment le français comme il avait passé vingt ans en France. Après tout, sa mère était Française. Quand l'officier reçut la lettre il fit venir John et il lui dit qu'il ne comprenait pas pourquoi il était si malheureux. Il lui demanda pourquoi il désirait retourner en France et ce qu'il voulait y faire.

LEÇON 27:

I. 1. La France était très pauvre à la fin de la guerre.
2. Aujourd'hui la France est prospère.
3. La France a quarante-cinq millions d'habitants.
4. Entre les deux guerres on craignait fort que la France ne vînt à se dépeupler sérieusement.
5. Oui, il y en a un.
6. La Communauté européenne est le Marché commun.
7. La France, l'Allemagne occidentale, l'Italie, la Belgique, la Hollande et le Luxembourg constituent le Marché commun à présent.
8. Le siège du Marché commun se trouve à Bruxelles.
9. Oui, je crois qu'elle est très dure.
10. La paix est toujours nécessaire pour qu'un pays prospère.

II. 1. *It seems that he has disappeared without trace.*
2. *Although we are tired we will set to work all the same.*
3. *In order that my list may be exact I shall have to know who is absent.*
4. *Unless he comes before three o'clock we shall not be able to leave today.*
5. *There was nobody who knew that.*
6. *If you have a thousand francs and if you are willing to lend them to me I shall be able to buy all that I need.*
7. *It is the most beautiful flower that I have ever seen.*
8. *It is quite obvious that you have learnt nothing.*
9. *I doubt whether she will be able to arrive today.*
10. *We shall not be happy before the war is ended.*
11. *He will be able to arrange things so that our enemies may not find out what has happened.*
12. *Look for a nail which is not rusty.*
13. *It seems to me that most of the apples are rotten.*
14. *It is better for John to go in first.*
15. *Would to Heaven that the king had acted thus!*

III. 1. **Qu'il ait, qu'il soit, qu'il porte, qu'il reçoive, qu'il sache, qu'il réponde, qu'il puisse, qu'il aille, qu'il dise, qu'il fasse, qu'il écrive, qu'il craigne, qu'il prenne, qu'il veuille, qu'il parte.**
2. **Que nous eussions, que nous fussions, que nous portassions, que nous reçussions, que nous sussions, que nous répondissions, que nous pussions, que nous allassions, que nous dissions, que nous fissions, que nous écrivissions, que nous craignissions, que nous prissions, que nous voulussions, que nous partissions.**

IV. **Il semble qu'une personne . . . possède**: after impersonal verb.
Il est possible qu'ils commencent . . . : after impersonal verb.
Le trait le plus marquant qu'on puisse . . . : relative after superlative.
On craignait que la France ne vînt . . . : after verb of emotion (fearing).
Qu'elle ne devînt . . . : after verb of emotion (fearing).
Cela n'étonne pas qu'il y ait . . . : after verb of emotion (astonishment).
Il est à regretter que . . . soient: after verb of emotion (regret).
Quel que soit le montant: relative after indefinite antecedent.
Il semble qu'on soit . . . : after impersonal verb.
Certains . . . craignent que . . . n'ait: after verb of emotion (fearing).
On ne trouverait personne qui osât . . . : relative after negative antecedent.
Avant que . . . ne vînt: after **avant que** clause.
Un homme qui . . . pût: relative after indefinite antecedent.

V. 1. Il semble qu'il ait perdu tout son argent.
  2. Pour que nous n'arrivions pas en retard l'autocar partira à deux heures et quart.
  3. Qu'ils reviennent à la fin de la semaine.
  4. Je ne croyais pas qu'il fût mort.
  5. Il demanda qu'on mît le voleur en prison.
  6. Elle regrette beaucoup que le travail ne soit pas fini.
  7. Il craignait que l'effort ne l'épuisât.
  8. Il faudra qu'on surveille les enfants toute la journée.
  9. C'est dommage que vous ayez perdu votre balle.
  10. C'est la seule personne que je reconnaisse.

VI. 1. Quoiqu'il soit jeune, il sait jouer du piano.
  2. Pour que vous compreniez ce que je vais dire je ferai un dessin au tableau noir.
  3. Il faut que vous arriviez à l'heure si vous ne voulez pas trouver la porte fermée.
  4. C'est dommage qu'ils n'aient plus d'argent.
  5. Avant qu'ils ne viennent, nettoyez le salon.
  6. Il me semble que vous vous trompez.
  7. Apportez-moi une serviette qui ne soit pas sale.
  8. Il est possible qu'ils aillent en Autriche à Pâques.
  9. Pourvu que vous soyez riche vous pouvez parcourir tout le monde.
  10. Veillez à ce que la porte soit bien fermée.

VII. Après la Seconde Guerre mondiale la situation économique de la France était déplorable. Le pays était très pauvre à cause du pillage organisé par l'ennemi. D'ailleurs, le réseau du chemin de fer, les routes et les ponts avaient subi des dégâts considérables. L'aide américaine permit à la France de commencer le travail de reconstruction. Aujourd'hui, cependant, le pays est très prospère. Les usines, les routes et les ponts ont été réparés et le revenu national va toujours croissant. Le chômage n'existe presque pas. On dit qu'une personne sur neuf possède une voiture. Quoique le pays soit si riche, la situation politique n'est pas très bonne. On craint quelquefois que la guerre civile n'éclate. Il faudra que le gouvernement suive une politique qui puisse unir le pays et lui rendre le calme. En effet, aucun pays sujet à des agitations politiques ne peut espérer rester prospère pendant longtemps. Pour que l'économie soit saine il est nécessaire que les travailleurs vivent en paix.

LEÇON 28:

1. HOW A DOG INSPIRED A LOVE OF MUSIC

Gaspard was a small black dog, thickset and not very attractive looking, but possessing two eyes full of life and warm friendship. I cannot remember how it came about that we had taken him in, but he spent several months with us during which time I loved him tenderly.

Now, during one winter evening walk, Gaspard had left me. They consoled me saying that he would certainly make his way home alone, and I came back to the house quite courageously. But when night fell, my heart sank.

My parents had invited to dinner that evening a talented violinist and I had been allowed to stay up to hear him. At the first sweeps of his bow, as soon as he had begun to play some sad, plaintive adagio, it was as though it conjured up for me dark paths through the woods, deep in the night when you feel yourself lost and forsaken; then I saw distinctly Gaspard wandering in the rain and coming to some sinister cross-roads, and failing to recognize his bearings, setting off into the unknown, never to return. . . . Then the tears came, and as nobody noticed them, the violin went on casting its sad plaint into the silence.

This was my first insight into music. Years went by before I understood anything fresh about it, for the little piano pieces, "remarkable for my age" they would say, which I used to play, were no more than soft, rhythmic sounds to my ears.

2. A HARD LIVING

And yet he had to find some means of livelihood. His salary from the orchestra was no longer sufficient. He gave lessons. His talent as a soloist, his reputation and above all the patronage of the prince attracted to him numerous pupils from the upper-middle classes. Every morning, from nine o'clock onwards, he gave piano lessons to young ladies — often older than himself — who frightened him by their flirtatiousness and who got on his nerves by the emptiness of their silly behaviour. They were utterly incompetent at music; on the other hand they all possessed, to a greater or lesser degree, a keen sense of the ridiculous, and their mocking glances showed no mercy for the least awkwardness in Christopher's behaviour. It was torture for him. Sitting beside them, on the edge of the chair, boiling with rage yet not daring to move, afraid of the sound of his own voice, he did his best to put on a serious expression, all the while feeling himself watched by them out of the corner of their eyes; he would lose countenance and, fearing to appear ridiculous, was so. He would lose his temper to the extent of making wounding reproaches. It was very easy for his pupils to get their revenge, and they did not fail to do so, embarrassing him by a certain way of looking at him, of asking him the simplest questions, which made him blush up to the eyes; or else they would ask him to do some little service — such as to go and fetch something they had left on a piece of furniture — for him this was the most painful test.

3. EATING OUT FOR THE FIRST TIME

As I said before, it was Eastertime. The holidays were marked by two memorable events. We went, one day, the three big ones, Joseph, Ferdinand and myself, on an outing in the country with Father. By following the rue Vercingetorix we were soon out of Paris. All we had to do then was to follow the western railway line to reach Meudon and the woods.

Once in sight of the wood, we came across a path with a signboard on which was written "No right of way." Ferdinand, at the head of the group, had stopped there in front, as though at the foot of a wall.

"We can't go any further," he shouted.

Father had a teasing expression, he was smiling. He stretched out his hand, touched the worm-eaten notice and suddenly snatching it he threw it far away into a ditch.

"There you are," he said with a smile. "The way is no longer barred. Go along, boys." I lagged behind, my soul deeply troubled.

The other event was a meal in a restaurant. We had been shopping all day long. Father said:

"There is nothing ready at home. We'll go and eat in a restaurant."

"Raymond," said mother, "this is madness."

Father replied:

"We shall see about that!"

The restaurant was almost empty and the green-painted room had a huge stovepipe running across it.

Mother said:

"I always find it surprising to be eating food that I have not prepared myself."

We found everything delicious and of a very unusual flavour.

"It's a very posh restaurant," muttered Joseph, gorging himself.

"No, it isn't," said father. "It's a twopenny-halfpenny restaurant."

Our great joy was shattered. Mother murmured:

"You shouldn't have told them that. They would not have noticed."

LEÇON 29:

1. Le lendemain matin Henri se leva plus tôt que d'habitude. Quand il eut fait sa toilette, il entra dans la chambre à coucher de sa mère. Elle était toujours très faible après sa maladie. Heureusement, sa sœur, Madame Villeneuve, avait

pu retarder son départ, et avait promis à Henri qu'elle resterait jusqu'à l'arrivée de la femme de ménage.

Henri dit à sa mère de ne pas s'inquiéter, l'embrassa et lui dit au revoir. Il lui restait à peine une demi-heure et il mangea à la hâte son petit déjeuner. Il était sur le point de partir quand le facteur frappa à la porte. Henri prit les lettres, y jetant un coup d'œil rapide pour voir s'il y en avait pour lui. En effet, il y en avait deux — une d'Allemagne — celle-ci venait probablement de son frère aîné Georges, qui faisait son service militaire à l'étranger — l'autre était évidemment de son nouveau patron.

Sans attendre pour les ouvrir, Henri les mit dans sa poche et laissa les autres sur la table de la salle à manger. Comme il se rendait à la gare, il entendit l'horloge de l'Hôtel de ville sonner huit heures. Il y avait peu de monde dans la rue à cette heure matinale. Henri s'arrêta au coin de la rue, acheta un journal, puis, hâtant un peu le pas, il traversa la rue et arriva, cinq minutes plus tard, devant l'immense entrée.

Au guichet il demanda un billet aller et retour. À la grille le contrôleur lui donna un sourire agréable et lui dit que le train attendait déjà au quai numéro six, et qu'il devait partir dans quatre minutes. Henri trouva un compartiment de deuxième classe, choisit une place au coin et s'assit. Le voilà, enfin, en route pour Londres pour commencer son nouvel emploi.

2. Quand je suis arrivé chez moi, maman avait l'air inquiet. Pendant quelques moments elle n'a rien dit, puis enfin, après avoir mis mon repas sur la table, elle s'est tournée vers moi et a dit:

"J'ai de mauvaises nouvelles pour toi. Ton père est tombé malade au bureau aujourd'hui et on l'a envoyé à l'hôpital. Dépêche-toi de manger; il nous faudra prendre l'autobus au coin de la rue à sept heures et demie pour aller le visiter."

Elle venait de finir de dire cela quand on a sonné à la porte. Maman est allée ouvrir, mais elle est revenue presque tout de suite, suivie de mon oncle Thomas, le frère de papa. Évidemment, il était venu offrir à nous aider.

"Ma voiture est devant la porte," a-t-il dit. "J'ai déjà téléphoné à l'hôpital. Ton père n'est pas trop malade pour recevoir des visiteurs. Nous devrions lui apporter quelques-unes de ses affaires et des livres. Peut-être voudra-t-il lire dans quelques jours. Voyons, Charles! Tu n'es pas obligé d'avoir l'air si triste. Tout ira bien avant peu. Aide ta maman à mettre son manteau. Nous partirons immédiatement."

3. Je sortis à la hâte de mon petit abri et, quand je me trouvai au grand air une fois de plus, j'eus la force d'essuyer mon front rouge et mouillé. Je m'appuyai un instant contre un arbre et, peu après, le chirurgien vint me bander le front. De grosses gouttes de pluie froide tombaient sur ma tête et semblaient me faire quelque bien.

"Je suis las de la guerre," dis-je au docteur — du moins je croyais parler au docteur.

"Et moi aussi," dit une voix basse que je semblais reconnaître.

Je soulevai le bandage de mes yeux et je vis, non pas le docteur, mais le général. Il était seul, triste, debout devant moi. Ses grosses bottes étaient enfoncées dans la boue, son habit était déchiré, la pluie ruisselait de son chapeau. Il me considéra un instant et dit:

"Je vous ai vu quelque part, n'est-ce pas?" Ces mots me firent comprendre que j'avais vieilli de visage plus que d'années.

"Je vous ai vu bien des fois, sans être vu moi-même," répondis-je.

"Voulez-vous de l'avancement?"

Je dis: "Il est trop tard."

Il croisa les bras un moment sans répondre, puis il dit:

"Vous avez raison. Dans quelques jours, vous et moi, nous serons probablement morts."

4. En arrivant au collège, j'entrai dans la salle de récréation et je m'assis à une table à quelque distance des élèves. Je les entendais rire et bavarder; j'aperçus, comme dans un rêve, le visage souriant de Dupré, et celui du petit Berger, et Lambert en train de proposer à Fauriat que, s'il neigeait jeudi ils pourraient organiser une bataille à boules de neige entre les classes de quatrième et de troisième. Tout à coup je me levai et fis le tour de la salle. Il me fallait trouver un moyen de rejoindre mon frère. Comment le faire? Je ne pouvais plus rester dans ce collège où j'avais honte et où j'étais trop malheureux pour travailler. Puis une idée me vint. "Je m'en irai," pensai-je. "Quand j'arriverai à Paris je chercherai l'appartement de mon frère. Je lui dirai. . . ." Une voix sévère interrompit mes pensées. "Monsieur," me disait le directeur, "prenez vos livres et suivez-moi."

5. Le garçon a fait demi-tour et s'est trouvé bientôt dans le quartier de la gare. Il marchait depuis deux heures; il commençait à avoir faim et pensait avec nostalgie à son lit chez lui. "Qu'est-il devenu, Jacques," s'est-il demandé.

Soudain, il a vu le café où ils avaient pris le petit déjeuner le matin. Il y est entré et s'est installé à une table près de la fenêtre. "Je devrais attendre ici," a-t-il pensé. "Je serai à l'abri de la pluie et je pourrai voir Jacques qui s'approche du côté de la ville."

Il venait de demander au garçon une tasse de café lorsqu'il a cru reconnaître son ami qui sortait en courant de la boulangerie en face. Mais il s'était trompé: ce n'était qu'un étranger qui portait un pain sous le bras.

6. Quand nous avions fini de manger, j'ai aidé Eliane à faire la vaisselle. Puis nous étions si fatigués que nous sommes allés nous coucher et nous avons dormi profondément jusqu'au lendemain matin. Au petit déjeuner nous n'avons pris qu'un petit pain avec une grande tasse de café, et puis nous nous sommes dépêchés pour aller attendre mon père qui devait quitter son bureau à onze heures et demie.

Il est arrivé un peu en retard, à midi moins vingt, en disant qu'un client difficile était entré au dernier moment et qu'il n'avait pas pu s'en aller. Nous sommes tous montés dans la petite voiture d'Eliane et filions bientôt vers la gare St. Lazare, pour prendre le train de midi.

Nous avons trouvé un compartiment vide de seconde classe. Mon père s'est laissé tomber dans un coin et a fermé les yeux, épuisé. Nous étions là depuis peu de temps lorsque nous ont rejoints un vieillard et un petit garçon, que j'avais aperçus au guichet, en train de fouiller dans leurs poches pour trouver le prix du voyage. Ils nous ont dit qu'ils allaient au Havre trouver le père du garçon qui revenait d'Amérique.

LEÇON 30:

1. UNE EXCURSION À LONDRES

Pendant les vacances de Pâques nous avons reçu un jour une invitation de notre tante Marie, qui habite Londres, d'y aller passer une journée entière. Nous nous sommes levés, ma sœur et moi, de très bonne heure et nous nous sommes rendus à la gare nous réjouissant à la pensée de faire, pour la première fois, ce voyage sans être accompagnés de nos parents.

Arrivés à la gare, nous n'avons pas dû attendre longtemps. Le train est arrivé à l'heure et nous avons trouvé deux places dans un compartiment tout près du wagon-restaurant. Papa nous avait donné assez d'argent pour nous permettre de déjeuner en route. On nous a servi un repas excellent. Comme il était agréable de manger et en même temps de pouvoir jeter un coup d'œil sur le paysage qui est si beau au printemps. À Londres notre tante nous attendait. Tout de suite nous avons fait une promenade en autobus et la circulation nous a vraiment enchantés. Nous avons visité la Tour de Londres, le Palais de la reine et quelques-uns des grands magasins. L'après-midi nous avons fait une promenade en bateau sur la Tamise jusqu'au Port de Londres. C'était une journée merveilleuse! Le soir nous avons repris le train pour retourner chez nous. Tous deux nous étions si fatigués que, pendant le voyage de retour, nous nous sommes endormis dans notre compartiment. Heureusement pour nous le chef de train nous a réveillés quelques minutes avant notre arrivée. Papa est venu nous trouver à la gare et il nous a conduits à la maison en voiture. Il va sans dire que, le lendemain, nous avons écrit pour remercier notre tante qui avait été si gentille.

2. Mon cher Jean,

Les vacances sont terminées et nous voici de nouveau au lycée. Il m'est difficile de croire que, il y a trois semaines, nous étions, la famille tout entière, au bord de la mer. Je me rappelle bien, cependant, le jour du départ. Nous devions mettre plus de huit heures pour faire le voyage en auto. En conséquence, nous nous sommes levés tous de très bonne heure. Nous avions fait nos valises la veille et avant sept heures du matin nous étions prêts à partir. Il faisait, ce jour-là, un temps splendide, et bientôt nous filions sur la grand'route vers la célèbre plage de Bournemouth. Vous savez combien j'aime faire de la vitesse en voiture et papa m'a beaucoup plu en faisant plus de soixante-dix kilomètres à l'heure! Heureusement il y avait peu de circulation à cette heure matinale. A mi-chemin nous nous sommes arrêtés et nous avons fait un pique-nique au bord d'un joli ruisseau. Vers quatre heures de l'après-midi nous sommes arrivés sains et saufs à notre hôtel qui se trouvait à une centaine de pas de la plage.

Pendant quinze jours nous nous sommes amusés d'une façon agréable. Le matin on se levait de bonne heure pour aller se baigner. L'eau était bien plus froide que dans le Midi de la France! Toute la matinée nous jouions sur la plage. L'après-midi nous avons fait quelques excursions en bateau. Une fois nous avons loué un bateau pour aller à la pêche en pleine mer. Malheureusement il a fait un orage épouvantable et nous avons failli nous noyer. J'ai été bien content de me retrouver sur la terre ferme! A l'hôtel nous avons fait la connaissance de trois jeunes gens que nous avons trouvés très sympathiques. Plusieurs fois nous sommes partis en excursion avec eux sans nos parents. Vous pouvez être sûr que, ces jours-là, on a bien ri. Comme le temps passe vite quand on est en vacances! Le retour était moins agréable. Nous avons fait panne en route et il fallait pousser la voiture jusqu'au garage le plus proche. En plein soleil c'était assez désagréable. En rentrant chez nous la seule consolation pour moi c'était de trouver les résultats de mes examens et d'apprendre que j'avais réussi. Comme récompense je me trouve maintenant en première — et j'ai encore plus de travail que jamais.

Bien des choses de ma part à vos parents.

Thomas

3. (Continuation of the story about Henri):

Henri ne resta pas longtemps seul dans le compartiment. Juste avant le départ du train, deux hommes ouvrirent la portière et s'élancèrent dans le compartiment. Quand ils avaient repris haleine le premier, qui était assis en face d'Henri, dit en souriant — "Nous avons failli le manquer aujourd'hui, mon vieux."

"Oui," répondit l'autre, "et à qui en était la faute? Tu as insisté t'arrêter pour acheter un journal que tu n'auras jamais, certes, le temps de lire."

"Mais si," répondit son compagnon, "comment veux-tu que je passe le temps entre midi et demi et deux heures? Tu sais bien que je sors assez rarement et j'aime occuper mes moments de loisir."

Henri avait bien envie de faire la conversation avec eux. Enfin, un peu timidement il demanda poliment — "Vous prenez tous les jours ce même train?"

"Mais oui," répondit le monsieur le plus âgé, "mais on ne vous a pas vu auparavant. Vous n'allez pas comme nous deux tous les jours à Londres, je pense?"

"C'est que je vais y commencer un nouvel emploi aujourd'hui. À partir de ce matin je prendrai, tous les jours, le train à cette heure-ci."

Les deux voyageurs lui expliquèrent qu'ils travaillaient dans une banque qui se trouvait, paraissait-il, à quelques centaines de pas du bureau où il devait se présenter, lui, à neuf heures. Au bout d'un quart d'heure ils avaient tout appris au sujet du nouvel emploi. Henri les trouvait très sympathiques et il était content de savoir qu'il aurait l'occasion de les voir très souvent. En descendant du train à Victoria ils lui expliquèrent vers quelle station de métro il devait se rendre. Henri les remercia chaudement et ils se dirent au revoir.

4. CAFÉ ET . . . SEL!

Michel et Jacques ont toujours de bonnes intentions à l'égard de leurs parents. Un jour, comme ceux-ci étaient sortis, les enfants ont décidé de leur préparer une grande surprise — de faire du café! Michel a mis l'eau à bouillir, et Jacques a eu l'intention de moudre le café. Mais c'est un petit garçon très maladroit. Ne faisant pas attention à ce qu'il faisait il a renversé le paquet de café, et, en même temps il a bousculé un gros paquet de sel. Quel gâchis! Grains de café et sel recouvraient le carrelage de la cuisine. "Ça ne fait rien," a dit Michel. "Faisons d'abord le café, ensuite nous séparerons les grains."

"Mais le sel . . ." a répondu Jacques.

"Avec beaucoup de sucre, ça ira," a répondu l'autre.

Sans avoir été tout à fait convaincu Jacques a moulu un peu de ce mélange, et bientôt l'odeur agréable s'est répandu dans la cuisine.

La joie qu'avaient ressentie les enfants en apportant le café a vite disparu! Papa et maman n'ont pas apprécié du tout ce café au goût plus ou moins étrange. "La prochaine fois," ont-ils dit, "nous préférerions que vous passiez le temps à faire le ménage. Il y a moins de danger!"

5. UNE PUNITION BIEN MÉRITÉE

Pierre n'est pas très fort en mathématiques; d'ailleurs, il déteste son professeur. La semaine dernière, Pierre, qui n'avait pas pu résoudre les problèmes qu'on lui avait donnés comme devoirs, a décidé de s'absenter de la classe. Ce jour-là, il est parti de chez lui comme d'habitude, mais il a passé son temps à errer dans la ville, à écrire des lettres assis sur la terrasse d'un café, et même à passer l'après-midi au cinéma!

Le lendemain, en classe, son professeur a voulu savoir pourquoi Pierre était absent la veille. Celui-ci a essayé de s'excuser en disant qu'il avait été malade

455

toute la journée, mais son professeur ne s'est pas laissé tromper. En tout cas Pierre, quand on lui a demandé de rapporter une lettre de ses parents, a rougi de honte. À son air coupable le professeur s'est aperçu que Pierre avait fait l'école buissonnière. Il lui a fait apporter son cahier de mathématiques: zéro sur vingt trois fois de suite! Voilà un garçon qui mérite une belle punition. Trois heures de retenue! Le pauvre Pierre! Il lui faudra expliquer à son père pourquoi il rentre si tard ce jour-là!

6. UNE AVENTURE À LA CAMPAGNE

Il y avait une fois deux petites filles qui aimaient se promener dans les prés. Un jour, accompagnées de leur chien Médor, elles sont parties faire une longue promenade à la campagne.

Soudain, en traversant un champ, elles ont vu un taureau qui s'approchait d'elles. Elles ont eu bien peur et se sont sauvées. Sachant qu'elles ne gagneraient pas la barrière elles ont grimpé dans un arbre. Mais le pauvre Médor n'a pas pu y grimper. Que faire? Au bout de quelques instants, Médor a pris du courage. Il a commencé à aboyer, et le taureau, fâché, s'est mis à le chasser. Pendant ce temps les deux filles sont descendues de l'arbre et se sont précipitées de l'autre côté de la barrière. Médor, qui courait plus vite que le taureau, les a suivies, et en quelques secondes il sautait, lui aussi, pardessus la barrière. Quelle chance!

LEÇON 31:

I. THE UNPOSTED LETTER

1. The medley of streets into which Eugène turned was behind the cross-roads Buci. He turned that way by accident, not looking where he was going.
2. When he saw the lady he was about to retrace his footsteps.
3. She could scarcely walk, her knees were giving way; she was wrapped in an old dressing gown, her head was bare, her hair all in disorder and she was very pale.
4. She seemed to be making her way to a near-by door; she leaned against the walls; she could hardly walk.
5. Eugène asked her where she was going, what she was looking for and if he could help her.
6. She gave no reply, recoiled with fear and pride.
7. She gathered her strength together, pointed to the post-box and said, "There!" She dragged herself back, clinging to the walls.
8. He offered to give her his arm and repeated his questions.
9. He felt a mixture of horror and compassion, was troubled and wished to know the secret of the old lady.
10. She was dying of hunger or poverty.

II. A DEAF-MUTE CHILD

1. Madame des Arcis se faisait comprendre à sa fille par des signes.
2. La mère de Madame des Arcis a dit, "Mieux eût valu pour elle ne pas être née."
3. L'oncle Giraud était maître maçon.
4. Il accusait sa femme d'avoir été très bavarde.
5. Il a dit que les vieux airs d'opéra sont tous pareils.
6. Les deux choses qui pourraient éveiller une femme qui dormait étaient quand son mari toussait et quand il se levait tôt pour aller surveiller ses ouvriers.
7. La petite pourrait apprendre à régler en comptant sur ses doigts.
8. La chose que l'oncle Giraud disait était difficile à apprendre était qu'il vaut mieux faire que dire.

III. CHILDHOOD MEMORIES OF A JOURNEY ON THE RHÔNE

1. He still recalls the ship, its passengers, crew, the noise of wheels and the whistle.
2. He stayed most of the time on deck near the anchor.
3. The bell sounded.
4. He had a parrot's cage between his legs.
5. He would have liked to be at sea.
6. It was fine weather. The waves were green.
7. That they were desert isles.
8. A thick mist came over the river and the sky darkened rapidly.
9. A large lantern was lit at the front of the boat.
10. He was excited.

IV. A GIRL LEAVES BOARDING SCHOOL

1. Elle les avait passées en pension.
2. Il a été gêné à cause de ses nattes et de sa vieille robe sale.
3. Il a montré une joie profonde parce qu'il s'est rendu compte que sa fille lui ressemblait.
4. Elle était d'une famille riche.
5. Elle aimait acheter des robes neuves, des disques, des livres, des fleurs.
6. Le trait le plus important de son caractère était son goût pour le plaisir.
7. A l'école elle lisait des livres d'instruction. À Paris, elle ne lisait pas du tout.
8. Ils étaient surpris parce qu'elle ignorait le nom des acteurs de cinéma.
9. Elle suivait des cours, puis allait au cinéma ou dans des cafés.
10. She remembers the smell of the linden trees in the playground.
11. He was embarrassed because she had plaits and wore an old, shabby dress.

12. He was overjoyed later to find that his daughter resembled him. He looked upon her as a precious plaything.
13. She belonged to a wealthy background.
14. Her love of pleasure is the most salient trait of her character.
15. She attended classes, went to the cinema and into cafés.
16. She went out with her father. This was unsuitable because she was too young. She amused her father's friends by her youth.

V. A FAITHFUL SERVANT FROM CHILDHOOD IS FOUND AGAIN

1. Jeanne était triste parce que sa tante venait d'être enterrée.
2. Une forte paysanne l'a saisie et l'a emportée.
3. Nous savons que la femme était forte car elle a emporté Jeanne comme elle eût fait d'un petit enfant.
4. Quand Jeanne s'est réveillée une femme dormait dans un fauteuil.
5. La mèche se trouvait flottant sur l'huile dans un verre de cuisine.
6. La femme endormie avait la tête inclinée sur l'épaule et le bonnet par terre.
7. Jeanne s'est approchée de la dormeuse sur la pointe des pieds.
8. La femme lui a ordonné d'aller se recoucher.
9. La servante s'appelait Rosalie.
10. Les deux femmes ont fini par sangloter toutes les deux.
11. She was tired because she had spent five nights by the bedside of her dying aunt.
12. The stranger handled her gently yet with authority.
13. Jeanne thought the stranger to be between forty and forty-five years of age.
14. It was near the middle of the night when Jeanne woke up.
15. She did not know where she had seen her before — or even when.
16. When the stranger saw Jeanne she sat up with a start.
17. She showed her affection by weeping and kissing her face and cheeks.
18. At the beginning of the story Jeanne was at the cemetery.
19. She cried because Jeanne could not recognise her as her old servant.
20. To make out who she was Jeanne leaned over her bed and stared hard.

VI. LISE

1. The love of a twelve-year-old boy for Lise.
2. He visited her in the evening when her mother had gone out.
3. He compared her to an angel, fairy and princess.
4. He continually asked her questions.
5. She used to avoid his dreamy eyes.
6. He showed his toys and his top, his knowledge of Latin.
7. He used to lean on her book to translate a psalm.

LEÇON 34:

1. (*a*) I ran for some time like a wounded goat. I felt lost. Where could I find some money? How could I get away and how could I find my brother again?

At last, overcome, worn out with fatigue and grief, I let myself drop into the snow at the foot of a chestnut tree. I might have stayed there until the next day, weeping, not having the energy to think, when suddenly, a long way off, I heard a bell ringing. It was the one at school. I had forgotten everything; that bell called me back to life; I had to go back and supervise the children's break in the hall. . . . Thinking of the hall, I suddenly had an idea. Straight away my tears stopped flowing; I felt stronger, calmer. I got up, and with the deliberate step of a man who has just made an irrevocable decision, I retraced my steps towards Sarlande.

If you want to know more about this important decision, follow me over that white plain, into the muddy streets of the town, into the main entrance of the school, and the children's recreation room. And read over my shoulder the letter I am now writing to my brother: "Forgive me, dear Roger, for the sorrow that I have just brought upon you. When you get this letter, your poor Dédé will be dead."

(*b*) For half a century, the middle-class ladies of Pont-l'Evêque envied Madame Aubain her servant, Felicity. For a hundred francs a year, she did the cooking and the housework, sewed, washed, ironed, could bridle a horse, fatten poultry, beat the butter, and she remained faithful to her mistress who nevertheless was not a pleasant person.

She had married a penniless young man who had died at the beginning of 1809, leaving her two very young children and a pile of debts. So she sold her furniture and left her house at Saint Melaine to live in a less pretentious one in an alley leading to the river.

She rose at dawn so as not to miss mass, and worked till evening without a break. Her face was thin and her voice shrill. At twenty-five one would have thought she was forty. From fifty onwards she was ageless, and always silent, with upright figure and calculated movements, she seemed to function automatically, like a woman of wood.

2. Dès qu'il eut reçu sa monnaie, Georges quitta le café et trouva un banc tout près sur le boulevard. Là, il sortit de sa poche l'argent qui lui restait et le compta. Il lui faudrait faire des économies jusqu'à la fin du mois, pensa-t-il. Avant de poursuivre son chemin, il y resta plusieurs minutes, regardant droit devant lui mais sans rien voir, pas même la foule qui se dépêchait sur le trottoir, ni les voitures, les taxis, les autobus en train de ramener des hommes plus heureux que lui vers la soupe qu'avaient préparée à la maison leurs femmes dévouées et affectueuses. Il se demanda pour la vingtième fois ce qu'il allait faire. Où se

coucherait-il? Il ne connaissait personne dans cette ville qui pourrait lui offrir un lit pour la nuit. S'il allait à l'hôtel il n'aurait pas assez d'argent pour payer son prochain repas.

Soudain, il sursauta. Il crut reconnaître le dos d'un jeune homme qui était sur le point d'entrer dans le café que Georges venait de quitter. Mais oui, c'était bien Bonvier, celui qui avait travaillé avec lui au bureau de poste il y a quelques années, et qui lui avait une fois emprunté 500 francs, qu'il n'avait jamais rendus. Georges se leva vite et suivit son ancien collègue à la table où il avait commandé un verre de bière.

3. 1. She wanted to know what games the boys across the road were playing.
2. She could have gone down into the street and entered behind the chemist's shop by a little door. She did not go that way because she was afraid of meeting grown-up persons in that unfamiliar house.
3. She used an ironing board.
4. She crossed on all-fours. She was three floors up.
5. She became giddy half-way across.
6. She saw the paving stones of the street and some men's shirts hanging out to dry.
7. She dug her nails into the plank to steady herself.
8. She heard the boys say that she had lost her nerve.

4. Michel est un jeune citadin qui habite une grande ville industrielle dans le nord de la France. Ses parents ont décidé de l'envoyer passer ses vacances chez des cousins à la campagne.

Michel a décidé d'apprendre tout ce qu'il pourrait sur la vie des fermiers. Lorsqu'il est arrivé dans le petit village de Normandie, tout de suite, il a pris de bonnes résolutions.

"Demain je vais me lever à la même heure que toi," a-t-il dit à son cousin. "Veux-tu me réveiller?"

"Très bien, à demain," a répondu son cousin. Le lendemain, à cinq heures du matin, Michel s'est levé en entendant la voix de son cousin qui l'appelait. Après avoir pris un petit déjeuner copieux, ils sont partis, accompagnés de Médor, un des jeunes chiens de la ferme.

Ils ont rejoint d'autres fermiers, et ont passé la matinée à couper le blé. À midi, tout le monde s'est dirigé vers de grands arbres pour prendre un repas bien mérité. Il faisait chaud et Michel a commencé à sentir les brûlures du soleil, mais il était heureux.

Une heure plus tard, ils ont repris le travail. Vers six heures du soir, ils sont revenus à la ferme. Michel a pensé que la journée de travail était finie, mais il se trompait. Son cousin l'entraînait vers l'étable pour traire les vaches.

Vers neuf heures, Michel s'est couché très fatigué, mais il était très fier: il avait travaillé autant que son cousin le fermier.

FRENCH-ENGLISH VOCABULARY

A

à [a] *to, at, on*
abandonner [abɑ̃dɔne] *to abandon*
un abattoir [abatwaːr] *slaughter-house*
abattre [abatr] *to knock down*
un abbé [abe] *abbot*
une abeille [abɛj] *bee*
un aboiement [abwamɑ̃] *barking*
l'abolition [abɔlisjɔ̃] (f.) *abolition*
une abomination [abɔminasjɔ̃] *abomination*
l'abondance [abɔ̃dɑ̃s] (f.) *abundance*
en abondance *in abundance*
abondant(e) [abɔ̃dɑ̃, -ɑ̃t] *plentiful*
d'abord [dabɔːr] *first of all, at first*
aboutissant(e) [abutisɑ̃, -ɑ̃t] *ending in*
aboyer [abwaye] *to bark*
abréger [abreʒe] *to cut short*
un abri [abri] *shelter*
un abricot [abriko] *apricot*
une absence [apsɑ̃ːs] *absence*
absolu(e) [apsɔly] *complete*
absurde [apsyrd] *absurd, preposterous*
un abus [aby] *abuse*
abuser de [abyse də] *to take advantage of*
accabler [akɑble] *to crush, overwhelm*
un accent [aksɑ̃] *accent*
accepter [aksɛpte] *to accept*
un accessit [aksɛsit] *certificate of merit*
un accident [aksidɑ̃] *accident*
accompagner [akɔ̃paɲe] *to accompany*
d'accord [dakɔːr] *agreed*
s'accoutumer à [sakutyme a] *to get used to*
accrocher [akrɔʃe] *to hang, hook up*
un accroissement [akrwasmɑ̃] *increase*
accroître [akrwaːtr] *to increase*
accueillir [akœjiːr] *to welcome*
un achat [aʃa] *purchase*
acheter [aʃte] *to buy*
un acheteur [aʃtœːr] *buyer*
achever [aʃve] *to complete*
un acide [asid] *acid*
l'acier [asje] (m.) *steel*
une aciérie [asjeri] *steel-works*
acquérir [akeriːr] *to acquire, purchase*
l'acteur [aktœːr] *actor*
actif, -ive [aktif, -iːv] *active*
l'activité [aktivite] (f.) *activity*
actuel, -elle [aktyɛl] *present*
une addition [adisjɔ̃] *bill, adding up*
adhérer à [adere a] *to join (party, etc.)*
admettre [admɛtr] *to admit*
administratif, -ive [administratif, -iːv] *administrative*
admirable [admirabl] *admirable*
admirer [admire] *to admire*
adoptif, -ive [adɔptif, -iːv] *adopted*
adorer [adɔre] *to adore*
une adresse [adrɛs] *address*
s'adresser à [sadrɛse a] *to address*
un(e) adversaire [advɛrsɛːr] *opponent*
un aérodrome [aɛrɔdroːm] *aerodrome*
affaiblir [afɛbliːr] *to weaken*
les affaires [afɛːr] *business*
faire des affaires d'or *to do a roaring [trade*
s'affairer [safɛre] *to bustle about*

s'affaisser [safɛse] *to be depressed, sink down*
affamé(e) [afame] *very hungry, famished*
l'affection [afɛksjɔ̃] (f.) *affection, fondness*
affectueux, -euse [afɛktyø, -øːz] *affectionate*
une affiche [afiʃ] *notice-board, poster*
afficher [afiʃe] *to display (a bill)*
affirmatif, -ive [afirmatif, -iːv] *affirmative*
une affluence [aflyɑ̃ːs] *flow, crowd, rush*
affreux, -euse [afrø, -øːz] *awful, horrible*
affronter [afrɔ̃te] *to face*
afin que [afɛ̃ kə] *in order that*
agacer [agase] *to annoy*
un âge [ɑːʒ] *age, period*
âgé (de) *aged, old*
d'un certain âge *middle-aged*
un agent [aʒɑ̃] *agent*
un agent de police [aʒɑ̃ də pɔlis] *policeman*
agile [aʒil] *agile, active*
agir [aʒiːr] *to act [matter of*
s'agir de [saʒiːr də] *to concern, be a*
l'agitation [aʒitasjɔ̃] (f.) *agitation*
agiter [aʒite] *to wave*
un agneau [aɲo] *lamb*
agréable [agreabl] *pleasant*
agréer [agree] *to agree to, accept*
un agresseur [agrɛsœːr] *aggressor*
agressif, -ive [agrɛsif, -iːv] *aggressive*
agricole [agrikɔl] *agricultural*
l'agriculture [agrikyltyːr] (f.) *agriculture*
l'aide [ɛd] (m.) *help*
à l'aide de *with the help of*
aider (à) [ɛde] *to help (to)*
aigu, -üe [ɛgy] *sharp, keen*
ailleurs [ajœːr] *elsewhere*
d'ailleurs [dajœːr] *moreover*
aimable [ɛmabl] *pleasant*
aimer [ɛme] *to like, love*
aimer mieux *to prefer*
aîné(e) [ɛne] *elder, eldest*
ainsi [ɛ̃si] *so, for example, thus, in this*
et ainsi de suite *and so forth [way*
ainsi que *as well as*
un air [ɛːr] *look, manner, tune*
à l'aise [a lɛːz] *comfortably*
à son aise *at one's leisure*
ajouter [aʒute] *to add*
ajuster [aʒyste] *to adjust*
un album [albɔm] *album*
l'Algérie [alʒeri] (f.) *Algeria*
l'algue [alg] *seaweed*
l'aliment [alimɑ̃] (m.) *food*
une allée [ale] *alley, garden path*
l'Allemagne [almaɲ] (f.) *Germany*
un Allemand [almɑ̃] *German*
aller [ale] *to go*
aller bien avec [ale bjɛ̃navɛk] *to match,*
s'en aller [sɑ̃nale] *to leave [go well with*
les Alliés [alje] *Allies*
allô [alo] *hallo*
une allocation [alɔkasjɔ̃] *allocation, grant*
une allocution [alɔkysjɔ̃] *short speech,*
allonger [alɔ̃ʒe] *to lengthen [address*

461

allumer [alyme] *to light*
une allumette [alymɛt] *match*
une allusion [allyzjɔ̃] *allusion*
    alors [alɔːr] *then*
une alouette [alwɛt] *skylark*
les Alpes [alp] (f.) *Alps*
    amasser [amɑse] *to gather*
une Amazone [amazoːn] *Amazon*
une ambition [ɑ̃bisjɔ̃] *ambition*
une âme [ɑːm] *soul*
    améliorer [ameljɔre] *to improve*
    américain(e) [amerikɛ̃, -ɛn] *American*
    l'Amérique [amerik] (f.) *America*
un ami, une amie [ami] *friend*
    l'amitié [amitje] (f.) *affection, friendship*
un amour [amuːr] *love*
un amoureux, une -euse [amurø, -øːz]
    ample [ɑ̃pl] *ample*   [*sweetheart*
    l'ampleur [ɑ̃plœːr] (f.) *fullness, scope*
    amusant(e) [amyzɑ̃, -ɑ̃t] *amusing*
    s'amuser bien [samyze bjɛ̃] *to have a good*
un ananas [ananɑ(ːs)] *pineapple*   [*time*
les ancêtres [ɑ̃sɛːtr] *ancestors*
    ancien, -ienne [ɑ̃sjɛ̃, -jɛn] *ancient, former*
    l'ancre [ɑ̃ːkr] *anchor*
un âne [ɑːn] *donkey*
un an, une année [ɑ̃, ane] *year*
    l'année scolaire *school year*
un ange [ɑ̃ːʒ] *angel*
    anglais(e) [ɑ̃glɛ, -ɛːz] *English*
    l'Anglais(e) *Englishman (-woman)*
un angle [ɑ̃ːgl] *corner*
    l'Angleterre [ɑ̃glətɛːr] (f.) *England*
un animal, -aux [animal, -mo] *animal(s)*
un anniversaire [anivɛrsɛːr] *birthday*
une annonce [anɔ̃ːs] *bid, advertisement*
    annoncer [anɔ̃se] *to announce*
    annuel, -le [an(n)yɛl] *annual*
une antenne [ɑ̃tɛn] *aerial*
    anxieux, -euse [ɑ̃ksjø, -øːz] *anxious*
    août [u] (m.) *August*
    apercevoir [apɛrsəvwaːr] *to catch sight*
un aperçu [apɛrsy] *outline, sketch*   [*of*
un apéritif [aperitif] *drink before a meal*
un appétit [apeti] *appetite*   [*moved*
    s'apitoyer [apitwaje] *to be emotionally*
un appareil [aparɛːj] *instrument, apparatus*
    un appareil photographique [aparɛːj
                    fɔtografik] *camera*
une apparition [aparisjɔ̃] *apparition*
un appartement [apartəmɑ̃] *flat*
    appartenir [apartəniːr] *to belong*
    appeler [aple] *to call*
    s'appeler [saple] *to be named, called*
une apostrophe [apɔstrɔf] *apostrophe*
    s'appliquer [saplike] *to apply oneself*
    apporter [apɔrte] *to bring*
    apprécier [apresje] *to value, appreciate*
    apprendre [aprɑ̃ːdr] *to learn*
    s'apprêter à [saprɛte] *to prepare to*
    approcher [aprɔʃe] *to come closer*
    s'approcher de [saprɔʃe də] *to approach*
    approuver [apruve] *to approve of*
    s'appuyer [sapɥije] *to lean*
    après [aprɛ] *after*
une après-midi [aprɛmidi] *afternoon*
une araignée [arɛɲe] *spider*
un arbre [arbr] *tree*
un arc [ark] *bow, arch*

un arc-en-ciel [arkɛ̃sjɛl] *rainbow*
un archet [arʃɛ] *bow*
    l'architecture [arʃitɛktyːr] (f.) *architecture*
    l'argent [arʒɑ̃] (m.) *silver, money*
une armée [arme] *army*
les armements [arməmɑ̃] (m.) *armaments*
    armer [arme] *to arm, to cock* (pistol)
un armistice [armistis] *armistice*
une armoire [armwaːr] *wardrobe, cupboard*
    arracher [araʃe] *to snatch*
    arranger [arɑ̃ʒe] *to arrange, fit up*
un arrêt [arɛ] *stop*
un arrêt d'autobus [arɛ dotɔbyːs] *bus-stop*
    s'arrêter [sarɛte] *to stop*
    en arrière [arjɛːr] *behind, backward, back*
une arrière-garde [arjɛːrgard] *rear-guard*
une arrivée [arive] *arrival*
    arriver [arive] *to arrive*
    arroser [aroze] *to water, to sprinkle*
un article [artikl] *article*
un as [ɑːs] *ace*
un ascenseur [asɑ̃sœːr] *lift*
un aspect [aspɛ] *appearance*
une asperge [aspɛrʒ] *asparagus*
    assaillir [asajiːr] *to attack*
un assassinat [asasina] *murder*
une assemblée [asɑ̃ble] *meeting*
    s'asseoir [saswaːr] *to sit*   [*sufficient*
    assez [ase] *sufficiently, rather, enough,*
    assidu(e) [asidy] *assiduous, hard* (work)
une assiette [asjɛt] *plate*
    assis(e) [asi, -iz] *seated, sitting*
un assistant [asistɑ̃] *assistant, person present*
    assister à [asiste a] *to watch, be present*
    assombrir [asɔ̃briːr] *to darken*   [*at*
    assourdissant(e) [asurdisɑ̃, -ɑ̃t] *deafening*
    assujettir [asyʒɛtiːr] *to subdue, fasten*
    assurer [asyre] *to assure*
un atelier [atəlje] *workshop*
    l'Atlantique [atlɑ̃tik] (m.) *Atlantic Ocean*
une atmosphère [atmɔsfɛːr] *air, atmosphere*
    atomique [atɔmik] *atomic*
    atroce [atrɔs] *atrocious*
    attabler [atable] *to sit down to table*
    attacher [ataʃe] *to tie*
une attaque [atak] *attack*
    atteindre [atɛ̃ːdr] *to reach*
    attendre [atɑ̃ːdr] *to wait (for)*
    s'attendre à [satɑ̃ːdr a] *to expect*
    attentif, -ive [atɑ̃tif, -iv] *attentive*
    l'attention [atɑ̃sjɔ̃] *attention*
        attention! *look out, careful!*
        faire attention *to be careful*
    attirer [atire] *to attract*
    attraper [atrape] *to catch*
    attrister [atriste] *to sadden*
    l'aube [oːb] (f.) *dawn*
une auberge [obɛrʒ] *inn*
    aucun(e) [okœ̃, -yn] *no (one)*
    au-dessous [odəsu] *below*
    au-dessus [odəsy] *above*
    augmenter [ɔgmɑ̃te] *to go up, increase*
    aujourd'hui [oʒurdɥi] *today*
    auparavant [oparavɑ̃] *previously*
une aurore [ɔrɔːr] *dawn*
    auquel, auxquel(le)s [okɛl] *to which*
    aussi [osi] *also, as*
    aussi (+ inverted verb) [osi] *so*
    aussi . . . que [osi k(ə)] *as . . . as*

462

aussitôt [osito] *immediately*
autant que [otã kə] *as much as*
un **autobus** [otɔbyːs] *bus*
l'**autocar** [otɔkaːr] *motor-coach*
un **automate** [otomat] *automaton*
automatique [otɔmatik] *automatic*
l'**automne** [otɔn] *autumn*
une **automobile** [otomɔbil] *motor-car*
l'**automobiliste** [otɔmɔbilist] *motorist*
une **autorité** [otɔrite] *authority*
un **autorail** [otoraːj] *diesel rail-car*
autoriser [otɔrize] *to authorise*
l'**autoroute** [otɔrut] *motorway, clearway*
un **auto-stoppeur** [otostɔpœːr] *hitch-hiker*
autour de [otuːr də] *around*
autre [otr] *other*
autrefois [otrəfwa] *formerly*
autrement [otrəmã] *otherwise*
l'**Autriche** [otriʃ] (f.) *Austria*
avaler [avale] *to swallow*
un **avancement** [avãsmã] *promotion*
avancer [avãse] *to advance*
avant [avã] *before*
  en avant *forward, to the front*
avantageusement [avãtaʒøsmã]
avare [avaːr] *miserly*   [*favourably*
avec [avɛk] *with*
une **avenue** [avny] *avenue*
l'**avenir** [avniːr] (m.) *future*
une **aventure** [avãtyːr] *adventure*
avertir [avɛrtiːr] *to warn*
aveugle [avœgl] *blind*
un **aviateur** [avjatœːr] *pilot*
un **avion** [avjõ] *aeroplane*
un **aviron** [avirõ] *oar*
un **avis** [avi] *opinion*
l'**avoine** [avwan] (f.) *oats*
avoir [avwaːr] *to have*
avoir à [avwaːr a] *to have to*
avoir beau [avwaːr bo] *to do in vain*
avoir lieu [avwaːr ljø] *to take place*
avouer [avwe] *to confess*
avril [avril] (m.) *April*

B

le **baba au rhum** [baba o rɔm] *rum-baba*
le **baccalauréat** [bakalɔrea] *school-leaving*
                          examination
le **bachot** [baʃo] *school-leaving examination*
les **bagages** [bagaːʒ] (m.) *luggage*
la **bagarre** [bagaːr] *brawl*
la **bague** [bag] *ring* (finger)
la **baguette** [bagɛt] *long loaf, stick*
la **baie** [bɛ] *bay*
se **baigner** [bɛɲe] *to bath, bathe*
le **baigneur** [bɛɲœːr] *bather*
la **baignoire** [bɛɲwaːr] *bath*
baiser [bɛze] *to kiss*
baisser [bɛse] *to lower*
se **baisser** [sə bɛse] *to stoop, bend down*
la **balance** [balãːs] *scales*
se **balancer** [sə balãse] *to sway*
balayer [balɛje] *to sweep*
balbutier [balbysje] *to stammer*
le **balcon** [balkõ] *balcony*
la **baleine** [balɛn] *whale*
la **balle** [bal] *ball, bullet*
le **ballon** [balõ] *ball, football, balloon*
la **banane** [banan] *banana*

le **banc** [bã] *seat, bench*
la **bande** [bãːd] *band*
la **banlieue** [bãljø] *suburbs*
la **banquette** [bãkɛt] *seat, bench, form*
la **barbe** [barb] *beard*
barbouiller [barbuje] *to besmear*
le **baron** [barõ] *baron*
la **barque** [bark] *boat*
la **barrière** [barjɛːr] *gate*
les **bas** [ba] (m.) *stockings*
bas, -sse [ba, bas] *low*
là-bas *down, over there*
en bas *downstairs*
basculer [baskyle] *to sway up and down*
la **basse-cour** [baskuːr] *farmyard*
le **bassin** [basɛ̃] *pool*
le **bateau** [bato] *boat*
le **bâtiment** [batimã] *building*
bâtir [batiːr] *to build*
le **bâton** [batõ] *stick, cane, wand*
battre [batr] *to beat*
se **battre** [sə batr] *to fight*
bavard(e) [bavaːr, -ard] *talkative*
bavarder [bavarde] *to chatter*
beau [bo] (m.), **belle** [bɛl] (f.) *fine,*
  avoir beau faire *to do in vain*   [*beautiful*
beaucoup [boku] *much, many, a lot*
le **beau-fils** [bofis] *step-son*
le **beau-frère** [bofrɛːr] *brother-in-law*
le **beau-père** [bopɛːr] *father-in-law*
la **beauté** [bote] *beauty*
le **bébé** [bebe] *baby*
la **bêche** [bɛʃ] *spade*
bêler [bɛle] *to bleat*
le **Belge** [bɛlʒ] *Belgian*
la **Belgique** [bɛlʒik] *Belgium*
la **belle-fille** [bɛlfij] *daughter-in-law*
la **belle-mère** [bɛlmɛːr] *mother-in-law*
la **belle-sœur** [bɛlsœːr] *sister-in-law*
la **béquille** [bekiːj] *crutch*
le **berceau** [bɛrzo] *cradle*
le **berger** [bɛrʒe] *shepherd*
la **besogne** [bzɔɲ] *task*
le **besoin** [bəzwɛ̃] *need*
  avoir besoin de *to need, have need of*
le **bétail** [betaːj] *cattle*
la **bête** [bɛt] *animal*
la **bêtise** [bɛtiːz] *silly thing, silliness,*
la **betterave** [bɛtrav] *beetroot*   [*stupidity*
la **betterave à sucre** [bɛtrav a sykr] *sugar-*
le **beurre** [bœːr] *butter*   [*beet*
la **bibliothèque** [bibliɔtɛk] *library*
la **bicyclette** [bisiklɛt] *bicycle*
le **bidon** [bidõ] *can*
bien [bjɛ̃] *well, good, much, many*
  Eh bien! *Well!*
  faire du bien à *to do good to*
  ou bien *or else*
  bien que *although*
bientôt [bjɛto] *soon*
la **bienvenue** [bjɛ̃vny] *welcome*
la **bière** [bjɛːr] *beer*
le **bijou(tier)** [biʒu(tje)] *jewel(ler)*
le **billet** [bijɛ] *ticket, bill, note*
le **billet de banque** [bijɛ də bãːk] *bank-note*
le **billet aller et retour** [bijɛ ale e rətuːr]
le **biscuit** [biskyi] *biscuit*   [*return ticket*
bizarre [bizaːr] *quaint, odd*
blâmer (de) [blame] *to blame (for)*

463

blanc, blanche [blɑ̃, blɑ̃ʃ] *white*
la blancheur [blɑ̃ʃœːr] *whiteness*
le blé [ble] *corn, wheat*
blessant [blɛsɑ̃] *offensive, cutting*
le blessé [blɛse] *wounded man* [(remark)
blesser [blɛse] *to hurt*
la blessure [blɛsyːr] *wound*
bleu(e) [blø] *blue*
blond(e) [blɔ̃, -ɔ̃ːd] *fair, blond*
la blouse [bluːz] *blouse, overall*
le blouson [bluzɔ̃] *windcheater*
le bœuf [bœf] *ox, bullock, beef*
boire [bwaːr] *to drink*
le bois [bwɑ] *wood*
boisé [bwɑze] *wooded*
la boisson [bwasɔ̃] *drink*
la boîte [bwat] *box, tin*
la boîte de conserves [bwat də kɔ̃sɛrv] *jar*
    of jam, tinned food
la boîte aux lettres [bwat o lɛtr] *post-box*
la boîte à ordure [bwat a ɔrdyːr] *litter-bin*
le bol [bɔl] *bowl*
bon, bonne [bɔ̃, bɔn] *good, right*
    à quoi bon? *what is the good of?*
le bonbon [bɔ̃bɔ̃] *sweet*
bondé(e) [bɔ̃de] *packed, full*
le bonheur [bɔnœːr] *happiness* [*snowman*
le bonhomme de neige [bɔnɔm də nɛːʒ]
le boniment [bɔnimɑ̃] *salesman's patter*
Bonjour! [bɔ̃ʒuːr] *Good day! Good*
la bonne [bɔn] *maid-servant* [*morning!* etc.
le bonnet [bɔnɛ] *cap, hat*
la bonté [bɔ̃te] *goodness*
le bord [bɔːr] *edge, side*
    à bord *on board*
border [bɔrde] *to border on*
la borne [bɔrn] *boundary, milestone*
borné(e) [bɔrne] *narrow, limited*
se borner à [sə bɔrne a] *to confine oneself to*
bossu(e) [bɔsy] *hunch-backed*
la botte [bɔt] *boot*
la bouche [buʃ] *mouth*
le boucher [buʃe] *butcher*
la boucherie [buʃri] *butcher's shop*
la boucle [bukl] *buckle*
le boueur [buœːr] *scavenger*
boueux, -euse [buø, -øːz] *muddy*
bouger [buʒe] *to stir, to move*
la bougie [buʒi] *candle, plug*
bouillir [bujiːr] *to boil*
la bouillotte [bujɔt] *hot-water bottle*
la boulangerie [bulɑ̃ʒri] *baker's shop*
le boulevard [bulvaːr] *boulevard*
la boule [bul] *ball*
le bouquet [bukɛ] *bouquet, bunch*
le bouquin [bukɛ̃] *old book*
le bouquiniste [bukinist] *secondhand*
le bourgeois [burʒwa] *citizen* [*bookseller*
la bourgeoisie [burʒwazi] *middle-classes*
bousculer [buskyle] *to jostle*
le bout [bu] *end*
    au bout de *after, at the end of*
la bouteille [butɛːj] *bottle*
la boutique [butik] *small shop*
le bouton [butɔ̃] *button*
la braise [brɛːz] *embers*
la branche [brɑ̃ːʃ] *branch of a tree*
brandir [brɑ̃ːdir] *to brandish*
le bras [brɑ] *arm*

brave [braːv] *brave, good, worthy*
braver [braːve] *to dare*
bref, brève [brɛf, brɛːv] *short, brief*
la Bretagne [brətaɲ] *Brittany*
les bretelles [brətɛl] *braces, straps*
brider [bride] *to bridle*
le bridge [bridʒ] *bridge* (card game)
le brigadier [brigadje] *corporal*
briller [brije] *to shine*
la brioche [briɔʃ] *bun, cake*
le briquet [brikɛ] *cigarette-lighter*
le brise-lames [brizlam] *breakwater*
briser [brize] *to break*
britannique [britanik] *British*
la brochure [brɔʃyːr] *pamphlet*
la brosse [brɔs] *brush*
la brouette [bruɛt] *wheelbarrow*
le brouillard [brujaːr] *fog, mist*
brouter [brute] *to browse*
broyer [brwaje] *to pound, to crush*
le bruit [bryi] *noise*
brûler [bryle] *to burn*
la brume [brym] *mist, thick fog*
brun(e) [brœ, bryn] *brown*
brusquement [bryskəmɑ̃] *abruptly*
le bûcher [byʃe] *wood-shed*
le bûcheron [byʃrɔ̃] *woodcutter*
le buffet [byfɛ] *sideboard*
le buisson [byisɔ̃] *bush, thicket, shrub*
buissonnier, -ière [byisɔnje, -jɛːr] *bush*
    faire l'école buissonnière *to play truant*
le bulletin [byltɛ̃] *report* [*luggage-ticket*
le bulletin de bagages [byltɛ̃ də bagaʒ]
le bureau [byro] *writing-desk, office*
le bureau de location [byro də lokasjɔ̃]
                                    box-office
le bureau de poste [byro də pɔst] *post office*
le bureau de renseignements [byro də
                    rɑ̃sɛɲmɑ̃] *enquiry office*
le but [by(t)] *target, mark, purpose*

C

ça [sa] *that* [*bathing-hut*
la cabine de plage [kabin də plaʒ]
la cabine téléphonique [kabin telefɔniːk]
                            telephone kiosk
le cabinet [kabinɛ] *water-closet, private*
cacher [kaʃe] *to hide* [*room*
le cachet [kaʃɛ] *stamp, seal*
la cachette [kaʃɛt] *hiding-place*
le cadavre [kadɑːvr] *corpse*
le cadeau [kado] *present, gift*
cadet, -ette [kadɛ, -ɛt] *younger, junior*
le café (crème) [kafekrɛm] *coffee* (*with*
la cage [kaːʒ] *cage* [*cream*)
le cahier [kaje] *exercise-book*
cailler [kaje] *to curdle*
le caillou [kaju] *pebble*
la caisse [kɛs] *packing-case, case, cash-box*
le calcul [kalkyl] *arithmetic, sum*
le caleçon de bain [kalsɔ̃ də bɛ̃] *bathing-*
le calendrier [kalɑ̃drje] *calendar* [*trunks*
calme [kalm] *calm*
le, la camarade [kamarad] (*school-*)*friend*
le cambrioleur [kɑ̃briɔlœːr] *burglar*
le camion [kamjɔ̃] *lorry*
la campagnarde [kɑ̃paɲard] *countrywoman*
la campagne [kɑ̃paɲ] *country*

le campeur [kɑ̃pœːr] *camper*
le camping [kɑ̃piŋ] *camping (site)*
le Canada [kanada] *Canada*
le canapé [kanape] *sofa, settee, couch*
le canard [kanaːr] *duck*
le candidat [kɑ̃dida] *candidate*
le canif [kanif] *pen-knife*
la canne [kan] *cane, stick*
le canoë [kanɔe] *canoe*
le canot [kano] *small boat*
le capitaine [kapitɛn] *captain*
la capitale [kapital] *capital* (city)
   car [kaːr] *for*
le car [kaːr] *motor-coach*
le caractère [karaktɛːr] *character*
la carafe [karaf] *decanter*
le carnet [karnɛ] *book* (of tickets, etc.)
le carnet de chèques [karnɛ də ʃɛk] *cheque*
la carotte [karɔt] *carrot*   [*book*
carré(e) [kare] *square*
le carreau [karo] *diamond* (cards), *check*
le carrefour [karfuːr] *cross-roads*
le carrelage [karlaːʒ] *tiled-floor*
la carte [kart] *card, map*   [*season ticket*
la carte d'abonnement [kart dabɔnmɑ̃]
la carte postale [kart pɔstal] *postcard*
le carton à chapeaux [kartɔ̃ a ʃapo] *hat-*
le cas [kɑ] *case*   [*box*
   en tout cas [ɑ̃ tu ka] *in any case*
la cascade [kaskad] *waterfall*
la caserne [kazɛrn] *barracks*
la casquette [kaskɛt] *cap*
casser [kase] *to break*
la casserole [kasrɔl] *sauce-pan*
la cathédrale [katedral] *cathedral*
la cause [koːz] *cause*
   à cause de *because of*
causer [koze] *to chat, cause*
la cave [kaːv] *cellar*
   ce, cet, cette, ces [sə, sɛt, se] *this, that,*
                     these, those
   ce qui, ce que [sə ki, sə kə] *what,*
   ceci [səsi] *this*   [*that which*
la ceinture [sɛ̃tyːr] *belt, waist*
   cela [s(ə)la] *that*
   célèbre [selɛbr] *famous*
   célébrer [selebre] *to celebrate*
   celui, celle [səlɥi, sɛl] *this one, that one*
   celui-ci [səlɥisi] *this one, the latter*
   celui-là [səlɥila] *that one, the former*
la cendre [sɑ̃dr] *ashes, cinders*
le cendrier [sɑ̃drije] *ash-tray*
   cent [sɑ̃] *hundred*
une centaine [sɑ̃tɛn] *group of about a*
le centime [sɑ̃tim] *centime*   [*hundred*
le centimètre [sɑ̃timɛtr] *centimetre*
le centre [sɑ̃ːtr] *centre*
   cependant [səpɑ̃dɑ̃] *however*
la céréale [sereal] *cereal*
la cérémonie [seremɔni] *ceremony*
le cerf [sɛːr] *deer, stag*
la cerise [s(ə)riːz] *cherry*
le cerisier [srizje] *cherry-tree*
   certain(e) [sɛrtɑ̃, -ɛn] *certain*
   certes [sɛrt] *most assuredly*
le cerveau [sɛrvo] *brain*
la cervelle [sɛrvɛl] *brain*
   cesser [sese] *to cease*
   ceux, celles [sø, sɛl] *these, those*

   chacun(e) [ʃakœ̃, -yn] *every, each one*
la chaîne [ʃɛn] *range, chain*
la chaise [ʃɛːz] *chair*
le chaland [ʃalɑ̃] *barge*
le chalet [ʃalɛ] *chalet*
la chaleur [ʃalœːr] *heat*
   chaleureusement [ʃalœrøːzmɑ̃] *warmly*
la chambre [ʃɑ̃ːbr] *room*   [*boxroom*
la chambre de débarras [ʃɑ̃ːbr də debara]
la chambre à coucher [ʃɑ̃ːbr a kuʃe] *bed-*
le chameau [ʃamo] *camel*   [*room*
le champ [ʃɑ̃] *field*
le champignon [ʃɑ̃piɲɔ̃] *mushroom*
la chance [ʃɑ̃ːs] *luck*
   bonne chance! *good luck!*
le chandail [ʃɑ̃daːj] *sweater*
   changer (de) [ʃɑ̃ʒe] *to change*
   pour changer [puːr ʃɑ̃ʒe] *for a change*
le chant [ʃɑ̃] *song, singing*
   chanter [ʃɑ̃te] *to sing*
le chapeau [ʃapo] *hat*
le chapeau melon [məlɔ̃] *bowler hat*
le chapitre [ʃapitr] *a chapter*
   chaque [ʃak] *each, every*
le charbon [ʃarbɔ̃] *coal*
la charcuterie [ʃarkytri] *pork butcher's*
la Charente [ʃarɑ̃t] *river and department*
   (i.e. county) *in south-west France*
   charger [ʃarʒe] *to charge, load*
le chariot [ʃarjo] *cart*
   charmant(e) [ʃarmɑ̃, -ɑ̃t] *charming*
le charme [ʃarm] *charm*
la charrette [ʃarɛt] *cart*
la charrue [ʃary] *plough*
   chasser [ʃase] *to drive away, sack*
le chat [ʃa] *cat*
le chataîgnier [ʃatɛɲje] *chestnut-tree*
le château [ʃato] *castle*
le château de sable [ʃato də sabl] *sand-*
   chaud(e) [ʃo, ʃoːd] *hot, warm*   [*castle*
   avoir chaud *to be hot*
la chaumière [ʃomjɛːr] *thatched cottage*
la chaussée [ʃose] *roadway*
   chausser [ʃose] *put on the feet*
la chaussette [ʃosɛt] *sock*
la chaussure [ʃosyːr] *shoes, footwear*
   chauve [ʃoːv] *bald*
la chauve-souris [ʃovsuri] *bat*
le chef [ʃɛf] *chief, leader, boss*
le chef de gare [ʃɛf də gaːr] *station-master*
le chef de train [ʃɛf də trɛ̃] *guard*
le chef-d'œuvre [ʃɛdœːvr] *masterpiece*
le chemin [ʃmɛ̃] *path*
   en chemin [ɑ̃ ʃmɛ̃] *on the way*
le chemin de fer [ʃəmɛ̃ də fɛːr] *railway*
la cheminée [ʃ(ə)mine] *fireplace, chimney*
la chemise [ʃmiːz] *shirt*
la chemise de nuit [ʃmiːz də nyi] *nightdress*
le chenapan [ʃnapɑ̃] *rogue, rascal*
le chêne [ʃɛn] *oak tree*
   en chêne [ɑ̃ ʃɛn] *in, made of, oak*
   cher, chère [ʃɛːr] *dear*
   chercher [ʃɛrʃe] *to seek, look for*
   chercher à [ʃɛrʃe] *to attempt to*
   chéri(e) [ʃeri] *dear, darling*
le cheval [ʃəval] *horse*
le chevalier [ʃəvalje] *horseman, knight*
le chevet [ʃ(ə)vɛ] *bed-head*
le cheveu [ʃəvø] *hair*

la cheville [ʃ(ə)viːj] *ankle-bone*
la chèvre [ʃɛːvr] *goat*
  chez [ʃe] *to (at) the house of*
  chic [ʃik] *smart*
le chien [ʃjɛ̃] *dog*
le chiffre [ʃifr] *figure, number*
le chignon [ʃiɲɔ̃] *coil (of hair)*
la Chine [ʃin] *China*
le Chinois [ʃinwa] *Chinese*
le chirurgien [ʃiryʒjɛ̃] *surgeon*
le choc [ʃɔk] *shock, impact*
le chocolat [ʃɔkɔla] *chocolate*
le chœur [kœːr] *choir*
  choisir [ʃwaziːr] *to choose*
le choix [ʃwa] *choice, selection*
le chômage [ʃomaːʒ] *unemployment*
la (société) chorale [(sɔsjete) kɔral] *choral*
la chose [ʃoːz] *thing*   [*society, choir*
le chou [ʃu] *cabbage*
le chou-fleur [ʃuflœːr] *cauliflower*
le chrétien [kretjɛ̃] *Christian*
  chuchoter [ʃyʃɔte] *to whisper*
la chute [ʃyt] *fall*
-ci [si] *this*
la cicatrice [sikatris] *scar*
le ciel [sjɛl] *sky*
la cigale [sigal] *grasshopper*
la cigarette [sigarɛt] *cigarette*
le cil [sil] *eyelash*
le cimetière [simtjɛːr] *cemetery*
le cinéma [sinɛma] *cinema*
  cinq [sɛ̃(k)] *five*
  cinquante [sɛ̃kãːt] *fifty*   [*fifty*
une cinquantaine [sɛ̃kãtɛn] *group of about*
la circonstance [sirkɔ̃stãːs] *circumstance*
la circulation [sirkylasjɔ̃] *traffic*
  circuler [sirkyle] *to circulate*
la cire à cacheter [siːr a kaʃte] *sealing-wax*
le cirque [sirk] *circus*
les ciseaux [sizo] *scissors*
le citadin [sitadɛ̃] *city-dweller, townsman*
la cité [site] *city*
le citoyen, la -enne [sitwajɛ̃, -ɛn] *citizen*
une Citroën [sitrɔɛn] *French make of car*
le citron [sitrɔ̃] *lemon*
la citronnade [sitrɔnad] *lemonade*
  civil(e) [sivil] *civil*
la civilisation [sivilizasjɔ̃] *civilization*
  clair(e) [klɛr] *clear, light (colour)*
le clair [klɛːr] *light*
  claquer [klake] *to slam (door), to flap*
la clarinette [klarinɛt] *clarinet*
la classe [klaːs] *class*
le classement [klasmã] *classification*
  classer [klase] *to file*
la clef [kle] *key*
le client, la -e [kliã, -ãt] *client, customer*
la clientèle [kliãtɛl] *business, customers*
le climat [klima] *climate*
un clin d'œil [klɛ̃ d œːj] *twinkling of an eye*
la cloche [klɔʃ] *bell*
le clocher [klɔʃe] *belfry*
la clôture [klotyːr] *fence*
le clou [klu] *nail*
le cochon [kɔʃɔ̃] *pig*
  cocorico or coquerico [kɔkɔriko]
le cœur [kœːr] *heart*   [*cock-a-doodle-doo*
  de bon cœur *heartily*
  au cœur tendre *tender-hearted*

le coffre [kɔfr] *chest, boot* (of car)
le coffre-fort [kɔfrfɔːr] *safe*
se cogner [sə kɔɲe] *to knock against*
  cohérent [kɔɛrã] *coherent*
la coiffure [kwafyːr] *hair-style, hair*
le coiffeur [kwafœːr] *hair-dresser*
la coiffeuse [kwafœːz] *hair-dresser,*
                      dressing-table
le coin [kwɛ̃] *corner*
  au coin du feu *by the fireside*
la colère [kɔlɛːr] *anger*
le colis [kɔli] *parcel*
  collaborer [kɔlabɔre] *to collaborate*
la colle [kɔl] *glue*
le collège [kɔlɛːʒ] *college*
le, la collègue [kɔlɛg] *colleague*
  coller [kɔle] *to stick*
  être collé *to fail*
le collier de perles [kɔlji də pɛrl] *pearl*
la colline [kɔlin] *hill*   [*necklace*
la colombe [kɔlɔ̃ːb] *dove*
le colonel [kɔlɔnɛl] *colonel*
le combat [kɔba] *fight*   [*many*
  combien (de) [kɔ̃bjɛ̃] *how much, how*
  comestible [kɔmɛstibl] *edible, eatable*
le commandant [kɔmãdã] *commander*
  commander [kɔmãde] *to order*
  comme [kɔm] *like, as*
  comme d'habitude *as usual*
le commencement [kɔmãsmã] *beginning*
  commencer (à) [kɔmãse] *to begin (to),*
                          start (to)
  comment [kɔmã] *how, in what way*
le commentaire [kɔmãtɛːr] *commentary,*
                          comment
le commerçant [kɔmɛrsã] *merchant, trades-*
le commerce [kɔmɛrs] *trade*   [*man*
  commercial(e) [kɔmɛrsjal] *commercial*
  commettre [kɔmɛtr] *to commit*
le commis [kɔmi] *clerk*
le commissariat [kɔmisarja] *police station*
la commission [kɔmisjɔ̃] *commission, order*
  faire ses commissions [kɔmisjɔ̃] *to do*
                          one's errands
  commode [kɔmɔd] *convenient*
la commode [kɔmɔd] *chest of drawers*
la commodité [kɔmɔdite] *convenience*
  commun(e) [kɔmœ̃, -yn] *common*
la communauté [kɔmynote] *community*
le communiqué [kɔmynike] *communica-*
                          tion, statement
  communiquer [kɔmynike] *to inform,*
                          communicate
le compagnon [kɔ̃paɲɔ̃] *friend*
la comparaison [kɔ̃parezɔ̃] *comparison*
le compartiment [kɔ̃partimã] *compartment*
la compassion [kɔ̃pasjɔ̃] *sympathy*
le compatriote [kɔ̃patriɔt] *compatriot*
  compenser [kɔ̃pãse] *to compensate*
le complet [kɔ̃plɛ] *suit*
  complètement [kɔ̃plɛtmã] *completely*
  composer [kɔ̃poze] *to sit (a written*
                      examination)
  comprendre [kɔ̃prãːdr] *to consist of,*
                          comprise,
                          understand,
                          include
le comptable [kɔ̃tabl] *book-keeper,*
                          accountant

la **comptabilité** [kɔ̃tabilite] *book-keeping*
le **comptant** [kɔ̃tɑ̃] *cash*
  au comptant [o kɔ̃tɑ̃] *for cash*
le **compte** [kɔ̃t] *account*
  sur son compte *on his account*
  compter [kɔ̃te] *to count*
le **comptoir** [kɔ̃twaːr] *counter*
  concerner [kɔ̃zɛrne] *to concern*
le **concert** [kɔ̃sɛːr] *concert*
la **concierge** [kɔ̃sjɛrʒ] *caretaker, concierge*
  conclure [kɔ̃klyːr] *to conclude, finish*
le **concombre** [kɔ̃kɔ̃ːbr] *cucumber*
la **condition** [kɔ̃disjɔ̃] *condition*
le **conducteur** [kɔdyktœːr] *driver*
  conduire [kɔ̃dyiːr] *to lead, drive* (car)
  se conduire [sə kɔ̃dyiːr] *to behave*
la **conduite** [kɔ̃dɥit] *conduct*
le **cône** [koːn] *cone*
la **conférence** [kɔ̃ferɑ̃ːs] *lecture*
la **confiance** [kɔ̃fjɑ̃ːs] *confidence*
  confier [kɔ̃fje] *to entrust*
  confiner (à) [kɔ̃fine a] *to border* (on)
  confire [kɔ̃fiːr] *conserve*
la **confiture** [kɔ̃fityːr] *jam*
le **conflit** [kɔ̃fli] *conflict*
le **confort** [kɔ̃fɔːr] *comfort*
  confortable [kɔ̃fɔrtabl] *comfortable*
  confus(e) [kɔ̃fy, -fyz] *confused*
le **congé** [kɔ̃ʒe] *leave, holiday*   [*tree*
le **conifère** [kɔnifɛːr] *conifer, cone-bearing*
la **connaissance** [kɔnɛsɑ̃ːs] *knowledge,*
      acquaintance
  connaître [kɔnɛːtr] *to know, to be*
le **conseil** [kɔ̃sɛːj] *advice* [*acquainted with*
  consentir [kɔ̃sɑ̃tiːr] *to consent*
la **conséquence** [kɔ̃sekɑ̃ːs] *consequence*
  en conséquence *consequently*
  par conséquent [kɔ̃sekɑ̃] *therefore, so*
les **conserves** [kɔ̃sɛːrv] (m.) *preserves,*
      tinned food
  considérable [kɔ̃sidɛrabl] *considerable*
  considérer [kɔ̃sidere] *to consider*
la **consigne** [kɔ̃siɲ] *left-luggage office*
  consister de [kɔ̃siste də] *to consist of*
  consoler [kɔ̃sɔle] *to console*
la **consommation** [kɔ̃sɔmasjɔ̃] *drink*
  constant(e) [kɔ̃stɑ̃,-ɑ̃t] *constant*
  constituer [kɔ̃stitɥe] *to constitute*
  construire [kɔ̃strɥiːr] *to construct, build*
  consulter [kɔ̃sylte] *to consult*
le **conte** [kɔ̃ːt] *story*
  contempler [kɔ̃tɑ̃ple] *to behold, reflect*
la **contenance** [kɔ̃tnɑ̃ːs] *countenance*
  contenir [kɔ̃tniːr] *to contain*
  content(e) [kɔ̃tɑ̃, -ɑ̃t] *pleased, happy*
  se contenter de [sə kɔ̃tɑ̃te də] *to be satisfied*
le **Continent** [kɔ̃tinɑ̃] *Continent* [*with*
  continuel(le) [kɔ̃tinyɛl] *continual*
  continuer [kɔ̃tinye] *to continue*
le **contraire** [kɔ̃trɛːr] *contrary*
  contre [kɔ̃ːtr] *against, near to*
  par contre *on the other hand*
le **contribuable** [kɔ̃tribɥabl] *taxpayer*
le **contrôle** [kɔ̃troːl] *inspection*
  contrôler [kɔ̃trole] *to check*
le **contrôleur** [kɔ̃trolœːr] *ticket-collector*
la **controverse** [kɔ̃trɔvɛrs] *controversy*
  convaincre [kɔ̃vɛ̃ːkr] *to convince*
  convenable [kɔ̃vnabl] *suitable*

  convenir de [kɔ̃vniːr də] *to agree to*
  convenu(e) [kɔ̃vny] *agreed, appointed*
la **conversation** [kɔ̃vɛrsasjɔ̃] *conversation,*
la **copie** [kɔpi] *copy*   [*chat*
  copieux, -euse [kɔpjø, -øːz] *copious*
le **coq** [kɔk] *cockerel*
  coquet, -ette [kɔkɛ, -ɛt] *pretty, attractive*
la **coquetterie** kɔkɛtri] *coquetry*
le **coquillage** [kɔkijaːʒ] *shell*
les **coquillages** [kɔkijaːʒ] *shells, shell-fish*
le **coquin** [kɔkɛ̃] *rogue, rascal*
le **corbeau** [kɔrbo] *crow*
la **corbeille à papier** [kɔrbɛːj a papje] *waste-*
la **corde** [kɔrd] *rope*   [*paper basket*
  cordial(e) [kɔrdjal] *sincere, friendly*
le **corps** [kɔːr] *body*
  correct(e) [kɔrɛkt] *correct, proper*
la **correspondance** [kɔrɛspɔ̃dɑ̃ːs]
    correspondence, connection (railway)
  corrompre [kɔrɔ̃ːpr] *to corrupt*
la **corvette** [kɔrvɛt] *sloop*
le **costume** [kɔstym] *costume, dress*
la **côte** [koːt] *coast*
le **côté** [kote] *side*
la **côtelette de porc** [kotlɛt də pɔːr] *pork*
le **coton** [kɔtɔ̃] *cotton*   [*cutlet*
le **cou** [ku] *neck*
la **couche** [kuʃ] *bed, couch*
  coucher [kuʃe] *to lodge, put to bed*
  se coucher [sə kuʃe] *to go to bed, lie down*
le **coude** [kud] *elbow*
  coudoyer [kudwaje] *to elbow*
  coudre [kudr] *to sew*
  couler [kule] *to flow*
la **couleur** [kulœːr] *colour, suit* (in cards)
le **couloir** [kulwaːr] *corridor*
le **coup** [ku] *blow, blast, etc.*
  tout à coup *suddenly*
  à coup sûr *doubtless*
  donner un coup de sifflet *to blow the*
le **coup de pied** [ku də pje] *kick* [*whistle*
le **coup d'œil** [ku dœːj] *glance*
  coupable [kupabl] *guilty*
la **coupe à champagne** [kup ɑ ʃapaɲ]
    champagne glass
le **coupe-papier** [kup papje] *paper-knife*
  couper [kupe] *to cut* (down)
le **couple** [kupl] *couple*
la **cour** [kuːr] *court-yard*
le **courage** [kuraːʒ] *courage* [*courageous*
  courageux, -euse [kuraʒø, -øz]
  couramment [kyramɑ̃] *fluently*
le **courant** [kurɑ̃] *current*
  courir [kuriːr] *to run*
le **courrier** [kurje] *mail, post*
la **courroie** [kurwa] *strap*
le **cours** [kuːr] *course, class*
  au cours de *during, in the course of*
la **course** [kurs] *errand, outing*
  court(e) [kuːr, kurt] *short*
  être à court de *to be short of*
les **cousin(e)s** [kuzɛ̃, -in] *cousins*
le **coussin** [kusɛ̃] *cushion*
le **couteau** [kuto] *knife*
la **coutellerie** [kutɛlri] *cutlery*
  coûter [kute] *to cost*
la **couture** [kutyːr] *dressmaking, needle-*
la **couturière** [kutyrjɛːr] *dressmaker* [*work*
  couvert(e) [kuvɛːr (-ɛrt)] *covered*

le couvert [kuvɛːr] *place at table*
   mettre le couvert *to lay the table*
la couverture [kuvɛrtyːr] *counterpane,*
   couvrir [kuvriːr] *to cover*   [*blanket*
le crabe [kraːb] *crab*
la craie [krɛ] *chalk*
   craindre [krɛ̃ːdr] *to fear*
la crainte [krɛ̃ːt] *fear*
   craintif, -ive [krɛ̃tif, -iːv] *fearful*
le crâne [kraːn] *skull*
la cravate [kravat] *tie*
le crayon [krɛjɔ̃] *pencil*
le crédit [kredi] *credit*
   à crédit *by instalments*
la crème [krɛm] *cream*
   crever [krəve] *to burst*
le cri [kri] *cry*
   crier [krie] *to shout*
le crime [krim] *crime*
la Crimée [krime] *Crimea*
le criminel [kriminɛl] *criminal*
la crise [kriːz] *crisis*
   critique [kritik] *critical*
   croire [kwaːr] *to believe, think*
   croiser [krwaze] *to cross, pass by*
la croissance [krwasɑ̃ːs] *growth*
le croissant [krwasɑ̃] *crescent roll*
   croître [krwaːtr] *to grow*
la croix [krwa] *cross*
la cruche [kryʃ] *jug*
   cueillir [kœjiːr] *to pick, gather, pluck*
   cuire [kɥiːr] *to cook*
la cuisine [kɥizin] *kitchen*
   faire la cuisine *to do the cooking*
la cuisinière [kɥizinjɛːr] *stove, woman cook*
la cuisse [kɥis] *the thigh*
le cuivre [kɥiːvr] *copper*
la culotte [kulɔt] *trousers, shorts*
   cultiver [kyltive] *to grow*   [*careful*
   curieux, -euse [kyrjø. -øːz] *curious, odd,*
la curiosité [kyrjɔzite] *curiosity, inquisitive-*
le cyclisme [siklism] *cycling*   [*ness*
le cygne [siɲ] *swan*

D

la dactylo [daktilo] *typist*
la dame [dam] *lady, queen* (cards)
le Danemark [danmark] *Denmark*
le danger [dɑ̃ʒe] *danger*
   dangereux, -euse [dɑ̃ʒrø, -øːz] *dangerous*
   dans [dɑ̃] *in*
   danser [dɑ̃se] *to dance*
la date [dat] *date*
   davantage [davɑ̃taːʒ] *more*
   de [də] *of, some*
   débarquer [debarke] *to disembark*
le débarquement [debarkmɑ̃] *disembarka-*
le débarras [debara] *lumber-room*   [*tion*
se débarrasser de [sə debarase də] *to get*
   debout [dəbu] *standing*   [*rid of*
   débrancher [debrɑ̃ʃe] *to disconnect*
le débris [debri] *remains, wreckage*
se débrouiller [sə debruje] *to shift for oneself,*
   to extricate oneself (from difficulties)
le début [deby] *beginning*
   décembre [desɑ̃ːbr] (m.) *December*
   décevoir [desəvwaːr] *to deceive, to*
   déchirer [deʃire] *to tear*   [*disappoint*
   décider (de) [deside] *to decide* (*to*)

   déclarer [deklare] *to declare*
   décoller [dekɔle] *to take off* (aeroplane)
   découper [dekupe] *to cut out*
   découvrir [dekuvriːr] *to discover, uncover*
   décrire [dekriːr] *to describe*
   décrocher [dekrɔʃe] *to unhook* (receiver)
le dédale [dedal] *maze*
   dedans [dədɑ̃] *in, into* (*it*)
   défait(e) [defɛ, -ɛt] *dishevelled*
la défaite [defɛt] *defeat*
le défaut [defo] *fault, defect*
   défendre [defɑ̃ːdr] *to defend*
la défense [defɑ̃ːs] *defence*
   défense de *it is forbidden to*
   défensif, -ive [defɑ̃sif, -iːv] *defensive, as a*
      defence
   défigurer [defigyre] *to disfigure, deface*
le défilé [defile] *parade*
les dégâts [dega] (m.) *damage*
   dégeler [deʒle] *to thaw*
   dégoûter [degute] *to disgust*
le degré [dəgre] *step*
   déguster [degyste] *to taste*
   dehors [dəɔːr] *outside*
   déjà [deʒa] *already*
le déjeuner [deʒœne] *lunch*
   délicieux, -euse [delisjø, -jøːz] *delicious*
   demain [dəmɛ̃] *tomorrow*
   demander [dəmɑ̃de] *to ask for*
   déménager [demenaʒe] *to move house*
   démesuré [demzyre] *enormous*
   demeurer [dəmœre] *to live, reside*
la demi-douzaine [dəmi duzɛn] *half dozen*
   demi(e) [dəmi] *half*   [*back*
   demi-tour (faire) [dəmituːr (fɛːr)] *to turn*
la demoiselle [dəmwazɛl] *young lady*
la démonstration [demɔ̃strasjɔ̃] *demonstra-*
   démontrer [demɔ̃tre] *to prove*   [*tion*
   démoraliser [demɔralize] *to demoralize*
la dent [dɑ̃] *tooth*
le départ [depaːr] *departure*
   dépasser [depase] *to exceed*
se dépêcher [sə depeʃe] *to hurry* (*up*)
   dépendre de [depɑ̃ːdr də] *to rely on*
   dépenser [depɑ̃se] *to spend* (money)
   faire des dépenses *to incur expenses*
se dépeupler [sə depœple] *to become depopu-*
le dépit [depi] *rancour, resentment*   [*lated*
   en dépit de *in spite of*
   déplorable [deplɔrabl] *deplorable*
   déplorer [deplɔre] *to deplore*
   déposer [depoze] *to put down*
   depuis [dəpɥi] *from, since*
   déraper [derape] *to skid*
   dernier, -ière [dɛrnje, -jɛːr] *last, latest*
la déroute [derut] *rout*
   en déroute *in flight*
   derrière [dɛrjɛːr] *behind*
   dès [dɛ] *from, as early as, as soon as*
   des [de] *of the, some*
   désagréable [dezagreabl] *unpleasant*
le désastre [dezastr] *disaster*   [*bring down*
   descendre [desɑ̃ːdr] *to come down, to*
   descendre à [desɑ̃ːdr a] *to put up at*
le désert [dezɛːr] *desert*
   désert(e) [dezɛːr, -ɛːrt] *deserted*
   désespéré(e) [dezɛspere] *desperate*
le désespoir [dezɛspwaːr] *despair*
   désigner [deziɲe] *to point out*

le désir [dezi:r] *desire*
  désirer [dezire] *to desire*
  désobéir (à) [dezɔbei:r] *to disobey*
  désobligeant(e) [dezɔbliʒɑ̃, -ɑ̃:t]
                    disagreeable, rude
  désolé(e) [dezɔle] *desolate, sorry, sad*
  désordonner [dezɔrdɔne] *to disturb, to
                    throw into confusion*
le désordre [dezɔrdr] *disorder*
le dessert [desɛ:r] *dessert*
  desservir [desɛrvi:r] *to serve, clear the*
le dessin [dɛsɛ̃] *drawing*   [*table*
  dessous [dəsu] *below, beneath, under-*
  dessus [desy] *on, upon, above*   [*neath*
le destin [dɛstɛ̃] *destiny*
la destination [dɛstinasjɔ̃] *destination*
    à destination de *going to, bound for*
  détacher [detaʃe] *to tear off*
le détail [deta:j] *detail*
    en détail *retail*
le détective [detɛkti:v] *detective*
  détendre [detɑ̃dr] *to relax, slacken*
  détester [detɛste] *to hate*
  détraquer [detrake] *to put out of order*
  détruire [detrɥi:r] *to destroy*
la dette [dɛt] *debt*
le deuil [dœ:j] *mourning*
  deux [dø] *two*
le deux-pièces [døpjɛs] (*ladies'*) *two-piece*
le deux-points [døpwɛ̃] *colon*   [*suit*
  devant [dəvɑ̃] *in front of*
le devant [dəvɑ̃] *front*
la devanture [d(ə)vɑ̃ty:r] *shop-front*
  devenir [dəv(ə)ni:r] *to become*
  deviner [d(ə)vine] *to guess*
  dévisager [devizaʒe] *to stare at*
  devoir [dəvwa:r] *to have to, be obliged to*
le devoir [dəvwa:r] *homework, duty*
  dévorer [devɔre] *to devour*
  dévoué(e) [devwe] *devoted*
la dictée [dikte] *dictation*
le dictionnaire [diksjɔnɛ:r] *dictionary*
  Dieu [djø] *God*
  différent(e) [difɛrɑ̃, -ɑ̃t] *different*
  difficile [difisil] *difficult, awkward*
la difficulté [difikylte] *difficulty*
  diffuser [difyze] *to diffuse, spread*
  digital(e) [diʒital] *finger* (adj.)
  digne [diɲ] *dignified, worthy*
la digression [digrɛsjɔ̃] *digression*
  diligent(e) [diliʒɑ̃, -ɑ̃t] *diligently*
  dimanche (m.) [dimɑ̃:ʃ] *Sunday*
la dimension [dimɑ̃sjɔ̃] *dimension*
le dindon [dɛ̃dɔ̃] *turkey*
  dîner [dine] *to dine*
le dîner [dine] *dinner, evening meal*
  dire [di:r] *to say, tell*   [*straight*
  directement [dirɛktəmɑ̃] *directly,*
la direction [dirɛksjɔ̃] *direction, manage-*
la directrice [dirɛktris] *headmistress* [*ment*
  diriger [diriʒe] *to direct*
  se diriger [sə diriʒe] *to make one's way*
la discipline [disiplin] *discipline*
le discours [disku:r] *speech*
  discret, -ète [diskrɛ, -ɛt] *discreet*
  discuter [diskyte] *to discuss*
  disparaître [disparɛ:tr] *to disappear*
  diposer [dispoze] *to have at one's disposal*
la dispute [dispyt] *dispute*

  se disputer [sə dispyte] *to contend for, argue*
le disque [disk] *record*
la distance [distɑ̃:s] *distance*
  distinctif, -ive [distɛ̃ktif, -i:v] *distinguish-*
  distinguer [distɛ̃ge] *to distinguish* [*ing*
  distrait(e) [distrɛ, -ɛt] *absent-minded*
  distribuer [distribɥe] *to deal, to deliver*
                                  (*letters*)
la distribution [distribysjɔ̃] *distribution*
le divan [divɑ̃] *divan*
  divers(e) [divɛ:r(s)] *various*
  divisé(e) [divize] *divided*
  dix [di(s)] *ten*
  dix-huit [dizɥi(t)] *eighteen*
  dix-neuf [diznœf] *nineteen*
  dix-sept [dizsɛt] *seventeen*
une dizaine [dizɛn] *group of about ten*
le docteur [dɔktœ:r] *doctor*
le document [dɔkymɑ̃] *document*
le doigt [dwa] *finger*
le domaine [dɔmɛn] *domain*
le domicile [dɔmisil] *private house*
  dominer [dɔmine] *to dominate, overlook*
le dommage [dɔma:ʒ] *damage, pity*
le don [dɔ̃] *gift*
  donc [dɔ̃:k] *so, therefore*
  donner [dɔne] *to give, deal*
  dont [dɔ̃] *of (from) whom, of which, whose*
  doré(e) [dɔre] *golden*
  dorer [dɔre] *to gild*
le dormeur, la -euse [dɔrmœ:r, -ø:z]
  dormir [dɔrmi:r] *to sleep*   [*sleeper*
le dos [do] *back*
le dot [dɔt] *dowry*
le douanier [dwanje] *customs officer*
  doubler [duble] *to overtake* (cars)
la douceur [dusœ:r] *sweetness, gentleness*
la douleur [dulœ:r] *pain*
le doute [dut] *doubt*
  se douter [sə dute] *to suspect*
  doux, douce [du, dus] *mild, gentle*
la douzaine [duzɛn] *dozen*
  douze [du:z] *twelve*
  dramatique [dramatik] *dramatic*
le drap [dra] *cloth, sheet*
le drapeau [drapo] *flag*
  drelin-drelin! [drəlɛ̃-drəlɛ̃] *ting-a-ling!*
  se dresser [sə drɛse] *to rise, stand*
  dresser [drɛse] *to set up, pitch* (tent)
  droit(e) [drwa, -at] *straight, right, direct*
le droit [drwa] *right, privilege*
la droite [drwat] *right* (hand side)
    à droite *to the right*
  drôle [dro:l] *funny*
  du [dy] *of the, some*
  duper [dype] *to dupe, impose on*
  duquel [dykɛl] *of which*
  dur(e) [dy:r] *hard*
  durer [dyre] *to last*
    sa vie durant *his whole life long*

E

  l'eau [o] (f.) *water*
  l'eau de vaisselle [o də vɛsɛl] *dish-water*
  éblouir [eblui:r] *to dazzle*
un échafaudage [eʃafoda:ʒ] *scaffolding*
  échapper [eʃape] *to escape*
une écharpe [eʃarp] *scarf*
un échec [eʃɛk] (m.) *check*

une **échelle** [eʃɛl] *ladder*
échoir [eʃwaːr] *to expire*
échouer [eʃwe] *to fail*
un **éclair** [eklɛːr] *flash of lightning*
éclairé(e) [eklɛre] *lit up*
un **éclat** [ekla] *burst, splinter*
éclater [eklate] *to burst, break out*
une **école** [ekɔl] *school*
un **écolier, une -ière** [ekɔlje, -jɛːr] *schoolboy,*
économe [ekɔnɔm] *thrifty* [*-girl*
économique [ekɔnɔmik] *economic*
économiser [ekɔnɔmize] *to economize*
l'**Écosse** (f.) [ekɔs] *Scotland*
s'écouler [sekule] *to elapse*
écouter [ekute] *to listen to*
un **écran** [ekrɑ̃] *screen*
écraser [ekrɑze] *to crush*
s'écrier [sekrie] *to cry out, exclaim*
écrire [ekriːr] *to write*
un **écriteau** [ekrito] *bill, notice*
un **écrivain** [ekrivɛ̃] *writer*
un **écureuil** [ekyrœːj] *squirrel*
une **écurie** [ekyri] *stable*
édifiant(e) [edifjɑ̃, -ɑ̃t] *edifying*
un **édifice** [edifis] *building*
un **effet** [ɛfɛ] *result*
en effet *indeed*
efficace [efikas] *effective*
s'efforcer [sefɔrse] *to force oneself,*
un **effort** [efɔːr] *effort, strain* [*endeavour*
effrayer [efrɛje] *to frighten*
effronté [efrɔ̃te] *shameless, cheeky*
effroyable [efrwajabl] *dreadful*
égal(e) [egal] *alike, equal*
égaler [egale] *to equal*
à l'égard de [a legaːr də] *with regard to*
égarer [egare] *to mislead, mislay*
s'égarer [segare] *to lose one's way*
une **église** [egliːz] *church*
s'élancer [selɑ̃se] *to rush*
l'**électricité** [elɛktrisite] (f.) *electricity*
électrique [elɛktrik] *electric*
un **électrophone** [elɛktrɔfɔn] *electric*
un **éléphant** [elɛfɑ̃] *elephant* [*gramophone*
l'**élevage** [ɛlvaːʒ] (m.) *stock-farming*
élevé(e) [elve] *educated*
un(e) **élève** [elɛːv] *pupil*
elle-même [ɛl mɛːm] *herself, itself*
elles [ɛl] *they* (f.)
s'éloigner [selwaɲe] *to recede*
s'embarquer [sɑ̃barke] *to embark*
un **embarras du choix** [ɑ̃bara dy ʃwa] *too*
[*much to choose from*
embarrasser [ɑ̃barase] *to embarrass*
embrasser [ɑ̃brase] *to embrace, kiss*
émettre [emɛtr] *to issue*
émigrer [emigre] *to emigrate*
emmener [ɑ̃mne] *to take away*
une **émotion** [emosjɔ̃] *emotion, feeling* [*of*
s'emparer de [sɑ̃pare də] *to take possession*
empêcher (de) [ɑ̃pɛʃe də] *to prevent (from)*
un **empereur** [ɑ̃prœːr] *emperor*
un **empire** [ɑ̃piːr] *empire*
une **emplette** [ɑ̃plɛt] *purchase*
faire des emplettes *to go shopping*
un **emploi** [ɑ̃plwa] *job*
employer [ɑ̃plwaje] *to use, to employ*
emporter [ɑ̃pɔrte] *to carry (take) away*
une **empreinte** [ɑ̃prɛ̃ːt] *print, imprint, mark*

emprunter [ɑ̃prœ̃te] *to borrow*
ému(e) [emy] *moved, touched, excited*
en [ɑ̃] *of it, of them* or *some, in, by*
enchanté(e) [ɑ̃ʃɑ̃te] *delighted*
l'**enchantement** [ɑ̃ʃɑ̃tmɑ̃] (m.) *enchantment*
encombré(e) [ɑ̃kɔ̃bre] *encumbered*
encore [ɑ̃kɔːr] *yet, still, again, besides*
encourager [ɑ̃kuraʒe] *to encourage*
l'**encre** [ɑ̃kr] (f.) *ink*
un **encrier** [ɑ̃krie] *ink-well*
endommager [ɑ̃dɔmaʒe] *to damage*
s'endormir [sɑ̃dɔrmiːr] *to go to sleep*
un **endroit** [ɑ̃drwa] *place, spot*
l'**énergie** [enɛrʒi] (f.) *energy*
l'**énergie hydro-électrique** [enɛrʒi
idrɔelɛktrik] *hydro-electric power*
énergiquement [enɛrzikmɑ̃] *energetically,*
l'**enfance** (f.) [ɑ̃fɑ̃ːs] *childhood* [*hard*
un(e) **enfant** [ɑ̃fɑ̃] *child*
enfantin(e) [ɑ̃fɑ̃tɛ̃, -in] *childish*
enfiler [ɑ̃file] *to put through*
enfin [ɑ̃fɛ̃] *at last, finally*
s'enflammer [sɑ̃flame] *to catch fire*
enfoncer [ɑ̃fɔ̃se] *to drive in, thrust*
s'engager [sɑ̃gaʒe] *to put oneself*
engageant [ɑ̃gaʒɑ̃] *engaging*
engraisser [ɑ̃grɛse] *to fatten*
une **énigme** [enigm] *puzzle*
enjamber [ɑ̃ʒɑ̃be] *to straddle*
enlever [ɑ̃ləve] *to carry off*
un **ennemi** [ɛnmi] *enemy*
l'**ennui** [ɑ̃nɥi] (m.) *trouble, boredom*
ennuyer [ɑ̃nɥije] *to annoy*
s'ennuyer [sɑ̃nɥije] *to be bored, weary*
ennuyeux, -euse [ɑ̃nɥijø, -øːz] *tiresome,*
énorme [enɔrm] *huge, enormous* [*boring*
enrager [ɑ̃raʒe] *to be enraged*
enregistrer [ɑ̃rəʒistre] *to send (luggage),*
enrhumé(e) [ɑ̃ryme] *having a cold* [*book*
s'enrichir [sɑ̃riʃiːr] *to get rich*
une **enseigne** [ɑ̃sɛɲ] *sign*
enseigner [ɑ̃sɛɲe] *to teach*
ensemble [ɑ̃sɑ̃ːbl] *together*
ensuite [ɑ̃sɥit] *then, next*
entamer [ɑ̃tame] *start* (a conversation)
entasser [ɑ̃tase] *to heap* or *pile up*
entendre [ɑ̃tɑ̃dr] *to hear, mean*
entendre raison [ɑ̃tɑ̃dr rɛzɔ̃] *to listen to*
bien entendu *of course* [*reason*
enterrer [ɑ̃tɛre] *to bury*
entêté(e) [ɑ̃tɛte] *obstinate*
un(e) **enthousiaste** [ɑ̃tuzjast] *enthusiast*
entier, -ière [ɑ̃tje, -jɛːr] *whole, entire*
entourer [ɑ̃ture] *to surround*
un **entr'acte** [ɑ̃trakt] *interval*
entraîner [ɑ̃trɛne] *to draw, to drag along*
entre [ɑ̃ːtr] *between*
une **entrée** [ɑ̃tre] *entrance*
entreprendre [ɑ̃trəprɑ̃ːdr] *to undertake*
entrer [ɑ̃tre] *to enter, go, come in*
entre-temps [ɑ̃trətɑ̃] *meanwhile*
une **entrevue** [ɑ̃trəvy] *interview*
envahir [ɑ̃vaiːr] *to invade*
un **envahisseur** [ɑ̃vaisœːr] *invader*
une **enveloppe** [ɑ̃vlɔp] *envelope*
envelopper [ɑ̃vlɔpe] *to wrap*
l'**envie** [ɑ̃vi] (f.) *envy, desire, longing*
avoir envie de *to have an inclination to*
envier [ɑ̃vje] *to envy*

environ [ãvirɔ̃] *about, near*   [*bourhood*
les environs [ãvirɔ̃] (m.) *surroundings, neigh-*
envisager [ãvizaʒe] *to envisage, face*
· envoyer [ãvwaje] *to send*
épais(se) [epɛ, -ɛːs] *thick*
une épaisseur [epɛsœːr] *thickness*
épargner [eparɲe] *to spare, to save up*
une épaule [epoːl] *shoulder*
une épée [epe] *sword*
une épicerie [episri] *grocer's shop*
les épinards [epinaːr] (m.) *spinach*
éplucher [eplyʃe] *to peel*
une époque [epɔk] *time, period, epoch*
une épouse [epuːz] *wife*
épouser [epuze] *to marry*
épouvantable [epuvãtabl] *dreadful*
un époux [epu] *husband*
une épreuve [eprœːv] *test, ordeal, sorrow*
l'épuisement [epɥizmã] *exhaustion*
épuiser [epɥize] *to exhaust*
un équilibre [ekilibr] *balance, equilibrium*
un équipage [ekipaːʒ] *crew*
une équipe [ekip] *team*
errer [ɛre] *to wander*
une erreur [ɛrœːr] *error*
escalader [ɛskalade] *to climb*
un escalier [ɛskalje] *staircase, stairs*
un escalier roulant [ɛskalje rulã] *escalator*
un escargot [ɛskargo] *snail*
un espace [ɛspas] *place* (in boat, etc.)
l'Espagne [ɛspaɲ] (f.) *Spain*
espagnol(e) [ɛspaɲɔl] *Spanish*
une espèce [ɛspɛs] *kind, species*
un espoir [ɛspwaːr] *hope*
un esprit [ɛspri] *spirit, mind, wit*
un essai [esɛ] *test, try*
essayer [esɛje] *to try* (*on*)
l'essence [esãːs] (f.) *petrol*
essentiel(le) [esãsjɛl] *important, essential*
essuyer [esɥije] *to wipe*
l'est [ɛst] (m.) *east*
estimer [ɛstime] *to estimate, appraise*
une estrade [ɛstrad] *stage*
et ... et [e ... e] *both ... and*
une étable [etabl] *cow-shed*
s'établir [setabliːr] *to establish oneself*
un établissement [etablismã] *establishment*
un étage [etaːʒ] *floor, storey*
une étagère [etaʒɛːr] *set of shelves*
un étalage [etalaːʒ] *stall*
étaler [etale] *to spread out*
un étang [etã] *pond, pool*
un état [eta] *state*
en état de *in a fit state to*   [*State*
l'État-Providence [eta prɔvidãːs] *Welfare*
les États-Unis [etazyni] (m.) *United States*
etcaetera [ɛtsetera] *etcetera*
un été [ete] *summer*
éteindre [etɛ̃ːdr] *to extinguish*
étendre [etãdr] *to extend, stretch*
éternel(le) [etɛrnel] *eternal*
une étiquette [etikɛt] *luggage label*
l'étonnement [etɔnmã] (m.) *astonishment*
étrange [etrãːʒ] *strange, foreign*
un étranger, -ère [etrãʒe, -ɛːr] *stranger,*
à l'étranger *abroad*   [*foreigner*
être [ɛːtr] *to be*
étreindre [etrɛ̃dr] *to hug*
étroit(e) [etrwa, -wat] *narrow*

étudier [etydje] *to study*
un étui [etɥi] *case*
l'Europe [ørɔp] (f.) *Europe*
européen(ne) [ørɔpeɛ̃, -ɛn] *European*
eux [ø] (m.) *them, they*
s'évaporer [sevapɔre] *to evaporate*
éveiller [evɛje] *to arouse*
s'éveiller [evɛje] *to awake*
un événement [evɛnmã] *event, occurrence*
évident(e) [evidã(t)] *plain, obvious*
évidemment [evidamã] *evidently*
un évier [evje] *sink*
éviter [evite] *to avoid*
une évocation [evɔkasjɔ̃] *conjuring up*
exact(e) [ɛgzakt] *exact*
un examen [ɛgzamɛ̃] *examination*
examiner [ɛgzamine] *to examine*
exaspérer [ɛgzaspere] *to exasperate*
l'excellence [ɛksɛlãːs] (f.) *excellence*
une exception [ɛksɛpsjɔ̃] *exception*
s'exclamer [sɛksklame] *to exclaim*
exclusif, -ive [ɛksklyzif, -iːv] *exclusive*
une excursion [ɛkskyrsjɔ̃] *excursion*
une excuse [ɛkskyːz] *excuse, apology*
s'excuser [sɛkskyze] *to apologize, excuse*
    oneself, decline an invitation
exécuter [ɛgzekyte] *to perform*
s'exécuter [segzekyte] *to comply, pay up*
l'exemple [egzãːpl] *example*
par exemple *for instance, for example*
exercer [ɛgzɛrse] *to exercise*
s'exercer [segzɛrse] *to practise*
une expérience [ɛksperjãːs] *experience*
expérimenté(e) [ɛksperimãte] *experienced*
expliquer [ɛksplike] *to explain*
un exploit [ɛksplwa] *exploit*
explorer [ɛksplɔre] *to explore*
une explosion [ɛksplozjɔ̃] *explosion*
un exportateur [ɛkspɔrtatœːr] *exporter*
exposer [ɛkspoze] *to display*
une exposition [ɛkspozisjɔ̃] *exhibition, show*
exprès [ɛksprɛ] *on purpose*
exprimer [ɛksprime] *to express*
une extase [ɛkstaːz] *ecstasy*
s'extasier [sɛkstazje] *to go into raptures*
extérieur(e) [ɛksterjœːr] *external, foreign*
l'extérieur [ɛksterjœːr] (m.) *outside*
un externe [ɛkstɛrn] *day pupil*
extraordinaire [ɛkstr(a)ɔrdinɛːr]
    extraordinary
extrême [ɛkstrɛːm] *extreme*

F

la fabrique [fabrik] *factory*
la façade [fasad] *front, facade*
la face [fas] *face*
en face de *facing*
faire face à *to face*
fâché(e) [faʃe] *angry*
se fâcher [sə faʃe] *to get angry*
facile [fasil] *easy*
la façon [fasɔ̃] *manner, way, kind, fuss*
de sa façon *of one's own making*
sans plus de façons *without more ado*
de toute façon *in any case*
le facteur [faktœːr] *postman*
faible [fɛbl] *weak*
la faiblesse [fɛblɛs] *weakness*
faillir [fajiːr] + inf. *nearly to*

la faim [fɛ̃] *hunger*
  avoir faim [avwaːr fɛ̃] *to be hungry*
faire [fɛːr] *to do, make, cause*
  que faire? *what is to be done?*
se faire [sə fɛːr] *to become, take place*
le faisan [fɛzɑ̃] *pheasant*
le fait [fɛ] *fact*
la falaise [falɛːz] *cliff*
falloir [falwaːr] *to be necessary to*
fameux, -euse [famø, -øːz] *famous*
familial(e) [familjal] *of the family* (adj.)
la famille [famiːj] *family*
la farine [farin] *flour*
fatal(e) [fatal] *fatal*
fatigué(e) [fatige] *tired*   [*tired*
se fatiguer [sə fatige] *to tire oneself, become*
il faut [fo] *it is necessary to*
la faute [foːt] *fault*
  sans faute *without fail*
le fauteuil [fotœːj] *armchair*
favori(te) [favɔri, -it] *favourite*
la fée [fe] *fairy*
féliciter (de) [felisite] *to congratulate* (*on*)
la femme [fam] *woman, wife*
fendre [fɑ̃ːdr] *to split*
la fenêtre [f(ə)nɛːtr] *window*
le fer [fɛːr] *iron*
férir [feriːr] *to strike*
ferme [fɛrm] *firm*
la ferme [fɛrm] *farm*
fermer [fɛrme] *to close, to shut*
se fermer [sə fɛrme] *to shut* (*itself*)
le fermier [fɛrmje] *farmer*
féroce [ferɔs] *ferocious*
la fête [fɛːt] *name-day, festival*
fêter [fɛte] *to celebrate, keep as festival*
le feu [fø] *fire*; (pl.) *traffic lights*
la feuille [fœːj] *leaf*
février [fevrie] (m.) *February*
le fiacre [fjakr] *hackney-carriage*
la ficelle [fisɛl] *string*
fidèle [fidɛl] *faithful*
fier, fière [fjɛːr] *proud*
la fierté [fjɛrte] *pride, boldness*
fiévreux, -euse [fjevrø, -øːz] *feverish*
la figue [fig] *fig*
la figure [figyːr] *face, picture-card*
figurer [figyre] *to appear, figure*
se figurer [sə figyre] *to imagine*
le fil [fil] *cotton, thread*
la filature [filatyːr] *spinning-mill*
filer [file] *to go along*
le filet [filɛ] *string-bag, net, luggage rack*
la fille [fiːj] *daughter*
  la petite fille *girl*
la fillette [fijɛt] *girl*
le film [film] *film*
le fils [fis] *son*
la fin [fɛ̃] *end*
fin(e) [fɛ̃, fin] *fine, delicate*
final(e) [final] *final*
finir [finiːr] *to finish*
fixement [fiksmɑ̃] *fixedly*
le flacon [flakɔ̃] *bottle*
la flamme [flaːm] *flame*
flatteur, -euse [flatœːr, -øːz] *flattering*
la flèche [flɛʃ] *church spire, arrow*
fléchir [fleʃiːr] *to bend*
la fleur [flœːr] *flower*

le, la fleuriste [flœrist] *florist*
le fleuve [flœːv] *river*
le flot [flo] *wave*
la flotte [flɔt] *fleet*
flotter [flɔte] *to float*
la flûte [flyːt] *flute*
la foi [fwa] *faith*
le foin [fwɛ̃] *hay*
la fois [fwa] *time, occasion*
  à la fois *at one and the same time*
  une fois de plus *once more*
la folie [fɔli] *madness*
follement [fɔlmɑ̃] *madly, wildly*
foncé(e) [fɔ̃se] *dark*
la fonction [fɔ̃ksjɔ̃] *function*
fonctionner [fɔ̃ksjɔne] *to function*
le fonctionnaire [fɔ̃ksjɔnɛːr] *civil servant*
le fond [fɔ̃] *bottom, far end, background*
  à fond [a fɔ̃] *thoroughly*
la fondrière [fɔ̃drjɛːr] *bog, ditch*
le fonds [fɔ̃] *funds, savings*
le football [futbɔl] *football*
la force [fɔrs] *force, strength*
forcer [fɔrse] *to force*
la forêt [fɔrɛ] *forest*
la formalité [fɔrmalite] *formality*
formidable [fɔrmidabl] *mighty, fearsome*
le formulaire [fɔrmylɛːr] *form*
la formule [fɔrmyl] (*printed*) *form*
fort(e) [fɔːr, fɔrt] *loud, strong, heavy*
fort [fɔr] *very* (*strongly*)   [(*rain*)
la fortification [fɔrtifikasjɔ̃] *fortification*
la fortune [fɔrtyn] *fortune*
fou, fol, folle [fu, fɔl] *mad*
la foudre [fudr] *lightning, thunderbolt*
le fouet [fwɛ] *whip*
fouetter [fwɛte] *to spank, whip*
fouiller [fuje] *to rummage, search*
le foulard [fulaːr] *silk scarf*
la foule [ful] *crowd*
fouler [fule] *to sprain*
se fouler [sə fule] *to put oneself out, take*
fournir [furniːr] *to provide*   [*pains*
la fourrure [furyːr] *fur*
le fourgon [furgɔ̃] *guard's van*
le foyer [fwaje] *foyer, entrance hall*
le fracas [frakɑ] *din*
frais, fraîche [frɛ, frɛʃ] *fresh, cool, chilly*
la fraise [frɛːz] *strawberry*
le franc [frɑ̃] *franc*
français(e) [frɑ̃sɛ, -ɛz] *French*
la France [frɑ̃ːs] *France*
franchement [frɑ̃ʃmɑ̃] *frankly*
franchir [frɑ̃ʃiːr] *to cross, to clear*
frapper [frape] *to strike*
frauder [frode] *to defraud*
le frein [frɛ̃] *brake*
fréquenter [frekɑ̃te] *to frequent, go to*
le frère [frɛːr] *brother*
les frites [frit] (f.) *chips* (food)
froid(e) [frwa, -ad] *cold*
  avoir froid *to be cold*
froisser [frwase] *to offend, hurt*
le fromage [frɔmaːʒ] *cheese*   [-*maker*
le fromager [frɔmaʒe] *cheesemonger,*
froncer [frɔ̃se] *to knit* (one's brow)
le front [frɔ̃] *forehead, brow*
la frontière [frɔ̃tɛːr] *frontier*
frotter [frɔte] *to rub, strike* (match)

la frousse [frus] *fright*
le fruit [frɥi] *fruit*
  fruitier, -ière [frɥitje, -jɛːr] *fruit* (adj.)
  fuir [fɥiːr] *to flee*
la fumée [fyme] *smoke*
  fumer [fyme] *to smoke*
  furieux, -euse [fyrjø, -øːz] *furious*
  furtif, -ive [fyrtif, -iːv] *furtive*
le fusil [fyzi] *gun*
  fusiller [fyzije] *to shoot*
le futur [fytyːr] *future* (tense)

G

le gâchis [gaʃi] *mess*
  gai(e) [ge] *gay*
  gagner [gaɲe] *to win, earn*
le gamin [gamɛ̃] *youngster, urchin*
le gant [gɑ̃] *glove*
le garage [garaːʒ] *garage*
  garantir [garɑ̃tiːr] *to guarantee*
le garçon [garsɔ̃] *boy, waiter*
le garçon de bureau [garsɔ̃ də byro] *office-*
le garçonet [garsɔne] *little boy*   [*boy*
le garde-manger [gard(ə)mɑ̃ʒe] *pantry* or
la garde-robe [gardərɔb] *wardrobe*   [*larder*
  garder [garde] *to keep, to guard*   [*to*
  se garder de [sə garde də] *to take care not*
la gare [gaːr] *station*   [*terminus*
la gare terminus [gaːr tɛrminys] *railway*
  gaspiller [gaspije] *to waste, squander*
le gâteau [gatø] *cake*
  gâter [gɑte] *to spoil*
la gauche [goːʃ] *left (hand side)*
  à gauche *to the left*
  gazouiller [gazuje] *to warble*
la gelée [ʒle] *frost*
  geler [ʒ(ə)le] *to freeze*
  gémir [ʒemiːr] *to moan*
le gendarme [ʒɑ̃darm] *constable*
la gendarmerie [ʒɑ̃darmri] *constabulary*
        headquarters
  gêné [ʒene] *inconvenienced, embarrassed,*
le gendre [ʒɑ̃ːdr] *son-in-law*   [*awkward*
  général(e) [ʒeneral] *general*
  en général *generally*
  généreux, -euse [ʒenerø, -øːz] *generous*
le genou [ʒənu] *knee*
les gens [ʒɑ̃] *people*
  gentil(le) [ʒɑ̃ti, -iːj] *pleasing, nice, kind*
la géographie [ʒeɔgrafi] *geography*
le gérant [ʒerɑ̃] *manager*
le geste [ʒɛst] *gesture*
  gesticuler [ʒɛstikyle] *to gesticulate*
le gilet [ʒilɛ] *waistcoat, vest*
le givre [ʒiːvr] *frost*
la glace [glas] *ice cream, ice, mirror*
  glacer [glase] *to freeze*
  glacial(e) [glasjal] *icy*
le gland [glɑ̃] *acorn*
  glissant(e) [glisɑ̃, -ɑ̃t] *slippery*
  glorieux, -euse [glɔrjø, -øːz] *glorious*
la gomme [gɔm] *rubber*
la gorge [gɔrʒ] *throat*
  gothique [gɔtik] *gothic*
  goudronner [gudrɔne] *to tar*
le gourmet [gurmɛ] *epicure*
le goût [gu] *taste, liking*
le goûter [gute] *afternoon tea*
la goutte [gut] *drop* (of water)

la gouttelette [gutlɛt] *drip, tiny drop*
la gouttière [gutjɛːr] *gutter of the roof*
le gouvernement [guvɛrnəmɑ̃] *government*
la grâce [graːs] *grace, thanks, mercy*
  gracieux, -euse [grasjo, -oːz] *graceful,*
la graine [grɛn] *seed*   [*gracious*
la Grande-Bretagne [grɑ̃ːdbrətaɲ] *Great*
  grand(e) [grɑ̃, -ɑ̃d] *big, large*   [*Britain*
le grand livre [grɑ̃ livr] *ledger*
la grand-mère [grɑ̃mɛːr] *grand-mother*
le grand-père [grɑ̃pɛːr] *grand-father*
les grands-parents [grɑ̃parɑ̃] *grand-parents*
la grand'route [grɑ̃rut] *highway*
la grand'rue [grɑ̃ ry] *main street*
  grandir [grɑ̃diːr] *to grow*
la grange [grɑ̃ːʒ] *barn*
la grappe [grap] *cluster*
  gras(se) [grɑ, grɑːs] *fat*
  gratuitement [gratɥitmɑ̃] *for nothing,*
la gravure [gravyːr] *print, picture*   [*free*
le gré [gre] *liking*
  savoir gré *to be grateful*
le grec [grɛk] *Greek*
  grêler [grɛle] *to hail*
le grenier [grənje] *loft, attic, warehouse*
la grenouille [grənuːj] *frog*
la grève [grɛːv] *strike, shore*
la grille d'égout [griːj degu] *drain*
la grimace [grimas] *face*
  faire la grimace *to pull a face*
  grimper [grɛpe] *to climb*
le grincement [grɛ̃smɑ̃] *screech, creaking*
la grippe [grip] *influenza*
  gris(e) [gri, griz] *grey*
  grommeler [grɔmle] *to mutter, grumble*
le grondement [grɔ̃dmɑ̃] *rumble*
  gronder [grɔ̃de] *to scold, shout at*
  gros(se) [gro, groːs] *big, fat*
  en gros [ɑ̃ gro] *wholesale*
le groupe [grup] *group*
la guêpe [gɛːp] *wasp*
ne ... guère [nə ... gɛːr] *hardly, scarcely*
la guerre [gɛːr] *war*
la guerre-éclair [gɛːreklɛːr] *lightning-war*
le guichet [giʃe] *ticket-office*
  guider [gide] *to guide*
les guillemets [gijmɛ] (m.) *inverted commas*

H (h = aspirated)

  habillé(e) de [abije də] *dressed in*
un habit [abi] *suit*
un habitant [abitɑ̃] *inhabitant*
une habitation [abitasjɔ̃] *dwelling-house*
les habitants [abitɑ̃] *people*
  habiter [abite] *to live in, dwell*
une habitude [abityd] *habit, custom*
  d'habitude *usually, generally*
  comme d'habitude *as usual*
  avoir l'habitude de *to be in the habit of*
la haie [ɛ] *hedge*
  haïr [aiːr] *to hate*
l'haleine [alɛn] *breathe*
  haleter [alte] *to pant*
la halle [al] *covered market*
la hanche [ɑ̃ːʃ] *hip*
le hangar [ɑ̃gaːr] *open shed*
les haricots verts [ariko vɛːr] *French beans*
  harmonieux, -euse [armɔnjø, -øːz]
le hasard [azaːr] *chance*   [*harmonious*

par **h**asard *by chance*
la **h**âte [ɑːt] *haste*
  à la **h**âte *in a hurry*
haut(e) [o, -ot] *high, above*
  là-**h**aut [lao] *up there*
  en **h**aut [ɑ̃ o] *upstairs*
  en **h**aut de [ɑ̃ o də] *at the top of*
  tout **h**aut [tu o] *aloud*
la **h**auteur [otœːr] *height*
le **h**aut-parleur [o parlœːr] *loudspeaker*
hélas [elaːs] *alas*
hennir [ɛniːr] *to neigh*
l'**h**erbe [ɛrb] (f.) *grass*
le **h**érisson [erisɔ̃] *hedgehog*
héroïque [erɔik] *heroic*
le **h**éron [erɔ̃] *heron*
le **h**éros [ero] *hero*
la **h**erse [ɛrs] *harrow*
hésiter [ezite] *to hesitate*
une **h**eure [œːr] *hour, time*
  de bonne **h**eure *early*
  à l'**h**eure pour *in time for*
  tout à l'**h**eure *just now, a few minutes*
heureux, -euse [œrø, -øːz] *happy*   [*ago*
heurter [œrte] *to run into, to hurt, jostle*
le **h**ibou [ibu] *owl*
hier [iɛr] *yesterday*
une **h**irondelle [irɔ̃dɛl] *swallow*
une **h**istoire [istwaːr] *history, story*
un **h**iver [ivɛːr] *winter*
la **H**ollande [ɔlɑ̃ːd] *Holland*
un **h**omme [ɔm] *man*
honnête [ɔnɛːt] *honest, reasonable*
l'**h**onnêteté [ɔnɛtte] *honesty, integrity*
la **h**onte [ɔ̃ːt] *shame*
  avoir **h**onte [avwaːr ɔ̃ːt] *to be ashamed*
un **h**ôpital [ɔpital] *hospital*
un **h**oraire [ɔrɛːr] *time-table*
un **h**orizon [ɔrizɔ̃] *horizon*
une **h**orloge [ɔrlɔːʒ] *clock*
une **h**orreur [ɔrrœːr] *horror*
horriblement [ɔrribləmɑ̃] *horribly*
hors de [ɔːr də] *out of, outside*
l'**h**ostilité [ɔstilite] (f.) *hostility*
un **h**ôtel [otɛl] *hotel*
un **h**ôtel de ville [otɛl də vil] *town hall*
la **h**ouille [uːj] *coal*
l'**h**uile [ɥil] (f.) *oil*
huit [ɥi(t)] *eight*
une **h**uitaine [ɥitɛn] *group of about eight,*
humain(e) [ymɛ̃, -ɛn] *human*   [*week*
humble [œ̃bl] *humble*
l'**h**umeur [ymœːr] (f.) *humour, mood,*
humide [ymid] *damp*   [*disposition*
hurler [yrle] *to yell*
la **h**utte [yt] *hut*   [*national anthem*
une **h**ymne nationale [im(n) nasjɔnal]

I

ici [isi] *here*
une idée [ide] *idea*
ignorant(e) [iɲɔrɑ̃, -ɑ̃ːt] *ignorant*
ignorer [iɲɔre] *not to know*
il [il] *he, it*
il y a [il ja] *there is, there are*
il y a un an [il j a œ̃nɑ̃] *a year ago*
une île [il] *island*
un illustré [illystre] *comic paper, picture*
ils [il] *they*   [*paper*

une image [imaʒ] *picture*
imaginer [imaʒine] *to imagine*
un(e) imbécile [ɛ̃besil] *fool*
imiter [imite] *to imitate, copy*
immense [immɑ̃ːs] *immense, huge*
un immeuble [immœbl] *property*
immobile [imɔbil] *motionless*
impatient(e) [ɛ̃pasjɑ̃, -ɑ̃t] *impatient*
impatienter [ɛ̃pasjɑ̃te] *to provoke*
s'impatienter [sɛ̃pasjɑ̃te] *to get impatient*
un imperméable [ɛ̃pɛrmeabl] *mackintosh,*
impoli(e) [ɛ̃pɔli] *rude*   [*raincoat*
une importance [ɛ̃pɔrtɑ̃ːs] *importance*
important(e) [ɛ̃pɔrtɑ̃, -ɑ̃ːt] *important*
importer [ɛ̃pɔrte] *to import, matter*
n'importe [nɛ̃pɔrt] *never mind*
impossible [ɛ̃pɔsibl] *impossible*
une impossibilité [ɛ̃pɔsibilite] *impossibility*
un impôt [ɛ̃po] *tax (income)*
une impression [ɛ̃prɛsjɔ̃] *impression*
un incident [ɛ̃sidɑ̃] *incident, occurrence*
incliner [ɛ̃kline] *to incline*
incompatible [ɛ̃kɔ̃patibl] *inconsistent*
inconnu(e) [ɛ̃kɔny] *unknown*
un inconnu [ɛ̃kɔny] *stranger*   [*dence*
l'indépendance [ɛ̃depɑ̃dɑ̃ːs] (f.) *indepen-*
un indicateur de vitesse [ɛ̃dikatœːr də vitɛs]
    speedometer
indigne [ɛ̃diɲ] *unworthy, undeserving*
indigné(e) [ɛ̃diɲe] *indignant*
un indigène [ɛ̃diʒɛn] *native*
indiquer [ɛ̃dike] *to point out*
un individu [ɛ̃dividy] *individual*
une industrie [ɛ̃dystri] *industry*
industriel(le) [ɛ̃dystriɛl] *industrial*
inégal(e) [inegal] *unequal*
infernal(e) [ɛ̃fɛrnal] *infernal*
infiniment [ɛ̃finimɑ̃] *extremely*
l'inflation [ɛ̃flasjɔ̃] (f.) *inflation*
informé(e) [ɛ̃fɔrme] *informed*
un ingénieur [ɛ̃ʒenjœːr] *engineer*
une initiation [inisjasjɔ̃] *initiation*
une injure [ɛ̃ʒyːr] *insult, injury*
innocent(e) [inɔsɑ̃, ɑ̃t] *innocent*
inquiet, -ète [ɛ̃kjɛ, -ɛt] *uneasy*
s'inquiéter [sɛ̃kjete] *to worry, be anxious*
inscrit(e) [ɛ̃skri, -it] *written, inscribed*
un insecte [ɛ̃sɛkt] *insect*
insister [ɛ̃siste] *to insist*
inspecter [ɛ̃spɛkte] *to inspect*
l'inspecteur [ɛ̃spɛktœːr] *inspector*
installer [ɛ̃stale] *to install*
s'installer [sɛ̃stale] *to establish oneself, to*
un instant [ɛ̃stɑ̃] *moment*   [*settle in*
  pour l'instant *for the moment*
une institutrice [ɛ̃stitytris] *school-mistress,*
    governess
instruit(e) [ɛ̃strɥi, -iːt] *educated*
à l'insu de [lɛ̃sy də] *unknown to*   [*her*
  à son insu [a sɔn ɛ̃sy] *unknown to him,*
une intention [ɛ̃tɑ̃sjɔ̃] *intention*   [*bewilder*
interdire [ɛ̃tɛrdiːr] *to prohibit, refuse,*
interdit(e) [ɛ̃tɛrdi, -it] *forbidden*
intéressant(e) [ɛ̃terɛsɑ̃, ɑ̃t] *interesting*
s'intéresser (à) [sɛ̃terɛse] *to take an*
un intérêt [ɛ̃terɛ] *interest*   [*interest (in)*
l'intérieur [ɛ̃terjœːr] (m.) *interior, home*
  à l'intérieur de *inside*
interminable [ɛ̃tɛrminabl] *endless*

un interne [ɛ̃tɛrn] *school-boarder*
interrompre [ɛ̃tɛrɔ̃:pr] *to interrupt*
une interruption [ɛ̃tɛrypsjɔ̃] *interruption*
un intervalle [ɛ̃tɛrval] *interval*
   dans l'intervalle *meanwhile*
intimider [ɛ̃timide] *to intimidate*
introduire [ɛ̃trɔdɥi:r] *to introduce*
s'introduire [sɛ̃trɔdɥi:r] *to worm one's way*
inutile [inytil] *useless*
invalide [ɛ̃valid] *invalid*
un invalide [ɛ̃valid] *disabled soldier*
une invasion [ɛ̃vazjɔ̃] *invasion*
inverse [ɛ̃vɛrs] *contrary, opposite*
une invitation [ɛ̃vitasjɔ̃] *invitation*
l'invité(e) [ɛ̃vite] *guest*
inviter [ɛ̃vite] *to invite*
involontairement [ɛ̃vɔlɔ̃tɛrmɑ̃] *involun-*
ironique [irɔnik] *ironic*   [*tarily*
irrévocable [irrevɔkabl] *irrevocable*
l'Italie [itali] (f.) *Italy*
l'Italien(ne) [italjɛ̃, -ɛn] *Italian*
ivre [i:vr] *drunk*

J

jaloux, -se [ʒalu, -u:z] *jealous*
jamais [ʒamɛ] *never*
ne .. jamais [nə . . . ʒame] *never*
la jambe [ʒɑ̃b] *leg* [*one's legs can carry one*
   à toutes jambes [a tut ʒɑ̃:b] *as fast as*
le jambon [ʒɑ̃bɔ̃] *ham*
janvier [ʒɑ̃vje] (m.) *January*
le Japon [ʒapɔ̃] *Japan*
le jardin [ʒardɛ̃] *garden*
le jargon [ʒargɔ̃] *jargon*
jaune [ʒo:n] *yellow*
je, j' [ʒ(ə)] *I*
la jetée [ʒəte] *jetty or pier*
jeter [ʒəte] *to throw (away)*
le jeu [ʒø] *game, sport, pack (of cards)*
jeudi [ʒødi] (m.) *Thursday*
jeune [ʒœn] *young*
les jeunes gens [ʒœn] *young men (people)*
la joie (ʒwa] *joy*
joli(e) [ʒɔli] *pretty*
joindre [ʒwɛ̃:dr] *to join*
le jonc [ʒɔ̃] *rush*
la joue [ʒu] *cheek*
jouer [ʒwe] *to play*   [*instrument*]
jouer de [ʒwe də] *to play (a musical*
jouer à [ʒwe a] *to play (a game)*
le jouet [ʒwɛ] *toy*
jouir de [ʒwir də] *to enjoy*
le jour [ʒu:r] *day*
   de jour en jour *from day to day, daily*
le journal [ʒurnal] *newspaper*
la journée [ʒurne] *day(time)*
joyeux, -euse [ʒwajø, -ø:z] *gay, joyful*
juger [ʒyʒe] *to judge*
le Juif, la Juive [ʒɥif, ʒɥi:v] *Jew, Jewess*
juillet [ʒɥijɛ] (m.) *July*
juin [ʒɥɛ̃] (m.) *June*
les jumeaux [ʒymo] *twin brothers, twins*
les jumelles [ʒymɛl] *twin sisters*
la jupe [ʒyp] *skirt*
le Jura [ʒyra] *Jura Mountains*
jurer [ʒyre] *to swear by*
le juron [ʒyrɔ̃] *swear-word*
jusqu'à [ʒyska] *until, up to, as far as*
jusque-là [ʒyskla] *so far, there*

jusqu'à ce que [ʒyskas(ə) kə] *until*
jusqu'ici [ʒyskisi] *up to now*
juste [ʒyst] *just, fair, right*
justement [ʒystəmɑ̃] *just, exactly*
juteux, -euse [ʒytø, -ø:z] *juicy*

K

le kilo(gramme) [kilɔgram] *French*
   measure = 2¼ lb. approximately
le kilomètre [kilɔmɛtr] *kilometre*
le kiosque [kjɔsk] *newspaper-stall*
le klaxon [klaksɔ̃] *hooter*

L

la [la] *the (f.), her, it*
là [la] *there*
-là [la] *that*
là-bas [labɑ] *down, over there*   [*laborious*
laborieux, -euse [labɔrjø, -ø:z] *toilsome,*
labourer [labure] *to work, plough*
le lac [lak] *lake*
lâche [lɑ:ʃ] *cowardly*
lâcher [lɑʃe] *to let go of, release*
lâcher prise [lɑʃe pri:z] *to let go*
là-dedans [ladədɑ̃] *in it*
là-haut [lao] *up there*
la laideur [lɛdœ:r] *ugliness*
la laine [lɛn] *wool*
laisser [lɛse] *to leave (a thing), to let*
le lait [lɛ] *milk*
la laiterie [lɛtri] *dairy*
la laitue [lɛty] *lettuce*
le lambeau [lɑ̃bo] *rag, scrap*
le lampadaire [lɑ̃padɛ:r] *standard lamp*
la lampe [lɑ̃:p] *lamp*
la lampe de bureau [lɑ̃p də buro]
lancer [lɑ̃se] *to throw*   [*reading-lamp*
la langue [lɑ̃:g] *tongue, language*
la lanterne [lɑ̃tɛrn] *lantern*
le lapin [lapɛ̃] *rabbit*
le lard [la:r] *bacon*
large [larʒ] *wide*
la largeur [larʒœ:r] *width*
la larme [larm] *tear*
las(se) de [la(s) də] *tired of*
se lasser [sə lɑse] *to tire*
le latin [latɛ̃] *Latin*
le lavabo [lavabo] *wash-basin*
laver [lave] *to wash*
le [lə] *the (m.), him, it*
la leçon [ləsɔ̃] *lesson*
le lecteur, la -trice [lɛktœ:r, -tris] *reader*
la lecture [lɛkty:r] *reading*
ledit, ladite [lədi, ladit] *the aforesaid*
légal(e) [legal] *legal*
léger, -ère [leʒe, -ɛ:r] *light, slight*
le légume [legym] *vegetable*
le lendemain (de) [lɑ̃dmɛ̃ (də)] *the next day,*
lent(e) [lɑ̃, lɑ̃:t] *slow*   [*day after*
lequel, laquelle [ləkɛl, lakɛl] *which*
les [lɛ] *the (plural), them*
la lettre [lɛtr] *letter*
leur [lœ(:)r] *their, to them*
le leur [lœ(:)r] etc., *theirs*
lever [ləve] *to raise*
se lever [sə ləve] *to get up, rise*
le lever du soleil [ləve dy sɔlɛ:j] *sunrise*
la lèvre [lɛ:vr] *lip*
la liberté [libɛrte] *liberty*

libre [libr] *free, liberated*
le lieu, les lieux [ljø] *place(s), scene(s)*
   avoir lieu *to take place*
   au lieu de *instead of*
le lièvre [ljɛːvr] *hare*
la ligne [liɲ] *line*
la limonade [limɔnad] *lemonade*
le lingot [lɛ̃go] *ingot, bullion*
le lion [ljɔ̃] *lion*
la liqueur [likœːr] *liqueur*
le liquide [likid] *liquid*
lire [liːr] *to read*
la liste [list] *list*
le lit [li] *bed*
la livraison [livrɛzɔ̃] *delivery*
livrer [livre] *to deliver*
se livrer à [sə livre a] *to engage in*
le livre [livr] *book*
le, la locataire [lɔkatɛːr] *tenant*
la locomotive [lɔkɔmɔtiːv] *engine, locomo-*
le logement [lɔʒmɑ̃] *accommodation* [*tive*
loger [lɔʒe] *to lodge, quarter*
loin de [lwɛ̃ də] *far from*
   de loin *from a distance*
le loisir [lwaziːr] *leisure*
long, -ue [lɔ̃, lɔ̃:g] *long*
le long [lɔ̃] *length*
   de long en large *up and down*
le long de [lɔ̃ də] *along*
longer [lɔ̃ʒe] *to run along (by)*
longtemps [lɔ̃tɑ̃] *(for) a long time*
longuement [lɔ̃gmɑ̃] *for a long time*
la longueur [lɔ̃gœːr] *length*
loquace [lɔkwas] *talkative*
lorsque [lɔrskə] *(at the moment) when*
louer [lwe] *to book, to let*
le loup [lu] *wolf*
lourd(e) [luːr, lurd] *heavy, close, sultry*
la louve [luːv] *she-wolf*
la lueur [lɥœːr] *gleam*
lui [lɥi] *to him, it, her*
lui-même [lɥi mɛːm] *himself*
luire [lɥiːr] *to shine*
luisant(e) [lɥisɑ̃, -ɑ̃t] *shiny, shining,*
la lumière [lymjɛːr] *light* [*gleaming*
lundi [lœ̃di] (m.) *Monday*
les lunettes [lynɛt] (f.) *spectacles*
la lutte [lyt] *struggle*
lutter [lyte] *to struggle*
le luxe [lyks] *luxury*
le Luxembourg [lyksɑ̃buːr] *Luxembourg*
le lycée [lise] *secondary school*
le lycéen [liseɛ̃] *secondary schoolboy*

M

ma [ma] (f.) *my*
la machine [maʃin] *piece of machinery*
la machine à coudre [maʃin a cudr]
         sewing-machine
la machine à écrire [maʃin a ekriːr] *type-*
la mâchoire [maʃwaːr] *jaw* [*writer*
le maçon [masɔ̃] *mason, bricklayer*
Madame [madam] *Mrs., madam*
Mademoiselle [madmwazel] *Miss*
le magasin [magazɛ̃] *large shop, store*
magique [maʒik] *magic*
magnifique [maɲifik] *magnificent*
mai [mɛ] (m.) *May*
maigre [mɛːgr] *thin*

le maillet [majɛ] *mallet*
le maillot de bain [majo də bɛ̃] *bathing*
la main [mɛ̃] *hand* [*costume*
maintenant [mɛ̃t(ə)nɑ̃] *now*
maintenir [mɛ̃tniːr] *to maintain*
le maire [mɛːr] *mayor*
la mairie [mɛri] *town-hall*
mais [mɛ] *but*
la maison [mɛzɔ̃] *house*
le maître [mɛːtr] *master*
la maîtresse [mɛtrɛs] *(school)mistress*
majeur(e) [maʒœːr] *major, greater*
mal (adverb) [mal] *badly, ill*
   mal à propos *at the wrong time*
   faire mal à *to hurt*
le mal [mal] *harm, hurt*
le mal du pays [mal dy pe(j)i] *homesickness*
malade [malad] *ill*
   avoir l'air malade *to look ill*
la maladie [maladi] *disease, illness, sickness*
la maladresse [maladrɛs] *clumsiness*
maladroit(e) [maladrwa, -wat] *clumsy*
malgré [malgre] *in spite of, despite*
le malheur [malœːr] *misfortune, accident*
malheureux, -euse [malœrø, -øːz]
        unfortunate, unlucky
la malle [mal] *cabin-trunk*
maman [mamɑ̃] *mother, mummy*
la Manche [mɑ̃ːʃ] *the Channel*
la manche [mɑ̃ːʃ] *sleeve*
le manche à balai [mɑ̃ːʃ a balɛ] *broomstick*
manger [mɑ̃ʒe] *to eat*
maniaque [manjak] *fussy, faddy, maniac,*
manier [manje] *to handle* [*raving mad*
la manière [manjɛːr] *manner, way*
le, la mannequin [mankɛ̃] *model, mannequin*
le manque [mɑ̃ːk] *lack*
manquer [mɑ̃ke] *to miss, lack*
le manteau [mɑ̃to] *coat*
le marbre [marbr] *marble*
marchand(e) [marʃɑ̃, -ɑ̃t] *saleable*
le marchand [marʃɑ̃] *merchant, tradesman*
le marchand des quatre saisons [marʃɑ̃ de,
    katr sɛzɔ̃] *costermonger*
la marchandise [marʃɑ̃diːz] *merchandise,*
        goods
la marche [marʃ] *step, walking, journey*
le marché [marʃe] *market*
   à bon marché *cheap(ly)*
   son marché *her shopping*
le Marché commun [lə marʃe kɔmœ̃]
        Common Market
marcher [marʃe] *to walk*
mardi [mardi] (m.) *Tuesday*
le maréchal [marɛʃal] *marshal*
la marge [marʒ] *margin*
le mari [mari] *husband*
marier [marje] *to marry*
Le Maroc [marɔk] *Morocco*
marquant(e) [markɑ̃, -ɑ̃:t] *prominent,*
        outstanding
la marque [mark] *mark, brand, make*
marquer [marke] *to mark, show*
mars [mars] (m.) *March*
le marteau [marto] *hammer*
massif [masif] *massive*
le matelas [matlɑ] *mattress*
le matelot [matlo] *sailor*
le matériel [materjɛl] *material, implements*

les **mathématiques** [matɛmatik] (f.)
    mathematics
la **matière** [matjɛːr] *subject, matter*
la **matière première** [matjɛːr prəmjɛːr]
le **matin** [matɛ̃] *morning*   [*raw material(s)*
  matinal(e) [matinal] *early morning*
  maudire [modiːr] *to curse*
  mauvais(e) [movɛ, -ɛz] *bad, wrong*
    de mauvaise grâce *grudgingly*
  me [m(ə)] *me, to me*   [*mechanic*
le **mécanicien** [mekanisjɛ̃] *engine-driver,*
  méchant(e) [meʃɑ̃, -ɑ̃t] *wicked, naughty*
la **mèche** [mɛʃ] *wick*
  mécontent(e) [mekɔ̃tɑ̃, -ɑ̃t] *displeased,*
le **médecin** [metsɛ̃, medsɛ̃] *doctor* [*annoyed*
la **Méditerranée** [mediterane]
    Mediterranean Sea
se **méfier (de)** [sə mefje] *to mistrust*
par **mégarde** [par megard] *inadvertently*
  meilleur(e) [mɛjœːr] *better, preferable*
  mélanger [melɑ̃ʒe] *to mix, shuffle* (cards)
le **mélange** [melɑ̃ːʒ] *mixture*
la **mêlée** [mele] *conflict, fray, scuffle*
  mêler [mele] *to mix*
le **melon** [məlɔ̃] *melon*
le **membre** [mɑ̃ːbr] *member, limb*
  même [mɛːm] *even, same*
la **mémoire** [memwaːr] *memory*
la **menace** [mənas] *threat*
  menacer [mənase] *to threaten*
le **ménage** [menaːʒ] *household, housework*
la **ménagère** [menaʒɛːr] *housewife*
  mener [məne] *to lead*
le **mensonge** [mɑ̃sɔ̃ːʒ] *untruth, lie*
-ment [mɑ̃] (adverbial ending) *-ly*
le **menteur** [mɑ̃tœːr] *liar*
la **mention** [mɑ̃sjɔ̃] *mention*
  mentionner [mɑ̃sjɔne] *mention*
  mentir [mɑ̃tiːr] *to tell lies*
le **menton** [mɑ̃tɔ̃] *chin*
le **menu** [məny] *menu*
la **mer** [mɛːr] *sea*
  merci [mɛrsi] *thank you*
  mercredi [mɛrkrədi] (m.) *Wednesday*
la **mère** [mɛːr] *mother*
le **mérite** [merit] *merit, worth, due*
le **merle** [mɛrl] *blackbird* [*lous, wonderful*
  merveilleux,-euse [mɛrvɛjø,-øːz] *marvel-*
mes [mɛ] *my* (plural)
le **mess** [mɛs] (*officers'*) *mess*
le **message** [mɛsaːʒ] *message*
le **messager** [mɛsaʒe] *messenger*
la **messe** [mɛs] *Mass*   [(tread, etc.)
  mesuré(e) [məzyre] *measured, regular*
la **mesure** [məzyːr] *extent, measure*
le **métal** [metal] *metal*
la **méthode** [metɔd] *method*
  méticuleux, -euse [metikylø, -øːz] *very*
    careful, particular
le **métier** [metje] *trade, profession*
le **mètre** [mɛtr] *metre*
le **métro** [metro] *underground railway*
  mettre [mɛtr] *to put, take* (time) [*angry*
se **mettre en colère** [sə mɛtr ɑ̃ kɔlɛːr] *to get*
se **mettre à** [sə mɛtr a] *to begin to*
se **mettre en route** [sə mɛtr ɑ̃ rut] *to start off*
le **meuble** [mœbl] *piece of furniture*
  meugler [møgle] *to low* (cow)
la **meule** [møːl] *stack, rick, millstone*

le **meurtre** [mœrtr] *murder*
le **miaulement** [mjolmɑ̃] *mewing, cater-*
à **mi-chemin** [a miʃmɛ̃] *half-way* [*wauling*
le **microbe** [mikrɔb] *germ*
  midi [midi] (m.) *noon*
le **Midi** [midi] *south of France*
le **miel** [mjɛl] *honey*
le **mien, la mienne** [mjɛ̃, mjɛn] *mine*
la **miette** [mjɛt] *crumb*
  mieux [mjø] *better* (adv.)
    le mieux *best*
  mil [mil] *thousand* (in dates)
le **milieu** [miljø] *middle, environment*
    au milieu de *in the middle of*
  militaire [militɛːr] *military*
  mille [mil] *thousand*
le **millier** [milje] *group of about a thousand*
le **million** [miljɔ̃] *million*
le **millionnaire** [miljɔnɛːr] *millionaire*
la **mine** [min] *appearance, mine*
le **ministre** [ministr] *minister*
  minuit [minɥi] (m.) *midnight*
la **minute** [minyt] *minute* (time)
le **miracle** [miraːkl] *miracle* [*miraculous*
  miraculeux, -euse [mirakylø, -øːz]
  misérable [mizɛrabl] *wretched, unhappy*
la **misère** [mizɛːr] *misery*
la **mission** [misjɔ̃] *mission*
la **mode** [mɔd] *style, fashion*
    à la mode *in the fashion*
  moderne [mɔdɛrn] *modern*
  modeste [mɔdɛst] *modest, unassuming*
  moi [mwa] *I, me, to me*
  moindre [mwɛ̃ːdr] *less, smaller, lesser*
    le moindre *smallest, least*
le **moineau** [mwano] *sparrow*
  moins [mwɛ̃] *less*
    au (du) moins *at least*
le **mois** [mwa] *month*
la **moisson** [mwasɔ̃] *harvest* (of cereals)
la **moitié** [mwatje] *half*
le **moment** [mɔmɑ̃] *moment*
  mon [mɔ̃] (m.) *my*
  Mon Dieu! [mɔ̃ djø] *Good heavens!*
la **monarchie** [mɔnarʃi] *monarchy*
le **monastère** [mɔnastɛːr] *monastery*
le **monde** [mɔ̃ːd] *world, people*
    tout le monde *everybody, everyone*
  mondial(e) [mɔ̃djal] *world-wide*
la **monnaie** [mɔnɛ] *money, change*
le **monologue** [mɔnɔlog] *monologue*
  monotone [mɔnɔtɔn] *monotonous*
  Monsieur [m(ə)sjø] *Mr., Sir* [*monstrous*
  monstrueux, -euse [mɔ̃stryø, -øːz]
  montagnard(e) [mɔ̃taɲaːr(d)] *mountain*
la **montagne** [mɔ̃taɲ] *mountain*
le **montant** [mɔ̃tɑ̃] *amount*
  monter [mɔ̃te] *to climb, go up, come up*
la **montre** [mɔ̃ːtr] *watch*
la **montre-bracelet** [mɔ̃trbraslɛ] *wristwatch*
  montrer [mɔ̃tre] *to show*
le **monument** [mɔnymɑ̃] *monument*
  moqueur, -euse [mɔkœːr, -øːz] *mocking*
se **moquer de** [sə mɔke də] *make fun of*
le **morceau** [mɔrso] *morsel, piece*
  mort(e) [mɔːr, mɔrt] *dead*
la **mort** [mɔːr] *death*
le **mot** [mo] *word*
le **moteur** [mɔtœːr] *engine*

la moto [mɔto] *motor-cycle*
le motocycliste [mɔtɔsiklist] *motor-cyclist*
mou, mol, molle [mu, mɔl] *soft*
la mouche [muʃ] *fly*
le mouchoir [muʃwaːr] *handkerchief*
moudre [mudr] *to grind*
la mouette [mwɛt] *sea-gull*
le moulin à vent [mulɛ̃navɑ̃] *windmill*
mourir [muriːr] *to die*
la mousse [mus] *moss, froth*
le mousse [mus] *cabin-boy*
la moustache [mustaʃ] *moustache*
le mouton [mutɔ̃] *sheep*
moyen, -enne [mwajɛ̃, -ɛn] *middle*
le moyen [mwajɛ̃] *means, manner*
le Moyen Âge [mwajɛnɑʒ] *Middle Ages*
moyennant [mwajɛnɑ̃] *in return for*
muet, muette [mɥɛ, -ɛt] *dumb*
multicolore [myltikɔlɔr] *many coloured*
le mur [myːr] *wall*
mur(e) [myːr] *ripe, careful* (thought)
la muraille [myraːj] *wall* (defensive)
le musée [myze] *museum*
la musique [myzik] *music*
le mutilé [mytile] *disabled person*
le mystère [mistɛːr] *mystery*   [*mysterious*
mystérieux, -euse [misterjø, -øːz]]

N

nager [naʒe] *to swim*
le nageur [naʒœːr] *the swimmer*
la naissance [nɛsɑ̃ːs] *birth*
naître [nɛːtr] *to be born*
la nappe [nap] *tablecloth*
natal(e) [natal] *native*
la natalité [natalite] *birth-rate*
la natation [natasjɔ̃] *swimming*
national(e) [nasjɔnal] *national*
la natte [nat] *mat, plait*
la nature [natyːr] *nature*
naturel, -elle [natyrɛl] *natural*
le naufrage [nofraːʒ] *shipwreck*
naval(e) [naval] *naval*
le navet [navɛ] *turnip*
le navire [naviːr] *ship, boat*   [*woe-begone*
navré(e) [nɑvre] *distressed, heart-broken,*
ne [nə] sign of negative
ne . . . pas [nə pɑ] *not*
ne . . . plus [nə ply] *no more*
ne . . . jamais [nə ʒamɛ] *never*
ne . . . point [nə pwɛ̃] *not at all*
ne . . . que [nə kə] *only*
néanmoins [neɑ̃mwɛ̃] *nevertheless*
négligé(e) [negliʒe] *neglected, slovenly*
négliger [negliʒe] *to neglect*
le Nègre, la Négresse [nɛːgr, negrɛs] *Negro,*
la neige [nɛːʒ] *snow*   [*Negress*
neiger [neʒe] *to snow*
le néon [neɔ̃] *neon*
net(te) [nɛt] *neat, clean, spotless*
nettoyer [nɛtwaje] *to clean, dust*
neuf [nœf] *nine*
neuf, neuve [nœf, nœv] *new, brand new*
neutre [nøːtr] *neutral, neuter* (in
neuvième [nœvjɛm] *ninth*   [grammar)
le neveu [nəvø] *nephew*
le nez [ne] *nose*
ni . . . ni [ni . . . ni] *neither . . . nor*
la niaiserie [niɛzri] *foolishness, nonsense*

le nid [ni] *nest*
la nièce [njɛs] *niece*
nier [nje] *to deny*
le niveau [nivo] *level*
le nœud [nø] *knot*
noir(e) [nwaːr] *black*
la noix [nwɑ] *nut*
le nom [nɔ̃] *name*
le nombre [nɔ̃ːbr] *number*
nombreux, -euse [nɔ̃mbrø, -øːz] *numerous*
nommer [nɔme] *to name*
non [nɔ̃] *no, not*   [*non-aggression*
le non-agression [nɔnagrɛsjɔ̃]
le nord [nɔːr] *north*
la Normandie [nɔrmɑ̃di] *Normandy*
la Norvège [nɔrvɛːʒ] *Norway*
nos [no] *our* (plural)
la nostalgie [nɔstalʒi] *home-sickness*
la note [nɔt] *mark, note*
notre [nɔːtr] *our*
le nôtre [noːtr], etc., *ours*
nouer [nwe, nue] *to knot, tie*
nourrir [nuriːr] *to nourish*
se nourrir [sə nuriːr] *to feed oneself*
la nourriture [nurityːr] *food*
nous [nu] *we, us, to us*
nouveau, -el, -elle [nuvo, -ɛl] *new, recent*
de nouveau [də nuvo] *again*
la nouvelle [nuvɛl] *news*
novembre [nɔvɑ̃ːbr] (m.) *November*
noyer [nwaje] *to drown*
nu(e) [ny] *naked, bare*
le nuage [nɥaːʒ] *cloud*
nuire [nɥiːr] *to harm*
nuisible [nɥizibl] *harmful*
la nuit [nɥi] *night*
le numéro [nymero] *number*
la nuque [nyk] *nape of the neck*
le nylon [nilɔ̃] *nylon*

O

obéir (à) [ɔbeiːr] *to obey*
objecter [ɔbʒɛkte] *to object*
une objection [ɔbʒɛksjɔ̃] *objection*
un objet d'art [ɔbʒɛ daːr] *work of art*
obliger [ɔbliʒe] *to oblige, compel*
obscur(e) [ɔpskyːr] *obscure*
l'obscurité (f.) [ɔpskyrite] *darkness,*
observer [ɔpsɛrve] *to observe*   [*obscurity*
un obstacle [ɔpstakl] *obstacle*
obtenir [ɔptəniːr] *to obtain, get*
une occasion [ɔkazjɔ̃] *occasion, bargain,*
    opportunity
occidental(e) [ɔksidɑ̃tal] *western*
une occupation [ɔkypasjɔ̃] *occupation*
occupé(e) [ɔkype] *busy*
s'occuper (à) [sɔkype a] *to be occupied* (at)
un océan [ɔseɑ̃] *ocean*
octobre [ɔktɔbr] (m.) *October*
une odeur [ɔdœːr] *smell*
odieux, -ieuse [ɔdjø, -øːz] *odious*
un œil [œːj] *eye*
le coup d'œil [ku dœːj] *glance*
un œillet [œjɛ] *carnation*
un œuf [œf] *egg*
une œuvre [œːvr] *work*
un officier [ɔfisje] *officer*
une offre [ɔfr] *offer*
offrir [ɔfriːr] *to offer*

478

un ogre [ɔgr] *ogre*
une oie [wa] *goose*
un oignon [ɔɲɔ̃] *onion*
un oiseau [wazo] *bird*
une olive [ɔliːv] *olive*
un olivier [ɔlivje] *olive-tree*
l'ombre [ɔ̃ːbr] (f.) *shade*
une ombrelle [ɔ̃brɛl] *parasol, sunshade* [*bus*
un omnibus [ɔmnibyːs] *slow (stopping) train,*
on [ɔ̃] *one, it, they*
un oncle [ɔ̃ːkl] *uncle*
une onde [ɔ̃ːd] *wave*
un ongle [ɔ̃ːgl] *finger nail*
onze [ɔ̃ːz] *eleven*
un opéra [ɔpera] *opera*
opérer [ɔpere] *to operate (on)*
une opinion [ɔpinjɔ̃] *opinion*
opposer [ɔpoze] *to oppose*
s'opposer à [sɔpoze a] *to be opposed to*
un oppresseur [ɔprɛsœːr] *oppressor*
opulent(e) [ɔpylɑ̃(t)] *wealthy*
or [ɔːr] *well, now* (conj.)
l'or [ɔːr] (m.) *gold*
un orage (m.) [ɔraːʒ] *thunderstorm*
une orange [ɔrɑ̃ːʒ] *orange*
un orateur [ɔratœːr] *speaker, orator*
un orchestre [ɔrkɛstr] *orchestra*
ordinaire [ɔrdinɛːr] *ordinary*
d'ordinaire *usually*
ordonner (à) [ɔrdɔne a] *to order*
un ordre [ɔrdr] *order*
en bon ordre [ɑ̃ bɔ̃nɔrdr] *tidy*
une oreille [ɔrɛːj] *ear*
un oreiller [ɔrɛje] *pillow*
une organisation [ɔrganizasjɔ̃] *organization*
organiser [ɔrganize] *to organize*
l'orge (f.) [ɔrʒ] *barley*
orner [ɔrne] *to decorate, to adorn*
un orphelin [ɔrfəlɛ̃] *orphan*
un orteil [ɔrtɛːj] *toe*
un os, des os [ɔs, o] *bone(s)*
oser [oze] *to dare*
ôter [ote] *to take off, away*
ou [u] *or*
ou . . . ou [u . . . u] *either . . . or*
ou bien [u bjɛ̃] *or else*
où [u] *where*
oublier [ublie] *to forget*
l'ouest [wɛst] (m.) *west*
oui [wi] *yes*
un ours [urs] *bear*
en outre [ɑ̃nuːtr] *besides*
une ouvreuse [uvrøːz] *usherette*
un ouvrier [uvrie] *worker, workman*
ouvrir [uvriːr] *to open*

P

pacifique [pasifik] *peace-loving,*
la page [paːʒ] *page* (book) [*peaceable*
la paille [paːj] *straw*
le pain [pɛ̃] *bread, loaf*
la paire [pɛːr] *pair*
paisible [pɛzibl] *peaceful*
la paix [pɛ] *peace*
le palais [palɛ] *palace*
pâle [paːl] *pale*
le palier [palje] *landing*
la palissade [palisad] *fence*
la pancarte [pɑ̃kart] *notice, placard*

le panier [panje] *basket*
la panique [panik] *panic*
la panne [pan] *breakdown*
le panneau [pano] *panel*
le panneau de signalisation *traffic-sign*
le pantalon [pɑ̃talɔ̃] *trousers*
la pantoufle [pɑ̃tufl] *slipper*
le paon [pɑ̃] *peacock*
papa [papa] *father, daddy*
le pape [pap] *pope*
la papeterie [paptri] *stationery*
le papier [papje] *paper*
le papier peint *wallpaper* [*paper*
le papier buvard [papje byvɑ̃] *blotting-*
le papier à lettres [papje a lɛtr] *writing-*
le papillon [papijɔ̃] *butterfly* [*paper*
le paquebot [pakbo] *packet-boat, steamer,*
Pâques [pɑːk] (m.) *Easter* [*liner*
le paquet [pakɛ] *parcel, packet*
par [par] *by, for, on*
le parachute [paraʃyt] *parachute*
le parachutiste [paraʃytist] *parachutist*
le paradis [paradi] *Paradise*
paraître [parɛːtr] *to appear*
le parapluie [paraplɥi] *umbrella*
le parasol [parasɔl] *parasol*
le parc [park] *park*
le parc de stationnement [parc də stasjɔnmɑ̃]
parce que [pars kə] *because* [*car park*
parcourir [parkuriːr] *to go all over*
le parcours [parkuːr] *run, trip*
pardessus [pardəsy] *over*
le pardessus [pardəsy] *overcoat*
le pardon [pardɔ̃] *forgiveness, pardon*
pardonner (à) [pardɔne] *to pardon*
le pare-brise [parbriz] *windscreen*
pareil, -ille [parɛːj] *similar, such*
le parent [parɑ̃] *parent*
la parenthèse [parɑ̃tɛːz] *bracket*
paresseux, -euse [parɛsø, -øːz] *lazy*
parfait(e) [parfɛ, -ɛt] *perfect, excellent*
parfois [parfwa] *sometimes, now and then*
le parfum [parfœ̃] *perfume, smell*
parfumé(e) [parfyme] *scented*
le Parisien [parizjɛ̃] *Parisian*
parler [parle] *to speak, to talk*
parler boutique [parle butik] (f.) *to talk*
le parloir [parlwaːr] *parlour* [*shop*
parmi [parmi] *among*
la parole [parɔl] *word*
la part [paːr] *part, behalf*
pour ma part *for myself, for my part*
particulier, -ière [partikylje, -jɛːr]
private, particular
en particulier *in particular*
la partie [parti] *part, game, portion*
faire partie de *to be a part of*
partir [partir] *to leave, depart*
partout [partu] *everywhere, all round*
parvenir [parvənir] *to reach, manage*
ne . . pas [pa] *not* [*a number of*
pas mal de [pɑ mal də] *quite a few, quite*
le pas [pɑ] *step* [*Dover*
le Pas de Calais [pɑ də kalɛ] *Straits of*
le passage [pɑsaːʒ] *passage, corridor*
le passage clouté [pasaːʒ klute] *pedestrian*
le passager [pɑsaʒe] *passenger* [*crossing*
le passage à niveau [pasaːʒ a nivo] *level*
crossing

479

le passe-partout [paspartu] *master-key*
le passeport [paspɔːr] *passport*
passer [pase] *to spend* (time)
se passer [sə pase] *to happen, occur*
se passer de [sə pase də] *to do without*
la passerelle [pasrɛl] *gangway*
le passe-temps [pastã] *pastime*
pastoral(e) [pastɔral] *pastoral*
la pâte dentifrice [paːt dãtifris] *toothpaste*
le pâté de foie [pate də fwa] *liver pâté*
paternel, -elle [patɛrnɛl] *fatherly, of the*
les pâtes [pat] *dough, macaroni*, etc. [*father*
la patience [pasjãːs] *patience*
patient(e) [pasjã, ãt] *patient*
patiner [patine] *to skate*
la pâtisserie [patisri] *cake shop*
le patron [patrɔ̃] *boss*
la patte [pat] *paw, foot*
la pâture [patyːr] *pasture*
la paume [poːm] *palm (of the hand)*
la paupière [popjɛːr] *eyelid*
pauvre [poːvr] *poor*
le pavé [pave] *paving-stone, paved road*
payer [pɛje] *to pay*
le pays [pe(j)i] *land, country, district*
les Pays-Bas [pe(j)iba] *Low Countries*
le paysage [peizaːʒ] *landscape, scenery*
le paysan, la -anne [peizã, -an] *peasant*
la peau [po] *skin*
la pêche [pɛːʃ] *fishing, peach*
pêcher [pɛʃe] *to fish*
le pêcheur [pɛʃœːr] *fisherman*
pédaler [pedale] *to pedal*
le peignoir [pɛɲwaːr] *dressing-gown*
le peignoir de bain [pɛɲwaːr də bɛ̃] *the*
peindre [pɛ̃ːdr] *to paint*
à peine [a pɛn] *scarcely*   [*bathing-wrap*
   n'être pas la peine *to be not worth while*
le peintre [pɛ̃tr] *painter*
la peinture [pɛ̃tyr] *painting*
pêle-mêle [pɛlmɛl] *higgledy-piggledy*
pêle-mêler [pɛlmɛle] *to jumble up*
la pelle [pɛl] *spade, shovel*
la pelouse [pəluːz] *lawn*
pencher [pãʃe] *to bend, lean*
pendant [pãdã] *during, while*
pendre [pãːdr] *to hang*
la pendule [pãdyl] *clock*
pénétrer [penetre] *to go into, to penetrate*
pénible [penibl] *painful, laborious* (task)
pénitent(e) [penitã,-ãt] *repentant, penitent*
penser [pãse] *to think*
pensif, -ive [pãsif,-iːv] *pensive, thoughtful*
la pension [pãsjɔ̃] *boarding house, boarding*
la pente [pãːt] *slope*   [*school*
   en pente [ã pãːt] *sloping*
perçant(e) [pɛrsã, -ãt] *shrill*
perché(e) [pɛrʃe] *perched*
perdre [pɛrdr] *to lose*
la perdrix [pɛrdri] *partridge*
le père [pɛr] *father*
le péri [peri] *fairy, genius*
la période [perjɔd] *period*
périr [periːr] *to perish*
permettre [pɛrmɛtr] *to permit*
le permis de conduire [pɛrmi də kɔ̃dɥiːr]
                                 driving licence
le perron [pɛrɔ̃] *flight of stone steps before*
le perroquet [pɛrɔkɛ] *parrot*   [*a house*

la personne [pɛrsɔn] *person*
ne ... personne *nobody*
persuader à [pɛrsɥade] *to persuade*
persuasif, -ive [pɛrsɥasif, -iv] *persuasive*
la perte [pɛrt] *loss*
son pesant d'or [sɔ̃ pəzã dɔr] *one's weight in*
peser [pəse] *to weigh*   [*gold*
petit(e) [pəti, -it] *small, little*
le petit-déjeuner [pətideʒœne] *breakfast*
le petit-fils [p(ə)tifis] *grandson*
la petite fille [pətit fiːj] *little girl*
la petite-fille [pətitfiːj] *grand-daughter*
la petite-nièce [la pətitnjɛs] *grand-niece*
le petit pain [pətipɛ̃] *roll*
les petits pois [pətipwa] *peas*
peu [pø] *not very, little, few*
sous peu *shortly*
à peu près *about, approximately*
peu à peu [pø a pø] *little by little*
le peuple [pœpl] *people, nation*
le peuplier [pœplie] *poplar tree*
la peur [pœːr] *fear*
avoir peur [avwaːr pœːr] *to be afraid*
peut-être [pøtɛːtr] *perhaps*
le phare [faːr] *headlamp, lighthouse*
la pharmacie [farmasi] *chemist's shop*
le phoque [fɔk] *seal* (animal)
la photo(graphie) [fɔtɔ(grafi)] *photograph*
le photographe [fɔtɔgraf] *photographer*
la phrase [fraːz] *sentence, phrase*
le piano [pjano] *piano*
la pièce [pjɛs] *room, coin, each, play, part*
le pied [pje] *foot*
à pied [apje] *on foot*
la pierre [pjɛːr] *stone*
piétiner [pjetine] *to trample, stamp on*
le piéton [pjetɔ̃] *pedestrian*
le pigeon [piʒɔ̃] *pigeon*
le pilier [pilje] *pillar*
le pillage [pijaːʒ] *pillage*
le pilote [pilɔt] *pilot*
la pilule [pilyl] *pill*
le pinceau [pɛ̃so] *paint-brush*
la pipe [pip] *pipe*
la pique [pik] *spade* (cards)
le piquet [pike] *peg*
pire [piːr] (adj) *worse*
le pire *the worst*
pis [pi] (adv.) *worse*
le pis *the worst*
la piscine [la pisin] *swimming pool*
la piste [pist] *track, ski-run*
le pistolet [pistɔlɛ] *pistol*
la pitié [pitje] *pity*
avoir pitié de *to be sorry for*
c'est pitié *it is pitiful*
pitier [pitje] *to pity*
pitoyable [pitwajabl] *wretched, pitiful*
pittoresque [pitɔrɛsk] *picturesque*
le placard [plakaːr] *cupboard*
la place [plas] *seat, public square*
faire place à *to make room for*
placer [plase] *to set, place*
le plafond [plafɔ̃] *ceiling*
la plage [plaːʒ] *beach, seaside resort*
plain(e) [plɛ̃, -ɛn] *flat*
la plaine [plɛn] *plain, level ground*
plaire (à) [plɛːr] *to please*
la plaisanterie [plɛzãtri] *joke*

le plaisir [plɛziːr] *pleasure*
  faire plaisir à *to please*
  s'il vous plaît *please*
le plan [plɑ̃] *plane, level ground*
la planche [plɑ̃ːʃ] *plank, board*
le plancher [plɑ̃ʃe] *floor* (boarded)
le plant, la plante [plɑ̃, -ɑ̃t] *plant, plantation*
  planter [plɑ̃te] *to plant*
le plastic [plastik] *plastic explosive*
le plat [pla] *dish*
le plateau [plato] *tray*
la plate-bande [platbɑ̃ːd] *flower-bed,*
plein(e) [plɛ̃, -ɛn] *full*　　[*grass-border*
  en plein air *in the open air*
  faire le plein de *to fill up with*
pleurer [plœre] *to cry*
pleuvoir [plœvwaːr] *to rain*
  il pleut à verse [il plœt a vɛrs] *it is*
　　　　　　　　　　　pouring with rain
le pli [pli] *trick* (cards)
plonger [plɔ̃ʒe] *to plunge, dive*
le plongeur [plɔ̃ʒœːr] *the diver*
la pluie [plɥi] *shower of rain*
la plume [plym] *pen*
le plumier [plymje] *pencil-box*
la plupart [plypaːr] *majority, most part*
plus [ply] *more*
  le plus *the most*
  ne . . . plus [ply] *no more*
  de plus *moreover*
  en plus *in addition*
plusieurs [plyzjœːr] *several*
plutôt [plyto] *rather, preferably*
le pneu [pnø] *tyre*
la poche [pɔʃ] *pocket*
le poêle [pwɑːl] *stove*
le poignet [pwaɲɛ] *wrist*
poinçonner [pwɛ̃sɔne] *to punch, clip*
le poing [pwɛ̃] *fist*
le point [pwɛ̃] *point, full-stop, dot*
le point d'exclamation [pwɛ̃ dɛksklamasjɔ̃]
　　　　　　　　exclamation mark
le point d'interrogation [pwɛ̃ dɛ̃tɛrɔgasjɔ̃]
　　　　　　　　question mark
  être sur le point de *to be about to*
  ne . . . point [pwɛ̃] *not at all*
le point-virgule [pwɛ̃ virgyl] *semi-colon*
la pointe [pwɛ̃ːt] *tip*
la poire [pwaːr] *pear*
le poireau [pwaro] *leek*
le poirier [pwarje] *pear-tree*
le poisson [pwasɔ̃] *fish*
la poissonnerie [pwasɔnri] *fish shop*
la poitrine [pwatrin] *breast, chest*
la poix [pwa] (*pine*) *pitch*
poli(e) [pɔli] *polite, polished*
le policier [pɔlisje] *policeman, detective*
polir [pɔliːr] *to polish*
le politicien [pɔlitisjɛ̃] *politician*
politique [pɔlitik] *political*
la politique [pɔlitik] *policy, politics*
la Pologne [pɔlɔɲ] *Poland*
polonais [pɔlɔnɛ] *Polish*
la pomme [pɔm] *apple*
la pomme de terre [pɔm də tɛːr] *potato*
le pommier [pɔmje] *apple-tree*
ponctuel, -elle [pɔ̃ktɥɛl] *punctual*
pondre [pɔ̃ːdr] *to lay* (eggs)
le pont [pɔ̃] *bridge, deck*

le pont-aqueduc [pɔ̃ akədyk] *aqueduct*
populaire [pɔpylɛːr] *popular*
la population [pɔpylasjɔ̃] *population*
le porc [pɔːr] *pig, pork*
la porcelaine [pɔrsəlɛn] *china*
le porche [pɔrʃ] *porch*
la porcherie [pɔrʃəri] *pigsty*
le port [pɔːr] *port, harbour*
la porte [pɔːrt] *door*
le porte-billet [pɔrt(ə)bijɛ] (*bank-*)*note case*
la porte d'entrée [pɔrt dɑ̃tre] *front door*
la porte-fenêtre [pɔrtfənɛːtr] *French*
le portefeuille [pɔrtəfœːj] *wallet*　[*window*
le porte-lettres [pɔrtəlɛtr] *letter-case*
le porte-manteau [pɔrtmɑ̃to] *hat-stand*
le porte-monnaie [pɔrtmɔnɛ] *purse*
porter [pɔrte] *to wear, carry*
le porteur [pɔrtœːr] *porter*
la portière [pɔrtjɛːr] *carriage-door, car door*
le portillon [pɔrtijɔ̃] *automatic gate,*
　　　　　　　　wicket gate
poser [poze] *to put, to ask* (*questions*)
la position [pozisjɔ̃] *position*
posséder [pɔsede] *to possess*
possible [pɔsibl] *possible*
  tout son possible *everything in one's*
le poste [pɔst] *post, set*　　　　[*power*
le poste d'essence [pɔst dɛsɑ̃ːs] *petrol*
　　　　　　　　station
le poste de télévision [pɔst də televizjɔ̃]
la postière [pɔstjɛːr] *postwoman*　[*TV set*
la posture [pɔstyːr] *posture*
le pot [po, pɔt] *jar, jug*
le potage [pɔtaːʒ] *soup*
le potager [pɔtaʒe] *kitchen-garden*
le poteau [pɔto] *post*
la poubelle [pubɛl] *dustbin*
le pouce [puːs] *thumb*
la poudre [puːdr] *powder*
le poudrier [pudrje] *powder-compact*
la poule [pul] *hen*
le poulet [pulɛ] *chicken*
le poumon [pumɔ̃] *lung*
la poupée [pupe] *doll*
pour [puːr] *for*
  pour que [puːr k(ə)] *in order that*
le pourboire [purbwaːr] *tip*
le pourcentage [pursɑ̃taːʒ] *percentage*
pourquoi [purkwa] *why?*
pourri(e) [puri] *rotten*
la poursuite [pursɥit] *chase*
poursuivre [pursɥiːvr] *to pursue, chase*
pourtant [purtɑ̃] *however*
pourvu que [purvy kə] *provided that*
pousser [puse] *to push, shove, heave*
la poussette [pusɛt] *push-chair*
la poussière [pusjɛːr] *dust*
le poussin [pusɛ̃] *spring chicken*
pouvoir [puvwaːr] *to be able to*
le pouvoir [puvwaːr] *power*
la prairie [prɛri] *meadow* or *grass-land*
pratique [pratik] *practical*
le pré [pre] *meadow*
la précaution [prekosjɔ̃] *precaution, care*
précéder [presede] *to precede*
précipiter [presipite] *to fling*
se précipiter [sə presipite] *to rush*
précipitamment [presipitamɑ̃]
　　　　　　　　precipitately

précis(e) [presi, -iz] *precise, precisely,*
        sharp (time)
la prédiction [prediksjɔ̃] *prediction, fore-*
préférable [prefɛrabl] *preferable [telling*
préférer [prefere] *to prefer*
premier, -ière [prəmje, -jɛːr] *first*
prendre [prɑ̃ːdr] *to take*
prendre garde [prɑ̃ːdr gard] *to take care*
prendre part à [prɑ̃ːdr paːr a] *to take*
le prénom [prenɔ̃] *Christian name [part in*
préparer [prɛpare] *to prepare*
près [prɛ] *near, close*
    de près [də prɛ] *closely, from close to*
la présence [prezɑ̃ːs] *presence*
à présent [a prezɑ̃] *nowadays*
présenter [prezɑ̃te] *to offer*
se présenter [sə prezɑ̃te] *to appear, call,*
            [occur (at), sit (for)
presque [prɛsk] *almost*
presser [prɛse] *to press, hurry*
se presser [sə prɛse] *to hurry, crowd around*
prêt(e) [prɛ, prɛt] *ready*
prétendre [pretɑ̃ːdr] *to claim*
prêter [prɛte] *to lend, pay* (attention)
la preuve [prœːv] *proof*
prévenir [prevənir] *to warn*
prévoir [prevwaːr] *to foresee, to prevent*
prier [prie] *to beg*
le prince [prɛ̃ːs] *prince*
la princesse [prɛ̃sɛs] *princess*
principal(e) [prɛ̃sipal] *principal*
le principe [prɛ̃sip] *principle*
le printemps [prɛ̃tɑ̃] *spring*
la priorité [priɔrite] *priority*
la prise [priːz] *taking, capture, catch*
la prise de courant [priːz də kurɑ̃] *electric*
la prison [prizɔ̃] *prison [wall-plug*
le prisonnier [prizɔnje] *prisoner*
privé(e) [prive] *private*
priver [prive] *to deprive*
le prix [pri] *prize, price*
    à prix fixe *at a fixed price*
    à tout prix *at all costs*
probable [prɔbabl] *probable*
le problème [prɔblɛm] *problem*
prochain(e) [prɔʃɛ̃, -ɛn] *next*
produire [prɔdɥiːr] *to produce*
le produit [prɔdɥi] *product [foodstuff*
le produit alimentaire [prɔdɥi alimɑ̃tɛːr]
le professeur [prɔfɛsœːr] *schoolmaster*
professionnel [prɔfɛsjɔnɛl] *professional*
profiter (de) [prɔfite] *to take advantage*
           of, to profit by
profond(e) [prɔfɔ̃, -ɔ̃d] *deep*
la profondeur [prɔfɔ̃dœːr] *depth*
le programme [prɔgram] *programme*
le progrès [prɔgrɛ] *progress*
le projectile [prɔʒɛktil] *missile*
prolonger [prɔlɔ̃ʒe] *to prolong*
la promenade [prɔmnad] *promenade*
    faire une promenade *to go for a walk*
se promener [sə prɔmne] *to go for a walk*
la promesse [prɔmɛs] *promise*
promettre [prɔmɛtr] *to promise*
le pronom [prɔnɔ̃] *pronoun [tion*
la prononciation [prɔnɔ̃sjasjɔ̃] *pronuncia-*
la propagande [prɔpagɑ̃ːd] *propaganda*
le propos [prɔpo] *purpose, matter*
propre [prɔpr] *clean, own*

prospère [prɔspɛːr] *prosperous*
la prospérité [prɔsperite] *prosperity*
le protecteur [prɔtɛktœːr] *patron*
la protection [prɔtɛksjɔ̃] *patronage*
protéger [prɔteʒe] *to protect*
la protestation [prɔtɛstasjɔ̃] *protest*
la prouesse [pruɛs] *feat, exploit*
la Provence [prɔvɑ̃ːs] *Provence*
la province [prɔvɛ̃ːs] *province(s)*
le proviseur [prɔvizœːr] *headmaster*
la provision [prɔvizjɔ̃] *provision*
    faire ses provisions *to do one's shopping*
provoquer [prɔvɔke] *to provoke*
prudent(e) [prydɑ̃, -ɑ̃ːt] *wise, cautious*
la prune [pryn] *plum*
le psaume [psoːm] *psalm*
public, -ique [pyblik] *public*
le public [pyblik] *public, audience*
publicitaire [pyblisitɛːr] (adj.) *advertising*
la publicité [pyblisite] *advertisement,*
puis [pɥi] *then, next [publicity*
puisque [pɥiskə] *since*
la puissance [pɥisɑ̃ːs] *power, authority*
puissant(e) [pɥisɑ̃, -ɑ̃t] *powerful*
le puits [pɥi] *well*
le pullover [pulovɛːr] *pullover*
punir [pyniːr] *to punish*
la punition [pynisjɔ̃] *punishment*
le pupitre [pypitr] *desk*
pur(e) [pyːr] *pure*
le pyjama [piʒama] *pair of pyjamas*
les Pyrénées [pirene] (f.) *Pyrenees*

Q

le quai [ke] *platform, quay*
la qualité [kalite] *quality*
quand [kɑ̃] *when*
    quand même [kɑ̃ mɛːm] *all the same,*
quant à [kɑ̃t a] *as for [even if*
la quantité [kɑ̃tite] *quantity*
la quarantaine [karɑ̃tɛn] *group of about*
quarante [karɑ̃t] *forty [forty*
le quart [kaːr] *quarter*
le quartier [kartje] *district, quarter*
quatorze [katɔrz] *fourteen*
quatre [katr] *four*
quatre-vingt-dix [katrvɛ̃dis] *ninety*
quatre-vingts [katrvɛ̃] *eighty*
en quatrième [ɑ̃ katriɛm] *in the third form*
que, qu' [kə, k] *that, whom, which*
que de [k(ə) də] *what a lot of*
    ne . . . que [kə] *only*
    qu'est-ce que [kɛs(ə)k(ə)] *what?*
quel, -le [kɛl] *What? Which?*
quelque(s) [kɛlkə] *some, a few*
quelquefois [kɛlkəfwa] *sometimes*
la querelle [kərɛl] *quarrel, dispute*
querelleur, -euse [kərɛlœːr, -øːz]
la question [kɛstjɔ̃] *question [quarrelsome*
la quête [la kɛt] *collection, search*
la queue [kø] *tail, queue*
    faire la queue [fɛːr la kø] *to queue up*
qui [ki] *who, whom, which, what, that*
la quinzaine [kɛ̃zɛn] *fortnight, group of*
quinze [kɛ̃ːz] *fifteen [fifteen*
quitter [kite] *to leave*
quoi [kwa] (pronoun) *what*
    de quoi *enough*

quoique [kwak(ə)] *although*
le quotidien [kɔtidjɛ̃] *daily paper*
quotidien, -ienne [kɔtidjɛ̃, -jɛn] *daily*

R

raccrocher [rakrɔʃe] *to hook up* (receiver)
raconter [rakɔ̃te] *to relate*
le radeau [rado] *raft*
le radiateur [radjatœːr] (*electric*) *fire*
la radio [radjo] *radio*
le rail [raːj] *rail*
le raisin [rɛzɛ̃] *grape*
la raison [rɛzɔ̃] *reason*
    à raison de *at the rate of*
    avoir raison *to be right*
raisonnable [rɛzɔnabl] *reasonable,*
ralentir [ralɑ̃tiːr] *to slow down* [*sensible*
ramasser [ramase] *to pick up*
ramer [rame] *to row*
la rampe [rɑ̃ːp] *stairs, banisters*
ramper [rɑ̃pe] *to crawl*
ranger [rɑ̃ʒe] *to set out, to display*
se ranger à [sə rɑ̃ʒe a] *to agree with*
le rapide [rapid] *express train*
se rappeler [sə raple] *to remember*
le rapprochement [raprɔʃmɑ̃] *coming*
                together, reconciliation
rarement [rarmɑ̃] *rarely*
se raser [sə raze] *to shave oneself*
rassembler [rasɑ̃ble] *to gather together*
se rassembler [sə rasɑ̃ble] *to assemble*
le rat [ra] *rat*
ravager [ravaʒe] *to devastate, to destroy*
le rayon [rɛjɔ̃] *ray, department*
récemment [resamɑ̃] *recently*
le receveur [rəsəvœːr] *conductor* (of bus)
recevoir [rəsəvwaːr] *to receive*
la recherche [rəʃɛrʃ] *searching*
    à la recherche de *in search of*
réciter [resite] *to recite, relate*
la réclamation [reklamasjɔ̃] *complaint*
la réclame [reklaːm] *advertisement*
réclamer [reklame] *to demand*
récolter [rekɔlte] *to harvest*
recommander [rəkɔmɑ̃de] *to advise*
reconduire [rəkɔ̃dɥiːr] *to take, lead back*
reconnaître [rəkɔnɛːtr] *to recognise*
se reconnaître [sə rəkɔnɛːtr] *to make out*
                where one is
le reconstruction [rəkɔ̃stryksjɔ̃]
                reconstruction
recopier [rəkɔpje] *to re-copy, duplicate*
recoucher [rəkuʃe] *to lay down again*
recouvrir [rəkuvriːr] *to cover*
la récréation [rekreasjɔ̃] *recreation*
reçu [rəsy] *received*
    être reçu *to pass* (*an examination*)
recueillir [rəkœjiːr] *to gather up*
reculer [rəkyle] *to draw back*
redouter [rədute] *to dread*
réduire [redɥiːr] *to reduce*
réel(le) [reɛl] *real, actual*
refaire [rəfɛːr] *to repair*
réfléchir [refleʃiːr] *to reflect, think*
refléter [rəflete] *to reflect*
la réflexion [reflɛksjɔ̃] *reflection*
le réfrigérateur [refriʒeratœːr] *refrigerator*
le refuge [rəfyːʒ] *refuge*
le réfugié [refyʒje] *refugee*

se réfugier [sə refyʒje] *to flee, take refuge*
refuser [rəfyze] *to refuse*
regagner [rəgaɲe] *to regain*
le regard [rəgaːr] *look, attention*
regarder [rəgarde] *to look at*
le régiment [reʒimɑ̃] *regiment*
la région [reʒjɔ̃] *region*
la règle [rɛgl] *ruler, rule*
régler [regle] *to arrange, put in order*
régner [rɛɲe] *to pervade, reign*
regretter [rəgrɛte] *to be sorry, to regret*
la reine [rɛn] *queen*
rejoindre [rəʒwɛ̃ːdr] *to join again*
réjouir [reʒwiːr] *to rejoice*
relâcher [rəlaʃe] *to loosen, release, slacken*
relever [rələve] *to raise*
relié(e) [rəlje] *bound*
relier [rəlje] *to link, connect*
la religieuse [rəliʒjøːz] *nun*
la reliure [rəljyːr] *binding*
reluire [rəlɥiːr] *to shine* (intrans.)
la remarque [rəmark] *remark*
remarquer [rəmarke] *to notice*
    faire remarquer *to point out*
remercier [rəmɛrsje] *to thank* [*back*
remettre [rəmɛtr] *to put on again, to put*
se remettre à [sə rəmɛtr a] *to resume*
remonter [rəmɔ̃te] *to go up again*
remplacer [rɑ̃plase] *to replace*
rempli(e) [rɑ̃pli] *full*
remplir [rɑ̃pliːr] *to fill in, fill up*
se remuer [sə rəmɥe] *to be busy*
le renard [rənaːr] *fox*
la rencontre [rɑ̃kɔ̃ːtr] *meeting*
rencontrer [rɑ̃kɔ̃tre] *to meet*
le rendez-vous [ːrɑ̃devu] *appointment*
se rendormir [sə rɑ̃dɔrmiːr] *to go back to*
rendre [rɑ̃ːdr] *to give* (*back*), *make* [*sleep*
se rendre [sə rɑ̃dr] *to surrender*
se rendre à [sə rɑ̃ːdr a] *to go to* [*realize*
se rendre compte de [sə rɑ̃ːdr kɔ̃t də] *to*
se rengorger [sə rɑ̃gɔrʒe] *to puff oneself up,*
renifler [rənifle] *to sniff* [*gorge oneself*
renoncer [rənɔ̃se] *to renounce*
renouveler [r(ə)nuvle] *to renew*
le renseignement [rɑ̃sɛɲmɑ̃] *information*
la rentrée [rɑ̃tre] *return* (*to school*)
rentrer [rɑ̃tre] *to return home, re-enter*
renverser [rɑ̃vɛrse] *to knock over, spill,*
renvoyer [rɑ̃vwaje] *send back* [*overturn*
répandre [repɑ̃ːdr] *to spread*
répandu(e) [repɑ̃dy] *rumoured*
réparer [repare] *to repair*
repartir [rəpartiːr] *to set out again*
le repas [rəpa] *meal*
repasser [rəpase] *to iron*
se repentir [sə rəpɑ̃tiːr] *to repent*
la répétition [repetisjɔ̃] *repetition*
le répit [repi] *respite*
répliquer [replike] *to reply, answer*
répondre [repɔ̃ːdr] *to reply*
répondre de [repɔ̃ːdr də] *to answer for*
la réponse [repɔ̃ːs] *answer, reply*
reporter [rəpɔrte] *to carry back*
reposer [rəpoze] *to rest*
reprendre [rəprɑ̃ːdr] *to resume, continue*
la représentation [rəprezɑ̃tasjɔ̃]
représenter [rəprezɑ̃te] *represent*
le reproche [rəprɔʃ] *reproach* [*performance*

la **république** [repyblik] *republic*
la **réputation** [repytasjɔ̃] *reputation*
le **réseau** [rezo] *network, system*
se **réserver** [sə resɛrve] *to reserve for oneself*
la **résignation** [reziɲasjɔ̃] *resignation*
se **résigner à** [sə reziɲe a] *to resign oneself to*
la **résistance** [rezistɑ̃ːs] *resistance*
                       (*movement*)
le **résistant** [rezistɑ̃] *member of the*
  résister [reziste] *to resist*   [*Resistance*
  résoudre [rezuːdr] *to solve*
  respirer [rɛspire] *to breathe*
  ressembler [rəsɑ̃ble] *to resemble*
les **ressources** (f.) [rəsurs] *resources*
le **restaurant** [rɛstɔrɑ̃] *restaurant*
le **reste** [rɛst] *remainder, remains*
  rester [rɛste] *to stay, remain*
  restreint(e) [rɛstrɛ̃, -ɛ̃ːt] *restricted*
le **résultat** [rezylta] *result*
  résumer [rezyme] *to summarize*
en **retard** [ɑ̃ rətaːr] *late*
  retarder [rətarde] *to delay*
  retenir [rətniːr] *to retain, keep, hold*
la **retenue** [rətny] *detention* (*school*)
se **retirer** [sə rətire] *to withdraw*
  retomber [rətɔ̃be] *to fall back*
le **retour** [rətuːr] *return*
  retourner [rəturne] *to return, go back*
se **retourner** [sə rəturne] *to turn round*
  retraverser [rətravɛrse] *to cross again*
  retrouver [rətruve] *to find again*
se **réunir** [sə reynir] *to join together*
  réussir [reysiːr] *to succeed, to pass*
la **revanche** [rəvɑ̃ːʃ] *revenge*
  en **revanche** *on the other hand, in return*
le **réveil** [revɛːj] *alarm clock*
  réveiller [revɛje] *to waken*
se **réveiller** [sə revɛje] *to awake, wake up*
  révéler [revele] *to reveal*
  revenir [rəvniːr] *to come back, return,*
le **revenu** [rəvəny] *income* [*cost, amount to*
  rêver [rɛve] *to dream*
le **réverbère** [revɛrbɛːr] *street-lamp*
  rêveur, -euse [rɛvœːr, -øːz] *dreamy*
  revoir [rəvwaːr] *to see again*
  au **revoir** [o rəvwaːr] *goodbye*
la **révolte** [revɔlt] *revolt*
le **revolver** [revɔlvɛːr] *revolver*   [*magazine*
la **revue** [rəvy] *inspection* (military),
le **rez-de-chaussée** [redʃose] *ground floor*
le **rhum** [rɔm] *rum*
le **rhume** [rym] *cold*
  riant(e) [rjɑ̃, -ɑ̃ːt] *pleasant, rosy*
  riche [riʃ] *rich*
la **richesse** [riʃɛs] *richness*
  ridé(e) [ride] *wrinkled*
le **rideau** [rido] *curtain*
  ridicule [ridikyl] *ridiculous*
  rien du tout [rjɛ̃ dy tu] *nothing at all*
  ne . . . rien *nothing*
la **rigueur** [rigœːr] *rigour*
  rire [riːr] *to laugh*
le **risque** [risk] *risk*
le **rival** [rival] *rival*
la **rive** [riːv] *shore, bank*
la **rivière** [rivjɛːr] *river*
le **riz** [ri] *rice*
la **robe** [rɔb] *dress*   [*dressing-gown*
la **robe de chambre** [rɔb də ʃɑ̃ːbr]

la **robe de fête** [rɔb də fɛːt] *best dress*
la **roche** [rɔʃ] *rock*
le **rocher** [rɔʃe] *rock*
le **roi** [rwa] *king*
le **rôle** [roːl] *role, part*
le **roman** [rɔmɑ̃] *novel*
  rompre [rɔ̃ːpr] *to break*
le **ronronnement** [rɔ̃rɔnmɑ̃] *purring,*
  rose [roːz] *pink*   [*humming*
la **rosée** [roze] *dew*
le **rossignol** [rɔsiɲɔl] *nightingale*
la **roue** [ru] *wheel*
  rouge [ruːʒ] *red*
le **rouge à lèvre** [ruːʒ a lɛːvr] *lip-stick*
  rougeâtre [ruʒaːtr] *reddish*
le **rouge-gorge** [ruʒgɔrʒ] *robin*
  rougir [ruʒiːr] *to blush*
  rouiller [ruje] *to rust*
  rouler [rule] *to roll, run along*
la **route** [rut] *road*
  en **route** [ɑ̃ rut] *on the way*
la **route nationale** [rut nasjɔnal] *main road*
  roux, rousse [ru, rus] *russet*
  royal(e) [rwajal] *royal*
le **Royaume-Uni** [rwajoːmyni] *United*
le **ruban** [rybɑ̃] *ribbon*   [*Kingdom*
  rudement [rydmɑ̃] *roughly*
la **rue** [ry] *street*
la **ruelle** [rɥɛl] *narrow street*
le **ruisseau** [rɥiso] *brook, stream*
  ruisseler [rɥisle] *to drip* (trickle)
la **ruse** [ryːz] *cunning*
  rural(e) [ryral] *rural, country*
le **russe** [rys] *Russian*
la **Russie** [rysi] *Russia*
le **rythme** [ritm] *rhythm*
  rythmé(e) [ritme] *rhythmic*

S

  sa [sa] (f.) *his, her, its*
le **sable** [saːbl] *sand*
le **sabotage** [sabɔtaːʒ] *sabotage*
  saboter [sabɔte] *to sabotage*
le **sac** [sak] *bag*
le **sac à main** [sak a mɛ̃] *handbag*
le **sac de montagne** [sak də mɔ̃taɲ] *rucksack*
le **sac de voyage** [sak də vwajaːʒ] *hold-all*
  sacré(e) [sakre] *confounded, sacred*
le **sacrifice** [sakrifis] *sacrifice*   [*sensible*
  sage [saːʒ] *good, well-behaved, wise,*
  sain(e) et sauf (-ve) [sɛ̃ (sɛn) e sof (soːv)]
le **saint** [sɛ̃] *saint*   [*safe and sound*
  saisir [seziːr] *to seize*
la **saison** [sɛzɔ̃] *season*
le **salaire** [salɛːr] *wage(s)*
le **salarié** [salarje] *wage-earner*
  sale [sal] *dirty*
se **salir** [sə saliːr] *to get dirty*
la **salle** [sal] *room*
la **salle d'attente** [sal datɑ̃t] *waiting-room*
la **salle de bain** [sal də bɛ̃] *bathroom*
la **salle à manger** [sal a mɑ̃ʒe] *dining-room*
le **salon** [salɔ̃] *sitting-room, cabin*
le **salon de coiffure** [salɔ̃ də kwafyːr]
           [*hairdressing saloon*
le **salon d'essayage** [salɔ̃ desɛjaːʒ] *fitting*
  saluer [salɥe] *to greet*   [*room*
le **salut** [saly] *greeting*
  samedi [samdi] (m.) *Saturday*

la sandale [sãdal] *sandal*
le sandwich [sãdwitʃ] *sandwich*
le sang [sã] *blood*
sangloter [sãglɔte] *to sob*
sans [sã] *without*
la santé [sãte] *health*
la satisfaction [satisfaksjɔ̃] *satisfaction*
satisfaire [satisfɛːr] *to satisfy*
satisfait(e) [satisfɛ, -ɛt] *satisfied*
la saucisse [sosis] *sausage*
le saucisson [sosisɔ̃] *German sausage*
sauf [sof] *except, safe*
le saule [soːl] *willow*
le saut à ski [so a ski] *ski-jump*
sauter [sote] *to jump*
sauver [sove] *to save*
se sauver [sə sove] *to run away*
savoir [savwaːr] *to know (how to)*
le savoir [savwaːr] *knowledge*
le savon [savɔ̃] *soap*
savourer [savure] *to taste*
le scandale [skãdal] *scandal*
le scarabée [skarabe] *beetle*
la scène [sɛn] *scene*
la scooter [skutɛːr] *motor-scooter*
scruter [skryte] *to scan, to scrutinize*
la séance [seãːs] *meeting, sitting*
le seau [so] *pail or bucket*
sec, sèche [sɛk, sɛʃ] *dry*
second(e) [səgɔ̃, zgɔ̃, -ɔ̃d] *second*
secouer [səkwe] *to shake*
le secours [s(ə)kuːr] *help*
le secret [səkrɛ] *secret, mystery*
le secrétaire [səkretɛːr] *writing-desk*
secrètement [səkrɛtmã] *secretly*
la section [sɛksjɔ̃] *section, division*
séduire [sedɥiːr] *to charm, lure*
seize [sɛːz] *sixteen*
le séjour [seʒuːr] *visit, stay*
le sel [sɛl] *salt*
selon [səlɔ̃] *according to*
la semaine [s(ə)mɛn] *week*
sembler [sãble] *to seem, appear*
faire semblant de *to pretend to*
la semelle [səmɛl] *sole (of shoe)*
semer [səme] *to sow*
le sénateur [sɛnatœːr] *senator*
sémillant(e) [semijã, -ãt] *sprightly, lively*
le sens [sãːs] *sense, direction, way*
sensationnel, -le [sãsasjɔnɛl] *sensational*
la sensibilité [sãsibilite] *sensibility*
sensible [sãsibl] *sensitive*
le sentier [sãtje] *path*
sentir [sãtiːr] *to feel, smell (of)*
séparer [sɛpare (də)] *to separate*
sept [sɛ(t)] *seven*
septembre [sɛptã:br] (m.) *September*
sérieux, -euse [serjø, -øːz] *serious*
le serpent [sɛrpã] *snake*
serrer [sɛre] *to grip, pull on, shake*
le servant, la -e [sɛrvã(t)] *servant*
serviable [sɛrvjabl] *obliging*
le service [sɛrvis] *service, favour*
la serviette [sɛrvjɛt] *brief-case, towel*
servir [sɛrviːr] *to serve*
servir à [sɛrviːr a] *to be useful (for)*
se servir de [sə sɛrviːr də] *to make use of*
ses [se] *his, her, its* (plural)
seul(e) [sœl] *alone*

sévère [sevɛːr] *severe, stern, harsh, strict*
si [si] *so, if*
si bien que [si bjɛ̃ k(ə)] *so that*
le siècle [sjɛkl] *century*
le siège [sjɛːʒ] *headquarters, seat*
le sien, la sienne [sjɛ̃, sjɛn] *his, hers, its*
le sifflet [siflɛ] *whistle*
signaler [siɲale] *to report*
le signe [siɲ] *mark*
le signe [siɲ] *mark, sign*
le silence [silãːs] *silence*
silencieux, -euse [silãsjø, -øːz] *silent*
le sillon [sijɔ̃] *furrow*
simplement [sɛ̃pləmã] *simply*
le singe [sɛ̃ːʒ] *monkey*
sinistre [sinistr] *sinister*
sinon [sinɔ̃] *except*
la situation [sitɥasjɔ̃] *situation*
situé(e) [sitɥe] *situated*
six [si(s)] *six*
le ski [ski] *ski*
faire du ski *to go ski-ing*
le skieur [skiœːr] *skier*
social(e) [sɔsjal] *social*
la sœur [sœːr] *sister*
soi [swa] *oneself*
la soie [swa] *silk*
le soif [swaf] *thirst*
avoir soif *to be thirsty*
soigné(e) [swaɲe] *neat, trim*
soigner [swaɲe] *to look after, care for*
soigneusement [swaɲøːzmã] *carefully*
le soin [swɛ̃] *care, attention*
le soir [swaːr] *evening*
la soirée [sware] *evening (party)*
soixante [swasãt] *sixty*
soixante-dix [swasãtdis] *seventy*
le sol [sɔl] *ground*
le soldat [sɔlda] *soldier*
le solde [sɔld] *remnant, sale*
solder [sɔlde] *to pay*
le soleil [sɔlɛːj] *sun*
le soleil couchant [sɔlɛːj kuʃã] *setting sun*
le soleil levant [sɔlɛːj ləvã] *rising sun*
solennel, -elle [sɔlanɛl] *solemn*
solennité [sɔlanite] *solemnity*
la solitude [sɔlityd] *solitude*
la solution [sɔlysjɔ̃] *solution, answer*
sombre [sɔ̃ːbr] *dull, dark, gloomy*
la somme [sɔm] *sum*
en somme [ã sɔm] *in short, on the*
le sommeil [sɔmɛj] *sleep*   [*whole*
le sommelier [sɔmǝlje] *wine-waiter*
le sommet [sɔmɛ] *summit*
son [sɔ̃] *his, her, its*
le son [sɔ̃] *sound*
sonner [sɔne] *to ring, sound*
la sonnette [sɔnɛt] *bell*
le sort [sɔːr] *fate, lot*
la sorte [sɔrt] *kind, sort*
la sortie [sɔrti] *exit, way out*
sortir [sɔrtiːr] *to go, come out, take out*
sot(te) [so, sɔt] *stupid, foolish*
le sou [su] *sou (coin of little value)*
se soucier (de) [sə susje] *to worry (about)*
la soucoupe [sukup] *saucer*
soudain [sudɛ̃] *suddenly*
souffler [sufle] *to blow*
la souffrance [sufrãːs] *suffering*

485

souffrir [sufriːr] *to suffer*
souhaiter [swɛte] *to wish*
le soulagement [sulaʒmɑ̃] *relief*
soulever [sulve] *to raise*
le soulier [sulje] *shoe*
souligner [suliɲe] *to underline, stress*
le soupçon [supsɔ̃] *suspicion*
la soupe [sup] *soup*
souper [supe] *to have supper*
le souper [supe] *supper*
le soupir [supiːr] *sigh*
la source [surs] *source, origin*
le sourcil [sursi] *eyebrow*
sourd(e) [suːr, -d] *deaf*
sourire [suriːr] *to smile*
la souris [suri] *mouse*
sous [su] *under*
sous peu *shortly*
le sous-marin [sumarɛ̃] *submarine*
soutenir [sutniːr] *to support*
souterrain(e) [sutɛrɛ̃, -ɛn] *underground*
se souvenir de [sə suvniːr də] *to remember*
souvent [suvɑ̃] *often*
la souveraineté [suvrɛnte] *sovereignty*
spacieux, -euse [spasjø, -øːz] *spacious*
spécial(e) [spesjal] *special*
la spécialité [spesjalite] *speciality*
les spectateurs [spɛktatœːr] (m.) *spectators*
les spiritueux [spiritɥø] (m.) *spirits*
le sport [spɔːr] *sport, game*
la station [stasjɔ̃] *station* [*resort*
la station balnéaire [stasjɔ̃ balneɛːr] *seaside*
le stationnement [stasjɔnmɑ̃] *stationing, standing still, parking*
la station-service [stasjɔ̃sɛrvis] *petrolstation*
le statisticien [statistisjɛ̃] *statistician*
stimuler [stimyle] *to stimulate*
stopper [stɔpe] *to stop*
stratégique [strateʒik] *strategic*
stupide [stypid] *stupid*
la stupidité [stypidite] *stupidity*
le stylo [stilo] *fountain-pen*
le stylo à bille [stilo a biːj] *ball-point pen*
subir [sybiːr] *to undergo, suffer*
subitement [sybitmɑ̃] *suddenly*
le subordonné [sybɔrdɔne] *subordinate*
la substance [sybstɑ̃ːs] *substance*
subvenir à [sybvəniːr a] *to provide for*
succéder [syksede] *to come after*
le succès [syksɛ] *success*
le sucre [sykr] *sugar*
le sud [syd] *south*
le sud-est [sydɛst] *south-east*
suffire [syfiːr] *to suffice, cope with*
suggérer [sygʒere] *to suggest*
suisse [sɥis] *Swiss*
la Suisse [sɥis] *Switzerland*
suite (tout de) [tu d(ə) sɥit] *at once*
à la suite *following*
suivant(e) [sɥivɑ̃, -ɑ̃t] *following*
suivre [sɥiːvr] *to follow*
le sujet [syʒɛ] *subject, topic*
sujet à *subject to*
au sujet de *about*
la superficie [sypɛrfisi] *area* [*superstitious*
superstitieux, -euse [sypɛrstisjø, -øːz]
supporter [sypɔrte] *to endure, put up with, support, bear*
supposé que [sypoz k(ə)] *supposing that*

la supposition [sypozisjɔ̃] *supposition*
sur [syr] *on*
sur-le-champ [syrlʃɑ̃] *at once*
sûr(e) [syːr] *certain, sure* [*Department*
la Sûreté [syrte] *Criminal Investigaːion*
surprenant(e) [syrprənɑ̃, -ɑ̃ːt] *surprising*
surprendre [syrprɑ̃ːdr] *to surprise*
surpris(e) [syrpri, -iːz] *surprised*
surtout [syrtu] *especially*
surveiller [syrvɛje] *to supervise, look after, watch*
survenir [syrvəniːr] *to occur*
survivre [syrviːvr] *to survive*
survoler [syrvɔle] *to fly over*
susciter [sysite] *to stir up*
le symbole [sɛ̃bɔl] *emblem, symbol*
sympathique [sɛ̃patik] *likeable, sympa-*
la symphonie [sɛ̃fɔni] *symphony* [*thetic*
le symptôme [sɛ̃ptoːm] *symptom*
le syndicat [sɛ̃dika] *syndicate, trade union*
systématique [sistɛmatik] *systematic*
le système [sistɛm] *system*

T

ta [ta] (f.) *your*
le tabac [taba] *tobacco*
la table [tabl] *table*
la table à ouvrage [tabl a uvraːʒ] *work-table*
la table de jeu [tabl də ʒø] *card-table*
la table de toilette [tabl də twalɛt] *dressing-*
le tableau [tablo] *picture* [*table*
le tableau noir [tablo nwaːr] *blackboard*
la tablette [tablɛt] *bar, block*
le tablier [tablie] *apron*
le tabouret [taburɛ] *stool*
la tâche [tɑːʃ] *task*
la tache [taʃ] *stain*
tacher [taʃe] *to stain*
taillader [tajade] *to gash*
la taille [taːj] *waist, figure, stature, fashion, shape, height*
le tailleur [tajœːr] *costume, tailor*
se taire [sə tɛːr] *to be silent*
le talent [talɑ̃] *talent*
le talon [talɔ̃] *heel*
le tambour [tɑ̃buːr] *drum*
La Tamise [tamiːz] *the Thames*
tandis que [tɑ̃di(s) kə] *whilst, while*
tant (de) [tɑ̃ də] *so much, so many*
tant pis [tɑ̃ pi] *so much the worse*
la tante [tɑ̃t] *aunt*
taper à la machine [tape a la maʃin] *to*
le tapis [tapi] *carpet* [*type*
taquin(e) [takɛ̃, -in] *teasing*
tard [taːr] *late*
tarder [tarde] *to delay, to be a long time*
le tarif [tarif] *tariff*
la tarte aux pommes [tart o pɔm] *apple tart*
la tartine [tartin] *slice of bread and butter*
le tas [tɑ] *heap, pile*
la tasse [tas] *cup*
le taureau [tɔro] *bull*
le taxi [taksi] *taxi*
te [tə] *you, to you*
le teint [tɛ̃] *complexion*
tel(le) [tɛl] *such*
un télégramme [telegram] *telegram*
le télégraphiste [telegrafist] *telegraph operator*

le téléphone [telefɔn] *the telephone*
la télévision [televizjɔ̃] *television*
tellement [tɛlmɑ̃] *to such a degree*
la tempête [tɑ̃pɛːt] *storm, wind*
le temps [tɑ̃] *weather, time*
  dans le temps *in times past*
tendrement [tɑ̃drəmɑ̃] *tenderly*
tenir [təniːr] *to hold, keep, take place*
le tennis [tɛnis] *tennis*
la tentation [tɑ̃tasjɔ̃] *temptation*
la tente [tɑ̃ːt] *tent*
tenu(e) [təny] *dressed*
la tenue de soirée [təny də sware] *evening* [*dress*
le terme [tɛrm] *term, end*
  terminer [tɛrmine] *to end, finish*
le terminus [tɛrminyːs] *terminus*
la terrasse [tɛras] *pavement, open-air cafe*
la terre [tɛːr] *land, earth, ground*
la terreur [tɛrœːr] *terror*
  terrible [tɛribl] *terrible*
le territoire [tɛritwaːr] *territory*
tes [te] (pl.) *your*
la tête [tɛːt] *head*
  faire une tête *to pull a long face*
le texte [tɛkst] *text, subject, matter*
le thé [te] *tea*
le théâtre [teɑːtr] *theatre*
la théière [tejɛːr] *teapot*
le thème [tɛm] *prose composition*
le thermos [tɛrmɔs] *Thermos flask*
le ticket [tikɛ] *ticket*
le tien, la tienne [tjɛ̃, tjɛn] *yours*
le tiers [tjɛːr] *third* (fraction)
le tigre [tigr] *tiger*
le tilleul [tijœl] *lime-tree*
le timbre [tɛ̃ːbr] *stamp*
le timbre-poste [tɛ̃brəpɔst] *postage stamp*
  timidement [timidmɑ̃] *timidly, shyly*
  tirer [tire] *to pull*
se tirer de [sə tire də] *to get out of*
le tiret [tirɛ] *dash*
le tiroir [tirwaːr] *drawer*
  toi [twa] *you, to you*
la toile [twal] *canvas, cloth, web*
la toilette [twalɛt] *dressing, dress*
  faire sa toilette *to wash and dress*
le toit [twa] *roof*
la tomate [tɔmat] *tomato*
la tombe [tɔ̃ːb] *tomb*
le tombeau [tɔ̃bo] *tomb, vault*
la tombée [tɔ̃be] *fall*
  tomber [tɔ̃be] *to fall*
ton [tɔ̃] (m.) *your*
le ton [tɔ̃] *tone (of voice)*
la tonne [tɔn] *ton (1,000 kilos)*
  tonner [tɔne] *to thunder*
le tonnerre [tɔnɛːr] *thunder*
la torche électrique [tɔrʃ elɛktrik] *electric*
le torchon [tɔrʃɔ̃] *duster* [*torch*
  tordre [tɔrdr] *to wring*
la torpeur [tɔrpœːr] *drowsiness*
le tort [tɔːr] *wrong*
  avoir tort *to be wrong*
la tortue [tɔrty] *tortoise*
la torture [tɔrtyːr] *torture*
  tôt [to] *soon*
  total(e) [tɔtal] *total*
  toucher [tuʃe] *to touch*
  touffu(e) [tufy] *bushy, thick*

toujours [tuʒuːr] *always, however, still*
la toupie [tupi] *spinning top, peg-top*
la tour [tuːr] *tower*
le tour [tuːr] *tour, turn*
  faire le tour de *to go round*
  faire un tour *to go for a stroll*
  à tour de rôle *in turn*
le tourisme [turism] *tourism*
le touriste [turist] *tourist*
le tournant [turnɑ̃] *turning*
  tourner [turne] *to turn*
  tousser [tuse] *to cough*
  tout [tu] *quite, entirely*
  tout(e) [tu, -t] *all, every*
  tout à coup [tut a ku] *suddenly*
  tout à fait [tut a fɛ] *absolutely*
  tout à l'heure [tut a lœːr] *just now*
  tout droit [tu drwa] *straight ahead*
  tout le monde [tu lə mɔ̃ːd] *everybody,*
                                    everyone
  tout de suite [tutsɥit] *immediately*
la trace [tras] *track*
le tracteur [traktœːr] *tractor*
la tradition [tradisjɔ̃] *tradition*
  traduire [tradɥiːr] *to translate*
  trahir [traiːr] *to betray, reveal*
le train [trɛ̃] *train*
  en train de *in the act of*
  en train *in one's stride*
le traîneau [trɛno] *sledge*
  traîner [trɛne] *to drag*
se traîner [sə trɛne] *to crawl*
  traire [trɛːr] *to milk*
le trait [trɛ] *feature*
le trait d'union [trɛ dyjɔ̃] *hyphen*
le traité [trɛte] *treaty*
le traitement [trɛtmɑ̃] *salary, treatment*
le trajet [traʒɛ] *journey, trip*
le tramway [tramwɛ] *tram*
la tranche [trɑ̃ːʃ] *slice*
  tranquillement [trɑ̃kilmɑ̃] *peacefully*
le transatlantique [trɑ̃zatlɑ̃tik] *transatlantic*
                                    liner, deck-chair
  transporter [trɑ̃spɔrte] *to transport*
  trapu(e) [trapy] *squat*
le travail [travaːj] *work*
  travailler [travaje] *to work*
  à travers [a travɛːr] *across*
  aller de travers [ale də travɛːr] *to go*
la traversée [travɛrse] *crossing* [*wrong*
  traverser [travɛrse] *to traverse, cross,*
                                    pass through
le trèfle [trɛfl] *club* (cards), *clover*
  treize [trɛːz] *thirteen*
le tremblement [trɑ̃bləmɑ̃] *trembling,*
  trembler [trɑ̃ːble] *to tremble* [*shaking*
  trembloter [trɑ̃blɔte] *to flicker*
  tremper [trɑ̃pe] *to soak*
le tremplin [trɑ̃plɛ̃] *spring-board*
la trentaine [trɑ̃tɛn] *group of about thirty*
  trente [trɑ̃t] *thirty*
  très [trɛ] *very*
le trésor [trezɔːr] *treasure*
le tribunal [tribynal] *tribunal*
  tricher [triʃe] *to cheat*
le trimestre [trimɛstr] *term*
  triomphale [triɔ̃fal] *triumphant*
  triomphant(e) [triɔ̃fɑ̃, -ɑ̃t] *triumphant*
le triomphe [triɔ̃ːf] *triumph*

triompher [triɔ̃fe] *to triumph*
triste [trist] *sad*
trois [trwɑ] *three*
se tromper [sə trɔ̃pe] *to make a mistake*
le tronc [trɔ̃] *trunk*
trop (de) [tro də] *too much, too many*
le trottoir [trɔtwɑːr] *pavement*
le trou [tru] *hole*
le trouble [trubl] *trouble*
troubler [truble] *to disturb*
troué(e) [true] *with holes*
la troupe [trup] *troop*
trouver [truve] *to find*
se trouver [sə truve] *to be situated*
tu [ty] *you*
tuer [tɥe] *to kill*
la tuile [tɥil] *tile*
la truite [trɥit] *trout*
La Tunisie [tynizi] *Tunisia*
le tunnel [tynɛl] *tunnel*
turc, turque [tyrk] *Turkish*
tutoyer [tytwaje] *to address familiarly*
le tuyau [tyjo] *pipe*
le type [tip] *type, fellow*
typique [tipik] *typical*
le tyran [tirɑ̃] *tyrant*

U

un(e) [œ̃, yn] *a, one*
un uniforme [ynifɔrm] *uniform*
l'union [ynjɔ̃] (f.) *union*
unique [ynik] *unique, one-way* (traffic)
unir [yniːr] *to unite*
universel(le) [ynivɛrsɛl] *universal*
l'université [ynivɛrsite] (f.) *university*
urgent(e) [yrʒɑ̃, -ãt] *urgent*
usé(e) [yze] *threadbare, worn out*
user [yze] *to wear out*
une usine [yzin] *factory*
un ustensile [ystɑ̃sil] *utensil*
utile [util] *useful*
utiliser [ytilize] *to make use of*

V

les vacances [vakɑ̃ːs] (f.) *holidays*
    les grandes vacances *summer holidays*
la vache [vaʃ] *cow*
vaciller [vasille] *to flicker, stagger, reel*
le vagabond [vagabɔ̃] *vagabond*
la vague [vag] *wave*
en vain [ɑ̃ vɛ̃] *in vain*
vaincre [vɛ̃ːkr] *to conquer*
vainement [vɛnmɑ̃] *vainly*
le vainqueur [vɛ̃kœːr] *victor*
la vaisselle [vɛsɛl] *dishes, crockery*
le valet [valɛ] *jack*
le valet de ferme [valɛ də fɛrm] *farm-*
la valeur [valœːr] *value*   [*labourer*
la valise [valiːz] *suitcase*
    faire une valise *to pack a suitcase*
la vallée [vale] *valley*
valoir [valwaːr] *to be worth*
se vanter [sə vɑ̃te] *to boast*
la variété [varjete] *variety, kind*
Varsovie [varsɔvi] (f.) *Warsaw*
le vase [vɑːz] *vase*
vaste [vast] *vast*
le vaurien [vorjɛ̃] *good-for-nothing*
le veau [vo] *calf*

la veille [vɛːj] *day before, eve*
veiller [vɛje] *to see to it, to sit up, stay*
la veilleuse [vɛjøːz] *night-light*   [*awake*
le velours [v(ə)luːr] *velvet*
le vendangeur [vɑ̃dɑ̃ʒœːr] *grape-gatherer*
le vendeur [vɑ̃dœːr] *salesman*
vendre [vɑ̃ːdr] *to sell*
vendredi [vɑ̃drədi] (m.) *Friday*
le Vendredi Saint [vɑ̃drədi sɛ̃] *Good Friday*
vénéneux, -euse [venenø, -øːz] *poisonous*
se venger [sə vɑ̃ʒe] *to avenge oneself*
venir [v(ə)niːr] *to come*
venir à [v(ə)niːr a] *to happen to*
venir de [v(ə)niːr də] *to come from,*
le vent [vɑ̃] *wind*   [*have just*
    faire du vent *to be windy*
le ventre [vɑ̃ːtr] *abdomen*
le ver [vɛːr] *worm*
le verger [vɛrʒe] *orchard*
véritable [veritabl] *regular, real, truly*
la vérité [verite] *truth*
vermoulu(e) [vɛrmuly] *worm-eaten*
le verre [vɛːr] *glass*
vers [vɛːr] *towards*
le vers [vɛːr] *line* (*of poetry*)
verser [vɛrse] *to pour, spill*
    à verse *pouring down, in torrents*
la version [vɛrsjɔ̃] *translation into mother*
vert(e) [vɛːr, -t] *green*   [*tongue*
le vertige [vɛrtiːʒ] *giddiness*
vertigineux, -euse [vɛrtiʒinø, -øːz] *dizzy*
la vertu [vɛrty] *virtue*
la veste [vɛst] *jacket*
le vestibule [vɛstibyl] *hall*
le veston [vɛstɔ̃] *jacket*
le vêtement [vɛtmɑ̃] *garment*
le vétérinaire [veterinɛːr] *veterinary*
vêtu(e) [vɛty] *dressed*   [*surgeon*
le veuf [vœf] *widower*
veuillez [vœːje] *be so good as to*
la veuve [vœːv] *widow*
le viaduc [vjadyk] *viaduct*
la viande [vjɑ̃ːd] *meat*
la victime [viktim] *victim*
vide [vid] *empty*
vider [vide] *to empty, vacate*
la vie [vi] *life*
le vieillard [vjɛjaːr] *old man*
vieillir [vjɛjiːr] *to grow old*
la vieillesse [vjɛjɛs] *old age*
vieux, vieille [vjø, vjɛj] *old*
vif, vive [vif, viːv] *lively*
vigoureux, -euse [vigurø, -øːz] *sturdy*
le vilain [vilɛ̃] *villain*
vilain(e) [vilɛ̃, -ɛn] *nasty*
le village [vilaːʒ] *village*
le villageois, la -oise [vilaʒwa, -waːz]
la ville [vil] *town, city*   [*villager*
le vin [vɛ̃] *wine*
le vin rosé [vɛ̃ roze] *light table-wine*
le vinaigre [vinɛːgr] *vinegar*
vingt [vɛ̃] *twenty*
la vingtaine [vɛ̃tɛn] *group of about twenty*
violent(e) [vjɔlɑ̃, -ɑ̃t] *violent*
le violon [vjɔlɔ̃] *violin*
le violoniste [vjɔlɔnist] *violinist*
la virgule [virgyl] *comma*
le virtuose [virtɥoːz] *virtuoso*
le visage [vizaːʒ] *face*

de **visage** [vizaʒ] *in looks*
visible [vizibl] *visible*
visiter [vizite] *to visit*
le **visiteur, la -euse** [vizitœːr, -œːz] *visitor*
vite [vit] *quickly*
la **vitesse** [vitɛs] *speed*
   à toute **vitesse** *at full speed*
la **vitrine** [vitrin] *shop-window*
vivant(e) [vivɑ̃, -ɑ̃t] *living, modern*
vivement [vivmɑ̃] *briskly*
vivre [viːvr] *to live*
le **vœu** [vø] *vow, wish*
voici [vwasi] *here is, here are*
la **voie** [vwa] *track*
voilà [vwala] *there is, there are*
le **voilier** [vwalje] *sailing-boat*
voir [vwaːr] *to see*
voisin(e) [vwazɛ̃, -in] *neighbouring*
le **voisin** [vwazɛ̃] *neighbour*
le **voisinage** [vwazinaːʒ] *neighbourhood*
la **voiture** [vwatyːr] *vehicle, car*   *[aboard!*
   en **voiture** [ɑ̃ vwatyːr] *by car, all*
la **voiture d'enfant** [vwatyːd dɑ̃fɑ̃]
la **voix** [vwa] *voice*   *[perambulator*
le **vol** [vɔl] *theft, flight*
la **volaille** [vɔlaːj] *poultry*
voler [vɔle] *to steal, fly*
le **volet** [vɔlɛ] *shutters*
le **voleur** [vɔlœːr] *robber*
volontiers [vɔlɔ̃tje] *willingly*
vos [vo] (pl.) *your*

votre [vɔtr] *your* (polite form)
le **vôtre** [votr] *yours*
vouloir [vulwaːr] *to wish, want*
vous [vu] *you, to you*
vous-même [vumɛːm] *yourself*
le **voyage** [vwajaːʒ] *journey*
voyager [vwajaʒe] *to travel*
le **voyageur** [vwajaʒœːr] *traveller*
vrai(e) [vrɛ] *true, real*
   à **vrai dire** *to tell the truth*
la **vue** [vy] *sight*
   en **vue de** *with a view to*
vulgaire [vylgɛːr] *vulgar, common*

W

le **wagon** [vagɔ̃] *railway coach*
le **wagon-lit** [vagɔ̃li] *sleeping-car*
le **wagon-restaurant** [vagɔ̃rɛstɔrɑ̃]
                 dining-car

Y

y [i] *to it, on it, in it,* etc.
le **yacht** [jat] *yacht*
les **yeux** [jø] (m.) *eyes*

Z

zéro [zero] *nought*
la **zone** [zoːn] *zone*
le **zoo** [zu] *zoo*
Zut! [zyt] *Oh bother*

PRONUNCIATION

THE pronunciations of French words are given only in the previous French-English vocabulary, and any French word should be consulted there for its appropriate pronunciation.

The Index should also be consulted for further guidance about the use and peculiarities of certain words.

ENGLISH-FRENCH VOCABULARY

A

a un(e)
abandon abandonner
able [*be*] pouvoir
aboard à bord
   all aboard! (train, etc.)
            en voiture!
about (concerning) au sujet de
   (nearly) environ
   (on the point of)
            sur le point de
   be about s'agir de
above au-dessus de
abroad à l'étranger
abrupt brusque
absence l'absence (f.)
absent-minded distrait(e)
abundance l'abondance (f.)
   in abundance en abondance
abuse un abus
accept accepter,
           agréer
accommodation le logement
accompany accompagner
according to selon
account le compte
   on his account sur son compte
accountant le comptable
ace un as
acquaintance [*make the*] *of*
      faire la connaissance de
acquainted [*be*] *with* connaître
across à travers
act une action
   in the act of en train de
actual réel(le)
add ajouter
addition l'addition (f.)
   in addition en plus
address (speech) une allocution
   (verb) s'adresser à
adjust ajuster
admit admettre
adopted adoptif, -ive
advantage [*take*] *of* abuser de,
          profiter de
adventure une aventure
advertisement la publicité
advertising (adj.) publicitaire
advise recommander
aerial une antenne
aeroplane un avion
affectionate affectueux, -euse
afford [*be able to*]
        avoir les moyens
afraid [*be*] avoir peur
after (time) après
   (place) derrière
   (at the end of) au bout de,
          dans
afternoon une après-midi
afterwards après
again de nouveau,
     encore
against contre

age l'âge (m.)
   (verb) vieillir
aged âgé(e) [de]
agitation les agitations (f.)
ago il y a . . .
agree to convenir de,
     accepter
agree with se ranger à
agreed! d'accord
aggressor un agresseur
air l'air (m.)
   l'atmosphère (m.)
   in the open air en plein air,
          au grand air
alarm-clock le réveil
alas hélas
all tout, etc.
allied allié(e)
allow [*someone*] *to*
     permettre [à quelqu'un] de
almost presque
alone seul(e)
along le long de
aloud à haute voix
already déjà
also aussi
although quoique
always toujours
a.m. du matin
America l'Amérique (f.)
American américain(e)
among parmi
amount le montant
amount to revenir à
ancient ancien, -ienne
and et
and so on et ainsi de suite
anger la colère
angry fâché(e)
   get angry se fâcher
animal la bête
announce annoncer
annoy ennuyer,
     agacer
answer la réponse
   (verb) répondre
anthem (*national*) une hymne
anxious anxieux, -euse
any du, etc.,
   tout, etc.,
   quelque(s),
   (whatever) n'import quel(le)
   (pron.) en
apartment un appartement
apologize s'excuser
apology une excuse
apparatus un appareil
appear paraître,
     figurer
   (seem) sembler
appearance la mine
     un aspect
apple la pomme
apple-tree le pommier
apply oneself s'appliquer
appointed convenu(e)

appointment le rendez-vous
appreciate apprécier
approach s'approcher de
approve of approuver,
     agréer
April avril (m.)
area la superficie
arithmetic le calcul
arm le bras
armaments les armements
armchair le fauteuil
army une armée
around autour (de)
   all around partout
   walk around faire le tour de
arouse éveiller
arrival une arrivée
arrive arriver
article un article
as . . . as aussi . . . que
as for quant à
ashamed [*be*] avoir honte
aside de côté
ask [*for*] demander
   (question) poser
assemble se rassembler
assiduous assidu(e)
astonish étonner
at à,
   devant (la porte, etc.)
at once tout de suite
Atlantic Ocean l'Atlantique(m.)
atrocious atroce
attack une attaque
attend (school, etc.) fréquenter
attention le soin,
     l'attention (f.),
     le regard
   pay attention to
        prêter attention à
attentive attentif, -ive
attract attirer
attractive coquet(te)
aunt la tante
August août (m.)
Austria l'Autriche (f.)
authority une autorité
autumn l'automne (m.)
avoid éviter
awake (se) réveiller
away absent(e)
   lead away emmener
awful affreux, -euse,
     terrible,
     épouvantable

B

back le dos
background le fond
bad mauvais(e)
baker's shop la boulangerie
balance un équilibre
balcony le balcon
bald chauve
ball le ballon,
   la balle

balloon **le ballon**
ball-point pen **le stylo à bille**
bandage **bander**
bank-note **le billet de banque**
bar **la tablette**
barely **à peine**
bargain **une occasion**
bark **aboyer**
barley **l'orge** (f.)
barn **la grange**
basket **le panier**
bath **la baignoire,**
  le bain
bathe **se baigner**
bathroom **la salle de bain**
be **être**
beach **la plage**
beautiful **beau, belle**
beauty **la beauté**
because **parce que**
because of **à cause de**
become **devenir**
bed **le lit**
  go to bed **se coucher**
bedroom **la chambre à coucher**
beef **le bœuf**
beer **la bière**
before (time) **avant**
  (place) **devant**
beg **prier de**
begin **commencer à,**
  débuter,
  se mettre à
beginning **le début,**
  le commencement
behind **derrière**
Belgium **la Belgique**
believe **croire**
bell **la cloche**
belongings **les affaires** (f.)
below **au-dessous de**
bench **le banc,**
  la banquette
bend down **se baisser**
besides **en outre,**
  d'ailleurs
betray **trahir**
better (adj.) **meilleur(e)**
  (adv.) **mieux**
between **entre**
bicycle **la bicyclette**
bid **une annonce,**
  une offre
big **gros(se),**
  grand(e)
bill **une addition**
bird **un oiseau**
birth **la naissance**
birthday **un anniversaire**
birth-rate **la natalité**
black **noir(e)**
blackboard **le tableau noir**
blast (of wind) **le coup**
blind **aveugle**
block **la tablette**
blood **le sang**
blow **le coup**
  (verb) **souffler**
blue **bleu(e)**

blue trout **la truite au bleu**
blush **rougir**
boarding house, school
  la pension
boat **le bateau**
  small boat **le canot**
boil **bouillir**
bone **un os**
book **le livre**
  (of tickets, etc.) **le carnet**
  old book **le bouquin**
book-keeper **le comptable**
book-keeping **la comptabilité**
boot **la botte**
  (car) **le coffre**
border [on] **border,**
  confiner à
bored [be] **s'ennuyer**
boring **ennuyeux, -euse**
born [be] **naître**
borrow **emprunter**
boss **le patron**
both **tous, etc., les deux**
both . . . and **et . . . et**
Bother! **Zut!**
bottle **la bouteille**
bottom **le fond**
bound (book) **relié(e)**
bound for **à destination de**
boulevard **le boulevard**
box **la boîte**
box-office **le bureau de location**
box-room **la chambre de**
boy **le garçon** [débarras
brake **le frein**
brand **la marque**
brandish **brandir**
brave **courageux, -euse**
brawl **la bagarre**
bread **le pain**
break **casser**
break out **éclater**
breakdown **la panne**
breakfast **le petit déjeuner**
  (verb) **prendre le**
    petit déjeuner
breathe **respirer**
bridge **le pont**
brief **bref, brève**
brief-case **la serviette**
bring **apporter**
bring down **descendre**
Britain **la Grande-Bretagne**
Brittany **la Bretagne**
brother **le frère**
brow **le front**
brown **brun(e)**
brush **la brosse**
build **bâtir**
building **un édifice,**
  le bâtiment
bullock **le bœuf**
bunch (flowers) **le bouquet**
bundle **le paquet**
burial **un enterrement**
burn **brûler**
burst **éclater**
bury **enterrer**
bus **un autobus**

bush **le buisson**
business **les affaires** (f.)
bustle about **s'affairer**
busy **occupé(e),**
  en train de
but **mais**
butter **le beurre**
button **le bouton**
buy **acheter**
buyer **un acheteur**
by **par,**
  de,
  en

C

cabbage **le chou**
cafe **le café**
cake **le gâteau**
calendar **le calendrier**
call **appeler**
call at **se présenter à**
calm **le calme**
  (adj.) **calme**
camper **le campeur**
camping **le camping**
can **pouvoir**
  (know how to) **savoir**
canvas **la toile**
capital (city) **la capitale**
car **la voiture,**
  une auto
  by car **en voiture**
card **la carte**
  pack of cards **le jeu de cartes**
card-table **la table de jeu**
care **le soin**
careful **méticuleux, -euse,**
  soigneux, -euse
carefully **soigneusement**
caretaker **la concierge**
carnation **l'œillet** (m.)
carpet **le tapis**
carriage (train) **le compartiment**
carriage-door **la portière**
carrot **la carotte**
carry **porter**
carry away **emporter**
carry on (continue) **continuer**
cart **la charrette**
case **le cas,**
  (suitcase) **la valise**
  in any case **en tout cas**
castle **le château**
catch **attraper,**
  prendre
catch sight of **apercevoir**
cathedral **la cathédrale**
cattle **le bétail**
ceaselessly **sans cesse**
celebrate **célébrer,**
  fêter
centre **le centre,**
  le milieu
certificate of merit **un accessit**
chair **la chaise**
chance **le hasard**
  by chance **par hasard**
change (money) **la monnaie**
  (verb) **changer**
  for a change **pour changer**

Channel [*English*] la Manche
charm le charme
    (verb) séduire
chase la poursuite
    la chasse
chat causer
chatter bavarder
chatterbox (adj.) bavard(e)
check (pattern) le carreau
cheek la joue
cheese le fromage
cheesemonger le fromager
chief le chef
cherry-tree le cerisier
chess les échecs (m.)
chest la poitrine
chest-cold le rhume de poitrine
chest of drawers la commode
chicken le poulet
child (m. or f.) un(e) enfant
childhood l'enfance (f.)
chilly frais, fraîche
chimney la cheminée
china la porcelaine
China la Chine
Chinese le Chinois
chocolate le chocolat
choice le choix
choose choisir
choral society or choir
    la [société] chorale
Christian name le prénom
church une église
cinema le cinéma
circumstance la circonstance
citizen le citoyen, la -enne
    le citadin
city la ville
civil civil(e)
civil servant le fonctionnaire
clarinet la clarinette
class la classe
clean propre
    (verb) nettoyer
clear clair(e)
    clear the table desservir
clerk le commis
clever intelligent(e)
cliff la falaise
climb grimper,
    escalader,
    monter
clip (tickets) poinçonner
cloak le manteau
clock la pendule
    (large) une horloge
close fermer
    (sultry) lourd(e)
closely (from close to) de près
closer [*come*] approcher
clothes les vêtements (m.),
    les habits (m.)
cloud le nuage
cloudless sans nuages
clover le trèfle
club (cards) le trèfle
coal la houille,
    le charbon

coat un manteau,
    un habit
coffee [*with cream*] le café
cold froid(e)   [(crème)
    be cold (persons) avoir froid
    (weather) faire froid
    with a cold enrhumé(e)
collaborate collaborer
colleague le (la) collègue
collection la collection
    take a collection
        faire la quête
colonel le colonel
colour la couleur
come venir,
    arriver
come in entrer
Come, come! Voyons!
comfort le confort
comfortably à l'aise,
    confortablement
comic paper un illustré
commanding officer
        le commandant
comment, commentary
        le commentaire
commit commettre
common commun(e)
common-sense le sens commun
comparison la comparaison
    in comparison with
        en comparaison de
compartment le compartiment
compatriot le (la) compatriote
complete complet, -ète
complexion le teint
comply s'exécuter,
    satisfaire à
comprise comprendre
concern s'agir de
condition la situation
conduct la conduite
conductor (of bus) le receveur
cone-bearing tree le conifère
confess avouer
confidence la confiance
confine oneself to se borner à
conflict le conflit
confounded sacré(e)
confused confus(e)
congratulate [*on*] féliciter [de]
conifer le conifère
connect relier
connection (railway)
        la correspondance
consent to consentir à
consequently par conséquent
consider considérer
considerable considérable
consist of comprendre,
    consister de,
    se composer de
construct construire
contain contenir
contend for se disputer
continue continuer
    (speaking) reprendre
convenience la commodité
convenient commode

convince convaincre
cook le cuisinier,
    la cuisinière
    (verb) cuire
cooking la cuisine
    do the cooking faire la cuisine
cool frais, fraîche
cope with faire face à
copper le cuivre
copy imiter
corn le blé
corner le coin
corpse le cadavre
correct correct(e)
corridor le couloir
corrupt corrompre
cost coûter,
    revenir à
cotton le coton
couch le canapé
cough tousser
count compter
counter le comptoir
country le pays
    Low Countries
        les Pays-Bas (m.)
country[*side*] la campagne
courage le courage
courageous courageux, -euse
course le cours
    in the course of au cours de
    of course bien entendu
court[*yard*] la cour
cover couvrir
cow la vache
cow-shed une étable
crawl ramper
creaking le grincement
cream-jug le pot à crème
criminal le criminel
    Criminal Investigation
        Department la Sûreté
crisis la crise
critical critique
cross la croix
    (verb) franchir,
    croiser,
    traverser
crossing la traversée
crowd la foule
crowd around se presser
crumb la miette
crush écraser
cry le cri
cry out s'écrier
cup la tasse
cupboard le placard,
    une armoire
curious curieux, -euse
customer le (la) client(e)
customs officer le douanier
cut [*down*] couper
cut short abréger
cutlery la coutellerie

D

daddy papa
daily quotidien, -ienne
daily help la femme de ménage

493

daily paper le quotidien,
le journal
damage les dégâts
(verb) endommager
damp mouillé(e)
danger le danger
dangerous dangereux, -euse
dare oser
dark sombre,
foncé(e)
darkness l'obscurité (f.)
darling chéri(e)
daughter la fille
dawn l'aube (f.),
l'aurore (f.)
day le jour
day[*time*] la journée
the day when le jour où
from day to day
de jour en jour
day before, eve la veille
next day le lendemain
dead mort(e)
deaf sourd(e)
deafening assourdissant(e)
deal distribuer
dear cher, chère,
chèri(e)
death la mort
decanter la carafe
December décembre (m.)
decide to décider de
deck le pont
declare déclarer
decorate orner
deep profond(e)
deep voice une voix basse
defect le défaut
defence la défense
defend défendre
delay (re)tarder
delighted enchanté(e)
deliver livrer
(letters) distribuer
delivery la livraison
demand réclamer
demoralize démoraliser
deny nier
depart partir
department le rayon
departure le départ
deplorable déplorable
depopulate dépeupler
become depopulated
se dépeupler
deprive of priver de
describe décrire
desire le désir
(verb) désirer
desperate désespéré(e)
despite malgré
destroy détruire
detective le détective,
le policier
detention (school) la retenue
detest détester
devastate ravager
devoted dévoué(e)
dew la rosée

diamond le diamant
(cards) le carreau
dictation la dictée
dictionary le dictionnaire
die mourir
diesel rail-car un autorail
difficult difficile
dignified digne
din le fracas
to dine [*out*] dîner [en ville]
dining-room la salle à manger
dinner-time l'heure du déjeuner
direction la direction,
le côté
dirty sale
get dirty se salir
disabled soldier un invalide
disagreeable désobligeant(e)
disappear disparaître
disaster le désastre
disconnect débrancher
discover découvrir
disease la maladie
disembark débarquer
disembarkation
le débarquement
dish le plat
dishes la vaisselle
wash the dishes
faire la vaisselle
dish-water l'eau (f.) de vaisselle
disobey désobéir à
display exposer
(a bill) afficher
displeased mécontent(e)
disposal la disposition
have at one's disposal disposer
dispute la querelle
distance la distance
from a distance de loin
in the distance au loin
distinguishing distinctif, -ive
district le quartier
disturb troubler,
déranger
divided divisé(e)
dizzy vertigineux, -euse
do faire
doctor le médecin,
le docteur
dog le chien
doll la poupée
dominate dominer
door la porte
front door la porte d'entrée
dot le point
doubt le doute
doubtless à coup sûr,
sans doute
down [*there*] là-bas
put down déposer
downstairs en bas
dozen la douzaine
half a dozen la demi-douzaine
drawing le dessin
dread redouter
dreadful effroyable
dream le rêve

dress la robe
(verb) s'habiller
best dress la robe de fête
dressed in vêtu(e) de,
habillé(e) de
dressing-table
la table de toilette
dressmaker la couturière
dress-making la couture
drink la consommation
(verb) boire
drip (trickle) ruisseler
drive conduire
drive away chasser
driver le conducteur
driving licence
le permis de conduire
drop la goutte
(verb) laisser tomber
drowsiness la torpeur
drum le tambour
dry sec, sèche
duck le canard
dumb muet(te)
during pendant
dust la poussière

E

each chaque
each one chacun(e)
each other se
early (adv.) tôt,
de bonne heure
as early as dès
easy facile
east l'est (m.)
Easter Pâques (m.)
eat manger
eatable comestible
earth la terre
economic économique
economize économiser,
faire des économies
economy l'économie (f.)
edge le bord
edible comestible
educate instruire
effective efficace
eight huit
eighteen dix-huit
eighty quatre-vingts
either . . . or soit . . . soit
elapse s'écouler
elbow le coude
(verb) coudoyer
elder aîné(e)
electricity l'électricité (f.)
eleven onze
elsewhere ailleurs
embark s'embarquer
emblem le symbole
embrace embrasser
emigrate émigrer
emotion une émotion
employer le patron
empty vide
(verb) vider
encumbered with
encombré(e) de

494

end le bout,
   la fin
   (verb) terminer
   at the far end au fond
endure supporter
enemy un ennemi
energetically énergiquement
engage in se livrer à
engine le moteur
engine-driver le mécanicien
England l'Angleterre (f.)
English anglais(e)
English Channel la Manche
enjoy jouir de
enough assez [de]
enter entrer dans
entirely tout,
         entièrement,
         tout à fait
enthusiast un(e) enthousiaste
enthusiastic enthousiaste
entrance une entrée
entrance hall le foyer
entrust confier
envelope une enveloppe
epicure le gourmet
equal égal(e)
equilibrium un équilibre
errands les commissions
   to do one's errands
         faire ses commissions
error la faute,
       une erreur
escalator un escalier roulant
especially surtout
essential essentiel(le)
establish oneself s'établir
establishment un établissement
evaporate s'évaporer
even (adv.) même
evening le soir,
        la soirée
   in the evening le soir
event évènement
ever jamais
every tout, etc.
everybody tout le monde,
          tous
everyone chacun(e)
everything tout
   everything in one's power
                 tout son possible
everywhere partout
evidently évidemment
examination un examen
   (inspection) le contrôle
examine examiner
example un exemple
   for example par exemple
excellent parfait(e)
           excellent(e)
except sauf
exception une exception
exclaim s'écrier,
        s'exclamer
excuse une excuse
       (verb) excuser
exemplary exemplaire

exercise exercer
exercise-book le cahier
exhaust épuiser
exhibition une exposition
exist exister
exit la sortie
expect s'attendre à
experienced expérimenté(e)
explain expliquer
explosion une explosion
express train le rapide
extend s'étendre
extent la mesure
extremely infiniment
eye, eyes un œil, des yeux
eyebrow le sourcil

F

face le visage,
      la figure
      (verb) faire face à,
            affronter
   pull a face faire la grimace
facing en face de
fact le fait
   in fact en effet
factory une usine,
        la fabrique
faddy maniaque
fair juste
faithful fidèle
fall tomber
fall asleep s'endormir
family la famille
famished affamé(e)
famous célèbre,
       fameux, -euse
far from loin de
   as far as jusqu'à
   so far jusque-là
farm la ferme
farmer le fermier
farmer's wife la fermière
farm-labourer le valet de ferme
farmyard la basse-cour
fashion la mode
fast vite
      (adj.) rapide
   *as fast as one's legs can
      carry one* à toutes jambes
fat gros(se)
fate le sort
father papa
fault la faute,
       le défaut
favourite favori, -ite
fear la peur
     (verb) craindre
fearsome formidable,
         effrayant(e)
February février (m.)
feed oneself se nourrir
feel like avoir envie de
feeling une émotion
fence la clôture,
       la palissade
feverish fiévreux, -euse

few peu [de]
   a few quelques
   quite a few pas mal de
field le champ
fifteen quinze
fifty cinquante
fight se battre
figure (number) le chiffre
file classer
fill in [up] remplir
fill up with faire le plein de
film le film
find trouver
fine beau, belle
finger le doigt
        (adj.) digital(e)
finger-prints
        les empreintes digitales (f.)
finish achever,
        finir,
        terminer
fire le feu
     (electric) le radiateur
fireplace la cheminée
   by the fireside au coin du feu
first premier, -ière
   at first d'abord
   first of all d'abord
fish le poisson
     (verb) pêcher
fishing la pêche
fist le poing
fitting room le salon d'essayage
five cinq
flat un appartement
      (adj.) plat(e)
flee se réfugier
fleet la flotte
floor le plancher
       (storey) un étage
florist le (la) fleuriste
flow une affluence
flower la fleur
flower-bed la plate-bande
fluently couramment
fly voler
fly over survoler
fog le brouillard
   be foggy faire du brouillard
fold [one's arms]
              croiser [les bras]
follow suivre
food la nourriture
foodstuff le produit alimentaire
fool un(e) imbécile
foolish things des bêtises (f.)
foot le pied
      (animal) la patte
   on foot à pied
football le ballon
for pour
     (giving reason) car
     (during) pendant
forbidden interdit(e)
   it is forbidden to défense de
forehead le front
foreigner l'étranger, -ère

foresee prévoir
forget oublier
forgive pardonner à
form (school) la classe,
   (bench) le banc
former celui-là, celle-là
   (adj.) ancien(ne)
formerly autrefois
fortnight la quinzaine
fortunate heureux, -euse
forty quarante
four quatre
fourteen quatorze
franc le franc
frankly franchement
free libre
French français(e)
French-window la porte-fenêtre
frequent fréquenter
fresh frais, fraîche
Friday vendredi (m.)
friend un ami, une amie,
   le compagnon
  school-friend le, la camarade
frightful affreux, -euse
frog la grenouille
from (away from) de
   (since) depuis
   (as early as) dès
   (as from) à partir de
front le devant
  in front of devant
frontier la frontière
frost le givre,
   la gelée
fruit le fruit
   (adj.) fruitier, -ière
full of rempli(e) de
fullness l'ampleur (f.)
full-stop le point
funds le fonds
funeral un enterrement
funny drôle
  make fun of se moquer de
fur coat le manteau de fourrure
furious furieux, -euse
furniture les meubles
  piece of furniture le meuble
furtive furtif, -ive
fussy maniaque,
   difficile
future l'avenir (m.)

G

game le jeu,
   la partie
gangway la passerelle
garden le jardin
garment le vêtement
gate (platform) la grille
   (automatic) le portillon
gather cueillir
gather together rassembler
gay joyeux, -euse
gaze regarder
general le général
generally généralement
gentle doux, douce

gentleman le monsieur
geography la géographie
germ le microbe
German (language)
        l'allemand (m.)
Germany l'Allemagne (f.)
gesture le geste
get obtenir,
   prendre
get up, rise se lever
get into monter dans
get out [*of*] descendre [de]
giddiness le vertige
gift le cadeau
gild dorer
girl la petite fille,
   la fillette
give donner
glance le coup d'œil
   (verb) jeter un coup d'œil
glass le verre
glove le gant
go aller,
   se rendre
go all over parcourir
go along filer
go away partir,
   s'en aller
go back retourner,
   revenir
go for a walk se promener
go in entrer
go into pénétrer
go to se rendre à
   (regularly) fréquenter
going to (bound for)
        à destination de
go up monter
gold l'or (m.)
golden doré(e)
good le bien
   (adj.) bon(ne)
   (well-behaved) sage
  do good to faire du bien à
  have a good time s'amuser bien
  what is the good of?
        à quoi bon?
good-bye au revoir
Good heavens! Mon Dieu!
goodness la bonté
goose une oie
governess une institutrice
government le gouvernement
graceful gracieux, -euse
grammar school le lycée
gramophone [*electric*]
        un électrophone
grass l'herbe (f.)
grass border la plate-bande
great grand(e),
   gros(se)
Great Britain
        la Grande-Bretagne
Greek le grec
green vert(e)
green peas les petits pois
greet saluer
greeting le salut
grey gris(e)

grind moudre
grip serrer
ground le sol,
   la terre
ground floor le rez-de-chaussée
group le groupe
grow (plant) cultiver
   (increase) croître
growth la croissance
grudgingly de mauvaise grâce
guarantee garantir
guide guider
guilty coupable
gullible facile à duper

H

habit l'habitude (f.)
  be in the habit of
        avoir l'habitude de
hair les cheveux (m.)
  cut hair couper les cheveux
hairdressing saloon
        le salon de coiffure
hair-style la coiffure
half la moitié
half-hour une demi-heure
half past et demi(e)
half-way à mi-chemin
ham le jambon
hammer le marteau
hand la main
handbag le sac à main
hang accrocher,
   pendre
happen se passer,
   arriver
happy content(e)
hard dur(e)
   (energetically)
        énergiquement
hardly ne . . . guère
harm le mal
   (verb) nuire à
        faire du mal à
harmful nuisible
harmonious harmonieux, -euse
harrow la herse
harvest la moisson
   (verb) récolter
haste la hâte
hasten se dépêcher,
   se hâter
hastily à la hâte
hat le chapeau
hate détester,
   haïr
have avoir
   posséder
have to devoir,
   avoir à
have just venir de
hay le foin
he il
   lui
head la tête
headlamp le phare
headmaster le proviseur
headmistress la directrice
headquarters le siège

healthy **sain(e)**
heap **le tas**
hear **entendre**
heart **le cœur**
heartily **cordialement**
heat **la chaleur**
heave a sigh **pousser un soupir**
heavy **lourd(e)**
heel **le talon**
   high-heeled **à hauts talons**
help **l'aide** (f.)
   (verb) **aider**
hen **la poule**
her **la,** *to her* **lui**
   (apart from verb) **elle**
   (adj.) **son, sa, ses**
here **ici**
here is, are **voici**
hero **le héros**
heroic **héroïque**
hers **le sien,** etc.
herself **elle-même**
hide **cacher**
higgledy-piggledy **pêle-mêle**
high **haut(e)**
high-heeled **à hauts talons**
highway **la grand'route**
hill **la colline**
him **le,** *to him* **lui**
   (apart from verb) **lui**
hire **louer**
his **son, sa, ses**
   (pron.) **le sien,** etc.
hitch-hiker **un auto-stoppeur**
hold **tenir, retenir**
holiday **le congé**
   summer holidays
      les grandes vacances
Holland **la Hollande**
home **un intérieur**
   [*at*] *home* **à la maison,**
      chez moi, etc.
homesickness **le mal du pays,**
      la nostalgie
homework **le devoir**
honey **le miel**
hook up (receiver) **raccrocher**
hooter **le klaxon**
hope **un espoir**
   (verb) **espérer**
horizon **l'horizon** (m.)
horrible **affreux, -euse**
horribly **horriblement**
horror **l'horreur** (f.)
horse **le cheval**
hospital **un hôpital**
hostility **hostilité**
hot **chaud(e)**
   be hot (persons) **avoir chaud**
      (weather) **faire chaud**
hour **une heure**
   early hour **une heure matinale**
   half an hour **une demi-heure**
house **la maison**
   private house **le domicile**
   to, at, the house of **chez**
household **le ménage**
housewife **la ménagère**
housework **le ménage**

how **comment**
how much, many **combien de**
however **cependant**
humming **le ronronnement**
hunch-backed **bossu(e)**
hundred **cent**
hungry **affamé(e)**
   to be hungry **avoir faim**
hurriedly **à la hâte**
hurry **se presser**
hurry up **se dépêcher**
hurt **faire mal à**
   (snub) **froisser**
husband **le mari,**
      un époux
hydro-electric power
   l'énergie (f.) **hydro-électrique**

I

I **je**
   (apart from verb) **moi**
icy **glacial(e)**
idea **une idée**
idiot **un imbécile**
if **si**
ill **malade**
illness **la maladie**
imitate **imiter**
immediately **tout de suite,**
      immédiatement
impact **le choc**
impatient **impatient(e)**
   get impatient **s'impatienter**
implements **le matériel**
important **essentiel, -ielle,**
      important(e)
impossible **impossible**
impression **une empreinte**
in **dans,**
   en
in it (there) **là-dedans**
in, into [*it*] **dedans**
inadvertently **par mégarde**
inclination **l'envie** (f.)
   have an inclination to
      avoir envie de
include **comprendre**
income **le revenu**
increase **un accroissement**
   (verb) **augmenter**
incur expenses **faire des dépenses**
indeed **en effet**
   (very) **bien**
independence **l'indépendance** (f.)
individual **un individu**
industrious **laborieux, -euse**
industry **une industrie**
influenza **la grippe**
inform **communiquer**
information
   le(s) renseignement(s)
informed **informé(e)**
inhabitant **un habitant**
ink **l'encre** (m.)
innocent **innocent(e)**
innocently **innocemment**
inscribed **inscrit(e)**
inside **à l'intérieur de,**
   dans

inspection **le contrôle**
   (military) **la revue**
instead of **au lieu de**
instrument **un appareil**
insult **une injure**
interest **un intérêt**
   be interested in **s'intéresser à**
interesting **intéressant(e)**
interrupt **interrompre**
interval (play) **un entr'acte**
interview **une entrevue**
invade **envahir**
invader **un envahisseur**
invite **inviter**
ironic **ironique**
-ish (colours) **-âtre**
island **une île**
issue **émettre**
it **il, elle, ce**
it is (+ noun) **c'est**
Italy **l'Italie** (f.)

J

jack (cards) **le valet**
jam **la confiture**
January **janvier** (m.)
jar **le pot**
Jew **le Juif**
Jewess **la Juive**
job **un emploi**
join (army) **s'engager dans**
   (party, scheme, etc.)
      adhérer à
joke **la plaisanterie**
jostle **bousculer**
journey **le voyage,**
      le trajet
joy **la joie**
joyful **joyeux, -euse**
judge **juger**
juicy **juteux, -euse**
July **juillet** (m.)
jump **sauter**
June **juin** (m.)
junior **cadet(te)**
just **juste**
   to have just **venir de**

K

keen **enthousiaste**
keep **garder,**
      tenir,
      retenir
key **la clef**
kick **le coup de pied**
kill **tuer**
kind **une espèce,**
      la variété,
   (adj.) **aimable**
   be so kind as to **veuillez**
king **le roi**
kiss **embrasser**
kitchen **la cuisine**
kitchen-garden **le potager**
knit one's brow
      froncer les sourcils
knock **frapper**
knock down **abattre**
knock over (spill) **renverser**

knot **nouer**
know [*that*] **savoir**
  (a person) **connaître**
know how to **savoir**

L

lack **le manque**
lady **la dame**
lake **le lac**
lamp **la lampe**
land **le pays,**
  la terre
landing **le palier**
landscape **le paysage**
language **la langue**
large **grand(e),**
  immense
last **dernier, -ière**
  (verb) **durer**
  at last **enfin**
late **tard,**
  en retard
  get late **se faire tard**
latter **celui-ci, celle-ci**
laugh **rire**
laughter **le rire**
lawn **la pelouse**
lead **mener,**
  conduire
lead away **emmener**
lead back **reconduire**
leader **le chef**
leaf **la feuille**
lean **s'appuyer,**
  se pencher
leaning **penché(e)**
learn **apprendre**
least (adj.) **le, la moindre**
  (adv.) **le moins**
  at least **au moins,**
    du moins
leave **le congé**
  (verb) **partir**
  (a thing) **laisser**
  (a place) **quitter**
ledger **le grand livre**
left **gauche**
left [*hand side*] **la gauche**
leg **la jambe**
legal **légal(e)**
leisure **le loisir**
  at one's leisure **à son aise**
lemonade **la citronnade**
length **la longueur**
lengthen **allonger**
less **moins** [**de**]
let go **lâcher prise**
let go of **lâcher**
letter **la lettre**
level **le niveau**
level crossing
  le passage à niveau
liberty **la liberté**
lie down **se coucher**
life **la vie**
lift **un ascenseur**
light **la lumière**
  (verb) **allumer**
  (adj.) **léger, -ère**

lighthouse **le phare**
lightning **la foudre**
  flash of lightning **un éclair**
like **comme**
  (verb) **aimer**
likeable **sympathique**
liking **le goût**
limb **le membre**
limited **borné(e)**
line **la ligne**
link **relier**
list **la liste**
listen to **écouter**
listen to reason **entendre raison**
lit up **éclairé(e)**
little (adj.) **petit(e)**
  (adv.) **peu** [**de**]
little by little **peu à peu**
little boy **le petit**
live **vivre**
  (reside) **demeurer,**
    habiter
loaf **le pain**
  long loaf **la baguette**
lodge **loger**
London **Londres** (m.)
long **long(ue)**
  for a long time **longtemps**
longingly **avec nostalgie**
look **le regard,**
  (appearance) **l'air**
  (verb) **avoir l'air**
look after **soigner**
look at **regarder**
look for **chercher**
look out! (*careful!*) **attention!**
lose **perdre**
loss **la perte**
lot (fate) **le sort**
lot [*of*] **beaucoup** [**de**]
loud **fort(e)**
loudspeaker **le haut-parleur**
love **un amour**
  (verb) **aimer**
low **bas(se)**
low (of cattle) **meugler**
lower (price, etc.) **baisser**
luck **la chance**
  good luck! **bonne chance!**
  be lucky **avoir de la chance**
lunch **le déjeuner**
  (verb) **déjeuner**
lung **le poumon**
lure **séduire**
-ly **-ment**

M

machinery **la machine**
mad **fou, fol, folle**
magic[*al*] **magique**
mail **le courrier**
maintain **maintenir**
majority **la plupart**
make (brand) **la marque**
  (verb) **faire,**
    rendre
make one's way **se diriger**
make use of **se servir de**
mallet **le maillet**

man **un homme**
manager **le gérant**
mannequin **le mannequin**
manner **la manière**
mantelpiece **la cheminée**
many **beaucoup,**
  bien des
map **la carte**
March **mars** (m.)
mark **le signe**
  (verb) **marquer**
  (brand) **la marque**
market **le marché**
  covered market **la halle**
marry **épouser,**
  se marier avec
marvellous **merveilleux, -euse**
master **le professeur,**
  le maître
masterpiece **le chef-d'œuvre**
match **une allumette**
  (verb) **aller bien avec**
material **le matériel**
matter of [*be a*] **s'agir de**
May **mai** (m.)
mayor **le maire**
me **me,**
  moi
meadow **le pré**
meal **le repas**
mean (signify) **vouloir dire**
means **le moyen**
meanwhile **entre-temps,**
  dans l'intervalle
Mediterranean Sea
  la Méditerranée
meet **rencontrer**
meeting **le rendez-vous,**
  la rencontre
melon **le melon**
member **le membre**
memory **la mémoire**
mention **mentionner**
merchant **le marchand**
messenger **le messager**
method **la méthode**
midday **midi** (m.)
midnight **minuit** (m.)
middle **le centre,**
  le milieu
  in the middle of **au milieu de**
mighty **formidable**
mild **doux, douce**
military **militaire**
milk **le lait**
  (verb) **traire**
mind **un esprit**
mine **le mien,** etc.
minute **la minute**
miracle **le miracle**
  by a miracle **par miracle**
miraculous **miraculeux, -euse**
miserly **avare**
miss **manquer**
missile **le projectile**
mistake **une erreur**
  make a mistake **se tromper**
mix **mélanger**
mixture **le mélange**

moan **gémir**
mocking **moqueur, -euse**
model **le mannequin**
modern **moderne**
    (languages) **vivant(e)**
moment **le moment,**
    un instant
    for the moment **pour l'instant**
Monday **lundi** (m.)
money **l'argent** (m.)
    (change) **la monnaie**
monkey **le singe**
month **le mois**
moon **la lune**
more **plus**
    (further) **davantage**
    more than once
        plus d'une fois
    once more **une fois de plus**
moreover **de plus,**
    d'ailleurs
morning **le matin**
    following morning
        le lendemain matin
most (+ adj.) **le, la plus**
    (adv.) **le plus**
mother **la mère**
motionless **immobile**
motor-car **une auto(mobile)**
motor-coach **un (auto)car**
motor-cycle **la moto**
motor-cyclist **le motocycliste**
mountain **la montagne**
mourning **le deuil**
much **beaucoup de**
    as much as **autant que**
    so much, so many **tant de**
    too much, too many **trop de**
mud **la boue**
muddy **boueux, -euse**
mummy **maman**
murder **un assassinat,**
    le meurtre
museum **le musée**
mushroom **le champignon**
music **la musique**
must **devoir,**
    il faut
my **mon, ma, mes**
mystery **le mystère**

N

nail **le clou**
name **le nom**
name-day **la fête**
narrow **étroit(e),**
    borné(e)
national **national(e)**
native **indigène**
natural **naturel(le)**
naturally **naturellement**
nature **la nature**
naughty **méchant(e)**
navy **la flotte,**
    la marine
near to **près de**
near by **tout près**
neat **soigné(e)**

necessary **nécessaire**
    it is necessary **il faut**
neck **le cou**
need **le besoin**
    (verb) **avoir besoin de**
needlework **la couture**
neglected **négligé(e)**
negro **le nègre**
neigh **hennir**
neighbour **le, la voisin(e)**
neighbourhood **le voisinage,**
    le quartier
neighbouring **voisin(e)**
neither . . . nor **ni . . . ni**
nephew **le neveu**
network **le réseau**
neutral **neutre**
never **ne . . . jamais**
nevertheless **néanmoins**
new **nouveau, nouvel, nouvelle**
    [brand] **neuf, neuve**
news **la nouvelle,**
    les informations (f.)
newspaper **le journal,**
    le quotidien
newspaper-stall **le kiosque**
next **prochain(e)**
    (then) **puis,**
    ensuite
niece **la nièce**
night **la nuit**
nine **neuf**
nineteen **dix-neuf**
ninety **quatre-vingt-dix**
no **non**
    (not any) **pas de**
    (adj.) **aucun(e),**
    nul(le)
nobody **personne**
noise **le bruit**
none **n'en . . . pas**
no one **ne . . . personne**
nor **ni**
north **le nord**
not **ne . . . pas**
nothing **ne . . . rien**
    for nothing **gratuitement**
notice **un écriteau**
    (verb) **remarquer,**
    apercevoir
notice-board **une affiche**
nought **zéro**
novel **le roman**
    detective novel
        le roman policier
November **novembre** (m.)
now **maintenant,**
    à présent
    just now **tout à l'heure**
    now and then **parfois**
nowadays **à présent**
nowhere **nulle part**
number **le nombre,**
    le numéro
numerous **nombreux, -euse**
nun **la religieuse**

O

oak **le chêne**

    made of oak **en chêne**
oats **l'avoine** (f.)
observe **observer**
obstinate **entêté(e)**
obtain **obtenir**
obvious **évident(e)**
obviously **évidemment**
occupy **occuper**
occur **survenir,**
    se passer
ocean **un océan**
October **octobre** (m.)
odd **bizarre**
of **de**
offer **une offre**
    (verb) **présenter,**
    offrir
offer to **s'offrir à**
offend **froisser**
office **le bureau**
    inquiry office
        le bureau de renseignements
officer **un officier**
often **souvent**
ogre **un ogre**
old **vieux, vieil, vieille,**
    âgé(e)
    grow old **se faire vieux, etc.**
    vieillir
old age **la vieillesse**
old man **le vieillard**
on **sur**
once **une fois**
    once again **encore une fois**
    at once **immédiatement,**
    sur-le-champ,
    tout de suite
one **un(e)**
    (pron.) **on**
one's son, **sa, ses**
one hundred **cent**
only **ne . . . que,**
    seulement
one-way (traffic) **le sens unique**
open **ouvrir**
opinion **un avis**
opponent **un(e) adversaire**
opportunity **une occasion**
oppose **s'opposer à**
opposite **en face**
    opposite direction
    le sens inverse
oppressor **un oppresseur**
or **ou**
orchard **le verger**
ordeal **une épreuve**
order **un ordre**
    (verb) **commander**
    in order that **pour que**
    in order to **pour**
ordinary **ordinaire**
organize **organiser**
orphan **un(e) orphelin(e)**
other **autre**
otherwise **autrement**
ought **devoir (je devrais, etc.)**
out of **hors de**
out of [get] **se tirer de**
outline **un aperçu**

outside l'extérieur (m.)
    (adv.) dehors
over sur,
    au-dessus de
over there là-bas
overcoat le pardessus
overlook dominer
overtake (cars) doubler
own propre
    [on his] à lui seul
    (verb) posséder
ox le bœuf

P

pack of cards le jeu de cartes
pack a suitcase faire une valise
packed (crowded) bondé(e)
packet le paquet
packing-case la caisse
pact le pacte
paint peindre
painter le peintre
painting la peinture
pair la paire
pamphlet la brochure
panic la panique
pant haleter
paper le papier
    (newspaper) le journal,
        le quotidien
parachute le parachute
    jump by parachute
        sauter en parachute
parade le défilé
Paradise le paradis
parcel le paquet,
    le colis
parent le parent
park le parc
parking le stationnement
part la partie
    (role) le rôle
    be a part of faire partie de
    most part la plupart
particular (careful)
        méticuleux, -euse
pass (time) passer,
    s'écouler
passport le passeport
pasture la pâture
path le chemin,
    le sentier
patience la patience
patient patient(e)
patiently patiemment
pavement le trottoir
paw la patte
peace la paix
peaceful paisible,
    tranquille
peace-loving pacifique
pear la poire
pear-tree le poirier
peas les petits pois
peasant le paysan, la paysanne
peel éplucher
peg le piquet
pen la plume

pencil le crayon
people les gens (m.)
    (inhabitants)
        les habitants
    (nation) le peuple
per cent pour cent
perched perché(e)
perfect parfait(e)
perform exécuter
performance la représentation
perhaps peut-être
persuasive persuasif, -ive
pervade régner,
    pénétrer
petrol l'essence (f.)
petrol station la station-service,
    le poste d'essence
phone le téléphone
    (verb) téléphoner
photograph la photo[graphie]
photographer le photographe
piano le piano
pick (gather) cueillir
pick up ramasser
picture-card (cards) la figure
picturesque pittoresque
pig le porc
pigsty la porcherie
pike le pique
pile le tas
pillage le pillage
pilot un aviateur,
    le pilote
pipe la pipe
pitiful pitoyable
pity la pitié
    it is a pity
        c'est dommage
placard la pancarte
place un endroit
    (in boat, etc.) un espace
    (scene) le lieu
    (verb) mettre
    lay a place (at table)
        mettre un couvert
    take place avoir lieu,
        se passer
plain (obvious) évident(e)
plan le plan
plane (level) le plan
plank la planche
plate une assiette
platform une estrade
    (railway) le quai
play jouer
    (game) jouer au, etc.
    (instrument) jouer du, etc.
pleasant agréable,
    (person) aimable
please faire plaisir à,
    plaire à
    (conversation)
        s'il vous plaît
pleased content(e)
pleasing (nice) gentil(le)
pleasure le plaisir
    take pleasure in se plaire à
plough la charrue
pluck (gather) cueillir

p.m. du soir,
    de l'après-midi
pocket la poche
point le point
point out indiquer,
    désigner,
    faire remarquer
point of view le point de vue
poisonous vénéneux, -euse
Poland la Pologne
police la police
policeman l'agent [de police],
    le policier
policy la politique
polish polir
polite poli(e)
political politique
politics la politique
poor pauvre
population la population
porter le porteur
possess posséder
    take possession of
        s'emparer de
poster une affiche
postman le facteur
post-office le bureau de poste
posture la posture
potato la pomme de terre
poultry la volaille
pour verser
pour with rain pleuvoir à verse
powder la poudre
power la puissance,
    le pouvoir
powerful puissant(e)
practical pratique
precious little fort peu de
precipitately précipitamment
precise précis(e)
    at three o'clock precisely
        à trois heures précises
prefer préférer
prepare to s'apprêter à
    (meal) préparer
present le cadeau
    (adj.) actuel(le)
    be present at assister à
pretend to faire semblant de
pretty joli(e),
    coquet(te)
prevent [from] empêcher [de]
previously auparavant
price le prix
prime minster
    le premier ministre
print une empreinte
    (engraving) la gravure
prison le prison
prisoner le prisonnier
private particulier, -ière
prize le prix
probably probablement
problem le problème
produce produire
product le produit
programme le programme
prominent marquant(e)
promise promettre

promotion l'avancement (m.)
proper correct(e)
prosperous prospère
protected protégé(e)
protest la protestation
prove démontrer
provide fournir
provide for subvenir à
provided that pourvu que
province[s] la province
provoke provoquer
pull tirer
pull on serrer
punch (ticket) poinçonner
punctual ponctuel(le)
punctually à l'heure
punish punir
punishment la punition
pupil un(e) élève
pure pur(e)
purpose le but
   on purpose exprès
purring le ronronnement
put [on] mettre
put on again remettre
put down déposer
put up with supporter
puzzle une énigme

Q

quaint bizarre
quality la qualité
quantity la quantité
quarrel la querelle
quarter [of an hour]
   le quart [d'heure]
quay le quai
queen la reine,
   (cards) la dame
question la question
   it is a question of il s'agit de
queue la queue
   (verb) faire la queue
quick rapide
quickly vite
   (lively) vivement
quiet tranquille
   keep quiet se taire
quite assez,
   tout
quite a few pas mal de

R

rail le rail
railway le chemin de fer
rain la pluie
   (verb) pleuvoir
raise lever,
   soulever
raptures [go into] s'extasier
rare rare
rascal le coquin
rather (very) assez
   (on the whole) plutôt
ray le rayon
reach (someone) rejoindre
   (place) arriver à
read lire
reader le lecteur, la lectrice

reading la lecture
ready prêt(e)
real réel(le),
   vrai(e)
realize se rendre compte de,
   comprendre
rear-guard une arrière-garde
reasonable raisonnable
recede s'éloigner
receive recevoir
recognize reconnaître
reconciliation le rapprochement
reconstruction la reconstruction
recreation la récréation
red rouge
reflect refléter
   (think) réfléchir
refuge [take] se réfugier
refuse refuser
regain regagner
regard l'estime (f.)
   with regard to à l'égard de,
      quant à
regiment le régiment
regular (real) véritable
reign régner
relate raconter
release lâcher
relief le soulagement
rely on dépendre de
remain rester
remark la remarque
remember se rappeler,
   se souvenir de
remnant le solde
repair refaire,
   réparer
repent of se repentir de
replace remplacer
reply répondre,
   répliquer
report le bulletin
   (verb) signaler
republic la république
reputation la réputation
reserve for oneself se réserver
reside demeurer,
   habiter
resistance la résistance
Resistance member le résistant
rest se reposer
restaurant le restaurant
restricted restreint(e)
result le résultat
resume reprendre
retain retenir
retire se retirer
return le retour
   (to school) la rentrée
   (verb) retourner,
      revenir
   (give back) rendre
   (home) rentrer
reveal révéler
review passer en revue
ribbon le ruban
rich riche
   get rich s'enrichir
rick la meule

rid of [get] se débarrasser de
ride (in a car) se promener
   en voiture
rifle le fusil
right le droit
   (side) la droite
   (correct) bon(ne)
  be right avoir raison
rigour la rigueur
ring sonner
   (telephone) téléphoner
rise se dresser,
   se lever
risk le risque
  at the risk of au risque de
river la rivière,
   le fleuve
road la route,
   la rue
  main road la route nationale
roadway la chaussée
rock le rocher
rogue le chenapan
role le rôle
roll rouler
   (bread) le petit pain
room la pièce,
   la salle
  lot of room
      beaucoup de place
rope la corde
rough rude
rout la déroute
row ramer
rowing boat le canot
rub [up] frotter
rude désobligeant(e)
rum-baba le baba au rhum
rumble le grondement
rummage fouiller
run le parcours
   (verb) courir
run away se sauver
run into heurter
rush une affluence
   (verb) se précipiter
Russia la Russie

S

sabotage le sabotage
   (verb) saboter
sack (discharge) chasser
sad triste
safe le coffre-fort
safe and sound
      sain(e) et sauf, -ve
sailor le matelot
sale le solde
salesman le vendeur
salesman's patter le boniment
same même
  all the same quand même
satisfied satisfait(e)
satisfied [be] with
      se contenter de
Saturday samedi (m.)
saucer la soucoupe
save sauver
  save up mettre de côté

501

say dire
scaffolding un échafaudage
scales la balance
scan scruter
scandal le scandale
scar la cicatrice
scarcely à peine,
        ne . . . guère
scenery le paysage
scented parfumé(e)
school une école
school friend le, la camarade
school year l'année scolaire
schoolboy, -girl
        un écolier, une -ière
schoolmaster le professeur
schoolmistress la maîtresse
scold gronder
scope l'ampleur (f.),
      l'étendue (f.)
Scotland l'Écosse (f.)
Scottish écossais(e)
screech le grincement
screen un écran
search chercher,
      fouiller
searching la recherche
  in search of à la recherche de
seaside le bord de la mer
seaside resort
        la station balnéaire
season la saison
seat (bench) le banc,
        la banquette
     (place) la place
seated assis(e)
second deuxième,
       second(e)
secondary school le lycée
secondary schoolboy le lycéen
secondhand bookseller
        le bouquiniste
secret le secret
     (adj.) secret, -ète
secretly secrètement
see voir
see again revoir
see to it that veillez à ce que
seed la graine
seek chercher
seem sembler,
      avoir l'air
seize saisir
-self -même
sell vendre
send envoyer
send back renvoyer
send for faire venir
sensible raisonnable
sensitive sensible
sentence la phrase
September septembre (m.)
serious sérieux, -euse
serve servir,
    desservir
service le service
set (television, etc.) le poste
set out (leave) partir
    (display) ranger

set up dresser
settee le canapé
settle in, down s'installer
seven sept
seventeen dix-sept
seventy soixante-dix
several plusieurs
shame la honte
shave se raser
shed le hangar
shelter un abri
  sheltered from à l'abri de
shelves [set of] une étagère
shift for oneself se débrouiller
shine reluire
ship le navire,
     le bateau
shirt la chemise
shock le choc
shoe le soulier
shop le magasin
  small shop la boutique
  at . . .'s shop chez
shopkeeper le marchand, la -e
  do one's shopping,
        faire ses provisions
shop-window la vitrine
short bref, brève,
      court(e)
  short of (money) à court de
  in short en somme
  cut short abréger
shortly sous peu
      avant peu
shorts la culotte
shot le coup de revolver
shout crier
shout at gronder
show une exposition
    (entertainment)
        le spectacle
    (verb) montrer
shrill perçant(e)
shuffle (cards) mélanger
shut fermer
sick (ill) malade
side le côté
sideboard le buffet
sigh le soupir
  heave a sigh
       pousser un soupir
sign le signe
sight la vue
  catch sight of apercevoir
  sights les monuments (m.)
silk la soie
silly thing la bêtise
silver l'argent (m.)
  of silver d'argent
similar pareil(le)
since (because) puisque
    (from) depuis
sincerely cordialement
sing chanter
singing le chant
sink un évier
    (verb) s'affaisser,
        se laisser tomber
sister la sœur

sit s'asseoir
sitting assis(e)
sitting-room le salon
situated situé(e)
  be situated se trouver
situation la situation
six six
sixteen seize
sixty soixante
sketch un aperçu
ski faire du ski
ski-jump le saut à ski
ski-run la piste
skid déraper
skin la peau
sky le ciel
slam (door) claquer
sleep dormir
  go to sleep s'endormir
  go back to sleep se rendormir
sleeper (person)
       le dormeur, la -euse
slice la tranche
slipper la pantoufle
slippery glissant(e)
slope la pente
slovenly négligé(e)
slow lent(e)
slow (stopping) train
       un omnibus
slow down ralentir
small petit(e)
smell une odeur
smell of sentir
smile le sourire
    (verb) sourire
smoke la fumée
    (verb) fumer
sniff renifler
snow la neige
    (verb) neiger
snowball la boule de neige
snowman
       le bonhomme de neige
so (therefore) donc
  aussi (+ inverted verb)
  (+ adj.) si
  (thus) ainsi
soak tremper
soap le savon
sock la chaussette
sofa le canapé
soldier le soldat
sole (of shoe) la semelle
solve résoudre
some du, etc.,
    quelque(s)
    (pron.) en
someone quelqu'un, etc.
something
    quelque chose de (+ m.)
sometimes quelquefois
somewhere quelque part
son le fils
song le chant
soon tôt,
    bientôt,
    avant peu
  as soon as dès que

502

sorry [*be*] **regretter**
   be sorry for **avoir pitié de**
sort **une espèce**
soul **une âme**
soundly (sleep) **profondément**
soup **le potage,**
      la soupe
south **le sud**
sovereignty **la souveraineté**
sow **semer**
spade **la bêche**
   (cards) **le pique**
Spain **l'Espagne** (f.)
spank **fouetter**
spare **épargner**
speak **parler**
special **spécial(e)**
species **une espèce**
speech **le discours**
   short speech **une allocution**
speed **la vitesse**
   (verb) **filer,**
        aller vite
   at full speed **à toute vitesse**
speedometer
     un indicateur de vitesse
spend (time) **passer**
   (money) **dépenser**
spill **renverser,**
     verser
spinach **les épinards** (m.)
spinning-mill **la filature**
spirit **un esprit**
spirits **les spiritueux** (m.)
spite of [*in*] **malgré**
spoil **gâter**
spot (place) **un endroit**
sprain (ankle, etc.) **fouler**
spread **répandre**
spread through **se répandre dans**
spring **le printemps**
spring-board **le tremplin**
squander **gaspiller**
square **carré(e)**
   (town) **la place**
stable **une écurie**
stack **la meule**
stage **une estrade,**
     la scène
stain **la tache**
   (verb) **tacher**
staircase, stairs **un escalier**
stall **un étalage**
stammer **balbutier**
stamp **le timbre**
stamp on **piétiner**
stand [*up*] **se dresser,**
     se lever
standing **debout**
stare at **considérer,**
     regarder fixement
start **commencer**
   (conversation) **entamer**
   (surprise) **sursauter**
state **un état,**
     la condition
   in a fit state to **en état de**
station **la gare**
station-master **le chef de gare**

stationery **la papeterie**
stay **le séjour**
   (verb) **rester**
steal **voler**
steel **l'acier** (m.)
steel-works **une aciérie**
step **le pas**
   (stairs) **la marche**
stern **sévère**
stick (glue) **coller**
still (yet) **encore**
stir up **susciter**
stock-farming **l'élevage** (m.)
stone **la pierre**
stoop **se baisser**
stop (bus) **un arrêt**
   (verb) **(s')arrêter**
   put a stop to **mettre fin à,**
       mettre un terme à
store (shop) **le magasin**
storm **la tempête**
story **une histoire**
stove **la cuisinière**
straight *ahead* **tout droit**
   put straight **mettre en ordre**
strange (odd) **curieux, -euse**
stranger **un inconnu,**
     un étranger
strap **la courroie**
stream **le ruisseau**
street **la rue**
   main street **la grand'rue**
street-lamp **le réverbère**
strength **la force**
stress **souligner**
stretch **étendre**
strict **sévère**
stride **le pas**
   in one's stride **en train**
strike (hit) **frapper**
   (matches) **frotter**
   (clock) **sonner**
strong **fort(e)**
struggle **la lutte**
   (verb) **lutter**
study **étudier**
style **la mode**
subject **la matière,**
     le sujet
subject to **sujet(te) à**
suburbs **la banlieue**
succeed (in) **réussir (à)**
such **tel(le)**
sudden **soudain(e)**
suddenly **tout à coup,**
     soudain
suffer (damage) **subir**
suffice **suffire**
sufficient(ly) **assez**
sugar **le sucre**
sugar-beet **la betterave à sucre**
suggest **suggérer,**
     proposer
suit **un habit**
   (cards) **la couleur**
suitable **convenable**
suitcase **la valise**
sultry **lourd(e)**
sum **la somme**

summer **l'été** (m.)
summit **le sommet**
sun **le soleil**
   rising sun **le soleil levant**
   setting sun **le soleil couchant**
Sunday **dimanche** (m.)
sunk(en) **enfoncé(e)**
sunrise **le lever du soleil**
supervise **surveiller**
supper **le souper**
sure **sûr(e)**
surgeon **le chirurgien**
surprise **surprendre**
surprising **surprenant(e)**
surrender **se rendre**
surround **entourer**
surroundings **les environs** (m.)
suspicion **le soupçon**
swallow **avaler**
swan **le cygne**
sway **se balancer**
swear **jurer**
swear-word **le juron**
sweater **le chandail**
sweetheart
     un amoureux, une -euse
swim **nager**
Swiss **suisse**
Switzerland **la Suisse**
sword **une épée**
symphony **la symphonie**
system **le système**

T

table **la table**
tail **la queue**
take **prendre**
   (time) **mettre**
take (lead) *back* **reconduire**
take away **emporter**
take by car
     transporter en voiture
take care not to **se garder de**
take off (aeroplane) **décoller**
take off, away **ôter**
take out **sortir**
take refuge **se réfugier**
talk **parler**
   (chatter) **bavarder**
talkative **loquace**
task **la tâche,**
     la besogne
taste **le goût**
   (verb) **déguster**
tax **un impôt**
taxi **le taxi**
taxpayer **le contribuable**
tea **le thé**
   afternoon tea **le goûter**
teach **enseigner**
teacher **le professeur,**
     l'instituteur, -trice
teapot **la théière**
tear **déchirer**
tear off **détacher**
teasing **taquin(e)**
telegram **le télégramme**
telegraph post
     le poteau télégraphique

telephone **le téléphone**
(verb) **téléphoner**
television **la télévision**
television set **le poste de**
tell **dire,** [télévision
raconter
ten **dix**
about ten **une dizaine de**
tenant **le, la locataire**
tender-hearted **au cœur tendre**
tennis **le tennis**
tent **la tente**
term (school) **le trimestre**
terminus **la gare terminus**
territory **le territoire**
test **une épreuve**
thank **remercier**
thank you **merci**
thanks to **grâce à**
that (conj.) **que**
(pron.) **cela, ça**
(adj.) **ce,** etc.
(that one) **celui-là,** etc.
that is to say **c'est à dire**
the **le, la, les**
theatre **le théâtre**
theft **le vol**
their **leur**
theirs **le leur,** etc.
them **les,** to them **leur**
then (at that time) **alors**
(next) **ensuite**
there **là,**
y
there is, are **il y a,**
voilà
up there **là-haut**
therefore **donc**
they **ils, elles, ce**
thick **épais(se)**
thief **le voleur**
thing **la chose**
think **réfléchir**
penser,
croire
think of, about **penser de, à**
thirteen **treize**
thirst **la soif**
be thirsty **avoir soif**
thirty **trente**
this (adj.) **ce,** etc.
(pron.) **ceci**
(this one) **celui-ci,** etc.
thoroughly **à fond**
thought **la pensée,**
la réflexion
Thursday **jeudi** (m.)
thousand **mille**
(dates) **mil**
thread **le fil**
threat **la menace**
three **trois**
thrifty **économe**
through **par**
throw **lancer,**
jeter
thumb **le pouce**
thunder **le tonnerre**
(verb) **tonner**

thunderbolt **la foudre**
thus **ainsi**
ticket **le billet**
single ticket **le billet simple**
return ticket
le billet aller et retour
ticket-collector **le contrôleur**
ticket-office **le guichet**
tidy **en bon ordre**
tie **la cravate**
tiled floor **le carrelage**
time **une époque,**
le temps,
la fois,
le moment
at one and the same time
à la fois
be a long time in **tarder à**
for a long time **longtemps,**
longuement
from time to time
de temps en temps
in time for **à l'heure pour**
time-table **un horaire**
(school) **l'emploi du temps**
ting-a-ling! **drelin-drelin!**
tip (gratuity) **le pourboire**
tire **se lasser,**
se fatiguer
tired **fatigué(e),**
las(se)
tiresome **ennuyeux, -euse**
to **à,**
vers
(in order to) **pour**
(fem. country) **en**
tobacco **le tabac**
today **aujourd'hui**
together **ensemble**
tomato **la tomate**
tomb **le tombeau**
tomorrow **demain**
ton **la tonne**
tongue **la langue**
too (also) **aussi**
too many, much **trop**
toothpaste **la pâte dentifrice**
top (mountain) **le sommet**
right at the top of
tout en haut de
torn **déchiré(e)**
tortoise **la tortue**
tour **le tour**
towards **vers**
towel **la serviette**
town **la ville**
in town **en ville**
town-hall **la mairie,**
un hôtel de ville
townsman **le citadin**
toy **le jouet**
track **la piste**
(railway) **la voie**
tractor **le tracteur**
trade **le commerce**
tradesman **le commerçant**
traffic **la circulation**
traffic lights **les feux** (m.)
(de circulation)

traffic-sign
le panneau de signalisation
train **le train**
trample **piétiner**
travel **voyager**
traveller **le voyageur**
tray **le plateau**
tree **un arbre**
tremble **trembler**
trim **soigné(e)**
trip (journey) **le trajet,**
le voyage
triumph over **triompher de**
troop **la troupe**
trouble **l'ennui** (m.),
la peine
be worth the trouble
valoir la peine
trousers **le pantalon**
trout **la truite**
true **vrai(e)**
trunk **le tronc**
truth **la vérité**
to tell the truth! **à vrai dire**
try [on] **essayer**
Tuesday **mardi** (m.)
turn **le tour**
in turn **à tour de rôle**
(verb) **(se) tourner**
turn back **faire demi-tour**
turn round **se retourner**
turnip **le navet**
twelve **douze**
twelve o'clock **midi** (m.),
minuit (m.)
twenty **vingt**
twice **deux fois**
two **deux**
two-piece **le deux-pièces**
type **taper à la machine**
typist **la dactylo**
tyrant **le tyran**
tyre **le pneu**

U

umbrella **le parapluie**
unable [be] **ne pas pouvoir**
uncle **un oncle**
under **sous,**
au-dessous de
undergo **subir**
underground **souterrain(e)**
underground railway **le métro**
underline **souligner**
understand **comprendre**
undertake **entreprendre**
undress **se déshabiller**
unemployment **le chômage**
unfortunate **malheureux, -euse**
unhappy **malheureux, -euse**
unhook (receiver) **décrocher**
uniform **un uniforme**
unite **unir**
United Kingdom
le Royaume-Uni
United States **les États-Unis**
(m.)

504

unknown **inconnu(e)**
  unknown to him, her
               à son insu
unpleasant **désagréable**
untidy **en désordre**
until **jusqu'à (ce que)**
up to **jusqu'à**
up and down **de long en large**
upset oneself **s'inquiéter**
upstairs **en haut**
use of [*make*] **se servir de**
used to (+ verb) **imperfect**
                   tense
used for [*be*] **servir à**
useless **inutile**
usherette **une ouvreuse**
usual **habituel(le)**
usually **d'habitude,**
      généralement
  as usual **comme d'habitude**
utensil **un ustensile**

V

vacate **vider,**
      quitter
vain [*in*] **vainement**
value **la valeur**
  (verb) **apprécier**
variety **la variété**
various **divers(e)**
vault **le tombeau**
vegetable **le légume**
vehicle **la voiture**
very **très**
  not very **peu**
veterinary surgeon **le vétérinaire**
victor **le vainqueur**
view **la vue**
  with a view to **en vue de**
village **le village**
villager **le, la villageois(e)**
violin **le violon**
visit **la visite**
  (verb) **visiter**
visitor **le visiteur**
voice **la voix**
vow **le vœu**

W

wage(s) **le salaire**
wage-earner **le salarié**
wait [*for*] **attendre**
waiter **le garçon**
waiting-room **la salle d'attente**
wake up **se réveiller**
waken **réveiller**
Wales **le Pays de Galles**
walk **marcher**
  go for a walk
          faire une promenade,
          se promener
walk round **faire le tour de**
wall **le mur**
wallet **le portefeuille**
want **vouloir,**
      désirer
war **la guerre**
wardrobe **une armoire**

warm **chaud(e)**
  be warm (persons)
              avoir chaud
  (greetings, etc.)
      chaleureux, -euse
  (weather)
          faire chaud
warn **avertir**
Warsaw **Varsovie** (f.)
wash **laver**
wash and dress **faire sa toilette**
wash up **faire la vaisselle**
wash-basin **le lavabo**
waste **gaspiller**
watch **la montre**
  (verb) **regarder,**
      observer
water **l'eau** (f.)
  (verb) **arroser**
water-closet **le cabinet**
wave **agiter**
way **la route,**
      le chemin
  on the way [*to*] **en chemin,**
      en route [*pour*]
  in this way **ainsi**
  make one's way **se rendre**
weak **faible**
weaken **affaiblir**
weakness **la faiblesse**
wear **porter**
wear out **user**
weather **le temps**
Wednesday **mercredi** (m.)
week **la semaine**
weigh **peser**
well **le puits**
  (adv.) **bien**
Well! **Eh bien!**
  as well as **ainsi que**
well up in **calé(e) en**
well-behaved **sage**
Welsh **gallois(e)**
west **l'ouest** (m.)
western **occidental(e)**
what (pron.) **qu'est-ce qui,** etc.
  (that which) **ce qui,** etc.
  (adj.) **quel,** etc.
whatever **n'importe quel(le),** etc.
wheat **le blé**
wheel **la roue**
when **quand,**
      lorsque
  the day when **le jour où**
where **où**
whether **si**
which (adj.) **quel,** etc.
  (pron.) **lequel,** etc.
  of which **dont**
while **pendant que,**
      quand
while away **passer**
whilst **tandis que**
whip **fouetter**
whisper **chuchoter**
whistle **le sifflet**
  (verb) **siffler**
white **blanc(he)**

who **qui,**
      qui est-ce qui?
whole **entier, -ière**
  his whole life long
             sa vie durant
whom **que,**
      qui,
      qui est-ce que?
  of whom **dont**
whose **dont** (= *of whom*)
why **pourquoi**
widow **la veuve**
widower **le veuf**
wife **la femme,**
      une épouse
wild **fou, fol, folle**
willingly **volontiers**
win **gagner**
wind **le vent**
window **la fenêtre**
windscreen **le pare-brise**
windy [*be*] **faire du vent**
wine **le vin**
  light table-wine **le vin rosé**
wine-waiter **le sommelier**
winter **l'hiver** (m.)
wipe **essuyer**
wish **souhaiter,**
      désirer,
      vouloir
wit **un esprit**
with **avec**
withdraw **se retirer**
within (time) **en**
      (place) **dans**
without **sans**
without fail **sans faute**
wolf **le loup**
woman **la femme**
wonder **se demander**
wood **le bois**
wood-shed **le bûcher**
wool **la laine**
word **le mot,**
      la parole
work **le travail,**
      l'emploi (m.)
  (verb) **travailler**
work of art **un objet d'art**
worker **un ouvrier,**
      le travailleur, la -euse
world **le monde**
  (adj.) **mondial(e)**
worm one's way **s'introduire**
worried **inquiet, -ète**
worry **s'inquiéter**
worry about **se soucier de**
worth **la valeur**
  it is not worth while
      ce n'est pas la peine
      ça ne vaut pas la peine
worthy **digne,**
      brave
wound **blesser**
wretched **misérable,**
      pitoyable
wrinkled **ridé(e)**
write **écrire**

writing-desk **le bureau,**
 le secrétaire
written **inscrit(e),**
 écrit(e)
wrong **mauvais(e)**
 go wrong **aller de travers**
 at the wrong time
 mal à propos
 be wrong **avoir tort**

Y

yard **la cour**
year **un an,**
 une année
yell **hurler**
yellow **jaune**
yes **oui**
yesterday **hier**
yet **encore**

you **tu, te, toi,**
 vous
young **jeune**
young lady **la demoiselle**
younger **cadet(te)**
your **ton, ta, tes,**
 votre, vos

Z

zone **la zone**

INDEX

à, 26, 134, 253-4
Actions as opposed to states, 353
Adjectives, + à with infinitive, 253-4
  agreement, 27
  colour, 44
  comparison, 214
  demonstrative, 55
  feminine forms, 215-6
  position, 28
  possessive, 44-5
Adverbs, comparison, 214-5
  formation, 63
Agreement of past participle, 78-9, 224-5, 354
  of subject and verb, 354
age, 139, 354
all, 354
aller, conditional, 154
  future, 106
  perfect, 88
  pluperfect, 172
  present, 37
  present subjunctive, 262
  use to form future, 107
  with infinitives, 232
an, année, 354
Animaux, les, 86
any, 38, 355
après, 355
arriver, perfect, 88
  pluperfect, 172
Articles, definite, 18
  indefinite, 18
  omission, 206-7
  partitive, 38, 207
  uses, 198-9
as, 355
s'asseoir, conditional, 154
  past historic, 191
auquel, 181
avoir, conditional, 154
  future, 106
  in expressions, 71
  past historic, 19, 191

  perfect, 78-79
  present, 17
  present subjunctive, 262

Bâtiments, les, 187
battre, future, 106
  perfect, 78
  present, 79
bien, 355
boire, imperfect subjunctive, 263
  past historic, 191
  present, 107
by, 356

can, 232
Carrefour, un, 221
carry, 356
ce, 55
celui, 146-7
c'est, 242, 359
Collectives, 163
colour, 356
Colours as adjectives, 44
Commands, 54, 358
commencer, imperfect, 138
Comparison of adjectives, 214
  adverbs, 214-5
Composition, 316-24
Comprehension, 325-38
Conditional tense, 154-5
  perfect, 226, 280
conduire, future, 106
  past historic, 191
  present, 70
connaître, future, 106
  past historic, 191
  perfect, 78
  present, 56
Consonants, 15-16
Conversation, 343-8
Corps humain, le, 103
courir, conditional, 154
  future, 106
  past historic, 191

perfect, 78
present, 79
craindre, future, 106
present, 70
croire, present, 107, 255
croître, present, 255
cueillir, conditional, 154
present, 107

danser, present, 27
Dates, 64, 356
Dative after verbs, 356
Days, 63, 356
de, 38, 254
Definite article, 18
demi, 356
Demonstrative adjectives, 55
pronouns, 146
dernier, 356
descendre, perfect, 88
pluperfect, 172
devoir, future, 106
perfect, 78
present, 56
with infinitives, 232-3
Dictation, 339-42
Dimensions, 173
dire, perfect, 78
Disjunctive pronouns, 114
donner, conditional, 154
imperfect, 137
imperfect subjunctive, 263
past historic, 190
perfect subjunctive, 262
pluperfect, 172
dont, 181
duquel, 181

écrire, future, 106
past historic, 191
perfect, 78
present, 63
en, 97, 356-7
entrer, perfect, 88
pluperfect, 172
envoyer, conditional, 154
espérer, 107
essuyer, 107
être, conditional, 154
future, 106

imperfect, 138
past historic, 191
perfect, 78
present, 17
present subjunctive, 262
verbs conjugated with, 88-9
Examination, 349-52
Expressions with **avoir**, 71
faire, 71

faire, conditional, 154
future, 106
perfect, 78
present, 37
present subjunctive, 263
use in expressions, 71
with infinitives, 233, 357
falloir, future, 106
perfect, 78
present, 56
present subjunctive, 263
Famille, la, 239
finir, conditional, 154
imperfect, 137
imperfect subjunctive, 263
past historic, 190
pluperfect, 172
present, 46
present subjunctive, 262
first, 357
fuir, present, 199
Future tense, 106
perfect, 225-6
use of **aller**, 107

go and, 357-8
Gender, 18

haïr, present, 255
have just, 155, 359

Idiomatic tense usage, 233-4
il est, 242, 359
il y a, 358
Imperative, 54, 358
Imperfect tense, 137-8, 358
first conjugation, 137
second conjugation, 137
third conjugation, 138
Impersonal verbs, 191

Indefinite article, 18
Indirect object personal pronouns, 97
Infinitive, 56
Insectes, les, 170
Inversion of verb, 19, 46, 55, 79, 88, 243-4, 292, 362-3
Irregular verbs, 27, 37, 46, 63, 78-9, 89, 106-7, 115, 173, 191, 199, 255, 286-7
  future, 106-7
  past historic, 191
it is, 242-3, 359

jeter, 107

late, 359
laver, se, 96
  pluperfect, 172
Learning a language, 9-10
lequel, 181
lever, 107
Liaison, 16, 28
lire, future, 106
  perfect, 78
  present, 46
little, 359
luire, present, 255

manger, imperfect, 138
Maison, la, 33
mentir, future, 106
  present, 70
mettre, future, 106
  perfect, 78
  present, 46
Meubles, les, 34
Miscellaneous sentences, 368
moi, 114
mon, 45
monter, perfect, 88
  pluperfect, 172
Months, 64, 359
mourir, conditional, 154
  future, 106
  perfect, 88-9
  pluperfect, 172
  present, 89
Movement, 359

naître, future, 106

  perfect, 88-9
  pluperfect, 172
  present, 89
Nasal vowels, 14
Negatives, 27, 360
  forms, 139
  forms as subject, 147
  with perfect tense, 147
nettoyer, present, 173
next, 360
Nouns, gender, 18
  plurals, 226
Nourriture, la, 104
nouveau, neuf, 360
nuire, present, 255
Numbers, cardinal, 18, 36, 162
    ordinal, 71, 163

Object pronouns, 64
Oiseaux, les, 170
on, 28
once upon a time, 361
Oral examination, 343
où, 181
ouvrir, future, 106
  present, 70

papeterie, la, 240
partir, perfect, 88
  pluperfect, 172
Partitive article (*some*), 38, 207
Passive, 225
Past anterior tense, 226
Past historic tense, 190-1
Past participle, 78
  agreement, 78-9, 224, 354
  as a clause, 361
  irregular verbs, 78
  with reflexive verbs, 225
paysage, le, 85
perdre, present, 62
Perfect tense, 78
  use in questions, 88
  with negative, 147
Perfect subjunctive, 263
personne, 361
peser, perfect, 78
peut-être, 361
Phonetic symbols, 12-16
Plage, la, 169

plaire, 115
pleuvoir, present subjunctive, 263
plus, 361
Pluperfect, 172
  subjunctive, 263
Plurals, 226
Poche, la, 52
Possession, 28
Possessive adjectives, 44-5
  pronouns, 208
pouvoir, conditional, 154
  perfect, 78
  present, 56
  present subjunctive, 263
  with infinitives, 232
prendre, future, 106
  perfect, 78
  present, 27
Prepositions, 44, 250-5, 361-2
  à, 26, 251-2, 254
  after verbs, 251-5
  de, 38, 251-2, 254
  governing verbs, 139
prochain, 356
Present tense, 27
Pronouns, demonstrative, 146-7
  disjunctive, 114
  in a command, 115
  indirect object personal, 97
  object, 64
  on, 28
  order of, 97
  personal, 115
  possessive, 208
  relative, 79, 180-1
  subject, 17, 19
  y and **en**, 97, 356-7
propre, 362
Pronunciation, 11-16
Punctuation, 339

quand, use of, 234
Questions, 19, 46, 55, 88, 243-4, 362-3
qui, 79, 180

recevoir, future, 106
  past historic, 191
  present, 70
Reflexive verbs, 96
Relative pronouns, 79, 180-1

rester, perfect, 88
  pluperfect, 172
rire, future, 106
  perfect, 78
  present, 63

's, 28
Sac à main, le, 52
savoir, conditional, 154
  future, 106
  perfect, 78
  present, 56
  present subjunctive, 263
  with infinitives, 232
Seasons, 363
Sequence of tenses, 266, 363
si, 234
so, 363
some, 38, 363-4
sortir, perfect, 88
  pluperfect, 172
Stress, 16
Subject pronouns, 17
Subject and verb, agreement, 354
Subjunctive, 262-6
  after conjunctions, 265-6
  imperfect, 263
  mood, 262
  perfect, 263
  pluperfect, 263
  sequence of tenses, 266
  uses, 263-6
suivre, future, 106
  perfect, 78
  present, 79

take, 364
tenir, conditional, 154
tense, idiomatic usage, 233
    sequence, 363
this and *that*, 55
Time, 36-7
time, 364
tomber, perfect, 88
  pluperfect, 172
tout, 79
Transport, le, 222

valoir, present, 116
  present subjunctive, 262

vendre, conditional, 154
  imperfect, 138
  imperfect subjunctive, 263
  past historic, 190
  pluperfect, 172
  present subjunctive, 262
venir, conditional, 154
  future, 106
  imperfect subjunctive, 263
  perfect, 88
  pluperfect, 172
  present, 37
  present subjunctive, 263
venir de, 155, 359
  future, 106
Verbs (see also individual verbs)
  + **à**, 251
  + **à** with infinitive, 253
  conditional, 154-5
  conditional perfect, 226
  conjugated with **être**, 88-9
  constructions with the infinitive, 253
  + **dans**, 251
  + **de**, 251, 254
  first conjugation, 27
  followed by different constructions, 252
  future, 106-7
  future perfect, 225-6
  idiomatic tense usage, 233-4
  imperative, 358
  imperfect, 137-8, 358
  impersonal, 191
  + indirect object, 250
  infinitive, 56
  inversion, 19, 46, 55, 79, 88, 243-4, 292, 362-3
  irregular, 27, 37, 46, 63, 78-9, 89, 106-7, 115, 173, 191, 199, 255, 286-7

  + no preposition, 250
  + **par**, 255
  past historic, 190-1
  past participles, 78-9, 224-5, 354, 361
  perfect, 78, 88-9, 147
  pluperfect, 172, 263
  + **pour**, 255
  + preposition, 250-5
  reflexive, 96
  second conjugation, 46
  sequence of tenses, 363
  subjunctive, 262-6, 354
  third conjugation, 62
  with infinitives, 232
Vêtements, les, 51
Vie quotidienne, la, 188
vieux, 216
vivre, future, 106
  perfect, 89
  present, 89
voir, future, 106
  imperfect subjunctive, 263
  perfect, 78
  present, 27
vouloir, conditional, 154
  future, 106
  perfect, 78
  present, 56
  present subjunctive, 262
  with infinitives, 232-3
Vowels, 12-14
Voyage, le, 188

Weather, 365
what, 365
while, 365
Words which look alike, 366-7

y, 97, 356-7

ACKNOWLEDGEMENTS

THE publishers wish to thank the following for the use of photographs on the pages indicated:

J. Allan Cash, 8, 293, 300, 347, 348. French Government Tourist Office, 307, 318, 335, 346. Paul Popper Ltd., 10, 297, 312, 329, 341, 342.

The publishers also wish to thank the following publishers and authors for the use of copyright text:

René Julliard: Françoise Sagan, *Bonjour Tristesse*, p. 335. Albin Michel: Romain Rolland, *Jean Christophe*, p. 301 and p. 342. Thomas Nelson: Pierre Loti, *Roman d'un Enfant*, p. 292 and p. 300.